Memory's Nation

John Seelye

Memory's Nation

The Place of Plymouth Rock

The University of North Carolina Press

Chapel Hill and London

© 1998
The University of North Carolina Press
All rights reserved
Set in Minion type by Keystone Typesetting, Inc.
Manufactured in the United States of America
The paper in this book meets the guidelines for
permanence and durability of the Committee on
Production Guidelines for Book Longevity of
the Council on Library Resources.
Library of Congress
Cataloging-in-Publication Data
Seelye, John D.
Memory's nation: the place of Plymouth Rock /
John Seelye.
      p.   cm.
Includes bibliographical references (p.   )
and index.
ISBN 0-8078-2415-1 (cloth: alk. paper)
1. Plymouth Rock (Plymouth, Mass.)
2. Pilgrims (New Plymouth Colony) I. Title.
F74.P8S44   1998
974.4'82—dc21   97-40784
CIP

02   01   00   99   98   5   4   3   2   1

The publication

of this book has

been aided by

generous support

from the

L. J. Skaggs and

Mary C. Skaggs

Foundation.

For Catherine, who was my rock;

For Alice, who has been my salvation.

You are here to listen to the voices of the dead;

To mediate anew the eternal truths

On which your fathers founded the State.

This imperial people, if it is to bear rule

Over a continent, must listen to the voice

Of which David spoke with dying lips:

"The Rock spoke to me."

You are here to hearken to the voice of the Rock.

—George Frisbie Hoar

CONTENTS

ILLUSTRATIONS

PREFACE

I must not detain you . . . nor will I detain you. . . .
I turn at once to what concerns this day and this hour.
—Robert C. Winthrop

Let me begin by saying that even I would wish this book no larger. At the start, it was to be a volume of several hundred pages, with a stress on visual iconography—graphics—not the rhetorical equivalent that now dominates the text. But that was the dilemma creating the problem: you cannot give adequate consideration to the changing meaning of the Pilgrims and their Rock down through the years without taking into consideration the many oratorical commemorations celebrating anniversaries of the Landing in 1620. And those performances belong to what has become a neglected, even forgotten literary form, forensic displays once regarded as classics of Anglo-American prose now seldom consulted save by scholars searching for a useful, illustrative quotation.

The orations of nineteenth-century America—like training in Latin and the classics that made up the literary education of (especially male) Americans during those years and provided the models and inspiration for their orations—are things very much in our past. Moreover, those forensic displays are ornate productions of considerable length, written during a period when the ear was one of the main instruments of intellectual and even sensual gratification and when an appreciation for the play of genius over the instrument of language was akin to an appreciation for music. Having been printed, these performances may still be read, but they must be hunted down and cannot be simply alluded to as if familiar to the reader. Moreover, they are complex vehicles of communication, utilizing rhetorical strategies that are codes to which we have lost the keys. And yet, if you wish to trace the changing meanings of the Pilgrims down through the years, you must do justice to their celebration by considering these forensic displays.

But why bother? What is it about the Pilgrims and their coming to America in 1620 that merits a detailed consideration? Perhaps some justification can be found in the fact that the Pilgrims and their Rock are still popular attractions in Plymouth, and though the Landing is seldom evoked in public discourse, as a subject for history painters it has inspired consideration in a number of recent studies of American iconography. The Columbian occasion certainly warranted an intensity of gaze on other landings, and the anniversary of the Statue of Liberty that preceded it sensitized scholars to the idea of Arrival, both subjects validating the iconic importance of the Pilgrims. But discussions of the Pilgrim advent in art have been limited to chapters or single essays, held within a much larger perspective. Is it a body of writing and art so substantial and noteworthy as to warrant a book-length study, and one of such size? What possible interest could such a subject have save to that marginalized class of persons who take pride in their descent from the *Mayflower* passengers? Or native New Englanders of Puritan ancestry? Both of these are diminished groups at a time when the history of the region is suspect, even politically incorrect. Who cares about New England these days, anyway? Well, frankly, that is just the point.

I was inspired at the start to undertake this project by an essentially frivolous motive, the result of reading a popular account of Plymouth Rock that illustrated the comedy implicit in the humblest and most boring of our national icons. First-time visitors to Plymouth routinely express their disillusionment at the smallness of the sacred boulder that they have imagined to be of epic dimensions. It is an encounter that by a process of deflation is the first step in dissipating a myth, an experience I take to be essential to what it means to be an American. The Rock is the central *figura* in what amounts to an ongoing hoax, underwritten by the perennial question as to whether or not the Pilgrims actually landed on it, a positive response to which is generally insisted upon by Plymouth antiquarians and tour guides but refuted or ignored by historians.

Moreover, without denying the Separatists a proper measure of due respect, we can detect in the Pilgrims a significant proportion of the Lilliputian element, which the Brobdingnagian brag of their nineteenth-century celebrants only emphasizes by contrast. I took it as a challenge, therefore, not only to convey the essential humor in the subject but to make what many might still regard as a negligible, even lifeless icon the subject of a book-length study. But along the way my own viewpoint gradually changed: without discounting the comic element, I discovered the extent to which celebrations of the Landing of 1620 were integral to the evolution of conflicting ideologies in New England during a time when that region still presumed to speak for the nation.

I must mention here Lawrence Buell's magisterial study, which appeared soon after I began this project, which by presuming to take seriously the many aspects and artifacts of New England's literary culture—an updating of Van Wyck Brooks's pioneering volumes—reinforced my own sense of the region's importance, even in decline. My focus is on one aspect of that culture, but it may be considered a paradigm of the whole, Plymouth Rock having been an instrument used to assert the region's moral hegemony even as its political and economic power waned. And to the extent that the moral implications of the Pilgrim Landing influenced national discourse, especially by underwriting the exceptionalness of the American experience, then the decline and demise of that paradigm should be of interest to a modern United States that seems to be following suit. As went New England, so goes the country.

Of especial interest in this regard is the evolution of the Republican Party, from its radical roots in the 1850s to a point at the start of the twentieth century when it resumed the burden of Federalist discourse. Descendants of the Puritans and their champions employed Plymouth Rock as an icon underwriting an exclusionist doctrine, employing language startlingly familiar to modern ears, now that the United States is once again threatened by an ungoverned tide of immigrants, objections to which are hardly limited to persons of Anglo-Saxon, Protestant origins.

But equally familiar to our own times are arguments of that day promoting an antithetical, inclusionist image of the Pilgrims, in an evolving dialectic the meaning of which is essentially contextual. The process is a multifaceted phenomenon that defines the received implication of the Pilgrims and the Rock over a century of rapid and to some exhilarating, to others frightening, change, inspiring both radical and reactionary ideologies. The major direction of iconic drift, however, was conservative, inspiring the title of this book, an obvious response to Perry Miller's Nature's Nation, in that it attempts to draw attention away from the liberal, transcendentalist message toward the conservative discourse to which Emerson and Thoreau were in part responding and, whether willing or not, to which they eventually contributed.

Memory's Nation, perhaps needless to say, is Nostalgia's Nation, inspiring an essentially male counterpart to the sentimentalism fashionable especially among women writers during Daniel Webster's heyday. The spirit of the jeremiad, as defined by Sacvan Bercovitch's refinement of Miller's use of that Puritan genre, maintains a concomitant vitality, even while exchanging the punitive for a celebratory emphasis, holding up the Forefathers not as impossible models for emulation but as the founders of a secular apostolic succession. But increasingly, following the Civil War, the celebrants of the Pilgrims found that their exhortations had little relevance to a new generation rising up in the United States, whose origins were not New England or Old England but other places.

By 1920, they had once again become radically redefined, but a redefinition that in effect spelled their doom as a useful ideological icon derived from a rhetorical continuity. That is why this book ends with the Tercentenary, which a literary critic of the day observed by noting that New England as a region was dead, by which he meant the culture generated by the Puritans and maintained ever more fitfully by their descendants. The rest is cellar holes and Robert Frost.

Memory's Nation

In my southern home . . . I too had nursed the heroic legend, and when I
made my reverent pilgrimage to Plymouth rock a cruel disillusion awaited
me. . . . It was as mythical as the Holy Stone of Mecca.
—*Moncure Conway*

"On Munday, they sounded ye harbor and found it fitt for shipping, and marched into ye land & found diverse cornfields & little running
brooks, a place (as they supposed) fit for situation." So writes William Bradford of the Pilgrims' first landing at the place they would call Plymouth.
Neither he nor any other contemporary witness mentions the specifics of their
coming ashore on December 11, 1620 (Old Style). Had it been otherwise, the
promoters of the sanctity of Plymouth Rock would have had a much easier
time of it, but it was not. A popular and recent authority has written that "the
story about the Rock, in fact, goes back only to 1769, when the First Comers
had been in their graves for a century or more. The Rock's almost universal
fame as a great national patriotic institution is of still more recent growth"
(Willison, 115). In fact, the story has no such point of origin, but our authority
does serve to establish an important distinction, between the Rock itself and
the "fame" of the Rock, which last, most certainly, dates from the epochal
moment in 1820 when it emerged from a local to a national eminence.

Literal minds are bothered by the absence of contemporary testimony as to
the Rock's authenticity, but that need not pester us here. It makes no difference, finally, whether or not the First Comers set their feet upon the Rock.
True, we can never sever the Rock from the Pilgrims, but Bradford and his
people, as Pilgrims, owe their first emergence not to the persecutions of Separatists and other reformers in the opening years of the seventeenth century in
England but to Patriot rhetoric in New England during the Revolution and,
most especially, to party battles in and around Boston at the turn of the
eighteenth into the nineteenth century.

Though often thought of as having a religious—or at least a spiritual—
significance, the Rock was from the start a political icon, and though an
ensuing century of conflict would further embue it with ecclesiastical associations, it would endure to the end as a statist symbol. That end, for purposes of
convenience, may be dated 1920, imposing a neat chronology that is violated
by the persistence of myth but is warranted by intellectual and political history.
As a political image, the Rock today is as dead as the proverbial stone.

Not since Calvin Coolidge has an American politician with presidential ambitions associated himself with it. More typically, as during the recent centennial celebration of the Statue of Liberty, presidents and presidential hopefuls have raised a campaigning arm in the shadow of Bartholdi's welcoming figure. The Rock, once a pietistic artifact, has become something of a joke; the Statue, once something of a joke, has become a pietistic artifact. The Statue has as a symbol finally merited the stature given it by Bartholdi; the Rock has shrunk to its actual size, dwarfed by the grandiose monument that shelters it. The reasons for this paradoxical transference and transfiguration are obvious and have to do with demography and demagoguery, factors clued by the neighboring presence of Ellis Island in New York harbor. By contrast, the Plymouth waterfront has its replicated *Mayflower*, which, despite the aura of the Compact, is hardly an ark of democratic inclusiveness.

And yet, as a symbol, Plymouth Rock has much in common with the Statue of Liberty, as a study of its iconic origins and evolution reveals. It stands in political terms for the same ideals as the Statue, differing only in a lack of specificity in allegorical outlines. Save for the chiseled date, 1620, there is nothing about the Rock that is different from any other large boulder found lying about Massachusetts. Most visitors express disillusionment over its size (a complaint seldom expressed by tourists to the Statue), but some of that disillusionment may stem from the grandiloquence of the rhetoric inspired by the Rock as well as from erroneous graphic depictions of the Landing, which put forward a pedestal threshold of considerable dimensions. These orators and artists seem never to have viewed the actual landfall in Plymouth, but whatever the facts, their inflations were clearly in the service of giving epic and ideological heft to the Landing, which actual encounter quickly dispels.

Where Bartholdi drew upon a conventional language of political symbols in creating his Statue, the creators of the Rock as an icon drew largely upon their imaginations. Scholarship has shown us that the public squares and iconographic archives of France are cluttered with equivalent versions of Bartholdi's statue, dating from the time of the French Revolution, but there is only one Rock. Like tiny Bedlowe's Island on which the Statue stands, Plymouth Rock was a chance creation of convenience, located at a strategic spot, where it served for more than a century as a podium for politicians, many of them dressed in preacher's clothing. On that Rock by means of rhetoric they erected a joint artifact, the lineaments of which, abstracted from their speeches and sermons, not a little resemble the outlines of Bartholdi's great Statue, a creation mirrored in the actual, though often ignored, monolith that crowns a modest height within the town of Plymouth, Hammatt Billings's granitic National Monument to the Forefathers.

But as a live, contemporary issue, Plymouth Rock is important mostly because it is dead. The issues that gave the Pilgrims vitality for more than a century are also dead and were dying even as the Rock received its penultimate accolade in 1920, the words spoken over it then being a kind of benediction, laying to rest the rhetoric that had first brought the Rock to life a century before. And yet Plymouth does attract modern pilgrims, who support a flourishing souvenir business. They wander through the bayside park, crowded with statuary and memorial tablets, perhaps pausing to imagine how it must have been for the First Comers, imaginings best undertaken in dreary December on the Massachusetts coast. At that season, looking out through the canopy over the Rock and past the empty yacht basin, one can easily imagine the little ship putting into the harbor, the shallop being lowered, the tiny figures bustling about.

It is a simple tableau, deceptively simple, as Governor Bradford pointed out, like the Rock itself. For the Pilgrims, certainly, did not find what they came seeking, but at the start most of them—the Saints if not the Strangers—knew what they wanted and shared fervently the same expectation. Although what they sought would be gainsaid by the events they set in motion, it is the very simplicity of their hopes that gives what followed their arrival particular point and poignancy. Not surprisingly, it is the tableau provided by the First Thanksgiving that has largely supplanted the Landing in the national imagination, with its emphasis on community, on sharing, and on feasting, a democratic gathering at a multicultural table.

By contrast, Plymouth Rock is so dead that it has become, so far as most intellectual historians are concerned, an invisible artifact. Our oldest monument—and it is surely that—has been bypassed by professors as well as politicians, who pause only to discount the "myth" of the Landing and then pass on to more pressing intellectual concerns, the relationship, say, of Separatism and Antinomianism or the overshadowing of Plymouth Plantation by the powerful Bay Colony to the north. Save for a handful of articles and essays, the complex posterity of the Rock has been largely ignored by historians. What follows is an attempt to rectify that massive omission, and if it is chiefly a calendar of errors, it is a sequence also that tells us a great deal about the way in which Americans regarded themselves, their institutions, and the changes threatening (or promising) to transform the nation at critical moments of uncertainty.

Those Americans, let it be said, were people who for the most part could claim New England antecedents, for the story of Plymouth Rock as a symbol is the story of the struggle by that region to retain its hegemony. By means of the press, the pulpit, and the public school system, the native-born and scattered generations of New England descent were able for the first century and a half of this nation's history to maintain a calculated grip on the national imagination. At about the time of the War of 1812, which had put the region into a defensive posture, New England Societies began to spring up in major urban centers across the United States, starting with New York City and spreading south to Charleston and New Orleans and as far west as San Francisco. From its founding, New England had cherished its position as the stronghold of an embattled minority, and that paranoid mentality profited the nation-within-a-nation over succeeding centuries. We cannot understand the prevalence of Plymouth Rock without taking into account New England's long tradition of self-justification, which intensified as region became section. The importance of Plymouth Rock, likewise, can be keyed to the diminishment of New England as an important zone of influence.

The Rock first heaved into view on the eve of the American Revolution and made its initial appearance in literature by means of a sermon that sought to promote the patriotic cause by associating it with the Pilgrim errand, dual events intimate with New England's decisive role in the War for Independence. The Rock next appeared in the armory of Federalist weapons, a rhetorical figure standing for New England's reactionary intransigency in the face of the victory of Jeffersonian Republicans, which took its most extreme position by threatening secession during the War of 1812. Plymouth Rock and New England were rescued from this destructive solipsism by Daniel Webster, who used the occasion of the bicentennial celebration of 1820 to elevate his region and its chief icon to national significance. It was an oration that would for many years associate Webster and the Rock in the popular imagination, the latter supporting the former as a pedestal uplifts a statue, a connection that the great Whig came to regret.

For the next three decades Webster would devote his political career to safeguarding New England's economic well-being even as he saw his presidential ambitions frustrated by New England's shrinking zone of influence. As early as 1830, Webster in his public orations had begun to stress national union over regional hegemony, but he would always be associated with his reification of Plymouth Rock. By 1850, the year in which Webster sacrificed for the sake of the Union his moral integrity and hence that of New England, the Rock was being perversely promoted by Garrisonian abolitionists as a symbol of regional sanctity. It served as the centerpiece of their efforts to effect a separation of free from slave states, which only the more emphasized New England's distance (and difference) from the rest of the world. And in 1920, the tercentenary address was delivered by Henry Cabot Lodge, the last and perhaps the loneliest of the Brahmin statesmen, cast in the shape of earnest futility prophesied by the career and writings of his mentor, Henry Adams, the personification of New England's final decline and withdrawal from modern America.

Henry Adams regarded himself and his generation as "lost," for his own value to himself seems to have resided in a quality of irrelevance, which gave his life what meaning it had. That would seem, finally, to be the meaning of Plymouth Rock also, whose story is linked inextricably to the history of New England's decline. It could be a tragic story, but it is not. It is comic, the kind of dry comedy in which Adams cast himself, a comedy of historical events that controlled the very men who conceived themselves in charge of those events. It is a comedy that began in 1620, when a boatload of men put ashore in a place to which they had been led by a sailor who mistook it for another place, much as the Pilgrims had first been set ashore on Cape Cod, not the banks of the Hudson River, toward which they had been heading. If Plymouth Rock is our oldest monument, it is also our most ludicrous icon, token of the vagaries of chance, the haphazardness of events that is essential to comedy.

Here again the factor of size plays its part. Much as the Pilgrims were forced by circumstances to revise their plans, certifying what would become the controlling thesis of Bradford's great history, crediting all things to the mysterious workings of Providence, so the Rock in its surprising smallness ever and again undercuts the myth of the Landing to which it loans its presence. If, as a century of orators would attest, the importance of the Rock borrows from event, then the emphasis reinforces the unlikeliness of the Rock as a cosmic signifier, when viewed with an eye uncluttered by history. Indeed, at such times the Rock seems the American cousin of that other famous stone, the one kicked by Doctor Johnson in refutation of Bishop Berkeley's notion of the world as idea. Yet it was as an idea that the Rock first emerged, and, even now, it is as an idea that our oldest icon continues to survive, a continuity that we shall be tracing in the pages that follow.

CHAPTER **I**

A Boat, a Ship, Some People

History is revelation.
—Calvin Coolidge

Let us pause here at the start to contemplate a familiar image, the rendering of the Pilgrims' landing at Plymouth by Charles Lucy, an English artist, a picture that was much circulated and adapted in popular engravings from about 1850 on. This is a static composition, monumental in its form and expression, and whatever its interest to us or lack thereof, it does serve to illustrate one overwhelming proposition: the Rock on which the Pilgrims stand is given meaning by their presence. Here, the iconography is overwhelmingly pacific, even prayerful, in keeping with the errand of the Pilgrims, but that is, as we will see, only one emphasis of several available. Still, we cannot separate the Rock from the Separatists. Viewing it, we must always remind ourselves of the Landing, for without the Landing, there is no subject meaning—no correlative—to the object.

Yet the Rock contributes to the Pilgrim experience also, signifying the obdurate stonescape that became their new home, a land of adversity that tallied so well with the obstinate Puritan ethos, like the anvil with the hammer. William Bradford provided for future generations an epitome of that hard prospect, the winter-blasted shore confronting the Forefathers when they first landed on the mainland: "The season it was winter, and they that know the winters of that country know them to be sharp and violent, and subject to cruel and fierce storms, dangerous to travel to known places, much more to search an unknown coast. . . . For summer being done, all things stand upon them with a weather-beaten face, and the whole country, full of woods and thickets, represented a wild and savage hue" (62).

There is, significantly, no particular Rock in Bradford's scene (nor, for that matter, any rocks at all), a lack borne out by the accounts written by the Pilgrims of their first days in North America. There, as in Bradford's *Of Plimoth Plantation*, the settlers simply "march into the land," as they had been doing

FIGURE 1. *The Landing of the Pilgrim Fathers*, a much-circulated engraving after a lost painting by the British artist Charles Lucy, ca. 1850. Note the skull-capped figure to the left supported by a staff, an elderly Elder Brewster, as well as the absence of armor and weapons. Instead, we have a figure to the right bearing a pick and shovel, forming a diagonal pointing to the *Mayflower*, suggesting, along with the presence of women, the Pilgrims' thoroughly domestic purpose. The mountain in the background is entirely imaginary and displaces a low-lying peninsula occupied by the town of Duxbury, now distinguished by a monument honoring its founder, Miles Standish. The captain is probably the figure in the far right corner of the triangular composition, seen carrying a woman, his ailing wife, Rose, who would soon die, becoming a significant icon for the age of sentimentality, elements discussed in chapter 16. (Courtesy Plimoth Plantation)

since wading ashore on the outermost point of Cape Cod a month before. We may not doubt that the Rock was there, having been deposited during the glacial age, but the exploring Pilgrims, who had waded ashore all along the Cape, would probably not have steered toward but away from any such hazard to navigation. And had a convenient natural pier been provided, surely their contemporary journals, filled with instances of providential aid, would have made some mention of it. Still, whatever the fact of the matter, the instrumentality of the Rock as a platform—or stage—does have considerable resonance, especially when taken in context with the "Pilgrim" designation, which, like the Rock's elevation, was the work of later generations of celebrants.

A contemporary anthropologist, Victor Turner, has studied the phenomenon of pilgrimage and come up with terms that Robert Arner has cited as relevant to the events of 1620. Drawing on numerous "root paradigms," from historical instances of insurrection to African rituals, Turner has derived a complex theory of liminality, regarded in effect as a communal rite of passage. By his definition, liminality is a "phenomen[on] of transition" that produces what Turner calls "communitas," an ideal state experienced (here quoting Martin Buber) by "'a multitude of persons,'" which, "'though it moves towards one goal, yet experiences everywhere a turning to, a dynamic facing of, the others, a flowing from *I* to *Thou*'" (*Ritual Process*, 112, 126–27). The result, in Turner's terms, is "a spontaneously generated relationship between leveled and equal total and individuated human beings, stripped of structural attributes" yet highly productive of new structures (*Dramas*, 202). For while communitas represents "a negation of many . . . of the features of preliminal social structure," it affirms "another order of things and relations. Social structure is *not* eliminated, rather it is radically simplified" (*Dramas*, 196). Moreover, though communitas "strains toward universalism and openness," its "historical fate . . . seems to have been to pass from openness to closure, from 'free' communitas to the solidarity given by bounded structure, from optation to obligation" (202).

Though the liminal instance is a "limbo of structure" inspiring a sense of "permanent revolution," such ideal moments are literally transitional, for the "'movement' becomes itself an institution among other institutions—often one more fanatical and militant than the rest, for the reason that it feels itself to be the unique bearer of universal human truths" (*Dramas*, 248, 252; *Ritual Process*, 112). Turner, whose influential works were published in 1969 and 1974, respectively, makes a number of references to parallel instances during the "age of Aquarius," when "many people, especially those under thirty, . . . tr[ied] to create a communitas and a style of life that [was] permanently contained within liminality," and it may have been to hippies that his essentially conservative message was addressed (*Dramas*, 261). If, as he opines, "yesterday's liminal becomes today's stabilized," he must be accounted a prophet, for yesterday's member of Woodstock Nation is often today's commuter from New Canaan to Wall Street (16).

And yet anyone familiar with the history of the Pilgrims in North America can detect the obvious parallel with Turner's programmatic movement from "*existential* or *spontaneous* communitas" to "*normative* communitas" and on to "*ideological* communitas." The Plymouth colonists would seem best assigned the middle modality, "where, under the influence of time, the need to mobilize and organize resources, and the necessity for social control among the members of the group in pursuance of these goals, the existential communitas is organized into a perduring social system" (*Ritual Process*, 132). Certainly the Pilgrims' failure to institute a primitive communism during their first year in the New World is well known. And William Bradford's great history of Plymouth Plantation took its initial impetus from the rising hope for continued (if modified) communitas experienced by him and his fellow colonists, while the falling action of the book reflects the author's dismay over and finally his stoic acceptance of the loss of the original spirit of the colony, as Christian idealism was replaced by commercial considerations.

We may doubt that as a group the Pilgrims ever experienced that intense euphoria Turner associates with the first modality or stage of communitas, for in the records they left behind, the Forefathers consistently insisted on conformity of the individual to community needs—as attested to, among many other documents, by the terms of the Mayflower Compact. And when it came to what Turner calls "the absolute communitas of unchanneled anarchy," we tend to think of Thomas Morton, the Pilgrims' archadversary in the New World, an opinion backed by revisionist historians, notably Richard Slotkin, for whom the Pilgrims as Puritans were repressive structure personified (Turner, *Dramas*, 171; Slotkin, 58–65).

When Turner speaks of "pilgrims," he most often has in mind the devout Muslims who journey to Mecca, yet in emphasizing the "passage quality of the religious life," he coincidentally detects "traces" of liminality in "formulations" also used by the Pilgrims of Plymouth. Thus when Turner notes that " 'the Christian is a stranger to the world, a pilgrim, a traveler, with no place to rest his head,' " he cites terms that bear comparison with Bradford's "they knew they were pilgrims, and looked not much on [worldly] things, but lift[ed] up their eyes to heaven, their dearest country," or with the "wandering wilderness" evoked by Robert Cushman in the first sermon associated with Plymouth Plantation (Turner, *Ritual Process*, 107; Bradford, 47; Cushman, 44).

Much else that Turner tells us about liminality likewise applies, including the marginal status of its avatars, their relatively low place on the social scale, and their sense of apartness and specialness—all qualities associated with the people we now call the Pilgrims but who were thought of at the time as Separatists, a fact to which the following quotation from Turner certainly applies: "The countless sects and schismatic movements in the history of religions have almost always asserted the values of communitas against those of structure and claimed that the major religions from which they have seceded have become totally structured and secularized, mere empty forms.

Significantly, such separatist movements have almost invariably adopted a cultural style dominated by the cultural idiom of indigence. In their first impetus, such movements often strip their members of the outward show of wealth or status, adopt a simple form of speech, and to a considerable extent strip their religious practices of ritualism and visual symbolism. Organizationally, they often abolish priestly hierarchies and substitute for them either prophetic charismatic leadership or democratic methods of representation" (*Dramas*, 266–67).

Then, too, as we consider the meaning of the Pilgrims to us, and the peculiar appeal of their experience to subsequent generations, something further might be derived from Turner's definition of "the power of the weak," by means of which a low social status is replaced by "sacred attributes" (*Ritual Process*, 109). Certainly the Pilgrims stand out from all the other early settlers of the North American continent, whether the French of Canada, the Spanish of Florida and Mexico, or the English at Roanoke and Jamestown, as remarkable exemplars of "pure" motives, distinct from the rest in having only a secondary interest in the commercial aspects of colonial enterprise. And though the settlers of Boston also knew great hardship during their first year in New England, the privileged birthright of John Winthrop and other leaders of the Bay Colony served to divorce them from that lowly state productive of a sacred status, much as the activities of John Endicott come down to us as structural repressiveness itself.

The popular images we have of the Pilgrims, whether gathered in tearful prayer as they prepare to depart from Leyden or in thoughtful congress as each in turn signs the Mayflower Compact, or posed on the threshold provided by Plymouth Rock, or making their solitary way to Sabbath service through snowy woods, or seated with Massasoit and other Indians at the Thanksgiving table, all of these promote a powerful image of pure, selfless integrity that is without equal in the icons of American experience. During their prolonged ordeals, the Pilgrims may indeed have taken on that deep inner spirituality described by Turner—certainly something similar sustained them during a lengthy experience of cultural alienation and powerlessness—but for those who would later celebrate them, the Pilgrims are sanctity itself.

And it is right here that we must establish an important distinction, again relying on Victor Turner for terminology but departing the realm of anthropology and archetypes for aesthetics. What the liminal experience of the Pilgrims may have been as they came ashore in 1620 is highly conjectural, but the forms inspired by that historic advent are not. They may tell us nothing about the facts of the experience, but they do inform us how that experience was regarded by makers of those artifacts—the icons—that have made the Landing so memorable a moment. And that will be the proper subject of this study.

Referring back now to Lucy's tableau, we can once again observe the static quality of the composition, even to the triangular form, enhanced by the (imaginary) mountain in the background. These are not people portrayed as in motion: they have been frozen, rather, at a key point in their passage, the moment they landed on the Rock. Behind them lies the *Mayflower*—their ark of passage from the Old World—before them is a vastness they will define by their presence. The moment is liminal, the Rock a literal threshold, but the execution conveys permanence, stability, structure. The perspective, as in virtually all depictions of the Landing, is *from* the shore the Pilgrims are contemplating and opens outward to the ocean. We never see what the Pilgrims are looking at; we are what they are looking at; we are the realized future. They are frozen in beholding us.

Look now at Henry Sargent's depiction of the Landing, a picture that antedates Lucy's by a half century. Here again the composition is static, although there is a significant drama being enacted. The Pilgrims are confronting an Indian, Samoset, at the moment of their arrival, a distortion of historical fact that Sargent resorted to in order to dovetail one scene of the drama to another, at the same time evoking the image of the ur-Arrival, already celebrated by Joel Barlow in his tercentenary production *The Vision of Columbus*. The Landing thereby becomes an encounter with the inhabitants of the New World, figured as a cringing supplicant, a posture regarded as proper to the occasion by a contemporary reviewer.

Sargent's picture is also enhanced by color, resulting in another difference: Governor Carver, like several of his male companions, is dressed in military wear, a helmet and, more significant, a scarlet jacket, a color associated with the agents of the British empire. The pious postures of Lucy's Pilgrims are largely missing: instead we have the determined front of British imperialism. But the same element of stability—of structure—is present, enhanced by the elements of the backdrop, those signifiers of adversity like the jagged tree stump and bits of rock and ice all contributing to the drama of the scene.

Discussions of the contexts from which Lucy's and Sargent's depictions emerged belong in subsequent chapters. But the point to be made here, drawing on both pictures, is that the traditional image of the Pilgrims in artistic depictions of the Landing, from early to late in the nineteenth century, is not one of passage but arrival, and not only of arrival, but endurance—prevalence. Notably, no prominent painting exists of the Pilgrims under way aboard the *Mayflower*, despite the stress given to that ordeal in Bradford's history. We have instead Edwin White's depiction of the pious passengers gathered in their cabin to sign the Compact, a moment that precedes the Landing at Plymouth and reinforces the idea of a stable social order, one given distinction by divine favor. Thus the liminalism of the Pilgrim experience, as conveyed by their

FIGURE 2. Henry Sargent's *Landing of the Fathers*, ca. 1815. Sargent's is a militant and Anglophiliac version of the Pilgrim advent, with Governor Carver in a red coat and sword in hand, facing a supplicating Samoset. To his right is Miles Standish, prominently displayed and armed to the teeth. He seems to be staring down a cowering Elder Brewster, and above him flies the British ensign. Women and children are present, but the painting is dominated by a male presence. The implications of these emphases are discussed in chapter 3. (Courtesy Pilgrim Society)

writings, is blocked out from the pictorial record, to which we can add Lucy's alternative icon, the departure from Leyden, another scene with a pyramidal structure, suggesting the cohesiveness of a common faith.

Taken together, these paintings do suggest a process, being moments that signal the uniqueness, pathos, and drama of the Pilgrim Pageant. They seem, however, not to have been imagined by the artists as forming a triptych or a series but as a sequence of discrete scenes. To use the language of the century that produced these pictures, they take the theatrical form of posed and frozen tableaux, a mute, summary moment occurring sometimes at midpoint, sometimes at the end of the play. Much as the Pilgrim experience resolved itself from millennial expectations into solidly institutionalized structures, so artistic interpretations of that experience during the course of the nineteenth century imposed a structure upon (or derived one from) that experience for the pur-

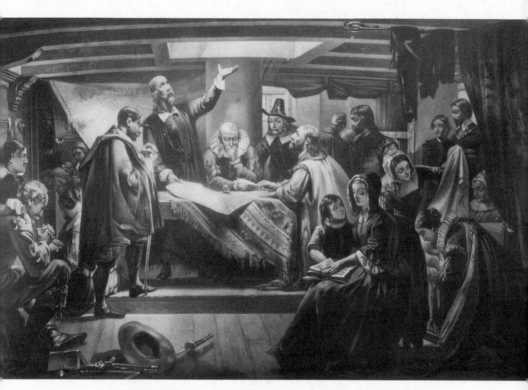

FIGURE 3. An engraving of Edwin White's *Signing the Compact in the Cabin of the May-flower*, 1867. The skylight illuminating the precious document suggests a providential witness, evoked as well by the elevated hand of Elder Brewster at the center of the composition. But note Miles Standish with his sword to Brewster's right and the sword and matchlock foregrounded on the deck, connoting the Puritan propensity for Christian soldiery. (Courtesy American Antiquarian Society)

poses of validating cultural stability by asserting the permanence of the past, in effect coining a rhetoric of conservative icons.

It is a gallery of pictures equivalent to the murals in the rotunda of our Capitol, save that they all derive from the single—and singular—experience of the Pilgrims, who are relegated to one panel in that national display. Notably, all of these icons hang in Pilgrim Hall, the templelike museum in Plymouth that contains dozens of mementos validating the sacredness of the Pilgrim experience and hence the exceptional nature of New England itself. It is a collection dominated by Sargent's Anglophiliac tableau, which testifies as well to the Anglo-Saxon continuity once considered so essential to the region's sense of its exclusive character. In sum, for celebrants of New England's sanctity, the Rock serves as a cornerstone, freighted with images garnered from a real and an imagined past upon which a nation will be built.

FIGURE 4. Lucy's *Departure of the Pilgrim Fathers*, 1853. An intensely pious tableau, dominated by the figure of Pastor John Robinson and, as in Lucy's version of the Landing, by the presence of women. Notably, Sargent's militant Carver is here shown with face covered by his hand in the left foreground, presumably in prayer. Bradford is the mustached young man reclining in the stock meditative posture of the era, and Miles Standish is the beardless youth to the right, comforting his wife, Rose, with his long hair virtually an androgyne. For the implications of all this, see chapter 16. (Courtesy Pilgrim Society)

We can here again refer to Robert Arner, who has written suggestively about the archetypical signification of stones in assessing the peculiar power of Plymouth Rock, whether as border markers, thresholds of liminality, or sacramental altars: "It is both the merest ledge of consciousness emerging from a great, gray unconsciousness of sea and a symbol of the sea itself," writes Arner of the Rock, "a vestige of the neutral zone so central to the rite of passage, and those who tread it belong temporarily neither to past nor future but are magico-religiously taken out of time" (32).

It may have been all of that, and more—one of the "thin places," celebrated by the Plymouth savant Peter Gomes, being a mystic zone where supernal

FIGURE 5. Design for an American bank note, ca. 1850, replete with imperial icons connoting national stability and blessedness.

spheres connect—but the signifying power of Plymouth Rock to its celebrants was also derived from symbolic constructs common not to the ancient but to what was in the late eighteenth and early nineteenth century the modern age. Without denying the subliminal power informing such artifacts, we can insist on the conscious and highly intellectual motives that led to their creation. They were part of the Enlightenment inheritance of the emerging United States, including such texts (soon enough icons themselves) as the Declaration of Independence and the Constitution.

We have here, for example, a design for a bank note engraved about 1850 that contains a retrospective gathering of such symbols, foregrounding Liberty with her pole and protecting shield, symbols adapted from British iconography of the prerevolutionary period. She is flanked on one side by a broken column betokening the destruction of a corrupt empire by the wrath of God (seen in the bolt of lightning) and on the other by a militant eagle (a symbol with both imperial Roman and Old Testament signification). The nation is represented by that figure dear to Christian idealism, a woman with child, but most important for our present concern, in the background we see a pyramid connoting durability divinely irradiated by providential favor and overarched by a rainbow sign promising peace and harmony. The mystic triangular shape, still associated with our national currency, is derived from the Freemasonic cabala that was a universal language among illuminati between 1750 and 1850. And that pyramid, an architectonic signifier of statist stability, emerged as a national icon at about the time that Patriots in Plymouth were discovering their Rock.

In 1776, immediately after Independence had been declared, a committee was convened in order to devise a Great Seal with which the documents of the new nation could be validated. Quite independent of each other, both Jefferson and Franklin came up with suggestions inspired by the Old Testament account of Exodus, dynamic tableaux emphasizing the liminal passage toward the land of Canaan (Jefferson) and the whelming of the Egyptian (Old World) army by the Red Sea (Franklin). Franklin also proposed incorporating the Freemasonic pyramid on the verso of the design, the only suggestion that survived, for by the time an acceptable iconic arrangement was adopted— about the time the Revolution was over—quite a different implication was involved. In the familiar spread eagle and shield, on the one side of the Great Seal, and the pyramid of empire, on the other, we have highly structured, statist symbols, connoting republican glory and divinely sanctioned imperial design, not revolutionary and liminal signifiers of departure and secessionism. And Plymouth Rock, as an icon, tends to share this consolidationalist signification, associated with the foundations of republican empire and embued with providential favor, an intellectual perhaps more than an archetypal construct. Sargent and Lucy subsequently arranged their otherwise quite different tableaux in pyramidal compositions, traditional in history paintings but also drawing validation from the national iconography.

Once again, the Pilgrims themselves—along with their counterparts in Puritan Boston—favored the image of Exodus for their experiences in the New World. But by the time of the Revolution, when the Exodus image was evoked for the Pilgrims, it was as a scriptural frame with which to give perspective to the crisis of the moment. The sufferings of the Fathers, as in the great sermon by Samuel Sherwood in 1776, validated the claims of the Sons to their inheritance of the New World republic, on the one hand, and on the other provided a high mark for emulation. The net result was to fix and simplify the experience of the Pilgrims in a series of symbolic moments, "sacred" in quite a different way from that intended by Victor Turner.

The process is identical to that encroachment of institutionalization over communitas that he describes, but the framing effect places the sacred moment in the past—identified with the national memory—and the composition as in the paintings by Sargent and Lucy is intended to give a positive shape not to the idea of transition or transformation but of stability. Notably, the emergence of the Mayflower Compact as essential to the idea of the Pilgrims attended the process of ratification of the Constitution, both documents being associated not with revolution but consolidation—statism.

That is why the Landing on the Rock as depicted by these artists gives the threshold less a liminal than a static function. The Pilgrims are frozen by conceptual time into a motionless aggregate, a point of reference—as well as reverence—for future ages to elicit whenever the occasion seems right. They are vibrant with potential but motionless. Their corporeal reality, so evident in their journals and histories, is gone; they are ossified into entablatures and statues, carved from the same substance as the Rock. They stand not for movement but stability, not the stability of the Pilgrims in 1620, so fragile in its dependence on their compact with each other and the very thin thread of support with England, but that massive, monolithic permanence desired by their descendants as they attempted to establish a republic whose foundation they fancied was laid by the Forefathers.

The Departure, the Landing, the Signing, these provide a statist trinity, a sacred triad of tableaux that would have as their equivalents the Declaration of Independence, the Revolution, the Constitution. At a later point would be added the Treaty with Massasoit, an icon associated with a pacific (if so often betrayed) policy of westward expansion, and the First Thanksgiving, an image that emerged as a national ritual during the Civil War, promoting an ideology of domestic tranquility, compensating for the tragedy of a national House Divided.

Eventually, as I have earlier suggested, the First Thanksgiving would displace the Landing as our dominant Pilgrim icon and occasion for celebration. There is a popular depiction of that feast by Jennie Brownscombe, which also hangs in Pilgrim Hall at Plymouth, but the painter gave us as well her version of the Landing, known only through a reproduction. The pyramidal composition and prayerful postures are carried over into the twentieth century, as is the emphasis on arms and the man, but the gendered aspect has been reversed: a woman now dominates the scene, much as women are essential to the notion of the First Thanksgiving. The primary place on the Rock is held by a pious figure with a definitive Botticelli quality, suggesting the complicity of shallop and scallop. Hers is a tender presence guarded by the advancing figures of Miles Standish with pikestaff and sword and a Pilgrim (probably John Carver) with a blunderbuss, but it reminds us that by the tercentenary year women in America were gathering political strength.

We will learn the identity of that woman in due time, but it suffices to say here that she is not Priscilla Mullins, who is placed slightly behind her in company with John Alden, in his carpenter's leather jerkin. They are figures not seen in the paintings by either Lucy or Sargent, for reasons we shall be learning as well. Perhaps most notable because so idiosyncratic, Brownscombe's tableau is resonant with postures and configurations associated with Roman Catholicism, and her emphasis on the prayerful woman suggests an element of Mariolatry, perhaps an attempt to rectify the imbalance in American iconography

FIGURE 6. *The Landing of the Pilgrims*, by Jenny Brownscombe, ca. 1920. This lithograph illustration, perhaps taken from a lost painting, is a version of the event derived from Botticelli that gives a feminist cast to the arrangement by having a woman dominate the composition, replacing Governor Carver in the usual iconic arrangement. Miles Standish is the dainty youth in armor with halberd, suggesting Edwardian origins. For further discussion of the iconography, including the identity of the central figure, see chapter 16.

detected by Henry Adams. Here, presumably, the Virgin *is* the Dynamo, and from her electric loins, as from the Rock, a nation will spring.

Specifics aside, these revisions reflect contextual shifts, clues to changing values in both region and nation, with their political and cultural manifestations. Let me say at this point that the contextual frame that has in recent years been placed around nineteenth-century depictions of historical subjects may be traced in terms of methodology to the landmark article by William H. Treuttner entitled "The Art of History," to which I was referred by the author himself at a critical point in the creation of this book. "We must 'read,'" writes

Treuttner, "our mid-century history paintings as broadly as we read the historians of the period, [for] the artists, like their literary colleagues, indeed had an eye on the present, regardless of the subject in which they chose to incorporate their message. . . . We must become more adept at interpreting historical subjects and think more carefully about what they meant in their own context. . . . And above all, we must keep in mind how the yardstick of history operated in the nineteenth century" (31). That yardstick is the basic unit of measure in *Memory's Nation*.

Which brings us to the image with which this initial discussion of iconography will end, a picture that marks a radical departure from the filiopietism of the depictions of the Pilgrims previously displayed. Here we have the Forefathers having their measurements taken for a line of men's clothing, a stark image of commodification that assures us the Pilgrims were not inevitably an object of piety for all Americans, most especially as the hegemony of Anglo-Saxon New England declined. This is a very funny picture and was intended as such surely, humor and hucksterism being close cousins. Needless to say, it does not hang in Pilgrim Hall.

Yet there is a serious dimension to this tableau, located in the specific liberties taken with an icon essential to the imagery of Liberty as an American ideal. Governor Carver remains frozen, but so does any man having his inseam measured, and a smile of pleasurable anticipation now plays beneath his beard. The woman to his left also smiles as she looks back at Standish and his ailing wife, and the formerly prayerful figure to his right now focuses his devotions on the three pairs of trousers he is removing from their box. The monumentality of the composition is gone, and we no longer focus on the Pilgrims posed at a pure moment of arrival, with the *Mayflower* in the background and the distant and entirely imaginary mountain conveying a sublime sense of critical mass. We are distracted by the bustling salesmen with their tape measures, movement connoting American enterprise and get-up-and-go, Emersonianism at its lowest common denominator.

The composition has been altered, the pyramidal form modified by adding the post office building and a line of Pilgrims waiting for their shipments, as another Pilgrim pulls on a pair of pants in a foreground littered with cartons. The Indians traditional to scenes of landing, missing from Lucy's tableau, have been added, their loincloths covered by mail-order trousers, a mismatch common to comic portrayals of the day, in which Native Americans are shown in awkward and unseemly attempts to adapt to the white man's costume. Even the Rock itself is desecrated, having been painted with an advertisement, a graffito not uncommon in the 1880s. Hilariously irreverent, this parody is entirely in keeping with the commercial spirit of the day, even to the conflation of the notions of "custom [that is, tailor] made" and mail-order delivery.

FIGURE 7. An enlightening lithographic travesty of the Lucy version of the Landing, ca. 1885, which validates the popularity of that image while laying impious hands on the Pilgrims. I am indebted to Georgia Barnhill, curator of graphic arts at the American Antiquarian Society, for having called my attention to this impudent display of commercialization. (Courtesy American Antiquarian Society)

In sum, despite the decline in sacredness of the Pilgrim idea, it obviously survives as a widely recognizable icon, and though entirely in the service here of the merchandising impulse, what is going on in this picture can stand for what had been happening for nearly a century. As a tableau, this advertisement is as accurate as the original by Lucy or the painting by Sargent, or even the later assemblage mounted by Brownscombe, for those "historical" images bear no resemblance to the actual arrival of the Pilgrims, either. These and other depictions of the Landing are shaped by artistic convention and contemporary ideologies. Always, the Pilgrims are having their measure taken for some purpose, are being assessed for ready-made garments, for stereotypical postures, rhetorical gestures, political platitudes. If the Rock takes its meaning from the Pilgrims, then the Pilgrims take their meaning from the ideological discourse of the moment. What they are, what they are looking toward, is entirely in the charge of whatever mode or impulse has control of the proceedings. The liminality of their passage is an illusion, was always an illusion. It is, finally, the consolidation into a negotiable icon that is the plastic element, not the experience of arrival. That is what changes over the years, not the Pilgrims in America, but our use of the Pilgrims in America.

At the start of their experience in the New World the founders of Plymouth gave those who wish to re-create those first days very little to go by. We have the early printed account of their American encounter, *Mourt's Relation*, but that experience was edited and shaped by the authors for certain effects. Bradford's omnium-gatherum provides detailed documentation of their commercial and other dealings, but the personal element is virtually absent, save for vivid descriptions of their adversaries, the Strangers among them. For Bradford's history is a lengthy legal brief on the Saints' behalf, whose moral integrity is intensified by the grim particulars of their intended traducers. In truth, the Puritan Separatists from Scrooby by way of Leyden were a commodity from the start. They became a commodity the moment they arrived, even as they drew up the document certfying their community, a kind of package warranting the praiseworthiness of their endeavor. They were advertisements for themselves, and what happened afterward was merely a signifying continuation of that initial process. Even now we are taking the measure of the Pilgrims for new garments precut to our specifications.

Do not be fooled by the living museum at Plimoth [*sic*] Plantation. What you see there is living rhetoric, theatrical equivalents to the semiotics of the democratic process, that ongoing liminal state. The Pilgrims, their sacred status removed, are presented as plain folks going about their daily business, no different from modern, everyday people, save in their quaint costumes and antique way of speaking. They have become democratized into an item of popular consumption, perhaps a more gritty comestible than the candified menu served up in Disneyland's version of the American past, but as a specimen preserve of a historical moment (1627) no less tailored by the needs of the present generation. We make a distinction between the living museum and the accumulation of well-dusted artifacts in Pilgrim Hall or the tawdry souvenirs for sale in Plymouth shops, but they all have much in common with each other and little connection to the reality of the Forefathers, whatever that may have been.

And yet we still seem to have a need to establish connections with those ancient people, whose arrival survives as a special moment, a zone available to anyone willing to effect a separation from the ongoing process of commodification at Plymouth. Return to that place and stand looking seaward on a wintry day. The image you behold is what you project upon that gray sea and sky and will be as true as any other. So long as there is a need for such an image, it will have the power of an icon, and you will not be alone upon that margin, nor will they, but for the moment there will be established a kind of communitas, that gathering of the living and the dead commemorated here as Memory's Nation. Look! Even now the ship is entering the harbor, the passengers clambering into the boat as oars gleam in the pale cold air. But do not expect as they step upon the shore to recognize them by their antique dress, for if that place is a liminal zone, so also does it transform the Pilgrims ever and again into persons not easily recognized as such by any exterior forms. You must not confuse the spirit with the thing.

CHAPTER 2

The Liberty Boys Hoist One for the Forefathers

Then from the pole's sublimest top
The active crew let down the rope.
—John Trumbull

I

In the words of the historian of Plymouth, Dr. James Thacher, it was in 1774 that "the inhabitants of this town, animated by the glorious spirit of liberty which pervaded the Province, and mindful of the precious relic of our forefathers, resolved to consecrate the rock on which they landed to the shrine of liberty" (*History*, 198). An earlier historian, Samuel Davis, set the date at 1775, but both are agreed that the Patriots of Plymouth, having already planted a Liberty Pole next to the courthouse, decided to place the sacred Rock in close proximity to that defiant signifier and for that purpose employed several screw jacks and (according to Thacher) thirty yoke of oxen. As an unintended consequence they managed to break the Rock in two, an accident that the Sons of Liberty, evincing Yankee ingenuity and a Puritan propensity for prophecy—along with that genius for symbolic displays we associate with their public activities—were able to spin to their advantage. Not only did the accident happily reduce the weight of what they finally hauled up into town, but they interpreted the splitting of the Rock as an omen foretelling "a division of the British empire." The larger, bottom part of the Rock was allowed to remain in its bed, at the center of a wharf sticking out into the bay, while the smaller, upper part, which still weighed many tons, was carried up from the beach. It was placed in "liberty pole square . . . where, we believe, waved over it a flag with the far-famed motto, 'Liberty or Death' "(199).

There is a certain humor to all this, in the Hudibrastic vein, but the Liberty Boys were quite serious. Ever since the furor over the Stamp Tax, Plymouth had been a busy, if somewhat removed, center of revolutionary activity. James Warren, the president of the Provincial Congress and identified with Sam

Adams as one of the Patriots who conceived the idea of Committees of Correspondence—the network of scribblers who kept subversive activities coordinated throughout New England—was a native of Plymouth and was the husband of Mercy Otis Warren, chronicler of the Revolution and a powerful literary satirist against the Tories. As early as March 1776, Sam Adams and John Hancock, writing as representatives of Boston, sent a letter to Plymouth praising its citizens for their activities against the Stamp Act, which had evinced the "truly noble spirit of our renowned Ancestors" (Adams, 1:71). The two men declared themselves filled "with deep Veneration" when they recalled "the ardent love of Religeon [sic] and Liberty" that had inspired those ancestors to escape the "oppressive Hand" of tyranny in "their Native Country, to forsake their fair Possessions and seek a Retreat in this distant Part of the earth" (71–72). Most important, "even in a Wilderness" the Forefathers took care "to lay a solid Foundation for learning . . . as the surest if not the only Means of preserving and cherishing the principles of Liberty and Virtue, and transmitting them to us their Posterity."

Clearly, the best way to "bless and revere" the "Memory" of their ancestors was to cherish their principles and throw off the oppressive Hand: after a paragraph detailing the perfidy of Great Britain over the past century in America, Adams and Hancock returned again to the "Spirit of our venerable Forefathers" and wished that it would be "revived and be defused [sic] through every Community in this Land," so that "Liberty Civil and Religeous, the grand Object of their View, may still be felt enjoy'd & vindicated by the present Generation, and the fair Inheritance transmitted to our latest Posterity" (73). Over the next ten years, Adams would several times write to or refer to the inhabitants of Plymouth, whose collective "pulse," as he informed Elbridge Gerry in 1782, "beat high and their resentment . . . is equal to that of any other Town. May God grant, that the Love of Liberty & a Zeal to support it may enkindle in every town. If the Enemies should see the flame bursting in different parts of the Country & distant from each other, it might discourage their attempts to damp & quench it. . . . I beg you would exert your utmost Influence in your neighboring towns and elsewhere. I hear nothing of old Salem" (2:349–50). Plymouth was once again foremost among the "candlesticks," the term favored by John Winthrop for the church-centered communities of New England.

Wesley Frank Craven and Alan Heimert, among others, have shown us the extent to which extolling the achievements of the Forefathers was a rhetorical convention during the decade preceding the Revolution, as a result of which Plymouth regained something of its elder glory, becoming the cynosure of (at least) New England's eyes, being (again in Sam Adams's words) "the most ancient town in New England." Late in December 1772, Adams wrote the

Committee of Correspondence in Plymouth, on which his friend Warren served, thanking its members for their "noble & patriotic Resolves" and once again praising the town for its readiness "to assert the natural religious & civil rights of the Colonists" (2:394). Adams this time coupled his praise for "the manly & becoming Spirit with which you have always expressed your selves on such Occasions" with "hearty" congratulations upon the occasion "of that great Anniversary, the landing of the first Settlers at Plymouth," most especially for "the religious & respectful Manner, in which it has been celebrated" (395). Writing to James Warren, in May 1774, Adams urged his fellow citizens of Plymouth to follow Newburyport in boycotting British imports, noting that "the heroes who first trod on your shore, fed on clams and muscles [sic], and were contented" (3:113).

Small wonder, then, that the Liberty Boys that same year decided to haul Forefathers' Rock (as it was called in Plymouth) up next to the Liberty Pole, so closely were their ancestors and the slogans of the Revolution coupled. Indeed, that "great Anniversary" of which Adams spoke had been celebrated in Plymouth only since 1769 and had initially been sponsored by a group of mostly younger inhabitants of the town, who had formed the Old Colony Club early that year, a social organization dedicated to civic and self-improvement and observations that honored the accomplishments of their ancestors. The club was avowedly (but futilely, as things turned out) apolitical, yet it can hardly be by chance that its founding and declared purpose coincided with the aftermath of the Stamp Act agitation and segues with the subsequent eruption against taxes and tea. We can better understand that moment in 1774 (or 1775) when Plymouth Rock was hoisted from its bed by considering, if only briefly, the activities and speeches of the Old Colony Club. Many ceremonies and much rhetoric later associated with the Rock can be found in embryo there.

The Forefathers had landed in Plymouth on December 11, 1620 (Old Style), but because of an error in converting the Old Style calendar date to the new, the young men of the Old Colony Club fixed on the 22d instead of the 21st, a mistake that would be perpetuated over the years to come. The event was thick with self-conscious symbolism, essential to the ideology-heavy demonstrations inspired by prerevolutionary activities, with their slogans, illuminations, parades, and like theatrical paraphernalia. The chief feature of the day was a banquet, the menu of which was intended to convey the hardships of the diners' ancestors, the "clams and muscles" alluded to by Sam Adams. As the Forefathers were forced to subsist on seafood and wild game, so dined their descendants, but what was necessity for the Fathers was largely a mother of culinary invention for the Sons. Thus the "decent repast . . . dressed in the plainest manner," as the minutes of the club tell us, consisted of nine courses, including dishes of clams and oysters, "a haunch of venison roasted by the first

[spit]jack brought to the Colony," succotash, seafowl, frostfish and eels, an apple pie, a "large baked Indian whortleberry pudding," and a final course of cranberry tarts (*Records of the Old Colony Club*, 400). The menu might seem contradictory to the club's stated intention of avoiding "all appearances of luxury and extravagance . . . in imitation of our worthy ancestors whose memory we shall ever respect," but only to someone not familiar with the gustatory habits of eighteenth-century Americans.

Other symbolic festivities followed, including a musket salute fired by certified descendants of the first settlers, and a song "very applicable to the day" was sung by a group of young gentlemen from the private academy kept by Mr. Peleg Wadsworth (401). But perhaps the most interesting aspect of the celebration may be found in the toasts proposed after the meal, all being led by the president of the club, Isaac Lothrop, as he sat in a chair of ancestral proportions that had once belonged to William Bradford.

Twelve in number, the toasts covered a generous variety of subjects, from "the memory of our brave and pious ancestors" to "a speedy and lasting union between Great Britain and her Colonies," a range of topics that managed to honor the heroes of the past while paying heed to the issues of the present—like the controversy over the detested Townshend Acts (403–5). But the tone was kept carefully conciliatory, with one possible exception, for a certain protopatriotism is detectable in the toast "May every person be possessed of the same noble sentiments against arbitrary power that our worthy ancestors were endowed with." From that dangling preposition, as from the Liberty Tree in Boston, can be seen hanging much of future moment.

When, a year later, Old Colony Day (as it was then called) was again celebrated, a few features were added to the usual course of dishes and toasts and "conversation upon the history of emigrate colonies and the constitution and declension of empires, ancient and modern" (415). Following the meal and toasts, the club members and their guests marched "in decent procession to Old Colony Hall," escorted "by a select company well skilled in the military arts." En route, they picked up another escort, "a company of children from the age of five to the age of twelve, whose natural ingenuity and the care and attention of their master had rendered them almost perfect military disciplinarians," and upon their arrival at the hall, members and guests were treated by their escorts to "a variety of maneuvres and firings, to the great satisfaction of every person present." This display of Lilliputian bellicosity was followed that evening by a bristling address by Edward Winslow Jr. that evoked the hardships suffered by the Forefathers and expressed the pious hope that the Sons would "act from the same principles and conduct [ourselves] with the same noble firmness and resolution when [our] holy religion or [our] civil liberties are invaded," remarks that were an expansion upon the protopatriotic toast of the previous year (417).

Though brief, Winslow's performance, a preview of Sam Adams's hortatory rhetoric, established a forensic precedent for future celebrations of what became known as Forefathers' Day. As in 1769, a song was composed for the occasion, which, though "set to the Tune of the British Hero," celebrated distinctly "Novanglian" heroics, and ended with a couplet evoking "Plymouth, the great mausoleum, / Famous for our forefathers' tomb!" (417–18). The poet, Alexander Scammell, then a local schoolteacher, would soon enough find opportunities to participate in the conversion of the British Hero to a hero of the Revolution: enlisting at the outbreak of the war, in 1781 he took command of a New Hampshire regiment and that same year was wounded and captured (or captured and wounded, the accounts differ) at Yorktown, dying two weeks later.

But Edward Winslow Jr., Scammell's fellow celebrant of Forefatherly courage, went a different way. In 1770, he was already an officer in the Royal Navy and would remain loyal to the Crown. At war's end, taking charge of a group of Tory exiles, Winslow emulated his Pilgrim Forefathers quite literally, setting sail for yet another wintry shore, in this case Nova Scotia, where he remained until his death in 1815. His case was hardly singular: by 1773, because of the defections of Patriot members, the Old Colony Club had become overwhelmingly Loyalist in its makeup, and following a quarrel with the local Committee of Correspondence, the club went out of existence. So much for the attempt to remain beyond politics during revolutionary times.

II

It will be remembered that in 1772 Sam Adams had praised the members of the Old Colony Club for "the religious & respectful Manner" in which they had observed the anniversary of the Landing that year. This was not a casual compound. The featured speaker was the Reverend Chandler Robbins, of the First Church in Plymouth, who had earlier attended the Old Colony celebrations and who was of the opinion, sent in a letter to the club late in 1771, that the nature of the occasion was such that a sermon extolling the Forefathers would be appropriate. He also recommended that a local clergyman be invited for the honor, and though he protested orotundly that he was not referring to himself, the members of the club duly extended Robbins his invitation. Thus it was that the ceremonies the next year, 1772, began with a hymn and a prayer, followed by Robbins's discourse, in which, according to the chronicles of the club, "after enumerating many of the virtues of our predecessors, he recounted their toils, their hazards, and their troubles, in their various attempts to shun the horrors of a despotic power and the curses of an ecclesiastical tyranny, and to obtain a land wherein they might enjoy their religion in its purity, and peace of conscience" (434).

The Reverend Robbins was, as Dr. Thacher notes in his history, a "strict Calvinist," who during his thirty-nine years of ministering to the town in its "ancient church" was at odds with most of his congregation, who drifted inexorably toward the latitudes of Unitarianism. This conflict will be examined in the proper place, but for now it is sufficient to note that Robbins never overlooked a chance to irradiate a public meeting with the light of the Gospels, most especially when the occasion allowed that the light be displayed in its ancient purity, and it was his evangelical spirit that established another major innovation in observances of the anniversary of the Landing. Hitherto, the celebration had been taking a secular direction, but thenceforth an ecclesiastical emphasis would be the rule.

In 1773, the featured speaker was the Reverend Charles Turner, of neighboring Duxbury, the second in a sequence of clergymen that would stretch into a long-lasting tradition, both in Plymouth and elsewhere. It was that scheduled event against which the intentions of the Committee of Correspondence came up the following November, eliciting from the club a disquisition on rights and privileges: "Your plans and proceedings, without advising with or consulting the other gentlemen of the town or the Club, appear to us so great an invasion of the liberty and privileges of the gentlemen of the town of Plymouth and the Old Colony Club, that we cannot approve of or comply with the same" (443). Thus the Liberty Boys were not always regarded as friendly to liberty, specifically defined, nor would their activities over the next several years modify this impression on residents of Massachusetts still loyal to the Crown.

The club had its way in 1773, and the Reverend Turner gave his discourse, but with the demise of the organization, succeeding ministers were sponsored by a public, not a private, agency for the next quarter century in Plymouth. The secular emphasis of the celebration of December 22 became supplanted by a pious one, but with no diminishment of its politicalization. As Alan Heimert and others have shown, the pulpit during the revolutionary period was a bully sounding board for patriotic ideology, and Forefathers' Day sermons of the era followed a similar line, eliciting the sufferings and triumphs of the Fathers in order to validate the radical activities of the Sons. Thus the Reverend Turner, in evoking the ghosts of the first settlers of Plymouth, had them address their descendants in sentiments that in effect gave warrant to the activities of the Committee of Correspondence, despite the sponsorship of his sermon by the Old Colony Club: " 'You are not insensible of the arduous difficulties we were called to encounter, the sea of troubles we waded through, as advocates for Heaven-born liberty; and that some of us lost our lives in freedom's sacred cause. It was, in a great measure, for your sakes, that we thus suffered'" (43). Though carefully subsumed to moral matters, Turner's subtext was written in the kind of characters that could be read on the run by departing members of the Old Colony Club.

Turner even managed to sound a paean to America's Rising Glory, the sort of thing that had been gracing college graduation exercises since 1770: marveling over the growth of civilization in North America following the arrival of the Forefathers, and granting some glimpses of its future greatness, Turner ended by alluding more or less evasively to "a prevalent spirit of inquiry [that] is among us . . . concerning the rights of the country and a prevalent disposition to assert them" (32). This tinkling cymbal became a sounding brass the following year, 1774, by which time the "prevalent spirit" had become loudly assertive, the first Continental Congress being then in session. For the minister presiding over the celebration of the Landing, the Reverend Gad Hitchcock, let fly a rhetorical broadside, identifying the common cause shared by the Forefathers and their descendants as an abiding love of Liberty, underwritten by the guarantees found in Scripture: "As far as the liberty of mankind has been impaired, and their rights invaded, and oppression and tyranny have prevailed in any kingdom or nation on earth; so far has there been a repugnance to, and a departure from the true spirit of the holy scriptures" (34).

Despite the ecclesiastical aegis, there is a certain legal logic in Hitchcock's sermon, equivalent to that in the Declaration of Independence, mounting an argument solidly based on precedent, found in both the example of the Forefathers and Holy Scripture. Nor was Hitchcock's discourse lacking in an awareness of contemporary political theory. In declaring that "Liberty is the cause of it all, and all should be ready to spend, and be spent in its service," the minister cited "Mr. Lock," who had defined Liberty as "a common cause and the right of nature," being a "self-evident" proposition that was not only supported by the Bible but witnessed in the "remarkable display of liberty in the great undertaking of our forefathers" (38, 39). In effect, Hitchcock was throwing up a wall of scriptural and historical authority, a rhetorical equivalent to the earthworks on Bunker Hill that were hastily constructed the following June.

By the time of the next celebration of the Landing, circumstances were such that the Reverend Samuel Baldwin seized the occasion to deliver a highly patriotic exercise, setting aside the ritual recital of the events that had brought the Leyden congregation to America for a chronicling of the events of the "Civil War" then in progress—the battles of Lexington, Concord, and Bunker Hill—to which he added a list of the colonists' grievances, the role of a benevolent Providence in directing their affairs, and an elaborate analogy between the fortunes of the embattled Patriots and the Israelites' sufferings while in Egypt.

Sacvan Bercovitch, following the lead of Perry Miller, has demonstrated the extent to which Puritan sermons utilize the ancient example of the Jews—whether as captives in Egypt or Babylon or marching across the wilderness toward their Promised Land—in order to direct, inform, or circumscribe the energies of their congregations. The Puritan jeremiad that emerges from this tradition frequently draws parallels between the original settlers of New England and their Israelite counterparts, and, like the prophet who gave his name to the genre, preachers like Cotton Mather drew unfavorable contrasts between those saintly colonists and the backsliding present generation. Bercovitch extends the purview of the jeremiad into the revolutionary generation of sermons, but it does seem as though a significant shift of emphasis occurred during the Revolution, namely a diminishment of the punitive, excoriating element.

Where an earlier generation of clerics had pointed to the Forefathers as exemplifying an ideal perhaps impossible to emulate, the revolutionary generation tended to set their auditors in the ancestral footsteps. They in effect put in motion a new version of the original errand, no longer defined in terms of gospel evangelism but political freedom. In summoning up the ghosts of the Forefathers, the Reverend Turner had them address their descendants directly, an intimacy of contact that may have provided the occasion for reminding the audience of the sacrifices of which they were the beneficiaries and a heritage of which they were the guardians, but which stressed an unbroken continuity, not that chasm between old and new generations that characterized the strategy of the jeremiad.

In effect, the sermons of the revolutionary period in New England provide a foretaste of the Fourth of July oration, in which ancestral accomplishments enhance the lives of the present generation, whose own achievements are likewise celebrated even as they are exhorted to strive all the harder to emulate their sires. Where the strategy of the jeremiad uses the past to berate the present, the tactics of the Forefathers' Day sermon establish an evolutionary, progressive sequence, tracing a continuous line from past to present instances. The Reverend Turner used the shades of the Forefathers primarily to warn against iniquity and sinfulness, but those kinds of ghosts were laid to rest in subsequent sermons, as preachers expanded on Turner's minority emphasis, increasingly citing the Forefathers as providing precedents warranting present actions. As in the instance of the Reverend Hitchcock's sermon, the frame becomes less eschatological than legalistic, in keeping with the lawyer-generated arguments by which the Patriot politicians asserted their rights, until Jefferson penned the most famous legal brief of all. It was quite consistent with the Enlightenment basis of the Revolution, which regarded history chiefly as a warrant for change.

A curious aspect of these celebratory and controversy-prone activities in

Plymouth is that we nowhere find a mention of Forefathers' Rock as the locus of the 1620 Landing. The elevation of the Rock in 1774 (or 1775) is without prelude in any of the highly symbolic ceremonies of the Old Colony Club, whose members were careful to bring forward whatever relics of the old time they could find—including Bradford's chair—but who, for whatever reason, neglected the Rock. And despite the presence in the Holy Scripture of equivalent monoliths, none of the early sermons sanctifying the anniversary allude to the local landmark by typological references. It was not until 1776, when the Reverend Sylvanus Conant was invited to preach upon the annual occasion, that an allusion graced by scriptural imagery can be found.

Conant devoted most of his sermon to developing the familiar analogy between the sufferings of the Forefathers and the insults then being endured by the American colonists, which, by way of the example of the Jews in the Old Testament, illustrated the doctrine that "afflictions" suffered by God's chosen people have a way of fostering "growth and increase." It is out of that extended argument that Conant's brief but for our purposes important allusion to the Rock emerged: "GOD . . . took them on the wings of his providence and wafted them over here. He set their feet upon a rock, and established them so firmly that none of the powers or machinations formed against them have been able to pluck them up; *but the more they afflicted them, the more they multiplied and grew*" (19).

Because Conant's figure is common enough in Scripture, its use may have been limited to a general reference to a rock as a symbol of endurance rather than a particularized allusion to the one in Plymouth. His passing reference to "the wings of providence" is expanded in a footnote, where he reveals his source in Deut. 32:11: "As an eagle fluttereth over her young, spreading abroad her wings, so the Lord alone did lead them." We can find in this same place in scripture a reference to God as "the Rock," whose work is "perfect," to the "Rock that begat thee," to "the Rock of his salvation" (32:4, 18, 15). But given the situation and the context, it is likely that Conant also had Forefathers' Rock in mind, as well as the *Mayflower*, perhaps, whose sails were here figured as the eaglelike wings of Providence. Notably, the Rock had a local relevance, while the sustaining Eagle was already a frequent and soon would become a standard symbol of the fledgling United States as well as a familiar figure for the aiding and abetting power of God.

If, as Bercovitch tells us, filiopietism is essential to the emerging signifiers of revolutionary sermons, then ancestor worship is inherent also to the emergence of Plymouth Rock as a sacred icon. Conant's sermon is filled with footnoted references to chroniclers of the Puritan experience, including Edward Johnson, Thomas Prince, and Thomas Hutchinson, whose histories become adjunct scriptures, further strengthening the filiopietistic connection. It is this regional particularism that recommends Conant to us, who can point to a specific "sacred point," "*this place*" as he emphasizes, and even more pointedly, if allusively, Forefathers' Rock (14). It is to that stone that he brings his providential eagle, the cruciform bird dear to much patriotic oratory to follow. Echoing John Winthrop's seamark sermon aboard the *Arbella*, Conant called upon "all Europe, and the whole world, [to] turn their eyes this way, and behold, and wonder to see these young American colonies set on fire at both ends and in the middle, and not consumed" (23). Out of such fire the Rock and Eagle first emerged, a pairing that identified the origins of the newly born United States with the advent of the Pilgrims in 1620, and out of the themes in Conant's sermon much oratory celebrating the Landing would come.

III

After 1780, no celebration of the Landing was held in Plymouth until 1793, the Pilgrims having served their purpose for the time. Unfortunately for our purposes, moreover, of the four sermons delivered between 1777 and 1779, only the first, by the Reverend Samuel West, was published. Because of this lacuna, we cannot make too much of West's failure to mention the Rock, despite his conventional association of the Forefathers with the providential history of the new nation, his American "Zion." For all we know, the other, unpublished sermons may have made up for West's neglect. More meaningful is the absence of the sacred stone from the anniversary discourse of Chandler Robbins in 1793, who broke the thirteen-year silence in Plymouth with a performance clearly calculated to rectify the hiatus, which gathered in all the established tropes of Forefathers' Day sermons.

As in his unpublished sermon of twenty-one years earlier, Robbins based his discourse on "the most noted historical facts, relative to the coming over of our forefathers," information taken by him from William Bradford's history of Plymouth as it had been transcribed by Nathaniel Morton in the manuscript "Plymouth Church Records," resulting in the first publication of what are now famous passages. Moreover, in taking his text from Psalm 77, "I will remember the works of the Lord; surely I will remember the wonders of old," and in his concomitant emphasis on God's providences in the history of New England, Robbins appears to have been self-consciously operating in the tradition of the Mathers. This textual antiquarianism is suggested also by his baroque style and his use of emphatic typographical tics, like the italics and capitalization fashionable a century earlier, along with his use of the *figura* central to the *Magnalia*: "Our history, from the *first landing* of our FATHERS in this town has been a history of wonders; and will furnish, to every generation, perhaps, as much matter for pious reflection and gratitude, as that of any nation or people that ever existed on earth. That of the children of Israel seems the nearest to resemble it: as any one may observe, who is acquainted with them both" (17). But though Robbins renders a detailed account of the Forefathers' arrival in Plymouth harbor, "here on this *very spot* which we now inhabit," perhaps because of the absence of any mention in his historical sources of the Rock, he is silent also regarding the specific feature of the "spot."

In contrast to Robbins's allusive shyness, when anniversary sermons were again commenced in Plymouth on a regular basis in 1798, both the Forefathers and their Rock appear as commonplaces, a date and emphasis we can associate with Timothy Dwight's personal testimony at the turn of the century. Climbing upon the Rock in 1800, Dwight avowed that "no New Englander who is willing to indulge his native feelings can stand upon the rock where our ancestors set the first foot after their arrival on the American shore without experiencing emotions entirely different from those which are excited by any common object of the same nature. No New Englander could be willing to have that rock buried and forgotten" (*Travels*, 3:73). These sentiments, famous in the nineteenth century, would not, however, be published for another twenty years but may be taken as typical of the emerging resolve, not only to point out Plymouth Rock but also to celebrate its singularity: "Let him reason as much, as coldly, and as ingeniously as he pleases, he will still regard this spot with emotions wholly different from those which are excited by other places of equal, or even superior importance." There is implicitly an element of ideology informing Dwight's sentimental paean, albeit an expression of a politics quite different from those of 1776, for if by 1800 the Landing had once again emerged as a political symbol, it was one with a very tight regional base, which warranted an emphasis on differences within the new nation, not revolutionary ardor.

Thus in 1801, the Reverend John Allyn ended his Forefathers' Day discourse in Plymouth with the following invocation: "May the rock of the pilgrims, and every vestige of antient times which they [of Plymouth] have among them, be associated with the recollection of those christian virtues by which their fathers were discriminated from the profane world" (34). In the following year, likewise, John Quincy Adams could deliver an oration in Plymouth—the first secular performance there on the occasion of Forefathers' Day since the brief address of Edward Winslow Jr.—in which he flattered his audience by comparing "this birth-date of your nation" (by which he meant December 22) to the obscure and often barbarous origins of other countries: "No Gothic scourge of God—No Vandal past of nations—No fabled fugitive from the flames of Troy— No bastard Norman tyrant appears among the list of worthies who first landed on the rock, which your veneration has preserved as a lasting monument of their achievement." (9).

We will consider Adams's oration at length in the next chapter, but it is necessary here to return to the activities of the Liberty Boys in Plymouth in

1774–75, which strenuously identified the Rock as the threshold of the Landing in 1620 yet which seems to have had little effect on the iconography of sermons of that period or during the quarter century following. By contrast, there is evidence that the "great rock" mentioned in a boundary description in the Plymouth town records in 1715 had been associated with the Landing well in advance of the attempts by the Patriots of Plymouth to haul it up into town. According to Dr. Thacher's history of Plymouth, it was in 1741 that the first testimony was given concerning the sanctity of the stone. Plans had been made that year to construct a wharf, made of masonry walls filled between with stones and dirt, that would surround and bury the large boulder located on the shore. News of this reached Thomas Faunce, known as Elder Faunce because of his position in the church but who was also ninety-five years old at the time. The tidings "impressed his mind with deep concern, and excited a strong desire to take a last farewell of the cherished object" (Thacher, 29).

Faunce was carried thence in a chair and bore testimony that the boulder in danger of being buried was the one "which his father had assured him was that, which had received the footsteps of our fathers on their first arrival, and which should be perpetuated to posterity." The ancient Elder then consecrated the rock with his tears "and bid to it an everlasting adieu." Since Faunce's father had come over in the *Ann* in 1623, and since Thomas himself was old enough to have known a number of the *Mayflower* passengers, his testimony was given considerable weight by later generations. It was, however, unrecorded at the time and had been conveyed to Thacher by the recollection of another resident of Plymouth, "the late venerable Deacon Spooner, who was then a boy and was present on the interesting occasion. Tradition says that Elder Faunce was in the habit on every anniversary [of the Landing] of placing his children and grand-children on the rock, and conversing with them respecting their forefathers."

Ephraim Spooner, in his turn, lived to the age of eighty-three and died one of the most beloved and respected citizens of the town. We cannot dismiss Spooner's testimony out of hand, even though the chronology indicates he was only six years old in 1741, and in Plymouth, at any rate, the passing on of this information from Elder to Deacon was regarded as equivalent to the succession of the Apostles. When, in 1817, the Reverend Horace Holley visited the town as the speaker of the day on the anniversary of the Landing, he made a point of visiting with the elderly Spooner, and in his address he noted that "Our venerable friend knew and conversed with Elder Faunce, who personally knew the first settlers, so Polycarp conversed with St. John, the beloved disciple of our Saviour" (Thacher, 229). Holley thereby gave the story of the Landing an authenticity validated by that of the Gospels.

Deacon Spooner, moreover, was the occasional guest of the Old Colony

Club and most likely shared his anecdote with the members as well as with Horace Holley fifty years later. It is all the more surprising, then, that it was not until 1774 that the Patriots of Plymouth focused the public's attention on the storied Rock by the shore. Furthermore, if the Liberty Boys were able to harness their oxen to it, then the Rock must have been for the most part exposed above the fill used to construct the wharf. This suggests that if the natives of Plymouth had not been sufficiently moved by Faunce's admonition in 1741 to locate their wharf elsewhere, they had at least kept the sacred relic elevated during the wharf's construction, where it remained in place thenceforth.

Of such compromises between commerce and piety is New England history made, and it was obviously to this half century of preservation that Dwight alluded when he declared that "no New Englander could be willing to have that rock buried and forgotten." Yet, once again, in terms of the written and published record, Plymouth Rock was for all intents and purposes a subterranean artifact until the turn of the century.

IV

To the thin filament of testimonial evidence we can add a set of secondary circumstances that surrounded the Rock in 1775. For we find that, aside from their use in Scripture, iconographic rocks had considerable contemporary ideological meaning at the start of the Revolution, specifically in the pages of the *Royal American*, a short-lived monthly published by Isaiah Thomas during that critical period. Thomas's periodical was misnamed, for it was outspokenly rebellious in its editorial policy, the Toryish look of its title providing a very thin disguise. What Sam Adams and his fellow Correspondents were accomplishing with pen and ink, Thomas gave even larger circulation in print, the items in his magazine serving to encourage and inform the efforts of the Liberty Boys throughout New England.

Nor was the past neglected in serving the immediate needs of the present, and during its single year of publication, first under the "seditious" Thomas, then under the somewhat less radical Joseph Greenleaf, the magazine serialized Thomas Hutchinson's *History of Massachusetts*, along with other material promoting "Instruction and Amusement," including patriotic poems in the "Rising Glory" vein and orations calculated to fuel the revolutionary cause. The magazine's index is a convenient gauge as well to the temper of the times, for in it we find "Corruption, the sad effects of" preceding (as cause precedes effect) "Congress, continental, list of delegates." Articles encouraging native agriculture and manufactures appear next to an essay by Dr. Franklin on waterspouts and whirlwinds. And along with Hutchinson's chronicle we have an ongoing calendar of contemporary political events, called a "history," as if the editor was aware of the cosmic signification of the times, even as he fed useful information to Patriot forces throughout the region, in effect contributing to the historical events his chronicle recorded.

But the most pertinent item for our concerns is a letter to the editor that appeared toward the end of the life of the *Royal American*, in the issue for December 1774:

> Sir,
>
> On a late excursion into the country, I met with a venerable old gentleman, on whose word I can confidently rely, who assured me, that about forty years past, a stone was dug out of a WELL in some part of the province with the following lines inscribed on it.
>
> > The EASTERN world it's glory ends
> > An empire rises where the sun DESCENDS.
>
> Upon hearing these lines repeated, I was naturally led to ask many questions relative to the place where this stone was found to have been long buried, whether it had not been preserved as a curiosity, &c., but could not obtain that satisfaction from my friend, as to the above circumstances that I wished for; that such a stone was found he well remembered, and repeatedly asserted also that it occasioned much conversation at the time.
>
> By publishing this narrative in your useful Magazine, you may be instrumental at bringing this matter further to light. It is probable that some of our inhabitants will remember the same occurrence, and be capable of giving us a more full account of it: which will be very agreeable to many of your readers, but to none more so than to your
>
> Obliged, Humble Servant.

In accordance with the correspondent's wish, further information was forthcoming in the next issue, but it turned out that what had been "dug up" was more in the way of an ossified chestnut than an ancient stone.

The response, again in the form of a letter, reached back to 1730, to yet another letter to an editor, Bartholomew Green of the *Boston News-Letter*. Green printed the letter as genuine, but according to the correspondent of 1775, it was patently a hoax, the writer having "in some dealings taken offence at Mr. Green, and probably upon that account took this method of retaliation, or perhaps he did it merely to divert himself, being a very facetious gentleman, and at that time (of controversy with Great-Britain about governor's salaries) if I remember right, a great liberty-man" (*Royal American*, 2:5). Refusing to reveal the name of the facetious gentleman, the correspondent of 1775 ends by including the letter of 1730 entire:

As your paper is the great devulgatory of all curious novelties, and as there hath been discovered in this fair town [of Plymouth] a very wonderful phenomenon, I have sent you an account thereof for the perusal of your curious readers.

Walking last week with a friend by a place where they were about to dig a seller [sic], we discovered a stone, on which there seemed to be engraved certain letters, which, when we had cleared from [them] the dirt, we read to our great astonishment, engraven very deep, the ensuing lines,

> The eastern world enslav'd, it's glory ends,
> And empire rises where the sun descends.

It seemeth to have been buried long in the earth, but as I intend to bring it with me to Boston so soon as the distemper [smallpox] is past and shew it to the curious and learned gentlemen in that place it seemeth unnecessary to give any further description thereof at present.

Your friend and servant, W. L.

We may suspect that the inquiry of December 1774 and the response in the following number of the *Royal American* may have been by the same hand. Still, the hoaxing letter of 1730 was real and seems to have had considerable contemporary and posterior fame. J. A. Leo Lemay, who discovered the original letter in the *Boston News-Letter*, notes that John Smibert, the English painter who accompanied George Berkeley to America in 1728, recorded the couplet with a brief notation of the accompanying story in his journal (*American Reader*, 39–40).

More important, Lemay observes that John Adams, in retirement, related the following anecdote in his correspondence with Dr. Benjamin Rush: having recalled the second line of a couplet, which ran, "And empire rises where the sun descends," Adams asked his brother-in-law, William Cranch, if he could recall the whole: "He paused a moment and said,—'The eastern nations sink, their glory ends, / And empire rises where the sun descends.'" Despite their similarity to George Berkeley's familiar lines, they were not, Cranch had declared, the bishop's work: "The tradition was, as he had heard it for sixty years, that these lines were inscribed, or rather drilled, into a rock on the shore of Monument Bay in our old colony of Plymouth, and were supposed to have been written and engraved there by some of the first emigrants from Leyden, who landed at Plymouth." Adams testified that he had "heard these verses for more than sixty years. I conjecture that Berkeley became connected with them, in my head, by some report that the bishop had copied them into some publication. There is nothing," concluded Adams, "in my little reading, more ancient in my memory that the observation that arts, sciences, and empire had travelled westward; and in conversation it was always added since I was a child, that their next leap would be over the Atlantic into America," obviously landing in the vicinity of Plymouth Rock (cf. *Works*, 9:599–600).

Kenneth Silverman in his cultural history of the American Revolution has enlarged at length upon this notion of westward passage—*translatio imperii*—which was common coinage in the eighteenth century, gaining considerable circulation through George Berkeley's famous lines, to which John Adams indirectly refers:

> Westward the Course of Empire takes its Way;
> The four first Acts already past,
> A fifth shall close the Drama with the Day:
> Time's noblest Offspring is the last. (*Works*, 7:373)

This stanza, though first published in 1752 as the conclusion to Berkeley's "On the Prospect of Planting Arts and Learning in America," was composed in 1726, as the then dean of Derry made plans for taking up residence in the New World, the first step in his projected plan to establish a college on Bermuda for the conversion and education of Native Americans. Perhaps Berkeley's manuscript poem advertising his plans for America had some advance circulation during and after his stay in this country, lending encouragement to the protonationalism then on the move.

On the other hand, the contents of Smibert's journal indicate that the notion of western progress was very much in the air in America when he and Berkeley arrived. Along with the "Plymouth" lines already mentioned, we find on the same page this set of couplets:

> Let lawles power in the East remain
> And never Cros the wide Atlantick main
> Here flourish learning trade & wealth increas
> The hapy fruits of liberty and peace. (102)

Smibert does not identify the source of these sentiments, less concerned with Virtue and the Muses than commercial transactions, but they seem of distinctly contemporary New England manufacture. They are in keeping with other doggerel copied down by Smibert, like those "fixed upon the Town House in Boston" or upon "the Meeting House door att Roxbury when the Assembly were Sitting there Anno 1733," which last contains these distinctly filiopietistic sentiments, prophetic of the rhetoric of 1774 and afterward:

> Our Fathers crost the wide Atlantick Sea
> And blest themselves, when in the desart free

And Shal their Sons thro treachery or fear
Give up that freedom which has Cost So dear? (103)

There was a considerable quantity of protopatriotic poetry and even drama generated in Boston during the early 1730s, inspired not by Berkeley's verses but by the ongoing quarrel between the legislature and royal governor over the matter of the gubernatorial salary. We can look back at the letter of 1730 and note the explanation of 1775, that the writer was of the "liberty party" during that dispute, which means that he was one in sentiments with the lines posted to the Roxbury Meeting House. David Shields has investigated in detail the pamphleteering war of the 1730s and has rendered in clear outlines the complex allegiances and politics of that troubled time. We may therefore say with some assurance that the author of the hoax letter was most likely an Old Charter man, who stood for the absolute authority (liberty) of the assembly in setting the governor's salary. Moreover, as John Adams's recollections attest, the couplet had a long patriotic life well beyond the issues that inspired it.

We should not exaggerate the importance of that decidedly occasional poem, but it is sufficient for our purpose to note the extent to which ancient rocks and libertarian sentiments were coupled in the minds of Massachusetts Patriots in 1774–75. In the same December issue of the *Royal American* that told the story of the fabulous stone in Plymouth, there was published a dream vision, an allegory in the revolutionary vein that featured a "stately fabrick" built upon "a rock which seemed to be placed there by nature" (471). The meaning of both the building and its foundation stone was given in the correspondence section of the following number of the magazine, along with the story behind the story of the rock dug up in Plymouth: The stately fabric, which combined both modern and ancient parts, was "the English constitution," whose "chief corner-stone, or greatest rock of safety," was "Magna Charta, or the natural liberties of the people," which, as the Patriots' argument went in 1774–75, included Englishmen in North America (4). In this number of the *Royal American* there also appeared a lengthy "view of the most remarkable sufferings and deliverances of our Ancestors [at Plymouth]; together with a brief account of the most singular interventions of divine providence in favour of English Americans down to the present day," along with a description of the way in which saltpeter, essential to the composition of gunpowder, can be made, "for the encouragement of arts, manufactures and commerce" (18).

These contingencies give added meaning to the self-conscious activities of the Liberty Boys of Plymouth during the same period, which in turn inspired the sentiments recorded in the journal of a young surgeon's mate who in 1775 was en route from his home in Barnstable to the encampment of Washington's army in Cambridge: passing through Plymouth, he paid a visit to Meeting

House Square and its Rock, which, "with its associations, would seem almost capable of imparting that love of country, and that moral virtue, which our times so much require. We seem holding converse with the celestial spirits, and receiving monition from those who are at rest in their graves. . . . Can we set our feet on their rock without swearing, by the spirit of our fathers, to defend it and our country?" (Thacher, *Journal*, 22). The man who wrote these words was the same whose history of Plymouth, published more than a half century later, would further memorialize Forefathers' Rock—by then called Plymouth Rock, and well on its way to becoming a national symbol.

But Dr. Thacher's remarks in 1775 attest (allowing always for the possibility that they were inserted in his journal at a later time) to the extent to which that landmark and its associated saints had already been politicized by the events preceding the outbreak of the Revolution. Though distinctly a local artifact, it was as an ideological icon with nationalistic significance that the Rock was lifted up and placed next to that undeniably political symbol, a Liberty Pole. At some point during this sacramentalizing process, the Patriots of Plymouth painted on their otherwise unadorned monument the date 1620, which gave the Rock its iconic identity. It thereby became an omphalos, a knot securing the present to the past, giving a new nation its vital connection with the power of memory, secured to a point identified with the initial settlement of Puritan New England.

Thenceforth, the Rock in Plymouth would serve future patriots as a noumenon, vibrant with historic and pious associations, borrowing power and meaning from both the past and the present moment. We may again quote John Adams, who at the time the Old Colony was founded was writing his influential dissertation on canon and feudal law, and who upon at least one occasion was the guest of the club. But it was other and subsequent associations that led him to proclaim in his autobiographical notes, written in 1805, that his dissertation should have been entitled "An essay on Forefathers' rock" (*Works*, 3:284). Because by 1805, thanks in part to his son's oratorical genius, the Rock had taken on a decidedly Federalist signification, as a subsequent generation took its turn at romancing that stone.

CHAPTER 3

The Federalists Take Their Stand on the Rock

*The Federalists stood upright, and their feet were firmly planted
on the rock of aristocracy, but that rock was bedded in the sands, or
rather was a boulder from the Old World, and the tide of democracy
was surely and swiftly undermining it.*
—*Catharine M. Sedgwick*

I

When the Great Awakening swept through New England in the
1740s, the members of the First Church (Congregational) in Plymouth were
especially hard hit by the evangelical virus, carried by a succession of the
"burning and shining lights" brought to a glare by the example and influence
of George Whitefield. The stock in trade of these itinerant preachers was a
lavish excoriation of their auditors for sinfulness, and there was apparently a
great hunger in New England for such abuse, no less so in the Old Colony than
elsewhere. For some, however, a sufficiency served as a feast, and a line was
crossed by the Reverend Andrew Croswell, whose antics in the service of grace
abounding included inviting women, children, and Negroes into the pulpit to
preach. Croswell was countenanced and encouraged by the local pastor, the
Reverend Nathaniel Leonard, but not all of his congregation were so affir-
matively minded. Eighty parishioners departed in 1744 and established the
Third Church of Plymouth, which remained separated from the First until the
furor and fervency of the Awakening had passed by.

According to James Thacher, among those who departed was the venerable
Thomas Faunce, who died the following year, and the coincidence of Faunce's
giving testimony at Forefathers' Rock just as the Great Awakening was erupting
suggests that the Elder may have been as much disturbed by this visible threat
to the Good Old Way as he was by the encroachments of commerce upon the
sacred stone. That Faunce resisted the blandishments of the New Lights does
not necessarily align him with any particular political group, though David
Shields maintains that in Boston many of the New Charter men were also Old

Light Congregationalists. Rather, it testifies that the Rock could serve as a signifier for the conservative impulse even as, thirty-five years later, it was seized by the Liberty Boys for radical purposes. After all, the gradual transformation of the Old Colony Club from protopatriots resisting the encroachment of the British Parliament on their freedoms to temporizers opposed to the extremes of those such as Sam Adams, an evolution accompanied by the co-opting by the Liberty Boys of the occasion first celebrated by the club, suggests the friability of both political allegiances and political symbols during the period preceding the Revolution.

Moreover, what happened to the constituency of the Old Colony Club during the revolutionary epoch was repeated throughout Massachusetts during the postrevolutionary years. That is, by the end of the century many of the radical Republicans of the earlier period had become reactionary Federalists. Like the Loyalist members of Winslow's club, they were unwilling to be carried any further by the popular impulse than their innately conservative instincts permitted. Though at the national level the Federalists were increasingly a minority, challenged by the Jeffersonian Republicans and turned out of office by Jefferson's victory of 1800, they remained powerful in New England, an embattled and increasingly embittered sectional majority. So it was that when Forefathers' Rock reemerged as a symbol, it was as a conservative, not a radical, icon. Much as Elder Faunce seems to have identified the Landing of the Fathers with the Good Old Way, so the Federalists of Massachusetts some sixty years later looked to the Rock as a symbol of the Grand Old Cause.

When in 1798 the celebration of December 22 once again went public in Plymouth, the Federalists were clearly in charge. The affair began on a high and disinterested plane, with a prayer offered up by Chandler Robbins, who, according to the *Columbian Centinel*, a Federalist paper in Boston, "in a reverential and impressive manner, peculiar to himself," gave thanks to "the Supreme Ruler of the Universe" for his providential aids to the small but heroic group of settlers "who at this inclement season began *here*" that community that "has scarcely a parallel in the annals of mankind" (Matthews, 309). Robbins was followed by Dr. Zacheus Bartlett, whose oration, according to the *Centinel*, "feelingly pointed out the striking events which distinguished the enterprise of our ancestors, and introduced and enforced many excellent political observations." Bartlett's speech was not published, and we can only guess at the drift of his "observations," but some hint of the temper of the times is provided by what occurred during and after the banquet that followed his performance.

The meal featured the traditional Old Colony Club menu of wild game and fish, but a newly added feature was "a piece of the *consecrated rock*," which decorated and helped to heighten "the pleasures of the social board." The banquet was further enhanced "by commemorating the eventful scenes of which our mother town has been the theatre," and a patriotic spirit was evinced by such songs as "Adams and Liberty" and "Hail Columbia," "sung with great animation and applause." Then the toasts began, starting with general and nonpolitical sentiments, like the one to the town of Plymouth: "May every view of the *consecrated rock*, excite in its inhabitants an emulation of the enterprize and industry of the first settlers." But soon enough Federalist bile began to surface, and Massasoit became the unlikely occasion for a Francophobic blast, his "unshaken adherence to treaties" providing "a dignified contrast to the 'punic faith' of modern Frenchmen" (310).

Toward the end of the evening in Plymouth, the toasts became even more sectionally partisan, celebrating "the Fisheries" (always a subject dear to New England and the Adamses) and awarding "unfading laurels to the able negotiators, who secured to the *United States* this incalculable source of wealth and nursery of seamen." And, finally, the celebrants hoisted glasses of pure vitriol to Jeffersonian Republicans, pledging the hope that Congress would soon "be purged from the unblushing perfidy of Mason, and the polluted saliva of Lyon." (Senator Stevens Thomson Mason of Virginia was one of the chief defenders of Matthew Lyon, a Vermont congressman and Jeffersonian Republican, who had recently been fined and sentenced to jail after infuriating Federalists by spitting in the face of Roger Griswold of Connecticut in response to an insult.) The *Centinel* reported this last toast without comment, but it did not go unremarked by the Republican press.

Two days later, the *Independent Chronicle*, having praised the performances of Robbins and Bartlett as doing "real honor to the memory of their departed worthies," thought otherwise of "the doings of some Federalists . . . *after* Dinner" (Matthews, 311). In the opinion of the *Chronicle*, it "is a melancholy discovery that in Plymouth as well as Boston, there are too many of their Posterity who dishonor them by their sentiments and practises, and are melancholy evidences that they are indeed the DEGENERATE *Plants of a* NOBLE VINE." The reference to Boston should be well taken, for it was in that same year of 1798 that Forefathers' Day was celebrated for the first time in that city, in emulation of the Plymouth custom, and the affair from the start was openly Federalist in sentiments and (to the *Chronicle*) offensively so.

The Boston celebration on December 22 was called the "Feast of Shells," a complex allusion referring to the prevalence of shellfish served, to the Ossianic poems of James Macpherson, in which shells are used for festive drinking, and to the symbolic scallop shell carried by early Christian pilgrims to the Holy Land. According to Albert Matthews, this was the first public occasion on which the founders of Plymouth received what became the customary designation. Thus the toasts began with " 'The Pilgrims of Leyden' . . . May the

Empire which has sprung from their labours be permanent as the *rock of their landing,*" a coupling of icons that was innocent enough perhaps but surely explains the appeal of Forefathers' Rock to the conservative sensibility (Matthews, 324).

Of a more pointedly Federalist kind was the toast to "the swords of *Endicott* and *Standish,* by which the first *Sedition Pole* in New-England was demolished," an allusion to Morton's Maypole on Merrymount and a suggestion that Liberty Poles were no longer welcome in Massachusetts. The allusion was further embellished by the wish that "all movers of Sedition, and lords of misrule, whether native or imported, meet the fate of Oldham and Morton, of Mount Wallaston!" There followed a flexing of "the strong arm of government," lifting not a sword but a glass against "*intriguing aliens* and *seditious citizens,*" pointed references to the Alien and Sedition Acts of 1798. A Federalist measure taken in direct response to the XYZ Affair, the acts were but the most potent evidence of the general paranoia frequently expressed by John Adams's party, whether in office or out.

From the start the Rock figured largely in the toasts, whether as in the literal reference quoted above or in contexts supporting elaborate allegories. Thus the federal Constitution was compared to "the shallop of our fathers," in the hope that it might "find a '*Rock*' and a shelter in *Old Colony* virtues and principles!" And Thomas Pickering, the rabid Francophobe then secretary of state, was toasted as "the rock of State, firm while Frenchmen froth around its base" (325). But the most extensive and meaningful evocation of the Rock of the Forefathers occurred in a song written for the Feast of Shells by "Mr. Thomas Paine" (this was the "Boston Paine," who shortly afterward, for obvious reasons, changed his name to Robert Treat Paine), in the second stanza of which the poet celebrated the sacred stone in transcendental terms:

> Round the consecrated ROCK,
> Convened the patriarchal stock,
> And there, while every lifted hand
> Affirmed the charter of the land,
> The storm was hush'd, and round the zone
> Of heaven the mystic *meteor* shone;
> Which, like that rainbow seen of yore,
> Proclaim'd that SLAVERY'S FLOOD was o'er,
> That pilgrim man, so long oppres'd,
> Had found his promis'd *place of rest.*

There is an essential, if intended, confusion here: Paine, by figuring the Pilgrims as "affirming the charter" while standing around the Rock, managed to conflate the Mayflower Compact with the document sacred to the Bay Colony. In another place in his song, Paine called upon the "Heirs of Pilgrims" to renew the Forefathers' Oath, another definably Boston touch that melded the founders of Plymouth with their Puritan compeers. Working toward the same end were the decorations of the hall, which included not only the "swords of CARVER and STANDISH," hanging at the ready should occasion provide a target of importunity, but a portrait of "the pious WILSON" (327). In effect, these acts of incorporation transported both the Pilgrims and their Rock to Boston, enlisting them in the service of the Federalist Party, as when the toasts to certified Pilgrim worthies, like Bradford, Brewster, and Carver, went on to include John Winthrop, "who had the honor of being calumniated by the *Jacobins* of his time."

The Boston papers differed dramatically (and predictably) in their accounts of the Feast of Shells. Thus the *Columbian Centinel*, in an account that used for the first time the designation "Plymouth Rock" (unnecessary in the town where it was located), assured its Federalist subscribers that the toasts delivered "evinced that the spirit of the *Old Colony* patriots had been bequeathed to the inheritors of their soil" (Matthews, 327). But the *Independent Chronicle* observed, quite to the contrary, that the custom of raising toasts was anathema to the "Heavenly Pilgrims": "To have *heard* 29 toasts given, must immediately have ended their journey through this then howling wilderness, and carried them strait [*sic*] to their desired home" (329).

This matter of toasts remained a sore point of contention for the next several years. The celebration in Boston in 1799 took a less partisan course, perhaps because the news of Washington's death came in the midst of the festivities and like the appearance of Banquo's ghost cast a fatal shadow over the banquet, serving as a reminder that in his farewell address he had spoken out against partisan and sectional bickering. But in 1800 and for a while thereafter party sentiments became increasingly outspoken, while the response in Republican newspapers grew all the more self-righteous concerning the inappropriateness of feasting and drinking to excess in the name of the Forefathers: "Oh! the rare sons of the pilgrims! eating and carousing to celebrate the *hardships*, *toils*, and *dangers* of their forefathers!" (341). In 1805, adding insult to inebriation, the celebrants broke into a spirited rendition of "Rule Britannia," which seemed to Republicans an outrageous profanation of the day sacred to the memory of the Separatists.

With that air of outraged morality dear to political pundits, the *Independent Chronicle* observed that the phenomenon of "a merchant [sitting] with composure to hear a song in praise of a nation which had interdicted almost the whole commerce of this country, is as remarkable as any narrative we could find in Mather's Magnalia" (Matthews, 346). Employing even stronger language, a letter to the *Chronicle* signed "Agricola" accused "the terrible party . . .

of colonel Hamilton" of seditious activities, singing the hymn "of one party in the European war" even as "we are contending for the important and enriching privileges of national nutrality [*sic*]" (347–48). The accusation of sedition was a well-aimed blow to the stomachs of the party that had framed the infamous acts, most particularly when its support of England was in part an attack on the French.

In 1805, as now, huffing leads to puffing, and a Federalist response to Agricola appeared in the pages of the *Centinel*: having accused his opponent of "wanton perversion of language" and a "malignant and unqualified calumny of good citizens and respectable men," the writer denigrated Agricola as an "occasional contributor . . . whose delirious effusions exhibit a melancholy picture of human extravagance and folly" (348). Still, it seems to have finally occurred to the Federalists that their hilarity at the expense of their political adversaries was having an adverse effect on their collective reputation. For whatever reason, the anniversary celebrations in Boston after 1805 became much more moderate in tone and less political in coloration, and the sobering custom of inviting a clerical speaker for the occasion was renewed.

It is notable that in attacking the Federalists, Republican writers paid at least lip service to the Forefathers, portrayed as sober, pious persons who would have been horrified at the goings-on during the Feasts of Shells. Still, it is also clear that at the turn of the century Plymouth Rock and the Pilgrims had been pretty much taken over as rhetorical tokens by the Federalists, though the invention of those iconic designations did not grant them a monopoly. Thus the Washington Society of Boston, a group of young men organized in 1805 for the purpose of challenging the Federalist hegemony when it came to celebrating the Fourth of July, devoted their toasts and celebratory odes for the most part to the heroes of the Revolution but took care as well to celebrate upon occasion "Plymouth's fam'd rock . . . impress'd" by the feet of "the Pilgrims . . . who from tyranny wander'd" to the American shore (*Historical View*, 89). The Washingtonians, however, were careful to resurrect the Liberty Pole so abhorrent to the Federalist muse, and in the same poem celebrating the Pilgrims and their Rock, they had the spirit of "Freedom" plant her standard on the sacred spot of the Landing.

There was perhaps a calculated impudence in imitating the Liberty Boys by raising a Pole in proximity to the Rock, and the Federalists' association of that libertarian symbol with Morton's defiant pagan erection was not entirely factitious. Though the Liberty Pole has a traceable iconographic genealogy, emerging from the cartoon wars in Great Britain during the heyday of John Wilkes, as Carla Mulford has discovered, radical intellectuals like Joel Barlow regarded it as obvious in its phallicism, at once a generative and an obscene signifier. So also Morton's pagan pole, which when coupled with the disruptive actions of the Master of the Revels at Merrymount—which included cohabiting with Indian women—made it over into an equivalent phallic token. We need not assume that Jeffersonian Republicans were familiar with Barlow's musings, which were in any event confided to his journal, nor with the arcane evolution he traced, in order to entertain the notion that the Liberty Pole had a phallic connotation. Hogarth's much circulated caricature of John Wilkes, which has the radical champion of Liberty holding a pole at the end of which is hung a chamber pot, gives the patriot a salacious grin that, along with the slant and placing of the pole, lends the picture an obvious sexual implication.

II

The contingency of May- and Liberty Poles observed by both the radical Republican Joel Barlow and New England Federalists is further developed in a play published in Boston in 1802. The author was Joseph Croswell, a merchant from Plymouth and the son of the evangelical minister who had caused so much ruckus there some sixty years earlier. Croswell as a young man had twice been a guest of the Old Colony Club, and his play is high on filiopietism; moreover, like the ceremonies celebrating Forefathers' Day in Plymouth and Boston at the turn of the century, it has a detectably Federalist bias. Entitled *A New World Planted; or, The Adventures of the Forefathers of New-England*, the drama is an interesting, if unlikely, hybrid produced by the marriage of Shakespeare's *The Tempest* and Bradford's account of the Pilgrims' first years in America, as told by his son-in-law, Nathaniel Morton.

Croswell's prologue draws the customary analogies between the Pilgrims and the Israelites, who under Moses fled the pharaoh, and then asks that Time "retrograde his flight" so as to carry the audience back to 1620, "Then o'er the far fam'd Rock . . . take his stand, / That we may see the worthy patriarchs land" (v–vi). The opening curtain reveals a representation of "Plymouth shore, the ship at anchor within the beach, the boat at the rock on which the passengers land," and with the entrance of the principal Pilgrims, the author abandoned rhymed couplets for blank verse (7). Again, Shakespeare is the model, for as in *The Tempest*, Croswell gives us a composite story of conspiracy overthrown and the imposition of a new order on the land, an action framed with Morton's *Memorial* in hand but the Alien and Sedition Acts in mind.

The play begins with a conversation between Carver, Bradford, Brewster, Warren, Winslow, and Standish, who give thanks to the "great disposer of events," including Brewster's acknowledgment of the divine wisdom that had separated New England from Old with a "vast sea" that will serve as "a barrier to screen us from our foes" and guarantee "a safe retreat from persecution's rage" (7). The notion of New World asylum is also emphasized by Winslow, who prophesies that the "friendly rock, projecting in the sea, / Affording us a safe and easy landing, / Will be remembered by our grateful sons," and the accommodating landscape is soon personified by the entrance of Samoset (with his familiar greeting) and Squanto (8). Things go swimmingly for a time between the Pilgrims and the Indians under Massasoit, harmony sped along by "Pocahonte," Massasoit's daughter and an aboriginal Miranda. Although she is dressed in civilized garb "that Samoset procur'd for her in England," it is the maiden's wild beauty that attracts a young man named Hampden, unrecorded among the *Mayflower* passengers but identified in the dramatis personae as "a young gentleman, who came to view the Country." The name Pocahonte suggests the early history of Virginia, not Plymouth Plantation, and when the young man announces his intention to marry Massasoit's daughter, he does so in a manner evoking Rolfe's famous deliberation on the consequences of his taking the hand of that other Indian princess. This anomalous matter takes up little room in the play, however: Pocahonte is no sooner introduced than she leaves the stage in search of her Ferdinand, who has likewise strayed off, and the two are inexplicably never seen or heard of again.

Instead, the burden of the play concerns the evil plot hatched by a band of conspirators, who are motivated by religious and personal concerns and seek "to overturn this mushroom government." Their names are familiar in the early record of the Puritans in America: Lyford, Oldham, Billington, and one "Molton," he of the Maypole having apparently had his name thus garbled to avoid confusion with Morton of the *Memorial*, from whom Croswell took his material. Predictably, the Pilgrims defeat the conspirators and in a concluding trial opt for leniency, banishing their enemies rather than putting them to death, another circumstance dictated by history but which Croswell makes much of. Once again, through Governor Carver the author evokes echoes of Shakespeare. This time it is the *Merchant of Venice*, for Carver defines Mercy as a "sublime and of a heavenly extract," the exercise of which elevates the soul "towards the exalted station of the Angels," diffusing "beneficence" through the landscape, thereby creating an equivalent heaven on earth: "O may this principle be fostered here. And always flourish with unfading lustre" (42).

Such sentiments modify the Federalist bias of Croswell's play, admitting a utopian note that seems more in keeping with Jeffersonian views. True, the author was held by historical accuracy to judicial leniency, yet Carver is given final lines in the drama that seem curiously out of line with the implication of the main story, with its paranoid emphasis on the idea of enemies working from within. Assuming the role of a prophet, he looks forward to the day when "this country may become a paradise, / Compared to the oppressed states of Europe," "halcyon days" to which the Forefathers "serve as humble 'stepping stones.'"

Of a similarly radical purport is the epilogue to the play, in which Elder

Brewster takes his turn as prophet, discerning "the future destinies of our new State": "Before my sight, new towns successive come, / Emerging from the forest's shady gloom." Brewster's vision in effect returns the scene to the present moment, making an obligatory mention of the Revolution and George Washington and ending on the brink of "the nineteenth century," where the "new blessings" enjoyed by the country "portend the great millennium is near" (45). In these concluding heroic couplets, Croswell seems to be borrowing prophetic fire from Joel Barlow's *The Vision of Columbus*, a poem associated with Jacobinism and Thomas Jefferson.

If Croswell's drama is not easy to parse politically, that is because he seems to be attempting to cover as many ideological bases as possible. Thus a kind of political balance between paranoia and promise is achieved in the opening lines of the play, spoken with the *Mayflower* and Plymouth Rock in the background, as the gathered Pilgrims wax enthusiastic about the opportunities for a profitable (because easily defended) settlement suggested by the surrounding landscape: Thus "towering" forests promise to provide timber for "navies in embryo" as well as lumber for "stately domes," while "These massy rocks, high cliffs and sounding shore, / Are fix'd as faithful centinels to check / The bold invasions of the encroaching sea" (8). The harboring fortress provided by nature keys the essentially defensive strategy of the play, which is a thoroughly statist drama, celebrating the establishment of authority over the forces of subversion from within and opposing force to armed attack from without. As for the "massy rocks," Croswell seems to have in mind another coastline, rather than Plymouth's, which in 1620 was a sandy beach with only one rock, though he was not the first (nor last) to depict the Landing in terms of a "sounding shore."

In the setting of his opening scene, Croswell may have been indebted to another drama produced in Boston that was also concerned with the Landing of the Forefathers. On April 12, 1799, there appeared in the *Massachusetts Mercury* an announcement of a new play, "Plymouth Rock; or, The Landing of our Forefathers," accompanied by a synopsis of the action that bears comparison with Croswell's: "In Scene l. A view of the Rock, and Plymouth Bay, and the landing of the Pilgrims in the year 1620, Dec. 22d, the first treaty with the Indians, their treachery in seizing two of the Pilgrims, and the ceremony used in cutting victims to death; their lives preserved by the arrival of the Captain and sailors, the cutting of the year and month on the Rock the naming of the place of their landing."

Again, there is a conflation of the Pilgrim experience with that of the Jamestown colony, capture and torture having no place in the early chronicles of Plymouth, but this negative emphasis was countered by staging "*An Indian Marriage and Nuptial Dance*" as an interlude between the first and second acts, followed in turn during the second act by the portrayal of "The Feast of our Forefathers," sans drinking shells we must assume, although the diners were treated to a rendition of "an ODE, on their landing, written by Thomas Paine." Following the feast, "the Goddess of Liberty appears to the Pilgrims," and she, like Brewster in Croswell's drama, foresees "the heroes that will fight for Liberty and Columbia."

In 1808, there opened in Boston on December 23, the day after Forefathers' Day, a "new Melodrama" entitled "The Pilgrims; or, The Landing of our Forefathers at Plymouth Bay, and the landing of the Pilgrims," making a distinction apparently between the vanguard led by Miles Standish and the main body of the settlers. The scene "represents Winter, with a snow storm. After returning thanks to Heaven for their safe arrival, Carver orders one of the Pilgrims to cut on the rock . . . the day of their landing." What follows is an expansion of the essential conflict in the play of 1799, namely hostilities between red men and white, this time involving the capture by Samoset of "Juliana," a situation and a heroine clearly borrowed from contemporary frontier literature.

The situation is resolved when Juliana, having "ascended a [not the] rock," crowns Samoset with her fusee, sending him "headlong down the precipice." As in the play of 1799, this mayhem was followed by a tableau, in which "*The Genius of Columbia descends in a Magnificent Temple, surrounded with Clouds*" (Matthews, 343–44). The chief importance here of this elaborate nonsense is the evidence it contains, first, of the tendency of dramatists of the period to ignore the historical record, and second, of the relatively rapid emergence of the formularization of the Landing as a standard set piece, with the *Mayflower* in the background and men carving the date on the Rock.

Because the Feasts of Shells seem to have inspired these productions—as the use of Paine's ode during the festivities of 1798 and the drama six months later suggest—this replicated stage set may possibly be traced to a work of art produced to accompany the celebrations in Boston, an invitation bearing a cartouche engraved by the Boston artist-illustrator Sam Hill that seems to date from 1798 (though the only recorded example bears the date December 22, 1800). Hill's engraving shows a small group of men dressed as sailors making the shallop fast to a rock bearing the date of the Landing. In the background sits a ship, obviously the *Mayflower*, but with the outlines of a contemporary square-rigger, while on a wintry and snowclad shore stand two Indians, awaiting their visitors' arrival. Below, there is another design, surrounding the rubric of the invitation, showing Plymouth Harbor in modern times, filled with shipping and a rock bearing the names of the principal Pilgrims. If not an allegory celebrating Columbia or Liberty, this is surely a tableau suggesting the blessings of same.

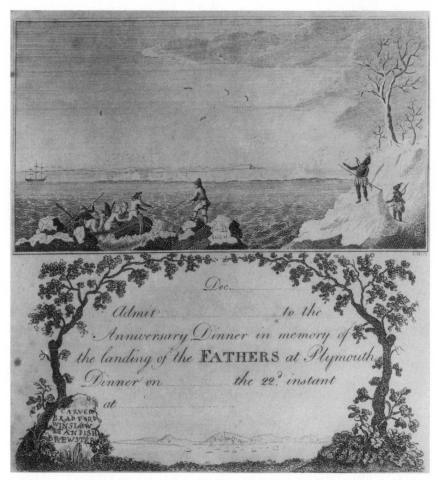

FIGURE 8. An engraved invitation to an early Feast of Shells in Boston, ca. 1798–1800. The work of Sam Hill, it was either derived from or inspired the painting by Michel Felice Corné, which follows. As in much of the rhetoric associated with the Landing, the past is underwritten by the present moment, the prosperity of which is the result of the Forefathers' sacrifices and is contrasted with the bleak scene in 1620. (Courtesy American Antiquarian Society)

Engravers of the eighteenth century (vide Paul Revere) were capable of creating their own designs, but there is a painting of the same period that bears close comparison with Hill's composition, a historical scene executed by the French émigré artist Michel Felice Corné (ca. 1752–1845), known for his marine scenes, landscapes, murals, panoramas, and portraits—and for having introduced the tomato to American cuisine. At least two versions exist of this picture, and it seems unlikely that a person of such talent would have sedulously copied out Hill's little design in large. It is also unlikely that either artist

FIGURE 9. Corné's first version of *The Landing of the Forefathers*, ca. 1798–1800. Note the rocky coast, not a feature of the Plymouth shore, and the witnessing Native Americans, a convention used in most depictions of landings, whether that of Columbus or later arrivals. (Courtesy Pilgrim Society)

ever viewed the beach at Plymouth, for as in Croswell's description (which they predate) their seascapes show the coast as rock-begirded.

This anomalousness was continued in a much more ambitious painting, first exhibited at the Feast of Shells in 1802, Henry Sargent's *The Landing of the Fathers*, a truly monumental composition executed in the grand historic manner of Benjamin West (see fig. 2). Once again, the landing site is depicted as rocky and desolate, with consequences of considerable duration, and Sargent's painting had further circulation by means of a colored print. I have earlier pointed to the scarlet coat worn by the governor, a touch that may well have been in the name of historical accuracy but between 1798 and 1815 had also a political coloration. That is, insisting on the allegiance in 1620 of the Pilgrims to the British Crown could hardly been viewed with disfavor by die-hard Federalists, who were apt to burst into "Rule, Brittania" at the drop of a tricorn.

Something of this is further suggested by a variation on his depiction of the Landing painted by Corné that recently came to light. It is similar to the other composition with two telling differences. Now the shallop is partly filled with

FIGURE 10. Corné's second version of the *Landing*, with a boat full of lobsterbacks in keeping with the spirit (and menu) of the Federalists' feasts, but the changed posture of the sailor on the Rock suggests that though the artist was a royalist émigré he retained the Frenchman's traditional Anglophobia. (Courtesy Vose Galleries; photo by Clive Ross)

men sitting in military postures and dressed in the famous red coats, a revision we might interpret as sympathetic to the Federalist position regarding Great Britain except for the second difference. For the sailor standing on the Rock has reversed his posture: instead of pulling on the line, he has turned around and is bending over. His hands are busy securing the rope, but his raised backside suggests something other than reverence for Old England. Still, the standing figure in the boat (looking forward not only to the New World but to Leutze's unforgettably unsailorlike winter Crossing) is wearing a costume with a Continental-army look. Moreover, many of the other passengers are dressed in civilian clothes, so we cannot draw hard and fast conclusions regarding the possibility of Republican (or Francophile) sympathies indicated here.

What is undeniable, however, is that the introduction of Plymouth Rock and the Landing to both art and literature was the direct result of its having been metaphorically transported from Plymouth to Boston, part and parcel of the Federalist attack on the Republican ascendancy. Thenceforth, the Rock and its Pilgrims were identified with the embattled New England hegemony. It would be a century-long (and losing) struggle to insist upon the region's edge on rectitude and intellect, as well as its priority in establishing those institutions identified with the new and rising Republic, including universal education and civil rights. If New England, in Lawrence Buell's terms, had a "culture," then central to its artifacts are the various celebrations and depictions of the Landing that emerge between 1798 and 1804, inspired by the Federalists' Feasts of Shells, an event that had its origins during the disputes with Great Britain that preceded the Revolution but which by 1800 were identified with maintaining British ties. This is less a contradiction than a continuity, attesting to the intensely political circumstances attending the emergence of the Pilgrims on their Rock as a popular icon.

III

A seal of sorts on the process by which the Landing took on a political coloration is provided by the history of New England written by Jedidiah Morse and Elijah Parish and published in the key year 1804. Buell has identified this as a definably conservative item in the ongoing debate between theological liberals and orthodox Calvinists, about which more will be heard later on. But there was certainly no harder-line a Federalist than Morse, whose pamphlets started brushfires of Francophobic paranoia during the last years of the eighteenth century. Equally assertive, if more in the optative vein, is Morse's digression on the celebrations of the anniversary of the Pilgrims' Landing, "observed by their immediate descendants at Plymouth, as a religious festival. A discourse is delivered adapted to the occasion; after public worship, more forcibly to impress their minds with the circumstances of their meritorious forefathers, clams, fish, ground nuts, and victims from the forest, constitute a part of their grateful repast.... It is a festival rational, and happy in its tendency. It reminds the guests of the virtues and sufferings of their fathers; by a comparison of circumstances it excites transports of gratitude, elevates the affections, and mends the hearts" (44–45). A Jeffersonian Republican might have enlarged upon the nature of the circumstances that "excited transports of gratitude," but Morse provided no opportunity in his book for a retaliatory response.

Morse further validated the importance of Forefathers' Day by including an appendix to his history that contains fifteen pages of "elegant and appropriate extracts and poetical pieces ... added as proper lessons for youth in academies and schools to commit to memory, and exhibit as oratorical exercises," all of which are taken from recent anniversary addresses. Included are extracts from the orations given in Plymouth by Judge John Davis in 1800, John Quincy

Adams in 1802, and the Reverend John T. Kirkland, then a Harvard professor but soon to become president of the college, in 1803. Of these three orations, only Adams's was printed elsewhere in full, and though we owe Morse a measure of gratitude for preserving at least in part the words of Davis and Kirkland, it is Adams's performance that would have the greatest future resonance.

Davis and Kirkland found the moment opportune to rehearse yet again the circumstances of the Landing, the sufferings and triumph of the Forefathers, and the wisdom of recurring to their "good old ways" as correctives to "modern degeneracy." But the son of John Adams and the heir apparent of New England Federalism took a somewhat different tack, interesting himself in the purely political aspect of the Pilgrims' arrival. Having pointed to the singularly bloodshedless chronicles of the Pilgrims as a unique inheritance and having emphasized their honest dealings with the Indians, Adams passed on to stress not the fact of arrival but the framing of the document known as the Mayflower Compact (24). This was a major departure from earlier (and much subsequent) practice, but then, as we have seen, Forefathers' Day discourse had been largely dominated by an ecclesiastical, not civil, venue. In effect, John Quincy Adams's political and legalistic stress was a logical extension of the sequence by which the Rock had become in Federalist rhetoric both a symbol of the Pilgrim advent and a *figura* for the Constitution. In time, moreover, the Mayflower Compact would displace Boston's "Magna Charta" as the document central to the process and would be celebrated as a prolegomenon to the Constitution itself.

Albert Matthews long ago credited Adams with having rescued the compact from historical obscurity, but Wesley Frank Craven has since pointed to a predecessor in the popular annalist George Chalmers, who in 1780 gave considerable emphasis to the compact in a discussion of New England's institutions that is sympathetic to the Pilgrims. And Chalmers inspired James Wilson of Philadelphia, who, in an influential series of lectures, referred to the compact as a singular document in the history of commonwealths (Craven, 53–57). We can also add here the information that Jedidiah Morse not only alluded to the compact in his *American Geography* of 1789 but printed the document entire and repeated the performance in his expanded *American Universal Geography* of 1793.

But Matthews's original claim certainly holds true regarding Forefathers' Day orations, and Adams's address therefore marks a return to the political cast of prerevolutionary ceremonies. Although he did not neglect the Pilgrims' religious motives for coming to America, he tended to give particular emphasis to the civil aspects of their experience. He stressed not only the legality of their dealings with the Indians but also the failure of their early attempt at primitive communism, contractual and anti-utopian emphases central to Federalist political theory. In effect, Adams's address of 1802 epitomizes the cooptative nature of those Feasts of Shells in which the Landing and the Rock played a signifying part.

But Adams took the high road, avoiding the nasty anti-Republican smears of those Boston occasions, and he would soon seem to such hard-liners as John Pickering imperfect in his loyalty to the Federalist Party, would indeed with his acceptance of certain Republican ideas put forth the shadowy outlines of the emerging Whig. Whatever the reason, John Quincy Adams's oration was a model of its kind and would long endure as an example of the powers that eventually earned him the Miltonic title "Old Man Eloquent," a distinction associated with his much later career as a congressman representing Plymouth County, which warranted an alternative epithet, "the representative from Plymouth Rock." But on December 22, 1802, Adams made only a passing mention of the Rock, "which your veneration has preserved as a lasting monument," and, pleading that the story was too familiar to bear repetition, he begged to be excused from carrying his audience "in imagination on board their bark at the first moment of her arrival in the bay; to accompany Carver, Winslow, Bradford and Standish, in all their excursions upon the desolate coast; to follow them into every rivulet and creek where they endeavored to find a firm footing, and to fix, with a pause of delight and exultation, the instant when the first of these heroic adventures alighted on the spot where you, their descendants, now enjoy the glorious and happy reward of their labors" (9–11). If Adams's account of the Pilgrims' first month in America was a short and accelerated one, it was not only because he sought to avoid the commonplaces of the occasion, but because he wanted to devote himself to the circumstances necessitating the compact.

Certainly it was fitting that the son of the man who claimed to have written his *Dissertation on the Feudal and Canon Law* on Forefathers' Rock was the orator who added the Mayflower Compact to the idea of the Landing. Mindful perhaps of the pious tradition within which he was working, Adams began by assuring his auditors that "the conviction of religious obligation" was the "sole and exclusive actuating cause" of the Pilgrims' settlement at Plymouth, that the "commands of conscience were the only *stimulus* to the emigrants from Leyden" (12). It was their religious motive that distinguished the Pilgrims from the other Europeans who had formed colonies in America, and similarly exceptional was the "instrument of government by which they formed themselves into a body-politic. . . . This is, perhaps, the only instance, in human history, of that positive, original social compact which speculative philosophers have imagined as the only legitimate source of government" (12, 17). A document made necessary by the exigencies of the moment, "the instrument of voluntary association, executed on board the Mayflower, testifies that the parties to it had anticipated the improvement of their nation" (20).

Not even George Bancroft would put the Compact in a more progressive frame of reference, coupling it by tacit association with the Declaration of Independence and the Constitution. But Adams in 1802, though increasingly under the sway of Jefferson, was still his father's boy, and it was through a Federalist frame that he viewed the Forefathers' utopianism, witnessed by their decision to "establish among them that community of goods and of labor, which fanciful politicians, from the days of Plato to those of Rousseau, have recommended as the fundamental law of a perfect republic." To mention Rousseau is tantamount to citing Jefferson, whose quixotism is being pointed to here, albeit by a hand sheathed with a kid glove: "To found principles of government upon too advantageous an estimate of the human character, is an error or inexperience, the source of which is so amiable, that it is impossible to censure it with severity. . . . Happily for our ancestors, their situation allowed them to repair it, before its effects had proved destructive" (20–22).

Adams also faced up to the censure-worthy charges of intolerance aimed at the Pilgrims, lining out a response that would be repeated with variations over the years: "Can we wonder, that men who felt their happiness here and their hopes of hereafter, their worldly welfare and the kingdom of Heaven at stake, should sometimes attach an importance beyond their instrinsic weight to collateral points if controversy, connected with the all-involving object of the reformation?" (27). Not only were the Pilgrims singular in the piety and order-liness of their enterprise, but they were, even when in error, part of the great progressive movement still going on in 1802, and they therefore provided worthy models for modern emulation: "Preserve, in all their purity, refine, if possible, from all their alloy, those virtues which we this day commemorate as the ornament of our forefathers" (31). And in that hopeful spirit, also, Adams closed with a quotation from the famous poem of Bishop Berkeley, "Westward the Star of empire takes its way," somewhat misremembered but thereby even more closely linked to his father's story about the lines of poetry inscribed "into a rock on the shore of Monument Bay in our old colony of Plymouth."

Published in an elegant pamphlet, Adams's oration served to lift the local occasion to a transcendent level, his mild version of Federalism and his gentle chiding of Jefferson making his views acceptable to various shades of fil-iopietistic partisanship. Equally important, Adams rescued Forefathers' Day from the ecclesiastical monopoly first established by Chandler Robbins, for having given a pious nod to the religious motives of the Forefathers, the burden of his oration emphasized the primacy of law in the actual founding of the Plymouth colony. And finally, as in his opening remarks, Adams insisted on the importance of the written (and spoken) word as agents of memory, for what distinguished the origins of New England from those of "other nations," who "have generally been compelled to plunge into the chaos of impenetrable antiquity" in search of their origins, was that "this birth-day [is] an event of which the principal actors are known to you familiarly as if belonging to your own age" (8). This singular intimacy of immediate recall made the founding of New England "an event of a magnitude before which imagination shrinks at the imperfection of her powers." Where recollection is so vivid, mere "imagination" slinks humbled into the background. What is most important about the Landing, therefore, is that it is literally an act of the memory as well as a memorable act.

Quite a different tone and emphasis was promoted by Alden Bradford, who delivered the address on Forefathers' Day in Plymouth in 1804. Bradford, whose given and surname recalled those "actors known to you familiarly," as Adams put it, was a liberal Congregational minister, who was forced by ill health to abandon his pastoral calling in 1795 and subsequently became clerk of court in Lincoln County. As a pastor manqué, therefore, he may have been chosen for the occasion as something of a compromise, but Bradford's Unitarian leanings in no way vitiated his Federalist convictions, and his oration was chiefly an attack aimed at the presence of "the Sceptic and the Athiest" in the "highest places of power" in the land (9–10). Bypassing Adams's observation that the Pilgrims had tried but then rejected primitive communism, Bradford insisted that although the Forefathers were "zealous advocates for *the rights of man*," they entertained "no fanatical sentiments, no ideas of the perfectability of human nature," and were primarily concerned with maintaining "the legitimate powers and the just restraint of government" (16). They were, in effect, primitive Federalists, as opposed to those "speculative politicians of the present age," Jacobin heretics like Thomas Paine and William Godwin, who deny religion its rightful place "in civil society" and insist "that the perfection of man consists in an entire freedom from authority and restraint." For his part, Bradford defined "government" as a mechanism "designed to save the people from the evils of their selfish and irregular passions."

Though mild, certainly, when compared with the excesses of the Feasts of Shells, Bradford's remarks hardly took Adams's high road of impartial discourse, and as he thrashed on through his oration, his lawyer's stock was wrenched askew and his clerical collar became increasingly visible. Despite Bradford's liberal theology, he yoked the jeremiad to his political philippic and dragged out the traditional specter of spiritual decline: "The character of the present inhabitants of New England is far below the degree of moral and christian excellence, for which our fathers were so justly celebrated" (17). And as for contemporary politics, "ambition has taken the place of patriotism, and base intrigue is substituted for true wisdom." Bradford's address, though published, did not survive its occasion, for what was increasingly wanted on Forefathers' Day was a performance, like Adams's, equivalent to a Fourth of

July oration, an exercise chiefly optative in emphasis, not denunciatory. This did not mean that the jeremiad would disappear from future celebrations, far from it, for the occasion of commemorating the Forefathers provided a choice opportunity to berate modern backsliders, but the genre was traditionally associated with the pulpit, not the political platform.

The forensic ideal was achieved by John Quincy Adams's carefully balanced discourse, which would provide the conservative model for much future high-toned but opaquely political discourse at Plymouth and elsewhere, ever and again echoed in statements sacramentalizing the Forefathers and celebrating the power of memory to certify their priority in North America. For if the United States was an exception among nations, it was because the Pilgrims were an exceptional group of people and the Landing and the Signing exceptional events, having no parallels in human history, a distinction often enforced by comparisons not with ancient history but colonial Virginia. It is this defining difference that is the emphasis of Adams's oration, and it is one that would be extended through the years by a great many more to come, whatever the specific coloration inspired by contemporary political events.

In 1824, the Federalists as a political party would be virtually extinct, and in an election chiefly defined by personalities and warring cliques, not parties, John Quincy Adams would be elevated to the presidency only by striking what seemed to be a corrupt bargain with Henry Clay, the emerging prophet of what would become the Whig Party. The appointment of Clay as Adams's secretary of state was an arrangement that tarnished what was until then a sterling reputation for probity. Through virtue of his frequent support of Republican policies and his service on Monroe's cabinet as secretary of state, Adams had long since lost the support of Federalists in New England, but he would hardly be identified with the emerging Democratic Party, and as a man with a party-less platform Adams was easily defeated by Jackson in 1828.

He would remain in politics for twenty more years, regaining as a congressman his earlier repute, his status as "the representative from Plymouth Rock" attesting not only to the county that elected him but to the firm, unyielding quality of his moral stance as he battled slavery interests. His was always a steadfastness to principle that appeared to some as disloyalty to party, and which may be traced back to a bedrock Federalism, the fealty to Law as the balance wheel of government that was the Adams inheritance and even the family fate. Thus the last of the Adams line with a high public profile was immortalized by an act of memory both profound and futile, nostalgic and vituperative, filiopietistic and infinitely sad, in all ways a final farewell to the Federalist faith, which like an ancient actor had made a long career of retiring from the stage.

CHAPTER 4

Webster and the Rock

You can commit no crime for they are created in their bone &
nature sentiments conscious of & hostile to it; unless you can suppress
the English tongue in America, & hinder boys from declaiming
Webster's Plymouth speech, & pass a law against libraries.
—Ralph Waldo Emerson

I

If John Adams, earlier in the century, had boasted that his dissertation on constitutions had been written while perched on Forefathers' Rock, if Timothy Dwight, at about the same time, had written of the marvelous sensations derived from that perch, standing in the very footprints of the Pilgrims, so over the succeeding decades the round world was seen in New England as radiating out in a vast circle from that central point. This eccentric concentricity was a complex phenomenon, resulting in part from a sincere faith among New Englanders in the sanctity of their regional origins but fueled also by a growing feeling, exacerbated by the embargo and the War of 1812, that they inhabited a world truly apart from the rest of the United States.

Western expansion, accelerated by the Louisiana Purchase, had brought another threat, the creation of additional territories and states that weakened the representative power of New England. Then, after the Compromise of 1820, the addition of new slave states threw the balance even more to the South and West. Thus to the paranoia of the Federalists regarding the incursion of Jacobinism under the cloak of Jeffersonian Republicanism there was added a territorial dimension, also associated with the policies of the Jefferson administration. Jedidiah Morse's *Compendious History* was a defensive product of this complex mood, insisting on the sanctity and singularity of his region.

But as the Bicentennial of the Pilgrim Landing approached, the fact of the moving western frontier was past remedy, much as the demise of the Federalist Party was now a certain thing. With characteristic Yankee ingenuity, poets and politicians asserted the regional hegemony and Puritan (hence Federalist) sanctity by connecting national expansion to the original impulse that had resulted in the arrival of the Forefathers. Once again, Plymouth Rock was a central point, pivotal to the idea of western progress.

"In whatever country we may be found, and in whatever circumstances," wrote Massachusetts-born William Gibbes Hunt late that year, "our sympathies will never cease to beat in unison with the feelings and congratulations which are inspired by the TWENTY SECOND OF DECEMBER" (285). Writing in the *Western Review*, published in Lexington, Kentucky, Hunt evoked the feelings of all westerners who could trace "the line of our ancestors to brave, pious, disinterested, and magnanimous men, who boldly leaped on Plymouth Rock in pursuit of Liberty, Religion, and Law." Most of the centenary celebrations were religious in nature, were in fact sermons read on Forefathers' Day. As Hunt expressed it, the event was such as to inspire "a JUBILEE, not of noisy mirth, or military pageantry, but of the triumphs of moral excellence, the victories and rewards of principle and truth" (286).

Like those entirely secular and patriotic occasions, the tour through New England of President James Monroe in 1817 and the subsequent tour of General Lafayette in 1824–25, like the Jubilee of Independence in 1826 and the subsequent memorial occasion necessitated by the coincidental deaths of Jefferson and Adams on that same sacred date, the Pilgrim bicentennial was an event that forcibly brought the present moment into confrontation with the record of the past. Hardly a speaker failed to call attention to the comfort, security, and ease that distinguished the modern scene from the bleak prospect confronting the Pilgrims on that cold day in December when they first stepped ashore. Again, this was a traditional perspective, but the celebratory frame gave it added weight, as assessed, once again, by editor Hunt, who credited the "peace and prosperity" of the present generation to "the virtues and institutions . . . transmitted" to the sons by their fathers.

Despite the celebratory moment, this divinely privileged legacy, with its well-worn analogy of the ancient Jews, gave warrant to a few pulpits for a revival of the old, fiery-tongued spirit of the jeremiad: if the present generation was urged to regard the Forefathers with gratitude, they were also exhorted to emulate their virtues, to follow the "Good Old Way." As always, the pastoral tendency was to elevate the first generation of Puritans until they became giants, the likes of which could no longer be found. "America has not seen a more manly and gigantic race than that which took possession of this western wilderness during the first century after the landing at Plymouth," pronounced Dr. Gardiner Spring before the New England Society in New York (*New England Society Orations*, 1:19–20). "We have," announced the Reverend Daniel Huntington in Bridgewater, Massachusetts, "lamentably declined from their simplicity and purity" (18). No preacher of the day was more enthusiastic in pointing out the golden trail left by the footsteps of God across New England than was Dr. Nathanael Emmons of Dedham, that stalwart champion of Calvinism, but Emmons also had a sharp eye for backsliders: "As we have been distinguished with divine favours like Israel, so our sins are aggravated like theirs," the present generation having sinned not only against God but "against the examples, the labours, the sufferings of our forefathers" (16).

In Albany, New York, the Reverend John Chester was able to demonstrate that the Pilgrims were directly responsible for the independence of the United States. But he encouraged his auditors to curb their own liberties for the sake of the "true subordination" that was such an admirable characteristic of Puritan (i.e., prerevolutionary) life: "Subordination and obedience were common in the family and school-room, the shop and the counting house, and order and happiness were the consequences"(21). Chester cast a sour eye on the rising generation and could detect an alarming "spirit of bold and licentious innovation" prevailing in the modern world (15). What was needed, he thought, was a return to the "*good old path* of duty," which on Chester's map led right past the good old whipping post and pillory: "Their laws were simple and intelligible, and they were executed with a promptness and a certainty, that made them terrible to the guilty:—of course public morals were pure" (22).

But where Chester drew upon the past to reinforce the wisdom that came with the "experience of age," the majority of celebrant ministers tended to use the past in order to measure the two centuries of progress that had followed the arrival of the Pilgrims: "Instead of the thinly scattered wigwams of the wild and wandering savage," observed the Reverend Alfred Ely of Monson, Massachusetts, "populous towns and cities have arisen, filled with the arts and blessings of civilized life" (24). Like Fourth of July celebrations, once again, the occasion of Forefathers' Day chiefly warranted something in the optative mode, and William Crafts, a southern lawyer of northern paternity, addressed the New England Society of Charleston, South Carolina, in terms that were positively congratulatory to descendants of the Pilgrims.

Borrowing a convention dating from Charles Turner's sermon in 1774, Crafts called up the ghost of one of the "Fathers of New England" so that he might convey his "emotions of joy and wonder" as he contemplated the modern scene: "In lieu of a wilderness, here and there interspersed with solitary cabins, where life was scarcely worth the danger of preserving it, he would behold joyful harvests, a population crowded even to satiety—villages, towns, cities, states, swarming with industrious inhabitants, hills graced with temples of devotion, and vallies [*sic*] vocal with the early lessons of virtue. . . . He would behold the little colony which he planted, grown into gigantic stature, and forming an honorable part of a glorious confederacy, the pride of the earth and the favorite of Heaven" (14).

Even Nathanael Emmons, like many another New England Jeremiah before him, could turn from castigating his backsliding neighbors to beholding a millennial prospect, observing that the "progenitors" who were "the instruments of raising us up to our present high and happy state" were best honored by "promoting the civil, religious, and literary interests of this rising empire. . . . God is opening to our view such future scenes and objects, as ought to encourage and animate us to employ all the means in our power, to build up the nation in every thing that is great and good" (21).

Emmons, one of the most effective—if reactionary—preachers of his day, liked to certify his Forefatherly connections by continuing to wear the knee breeches and cocked hat of his youth, and he reached back likewise in his sermon to the rhetoric of the revolutionary era—his own generation—in order to assure his auditors of continuing providential favor: "God has carried us," he declared, "as on eagles' wings, through every period of our national existence," a figure of speech harking back to the Reverend Conant's sermon in 1776 that was used by several other ministers as well on the occasion of the bicentennial celebration (Emmons, 10; cf. Rowland, 5; *New England Society Orations*, 1:13; Woodbridge, 21).

Given this reservoir of already familiar tropes and conventions, it is somewhat surprising to note the virtual absence of Plymouth Rock from the nearly twenty bicentenary addresses that were published. A few of the accounts of the Pilgrims' arrival do make a ritualistic mention of "the memorable rock," but many more speakers preferred to ignore the Rock for an elaboration of the bleak scene that confronted the Pilgrims as they (presumably) stood upon it (*New England Society Orations*, 1:10; Wilbur, 9; Porter, 6; French, 11). For whatever reason, it was not a minister but a layman, Benjamin Faneuil Dunkin, Esq., who, in addressing the New England Society of Charleston, on Forefathers' Day a year before the bicentennial occasion was observed by William Crafts in that city, made most of the Rock in his oration.

Dunkin stated his hope that "the Rock of Plymouth" would be to the posterity of the Pilgrims "a perpetual monument, of hardihood that knew not fear, of independence that would not succumb, of conscientious Christianity that dared not temporize" (8). His figure—to say nothing of his middle name— evokes the embattled Federalist toasts of a generation earlier, suggesting that like many another transplanted emigrant he continued to observe fashions no longer current back home. Perhaps something similar inspired editor Hunt's mention of the Rock in the *Western Review*, along with a lengthy quote from the "*Massachusetts Historical Collections*" concerning its history and validity. Or perhaps it was that Dunkin and Hunt felt called upon to enlighten their southern and western audiences concerning a subject too well worn in New England to warrant mentioning there.

And yet, in 1822, in a Forefathers' Day address by the Reverend P. M. Whelpley, read before the New England Society in the City of New York, we find the speaker placing himself in his imagination "upon the rock where [the Pilgrims] first rested from their wanderings," and from there "looking abroad upon this wide and now populous region" to gain a proper perspective (*New England Society Orations*, 1:106). What follows is the familiar comparison between "a waste howling wilderness" and "a great and extending empire," but what is now once again in place is the centrality of the Rock to the composition. Moreover, Whelpley returned twice again to the omphalos of New England in the course of his tribute to the Pilgrims, concluding his discourse by inviting his auditors "back to the rock where the Pilgrims first stood," for a final glance at "this wide and happy land, so full of their lineal or adopted sons," and a reminder as to whom the descendants of the Fathers owed their present prosperity (134). For Whelpley, the Rock was pedestal, pulpit, and perspective point from which to view the world around, a world that owed its present greatness to the Pilgrims, who were the first to stand upon it. Given the reticence of Whelpley's clerical brothers to make much of the Rock in their observances two years earlier, we may wonder what had happened in the interval to inspire him to make it a central feature in his own address.

What had happened was Daniel Webster, as Whelpley himself acknowledges, giving not only a central place to the Rock but a lengthy quotation from Webster's bicentennial oration, the words of the man who was the Pilgrims' "most eloquent panegyrist" (118). William Hunt in 1820 had announced the selection of Webster as the speaker in Plymouth as the best possible choice, "whether we consider the personal virtues of the man, the talents which distinguish him in his profession, or the attainments and abilities which he displayed in Congress. . . . No man is better qualified to trace the influence of the Fathers and their policy through successive generations down to the present hour" (297).

Hunt observed that the line of speakers who had preceded Webster on Forefathers' Day in Plymouth were "among the most distinguished of New England, both clergymen and laymen." Since the "interest" of the event had increased over the years, the occasion would, because of the "present anniversary," be the "most important that has ever yet occurred" and would require someone of Webster's talents. Hunt was glad to announce, therefore, that "the orator has, as the papers tell us, met public expectation, and to do this is assuredly no small task" (300). To paraphrase Emerson, regarding another but similar occasion, here was Webster and there was the Rock, and neither Webster nor the Rock would be quite what each had been before the two were brought into such electrical conjunction.

II

In placing Webster's bicentennial oration into context, we should remember that the speaker was still a Federalist politician and that his party was on the verge of extinction. Those defiant toasts during the Feasts of Shells were a thing of the past, and the injuries suffered by the Federalists because of their stand regarding the War of 1812 had only recently been patched over by President Monroe's eastern tour. Federalism would have a brief, if strategically modified, resurgence with the election of John Quincy Adams to the presidency, but the muddied terms of that arrangement gave the Federalists' Great Man theory of government the look of private dealings and privileged power. Much as key elements of Federalist ideology would survive in the platforms of the Whig Party, so the Whigs would never rid themselves of complicity, real or imagined, with monied interests. The Whig Party, it might be said, had the eaglelike features of Calhoun, but it walked on the feet of Clay.

The Whigs, it can also be said, spoke with the voice of Webster, whose pronouncements regarding the absence of any Alleghenies in his politics had to be balanced off against his regional allegiances and were generally found lacking. There is some irony in Webster's cherishing, as a politician and gentleman farmer, his humble New Hampshire origins, given his move from Portsmouth to Boston in 1816. His New Hampshire associations were intensified publicly during his famous argument on behalf of Dartmouth College before the Supreme Court in 1819, but Webster would increasingly identify himself with mills and money in Massachusetts.

By 1820, he had given up his seat in Congress and gone into private—and lucrative—practice, although he managed also to maintain a fine sense of political balance, speaking out against the Missouri Compromise while supporting free trade, an antislavery, antitariff stance that in Massachusetts was still firmly footed upon the status quo. Well known since his college days for his oratorical powers, Webster had been called upon from time to time for Fourth of July speeches, and his forensic display on behalf of Dartmouth was supposed to have brought tears to the eyes of Supreme Court justices, a miracle of Mosaic proportions. As editor Hunt testified, Webster was the natural choice as speaker of the day in Plymouth on the bicentennial occasion, but no one, perhaps, quite anticipated the intensity of the result.

The only firsthand, contemporary account we have of the effect of Webster's speech is that of George Ticknor, who in a letter written to his parents virtually on the spot spoke of having "run away from a great levee . . . thronging in admiration round Mr. Webster, to tell you a little word about his oration" (*Life, Letters, and Journals*, 1:329). As the orator of the day was having a symbolic scallop shell hung around his neck by adoring young daughters of the Pilgrims,

Ticknor admitted that he wasn't quite sure as yet of his opinion concerning the actual content of the address, having been so carried away by "the immediate influence of his presence, of his tones, of his looks" (330): "I was never so excited by public speaking before in my life. Three or four times I thought my temples would burst with the gush of blood; for, after all, you must know that I am aware [that his speech] is no connected and compacted whole, but a collection of wonderful fragments of burning eloquence, to which his manner gave ten-fold force. When I came out I was almost afraid to come near to him. It seemed to me as if he was like the mount that might not be touched, and that burned with fire." Ticknor added that he would have to read the oration before delivering a final opinion as to its worth (he would have to wait nearly a year before it was printed), and modern commentators for the most part find the speech something less than Webster's subsequent and equally famous oration at the laying of the cornerstone of the Bunker Hill Monument. Nor was Ticknor, at the time, an unbiased witness, having personal associations with Webster and having accompanied his party from Boston to Plymouth.

Ticknor had, moreover, prepared himself to be in a receptive mood prior to the event. Immediately upon his arrival in Plymouth, he went to Forefathers' Rock and, standing upon it, recorded emotions not much different from those of Timothy Dwight in 1800: "I have seldom had more lively feelings from the associations of place than I had when I stood on this blessed rock; and I doubt whether there be a place in the world where a New England man should feel more gratitude, pride, and veneration than when he stands where the first man stood who began the population and glory of his country. The Colosseum, the Alps, and Westminster Abbey have nothing more truly classical, to one who feels as he ought to feel, than this rude and bare rock" (328). In making this comparison Ticknor would seem to be moving from the sublime to the silly, but even while making necessary allowances for regional chauvinism aroused by the intensity of the moment, we should pay it some heed, for it provides a convenient key to the sensibilities of the age. Ticknor knew whereof he spoke, in terms both of allusions and aesthetics.

Having graduated from Dartmouth in 1807, George Ticknor had subsequently determined that his interest in literature made it necessary for him to study abroad. He departed for Germany in 1815 in the company of Edward Everett, late the brilliant and very young minister of the prestigious Brattle Street Church, but who would return to fill the newly created chair of Greek literature at Harvard. For his part, Ticknor had been invited while he was still traveling in Europe to become the new Smith Professor of French and Spanish at Harvard, and after an additional year touring Spain, France, and Italy, he returned to Cambridge in 1819, reuniting with his fellow cosmopolite, Everett.

Ticknor's journals reveal the extent to which he sought out famous places in order to experience the intellectual frisson of historic events, those "storied associations" for the sake of which Irving's Geoffrey Crayon would set sail in *The Sketch Book*. On entering Rome, having passed through the Alps via the Simplon Pass, Ticknor lost no time before he visited the Colosseum, where "every pillar and every portal [was] a monument that recalled ages now gone by forever, and every fragment full of religion and poetry,—all this . . . was enough to excite the feelings and fancy, till the present and immediate seemed to disappear in the long glories and recollections of the past" (1:170).

It was in similar language that Ticknor reported his feelings while standing on Plymouth Rock, a coincidence incomprehensible to modern sensibilities, but persons of his generation would have seen no diminishment but rather an increase in proportion when comparing the New World, natural monument to the Old World symbol of decline and fall. For sons of New England like Ticknor, Plymouth was "a spot to which more recollections tend than to any other in America. . . . It was like coming upon classic ground, where every object was a recollection and almost a history" (328). Having been introduced to Sam Davis, the Plymouth historian—who was himself something of a local landmark and living chronicle—Ticknor saw him as "uniting in his person all the attributes of a forefather, and all the recollections, traditions, and feelings of one of their descendants, so that I look upon him as a kind of ghost, come down from the seventeenth century to preserve for us what without him would certainly have been forever lost" (329). As William Craft's conjured spirit and the popularity of Irving's "Rip Van Winkle" testify, such figments of the past were contemporary literary currency in 1820, antiquarian dress rehearsals for the advent of Lafayette, who in his American tour would be celebrated as the revolutionary era incarnate.

Fred Somkin has set the advent of the resurrected marquise in the context of the Era of Good Feelings, a version of popular hysteria that conflated emotions of joy and grief, suggesting deep reservations and insecurity now that the generation of Great Men was passing away. It is perhaps impossible otherwise to understand the heightened reactions of Ticknor's generation to those places (and persons) where the past and present seemed to be contingent, a fourth dimension filled with spirits from older worlds. But when Americans like Ticknor expressed such depths of feeling in confronting historical sites, they did so in language prepared for them by Archibald Alison, the English aesthetician (and curate) who in 1790 published his *Essays on the Nature and Principles of Taste*. In his account of the impact of aesthetics on the rise of tourism in the United States, John Sears has stated that Alison's book would have considerable impact on Americans for the next half century, instructing them how "to feel as they ought to feel" in the presence of the past.

Where Edmund Burke in 1746 had set down the terms of aesthetic discourse for the Enlightenment and the subsequent romantic generation, establishing the Sublime and the Beautiful as complementary but quite different aspects of Nature, Alison further refined those terms by insisting that natural prospects alone, whether mountains or waterfalls or peaceful valleys, were not sufficient for maximum effect or impact. His close contemporary, William Gilpin, had developed an intermediary term, the Picturesque, which he associated with pleasing combinations of scenic attributes, juxtapositions of foliage and open areas, winding rivers and cliffs, with an occasional ruin thrown in for contrast, but Alison thought that such arrangements, however pleasing to the senses, were bereft of any "moral" element. What a landscape needed to be properly picturesque were historical associations.

A mountain associated with human chronicles was *more* sublime than a mere peak, however grand, and the glimpse we might have of a ruin glorified a natural landscape because it informed the prospect with our awareness of the historical circumstances of which that ruin was a relic. Any aesthetic reaction, according to Alison, is invariably inspired by associations, whether personal or those informed by reading—by education. The more educated we are, he stated, the better equipped for aesthetic responses to sublime or beautiful vistas. Similarly, the more history a country has, the more likely it is to have scenery that elicits the emotions inspired by the sublime or the beautiful.

These principles of taste were not easy to swallow in the United States, which was relatively impoverished in matters of historical association. Crève-coeur had anticipated the reaction to Alison, and his *Letters from an American Farmer* (1782) had extolled the aesthetic thrill of beholding new settlements springing up in the western wilderness, far superior he claimed in positive morality than the sight of a decaying ruin in the midst of a European swamp. Fenimore Cooper, in *Notions of the Americans* (1828), likewise argued through his American spokesman that the United States had both sublimity and beauty in its *future* promise, that we should leave ruins and their associations to Europe and focus instead on the exciting prospects of building a new nation.

Still, in his historical romances, modeled after Scott, Cooper the novelist did his best to farm the thin soil of American chronicles, and Rufus Choate, one of the founders of the Whig Party, in 1833 launched his own career as an orator by delivering in Salem, Massachusetts, a lecture entitled "The Importance of Illustrating New-England History by a Series of Romances like the Waverley Novels." Lawrence Buell regards this as a document central to an emerging New England literature, in which Choate urged regional writers to give "to the natural scenery of the New World, and to the celebrated personages and grand incidents of its early annals, the same kind and degree of interest which Scott has given to the Highlands, to the Reformation, the Crusades, to Richard the Lion-hearted, and to Louis XI" (*Addresses and Orations*, 2). If, as an aesthetic exercise, Choate's oration was Alisonian in emphasis, it was underwritten by a sectional strategy.

For Choate, an ardent promoter of a future made better by tariffs, banks, and internal improvements—in sum, an America along the lines of Clay's American Plan—resurrecting the heroes of the past would not only act as a superior kind of history lesson but would throw the accomplishments of the present generation into proper relief: New England was both "the dwelling place of the Pilgrims, and of the children of the Pilgrims" (16). The arrival of the *Mayflower* and the debarking of the Pilgrims "on the bleak sea-shore and beneath the dark pine-forest of New England" provided "an incident of . . . moral sublimity" unmatched in the records of "history, fiction, literature," but the historical romancer would achieve his greatest effects by spreading out "before you the external aspects and scenery of that New England, and con- trast them with those which our eyes are permitted to see, but which our fathers died without beholding. And what a contrast!" (24, 14). By such means did Whig orators maintain a glib balance between the past, the present, and the future, jugglery at which Webster was the grand master.

It is perhaps unnecessary to point out that by 1833 Fenimore Cooper had already become the American Scott, and Catharine Maria Sedgwick, among others, had already written historical romances in the manner of the Waverley Novels about early New England history. With Buell, I cite Choate not as particularly prophetic but as symptomatic of his age and to demonstrate that the Whigs, even in celebrating historical associations, could keep a level eye on the present advantage and the future profits in so doing. They were in this regard, as Buell has demonstrated, hand in glove with the Unitarians, whose interest in history was, like Choate's, of a literary kind and who generally hastened back from the past to celebrate the modern moment.

In 1815, when it had been the Reverend James Flint's turn to deliver the Forefathers' Day sermon in Plymouth, he had devoted two long paragraphs to "*the rock of the Pilgrims*" and the "crowd of kindred ideas [that] throng into the mind" when one beholds it: "If this rock bears no written record of the names and achievements of these modest and much enduring soldiers of the cross, it needs only to be touched by the magic wand of imagination and memory, and more miraculous than the effect produced upon the rock in the wilderness by the rod of Moses, there issues from it a fountain of instruction, of ancient and affecting recollections; it becomes animate and eloquent, and verifies the assertion of the poet, that there may be 'sermons in stones' " (5). And the sermon wrought by Flint from the stone at Plymouth was an ornate proof that the Pilgrims' religion was "a rational and spiritual worship of the true God," was, in effect, the wellspring of modern Unitarianism (5).

Flint's claim will at a later point be put into the context of the ongoing

FRONTISPIECE

MR. and Mrs WEST, Viewing the Rock on which our Fore-Father's Landed at Plymouth.

FIGURE 11.
Woodcut frontispiece to *The Awful Beacon* (1816). Lucy and her bridegroom contemplate the Rock, which is carefully depicted so as to conceal its actual size, irrelevant in any event according to Mr. West's Alisonian dialectic. (Courtesy American Antiquarian Society)

debate between Unitarians and Trinitarian Congregationalists regarding the true line of doctrinal descent from the Pilgrims. I cite it here only to reinforce my point that by 1820 the beauties of antiquity were often viewed through an ideological frame, which does not necessarily gainsay the power of historical associations to excite people like George Ticknor. At the same time, Plymouth Rock even in 1820 needed all the help it could get from whatever source. When the fictitious Miss Lucy Brewer in the anonymous *The Awful Beacon* (1816) visited Plymouth with her intended, a Mr. West of New York, she expressed a certain uneasiness about bringing her fiancé to the "celebrated rock . . . on which our Forefathers were said first to have landed" (9). Though a native of Plymouth, Lucy admitted that there was "nothing peculiar in the appearance of this gray coloured stone, which, remaining in its natural state, I viewed with an eye of indifference" (21). But what Lucy could not appreciate, her fiancé, though from New York, was able to expiate on at length, being "much more of an Antiquary" than his bride and therefore aroused to a high degree "of philosophical satisfaction" by beholding the historic Rock.

Placing his hand upon it, and presumably drawing inspiration therefrom, Mr. West corrected his fiancée's thinking regarding the unadorned boulder: "'This rock, Lucy, in the appearance of which you may indeed perceive nothing very peculiar, and which you may conceive as unworthy the notice of the passing stranger, I do indeed view, with inexpressible satisfaction—it was the first firm foundation on which the worthy Pilgrims set their feet in this now thickly inhabited quarter of the new world' " (22). The well-informed, if condescending, bridegroom then goes on for two pages more to describe the scenes that greeted the " 'little band of Puritans' " and the changes they subsequently made in the landscape, introducing " 'symmetry by the assistance of all the instruments of art,' " until " 'the coasts were covered with towns, and the bays with ships—and thus the new world like the old became subject to man.' " Mr. West concludes his peroration with the observation that " 'these were events worthy of commemoration, and ought to have been perpetuated by a suitable inscription upon the rock' " (23).

Daniel Cohen, who first called my attention to this passage, regards Mr. West's account of the energetic, transformational Pilgrims as a sign of the times, registering the delayed emergence of a "modern America" occasioned by the final break from England and the eighteenth century caused by the War of 1812. He notes that Mr. West's is a misreading of the Puritan spirit, one that ignores its "humble dependence on a sovereign God," and certainly Providence plays no part in the New Yorker's abbreviated history of New England (Cohen, 382). But Mr. West's account of the Puritans' transformational role is very much in keeping both with contemporary celebrations of progress and with Alisonian aesthetics. By putting his hand on the Rock, the bridegroom put his finger on the problem—and the solution: standing bereft of information detailing the history with which it is associated (the "suitable inscription"), the boulder was no different from any other. What gave it meaning and importance were the associations it called up in the mind of an informed beholder. The essential component of a memorial is its connection with a national memory.

But what gave the historical context most meaning for the American viewer, as Mr. West also makes clear, were the events subsequent to the Landing. With his free hand, as it were, Mr. West gave an emphasis to the historic associations of the Rock by pointing to the bustling scene that now filled the once barren landscape. Where romantics like Washington Irving were offended by the incursions of commerce and technology into the natural landscape, Whiggish champions of change like William Crafts, Rufus Choate, and Mr. West derived strong feelings of aesthetic pleasure from beholding the visible record of linear progress, an aesthetic of the new we can trace back to Crévecoeur's appreciation of settlements springing up in a wilderness. In such a view, historical associations gather even more power by means of the differences imposed on the landscape in the interval between "then" and "now."

Though a favorite theme of the Whigs, this emphasis on the beauties of Progress was without political party, and to the recipe for historical fiction served up by Rufus Choate, we can add the formula followed by the Demo-

FIGURE 12. Engraved certificate of membership issued by the Pilgrim Society, created in 1820, the bicentennial year. Like Sam Hill twenty years earlier, the artist shared Webster's emphasis on Progress and included a view of the "modern" Plymouth in 1820 below the scene of the Landing. Rather than stressing the element of adversity, as in the pictures by Corné and Sargent, the emphasis here is on domesticity (a cooking pot and a woman unpacking a trunk), and the Rock extends an accommodating shape out into the harbor. (Courtesy American Antiquarian Society)

cratic historian George Bancroft. In the first volume of his epic history, published in 1834, Bancroft certified the Rock rather cautiously as standing "near" where the Pilgrims landed, which makes it no less sacred to "a grateful posterity," who celebrate the anniversary of the Landing "as the origin of New England, the planting of its institutions. Historians love to trace every vestige of the pilgrims; poets commemorate their virtues; the noblest genius has been called into exercise to display their merits worthily, and to trace the consequences of their enterprise" (1:246). It is the last phrase that needs stressing, for if the Rock was important because the Pilgrims landed on (or near) it, the Pilgrims were important because of what they set in motion—the present moment and the more glorious (because indefinite) future.

It is notable that the cartouches decorating the certificate of membership first issued by the newly formed Pilgrim Society in 1820—a group formed with an antiquarian as well as a bicentennial mandate—follow Sam Hill's precedent of 1800 by complementing a scene depicting the Landing of the Pilgrims with another showing Plymouth harbor two centuries later, filled with signs of a bustling commerce. This was in all senses Mr. West's view of history, in which the past is validated by the prosperity of the present, and it is the context out of which Daniel Webster spun his great oration in 1820.

III

As a squat gnomon, Plymouth Rock threw a shadow moving between past, present, and the future, and those who perched upon it, whether in reality or in metaphor, were caught inescapably in that trinitarian necessity. Bearing witness to providentially dictated progress, the record of which was the story of the Pilgrims' triumph and the accomplishments of their descendants, meant casting a look, however momentary, into the future, with sentiments of an anticipatory and generally hopeful kind. So also Daniel Webster, in Ticknor's synopsis of his oration at Plymouth:

> It was on the point of time where we now stand, both in relation to our ancestors and to posterity; and he discussed it, first, as to the Pilgrims who came here, what they suffered at home and on their arrival, and how different were the principles of colonization from those in Greece, Rome, and the East and West Indies; secondly, as to the progress of the country, and its situation an hundred years ago, compared with what it is now, in which he drew a fine character of President [John] Adams; thirdly, as to the principles of our governments, as free governments,—where he had a tremendous passage about slavery,—as governments that encourage education,—where there was a delightful compliment to President Kirkland [of Harvard],—and as governments founded on property. . . . And finally, in the fourth place, as a great people welcoming its posterity to the enjoyment of blessings which all the rest of the world cannot offer, with which he ended in a magnificent flood of eloquence. (*Life*, 1:330)

In sum, if Webster's was a rhetorical equivalent to the annihilation of "time and space . . . by the power of genius" of which Rufus Choate was to speak, it also testified to the family connection between the millennialist aspects of the Puritan jeremiad and the Fourth of July oration.

Webster opened his oration with forensic pyrotechnics, alluding to "the bright and happy breaking of the auspicious morn, which commences the third century of the history of New England," a new day filled with "present joy," which gilded "with bright beams the prospect of futurity" (*Writings and Speeches*, 1:181). His was a figure that set his theme in an optative burst of light, celebrating the historic occasion by irradiating the moment with hope for a glorious future. And in the first sentence of his second paragraph, Webster delineated the mystic bond between the three stages of time: "Living in an epoch which naturally marks the progress of the history of our native land, we have come hither to celebrate the great event with which that history commenced. For ever honored be this, the place of our fathers' refuge." Then, having staked out the parameters of time and place, Webster began his third paragraph by evoking Alison's theory of associations in terms of filial piety: "It is a noble faculty of our nature which enables us to connect our thoughts, our sympathies, and our happiness with what is distant in place or time, and looking before and after, to hold communion at once with our ancestors and our posterity."

This was that pivotal "point in time" to which Ticknor referred, an Alisonian "spot of earth" in which the past and futurity come together through the power of "our rational and intellectual enjoyments. We live in the past by a knowledge of its history; and in the future by hope and anticipation." Here again is that optative use of memory, the anticipatory note so typical of American retrospective views, which in patriotic oratory differs from the jeremiad in both going and coming. Where hard-line Congregationalists like the Reverend Chester regarded the Pilgrims as a breed of giants and their descendants as a bunch of moral midgets, Webster chose to view the chronicles and achievements of the Forefathers as a continuum in which his auditors could participate, building ever more stately accommodations on ancestral foundations.

Hence his assertion that by studying history we can establish certain points that resolve into a vector pointing forward, "running along the line of future time," leading to a contemplation of "the probable fortunes of those who are coming after us. . . . We protract our own earthly being, and seem to crowd whatever is future, as well as all that is past, into the narrow compass of our earthly existence" (182). That is, we may ensure for ourselves a certain immortality, equivalent to that of the Forefathers, "by attempting something which may promote [the] happiness" of those who come after us, and "leave some not dishonorable memorial of ourselves for their regard, when we shall sleep with the fathers." We can only speculate what the Reverend Chester would have thought of such bedfellows, but the prospect was not unlike Rufus Choate's subsequent description of a congregation brought by a Patriot minister of the Revolution into an evangelical enthusiasm, so that "one universal and sublime expression of religion and patriotism diffuses itself over all countenances alike, as sunshine upon a late disturbed sea" (35). So also the expressions on the faces of Webster's audience, if we may believe the testimony of Ticknor, as the mighty Daniel judged them potential equals to their ancestors, fellow citizens in a vast Republic, extended both in terms of time (memory) and space (anticipation).

As a "point of time," finally, Webster's pivotal position was identified with Plymouth Rock: "We have come to this Rock, to record here our homage for our Pilgrim Fathers. . . . And we would leave here, also, for the generations which are rising up rapidly to fill our places, some proof that we have endeavored to transmit the great inheritance unimpaired" (183). Where earlier sermons and orations had generally evoked the image of the Pilgrims coming ashore in the past tense, Webster reinforced the continuity between the historic and contemporary moments by mounting a "vision," defined by a contemporary as a rhetorical means of "describing events as passing before the reader" (*Out-Line*, 5) Rather than call up the ghost of a specimen Forefather, Webster practiced necromancy on a massive scale, summoning back to Plymouth Rock the sacred band entire, an experiment in associationism that approximated a diorama or a theatrical tableau:

> There is a local feeling connected with this occasion, too strong to be resisted; a sort of *genius of the place*, which inspires and awes us. We feel that we are on the spot where the first scene of our history was laid; where the hearths and altars of New England were first placed; where Christianity, and civilization, and letters made their first lodgement, in a vast extent of country, covered with a wilderness, and peopled by roving barbarians. We are here, at the season of the year at which the event took place. The imagination irresistibly and rapidly draws round us the principal features and the leading characters in the original scene. We cast our eyes abroad on the oceans, and we see where the little bark, with the interesting group upon its deck, made its slow progress to the shore. We look around us, and behold the hills and promontories where the anxious eyes of our fathers first saw the places of habitation and of rest. We feel the cold which benumbed, and listen to the winds which pierced them. Beneath us is the Rock, on which New England received the feet of the Pilgrims. We seem even to behold them, as they struggled with the elements, and, with toilsome efforts, gain the shore. We listen to the chiefs in council; we see the unexampled exhibition of female fortitude and resignation; we hear the whisperings of youthful impatience, and we see what a painter of our own has represented by his pencil, chilled and shivering childhood, houseless, but for a mother's arms; couchless, but for a mother's breast, till our own blood almost freezes. (183–84)

By segueing from his own word picture to the painting by Henry Sargent, Webster gained added vividness for his participatory evocation of the Landing, which was delivered inside the confines of the First Congregational Church, not at the site of the Landing. Like the artist, his task was to "kindle the imagination" by means of a "retrospect," a long look backward at the event, and with the power of description to transport his audience through space and time "to the interesting moment" itself (186). And it must be an *interesting* moment, by which Webster meant one with something more than picturesque power. Such a point in time must be one on which great consequences were dependent, for the power of historical associations, in Webster's as in Flint's and Choate's view, is greatly increased by our awareness of the extent to which a given event has consequences extending into subsequent eras: "On these causes and consequences, more than on its immediately attendant circumstances, its importance, as an historical event, depends" (185). So the peculiar power of Plymouth Rock, the specific locus of a moment from which the future greatness of New England sprang.

We have already seen how the fictional "Mr. West" came up with a similar truth, similarly derived from Alison, but there is a definitive difference in proportion, Webster giving greater emphasis to the extent to which the *future* consequences of a historic action determine its associative power, a Whiggish dimension virtually missing from Alison's theory, even if implicit in it. Reinforcing this element, Webster at a later point conjured up the Pilgrims once again, so that they might through him deliver a prophecy the moment "they landed upon [the] rock," a fictive occasion that recalls the scene in Croswell's play when Elder Brewster casts a long look forward in time. Such tricks of forensic ventriloquism were hardly original with Webster, but they would become his famous stock in trade, as when, in 1826, he put into the dead John Adams's mouth an eloquent speech at the signing of the Declaration of Independence that would in time be taken for Adams's own. It was a device that added heft to the "vision" mode of rhetorical expression and had the additional virtue of permitting Webster to assume the identity of the putative speaker, in this case the corporate body of the Forefathers:

> If God prosper us . . . we shall here begin a work which shall last for ages; we shall plant here a new society, in the principles of the fullest liberty and the purest religion; we shall subdue this wilderness which is before us; we shall fill this region of the great continent, which stretches almost from pole to pole, with civilization and Christianity; the temples of the true God shall rise, where now ascends the smoke of idolatrous sacrifice; fields and gardens, the flowers of summer, and the waving and golden harvest of autumn, shall spread over a thousand hills, and stretch along a thousand valleys, never yet, since the creation, reclaimed to the use of civilized man. We shall whiten this coast with the canvas of a prosperous commerce; we shall stud the long and winding shore with a hundred cities. That which we sow in weakness shall be raised in strength. From our sincere, but houseless worship, there shall spring splendid temples to record God's goodness; from the

simplicity of our social union, there shall arise wise and politic constitutions of government, full of the liberty which we ourselves bring and breathe; from our zeal for learning, institutions shall spring which shall scatter the light of knowledge throughout the land, and, in time, paying back where they have borrowed, shall contribute their part to the great aggregate of human knowledge; and our descendants, through all generations, shall look back to this spot, and to this hour, with unabated affection and regard. (186–87)

In 1620 the Pilgrims were more concerned with filling their immediate needs than in prophesying a glorious future for their colony, and their eyes, as Bradford famously observed, were fixed on heaven, not on an earthly horizon. But Webster's use of the Pilgrims, like Croswell's before him, is in the optative mode of the Enlightenment, and by granting them a power of foresight they did not have, he adds an element of intentionality, lending a purpose derived from the consequences of the Landing to the act itself. It is not only a celebration of an emerging Whig vision that is irrelevant to the experience of the Forefathers, but by casting it as prophecy Webster makes present-day New England the realization of the Pilgrim hope.

At a later point, about halfway through his discourse, Webster once again had recourse to the Rock, this time as a spatial locus, not a chronological punctuation mark, and seized the moment of contact with the sacred stone for a bit of prophecy of his own: "Two thousand miles, westward from the rock where their fathers landed, may now be found the sons of the Pilgrims, cultivating smiling fields, rearing towns and villages, and cherishing, we trust, the patriarchal blessings of wise institutions, of liberty and religion. . . . Ere long, the sons of the Pilgrims will be on the shores of the Pacific. The imagination hardly keeps up with the progress of population, improvement, and civilization" (206–7). What Sylvanus Conant and his generation credited to Providence, Webster, following John Quincy Adams, gave to Progress, the regnant spirit of his own generation. Like a navigator on a ship, Webster first took his bearings on the past, then swung his instrument westward toward the future. He thereby established a vector that moved out from Plymouth Rock, once again certifying its signification to the birth of a nation, as the benchmark for a baseline along which an orderly empire would extend.

At the end of his oration, Webster returned a final time to the Rock, once more taking the place of the Pilgrims, like them basking in the anticipated praise of future generations: "Who[ever] shall stand here, a hundred years hence, to trace through us their descent from the Pilgrims, and to survey, as we have now surveyed, the progress of their country, during the lapse of a century," such a one, Webster was sure, would lift up a "voice of acclamation and gratitude," the which, "commencing on the Rock of Plymouth[,] . . . shall be transmitted through millions of the sons of the Pilgrims" until "it lose itself in the murmurs of the Pacific seas" (225).

Webster's repeated returns to Plymouth Rock, like the rubbing of a piece of amber, endowed it with a certain electricity, lending that rather loose aggregate of ideas that was his oration a unity and a force that so impressed George Ticknor. Small wonder that the first thing Ticknor did after the oration was over was to visit yet again the sacred Rock, "with all our recollections, all our burning feelings . . . and stood here, just two centuries from the moment when the first Pilgrims landed" (330). At that moment, recorded by Ticknor, the Rock itself had also arrived, and Webster may be said to have placed himself upon it with his toast during the dinner that followed his oration: "The Rock of Plymouth—May it be trodden two thousand years hence, by as worthy feet as leaped upon it 'two hundred years ago'" (*Columbian Centinel*, December 27, 1820).

"The Rock on which the Pilgrims disembarked," wrote Tocqueville in his great work on American democracy, "is still shown [and] has become an object of veneration in the United States. I have seen fragments carefully preserved in several American cities. Does that not clearly prove that man's power and greatness resides entirely in his soul? A few poor souls trod for an instant on this rock, and it has become famous, it is prized by a great nation; fragments are venerated, and tiny pieces distributed far and wide. What has become of the doorsteps of a thousand palaces? Who cares for them?" (238). Tocqueville's source for his information about the landing of the Pilgrims was Nathaniel Morton's *New England's Memorial*, a new edition of which, edited by Judge John Davis of Plymouth, had appeared in 1826—a delayed bicentennial event. Morton, of course, depending on his uncle's history, makes no mention of the Rock, but Davis made up for the omission by means of a footnote, identifying "the place of [their] first landing" as "a large rock, at the foot of the cliff near the termination of the north street leading to the water," and which remains "as a precious memorial of that interesting event" (48). Davis, however, does not mention the traffic in fragments of the rock, which seems to have commenced at some point during the 1820s. We can credit only so much to the power of Webster's oration, unassisted by his magnetic presence, but it is perhaps no coincidence that the national distribution of the published version predates by a very short time the spread of those fragments out from Plymouth, like pebbles distributed from a ledge of rock by the New England glacier. It was a kind of talus associated with the western migration of Webster's fellow Yankees, whose presence was thought oppressive by many and which certainly left its mark upon the land.

IV

In 1820, Daniel Webster was a prominent New England lawyer and Federalist politician, but after his speech on December 22 he was much more than that; he was on his way to apotheosis as the godlike Daniel, having delivered a patriotic equivalent to the Sermon on the Mount. For Webster had seized the occasion of Forefathers' Day to depart law and local politics for the high plane of literature, with an oration that is magisterial in diction, elevated in tone, epical in scope, dramatic in evocative intensity, and, to all obvious appearances, above party and faction in stance. Delivered on the threshold of what has been called the "Era of Good Feelings," Webster's great speech is one of the decade's happiest moments, for if America did feel good, it was because its citizens were sure they had a destiny and that it was carrying them forward at a great rate of speed. And if America in 1820 believed in universal Progress, then Daniel Webster was the American prophet, for in his bicentennial speech we are made to behold the still young nation as part of a vast continuity, spreading westward from the rock upon which the Pilgrims landed.

At the same time, Webster's attempts to remain above party and faction were imperfect. Perhaps the longest and most detailed account of the festivities at Plymouth appeared in the *Columbian Centinel*, still staunch in its Federalism, which rendered in full the toasts offered at the celebratory dinner and pronounced Webster's oration "every thing which had been anticipated . . . by those who best knew him" (December 27). Likewise, the *Boston Daily Advertiser and Repertory*, another Federalist paper, edited by Nathan Hale, gave a long and detailed account of Webster's speech. By contrast, the *Independent Chronicle and Boston Patriot*, a Republican organ, managed to render an account of the celebration that made no derogatory remarks about the number of toasts consumed but failed as well to mention either Webster's oration or the orator himself. This omission occurred despite the fact that the *Patriot*'s story was abstracted from the *Boston Palladium*, which had devoted a paragraph to Webster's performance, judged as "correct in its historical statements, powerful in argument, rich in description, and pathetic and eloquent in appeal" (December 25).

It needs also to be noted that after Webster left Plymouth, he would return to a state convention that was revising the Massachusetts constitution, an ongoing event that provides a framing context for his oration. Perhaps the two hottest issues under debate were the attempts to discontinue state support of the Congregational Church—the so-called Standing Order—and the effort to remove the property basis for the qualification of state senators, substituting instead a popular vote. Not surprisingly, the *Independent Chronicle* opposed state support of "the Privileged Order" (a calculated swipe at Harvard) and stood for senatorial elections. By contrast, the prevailing sentiments at the bicentennial celebration were warmly Federalist: "Judge Thomas," a state senator from Plymouth County, raised his glass to the sentiment "Our Forefathers' creed; Law, Liberty and Religion: If their descendants would preserve the two first, let them not expunge the 'third article' "—the section of the state constitution establishing the "Standing Order." The judge's toast was (as the *Centinel* noted with satisfaction) "received with great approbation; and the cry of 'encore, encore,' was repeated from every part of the hall." Such was the window of political opportunity through which Webster's "disinterested" performance of December 22 should be viewed.

Of his several contributions to the constitutional convention, the chief was a successful defense of the property qualification for state senators, which Webster regarded as giving stability to that legislative body, hence to the government entire. And though Webster in his Plymouth oration, as the Reverend Whelpley would complain, scanted the religious aspect of the Pilgrim experience, which enabled him also to avoid any mention of the "third article," Webster did speak on the reverence for property felt by the Forefathers, rendering a paraphrase and précis of his much longer speech on the subject at the state convention. "Their situation," said Webster of the Pilgrims, "demanded a parcelling out and division of the lands, and it may be fairly said, that this necessary act *fixed the future frame and form of their government*. The character of their political institutions was determined by the fundamental laws respecting property" (211). In celebrating the ownership of property as essential to a well-ordered society, Webster was echoing the wisdom not only of the Pilgrims but also of the Founding Fathers, when they established property as the bedrock of the Constitution. But he was speaking as well on behalf of the privileged class of Americans, for whom he would increasingly be a spokesman. Despite his Whiggish emphasis on progress, Webster was still a Federalist at heart, and his frequent returns to Plymouth Rock during his speech should remind us of the association that emerges from those Feasts of Shells during the opening years of the century between the sacred stone and the Constitution.

There is some additional interest, therefore, in what would become Webster's most famous use of the Rock in his oration of 1820, a year chiefly associated in the national mind with the Missouri Compromise, the result of which was a line riven across the Louisiana Territory that was perceived either as a threat to national union or a logical extension of the sanction of slavery by the Constitution. Like most New Englanders, who regarded slavery as immoral and perceived the compromise as a threat to their region's hegemony, Webster was against the admission of Missouri as a slave state and in December 1819 had given a speech in Boston that had become the basis for a memorial to Congress on the thorny subject. It was a lengthy discourse on the constitutional right of the U.S. government to determine whether new states would be slave or free and ended with an "appeal to the justice and wisdom of the national councils to prevent the further progress of a great and serious evil" (*Writings and Speeches*, 15:71).

Justice Joseph Story, the independent-minded Jeffersonian Republican from Massachusetts who had been appointed to the Supreme Court in 1811, was also opposed to the compromise and in May 1820 had delivered a charge to the first grand jury assembled in the newly established state of Maine (created as a geopolitical counterweight to Missouri) that contained a long and emotional attack on the slave system. Published later that year, Story's charge ended with sentiments that would become familiar rhetorical items in the emerging arguments for abolition: "Our constitutions of government have declared that all men are born free and equal, and have certain unalienable rights, among which are the right of enjoying their lives, liberties and property, and of seeking and obtaining their own safety and happiness. May not the miserable African ask 'Am I not a man and a brother?'" (*Charge*, 16). The "traffic" in human beings was "inhuman," emphasized Story, and he rendered in painful detail the sufferings of Africans during the infamous "middle passage," devoting three closely packed pages to horrific descriptions rendering "a picture of human wretchedness and human depravity, which the boldest imagination would hardly have dared to pourtray [*sic*], and from which . . . the most abandoned profligate would shrink with horror" (17–21).

It was against this dark background, then, that Webster, toward the end of his Plymouth oration later that same year, finally admitted that the long and shining record of American progress did have one blot upon it, caused by the "traffic" whose "contamination" inspired the "revolt" of every "feeling of humanity. . . . I mean the African slave trade" (221). He called upon "all the true sons of New-England, to cooperate with the laws of man, and the justice of heaven. If there be, within the extent of our knowledge or influence, any participation in this traffic, let us pledge ourselves here, upon the Rock of Plymouth, to extirpate and destroy it. It is not fit, that the land of the Pilgrims, should bear the shame longer." This was the "tremendous passage about slavery" to which Ticknor had alluded in his synopsis, immediately following his note regarding the speaker's emphasis on "the principles of our governments, as free governments."

Indeed, one of Webster's major themes in his oration was a generic map tracing the evolution in America of the spirit of "liberty," from the "love of religious liberty" associated with the Pilgrims to a love of "freedom" in its most exalted form, which gives men of "conscience" the courage to resist the "hand of power" when it becomes restrictive: "Nothing can stop it, but to give way to it; nothing can check it, but indulgence" (187–88). As John Quincy Adams had suggested, the Pilgrims were "republicans in principle," whose love of "religion and civil liberty" was what endowed the Rock with its peculiar power, being an association unique in the colonial annals of America: "Thanks be to God, that this spot was honored as the asylum of religious liberty!" (190).

Since America's "genealogy" began with "the inspiration of liberty," Webster could hardly avoid the contradiction of slavery: "We are bound to maintain public liberty, and by the example of our own systems, to convince the world that order and law, religion and morality, the rights of conscience, the rights of persons, and the rights of property, may all be preserved and secured, in the most perfect manner, by a government entirely and purely elective" (220–21). Implicit in this system was the necessity of "correcting" any "errors in our establishments" that "experience may show" during the passage of time: "If any practices exist contrary to the principles of justice and humanity within the reach of our laws or our influence, we are inexcusable if we do not exert ourselves to restrain and abolish them" (220). It is in the very next sentence, in a new paragraph, that Webster began his "tremendous passage" excoriating the "African slave-trade."

The association of the Pilgrims with religious, hence civil, liberty was a Forefathers' Day convention dating from the time of the Revolution. John Quincy Adams in 1802 had certified the connection between the compact and the Constitution, and in 1816 James Flint referred back to Adams in calling the *Mayflower* a "floating republic" and celebrating the Pilgrims as apostles of "religious and political liberty" and "rights of conscience" (11, 14). In the bicentennial sermons of 1820, a number of Protestant ministers made similar connections, along the lines of those laid down by Heman Humphrey: "Let us not forget, that we are . . . indebted to the fathers, who counseled and prayed and acted for us, a century before Washington and Adams were born. . . . [They were] the active promoters, and the fearless champions of civil liberty" (*Character*, 31). But of all the pious celebrants of American liberties on Forefathers' Day, 1820, only one, the Reverend Stephen Chapin, a Baptist whose parish was not coincidentally in the neighborhood of Portland, Maine, and thereby within the range of the outraged voice of Justice Story, spoke out against the slave trade.

Not only did Chapin refer to Story's explosive "charge" of May 8, but he appended to his sermon a lengthy note that rendered the horrendous "details, which are the ordinary attendants upon this trade" (45). The whole, at times problematic and conflicted matter of the relationship between the Pilgrims as ideological icons and abolition as a political and religious movement in New England will be the subject of a subsequent chapter. It is necessary at this point only to state the obvious, that in 1820, despite the protests in Boston and Salem in 1819, there was no universal sentiment being expressed from New England pulpits against the illegal traffic in slaves even then being carried on in vessels manned and captained by Yankee seamen. Nor would there be for many years any major politician who would call for the immediate abolition of slavery nationwide. Nor had Webster in 1820. The extension of slavery was one thing, which because of the notorious two-thirds provision gave southern states added power with added slaves; and the traffic in slaves had been forbidden by an act of Congress in 1808. But the abolition of slavery was quite another matter, on which the most reasonable of men could (and surely would) differ.

Newspapers protested Story's impassioned language in his charge to the grand jury, and it took courage for Webster to echo his language. At the same time, neither Webster's fellow New Englanders nor the rest of his fellow Americans—including those who were even then (as in Missouri) "making for the extension of this trade"—would ever again hear him speak out in such strong terms on this difficult and painful matter (221). Because of his increasingly snug ties to mercantile interests in Massachusetts, which were increasingly dependent on the raw cotton shipped north from states whose economy was increasingly supported by slave labor, Webster would thenceforth begin his long decline from grace. He would in the future for the most part evoke the Constitution not for its having granted to the central government the power to determine whether states were free or slave but for its mystical connection with the idea of national union and for its foundation on the bedrock of property— including that which took human form.

But in 1820, Webster demanded that the slave trade be eradicated from "the land of the Pilgrims," and wherever it was found, "let that spot be purified, or let it cease to be of New England. Let it be purified, or let it be set aside from the Christian world; let it be put out of the circle of human sympathies and human regards, and let civilized man henceforth have no communion with it" (222). This is language absolute in demands, immediate in applicability, and ultimately secessionist in spirit. As such, it is in harmony with the proclamations soon to be heard from ultra-abolitionists like William Lloyd Garrison, who would not limit themselves to excoriating the traffic in slaves but would press for immediate emancipation and who would become the kinds of motes that were a beam in the eye of such publicans and politicians as made up the Whig Party, for whom extremism in the name of universal liberty was a threat to the stability and well-being of the national union.

Stability in Plymouth in 1620 had been given legal form by the Compact, which "established the elements of a social system" even before the Forefathers came ashore on the Rock: "At the moment of their landing . . . they possessed institutions of government, and institutions of religion; and friends and families, and social and religious institutions, framed by consent, founded on choice and preference, how nearly do these fill up our whole idea of country!"

(198). Though the Pilgrims were "already *at home*" when they landed, their new locality was transformed by the passage of time, associating it with "interesting scenes and high efforts," lending it thereby a power to take "a hold on human feeling" and demand "from the heart a sort of recognition and regard." For Webster, the politics of nostalgia are separatist in impulse once a new home feeling is born, and the history of New England, to which he devoted ten of more than a hundred pages, is a chronicle and a sequence that resulted in a nascent patriotism, the which, "shutting out from its embraces the parent realm, became *local* to America" (202). In effect, the regional, hence national, memory begins with 1620 and is identified with Plymouth and its Rock.

Webster added the heft of conservative authority to his regional emphasis by quoting Burke's great speech on the eve of the American Revolution, citing his reference to "that little speck, scarce visible in the mass of national interest, a small seminal principle, rather than a formed body," which gave such engendering power to the arrival of the Pilgrims (207). That speck was best pinpointed as Plymouth Rock, being the kind of stone associated with procreation as well as stability. But because it was also associated with "the ashes" of the Forefathers, the presence of which at Plymouth also drew "strong emotions to the spot," the Rock was something of a gravestone, also, a dual symbol therefore of birth and death (199). Finally, given Webster's role in promoting the Rock as a national symbol with a local (regional) base, we may imagine it as a kind of pedestal, with Webster standing upon it, one hand pointing westward in an oratorical gesture, the other clutching the Constitution to his bosom.

It was in such a posture, certainly, that a grateful posterity would seek to place Webster after his death. The formal eulogy honoring Webster at the memorial ceremonies in Boston in 1852 was delivered by George S. Hillard, friend and law partner of Charles Sumner, friend and adviser of Hawthorne. Hillard was also a steadfast Whig who would cling to his party as it went down beneath the waves of insurgent Republicanism, holding on, as it were, to Webster's sinking coffin. The loyal Hillard spoke of many things that were still to Webster's declining credit, including his stand against Hayne and nullification in 1830, when the orator fixed forever his political identity in association with Union and the Constitution. When he came to the great man's "occasional discourses," Hillard compared them in relation to the speeches of other men to the monument on Bunker Hill, which "soars above the objects around it" (*Memorial of Daniel Webster*, 260).

But it was not the famous Bunker Hill oration Hillard chose to single out "as a production which all, who have followed in the same path, must ever look upon with admiration, and despair." It was the "Plymouth Oration," defined by Hillard as "the beginning of a new era in that department of literature. It was the first and greatest of its class; and has naturally fixed a standard of excellence which has been felt in the efforts of all who have come after him. Its merits of style and treatment are of the highest order, and it is marked throughout by that dignity of sentiment and that elevating and stirring tone of moral feeling which lift the mind into regions higher than can be reached by eloquence alone." Yet, with what must have been unconscious irony, Hillard's elevation of Webster's oration of 1820 as a rhetorical monument that must forever be looked upon "with admiration, and despair," contains a compound irony that epitomizes the paradox of Webster as a public man.

The despair to which Hillard referred was that of the orators condemned to follow Webster to the podium in Plymouth on Forefathers' Day or in other ways beg comparison with Webster's priority as eloquence personified. But there was another kind of despair, felt by persons who in 1820 had heard or who afterward had read Webster's stirring condemnation of slavery and for whom admiration by 1850 had turned to the bitterness of betrayal. For such persons, Webster's godlike stature had by the time of his death become reduced to something akin to Plymouth Rock with its historical associations removed—a lowly, featureless lump resembling a toad.

Thus, we can balance Hillard's funeral oration with Theodore Parker's sermon preached on the occasion of Webster's death, which returned again and again to that moment in 1820 when "the orator of Plymouth Rock" had spoken out against slavery only to become thereafter an "advocate" of compromise with the slave power. If the power of Webster's rhetoric energized the Rock, elevating it and the events associated with it to prominence in the national gaze, its perpetuity ensured by the oration having been published and excerpted in part in countless school readers, the Rock, like Webster, was a profoundly ambivalent icon. Having provided a pedestal that elevated him to national attention, it would eventually in the eyes of many serve as his tombstone.

CHAPTER 5

Wherein Tears Are Struck from the Rock

*Whilst speculators consider the steady growth from savage need to the
wealth & strength & joys of civilized society & remember the fearful
odds against which they have succeeded & the apparent aid of an
omnipotent Providence so often rescuing or fortifying their littleness—
in the view of it all, they blot out the sweet harmony & tint of the
picture in the mind, thrust in the blank & shapeless agency of Chance
instead, and behold, say they how* fortunate *is man!*
—Ralph Waldo Emerson

I

The Forefathers' Day oration in Plymouth in 1824 was delivered by
Edward Everett, the first in that town since the bicentennial celebration. It is a
tribute to Everett's great gift for elegant, if not always original, discourse that
his performance is generally regarded as second only to Webster's among the
many that followed, a posterior position that Webster's protégé and fellow
Whig would in the future have frequent opportunities to fill. As an orator,
Everett was famous for his learnedness and polish, but his performances,
though distinguished by high intellect and rhetorical grace, lacked Webster's
force of expression, much as Everett did not have the sheer physical energy of
the older man, nor did his many orations long survive their moment by means
of memorable quotations.

Everett's shadow fame is reinforced early and late: shortly before his death,
he was the featured orator at the dedication of the Civil War graveyard at
Gettysburg, whose deeply researched and soul-searching performance of two
hours was followed by Lincoln's few well-chosen words, the superiority of
which Everett had the intelligence and grace (his two chief virtues) to acknowledge. And yet, in his day Everett's career was a progress that cut a substantial

wake in public waters even if his draft was shallow. In 1867, Emerson, in recounting the history of New England letters during his lifetime, chose to begin his chronicle with 1820, not because of Webster's great oration but because that was the year associated with Everett's return to Harvard from Germany, bringing with him the New Thought of the age.

Everett's career up to that point had been brilliant and rapid. Following his graduation from Harvard and four years of divinity studies there, he had been installed in 1814 at the age of twenty as the minister of the Brattle Street Church, a Unitarian stronghold with a wealthy congregation. With his great forensic and literary gifts, a personal beauty of almost classical perfection, and a charming manner, Everett was an immensely popular preacher, but within a year he had accepted an appointment in Greek literature at Harvard. There followed his departure for Europe with George Ticknor, an interlude of post-graduate studies abroad to prepare himself for the teaching post, and the epochal return celebrated by Emerson.

Everett brought his characteristic intelligence and charm into the classroom, but by 1824 the professor had decided to test his talents on a wider audience: he departed the academy for politics, and by the time he made his appearance in Plymouth, had been elected to the U.S. Congress. Only thirty years old in 1824 and already the editor of the prestigious *North American Review*, he would go on to a career whose many facets permitted the display of Everett's brilliance, but his was a prismatic spectrum the colors from which tended to fade with the occasions that inspired it.

Earlier that year Everett had delivered his first public oration, marking the high point of his brief tenure at Harvard by a spellbinding Phi Beta Kappa address. Speaking on the prospects for an American literature, at a time when that seemed an oxymoron, Everett in closing his remarks took dramatic advantage of the presence in his audience of General Lafayette, and though the connection between Lafayette and American literature was not obvious, Everett made it so. His eloquent gesture of welcome brought thunderous applause, thus ending Everett's performance by an adroit sharing of Lafayette's fame and giving a powerful impetus to his public career, carrying him not only to the U.S. Congress but to Plymouth.

Clearly, the man invited to succeed Webster was worthy of his hire but was in all ways the older man's counterpart, not his match; son of a clergyman, not a farmer; and an urbane minister-scholar, not a country-born lawyer, whose career over the past ten years had been a pyrotechnic display of abilities, not a slow, single-minded climb to wealth and social prominence. Even by 1824, Webster had traveled no farther from New England than Washington, D.C., while his counterpart and protégé had visited the storied sites of the Old

World. Everett, in sum, was a Brahmin, Webster a bull of the ordinary (if exceptional) Yankee breed, yet both men came to Plymouth at an important turning point in their lives.

In 1820, Everett had been scheduled to read an original poem following Webster's performance, but, having first accepted the invitation, he subsequently (and wisely) declined the doubtful honor. Even as late as 1824, Everett's willingness to be compared to Webster is to his credit, and the contemporary fame of his Plymouth oration that year was regarded as a serious challenge to the other man's achievement. But Webster followed in 1825 with his Bunker Hill address and in 1830 gave triangular strength to his reputation by his response in the U.S. Senate to Robert Hayne, assuring his dominance in American oratory forever. And in time, Everett's speech would be likened to the iridescence of the rainbow, as compared with the thunder and lightning of the storm that it followed (Davis, *Memories*, 360). It is an evaluation obviously conditioned by his subsequent political career, not only as a member of Congress but as a U.S. Senator and governor of Massachusetts, which continued to suffer by comparison to Webster and from attacks by abolitionists for his vacillations regarding slavery and his statements of sympathy for the South, all made in the name of Webster's sanctified Union. During his ripest years he was held in contempt by his formerly adoring student, Emerson.

All of this lay ahead of Everett in 1824, and however ambitious he may have been regarding his future career, his eyes were fixed for the occasion upon the past, not only the Pilgrim moment but the celebrations of the Landing that preceded his own. Thus Everett's opening words made frequent references to "familiar commonplaces," to "sentiments so often uttered and welcomed on these anniversaries," and he observed the conventional necessity of "dwelling on the circumstances under which their memorable enterprise was executed" (*Orations and Speeches*, 1:45–46). Whatever his faults, Everett could never be accused of lacking a sense of dutifulness, nor, for all his agility, could he avoid treading on the toes of Webster's great speech, as when he pointed to the "peculiarity in the nature of [the Pilgrims'] enterprise, that its grand and beneficent consequences are, with the lapse of time, constantly unfolding themselves" (47).

Indeed, given the day and his own Unitarian-Whig ideology, it was virtually impossible for Everett to speak of the Pilgrims without associating them with the spirit of Progress of which they were such an integral, even influential part, "which led them across the ocean, and guided them to the spot where we stand" (46). But where Webster had dwelt on the beauties of Progress, chiefly, Everett concentrated on the blessings of Space, conceived in political terms. His emphasis was on the importance of the distance between New England and the Mother Country to the success of the Puritan experiment. Only the vast ocean and difficult passage made the success of the Separatist venture possible. This was the spacial factor permitting the "benign neglect" celebrated in Burke's famous defense of the colonialists' cause during the revolutionary era, a speech to which Webster had referred in 1820, but beneficial isolation was only part of Everett's equation.

For of like importance was the element of hardship. In 1820, at the bicentennial dinner, Everett had proposed a toast to the Puritan magistrate, William Stoughton, who first coined the notion that " 'God sifted a whole Kingdom for the wheat to sow in this western land,' " a winnowing process that was the subject of Everett's subsequent discourse (*Palladium*, December 22, 1820). According to this logic of adversity, it was the persecution the Pilgrims endured before coming to America that prepared them by purifying "the ranks of the settlers" for the even greater ordeal to come (67). Filtered out by hardship was "all patrician softness, all hereditary claim to preeminence. No effeminate nobility crowded into the dark and austere ranks of the pilgrims." The dangerous and nearly disastrous voyage of the *Mayflower* was an extension of the winnowing process, as was the suffering that awaited the exiles in America, for "these trials of wandering and exile of the oceans, the winter, the wilderness and the savage foe were the final assurance of success . . . all wrought together for good."

Taken as a sum of adverse conditions paradoxically promoting their welfare, the record of the Pilgrims' experience was one of "extraordinary good fortune" (50). A key to his melioristic view of the world, "fortunate" was Everett's definitive word in his summary of the Forefathers' troubled history: "Their banishment to Holland was fortunate; the decline of their little company in the strange land was fortunate; the difficulties which they experienced in getting the royal consent to banish themselves to this wilderness were fortunate; all the tears and heart-breakings of that ever-memorable parting at Delfthaven had the happiest influence on the rising destinies of New England" (66–67). "Happy," as here, was another favorite word in Everett's description of the Pilgrims' sufferings: "Happy, that our foundations were silently and deeply cast in quiet insignificance, beneath a charter of banishment, persecution, and contempt; so that, when the royal arm was at length outstretched against us, instead of a submissive child, tied down by former graces, it found a youthful giant in the land, born amidst hardships, and nourished on the rocks, indebted for no favors, and owing no duty" (66).

Here again was Burke's great precedent, and Webster's as well, for though steering well clear of Plymouth Rock, which Webster had for the time made his own, Everett referred frequently to the rockiness of New England in general, a landscape that enhanced the blessings of adversity, with its "austere sky," its "hard, unyielding soil" (61). Thus it was to an "iron-bound coast" that the

Pilgrims came, their "long, cold, and dangerous autumnal passage" ending with their "landing on the inhospitable rocks at this dismal season," a hard place but one suitable, indeed highly appropriate, to "the dark and austere ranks of the Pilgrims" who clambered ashore upon it (62, 67). From this "happy" concatenation of rocks and a people hardened by adversity there emerged the "industry and frugality, on which alone the prosperity of the colony could be secured" (60).

Approximating Milton's Fortunate Fall, albeit filtered through a Unitarian sieve, Everett's account of the Pilgrims' flight from the Old World derived from the Puritan's emphatic connection between privation and virtue and his own theological propensity to emphasize happy concatenations of event. He compared New England to those tropic zones where an easy fertility resulted in quick riches but also in disease and early death, being a "lucrative desolation," where by contrast the land of the Pilgrims now puts forth "the smiling aspect of . . . busy, thriving villages" (61). We can have no doubt that in speaking of the West Indies Everett was alluding as well to the southern colonies, put forth in terms of landscape, however, not the institution of slavery, which the speaker avoided along with the Rock, perhaps because of Webster's priority also. "The rocks and the sands, which would yield us neither the cane nor the coffee-tree, have yielded us, not only an abundance and a steadiness in resources, rarely enjoyed amidst the treacherous profusion of tropical colonies, but the habits, the manners, the industrious population, the schools and the churches, precious beyond the wealth of all the Indies" (62).

Everett in effect managed to evoke Webster's Rock without mentioning it, sublimating it within the terms of hardship and deprivation, those disguised blessings that nurtured the Pilgrim seed until it became the Liberty Tree. But he could not avoid the necessity of the other Forefathers' Day trope, and toward the end of his oration Everett summoned up a "vision" of the Landing, a justly famous evocation that expanded even as it challenged Webster's relatively brief account and gave further point to his own emphasis on the blessings of adversity:

> Methinks I see it now, that one solitary, adventurous vessel, the Mayflower of a forlorn hope, freighted with the prospects of a future state, and bound across the unknown sea. I behold it pursuing, with a thousand misgivings, the uncertain, the tedious voyage. . . . I see them now, scantily supplied with provisions, crowded almost to suffocation in their ill-stored prison, delayed by calms, pursuing a circuitous route; and now, driven in fury before the raging tempest, in their scarcely seaworthy vessel. . . . The laboring masts seem straining from their base; the dismal sound of the pumps is heard; the ship leaps, as it were, madly from billow to billow; the ocean breaks, and

settles with ingulfing floods over the floating deck, and beats with deadening weight against the staggered vessel. I see them, escaped from these perils, pursuing their all but desperate undertaking, and landed at last, after a five-months' passage, on the ice-clad rocks of Plymouth, weak and exhausted from the voyage, poorly armed, scantily provisioned, [and] surrounded by hostile tribes. Shut now the volume of history, and tell me, on any principle of human probability, what shall be the fate of this handful of adventurers . . . ? Is it possible, that from a beginning so feeble, so frail, so worthy, not so much of admiration as of pity, there have gone forth a progress so steady, a growth so wonderful, a reality so important, a promise yet to be fulfilled so glorious? (68–69)

This is surely a literary exercise of an impressive kind, but the very bookishness of the effort, clued by that metaphorical closure of "the volume of history," is betrayed by a thing so small as to have escaped attention: Everett has the Pilgrims landing on "the ice-clad rocks of Plymouth," when only one rock was there, a landscape perhaps traceable to his efforts to honor even while avoiding Webster's precedence, but one bearing no resemblance to the geological fact. By 1824, as we have seen, this was an error already perpetuated in literary and graphic depictions of the landing, and it is in keeping after all with Everett's emphasis throughout on the hardness of New England's landscape and its beneficent effect on the inhabitants. Moreover, Everett's anomalous shoreline, enhanced by his image of an iron-bound coast, would have a considerable reach, thanks to a circumstantial chain of subsequent events.

Within months of its publication, stray sheets of Everett's speech, so the story goes, somehow ended up in a British bookstore. They were used to wrap a packet of books for a famous poet, who was inspired by the words they contained to write lines in praise of the Pilgrim Fathers. Set to music by her sister, the verses would become a perennial favorite during festivities celebrating Forefathers' Day in New England and elsewhere, and as an evocation of the Pilgrims' sufferings and triumphs they endured well into this century, long after the oration itself had lost its luster and the annual celebration had lapsed into neglect. Ironically, it was Everett's anomalous citations of "iron-bound shores" and "ice-clad rocks" that would inspire the most memorable phrase in the poem, the "stern and rock-bound coast," which even now survives as a conventional cliché evoked when describing the upper reaches of the New England shore.

II

When she suffered an untimely but thereby appropriate demise in 1835, Felicia Hemans was perhaps the most popular and highly esteemed woman poet writing in England, who enjoyed an equally high regard in the United States. Born Felicia Browne in 1794, she was an exact contemporary of Edward Everett, and her career strangely mirrored his own. About the time Everett matriculated at Harvard, she became "Mrs. Hemans," as she would be famously known, having at fifteen married an army captain, who, after giving her five sons over the first six years of their marriage, departed for Italy on the grounds of ill health, never to return. He did not die, however; he simply did not return. This was in 1818, as Everett was completing his studies in Germany, and of Felicia Hemans it may be said that the loss of her husband provided an equivalent education: From the captain's departure until her death, she made an art of her forlorn state, with considerable public success. By 1825, when Everett spoke at Plymouth, the poet had seen into print a total of thirteen books, all characterized by a lacrimose spirit.

"Melancholy," intoned Sir Archibald Alison, the historian son of the aesthetician, "had marked her for its own" (Allibone, 1:819). He compared her to Coleridge, "if not in depth of thought, at least in tenderness of feeling and beauty of expression." Byron praised her work, as did sundry Scotch reviewers, and Scott himself was an aging admirer, along with Wordsworth, to whom the lovely Hemans played flirtatious daughter. To her contemporaries, Felicia Hemans was a perfect example of what a woman poet should be: the great Jeffrey pronounced "the poetry of Mrs. Hemans a fine exemplification of Female Poetry; and we think it has much of the perfection which we have ventured to ascribe to the happier productions of female genius." In the United States, George Bancroft observed that "in her pursuit of literary renown, she never forgets what is due to feminine reserve." Hemans would be frequently published in American magazines and annuals and would be the role model for Lydia Sigourney as well as for many lesser-known women ambitious as poets.

As Ann Douglas has noted, Hemans was a particular favorite of Unitarian belletrists, and in 1826, the eminent Harvard theologian Andrews Norton saw through the press the first collected edition of Hemans's works. Norton and his fellow Unitarians rated Hemans above Homer and Milton because of her "heart sorrow" (lacking in Homer) and the purity of her "human sympathy," of which Milton was devoid (Douglas, 113). Ideology as well as contemporary aesthetics surely played its part in what Douglas calls an "absurd judgment": Homer's godlike "indifference" was essential to the transcendental theory of literature, whereas Milton was beloved of orthodox Calvinists for his severe celebration of divine omnipotence. "Human sympathy" was by contrast a major tenet of Unitarianism, which elevated sentimentality to a par with the workings of grace. Moreover, as Jane Tompkins has demonstrated, American literature of the kind inspired by Hemans's example empowered women by displaying their Christ-like suffering to advantage.

Yet within four years Norton was urging restraint on the poet of human hurt, perhaps having come to the realization that tears shed for their own sake were the kind Tennyson would celebrate as "idle." With his New England practicality, Norton wanted water that worked, in his case for the greater glory of God. He therefore strove to channel Hemans's genius into what he conceived would be a more productive exercise of her "influence"—a key word in the liaison between Unitarian ministers and their women co-workers for Christ. In a letter to her in 1829, Norton wrote that he was "almost persuaded that the power of your poetry would be even more extensively felt and acknowledged; and with better influence perhaps upon many hearts" if she undertook to write verses "strictly devotional," thereby expressing "the feelings of a mind truly penetrated and elevated with just apprehensions of the character of God." (Letterbook C, 58). Norton represented the most conservative wing of the revolt against Trinitarian Congregationalism, and his gentle urging reveals perhaps some uneasiness over the specter of a woman who was evincing considerable self-empowerment outside the benefit of clergy, female sufferance recalling the bad example of Anne Hutchinson.

But the liberal Unitarian William Ellery Channing shared Norton's reservations, and in reading his colleague's edition of Hemans's works in 1827 he confided to his diary that her "sense of the evils of life is too keen and colors her views too much. I love to be touched, moved, but not depressed" (*Memoir*, 415). Like Norton, Channing wished for the kind of suffering that "purifies and exalts the soul," the Christological agon that is "the occasion of moral strength and victory," a reconciliation of "intense sensibility with peace and energy." In sum, Felicia Hemans would be a better poet if she were *more* like Milton— more, that is to say, like a man. Like Edward Everett, say, from whose Unitarian conviction that suffering is a moral force came his depiction of the Pilgrims as twice-purified Puritans.

It is not surprising, then, that according to tradition, Hemans was inspired by having read Everett's description in 1824 of the arrival of the Forefathers to write a poem in praise of the Pilgrims that achieves just the kind of balance between suffering and moral triumph that Norton and Channing desired:

> The breaking waves dash'd high
>   On a stern and rock-bound coast
> And the woods, against a stormy sky,
>   Their giant branches tost;
>
> And the heavy night hung dark
>   The hills and waters o'er,
> When a band of exiles moor'd their bark
>   On the wild New England shore.

Not as the conqueror comes,
　　They, the true-hearted came,
Not with the roll of the stirring drums,
　　And the trumpet that sings of fame;

Not as the flying come,
　　In silence and in fear,—
They shook the depths of the desert's gloom,
　　With their hymns of lofty cheer.

Amidst the storm they sang,
　　And the stars heard and the sea!
And the sounding aisles of the dim woods rang
　　To the anthem of the free! (*Poems*, 1:25–26)

Hemans went on for another five stanzas to celebrate the errand of the Pilgrim Fathers, which had brought old men "with hoary hair" and women with "fearless eye" to a storm-wracked coast and which was not a quest for treasure but for "a faith's pure shrine!" "Ay, call it holy ground," Hemans ended famously, "The soil where first they trod! / They have left unstain'd what there they found / —Freedom to worship God!" (27). Norton gave the poem a place of honor in his edition, second only to Hemans's celebration of Swiss freedom, "The League of the Alps," and introduced it with an admiring note: "Every one must feel the sublimity and poetical truth, with which she has conceived the scene presented, and the inspiration of that deep and holy strain of sentiment, which sounds forth like the pealing of an organ" (27). Norton, however, did not touch on the genesis of the poem, which was only made public after the death of both the poet and her editor.

The testimony was that of the Reverend Charles Brooks, who chose the occasion of the first meeting of the Cape Cod Association in 1851 to recount an interview with the poet many years earlier. The association had been formed to call attention to the fact that the Pilgrims had first landed in the vicinity of Provincetown, not Plymouth, and though the natives of the rival town had the Rock, the people of the Cape had the recorded priority of arrival, as well as sundry relics, including the blanket "in which Peregrine White, the first born of Cape Cod, was wrapped" (*Constitution*, 17). These objects were exhibited in Assembly Hall on December 11, along with "portraits of distinguished natives of Cape Cod" and a suspended fish of that designation.

The main orator of the day was Henry A. Scudder, lawyer of local note, who, while admitting that the earliest chronicles of the Cape were bare of event, managed to fill two hours in honoring the Forefathers, giving great stress to the importance of the Compact, which had been written while the *Mayflower* lay at anchor in Provincetown harbor. There then followed the usual dinner, followed by the traditional poetry, jests, and toasts, the most interesting of which was given by the Reverend Brooks. Responding to "The Clergy," he recalled his meeting with Felicia Hemans in 1834, during which the poet had related the occasion of the inspiration and composition of her famous hymn:

> I purchased two volumes at the book-store and brought them home, and as I laid them on my table my eye was attracted by their envelope, which proved to be eight pages 8vo, of an address delivered at Plymouth on some anniversary. There was no title page and no date. The excellence of the paper and the beauty of the type first arrested my attention; but, how this stray fragment got to Ireland, I could never ascertain. I began to read, and I found it contained an entire description of the fact of landing, and so beautiful was the painting and so thrilling the fact, that I could not rest till I had thrown them into verse. . . . I caught the fire from this transatlantic torch and began to write, and before I was aware I had finished my poem. (75–76)

The Reverend Brooks ended his story by praising "*the truth*" that "*makes the poetry*," for "so true is that poem to the facts and feelings of the case, that this fortunate lady has connected her name forever with the shore of Plymouth and the landing of our fathers; yes, so long as 'the breaking waves dash high on that stern and rock-bound coast,' to chant their ocean dirge at the grave of the Pilgrim, so long shall be joined in the sacred requiem the name of Felicia Hemans." But in gushing over the "truth" to be found in Hemans's poem, the Reverend Brooks generously overlooked a certain poetic license. As any number of scholars and orators were to observe, the first landing at Plymouth was made by ten men in a boat, not the entire passenger list of the *Mayflower*. Then, too, no contemporary account of the Pilgrims' arrival, either on the Cape or at Plymouth, records the singing of grateful hymns. Finally, there is that howler that can be heard above the sound of the waves breaking high, for, once again, the coast of Massachusetts near Plymouth is chiefly sand.

Not all of Felicia Hemans's American visitors were quite so considerate as Mr. Brooks claimed to have been. Moncure Conway's *Autobiography* records a visit paid to her by "the elder Channing" when he was in Europe: "He spoke of her hymn on 'The Landing of the Pilgrim Fathers in New England,' and told her that he had heard it sung by a great multitude on the spot where the Pilgrims landed. But when, in answer to her questions, he was compelled to inform her that the coast described in her hymn as 'stern and rock-bound' was lacking the definitive article, she burst into tears" (1:161).

There are, however, some problems detectable in Conway's account. William Ellery (the elder) Channing made his European visit in 1822–23, before his correspondence with Felicia Hemans began and most certainly before her famous song was written. On the other hand, Andrews Norton (the "elder" Norton, father of Charles Eliot) did visit his ideal poetess while abroad in 1827, and it may have been he who caused further hardship and sorrow on the part of the long-suffering "authoress." If such was the case, the two contemporary biographies of Hemans are silent on the matter.

Moreover, the Reverend Brooks recalled having told his hostess "how I had stood with a thousand persons in the old Pilgrim Church, at Plymouth, on 'Forefathers' Day,' and sung with them her exquisite hymn," a remark that caused "a tear to steal into her eye" (76). This part of his recollection audibly resonates with Conway's anecdote, so perhaps it was Brooks who broke the bad news. He was certainly guilty of a crime of omission, for nowhere does he reveal the identity of the author of the inspirational passage that got Felicia Hemans's pen flowing fast. Edward Everett's name first appears in connection with the episode in 1852, the year after Brooks told his story in Boston, in a Forefathers' Day sermon delivered by the Reverend Alvan Lamson in Dedham, Massachusetts. The minister in a footnote credited the oration to "the Hon. Edward Everett . . . judging from what the author of the poem says of the beauty of the typography, taken in connection with the very graphic description of the voyage and landing" (36).

But Webster's oration of 1820 fits both characteristics also, and John Quincy Adams's address of 1802, reprinted in 1819 in anticipation of the Bicentennial, not only fits the physical description given by Hemans of the text but contains the main thrust of her poem, that the Pilgrims came in peace, not war. And yet Everett's description of the Landing comes closest in spirit and language to the poem, and, most conclusively, it is in his oration that the image of an "iron-bound coast" appears, which, with his evocation of the icy rockiness of the Plymouth shore, may have inspired Hemans's equally anomalous, if much more famous, phrase. And it was Everett who used the phrase, stolen from Joseph Addison, in association with the "footsteps of our suffering fathers . . . a classic, yea, a holy land," which had been translated by Hemans into "holy ground," though Everett was speaking of Old England, the celebrated place of the Pilgrims' origin, not New, and Addison of Italy (65). Still, that unbound sheets of an oration published early in 1825 should have reached Hemans in time to inspire a poem that would have arrived in America to be included in her collected works later that same year suggests another "happy" concatenation of events close to the miraculous.

Whatever its source, Hemans's hymn would be frequently sung on Forefathers' Day across America and was regularly quoted in oratorical celebrations of the Pilgrims. There was something in the idea of a stormy landing on a rocky shore that enhanced the event, reinforcing even if it was not derived from Everett's ideology of adversity. Thus, in 1820, William Crafts had anticipated Everett by bringing the Pilgrims "in a little barque, across the perilous ocean, to an ice-bound rocky shore" (6). And as late as 1851, Alfred B. Street entertained the Phi Beta Kappa Society at Yale with a poem in which he rendered a virtual paraphrase of Hemans's opening lines, a description given through the mouth of a participating Pilgrim, who told "How the dark surges burst in thundering shocks / Upon the wintry whiteness of the rocks" (13).

From the beginning, as we have seen, painters starting with Corné preferred a hard-faced vista against which to set the Landing, and Sargent's dramatic depiction used cliffs and a splintered tree trunk to lend force and images of adversity to his setting. By means of a lithograph, Sargent's picture was circulated widely, giving validity to Everett's image, perhaps even inspiring it. In 1854, Peter F. Rothermel gave further impetus to this tradition with his *The Landing of the Pilgrims on Plymouth Rock*, a Gothicized version of the event that would seem to have been inspired by Hemans's lines. But a pamphlet published to advertise an engraved version of Rothermel's work quotes an equivalent work by William Cullen Bryant, first read before the New England Society in the City of New York in 1829, which begins:

Wild was the day, the wintry sea
   Moaned sadly on New England's strand,
When first the thoughtful and the free,
   Our fathers, trod the desert land. (*New England Society Orations*, 1:142)

It is notable that Bryant avoided rocks for the general and ambiguous "strand," and the pamphlet quotes William Russell, the Plymouth antiquarian, to the effect that " 'there is not known in the township a single ledge save those the fisherman reaches with his lead at various points of the coast' " (*Description*, 7). But that is not the impression conveyed by Rothermel's rendering of the scene, which is of a considerable ledge against which the shallop is "being held, with rope and pole, by the strong arms of the Pilgrim band," at the center of which is "the erect and manly form of Isaac Allerton . . . grasping a long pole, by means of which, with energetic firmness, he is shoving or holding the boat in its position" (11).

We shall be returning to Rothermel's painting in quite another context, but the point to be made here is that the aesthetic preference operating in England and America during the first half of the nineteenth century demanded something as a backdrop to the Landing in keeping with contemporary notions of the Picturesque, which in terms of heroism required an element of the Sublime. It will be remembered that Alison's theory of association posited histor-

FIGURE 13. Peter Rothermel's *Landing of the Pilgrims at Plymouth Rock* (1854). Though apparently inspired by Bryant's poem of 1829, this Gothicized tableau lent massive sanction to Mrs. Hemans's image of breaking waves. But Rothermel added an element of pathos by giving the center of his composition to Rose Standish—shown being handed ashore by her husband, who lacks the armaments so often associated with the man. (See also figs. 1, 4, 16.) (Courtesy Lafayette College)

ical events as enhancing that element, but it did not discount the benefits of an awe-inspiring natural setting, which Everett derived from Burke along with his spatial theory of survival.

Given Everett's complicity in promoting the Landing in adversarial terms, it is interesting that in a later speech he rendered a description of the *Mayflower*'s arrival that was antithetical in imagery and implication, but as effective in its way as his earlier "vision." The occasion was the Bicentennial in 1839 of the founding of Barnstable, a town on outermost Cape Cod. Everett was not the featured speaker of the day but rose to give an extended response to "The Pilgrim Fathers," which would have almost as much currency over the years as his version of the Landing in 1824. Varying from his usual habit, he delivered not a prepared but an impromptu speech, at the center of which was a metaphor that extends the idea of "the everlasting rock of liberty" to a much grander iconographic reach, while still keeping it within the geopolitical confines of Massachusetts (*Orations and Speeches*, 2:329).

Everett's metaphor can be explained by the occasion, which was to celebrate the Cape Cod priority, but it also was dictated by his desire to remedy the emphasis of his oration in 1824 on good fortune as shaping the destiny and character of the Pilgrims. We can find several references to Providence in his Plymouth address, but in the view of his former student, Emerson, they did not sufficiently dominate the historical context. Having read "Everett's rich strains at Plymouth" and approved in general of "the auspicious promise of the times" held out by "*our Cicero*," Emerson went on to grumble in his journal about the contrast between the Pilgrims "in their tribulation kneeling to God" and Everett in the midst of modern "prosperity" deeming that "the settlement at Plymouth (the most conspicuous interposition of God's Providence in these latter days) [was] *fortunate*" (*Journals*, II:318–19).

Emerson is here in sympathy with the Reverend William Torrey of Plymouth's Third Church, who in 1821 had mounted a pointed attempt to rectify what he regarded as Webster's glib expressions of "joy" in 1820, a mood that was not, as Torrey saw it, "universal" throughout New England, or Philip Melancthon Whelpley, the orthodox minister who had objected in 1822 that the rhetoric celebrating the Landing had drifted too far into secular and political considerations and ignored the religious, even divine nature of the event (Torrey, 18; *New England Society Orations*, 1:126). We may assume that other clerics also objected to "the scepticism of prosperity, the scepticism of knowledge, the darkness of light" that had radiated from Everett's "Sun" until Emerson's "eyes [we]re blurred." In 1839, therefore, Everett took especial pains to trace the clear lines of providential favor that blessed the advent of the Pilgrims in America. He retained the main thrust of his earlier argument, that the "founders of the new republic beyond the sea" were being trained "for their illustrious mission" by an extended experience of "obscurity, hardship, and weary exile" in the Old World, but it was something more than the winds of secular progress that blew them to the Massachusetts coast (331).

For when Everett got to the centerpiece of his impromptu performance, that traditional "vision" of the *Mayflower*'s arrival—now displaced from Plymouth to Provincetown—he magnified the "single dark speck, just discernible through the perspective glass, on the waste of waters" (yet another borrowing from Burke via Webster) into a vessel of the divine will: "I dare not call it a mere piece of good fortune, that the . . . shore of New England should be broken by this extraordinary projection of the Cape, running out into the ocean a hundred miles, as if on purpose to receive and encircle the precious vessel" (331). Everett went on to provide an immense set of God-given geographic brackets within which to place the arrival of the Forefathers, a revisionary vision keyed by the phrase "As I *now* see her": "As I now see her, freighted with the destinies of a continent, barely escaped from the perils of the deep, approaching the shore precisely where the broad sweep of this most remarkable headland presents almost the only point at which, for hundreds of miles, she could with any ease have made a harbor, and this perhaps the very best on the seaboard, I feel my spirit raised above the sphere of mere natural agencies. . . . Yes, the everlasting God himself stretches out the arm of his mercy and his power in substantial manifestation, and gathers the meek company of his worshippers in the hollow of his hand" (331–32). This passage was singled out by newspaper editors of the day for quotation and enjoyed considerable circulation thereafter. As a regional expression, moreover, Everett's encircling Cape is integral to the centripetal emphasis of New England's original Separatist errand and its continuing geopolitical role. It is an essentially conservative metaphor, which evokes the imagery of asylum and stasis, not territorial expansion, which in New England was regarded as a perpetual threat to regional—and moral—integrity.

Everett's imagery was sanctioned, if not inspired, by the picture decorating the certificates of membership first issued by the Pilgrim Society in Plymouth in time for the celebration of 1820 (see fig. 12). There, the Rock is shown as a modest but definably accommodating arm extending into the bay, as the recently arrived Pilgrims set about what are clearly domestic, not heroic, chores. The family-friendly composition includes in the foreground a woman removing articles from a trunk, as her male companions point toward an Indian who is presumably Samoset with his welcoming words. As Everett reminded his audience, it was the soft, even matronly shore of the Cape that was "pressed by the feet of the Pilgrims before they rested on Plymouth Rock," this in a discourse that began with a gracious tribute to "those excellent, noble-hearted women, the MOTHERS of Plymouth and Massachusetts, who bore their full share of the hardships and afflictions of the first settlement" (334, 325). Here again we find a note in harmony with the female figure in the foreground of the Pilgrim Society certificate, although it would be almost twenty more years before the image of the Pilgrims would be feminized.

Still, by 1839 there were forces already at work in New England that would result in such gender revisions with which Everett was obviously in synchronization and for which he should be given due credit. Equally important was his emphasis on the arrival of the *Mayflower* as an event enclosed by sheltering, providential arms, a configuration enhancing the idea of New England as a special, divinely sanctioned asylum, which would by 1839 be lending a righteous impulse to forces that would drive Everett permanently from his long career of public service. In the view of his opponents New England's embrace was as yet not wide enough, and the exceptionalism associated with providential intervention promoted the antithetical notions of exclusivism and exclusionism as well.

CHAPTER 6

Circumferential Matters Relating to the Rock

We trace the mount *which gently soars,*
Above the sea and circling shores,
Where Standish, first of martial name,
Who dauntless won heroic fame . . .
Was wont to gaze on every side,
And scan the sail of every tide.
—*William S. Russell*

I

We have and will continue to put a stress on Forefathers' Day sermons and orations as the main vehicle by which the sacramentalization of Plymouth Rock was effected. But perhaps because of the example of Webster and Everett, during the 1820s speakers on other formal New England occasions began to evoke the Pilgrims also, two notable examples of which are worth considering here, the Reverend F. W. P. Greenwood's sermon before the Artillery Company of Boston in 1826, and the Reverend Orville Dewey's election sermon honoring Governor Levi Lincoln that same year. Their sermons were distinct from Forefathers' Day orations, in that they were not specifically framed to honor an anniversary, but because the occasions and genres stretched back to the very beginnings of the Bay Colony, in 1826 both Dewey and Greenwood were earnest in pressing the matter of historic continuity. Such an emphasis necessarily took them back to the Pilgrims and their Rock, permitting opportunities to honor even while skirting Webster's priority, in effect heeding Everett's example.

Thus Greenwood, a Unitarian and associate pastor of King's Chapel in Boston, noted that the first "train band"—the predecessor of the citizen militia made famous by events at Lexington and Bunker Hill—"was gathered a few years only after the landing of our pilgrim fathers on the rocks of Plymouth," a fact that necessitated a commemoration of "the spirit, the principles and the deeds of men, from whom we boast, and have reason to boast, that we are descended" (3–4). Greenwood's "rocks" clearly derive from Everett, as did his rehearsal of the "old tale," the perilous crossing that ended on "a hard and wintry coast, unfruitful and desolate" but empty also of persecutors: "They saw that they were free, and the desert smiled" (6–7). Emphasizing with Everett the blessings of space, Greenwood, like so many other Burke-inspired celebrants of the Pilgrims, traced back to them "the beginnings of the revolution" (8).

Greenwood also felt called upon to respond to the reputation of the Puritans as "dark, deluded enthusiasts" and went on to justify each "fault" in turn as the result of "their piety and sense of religious obligation" (9). This necessity of Puritan celebrants to defend the Forefathers against charges of bigotry and superstition dates from John Quincy Adams's oration in 1802, and having admitted the Forefathers were hardly without their flaws, Greenwood went on to echo Adams in urging his auditors "to preserve whatever was excellent in the manners and lives of the puritans, while we forsake what was inconsistent or unreasonable; and then we shall hardly fail to be wiser and happier, and even better than they were" (22).

"Better than they were" clues Greenwood's doctrinal bias, an Enlightenment faith in the inevitability of Progress. Orville Dewey, also a Unitarian minister, followed a similar line in stating *The Claims of Puritanism*. He started with a retrospective frame that emphasized the traditional aspect of the occasion, which necessarily "reminded" him of "the days of the Puritans," establishing an immediate line of continuity (3). Like Greenwood, Dewey felt it incumbent on him to "vindicate the Forefathers from some portion of the unmeasured obloquy and abuse . . . heaped upon their memory" (6). But where Greenwood's Unitarianism was conservative and posited the strictness of the Fathers as a salutary antidote to contemporary "softness, and indulgences, and foreign fashions," Dewey, the protégé of William Ellery Channing, took a somewhat more liberal tack (Greenwood, 20).

In effect championing the qualities of the Fathers that Greenwood had cited in their disfavor, Dewey translated them into terms agreeable to "the general liberality of the age," beginning with a lengthy examination of "the first crime of which they were guilty," namely "dissent," a crime only in the ironic sense: "How has the cause of knowledge, liberty or religion ever advanced in the world, but by this same hated dissent? . . . The very watchwords of the more improved and liberal systems of these times are—if I may venture so to denominate them—'no dissent, no improvement!' Forbid the one, and you effectively exclude the other. . . . Break up this necessary dependency of things, and the march of civilization, of the arts, of knowledge, liberty and religion is at a stand" (4, 6, 8). These were brave words in 1826, surely, of the same order as Webster's stand on the slave trade, and like Webster Dewey would live to regret them.

Greenwood had ended his sermon with a retrospective emphasis, urging his auditors to look back down the long line of Puritan soldiers in whose ranks they were now standing and to "regard those old members as still in the midst of you . . . to keep alive in your bosoms the pure calm flame of freedom" (22). He thereby enlisted his Artillery Company among the eternal ranks of New England's defenders, but Dewey worked in the opposite direction, making of the Puritans not a sheet anchor of conservative continuity but early equivalents to the kind of modern workers for improvements with whom the age was blest: "The only possible method of advancement . . . is for some minds to take the lead, to become enlighteners and guides for the rest—to become *dissenters*" (7–8). Reform in 1826 was to the Unitarians what internal improvements were to the emerging Whigs, and given the interlock Lawrence Buell has demonstrated between the Unitarian Church and the Whig Party, both issues can be seen as congruent parts of the contemporary faith in Progress. Rather than linking his auditors to the Pilgrims and thereby making them part of a vast historical continuity, Dewey made over the Pilgrims into replicas of modern reformers.

In time, establishment Whigs and their clerical counterparts would not be happy with any such coupling of the Forefathers with modern dissent, but in 1826 Dewey was caught up in the euphoria generated by the movement toward moral reform that characterized the decade. He cited the "first printed Sermon" preached in Plymouth by John Cushman, which urged the Pilgrims "not to live for themselves, alone or only for one another, but for their posterity" (21). And in language reminiscent of Webster's, although traceable as well to Archibald Alison's associationist aesthetic, Dewey insisted upon the importance of "consecrated spots: places, the bare mention of which, is enough to awaken, in all ages, the reverence and enthusiasm of mankind." With an allusion to the monument designed for Bunker Hill, Dewey noted that "the structures of art that shall rise upon" these sacred places "shall only *point them out* to other times, as holy." But battlefields are not the only scenes of ideological struggle, and "harder contests than those of blood and battle have been sustained in this land," a reflection that brought Dewey finally to "the Rock of Plymouth," not an artificial but a natural memorial marking the place "where a handful of men held conflict with ghastly famine, and sweeping pestilence, and the wintry storm; held conflict, and were not conquered" (25).

Dewey urged his auditors "to gather around that shrine of our Father's virtues, that monument of their toils and sufferings, which the chafing billows of the ocean shall never wear away." And in making "a holy pilgrimage to that sacred spot," in listening to "gifted orators and statesmen proclaim our enthusiasm and our gratitude," we should always bear in mind that modern pilgrims do not go "through the solitary glooms and howling storms of the wilderness . . . not amidst poverty, and peril, and sickness . . . but through rich plantations and happy villages, with chariots and horses, and equipages and state, with social mirth and joyful minstrelsy and music" (25–26). Such remembrance should foster not only gratitude but emulation of the Pilgrims' virtues, for there are "dangers" in the modern day, not those of a fanged wilderness but of "comparative ease and safety, of sensuality, of intemperance and effeminacy," most especially the "single evil of intemperance . . . more to be dreaded in the land than all the hardships and perils of the sea and the wilderness" (29).

So also Greenwood. But Dewey's emphasis was chiefly on the happy modern moment, as opposed to the dark mood of election-day gatherings in the time of the Puritans, "when fear, and perplexity, and gloom sat heavily on the general mind and countenance" (31). He ended his sermon, in effect, on relatively safe ground, having retreated from his opening celebration of the Puritans as dissenters to the heights of self-congratulation on the blessings of the modern age. But along the way he had revealed a disjunction deeply embedded in the Unitarian consciousness, which in forswearing the divinity of Christ made Him over into a modern reformer, yet as a Man of Peace the Unitarian Savior was given a happy face. Not from Him (or His celebrants) could we expect dissent of the kind disturbing to the status quo.

Moreover, although both Greenwood and Dewey, like Everett, gave relatively short shrift to Webster's Rock, they shared with their predecessor orators the sense that the site of the Pilgrim Landing is a sacred spot. Equally important, in urging their auditors to make a pilgrimage to the site, all four speakers mounted complex figures intended to effect a union between the living auditors and the saintly dead. Thus Webster and Everett summoned their audiences to the shore as witnesses to the Pilgrims' arrival; Greenwood suggested that the living ranks of the Artillery Company are but the end of a long thin line of soldiers still standing in ghostly readiness to defend New England's liberties; and Dewey strove to remind modern visitors to Plymouth that their happiness was both a stark contrast to and a result of the sufferings of the first visitors to that place two centuries ago. These emphases are not new to Forefathers' Day addresses, which from the very beginning tended to stress an optative mood, but they are, even in the performances of the ministers, overwhelmingly statist in emphasis, once again in harmony with the Era of Good Feelings.

And yet something of the evangelical spirit can be detected in these orations and sermons also, an emphasis on community and witness, by means of which the historical moment becomes a kind of text in which the audience is invited to participate, to join, as it were, the whole body of the Forefathers. Gratitude, as Dewey suggested, should inspire emulation, making dissent an ongoing heritage of the Pilgrims. This hortatory emphasis should remind us of the wave of revivals then in motion, which was to gain terrific momentum during the next decade, with spun-off dervishes who would give new meaning to the idea of dissent. That the four speakers were Unitarians, while evangelism was a Trinitarian Congregationalist article of faith, suggests that there was a spirit of the age at work here, much as the Whig Party during the succeeding decades would utilize a secular version of the mechanics of revivalism in order to arouse popular enthusiasm for their candidates, a calculated response to the changing demographics of democracy.

II

There is, of course, that more immediate analogy, the Fourth of July oration, which provided a secular scripture and promoted a version of the Aenean piety. These forensic efforts, which emerged with and shared the conventions of Forefathers' Day orations, began to crowd election-day sermons in Massachusetts as the chief venue for regional pieties, if only because they tended to expand local matters into national significance, becoming yet another agency reinforcing New England's need for a sense of self-importance. To a foreign eye, such chauvinistic exercises could be the source of amusement. In 1827 there appeared in London a book entitled *American Sketches*, whose anonymous author was identified as "a Native of the United States," by which was meant a person of Native American origin. The identity was obviously assumed, for though the writer demonstrated a genuine familiarity with America, especially the South, he seems likely to have been yet one more English traveler disenchanted with the progress of democracy. And in a humorous parody, "Visions of the Fourth of July," which followed his wry account of Lafayette's worshipful reception in the United States, the writer rendered an epitome of what was becoming a predictable and therefore boring annual rite.

The author mockingly runs through the entire gamut of well-worn patriotic "visions," concluding with this sneer: "For my own part, I do not see what necessity or even propriety there can be in continuing these orations. The Declaration of Independence is all that is worth reading on the subject" (116). Such ritual performances he noted are predictable even to the chronological necessity: they always begin at the beginning, with the Landing of 1620, providing the orator an occasion for informing his "astonished audience" about the Pilgrims' advent:

They came a set of noble adventurers, a band of brothers, in a little boat over the angry waters of the Atlantic; and, after experiencing, like all other boats, great and small, the sunshine and the storm of old Ocean, touched, at length, upon the rocky shores of New England—great stress generally laid upon the circumstance of the shores being rocky—because all shores are not. Then follows a compliment to the New Englander—because the pilgrims landed at Plymouth, instead of Staten Island, the Virginia, or Delaware Capes—to which, perhaps, the wind happened not to be blowing at that time. The situation of the pilgrims upon the memorable rock, which they afterwards removed to the centre of the town, where it is to be seen to this day—what had they to do upon this rock? Why, they first managed to kindle a fire in that frozen clime, a very wise precaution on the part of the pilgrims. (100–101)

The parodist then passes on to the convention of citing the amazing record of American progress consequent upon the arrival of the *Mayflower*: "Plymouth was then a barren rock—it has now four or five thousand inhabitants! extraordinary fact, this" (102). Obviously, then, not all English readers were as impressed by American oratory as was Felicia Hemans, but even parodies serve a useful function, assuring us of the mandatory evocation of the Pilgrims and their Landing—and a rocky coast—in patriotic discourse, clear evidence of the influence not only of Webster but also of Everett, whose emphasis on happy chance is mocked in this passage.

These repetitions were reinforced in other ways, as well. In 1827, also, John Pierpont, a poet, Unitarian minister, and compiler of textbooks, entered for copyright his *National Reader; a Selection of Exercises in Reading and Speaking, Designed to Fill the Same Place in the Schools of the United States, That Is Held in Those of Great Britain by the Compilations of Murray, Scott, Enfield, Mylius, Thompson, Ewing, and Others*, the self-advertising title of which reveals its purpose. Having already published with great success his *American First Class Book* in 1823, Pierpont determined there was a need in the United States for a reader "*designed* for American schools." His textbooks were part and parcel of the jubilee mood of the 1820s and reflected as well the literary nationalism of the period, which produced Noah Webster's dictionary of the "American language" the following year, as well as *Rachel Dyer*, a self-consciously "American" work of fiction by John Neal, Pierpont's former business partner and his lifelong correspondent.

We have, reasoned Pierpont in his preface, our own political institutions and our own history, in which our children need to be instructed. Likewise, "our country, both physically and morally, has a character of its own," in which American children should be instructed, in order to make them better citizens:

"Its mountains, and prairies, and lakes, and rivers, and cataracts—its shores and hill-tops, that were early made sacred by the dangers, and sacrifices, and deaths, of the devout and the daring—it does seem as if these were worthy of being held up, as objects of interest, to the young eyes that . . . are opening upon them, and worthy of being linked, with all their sacred associations, to the young affections, which sooner or later, *must* be bound to them, or they must cease to be . . . the inheritance and abode of a free people" (iii–iv). The operative influence, clearly, was that of Archibald Alison, hinted at by the notion of a "moral" landscape, made "sacred" by "associations," and it is notable that the penultimate selection in the *American First Class Book* is an excerpt from Alison extolling the moral influence of natural scenery.

Not surprisingly, many of the orations we have been concerned with here were included by means of excerpts by Pierpont in his *Reader*: Everett, Greenwood, and Dewey are represented by their descriptions of the Pilgrims' arrival, all of which continued to celebrate the exceptionalist nature of the American experience, just the emphasis that the author of *American Sketches* found so amusing and jejune. Webster's Plymouth oration is not represented in Pierpont's *Reader* for the simple reason that it provided two generous selections for his earlier *First Class Book*; and instead it is the Bunker Hill address that increased the chauvinist fervor and regional bias of the 1827 textbook.

Though Pierpont in his preface noted that the selections chosen were not "entirely . . . American productions," for "a national spirit" is not "an exclusive spirit," he gave New England authors a virtual monopoly among those Americans whose names appear in the table of contents. While Felicia Hemans's lines to the Pilgrims appear in the poetry section, so does Pierpont's own "The Pilgrim Fathers," written for the Forefathers' Day exercises in Plymouth the year before. By its inclusion, Pierpont answered his own poetic refrain, "The Pilgrim Fathers, where are they?" ensuring that they would be permanently installed in schoolrooms across the land and by repetition installed in youthful memories as well. True, in 1827 New England certainly had precedence in numbers where American authorship was concerned, but Pierpont's attempt at producing a "national" reader was so successful that it was kept in print for more than a quarter century before being revised, thereby guaranteeing that sanctity of place would be closely identified with his native region by the rising generation.

In 1804, as we have seen, Jedidiah Morse had anticipated Pierpont's logic by appending to his *History of New England* selections from three Forefathers' Day addresses, and Morse was in other ways anticipatory of later, more detailed efforts to celebrate and extend his region's influence. In his *American Gazeteer*, first published in 1797, he made up by means of an expanded entry for "Plymouth" in the appendix for his remissness in his *Geography* of 1789, noting that "the *rock* on which their forefathers first landed, was conveyed, in 1774, from the shore to a square in the centre of the town. The sentimental traveller will not fail to view it." Notably, this entry predates the first of the Feasts of Shells in Boston, as well as Timothy Dwight's "sentimental" visit to the Rock in 1800, which was not made available to the public until the four volumes of his *Travels* were published in 1822. As John Sears has shown us, Dwight's work contributed to the growing phenomenon of tourism, aided and abetted by the urging of Orville Dewey and others that patriotism required visits to the sites made sacred by the sacrifices of the Forefathers.

When in 1828 Theodore Dwight, the elder Dwight's nephew, revised and expanded his popular guide book, *The Northern Traveler*, he acknowledged the primacy of that mystic stone on which his revered uncle and tutor had perched nearly thirty years earlier. Like Pierpont, the younger Dwight relied on Alison in defining the town of Plymouth as being "highly interesting" because of its "history, being the site of the first settlement made by the New-England Pilgrims in 1620. . . . A mass of granite rock is still shown on which those stepped who first landed. It has been divided, and a part of it remains buried near the shore in its natural location, while the upper part is removed into the centre of the village" (304). Dwight was carefully circumspect in his description, "mass" being sufficiently ambivalent for his purposes, conveying the impression of monumentality without being specific.

In a subsequent volume of travel sketches, *Things as They Are* (1834), Dwight expanded on his earlier entry, along the sentimental lines laid down by his uncle, and recorded his own visit to Plymouth, undertaken "with becoming reverence, on account of the memory of our forefathers. What a dreary scene must the coast have presented to them when they landed on this spot in December, 1620!" (166–67). With a careful, even a topographical eye, Dwight reduced Felicia Hemans's sublime scene to "a range of low hills" that gave an unpicturesque "uniformity to the shore, to which nothing but some important historic event could have given interest" (167). As Dwight attested, the rim of Massachusetts Bay is covered with an "undulating surface of light sand, intermingled with loose primitive rocks," including the shore of Cape Cod, "on which the Pilgrims first affected a landing," and the beach at Plymouth around "Carver's rock, on which tradition says they first stepped from their boat." Dwight's uninspiring vista and idiosyncratic nomenclature notwithstanding, he rehearsed the pieties of the place, from which "we can trace the operations of their principles among our countrymen, [and] find that we owe to them almost every thing we are and have and hope for."

In 1834 also was published the first volume of George Bancroft's magisterial history of the United States, animated throughout with the faith in Progress that characterized so much patriotic rhetoric of the previous decade. Though

Bancroft hedged on the function of "the rock marked by a grateful posterity . . . near which they landed," he did not hold back regarding the "day" of the Landing, celebrated as "the origin of New England, the planting of its institutions. Historians love to trace every vestige of the pilgrims; poets commemorate their virtues; the noblest genius has been called into exercise to display their merits worthily, and to trace the consequences of their enterprise," to which Bancroft's next nine volumes were devoted (1:246). A Jacksonian Democrat, Bancroft serves here to move us from the jubilant 1820s into an era seldom characterized as one of good feelings. Though Bancroft shared with the emerging Whigs a belief that the United States was an avatar of Western progress, his terms were often different from the view promoted by Webster and Everett.

We shall in time, like Orville Dewey, have our fill of dissent, but let us here take brief note of a contrariwise reading of New England history that was delivered as an oration in 1836 by William Apess, a Pequot Indian. Choosing as his occasion the 160th anniversary of the death of King Philip, Apess mocked the conventions of the Forefathers' Day address toward a much more serious end than that of the pseudo-Amerindian who wrote *American Sketches*. His own people having been massacred by the people celebrated on December 22, he presented himself as one of a very few "descendants who now remain as the monument of those who came to improve our race and correct our errors" (277). For Apess, the "American Pilgrims" were guilty of "the most daring robberies and barbarous deeds of death," all of which were borne "with patience and resignation" by the native peoples of New England, "in a manner that would do justice to any Christian nation or being in the world" (278).

From Apess's point of view, the day in December associated with the Pilgrim Landing was not sacred to the idea of Liberty, quite the reverse: "The Pilgrims landed at Plymouth, and without asking liberty from anyone they possessed themselves of the country, and built themselves houses, and then made a treaty, and commanded [the people of Massasoit] to accede to it. This, if now done, it would be called an insult, and every white man would be called to go out and act the part of a patriot, to defend their country's rights" (280). Apess went on to render in detail the "injuries upon injuries" inflicted on the region's inhabitants by the Pilgrims, concluding that the "22nd day of December, 1622" should not be a day to celebrate but rather one to mourn: "Let the children of the Pilgrims blush, while the son of the forest drops a tear and groans over the fate of his murdered and departed fathers. He would say to the sons of the Pilgrims . . . let the day be dark . . . let it be forgotten in your celebration, in your speeches, and by the burying of the rock that your fathers first put their foot upon" (288). This last insult was a reference to Dwight's famous caveat against burying the Rock, in turn a reference to Elder Faunce's plea, but the burden of Apess's oration was necessarily on King Philip's War. He undoubtedly took a measure of strength from Washington Irving's sympathetic account of both the Native American and Metacomet in *The Sketch Book*, but his rhetoric borrowed the strategy of the burgeoning abolition movement.

"We say," declared Apess, "let every man of color wrap himself in mourning, for the 22nd of December and the 4th of July are days of mourning and not of joy. . . . Let them rather fast and pray to the great Spirit, the Indian's God, who deals out mercy to his red children, and not destruction." These words echo William Lloyd Garrison's sentiments aimed at persons "of color" (albeit not red) in America and are but a small part of a much larger rhetorical tradition associated with the emergence of the abolition movement, with which we shall concern ourselves at a later point. They are included here as a specimen example of sentiments contrary to those ritual expressions of celebration associated with days sacred to the Landing and the Declaration of Independence, marginal and in the minority, but providing a necessary antiphony to the dominant chorus of affirmation. By 1830, moreover, other voices were heard in New England that prophesied doom rather than a glorious future for the sons of the Pilgrims, signaling that the Era of Good Feelings was indeed over and that troubling times lay ahead. Webster's example loomed over the 1820s, nor would it ever be ignored, but by the end of the decade a number of orators would regard his optimism as unwarranted.

III

The oration on Forefathers' Day in Plymouth in 1829 was delivered by William Sullivan, a Federalist who had served for a quarter century in the Massachusetts legislature but was about to step down. Sullivan's decision to retire was facilitated by his wife's having come into a sizable inheritance, but it was undoubtedly inspired as well by the advent of Andrew Jackson, for his oration is dark with the shadow cast by the Democratic ascendancy and his overview burdened with the grim prospects facing the United States. Gone from the contemporary scene were men like George Washington, from whose "elevated standard" the stature of the country's leaders had declined, to the point where "the surest means to recommend [a man] to office" was a mixture of "disgusting adulation . . . and odious crimination" (26). So bad was the state of politics in the United States that Sullivan wondered aloud if "this country will continue as free, and as happy, as the Pilgrims intended it to be?" (15).

He therefore, like Apess but for quite different reasons, felt himself unable to follow the usual (i.e., Whig/Unitarian) custom on such occasions, to speak "of American happiness . . . with high sounding praise . . . to announce, with prophetic confidence the unceasing glories of civil liberty, through successive ages" (13). He stressed at the start the extent to which the fortunes of the Pilgrims "seem to have hung upon some incident, which turning, ever so little, one way or the other, might be favorable or fatal" (9). Sullivan was thereby echoing Everett's theme in 1824 but with no emphasis on the Panglossian winds of Progress that directed all things to the good. Sullivan's is a tragic view of life, and in evoking "the familiar knowledge" of what occurred and what followed in "this interesting place," he hints that things might have gone in a different and darker direction (8).

Nor may the sons of the Pilgrims rest assured that the fortunate sequence will continue, the Democrats having "set up an imaginary being called 'THE PEOPLE.' This being is wise, infallible, sacred. . . . The rest are the *minority*, that is, *nobody*" (50). Though the Pilgrims may have set in motion the forces that brought about the Revolution and the ideals embodied in the Constitution, the certainties of the past are forever threatened by unpredictable shifts and changes in the body politic: "The administration of such a government [as ours] is truly difficult, even when the highest minds, governed by the purist motives, are called to it. What then may it become, when the object is to carry men and measures; or to raise a rampart around a usurped authority?" (29). Here again we have the familiar Federalist paranoia expressing itself, not in terms of Jacobin infiltration but by the threat of a military presence in the White House. Sullivan spoke darkly of the "well-grounded fear . . . that a commander returning victorious from some conquered province, or republic, will attempt to conquer his own country" (36–37). General Jackson as an American Napoleon seems to cohere from this nebulous hint, in stark contrast to the godlike disinterestedness of General Washington.

These apprehensions may explain the rhetorical nervousness with which Sullivan began his discourse: "At first," on such occasions, "the mind rests on the great event in which you are associated to commemorate; but soon it is drawn away, and attracted [back] through the centuries, which slowly produced that event. It returns to the memorable scene of the landing; and again it is hurried away, and finds itself descending in the course of time to the existing day and generation" (4). For Sullivan, "the mind" is poised trembling on the threatening verge of temporality: "It stands, fearfully, on that ever advancing boundary, which separates time that has been, from time that shall be; and holding up the lights which numbered years have left, it vainly attempts to discern, what unnumbered years must unfold." This is hardly the optimistic stance of a Webster or an Everett, with feet firmly planted on the rock of historic precedent, from which one can look back down the ages from the present glorious moment and then on to an even more shining future.

Sullivan's description of the *Mayflower* with which he opened his oration is also idiosyncratic, and though he employed the traditional "vision" and invited his audience to join him on the shore to await the Pilgrims' landing, it was not so much as a welcoming committee than as witnesses to the boundless wilderness on one side of the strand and the great ocean on the other, a vastness of primeval solitude into which would stray "that proud result of human genius, which finds its way where it leaves no trace of itself, yet connects the severed continents of the globe" (7). Sullivan's conundrumlike definition of the *Mayflower* is a suggestive metaphor, yet in asserting with Everett the importance of the ocean voyage, his image suggests the impermanence of all human activity. And it is this emphasis on cosmic uncertainty that gives special force to his assertion at the close of his oration of the noumenality of the place on which they stood:

> The ground on which we move, and on which they moved, seems to be sacred, and not that of our accustomed existence.... We are unconsciously drawn into the presence of the Pilgrims—they seem to have descended among us, to receive our tributes, with encouraging, and approving smiles. We are transferred to the days in which they, *and they only*, were here. We touch the cherished relics, which were their own. We enter their humble dwellings; we are present with them in their humble dwellings; we are present with them in their sincere devotions. . . . We hear them encourage each other in the faith, that their CREATOR will uphold them in their efforts to secure the blessings of rational liberty. (43–44)

Sullivan ended this sacramental communion with a reference to Peregrene White, "the first born in the new world," whose life, when conjoined with "the life of his immediate descendant; and the years of one, yet living, to whom that descendant was known," provides a magic chain linking the Landing with the present moment of celebration. For the visionary act of the imagination is substantiated by the presence of the Pilgrims' descendants, to whom may be traced "the lines of direct descent from these munificent benefactors. . . . We rejoice to be assured, that their blood now warms the hearts of men, who are worthily conscious of being the lineal representatives of the Pilgrims" (44). This is a transubstantiative exercise that spiritualizes the Alisonian element, urging the audience past the line of merely passive witness into history itself as participatory actors. Instead of summoning the ghost of a dead Pilgrim, Sullivan asks, "Is there nothing of themselves *below*?"—that is, still present among the living—then he points to the audience itself as flesh-and-blood replicas of the Forefathers. It was perhaps a desperate hope, but in the minds of diehard Federalists like William Sullivan, his were desperate times.

Sullivan's mystical celebration of union between past and present follows the lead of Greenwood and Dewey, and like Dewey, Sullivan played down the need for monuments, however sublime in concept and execution, and stressed the importance of anniversary celebrations of the Landing, which serve as "hallowed conservators of these words of gratitude" (42). This was Webster's emphasis also in his great oration at Bunker Hill in 1825, but where Webster's words radiated confidence in the popular memory, Sullivan expressed a fear that New England would forget the intimate connection to the Pilgrims that his concluding words sought to establish, that at some future time the annual commemorations, the ritual days "of national accounting shall be no more" (43). At that time, he somberly instructed, there would no longer be a need for a "pathway to the ROCK OF THE PILGRIMS, nor anything to tell where their ASHES sleep."

It was to prevent that loss of memory that Sullivan turned to the compiling of class books and the writing of history. To keep the recollection of the Pilgrims alive it was necessary to reinforce that electric chain of recall by which the present moment becomes a vivified past by standing on soil made sacred by the Pilgrim presence. This suggests that William Sullivan's oration brought a fitting, if uncertain, close to a decade that saw the publication of Felicia Hemans's poem and song, which likewise sought to sanctify the landing place of the Forefathers by defining it as holy ground, in effect providing the national anthem for celebrants of New England's sectional exceptionalism. But if Sullivan caught the common chord found in those orations excerpted in Pierpont's readers, so he sounded a dissonant note that was already audible by the decade's end in Forefathers' Day performances, a recrudescence of the old Federalist paranoia that regarded with fear the consequences of the progress associated with the Pilgrim Landing.

CHAPTER 7

The Great Trinitarian-Unitarian-Congregational Battle over the Ownership of the Pilgrims and Their Rock

And the parson was sitting upon a rock,
At half-past nine by the meet'n house clock.
—O. W. Holmes

I

By 1830, it might be said, the Unitarians had Mrs. Hemans, her poem and song, but their rights to the Pilgrims and Plymouth Rock were not thereby exclusive. As I have earlier suggested, celebrants of the Landing framed orations inextricable not only from the emerging Whig ideal of universal progress but from the ongoing wrangle between Trinitarian Congregationalists and Unitarians. Though associated with Boston and Cambridge—especially that bastion of liberal theology, Harvard College—the struggle had a provincial locus in Plymouth, nonetheless ardent and protracted for its rural setting. From colonial days, there was a complex interlock between ecclesiastical and statist matters in New England—implicit in a theocracy—and we have seen where the New Lights/Old Lights controversy in Plymouth may have been in part responsible for Elder Faunce's pointing to the Rock as the site of the Forefathers' Landing.

It was Faunce, once again, who was among those who left the First Church in Plymouth, outraged at the goings-on sanctioned by their minister, Mr. Leonard. The departure of Old Light "liberals" in 1744 to found the Third Church in Plymouth left the New Lights in charge at the First, a doctrinal unanimity that may not have been perfect. For when Leonard requested dismission in 1755, his health having failed, the congregation was only with difficulty able to find a minister acceptable to them, a process that took five years. Their Dalai Lama, Chandler Robbins, was a man with all the right markings, being the son of a leading New Lights minister, Philomen Robbins of Connect-icut, who reinforced the paternal and doctrinal connection by preaching the sermon at his son's ordination in Plymouth.

To this sermon, when it was published, was attached a history of the First Church, written by the Reverend John Cotton, who bore his famous great-grandfather's name and calling but who because of a "weakness of the voice" had been forced to resign his pulpit. Returning to Plymouth, John in 1755 had succeeded his father, Josiah, as the register of deeds, a post leaving him suffi-cient leisure to recover his ministerial voice at least in printed form. Josiah Cotton had been a prime mover in the formation of the Third Church, but the passing away of the Great Awakening and the Reverend Leonard having re-moved the sources of discontent, that congregation would subsequently de-cline, its remnant by 1776 rejoining the First. Apparently John by 1760 had become a member of the church his father had deserted, for the mood at Robbins's installation was conciliatory, and the sermon of Philomen when coupled with John Cotton's history provides a remarkable document of filio- and patriopietism.

The elder Robbins's sermon is for the most part a general treatment of "the Duty and Business of Gospel Ministers," but it ends with a personal address to his son, an emotional charge to "keep my Words and write them on the Table of thy Heart," and he likewise turned to the congregation, and asked their "Candor and Charity" toward Chandler, for "he is but a Child—an earthen Vessel: and no other is to be expected but that Weakness and Failings will be manifest in him. . . . Sympathize with him under such Troubles and Trials as may occur to him; and in . . . your Affection encourage his Heart" (17–20). The Plymouth congregation would need plenty of both candor and charity in the years to come regarding the Reverend Robbins, though the word "weakness" was seldom associated with his rule, certainly not by John Cotton.

Most important here, Cotton's history as a product of 1760 was not only a pioneering Plymouth chronicle—the first since Morton's *Memorial* of a cen-tury earlier—but it brought to Chandler Robbins's ordination the entire weight of the Pilgrim continuity. Notably, Cotton's narrative is firmly based on "Dr. Mather's Magnalia [and] Mr. Morton's New England Memorial" and recounts the familiar list of hardships encountered by the Pilgrims in the New World. Not surprisingly, given the tendency of historians to bend their texts to con-temporary occasions, much of his account deals with the difficulties of the early settlers in finding a suitable minister. It likewise emphasizes the subsequent tensions and divisions in the congregation thereafter, though the thirty years of the Reverend Leonard's controversial pastorate are passed over quickly— "tactfully" might be a better word—with only a brief mention of the formation of the Third Church in 1744. Cotton moved on to the search for Leonard's successor, "Endeavours for the Resettlement of Gospel-ordinances among them," a lengthy process that finally ended when "Providence led them to the Choice of Mr. Chandler Robbins" (Robbins, 26).

Devoting several more pages to particulars of the ancient church's "*Principles and Practices*," Cotton delivered an encomium to the Fathers for their high "*Regard to Religion and practical Godliness*" for which they "were held in Renown . . . coming as nigh the primitive Pattern of the first Churches, as any Church in these latter Ages has done" (27, 32). He ended his history by thanking God "for his Presence with them, and Protection over them—for putting it into their Hearts to transplant themselves, over the Ocean, into this then hideous Wilderness—for keeping them in their Way, and preparing a Place for them—for settling them here in Peace, and providing for them in their low Estate—for defending them from the Insults of the natives, and preserving their civil and religious Privileges, notwithstanding the many Attempts of Enemies to overthrow them—for increasing their Numbers, and causing them to take deep Root" (34).

This document, given further circulation by the Massachusetts Historical Society in 1795 (and 1835), continues and forwards the providential emphasis of the Mather tradition that lent such force to sermons of the revolutionary era. Cotton ended his *Account* with a comparison traditional to the jeremiad between the "blessed Ancestors" and their descendants, who "fall so short of their heavenly Pattern," and it is worth mentioning that this censorious note was dropped from the version published under the auspice of the Massachusetts Historical Society in 1795 (35; cf. *Collections*, First Series, 1835 ed., 4:141). By then, Cotton's backsliding contemporaries were undoubtedly thought to be in the company of those "blessed Ancestors" and absorbed thereby into that "heavenly Pattern" forever associated with a retreating Golden Age in New England. In any event, as we have already seen, the jeremiad was no longer much in favor when celebrating ancestral accomplishments.

Cotton makes no mention of the Rock that would emerge so prominently in the last years of the century, nor does he style the original settlers of Plymouth as "Pilgrims" or even "Fathers," preferring "Ancestors" and "these People." Yet his renewal of the convention of holding up the first settlers of Plymouth as providentially directed to the New World, and as having thenceforth enjoyed God's favor, despite their setbacks and suffering, points directly forward to the purport of the first of several celebrations of Forefathers' Day by the Old Colony Club in 1769. Given the intimate association of Cotton's chronicle with Chandler Robbins's ordination, we may hardly doubt why he thought of himself as the ideal "choice" for a minister to preside over the festivities as the tradition continued into a second year.

A preacher of considerable force and charm and an outspoken champion of the rights of New Englanders, who during the Revolution served as an army chaplain, Robbins was also a hard-line Calvinist, whose attempts to force his conservative convictions upon his congregation led to even more controversy. And one of his chief rivals for the hearts and minds of the First Church would be the same John Cotton whose history of that body was appended to Philomen Robbins's sermon.

Though Robbins was a popular minister, whose devotion to the Patriot cause was matched by his religious zeal, during the course of his long pastorate he took an increasingly intransigent line on the matter of church membership for the children of parishioners and opposed the Half-Way Covenant that had been instituted in Massachusetts, siding with Jonathan Edwards, not the Boston theocracy. As a New Light minister, Robbins also shared Edwards's faith in the efficacy of revivals as an instrument for reawakening the zeal of the Forefathers, but his attempts to impose Edwards's doctrines by means of a formal creed were met with objections by John Cotton. Following the Old Light line, Cotton's argument reached back to the ancient practice, so much like "the primitive pattern of the first churches" he had praised in his earlier history, which allowed for the baptism of infant children of members in good standing, with their confirmation coming only after they had reached the age of discretion.

This dispute, which centered on community and family solidarity versus doctrinal rigidity, was never resolved in Plymouth (or elsewhere) but hung in the air like wrestling angels over the First Church for many years thereafter, until displaced by other doctrinal tangles, which emerged soon after the death of Robbins in 1799. For that hard-nosed Calvinist was succeeded in his pulpit by the Reverend James Kendall, a recent Harvard graduate who brought to Plymouth the easterly winds of change: in effect a Unitarian, Kendall preached a line that was much more in sympathy with the liberalizing tendency set in motion by the Enlightenment than his predecessor had been, and was spotted as an "Arminian in full" by a nephew of Chandler Robbins in his very first sermon (*Plymouth Church Records*, xlii). Kendall's ordination ushered in at the turn of the century quite a different dispensation, one that despite its latitudinarianism realigned the old quarrels.

The emphasis on "works" identified with Arminianism was a very old bone of contention among Congregationalists, and even liberal New Light church members would close ranks with the more conservative in resisting any such encroachment upon the purity of Grace as signifying Election. The result could be predicted. As in 1743, a minority of the congregation was made uncomfortable by the relaxing of doctrinal rigor—which now included the evangelism that was the heritage of the New Lights—and departed to revive the old Third Church in name, if not in spirit.

Like Robbins's entrenched Calvinists, these new separatists brought to their church a succession of pastors who were as determinedly of the Trinitarian Congregational allegiance as Kendall was in sympathy with the emerging palliations of Unitarianism. Insisting that it was the true vessel of the Pilgrim faith, the new Third Church congregation took with it a grievance given point by the First Church having retained as its rightful "furniture" the silver communion service, associated with that ceremony of convenantal integrity shared by the faithful in Plymouth for so many generations.

Moreover, the half-century-old stalemate between John Cotton and Chandler Robbins over who had the right to evoke the example of the Forefathers in celebrating the purity of their doctrines was hardly dead. Forces were gathering on opposite sides of the question regarding the inheritance of the Pilgrim Fathers, and Plymouth Rock soon displaced the silver communion service kept by the First Church as the chief item of furniture in dispute. In general, the emerging Unitarians tended to emulate the serpent and dove in promoting their liberal agenda and tried to avoid open conflict, fearing (correctly) that internecine warfare would further weaken Congregationalism. It was the Calvinists who tended to take the aggressive side, blasting the liberals as degenerate derelicts from the Good Old Way.

Most, if not all, of these shifts of allegiances and doctrines in Plymouth were identical to similar disputes going on all over New England during the same period, but, perhaps because of the town's congregate sense that it occupied a special place in Puritan history, the wrangles there regularly sought the sanction of the past. They were also upon occasion as Byzantine in complexity as a modern tax code, yet it is not difficult to trace patterns in the sermons celebrating the Forefathers from both sides of the dispute that provide clues to the changing meaning of both the Pilgrims and their Rock.

II

In 1805, that warhorse of orthodoxy, Jedidiah Morse—the Federalist agitator who as a Congregational minister continued to maintain his fealty to old New Light doctrine—took it upon himself to dispute the election that year of the Unitarian minister Henry Ware as Harvard's Hollis Professor of Divinity. This distracted the geographer's immediate attention away from the threat to the United States posed by French Jacobins and Jefferson, but it created an open doctrinal schism that threatened the Sunday peace of his beloved region. In effect, Morse licensed the expression of the repressed outrage felt by Trinitarians over the betrayals of Congregationalism by ministers who concealed Unitarian heresies under their robes. Once again, though the epicenter of the quake was identified with Harvard Yard, Plymouth was shaken by the doctrinal shock waves.

A convenient starting point is provided by the Forefathers' Day sermon read in Plymouth in 1801 by the Reverend John Allyn, who had been brought up in Arminianism and was already a prominent Unitarian. For Allyn established a precedent that would have a considerable progeny by quoting the "wholesome counsel" of John Robinson, the Pilgrims' pastor in Leyden, as his parishioners set sail for the New World. Robinson, who remained behind with the greater number of his congregation, was to join the Separatists in America, but he died before that could happen, and his parting words were all the more precious therefore.

Allyn thought of Robinson's advice as breathing "a noble spirit of liberty," which he identified with the Unitarian faith, and called it to the particular attention of "reformed churches and ministers," an association that would not go unchallenged in the years to come (23). Though associated not with the arrival of the Pilgrims in the New World but their departure from the Old, Robinson's words of advice were seen by Allyn as defining the Forefathers' errand, hence as having determined the doctrinal direction of their descendants in America. Moreover, because Allyn in this same sermon delivered one of the first evocations of Plymouth Rock, he proved to be an innovator in both regards, establishing twin rhetorical tropes that would be associated with Unitarian discourse thenceforth. The pertinent passages follow:

> He charged us, before God and his blessed angels, to follow him no further than he followed Christ: and if God should reveal anything to us by any instrument of his, to be as ready to receive it as ever we were to receive any truth by his ministry. For he was very confident the Lord had more truth and light yet to break forth out of his holy Word. He took occasion also to bewail the state and condition of the reformed churches, who were come to a period in religion, and would go no further than the Instruments of their Reformation. As for example, the Lutherans could not be drawn to go beyond what Luther said; for whatever part of Gods word He had further imparted and revealed to Calvin, they had rather die than embrace it; and so, said he, you see the Calvinists, they stick where he left them—a misery much to be lamented: For though they were precious, shining lights in their times; yet God had not revealed his whole will to them: And were they alive now, they would be as ready to embrace further light as that they had received. Here also he put us in mind of our church covenant; whereby we engaged with God and one another to receive whatever light or truth should be made known to us from His *written word*. (22; cf. Young, 396–97)

Allyn quoted Robinson's stirring words from Thomas Prince's *Chronological History of New England* (1736), a filiopietistic text dear to Pilgrim celebrants, and acknowledged that they had first been set down in Edward Winslow's *Good*

Newes from New England in 1624, from the author's recollection of what Robinson had said. Like other gospels, the words may have been somewhat recast to suit changing doctrinal needs, including the direction Puritanism took in America thanks to the influence of the Separatists of Plymouth. But the admonition to seek "new light" not only underwrote the historical Separatist occasion, it provided encouragement for modern Unitarians also and gave them a powerful validation, given the source. It would be a number of years before the Unitarian claim to both Robinson's sermon and Plymouth Rock would be openly challenged, although rumblings of the Trinitarians' reluctance to countenance the appropriation of such sacred furniture were soon heard.

The year following, in delivering his own Forefathers' Day sermon in Plymouth, the Reverend Adoniram Judson anticipated the future fireworks. The speaker at the official celebration of the Landing was John Quincy Adams, who, as we have seen, devoted his address to the secular and civil consequences of the Pilgrims' arrival, emphasizing the Mayflower Compact. Judson's auspices were ecclesiastical, in specific the congregation of the Third Church, which had so recently set up its own meetinghouse. As the minister of the newly created tabernacle, Judson's mission was twofold: to balance Adams's stress on statist matters, and to redress (if indirectly) the effects of the schism of which the Third Church had been the reluctant creation. His tack was overwhelmingly Calvinist in burden and aggressive in tenor, befitting his errand in what he regarded as a wilderness of secularization and impiety.

Typically—even typologically—Judson began by drawing the usual analogy between the Forefathers and the Old Testament Jews and sounded the Grand Old Puritan note of Separation. But the analogy was obviously intended to reach into an even newer dispensation, to wit, the doctrinal implication of his congregation's departure from the church of the Reverend Kendall: "All, who obey the call of the gospel, and love the doctrines and duties of religion, will come out of Babylon, deny themselves, and take up the cross. This is confirmed by the example of the primitive Christians, and by all the conduct of the virtuous and good" (14). As "primitive Christians," according to Judson's definition, the Pilgrim Fathers espoused doctrines entirely in harmony with the contemporary Calvinist formulation espoused by the Third Church of Christ in Plymouth, including such key items as "the divinity of Christ, and . . . the total depravity of man. . . . All this appears from their records, confessions of faith, and articles of the church" (10). Judson went so far as to impersonate "one of our pious ancestors," a device that had some prior and would have much subsequent use in various contexts, and through his mouthpiece addressed his auditors in quotation marks, asking them to " 'reflect on our hardships, our sufferings, and our ardent desire to promote the interest of

Christ. . . . For you we planted fields and vineyards; that you might enter into our labors, be a free people, and enjoy the gospel of God' " (18).

Where later, chiefly Unitarian ministers (like Greenwood and Dewey) would attempt to conjoin the Pilgrims with their descendants, in effect updating the Fathers so that they could move forward in step with the Sons, Judson (like the Trinitarians Chester and Emmons) ended by bidding his people to walk backward, to "tread in the footsteps of our pious fathers. . . . Let us seek the good old way, and go forth in the footsteps of the flock" (22). In 1802, as in 1620, those retrograde footsteps led out of the modern corruptions of the church back toward a primitive simplicity, a movement essential to Separatism and one that Judson equated with the departure of his congregation from the First Church.

It is all the more surprising, then, that in 1817 Judson asked dismission from his congregation that he might take orders as a Baptist minister, joining a sect not often equated with the specifics of the Pilgrim faith and which had been much persecuted by the Puritans (Davis, *Memories*, 305). Indeed, the Reverend Judson was not following in the footsteps of the Fathers but in those of his son, also Adoniram, who had in 1812 joined the Baptist faith and become a force in missionary work in India. More consistent with tradition, perhaps, is the information provided by the chronicler of nineteenth-century Plymouth, William Davis, that the Reverend Judson, while occupied in tracing back the doctrinal path in its apostolic purity to the Forefathers, managed to acquire "all the lots of land on the west wide of Pleasant Street," a binary preoccupation not at all at odds with the activities of the Forefathers, as they appear in the town records of deeds and like articles of legal transaction.

The following year, 1803, the premier speaker on Forefathers' Day in Plymouth was the Reverend John Thornton Kirkland, a tutor in logic and metaphysics at Harvard and a member of the group that had just established the *Monthly Anthology* and the Boston Athenaeum, a journal and institution soon to be the aorta and ventricle of the liberal and ultimately the Unitarian wing of the Congregational Church. Urbane, plumply handsome, witty, and skillful in public address, Kirkland would go on to become president of Harvard in 1810 and would be responsible for expanding its professional schools into a bona fide university and attracting to its liberal arts college a nationally, even internationally famed faculty, including George Ticknor and Edward Everett. It is something of an irony, therefore, that what survives of Kirkland's address are the excerpts included in the appendix to Jedidiah Morse's history of New England, because, as we have seen, Morse would emerge as a ferocious adversary of Harvard's increasingly liberal tendencies.

But then, judging from the excerpts published by Morse, Kirkland, as befitted a Unitarian and a future academic administrator, shunned controversy as if it were the ague. His oration was chiefly historical, not religious, in emphasis, as were the two other addresses with which it kept company, those of John Davis—lawyer, judge, and Plymouth historian—and John Quincy Adams. They thereby contained nothing to alert the Calvinist paranoia of the editor. Kirkland necessarily stressed the pious character of the Pilgrims, but his emphasis was on those of their institutions that resulted in the prosperity and enlightened happiness of future generations: "The country, which they planted, advanced in all those things, which make nations great and happy, with a rapidity unexampled in the annals of mankind" (Morse and Parish, 384). Who of whatever dispensation could quarrel with such universally benign sentiments? Yet within such bland fruit we can detect that complex seed whereby Unitarianism and the Whig Party would emerge intertwined by a mutual faith in Progress.

On the other hand, anyone seeking to establish doctrinal balance assuredly found it on Forefathers' Day in Plymouth in 1803, for sharing the pulpit with Kirkland on that occasion was the Reverend Jonathan Strong, and the contrast between the college professor and the preacher provides a virtual allegory of the soon-to-emerge differences between the "new" liberal and conservative division in the Congregational Church. As opposed to the blandly intellectual, smoothly conciliatory Kirkland, Strong was a man whose character and delivery are suggested by his name. A rural pastor, who divided his time between his parish duties and his farm, he was a large-bodied and lion-voiced preacher, and his doctrines were of the undiluted Calvinist strain. Strong took the same tack as Adoniram Judson, indeed sailed forth under even stronger winds, for not only did he cite the Fathers as being worthy of pious emulation, but he attacked the modern generation in the denunciatory language of the jeremiad, that genre dear to defenders of the orthodox faith.

Stressing the providential history of New England by means of the familiar analogy with ancient Israel, Strong provided a list of the "religious sentiments" of the Pilgrims that followed Judson's menu while increasing the element of severity. His were doctrinal points not only Calvinist to the extreme but shaped to the narrowness of a punishing rod aimed at the backslidings of liberal apostates from the Good Old Dogma, threatening "endless punishment [to] the finally impenitent" (15). Like Judson also, he assured his auditors that the "religious tenets" of the Pilgrim Fathers could be found in "their confessions of faith and other theological writings," documentation the specifics of which were otherwise lacking.

Strong went on to emphasize the providential aspects of the Pilgrim experience, God having prepared "the way for their settlement, by that devouring pestilence which had almost depopulated . . . the wilderness to which they were directed." The same divine dispensation provided "a convoy of guardian angels" that attended the Forefathers "across the tempestuous ocean, to that memorable rock, on which their feet were first placed!" (18–19). Having planted the Pilgrims on their Rock, Strong devoted the remaining six pages of his sermon to the "very great and awful declension among their descendants, in things of a moral and religious nature," a decline not coincidentally illustrated by points associated with Unitarianism: "Do not some boldly deny the very first principles of natural religion? Do they not disown the existence of the Supreme Being, the accountability of mankind, and a future state of retribution? . . . Do not a much larger number call into question the truth of the Holy Scriptures?" (29–31).

We may at this point picture a slight measure of discomfort and shifting of feet among those of Strong's auditors who were members of the First Church. What followed, moreover, must have caused considerable ear burnings, if not conflagrations of the heart, for Strong reminded his auditors of the kinds of retribution an angry God is capable of inflicting, part and parcel of the jeremiad's punitive emphasis. And in encouraging the people of Plymouth "to imitate those pious pilgrims . . . whose virtues we this day celebrate," he employed a strategy similar to that used by the Federalists when lambasting the Jeffersonians by evoking the ghost of the Puritan past (25).

Still, the orthodox did not have a monopoly on reaction, for some theological liberals had their limits as well. Thus, the next Forefathers' Day orator would be Alden Bradford, who, though a Unitarian, would, as we have seen, use the occasion to belabor the modern generation for having elevated "the *Sceptic* and *Athiest* to the highest places of power in a christian country" (10). There was clearly in some conservative minds at the turn of the century a connection between the liberalizing influence of the Enlightenment—"indifferentism" Bradford called it—and the contemporary drift of both religion and politics toward less rigorous applications of ideological principles.

Though hardly as outrageously outspoken in their sentiments as the Federalist toasts during the Feasts of Shells, Strong and Bradford may have been perceived nonetheless as conveying a spirit of contention no longer welcome at Forefathers' Day celebrations, whose audiences were presumably mixed in their own religious and political affiliations and who may have been impatient over having to sit through a torrent of abuse, albeit high principled, awash with sneering references to Voltaire, Tom Paine, and William Godwin. Perhaps by way of righting the balance, the speaker on Forefathers' Day in 1805 was the Reverend James Kendall of the First Church, whose sermon did not survive but which we may be sure studiously avoided controversial matters, the sort of Unitarian performance that generally infuriated conservative Congregationalists, who were quick to equate neutrality with equivocation.

Then, in 1806, the Plymouth committee for arrangements hit upon a perfect choice as speaker for the anniversary event, the Reverend Abiel Holmes, an orthodox Calvinist who had recently gained considerable renown as a scholar of early New England history, having the year before produced a chronology intended to displace Prince's monumental but outdated work. Holmes was no Judson or Strong, no fundamentalist zealot, and as the minister of the First Church in Cambridge, he came out of the same learned environs as Dr. Kirkland. Like Kirkland, he was as much a historian as a minister, and though a conservative Congregationalist, like the Harvard professor he avoided theological controversy. Indeed, over the next quarter century the Reverend Holmes would strive to be a moderating influence among the Trinitarian Congregationalists, even while espousing a remnant Calvinism that would prove so repugnant to his sensitive son, Oliver Wendell, as to drive him into the always open arms of the Unitarians.

In 1806, none of this could have been foreseen, yet prescience was certainly involved in choosing Holmes as the speaker for the day. For his reputation as a historian, along with his accommodating temper, inspired him to deliver a learned discourse, not an impassioned sermon, with which no one could have found fault. Indeed, Holmes's greatest fear of giving offense involved his apologetic use of well-worn material, and in telling yet one more time the story of the Pilgrims, Holmes asked pardon for repeating the account of "occurences too familiar to your minds to require recital" (*A Discourse*, 15). Like Everett almost twenty years later, Holmes was compelled to emulate Pope by giving better expression to what had so many times been said before, and he too rose handily to the occasion.

He expanded upon a device borrowed from John Quincy Adams's Forefathers' Day address that both Webster and Everett would use in their turn, not a "vision" in the strictest sense, but an enlistment of his auditors in the company of that exploring band that turned the familiar terms of the story into high, participatory drama: "The footsteps of the Pilgrims have been traced out with mingled curiosity and veneration. Every thicket which they penetrated, every danger which they encountered, every obstacle which they overcame, and every solace which they received, are faithfully registered in your memories. You have often, in imagination, accompanied the shallop, which was sent out with Carver, Bradford, Winslow, Standish, and a few seamen, to sail around the bay, in search of a place for settlement. . . . But how great was your terror, when the night approaching, the mast breaking, the sail at the same instant falling overboard into the sea!" (15–16).

Where Webster in 1820, and Everett four years later, would place their auditors on the shore, watching as the shallop came ashore at Plymouth, Holmes in 1806 put them in the boat with the exploring party, narrowly escaping destruction in a storm and spending the following Sabbath on Clark's Island: "The day following, you remember it was, they sounded the harbour, lying before us, and came on shore. The feet of the Pilgrims then first stepped on that ROCK, which your filial piety, Sons of the Pilgrims, has sacredly preserved; and which will be at once a memorial of the event, and a monument of their honour, to the latest generation" (16).

From his melodramatic evocation of the Landing, Abiel Holmes moved on to a more sober, objective consideration of the character and religious principles of the Pilgrims and the "privilege" of being descended from those "Fathers," not unlike that which endows the descendants of the "illustrious ancestors of the Hebrew nation" (24). He was not, however, as exemplary in his tolerance as this reference might suggest, for he hastened to distinguish his auditors from their contemporary Jewish equivalents: "Instead of boasting with Pharisaic pride, *We have Abraham to our father*, let us prove ourselves worthy of our high and honourable descent, by conducting [ourselves] as becomes *the children of Abraham*," and not only boast of but "imitate the examples of our Fathers" (27–28).

Holmes also took the opportunity to scorn the followers of Mohammed, "the disciples of the Arabian Imposter [who] visit the tomb of their prophet, to offer the sacrilegious homage, or to confirm their fallacious hopes," as well as "the devotees of the Romish church [who] search the graves of the saints for holy relics" (28). He seems to have taken this bigoted tack as a substitute for contemporary sectarian controversy, for flogging the straw horses of Mohammedism and Roman Catholicism could cause little pain in Plymouth. And yet something of a subtext can be detected in pairing the "right of free inquiry," the "catholic and liberal spirit" that the Pilgrims "nobly asserted and maintained," with those "evangelical doctrines, which had the sanction of their judgment," thereby validating one of the distinguishing tenets of Trinitarian Congregationalism even while celebrating the Unitarian's love of liberated discourse (26–27).

Certainly the Reverend Holmes's address was intended to avoid an exclusivist, perfectionist Separatist spirit and express instead an inclusive outreach, seeking only to dismiss from the Protestant ideal the kinds of superstitions associated with the Muslim and Roman Catholic faiths. What is found and celebrated at Plymouth promotes only "exalted views" and "sublime purpose." Thus, in honoring the Pilgrims, "we come on no pilgrimage. We seek no relics, to aid credulous superstition. We come to visit the graves of our Forefathers, to commemorate their virtues, and to learn from them lessons of wisdom. Sons of the Pilgrims! Look at yonder rock, on which your Fathers first stepped; look at that brook, of which they first drank; look at the cold ground, on which they first lay; look at the hill, where they first met the aboriginal prince; look at this eminence, which they first fortified; look at the lots, which they first enclosed; look on the earth, which covers their remains; and while ye exclaim, THESE ARE THE MEMORIALS OF OUR FATHERS, imbibe their spirit, and follow their examples, and ye shall hereafter enter into their rest, and sit down with them and with all the holy fathers in the kingdom of heaven" (28). This concluding invocation is integral to that earlier moment when Abiel Holmes placed his auditors beside their Forefathers, and works toward the conservative goal of reifying the simple virtues of the Pilgrims. But his language at times echoed the Unitarian emphasis on continuity and community, welding past and present into one inseparable whole.

Even as Holmes spoke as the invited guest on Forefathers' Day, less inclusive sentiments could be heard nearby. In the neighboring community of Manomet was located the "Second Church" of Plymouth, by actual count the sixth that had departed from the First by 1738, the year of its founding. This was a separation of convenience more than doctrine, but the Second had gone its own clearly Calvinist way, and on Forefathers' Day in 1806 the Reverend Seth Stetson was busy rectifying the perfect balance achieved in the discourse of the orator of the day. At one point in his oration, Holmes had made a modest plea for tolerance, excusing his hearers from having to embrace "the dogmas of Calvin or of Robinson," the Pilgrims' preacher in Leyden, so long as they strove to follow "what we apprehend to be *the truth as it is in Jesus*" (27). Stetson also made reference to John Robinson's farewell to his parishioners: "They should," paraphrased Stetson from Robinson's farewell sermon, " 'expect greater light in the church, and ought not to be divided from their brethren because they had different degrees of light in divine things,' " sentiments that gave a conciliatory spin to the actual words but were hardly true to the original (20). In the same manner, Stetson rendered a virtual paraphrase not of Robinson but of Holmes, stating that "so far as our forefathers followed Christ, so far we should follow them."

But then Stetson got down to particulars of the sort avoided by Holmes, adding that "our forefathers believed the doctrines of grace," which was "the same system of truth" as was held by "Luther, Melancthon, and Calvin, and the other reformers," which included "predestination, election, reprobation; total depravity of the human will; regeneration by faith alone, and that faith the gift of God; by grace, not of works, through the atoning blood of Christ," a list not much different in kind though perhaps something less in hellfire than that compiled by Jonathan Strong (21). And Stetson likewise shared the traditional orthodox view that "no nation under heaven resembles God's chosen people Israel, more than the United States of America; especially New England" (4). On the other hand, though he ended his sermon with the traditional call for repentance, Stetson did not extend the blame to modern "degeneracies" in doctrine. Still, his sermon was hardly as moderate as Holmes's performance and must be accounted a classic Trinitarian production, in its restraint more a complement than a counterpart to Holmes's oration.

It does come as a shock, therefore, to learn that in 1817 the Reverend Seth Stetson led a significant part of his Manomet congregation into the ready embrace of Unitarianism and was something of a pioneer in that regard, his being the kind of separatist gesture previously associated with seceding clusters of reactionary Congregationalists. By that time, perhaps, the meaning of Robinson's farewell sermon had begun to take on a different urgency for Stetson, so that he could regard separatism as a way of advancing, not turning back. As we shall presently learn, that was certainly the use to which Robinson's words would be put in sermons read at Plymouth by Unitarian ministers on Forefathers' Day.

For Holmes's coupling of John Calvin with John Robinson would have a long and troublesome reach into the future and would emerge as a central point of contention in the debate between conservative and liberal Congregationalists. By that time, the hold of the orthodox upon Plymouth Rock had become slippery, challenged by questioning the logic of citing Robinson's open-ended discourse in the defense of their rigidly exclusive, dogma-ridden claim to the Pilgrims, just such a tactic that Abiel Holmes carefully avoided but which Seth Stetson as purposefully did not.

III

It perhaps needs to be pointed out, once again, that the drift among enlightened Congregationalists toward Unitarianism does not easily translate into modern notions of liberalism. Questioning the divinity of Christ and emphasizing the importance of good works alleviated the stringencies of Calvinist doctrine, and signing off on the literalness of the certainty of hellfire (especially infant damnation) mitigated the moroseness of Calvinism also. But although Unitarianism was the child of the Enlightenment, in its arguments appealing to the mechanics of human reason, it was also the faith of the merchant and professional class. It was therefore the religion of the wealthy and privileged, which is to say it was an urban phenomenon generally while conservative Calvinism remained strong in the country. Politically, as in the person of Jedidiah Morse, Trinitarianism tended to meld with Federalism, while Unitarianism imbued the emerging Whig Party with an eschatological equivalent of its optimistic, open-ended belief in progress. This did not, however, include radicalism in its embrace.

It is a helpful corrective to note that as a Harvard undergraduate John Kirkland volunteered to serve in the army that put down Shay's Rebellion, and upon assuming the pulpit in Boston's New South Church in 1793, he preached a series of sermons against the infidelity of the French (i.e., Jeffersonian Republicans). It was a message that provided the substance of Kirkland's Phi Beta Kappa oration at Harvard in 1798, by then given urgent point by Jefferson's near win in the presidential election that year. Unitarians may, in the minds of orthodox Congregationalists, have been guilty of degenerating from the Good Old Way, but as Alden Bradford angrily testified, they were not necessarily to be equated with Democratic Republicans.

Therefore, when we observe that Stetson's sermon was the last gasp of Calvinism during Forefathers' Day celebrations in Plymouth for many years, we must not interpret this as a sign of any burgeoning democratic spirit in that town. Rather, the avoidance thenceforth of Calvinist jeremiads for the usual bland affirmations of Unitarian ministers indicates if anything a move toward a centrist and establishmentarian stability. It was part and parcel of an increase in assertions of New England's importance as the original source of the democratic spirit, a direction epitomized by Webster's performance in 1820. Nor can we discount the predilection of committees appointed to stage celebrations to accentuate the positive. Unitarians, moreover, were inclined toward polite (and that is the word) letters as part of their coda, if not creed, and even the most cursory comparison of the performances of John Kirkland and Jonathan Strong indicates the superiority of the former in terms of literary qualities. In sum, you could count on a Unitarian to provide the right mix of high style and affirmation proper to the self-gratulatory mood of Forefathers' Day, performances that, prior to 1820, clearly point the way toward Webster's epitome of the genre.

Typical was a sermon read in Plymouth on the anniversary occasion in 1809 by the Reverend Abiel Abbott, pastor of the First Church in Beverley and a minister with decided Unitarian tendencies. He chose as his text the passage from Deuteronomy that had graced the Reverend Conant's patriotic exercise on the eve of the Revolution, with its reference to the sheltering eagle's wings of divine favor. But in encouraging his auditors to model their behavior after that of the providentially blessed Forefathers, Abbott in his closing words took a moderating, even mollifying position. Thus the "Divine Being" by his account was neither Jonathan Edwards's absolute monarch nor the disinterested clock maker of the Enlightenment, but a fond parent "in the midst of his family, provident of their welfare," and concerned with promoting the means, "rugged and painful perhaps, yet the best to insure their greatest ultimate perfection and happiness" (20). And Abbott pictured the Forefathers not as formidable paragons of Christian virtue but as pursuing "laborious researches after divine truth," for though "they studied the scriptures and were mighty in them; yet [they] did not imagine that *they had already attained, or were already perfect*" (22).

As the italicized emphasis suggests, Abbott depended upon the farewell sermon of "the learned Robinson" as the authority for his liberal reading of the Pilgrims' faith. In this, he was following the lead of the Reverend Allyn in 1801 and thereby attesting to the Unitarian monopoly regarding those progressive sentiments. But Abbott, unlike Allyn, neglected to mention the source of Robinson's words, and he revised the original text so that it is phrased not in the primarily third-person voice of Winslow's recollection but in the direct, first-person address throughout. He likewise took other liberties that gave added force to the admonition and increased the sectarian bias, as a comparison with Allyn's version will show:

> I charge you before God and his blessed angels that you follow me no farther than you have seen me follow the Lord Jesus Christ. If God reveal any thing to you, by any other instrument of his, be as ready to receive it, as ever you were to receive any truth by my ministry; for I am verily persuaded—I am very confident that the Lord hath more truth yet to break forth out of his word. For my part I cannot sufficiently bewail the condition of the reformed churches who are come to a period in religion, and will go, at present, no farther than the instruments of the reformation. The Lutherans cannot be drawn to go beyond what Luther saw: whatever part of his will our good God has revealed to Calvin, they will rather die than embrace it. And the Calvinists, you see, stick fast, where they were left by that great man of God, who yet saw not all things. (23)

It is not difficult to see why both Holmes and Stetson handled this passage so gingerly and sparingly and why it would be waved about by Unitarian celebrants of the Pilgrims with the same reverence with which political celebrants waved the Mayflower Compact. In urging his hearers to "breathe . . . the large spirit of the enlightened Robinson," and in effect resurrecting the Pilgrims' minister by using the first-person voice, Abbott was bringing something else ashore with those ancestors who "stepped from their shallop upon the rock of Plymouth" than that Calvinism preserved in aspic celebrated by conservative Congregationalists like Strong and Judson. By Abbott's account the chief cargo of the *Mayflower* was "the quickening influence of the same holy zeal for the advancement of our people in light, grace, and virtue," which gave impulse to "an enterprize, the magnitude and importance of which to their posterity and mankind we can now estimate," declarations not much different in emphasis from Webster's celebration of the Pilgrims and Progress in 1820 (24, 23).

During the troubled times engendered by Jefferson's embargo and the War of 1812, there was only one sermon delivered in Plymouth on Forefathers' Day, and that went unpublished. But once the Treaty of Ghent had been signed, certifying for good and all American independence from Great Britain (and the resumption of trade with same), the Reverend James Flint was free to renew the tradition, and his sermon acted to solidify the Unitarian monopoly. Indeed, if his hosts had expected the usual kind of understated Unitarian performance, what they received was quite a different article, for by 1815 liberal Congregationalists were uncloseting themselves all over New England, and it would be two years later that Stetson took his walk. Indirection and equivocation were no longer necessary, and Flint was outspoken in his opinions.

But in terms of literary qualities, his sermon was very much in the Unitarian tradition, Flint being, in the words of a contemporary, "of a poetical turn of mind," being a man of the study and "not at all fitted for the cares of life" (Sprague, 409). This is the testimony of Elizabeth Peabody of Salem, where Flint served for many years as a pastor—from 1821 until his death in 1855—and who was regarded by her brother-in-law, Nathaniel Hawthorne, as being often out of touch with reality herself.

But Peabody's characterization is reinforced by that of another contemporary, who testified that Flint had "the graces and with them some of the unfortunate liabilities of a highly poetic temper." This sensitive soul would compose the ode for the bicentennial celebration in Plymouth that Everett declined to write, "Two Hundred Years Ago," which would long remain popular, regularly recited on similar occasions.

We have already seen how Flint rose to the occasion in 1815, comparing Plymouth Rock to the rock in the wilderness made a fountain by Moses' rod, a milestone on the way toward Webster's extended use of the natural monument at Plymouth several years later. Flint noted the similarity of the Rock to the Pilgrims themselves, in terms of unadorned simplicity, yet the conjunction of the twain in 1620 signaled "the dawn of a new day upon this world" (3). Like Holmes a decade earlier and so many speakers thereafter, Flint devoted a long passage to an elaboration upon his audience's intimate knowledge of the Pilgrim advent: "You have exulted with them in their discovery of that quiet harbour, and this sheltered spot, on which they, and you, and the generations that sleep with them, have drank the portions alotted to each of bitter and of sweet in the cup of existence. You have paused with them, when first disembarked upon this spot, to contrast, for a moment what they had come from, with what was before them" (9).

Flint also made what was becoming the obligatory Unitarian citation from Robinson's sermon, with the added observation that the Pilgrims "would lament the condition of not a few of our churches at the present day," not because of their declension from the church of the Fathers but because, in Robinson's own words, they "'remained at a stand in religion'" (13). This was a marked departure from customary Unitarian practice, in effect throwing Robinson's words into the faces of conservative Congregationalists, those orthodox Calvinists who regularly referred "to the sentiments of our fathers, as affording authority and sanction for abiding unalterably by the articles of their creed, for setting up the orthodoxy of their day, as an infallible standard of faith, to which every Christian must conform" (23).

In a footnote to the published version of his sermon, Flint rendered an account of the "agitation" between those two parties of Massachusetts clergy known as "liberal and orthodox," which he viewed as a contest between those (the Unitarians) who were "in support of the very principles and rights, asserted and maintained by the first fathers of New England, and on the other, in opposition to them" (23). While calling for the "pious Unitarian and Trinitarian, Calvinist and Arminian . . . amicably [to] agree and to love one another," Flint provided few grounds for such a resolution, in effect calling the actions of the Trinitarians not only a betrayal of the Pilgrim faith as defined by John Robinson but an offense in the eyes of Christ (24). It is hard to reconcile this combative posture with that scholarly recluse described by Elizabeth Peabody, but perhaps by 1821 Flint had discovered that there were very good reasons why his Unitarian brethren chose not to confront their orthodox counterparts head-on, whose capacity for rage could out Herod the heathen.

Peabody also noted that the Reverend Flint "felt very much the imperfections" of this mortal world, and we can detect that darker side early on in his sermon, when he invited his auditors to join him in (figuratively) standing upon Plymouth Rock. Beneath their feet lay open "not indeed a vein of silver or of gold, but a mine of solemn and salutary reflection upon the days that are past, the rapidity of the flight of time, the feebleness and transient existence of man, the successive generations, that have gone before us, the origin, growth, revolutions, and decay of nations, the changes in human opinions and forms in government and religion, and the vanity of all else, but virtue, peity, confidence in God" (4–5). Having celebrated the Rock as a virtual fountain of poetic associations, Flint now presented it as a signifier of carpe diem, inspiring sobering reflections on the transience of all mortal ambitions and ending with a conventional assertion of reliance on deity and the " 'sure and certain hope' of immortality and heaven" by those who are reborn by their faith in the resurrection of Jesus Christ. These sentiments could hardly have given offense to orthodox auditors, and they gave Plymouth Rock a doctrinal certitude in keeping with its heft and permanence as an icon.

This conservative position is in marked contrast to Flint's concluding words, which refer not to the Rock but to Robinson's sermon, the words of which promote an antithetical message, emphasizing the progressive spread of enlightenment, not the static certitude of reliance on "immortality and heaven" that Flint associated with the Rock. Like Orville Dewey a decade later, Flint's divided emphasis reveals both the doctrinal liberalism and the statist conservatism of the Unitarians, calling for open-mindedness concerning the light of revelation yet acknowledging the temporal nature of institutions.

Still, the effect of those closing sentiments was to seize the Pilgrims for the Unitarians and with them their Rock, an act equivalent to the First Church's maintaining possession of the communion vessels associated with the primitive faith of the Fathers. At last the Unitarian voice in Massachusetts was raised above a polite demurrer, at a moment, moreover, when the end of the War of 1812 brought a closure of sorts to the feud between Federalist celebrants of Forefathers' Day and their Republican critics, a major cause of discontent having been removed. It was as if New England needed some kind of adversarial controversy in order to be true to the Puritan heritage, as over the dying embers of the Federalist/Republican conflagration the flames of the Trinitarian/Unitarian ground fire suddenly leaped up.

In the year Flint read his sermon, the *Monthly Anthology* became the *North American Review*, suggesting the increase of national ambition in what had been previously a regional movement. Then, in 1819 William Ellery Channing would deliver his epochal *Baltimore Sermon*, the most famous crack in the Congregational facade of unity. In that same year, Professor Ware, whose appointment to his Harvard chair had so enraged Jedidiah Morse, fulfilled Morse's worst fears by founding the Harvard Divinity School, the future stronghold of Unitarianism, suggesting that not all paranoia is without reason. In sum, the Reverend Flint's poetic periods may have been underwritten by the querulousness of a man more comfortable in his study than confronting the harsher facts of life, yet his grumblings about the failings of orthodox Congregationalists certainly proved to be prophetic of the coming schism.

IV

Given the widening breach in Congregationalism, it is not surprising that a number of the ministers who observed the Bicentennial of 1820 used the opportunity to address the matter, an "opening vein" quite different from that evoked by Flint's magic touch on Plymouth Rock in 1816 but certainly productive of much outpouring. Thus the jeremiadlike tendency was, as we have earlier noted, mostly found in sermons by ministers of the orthodox persuasion, chief among whom was Nathanael Emmons. A stalwart (if short-statured) defender of the Trinitarian faith, Emmons, like President Monroe, preferred to dress in the costume of the late eighteenth century but shared little else with the Virginia Democrat. With that idiosyncrasy that gave his sermons a definable edge, Emmons chose as the subject for his bicentennial observations not the Landing but the first Sabbath observed in Plymouth and used it as a stick with which to belabor the "errorists" of the day (12).

Noah Porter, the equally reactionary minister of the Congregational church in Farmington, Connecticut, paused in his jeremiad against the "present degeneracy" of New England to ask rhetorically, "Could [the Puritans] have imagined that within two centuries after their flight to these shores, for the express purpose of advancing the Christian faith, the very churches which they first formed, would have 'denied the Lord that brought them'?" (18). Heman Humphrey, pastor of Pittsfield's Congregational church, assured his auditors that "in discipline, the founders of the New-England churches were strictly *congregational*," and the speaker before the New England Society in the City of New York, the Reverend Gardiner Spring of the Brick Church in Manhattan, celebrated the day by leveling a barrage against the Unitarians in their Boston stronghold (Humphrey, *Character*, 26).

In response, a delegation of Unitarians from the city called on Spring as "descendants of the Pilgrims" to express polite dismay that he had employed an occasion so solemn and so delightful for such an unpleasant performance, "theological contention" being "of all subjects the harshest, most dissocial, and discordant" (*New England Society Orations*, 1:58). By contrast, they pointed to recent sermons of Channing and "Professor Everett" as examples of the kind of polite discourse habitual to Unitarians, calculated not to give offense. But Everett's performance in 1824 could hardly have given comfort to the party of gloom then contending for spiritual empire in New England, and when in 1826 Forefathers' Day in Plymouth was observed by the Reverend Richard Salter Storrs of Braintree, Spring's emphasis was reinforced.

Storrs, protégé of Lyman Beecher and founder of the American Tract Society and other instruments of orthodoxy, objected that the "ready pen" of the "mere historian" and the "tongue of the eloquent orator" were incapable of expressing the religious basis of the Pilgrim advent, when the Forefathers "in the depths of winter planted their feet on yonder rocks [*sic*], and there laid the broad foundations of an empire" (*Spirit of the Pilgrims*, 10–11). In Storrs's view, the secret of the Pilgrims' success was their "Exclusive Spirit," that covenantal enclosure that "shuts out from heaven all but the 'pure in heart,' and which explains "the voluntary expatriation of our fathers. . . . They braved every danger, they plunged into sufferings as severe as any that flesh is heir to, with their eyes open, for the vindication and defense of this very peculiarity of our religion, so much reprobated by many of their descendants" (16–17). Storrs took the Unitarians to task for blindsiding the "pure and heroic spirit" of orthodoxy, which could be traced by means of "that long series of religious revivals by which our country has been preeminently blessed from the beginning" (29).

For Storrs, the "Exclusive Spirit" was a bulwark of "fixed religious principle" that stood fast against error and lax clerical practice (31–32). The price of doctrinal purity was eternal vigilance, and only those clergy who demonstrated the "the firmness of a Robinson and the boldness of a Paul" were worthy to be called "the sons of the puritans." Such a one was Storrs's mentor, Lyman Beecher, who had been waging a long and ultimately successful campaign in Litchfield, Connecticut, against intemperance, bolstered by a series of revivals, victories that resulted in this young lion of orthodoxy being invited out of the West to Boston. Arriving in 1826, the year of Storrs's Forefathers' Day sermon, Beecher was installed in the newly formed Hanover Street Church with the hope he would lead the fight against the Unitarian menace. He met all expectations and soon animated Boston with his pulpit performances, leading to a series of revivals of increasing force.

It is not surprising, then, that Beecher followed Storrs to Plymouth and in 1827 delivered the Forefathers' Day sermon in his turn. Perhaps because of his recent whirlwind of activities on behalf of the orthodox, he dusted off for that occasion an address earlier read before the General Assembly in Connecticut, adding a few touches appropriate to the day. Proud of his heritage as the son and grandson of blacksmiths, whose physical sturdiness he shared and which he carried into the pulpit—in terms both of gestures and bold expressiveness—Beecher also drew strength from his rural background, which had suited him well in Litchfield but perhaps made him a bit defensive in Boston. There is plainly detectable in his Forefathers' Day sermon a self-referential note, as when he mounted an extended comparison between modern New Englanders and their rough-hewn forefathers, who were "not as expert in the graces of dress and the etiquette of the drawing room, as some of their descendants" (19).

Such men were, however, skilled in the then necessary arts of felling trees, ploughing fields, sailing the seas, and, very much to the point, killing Indians. Such talents, clearly, were lacking in modern Boston, being more suited to a frontier than an urban existence, and Beecher conjectured for the amusement of the orthodox what would have happened had not the stalwart Pilgrims but a well-mannered group of drawing-room habitués "stepped upon Plymouth rock" (19). The Indians, he suggested, "never would have mourned their wilderness lost, but would have brushed them from the land, as they would brush the puny insect from their face." We may well assume that the weaklings Beecher had in mind were reasonable equivalents of the editorial board of the *North American Review*, while he stood before his auditors a close facsimile of the sturdy Pilgrims he was extolling. The following year Beecher launched in Boston his own periodical, the *Spirit of the Pilgrims*, dedicated to combating the errors being spread by Unitarians and declaring in the first number that "the orthodox feel themselves to be *the proper and legitimate representatives of their pilgrim fathers*" (8).

In his Forefathers' Day sermon, Beecher echoed Storrs's point that in "many of the discourses and orations which commemorate the deeds of our Fathers, their character, as the apostles of civil liberty," had perhaps been overemphasized, while "their doctrines, their piety, their church order, and the other peculiarities of their religious institutions are passed off with cold commendations, or perhaps palliated and excused as the defects of the age" (19). For Beecher, the "defects" of his own age included just those kinds of "improvements" promoted by Whigs like Webster, for "the tide of business and pleasure, bursting from our cities, rolling on our seacoast, and flowing in our canals, will soon sweep away the Sabbath, unless a vigorous public sentiment, by preaching of the Gospel, and the power of the Spirit, can be arrayed for its preservation" (20).

Beecher was followed in Plymouth in the succession of Forefathers' Day celebrations by other prominent Trinitarians, like the Reverend Samuel Green, who combined praise of the Pilgrims with condemnation of the "withering influence" of Unitarianism, traceable to the flourishing of "deistical publications" during the Revolution (32, 30). Green accused the early champions of liberalism of having masked their opinions under the cloak of orthodoxy, only gradually insinuating into their sermons, "though with great caution, first high Arianism, then Unitarianism, down to its lowest grades" (28). But this steady parade of the orthodox in Plymouth was sponsored, we should note, not by the Pilgrim Society but by the Third Church, whose Calvinism had never flagged, and in 1831, as if to testify to its adherence to the Good Old Way beyond the call of duty, the Third Church sponsored two Trinitarians to assist in their commemoration of the Landing.

The Reverend Alvan Cobb delivered a hard-line, tightly reasoned exercise, in which he substituted for Plymouth Rock the doctrinal "ROCK on which [the Pilgrim Fathers] set their foot, and on which they built their hopes for eternity" (20). And John Codman, D.D., avoided the historic Rock as well, but in establishing his main point, that the Pilgrims were "the most decidedly orthodox" of Calvinists, he took issue with the favorite Unitarian argument that "the farewell advice of the beloved Robinson is . . . an excuse for a wide departure from his faith" (5, 18). Codman was hostile to any such concession and was scandalized that anyone would attribute "the denial of the Lord's Divinity and atonement" to Robinson (not that anyone had), and he dismissed any such allegations as "strangely, if not perversely, ignorant. . . . Let not that truly Catholic and excellent valedictory of the pious Robinson any longer be perverted to favor religious views, which would have filled his holy soul with grief and with horror" (19–20). Thus the thirty years' tradition of tacitly allowing the Unitarians the sanction of Robinson's farewell words was here revoked: clearly, the time for the reconciliation of differences between the two groups of Congregationalists for which the Reverend Flint had called was long past.

The sort of thing that got the orthodox in an uproar was demonstrated in

Plymouth the following year, 1832, when the First Church took over the public ceremonies on Forefathers' Day. They invited the scholarly Unitarian Convers Francis, author of a history of Watertown and a memorial of his father-in-law, the Reverend John Allyn, as well as the mentor of his sister, Lydia Maria Child, who was already emerging as a force in the antislavery and other radical movements. With that smoothness of manner and sweet reasonableness that advocates of orthodoxy like Samuel Green regarded as seductively subtle, Francis followed the lead of Orville Dewey in 1826 and put forth the Pilgrims as advocates of reform, champions of civil liberty, and apostles of Progress, and while scanting the Rock itself, he did evoke the "barren coast" that had greeted the Forefathers in 1620: "Here at least the genius of the place will not permit the toil and sufferings of the pilgrims to be forgotten" (26). Like Everett in 1824, Francis emphasized the iconic *Mayflower*, "that solitary vessel" pursuing her lonely and "cheerless course over the wide waste of waters" (25, 22). He compared the Pilgrim ark in terms of associations to "the little and crazy fleet of that wonderful man" Christopher Columbus, for upon both voyages there hung "a great experiment for humanity" (22–23).

Columbus was a figure often evoked by Whig champions of improvement, his voyage having been contemporary with the introduction of the printing press and compass to the Western world, and whose ships carried in their wake the visible spirit of Progress. And Francis went on to associate the Pilgrim "spirit"—which the orthodox identified with Calvinism—with the purposes of reform, so "dear to the friends of improvement" in modern times, whose voices may be heard "announcing that man has learned to read better than before," not the mysteries of Scripture but "the design of God in the purposes of the social state" (39). Francis could not have provided a more apt illustration of just what the orthodox were preaching against, his sermon a performance entirely secular in emphasis, identifying the Pilgrim advent as just another episode in the waves of "improvement" against which preachers like Lyman Beecher were arousing the apprehension of their congregations. In harmony with Webster's vision of the meaning of 1620 and Dewey's notion of the Pilgrims as agitators for reform, Francis's sermon was a pluperfect example of what Trinitarian preachers thought was wrong with Unitarian Congregationalism—and the modern world of which it was a symptom.

The debate between Trinitarians and Unitarians continued on sequential Forefathers' Day celebrations in Plymouth until the emerging tensions between North and South necessitated other concerns. A running argument predictable in its outlines and unvarying in emphases and tropes, it need not occupy our attention here much longer, though it was perhaps more important than a modern reader might imagine. The conservative argument put forth a consolidationist, reactionary view toward history, advocating a return to a simpler, more authoritarian time, while the liberals expressed an expansionist, progressive view, in which the past was but the foundation of the present. The poem by Abiel Holmes's famous son about the chambered nautilus pretty much summed up the progressive Unitarian idea, while his poem about the deacon's deconstructed shay provides a humorous version of the Trinitarian dependence on tradition. It was a schism not unlike its geopolitical counterpart, the division between the Northern and the Southern states, though hardly as serious in its consequences. As we shall see, secession is country cousin to separation.

For our part, we can put a period to this lengthy and to some a Lilliputian wrangle by turning to another celebratory moment in Plymouth, namely the fiftieth anniversary of the assumption by James Kendall of the pulpit in the First Church of Christ, held on New Year's Day in 1850. In the sermon he read on that occasion, the Reverend Kendall breathed a few relatively harmless homilies, worn smooth by previous handling, as when he attributed the universal system of education in the United States to the Pilgrim Fathers, to whom could likewise be credited American progress in general. Standing as he did at midcentury, Kendall was able to record the wonders of the past fifty years of his pastorate, which included not only missionary work and temperance reform but steam power, peace societies, and the marvel of electricity, by means of which with "*lightning speed*... a telegraphic dispatch is sent from the heart of the nation to its extreme boundary. For example;—an incident occurs at the city of Washington, and, early in the evening of the same day, we read it quietly in a printed sheet by the Rock of Plymouth" (17–18).]

Kendall in praising improvements in communication may have had Lyman Beecher's jeremiad of 1827 in mind over the years, for though he was willing to admit that the technological "facilities and accommodations" of the modern day might well have their attendant evils, he argued that the advantages clearly outweighed them (18). But in taking care to cover himself in one direction, Kendall left his other flank unguarded, and ignoring or perhaps forgetting the caveat of the Reverend Codman twenty years earlier, he blandly cited Pastor Robinson's parting sentiments to the Pilgrims concerning the progressive light of the Gospels—so evocative of the progressive spirit of both the Pilgrims and their descendants—in terms comforting to the Unitarians in his audience: "What he wanted, what he earnestly desired, what he fervently prayed for was progress—progress in Christian knowledge, grace, and truth; progress in imbibing the spirit, and attaining the temper and character of Jesus" (5). Kendall went on to speak condescendingly of Robinson's successors in America, his own predecessor "pastors of the Plymouth church" who were "no doubt pious men, and earnest and devoted laborers in the vineyard of their lord . . . although with less of the spirit of free enquiry and Christian liberty than

Robinson," being content to rest secure in "the opinions" of John Calvin, "the Genevan Professor, who with all his attainments, in the judgment of Mr. Robinson, SAW NOT ALL THINGS" (7).

"The Pilgrim Fathers of New England," thundered the Reverend Charles S. Porter, of the Third Church in Plymouth, "were . . . Puritans," who "had heard the voice of the Son of God out of the midst of the fire on Sinai, from amid the convulsions of nature on Calvary, and he became their law and Lord" (14). The occasion for these volcanics was the fiftieth anniversary not of Kendall's ministry but the consequent formation of the Third Church, celebrated on October 1, 1851. The Reverend Porter therefore dwelled on the "secession [sic] . . . for conscience's sake," not only of the departing members of Kendall's congregation in 1800 but that ensuing series of "Evangelical" seceders from Unitarianism that had taken place afterward, of which "the original members of this church were the first" (27). Like the Pilgrims, they were "pioneers" who left "the sanctuary of their fathers" to heed the paramount claims of the gospel. . . . They were constrained to leave all behind, sanctuary, funds, communion furniture, to seek for themselves and theirs a place of worship and the preaching of a gospel that neither denied their faith or belied their hopes."

The Third Church obviously had a long memory and still cherished not only their lost silverware but the similarities of their "separation" to that of the Pilgrims, evoked by Porter at the moment of their "embarking . . . at Delft-Haven, on board the Mayflower" (34). And the departure of the Pilgrims from Holland naturally brought to mind the parting words of their pastor and by necessity the recent assertion of "the venerable senior pastor of the First Church," the Reverend Kendall, concerning those well-known sentiments.

"Admirable charge!" said Porter of Robinson's farewell words, well becoming to "a protestant Christian and a Puritan pastor . . . ! But what one word is there in it, that commends or justifies the rejection of all the great and essential doctrines of the cross, faith in which moored the soul of the old Puritan to God and heaven! Shades of the Pilgrims . . . ! Do you hear it? That old Puritan, John Robinson, the erudite scholar and venerable pastor, is made the herald and prophet of Unitarianism!" (35). That, of course, was not what Kendall had claimed, but in associating Robinson's parting words with the spirit of Progress and his successors in Plymouth with something less than Robinson's openness of vision, Kendall in effect spoke in a code Porter was quick to decipher, when he "read it . . . in a printed sheet by the Rock of Plymouth."

A descendant of John Carver, the Reverend Porter found that the "drop of Puritan blood" in his veins was brought to a boil by Kendall's "assumption," which had become a traditional Unitarian exercise, "paraded before the public till, always senseless, it has become offensive to those who perceive the wide stretch the premises must have, to begin to make good the conclusion. It is too absurd to be made, or believed, by those whose home is by the 'Rock,' and with whom are the sepulchres of the Pilgrims!" (35–36). Porter then moved on to an indictment of Unitarianism, "at first an insidious and, in the end, a bold and determined assault upon Puritan faith, on Puritan soil, by means of resources gathered and garnered by, Puritan labor and sacrifice" (45). How the memory of that lost "furniture" both endured and long rankled!

But Porter ended by returning to his main point, that it was the orthodox of Massachusetts who were the true inheritors of the Pilgrim idea, there being no "older faith than ours, here at Plymouth Rock, except the faith of devils," which last was not a reference to witchcraft (or Unitarianism) but to the religion of Native Americans (45). Where Kendall made but passing mention of the Rock, as a chronological waymark from which to measure the succession of his clerical predecessors in the First Church of Plymouth, Porter elevated it as a supremely "significant symbol of all that is great, best, most desirable for man, in this world and the next. . . . How many, from the ends of the earth, have sent their thoughts to the Pilgrim Boulder, rounded and smoothed by its own unregistered migrations, save by Him who numbered the ripples that gamboled about it in calms, and the waves that rolled over it in storms, and at length, planting it here, mid sea and shore, made it a stepping-stone to a new order of things, both in church and state. How many have visited it, gazed upon it, stood upon it" (18).

Porter continued on in this vein, but it is sufficient for our purposes to record that as the waves of disbelief rose higher, it was the orthodox who clung to the Rock, while the liberals used it as a point demarking a fast-retreating point in time, encapsulated in Kendall's image of modern man reading the latest news from the nation's capital "by the Rock of Plymouth," the new and the old brought not together but into picturesque juxtaposition.

V

In 1855, the Reverend Joseph S. Clark, like Abiel Holmes an orthodox but conciliatory Congregationalist, attempted, as the title of his discourse tells us, to "Repair the Breach" within his church. Though an advocate of the Trinitarian line, to which he would devote a scholarly and still useful volume, published in 1858, Clark felt that there was yet hope for Congregationalism, which had "a remarkable power of self recovery" (27). He declared his faith in the power of the church's "past history" as holding out "the most animating hope of [its] future progress, and is itself a mighty means of securing it. The remembrance of John Robinson and his achievements; of New England's founders and their fortitude; of the first Congregational churches in this country, and their invincible faith, will act on their descendants through all coming time as an incentive to piety and a rebuke to degeneracy" (28). Clark was clearly of the party of Memory and traced modern evangelical Congregationalism back to the Pilgrims and their Rock, but his celebration of John Robinson, styled the American Moses, coincides with that of the Unitarians: "The practices and opinions of JOHN ROBINSON, more than those of any other man, have shaped the institutions of New England, though he never set foot on her soil" (3).

Doctrinal specifics aside, it was the figure of Pastor Robinson that emerged as the central focus of the theological wrangles between the two Congregational factions. Perhaps because of the ministerial connection, perhaps because, despite the claims of Judson and Strong, the Pilgrim annals after John Cushman's sermon of 1621 are bare of theological discourse, Robinson became central to the orthodox/liberal dispute, his writings providing the necessary documentation. To this we can add the Christology inherent in American Protestantism, which seeks out messiahs for whatever sectarian dispute is in progress—a tendency to which the evangelical impulse and the advocacy of moral reform would give added force.

As late as 1895, John Robinson would serve the champions of reform, by then widened to include civil rights, as a prophet, and in his Forefathers' Day address of that year—the 275th anniversary of the Landing—Senator George Frisbie Hoar of Massachusetts, who had devoted his career to radical causes, argued that Robinson's farewell address applied not only to theological doctrine but political theory: "When religious liberty set her foot on the rock at Plymouth, her inseparable sister, political freedom, came with her" (*Proceedings*, 28). As we shall see, this pairing would lead the celebrants of the Pilgrims into troubled waters in the years preceding the Civil War, but for persons who pushed the principles of Unitarianism to their logical conclusions, the tableau of the Embarkation was seen as providing doctrinal sanction for what followed the Landing, with its necessarily secular emphasis. As in Lucy's twin tableaux (see figs. 4 and 1), Robinson dominates the first, Governor Carver the second, but the two are part of one whole, to which would be added a third part, typified by (among many such depictions) White's *Signing the Compact* (see fig. 3), providing the triptych upon which the liberal tradition in the United States—as seen from New England—would draw.

There are other reasons for the emerging emphasis on the Departure as a matching icon to the Landing, and these will be discussed in a later chapter, but the central place of Robinson in the tableau could hardly be opposed by clergymen, whose own profession it validated. The shyness of liberal ministers regarding the Rock may possibly be traced to Webster's eloquent use, a complex reaction involving something more than literary considerations, as the following chapter will suggest. Among the Unitarian clergy, the gifted but idiosyncratic James Flint drew from Plymouth Rock a seminal, sustained flow of images, but after Webster's famous reference to that epochal threshold of American freedom, nothing similar came from a liberal minister's pen. As we have seen, Webster's priority was in part also responsible for the emergence of a third icon, Everett's celebration of the *Mayflower*. Acceptable to ministers and politicians alike, a figure with both covenantal and statist implications, over the years after 1824 the *Mayflower* would become an important rhetorical and artistic symbol with complex implications, essential to the idea both of Departure and Arrival, and lending its name to the sacred Compact.

Moreover, the *Mayflower* was as important for what it was not as for what it was, an exclusionary quality essential to the exceptionalism of the Pilgrims. As Terence Martin has shown, the differences obtaining in the United States were essential to the rhetorical tropes of Fourth of July orations, and the same may be said of Forefathers' Day sermons and addresses. Thus Everett had empha- sized that the *Mayflower* carried Englishmen to America, who brought with them British traditions of civil and religious liberty, which flourished excep- tionally in New England, thanks to the isolating distance from the Old. And as many speakers would subsequently point out, what the Pilgrims did not bring with them on their sacred ark was slavery, a declaration of fact that was seldom as simple in implication as it might at first appear, nor was the libertarianism of the Pilgrims without its contradictions as well, a paradox with which the following chapter is chiefly concerned.

CHAPTER 8

Concerning Certain Flaws in the Rock

The Puritans of 1620 had not a rash or visionary thought about
them. No orders of nobility, no enslaving of captives, no digging
for gold, no community of goods, no agrarian laws. They erred after
as bigots & erred on virtue's side.
—Ralph Waldo Emerson

I

In his *History of the Town of Plymouth* of 1885, William T. Davis in describing the bicentennial celebration in 1829 deferred to Dr. Thacher's account, but he did add one significant detail, "described to the author by a gentleman who was present" (102). According to this story, "several clergymen, among whom was Dr. Kirkland, took part in the exercises, and during the oration stood leaning over the rail of the pulpit looking down on Mr. Webster and catching every word of his impassioned oratory." But when Webster reached the end of his attack on the slave traffic and declared, " 'if the pulpit be silent whenever or wherever there may be a sinner bloody with this guilt within the hearing of its voice, the pulpit is false to its trust,' . . . he turned his face upward and backward, and the clergymen, whose silence on the subject was one of the extraordinary phenomena of the times, slunk back to their seats mortified and chagrined." Born in 1822, Davis had to rely on the testimony of another for the specific anecdote, but having filled a number of public offices in his native Plymouth during his long career as a lawyer and merchant, he certainly could testify as to the prevailing position of the clerisy during the subsequent period when the abolitionist debate was raging. Nor were clerics the only persons of authority in New England who shrank from any mention of the "peculiar institution."

Parody is always a welcome guide to the conventions of an era, instance the *American Sketches* on Fourth of July orations, and for an updated example we can turn to Artemus Ward, who in addressing his "Feller Sitterzens" in Wethersfield, Connecticut, on July 4, 1859, observed in passing "the grow'th of Ameriky from the time when the Mayflowers cum over in the Pilgrim and brawt Plymmuth Rock with them" (Browne, 167). The showman was from Indiana and could therefore be pardoned his confusion in lieu of the power of his testimony to the universality of his allusion. A collection of Ward's public pronouncements delivered in the late 1850s is a scrapbook of oratorical conventions of the day—not excluding secessionist sentiments, when Ward happened to be in the South. What he was *for* depended on his audience—"my perliteral sentiments agree with yourn exactly"—but what he was *against* was as consistent as his opportunism: except for temperance, the adversaries of which seldom sought (or were able to reach) public platforms, Ward was unanimous in his antagonism toward reform in the many rainbow hues displayed in the decades before the Civil War. Women's rights, free love, and abolition were targets of his ridicule, along with the eccentricities of emerging religious sects as he saw them. In this generous opposition to currents of change, Ward was in perfect tune with most of those conservative Americans who had easy access to the public ear.

As the manager of a traveling circus and waxworks, Ward shared a number of P. T. Barnum's characteristics, but his politics were of the language, if not the party, of Webster: "I'm a Union man. I luv the Union. . . . I'm for the Union as she air, and withered be the arm of every ornery cuss who attempts to bust her up" (167). As the threat of war loomed in 1859, Ward addressed himself to the "Krysis," which he traced to "our Afrikan Brother," a kinship Ward devoutly renounced, wishing "Cuffy" as he called him back to "Afriky's burnin shores" (78). And yet the "Krysis," he acknowledged, was not the fault of the African but could be laid to "inflammertory individooals," a few "hily respectyble gentlemen and sum talentid females. . . . He wooden be sich an infernal noosanse if white peple would let him alone. . . . What's the good of continnerly stirin him up with a ten foot pole?"

Twenty years earlier, in his Forefathers' Day oration in Plymouth, William Sullivan had likewise regarded slavery from the end of a lengthy stick, but with no desire to agitate the subject. After Webster, Sullivan was the first speaker on that occasion and in that place to mention slavery, adding it to his list of problems darkening the political horizon in 1829. While "commending that philanthropy, which seeks to emancipate millions from slavery," Sullivan noted that such an endeavor was "dangerous, difficult, and impractical": it not only violated the right guaranteed by the "national contract" to hold our fellow humans in bondage, but, when voiced by persons not resident in those regions where that "right" was law, it only "aggravated the evil by interfering" in the internal affairs of other states (35).

Moreover, even if the abolitionists' purpose could be "accomplished in a single day, what is to be done with two millions of persons, who are without knowledge, without property, without skill, and who cannot, from complexion . . . mingle with and disappear, in the mass of population?" (34). Sullivan favored a gradual, not an immediate, solution to the problem: "The only cure for slavery is interest; at best a partial one. Interest has moved the line of slavery, from Maine to Pennsylvania. It will remove it, onward, until it comes to a wide expanse where it will remain until the inscrutable designs of Providence have been accomplished." This was a view that would hold among well-meaning but cautious and careful persons in New England for the next twenty years, producing a voluminous literature the main points of which were stated with admirable concision by Sullivan in 1829.

The Whigs who emerged during the subsequent decade shared the old Federalist's concerns and espoused a gradualist and hopefully providential "solution," a position not much different from that of the Democrats save perhaps in the degree of emphasis on the desirability of abolition, for which the Jacksonians had less sympathy. Like Sullivan, the Whigs felt that emancipation was a good idea but not one that should be implemented too hastily or championed in a censorious manner, thus angering and thereby alienating Southerners, who had in 1820 indicated their hostility to outside interference.

For Sullivan and Daniel Webster, disunion was a far greater threat to the nation than was the moral taint of the slave system. Such was not the case, as New England was soon to discover, among an outspoken, even strident minority of Americans, but most public persons of high (and noble) profile, like President Kirkland of Harvard, preferred to remain seated when the subject of slavery was mentioned. As for those representatives of the establishment who wished, like Sullivan, to address the snarling beast of slavery, the ten-foot pole of Artemus Ward seemed the best implement with which to address it.

Given this conservative position espoused by prominent New Englanders, it is to be expected that Plymouth Rock and the Pilgrims were not much associated in public places with immediate abolition in the 1820s or the decades following. "The soil of New England," proudly intoned President Josiah Quincy of Harvard University on the occasion of Boston's bicentennial celebration, "is trodden by no slave" (49). But in celebrating the spirit of Liberty, "civil and religious," that the Forefathers brought to America, the son and namesake of a great revolutionary patriot made no suggestion that New England should foist its institutions—or lack of them—upon other regions (16). Quincy, who in his youth had actively opposed the Louisiana Purchase as a threat to the sanctity and solidity of the Union, in 1830 preferred that New England serve passively as an inspirational beacon to benighted regions and "be an example to the world, of the blessings of a free government, and of the means and capacity of man to maintain it" (54). This was substantially Webster's message at Bunker Hill in 1825, and we may assume that, like Webster, Quincy was referring to dark places in Europe, not the United States.

All such public pronouncements of Puritan virtue in New England were gauged at least in part to assert regional hegemony, with the intention of compensating for the loss of proportionate national representation by taking the moral high ground. As a Federalist, Quincy had opposed in Congress the two-thirds provision for slave representation (which gave Southern states unfair advantage in terms of sectional weight), and during his five-year term as Boston's mayor in the 1820s, he had instituted civic reforms—including the establishment of a board of selectmen—that, as he noted in his bicentennial address, had helped make that city "among the foremost and the boldest to exemplify and uphold whatever constitutes the prosperity, the happiness, and the glory of New England" (5).

But reform for Josiah Quincy, once again, was a matter mostly of elevating and brightening Boston's moral beacon, activities perfectly consistent with his loyalty to the Federalist ideology, which long outlived the party itself. He continued at Harvard the good work of his predecessor, President Kirkland—if with something more by way of administrative rigor—hiring notable historians and teachers of literature as well as building a new university library. But like so many Unitarians of high profile, though expressing in private his opposition to the extension of slavery, Quincy began to speak out in favor of abolition only after the passage of the Fugitive Slave Law brought slavery into close proximity to Faneuil Hall. By that late period, the pole of Artemus Ward had become a splintery matter of inches.

By contrast, Josiah's son Edmund Quincy, though like his father a Federalist, enlisted himself early on in the agitation to bring about the immediate abolition of slavery, becoming a loyal member of the clique that was clustered around William Lloyd Garrison. But Quincy's other son and namesake, Josiah Jr., became an outspoken Whig and expended his energies building railroads and other institutions and improvements that Whigs saw as strengthening New England's parity in the sectional rivalry with the South and West. The Quincy family provides a virtual diagram of New England between 1830 and 1860, being a literal example of Lincoln's figure of a "house divided." Somehow it remained standing, a balance exemplified by the equilibrist efforts of the father who stood between his sons, if often in a Laocoön pose, all three struggling with that serpentine proposition that because of the Puritan connection New England had an exclusive monopoly on virtue, the exercise of which, however, was variously applied.

II

With occasional exceptions, persons who took up the cause of the slave in New England in the 1820s tended not to have much stake in the commercial life of the region. Among the clergy, they tended also to be associated with de-

nominations other than Unitarian—with, in fact, orthodox Congregationalism and the Baptists. Even as William Ellery Channing, in his lecture on
Milton, was praising a cloistered virtue, the evangelical spirit was moving out
from temperance reform toward abolition. In 1824, young Leonard Bacon, a
minister's son fresh from that citadel of Trinitarianism, the Andover Theological Seminary, read before a Boston audience a Fourth of July oration entitled *A
Plea for Africa*. It was in effect an appeal on behalf of the American Colonization Society, whose proposed solution to slavery William Sullivan in 1829
would question. An institution "originating among the planters" of the South,
the society sought to transport free people of color back to Africa, with the expectation that American Negroes, "skilled in arts, and well instructed, moral,
and christianized, must have an influence on the millions of that unfortunate
country" (36). But while acknowledging the "respectable and worthy" motives
of the society's members, Sullivan found it "difficult to discern, how their
measures, with whatever success they may be attended, are to effect a general
manumission. They dip from an ocean which fills up faster than they can
diminish it" (35).

When Channing eloquently broke his long silence regarding slavery in 1836,
he came to much the same conclusion as the old Federalist regarding the
efficacy of establishing a colony of freed blacks in Africa. But "whatever good it
may do abroad—and I trust it will do much," wrote Channing, "it promises
little at home," and in a subsequent writing, he used language remarkably
similar to Sullivan's: colonization as a solution to the problem of slavery, he
observed, was "a process about as reasonable as that of draining the Atlantic"
(*Works*, 729, 784). Yet the idea of colonization seemed to many Americans not
of color an ideal solution to the problem, for reasons that Leonard Bacon's
oration in 1824 reveals.

He began with a ritual reference to the effect upon the New England wilderness of the arrival of "our Pilgrim fathers," who erected "the ensigns of their
freedom and altars of their religion" and "in the midst of peril . . . became the
founders of an empire" the prosperity of which is evidenced everywhere (62).
He likewise observed the convention of attributing the success of the Pilgrims
and the consequent prosperity of New England to "the doing of Jehovah": "It is
God who hath spread out our land like the garden of Eden, who hath made it
free as its winds and its waters, and filled it with the light of science and the
glories of his own eternal truth!" (62–63). But Bacon then went on to suggest
that if present prosperity was traceable to the "grand purposes of God's benevolence" both to the Pilgrims and their descendants, then it was fitting that
modern Americans should think benevolent thoughts and undertake benevolent acts themselves.

Bacon described the deplorable condition of Africa, the result not only of perpetual warfare by a "barbaric" people but of the traffic in humans being carried on despite "the abolition of this traffic" by Great Britain and the United States (65). He devoted a page or two to the horrors of the slave trade and its wretched victims, echoing Story's "Charge" of 1819, and acknowledged that any "plea" for Africa must include those "children of Africa" now held as slaves in America: "They are one nation—a separate-distinct-peculiar people" (66). The beauty of the plan advanced by the American Colonization Society is that it would benefit both kinds of Africans, bringing "peace and happiness to the continent of Africa" while elevating "all her children to the rank which God has given them in the scale of existence," meanwhile enabling them to "cover Africa with the institutions of civilized freedom and fill it with the light of knowledge and religion" (67).

The scheme of the society was Separatism in reverse—exile—and it was natural for young Bacon, brimming with good will and humanity and fired with an evangelical zeal to bring light to the Dark Continent, to compare those American Negroes who were to be "trained up and sent to Africa" to "the Pilgrims of Plymouth or the Puritans of New Haven—men with all that wisdom and all that dauntless piety—which gave renown to the Winthrops and the Winslows—the Davenports and Hookers of our early history!" (70–71). But the solution and the simile simply wouldn't stick with certain people in "Plymouth or New Haven," or Boston for all of that. If hardheaded Federalists like William Sullivan regarded the plan of the society as well intentioned but inadequate to the complexity of the problem, even harder-headed Federalists like Edmund Quincy dismissed it out of hand as hypocritical. For it did not escape some Americans that "the plans, the history, the prospects" of the society were uniformly aimed at ridding the United States of free persons of color, regarded as undesirable elements of society in both the Northern and Southern states (71). Though these last were a minority, they were highly vocal and were determined that they would be heard—and hear from them we shall in chapters yet to come.

Bacon's anomalous reference to the "Puritans of New Haven" in a speech given in Boston is a textual aberration resulting from his having given the same sermon a year later in that Connecticut city, a place with which he would be identified for the rest of his long and productive career. Bacon left Andover intending to carry the light of orthodoxy into the darkness not of Africa but the western frontier, but his errand got him no farther than New Haven, where he delivered his appeal on behalf of the American Colonization Society on the Fourth of July, 1825, and so impressed his auditors that he was invited to assume the vacant pulpit of the First Church of New Haven. The congregation was made up of the most prominent people of that community, a heady assignment for such a young man, and though Bacon continued to speak out on behalf of African Americans and devoted himself to improving their opportunities for education in New Haven, not much more was heard from him regarding the Euclidean beauty of the plan of the American Colonization Society. By 1848 he had become active in the free-soil movement.

Bacon's post in New Haven provided the leisure and his proximity to Yale the impetus to begin the work for which he is best known, *The Genesis of the New England Churches*, not published until 1874 but commenced at the height of the Trinitarian-Unitarian debate and intended to demonstrate that the truly "American way" was the way of Separation (including church from state), which was, of course, the Good Old Pilgrim Way. In 1838, before committing himself to the cause of abolition, Bacon published his *Thirteen Historical Discourses on the New England Churches*, the prolegomenon to his later, more comprehensive chronicle, and it was undoubtedly his growing reputation as a young orthodox clergyman-scholar that had resulted in his being invited, the previous year, to give the annual Forefathers' Day address before the New England Society in the City of New York. Founded in 1805, this was the oldest of such organizations, made up of men from the eastern states who had traveled toward the West (and South) in search of fortune, their progress marked by the establishment of similar societies all the way (by 1850) to San Francisco. These were conservative groups, being of the parties of commerce and nostalgia for the most part, and the society in New York had been the sponsor of Gardiner Spring's attack on Unitarians as well as the Reverend Whelpley's revisionist sequel to Webster's oration of 1820.

Leonard Bacon did not disappoint his auditors and gave them a lengthy dose of historical discourse, beginning by tracing the Reformation from its beginnings down to that moment when "one hundred . . . Pilgrims, including men, women, and little children, landed from the Mayflower on the rock of Plymouth" (*New England Society Orations*, 1:179). Much of his address, however, was devoted to defending the Puritans from charges of intolerance and fanaticism, and when Bacon came to their treatment of Quakers, he gave the problematics of persecution a novel twist by referring to "the conduct of some in our more enlightened and free thinking age" (195). We should not, Bacon pointed out, confuse the Quakers of the seventeenth century with their modern equivalents: "No, if you would find the true successors of the Quakers of 1650, you must look elsewhere. The Anti-slavery agitators of our day, are extensively regarded very much as the Quakers were regarded by our ancestors."

Bacon had followed the lead of previous Forefathers' Day speakers in New York and avoided the troublesome subject of slavery for the tranquil topic of the Pilgrim/Puritan advent. But in attempting to put a contemporary slant on historical matters, he framed an analogy that was as deeply conflicted as the controversy that engendered it. For in New England and New York in 1837 the agitation against slavery was perhaps a more painful subject than was slavery itself: "Some of [the abolitionists] execrate our constitution and our laws, and revile our magistrates, and utter all manner of reproach against our ministers and our churches. Some of them go about preaching doctrines which tend not only to the extinction of the 'peculiar institutions' of one part of our country, and the subversion of our 'glorious union,' but to absolute and universal anarchy. We cannot indeed charge upon them everything that was charged upon the ancient Quakers . . . but they have published doctrines highly offensive to public opinion, and as is commonly believed highly dangerous to society" (195–96). And what has been the reaction of their fellow citizens "in our age of toleration and free inquiry" to these excesses of reformational zeal? "The answer is found in the roar of mobs and the smoke of smouldering ruins," mob violence against antislavery agitators, carried out by men who in Bacon's terms had been "fiercely liberal" in condemning "our ancestors, for persecuting the Quakers."

It is tempting to read into Bacon's prose a fine irony, but his temper was otherwise. He was no friend to radical abolitionists but was willing to use their sufferings at the hands of the mob, with which he had no sympathy either, in order to make a point about persecution in Puritan Massachusetts. The Forefathers, Bacon pointed out, "made laws against the fanatics with whom they had to do," whereas, because of the "enlightened and liberal maxims" of modern day lawmakers, there can be no legislation "to limit freedom of opinion and discussion," and persons opposed to abolitionists are therefore obligated to act "without law and against law" (197). His was, in effect, an apologia for vigilantism, albeit read backward from the Puritan example.

By Bacon's accounting, the more democratic American institutions become, the fiercer would be the reaction against radicals who take shelter behind those institutions. He thereby gave a paradoxical turn to Orville Dewey's effort ten years earlier to spin Puritan "dissent" into an equivalent to modern reform, for Bacon's was a conservative use of early American history. By his lights, it was not the dissent of the Puritans that was praiseworthy but their government of laws, and it was the Quakers who occupied the dissenting (hence reforming and troublemaking) position. The Forefathers' fealty to law was one of their most admirable characteristics and reinforced the positive aspect of their heritage: what was needed was not less persecution of ultra-abolitionists, Bacon implies, but prosecution through legal means, thereby obviating the need for lawless mobs.

In giving new meaning to both the Puritans' harsh treatment of Quakers and the mob action against agitators, Bacon accomplished a rhetorical feat not unlike those attempts by Abiel Holmes, James Flint, Webster, Everett, Greenwood, and Dewey to place their auditors in the midst of the Pilgrims. "*You are the they of them*" is the consistent subtext, despite the changing context, though neither group in Bacon's instance could take much comfort from the mutual association. Aside from his contemporary reference, Bacon's clever use of the past is one more reminder that the tradition of the Pilgrim Fathers as having originated the "free institutions" of the United States was a problematic proposition, given the Puritan propensity for punishing dissenters. As we have already seen, Forefathers' Day orators and other Pilgrim celebrants during the first thirty years of the nineteenth century found it necessary again and again to explain away that dark stain on the gleaming fabric of New England's early history, a spot that not a little resembled dried blood.

Before pursuing the abolitionist controversy further in succeeding chapters, we need to pay deferred attention to that necessity, which helps to explain the often self-contradictory role that the Puritans would play as the agitation for emancipation and its opposition increased. Thus Artemus Ward on the Fourth of July, 1859, was willing to flatter his Connecticut audience by a ritual evocation of the Pilgrims and Plymouth Rock, but he begged to be excused for not praising "the early settlers of the Colonies. People which hung idiotic old wimin for witches, burnt holes in Quakers' tongues, and consined their feller critters to the tredmill and pillery on the slitest provocashun may have bin very nice folks in their way, but I must confess I don't admire their stile, and will pass them by" (167–68).

The Puritans may have "ment well," but the Indiana showman preferred to extend his fullest sympathies to America's Indians, who "were innocent of secession, rum, draw-poker, and sinfulness ginrally. They had no Congress . . . or Associated Press. . . . I say, in view of the mess we are makin of things, it would have been better for us if Columbus had staid to home" (217–18). Ward in effect classed the Puritans with that modern moral pestilence, reformers, being persons whose advocacy of societal perfection more often than not brought "improvements" of the destructive kind.

As Ward's dismissiveness suggests, the opposition of Protestant clergy in New England to the extreme views and disruptive actions of radical abolitionists can be read as another assertion of memory, Puritanism itself having in the manner of a recessive gene a deep history of radicalism in the name of virtue gone bad. For Bacon, what was happening in the late 1830s was a lesson in the cyclical nature of history, which had for the unwary a boomerang effect. Thus modern reformers in their excess of zeal were facsimile Puritans; but as victims of persecution, they resembled those other reformers, the Quakers, who accused the Puritans of sinfulness and were flogged and hanged for their pains. From either viewpoint, the Puritans were not entirely pure, whether regarded as narrow-minded zealots or as the repressors of excess zeal in others.

But if New England wished to preserve its moral hegemony, which it regarded genealogically as descending from the Separatists of 1620, then its churchmen and other moral agents had to come to terms with that problematic Puritan past, especially since it seemed to be taking new and alarming forms, engendered by the abolitionist controversy. It was one thing to celebrate the Pilgrim Separatists, but what was one to do with their modern equivalents, abolitionists calling for New England to secede from the other states, which by the radicals' definition were corrupt as any Old World tyranny?

That is, where radical moralists had a simple, Alexandrine solution to the Gordian knot of an iniquitous system supported by the Constitution, conservative churchmen (encouraged, shall we say, by their wealthy parishioners) preferred to pick away at it in the hope that in God's good time it would unravel itself. Though contemporary commercial considerations undoubtedly influenced their temporizing, they could certainly draw upon New England's history to illustrate the dangers of actions impelled by thoughtless zeal.

Again, even liberal Unitarians like Channing did not champion ultra-abolition and put their faith in the power of prayer to change Southern hearts and the power of reason to change Southern minds. And although Trinitarians like Lyman Beecher were outspoken in their attacks on slavery, theirs was a halfway platform of abolition and stopped well short of immediate emancipation. Beecher himself was a champion of African colonization, as was his novelist daughter. But whatever the program preached to the South, New England Protestantism needed to set its own house of memory in order, for in all the wrangles over whether the Unitarians or Trinitarians were the "true" inheritors of the Good Old Way, there seemed to be general agreement that something needed to be said by way of explanation, if not apology, about the Bad Old Way of handling dissent.

Whether the matter at hand was simply a celebration of modern blessings credited to the Forefathers or a hortatory exercise urging reforms that would continue the Pilgrim/Puritan tradition, the flaws in the record of tolerance in early New England needed addressing before the speaker could draw strength from the past in facing contemporary matters. And so, before resuming in the next chapter further considerations of the tar baby that celebrants of the Pilgrims found sitting in the middle of whatever roadway they took leading forward from Plymouth Rock, we need to explore the brier patch that the same celebrants were forced to confront whenever they dealt with those parts of the Puritan past that were exceptionally prickly to the modern touch.

III

As early as 1789, Jedidiah Morse, that militant Calvinist and Federalist gadfly, had used his *American Geography* to square away the untidy aspects of the Puritan myth. His section on New England begins by celebrating his countrymen in language evocative of Forefathers' Day orations well before that genre became conventionalized. New England, he proudly announced, was "a nursery of men," a virtual hive that sent swarms yearly "into other parts of the United States" (144). New Englanders by Morse's account are a heroic people, who "glory, and perhaps with justice, in possessing that spirit of freedom, which induced their ancestors to leave their native country, and to brave the dangers of the ocean and the hardships of settling a wilderness. Their education, laws, and situation, serve to inspire them with high notions of liberty" (145). Indeed, if New Englanders have a fault, it is that they are "often jealous to excess," imagining grievances and nursing "groundless suspicions, and unjust complaints against government."

But Morse insisted that the habitual suspicion endemic to the New England character had its positive side, for though "productive of some political evils," it demonstrated "that the essence of true liberty exists in New England; for jealousy is the guardian of liberty, and a characteristic of free republicans," a notion that suggests a certain continuity in the politics of reaction in the United States. A similar logic governs Morse's account of the Puritans in New England, which begins with a lengthy history of the Pilgrims (including the signing of the Compact, which is reproduced entire) and the Landing, absent (typically in 1789) an account of Forefathers' Rock. Morse also noted that the Plymouth settlers, though "rigid" in their Separatist faith, "never discovered that persecuting spirit which we have seen in Massachusetts" and provided refuge within their borders not only for Anne Hutchinson but for fugitive Quakers and Baptists (156).

This distinction, as we have seen, tended to be neglected thereafter, especially in Boston, where Pilgrims and Puritans were conflated, but Morse gave it great emphasis, so much so that the history of Salem and Boston is detached from his account of New England and is found in the entry for "Massachusetts." There he rendered a full account of the trial of Hutchinson, the persecution of Samuel Gorton, the harsh handling of the Quakers and other dissidents, and the witchcraft scare, along with an apologetic emphasis on the moral "scrupulousness" of the Puritans, which he was quick to pronounce "ridiculous" when it descended to the cut of hair and the use of tobacco (187).

As for the much more serious matter of the witchcraft "delusion," Morse dismissed it as in no way unique to New England but rather as part and parcel of "the spirit of the times" (186). In like fashion, he ascribed the rough treatment of the Quakers to their "rude and contemptuous" behavior, which included invading churches and insulting ministers with the "grossest railings" (188). At the same time, Morse noted that the passage of "severe laws" against the Quakers by the Puritan magistrates had an effect opposite to the one intended: "The persecution of any religious sect ever has had, and ever will have a tendency to increase their number" (188).

The result was an escalation of retribution ending with a law punishing with death Quakers who returned to Massachusetts after being banished, an "impolitic" as well as "unjust" measure: "The most that can be said for our ancestors is that they tried gentler means at first, which they found utterly ineffectual, and that they followed the examples of the authorities in most other states and in most ages of the world, who with the like absurdity have supposed every person could and ought to think as they did, and with the like cruelty have punished such as appeared to differ from them."

Morse's was the higher wisdom, as relevant today as it was two centuries ago, but that folly is the ruling principle of humankind is suggested by his subsequent behavior. Otherwise it is hard to reconcile this apostle of Reason with the hysterical Federalist who within ten years would advocate the passage of alien and sedition laws to suppress "Jacobin" ideas in the United States and who was willing to block the appointment of a known Unitarian to a prestigious chair at Harvard, expressions of New England's traditional "jealousy" that approximated the Puritan repressions of the seventeenth century.

We must not confuse Morse even in 1789 with liberal thinkers like Jefferson, and he was quick to censure the Quakers of the early period, whose "imprudent, indelicate, and infatuated conduct" was offensive to any well-ordered community. Still, Morse went on to admit, the perpetrators of such aberrant behavior were more properly "subjects of a mad-house, or a house of correction; and it is to be lamented that ever any greater severities were used" (189). And Morse anticipated Leonard Bacon's distinguishing between the crazy Quakers of Endicott's day and those of modern times, "a moral, friendly, and benevolent people."

There is, because of Bacon's later context, some irony in Morse's further praise of the Quakers of his day for, among other social virtues, their "hospitality, and particularly for their engagements in the abolition of the slavery of the Negroes. In this land of civil and religious freedom, it is hoped, that persecution will never again lift its direful head against any religious denomination of people, whose sentiments and conduct are consistent with the peace and happiness of society" (189). In that bracketing of "abolition" with "persecution" and the "peace and happiness of society," Morse, despite his optative prose, provided a dark look forward into the next century, a perspective that more than one person would use from an apposite but antithetical point of view. All of which suggests that Morse, so often honored as the Father of American Geography, perhaps needs more attention as a cultural historian — and prophet—than he has hitherto been given.

It is difficult to turn anywhere in Morse's *Geography* and not find the seeds of much that was to characterize the elements not only of Forefathers' Day sermons and addresses but Fourth of July orations in New England as well, from the argument for the necessity of the Union—which guaranteed the strength of an expanding empire—to the pantheon of American heroes produced by the Revolution. From temperance (he was for it) to tariffs (against), Morse covered an amazing variety of moral and political topics, and his opinions would be echoed by prominent persons for a considerable period of time to come.

Even from our enlightened place in history, Morse's opinions must be accounted balanced and fair, as when he attributed the "spirit of infatuation respecting witchcraft" that broke out in 1692 to "a scene of fraud and imposture, began by young girls, who at first thought of nothing more than exciting pity and indulgence, and continued by adult persons, who were afraid of being accused themselves" (191). Morse noted that, as with the persecution of Quakers, "the same infatuation was at this time current in England," and "the law by which the witches were condemned, was a copy of the statute in England," so "the odium of this tragic conduct" should not rest on New England alone (192). As we shall see, the contextual argument will hold for a century of apologias regarding the Puritan persecution of religious dissent and the witchcraft delusion. Likewise, Morse's enlightened argument that the Quakers who disturbed the public peace in the 1650s were best treated as insane will surface again in the writings of the most liberal intellectuals and writers of the 1840s and 1850s.

Where Morse was specific about the faults of the Puritans, John Quincy Adams, the first Forefathers' Day orator who felt called upon to explain away the unpleasant aspects of the ancestral character, was rather general, nor did he bother to distinguish the founders of Plymouth from their Boston neighbors. Noting in 1802 that "an enlightened age" regards with contempt persons who engage in "controversies about trifles," Adams conceded that the zeal of the Puritans "was kindled by subjects of trivial importance" and admitted also that while "aggrieved by the intolerance of others" toward themselves, "they were alike intolerant" of others (26). Avoiding nasty particulars, Adams justified the bigotry of the Pilgrim Fathers by pointing out that their "sufferance" even in the New World was not guaranteed, as a consequence of which they tended "to look upon every dissenter among themselves with a jealous eye" (26, 29). Finally, if "their zeal might sometimes be too ardent . . . it was always sincere" (29).

With that characteristic Adams skepticism regarding human motives, in which Calvinism was filtered through an Enlightenment sieve, he observed wryly that even in modern times, when "religious indulgence" is the ideal—a "right" written into the Constitution—mankind remains imperfect. Thus those who are contemptuous toward controversy over trifles make an exception regarding small matters "such as inflame their own passions" (26). And if modern Christians have "triumphed over the prejudices of a former generation," they have yet to be "victorious over the malignant passions of our own," suggesting that Adams was aware of the kinds of self-contradictions found in fellow Federalists like Morse (29–30). Humility, finally, is the best posture from which to honor the memory while numbering the faults of the Forefathers, a position that was shared by few apologists for the Puritans in Plymouth and elsewhere.

The Bicentennial provided a special venue for an honest theological appraisal of the Forefathers, the occasion demanding some account of and explanation for the failings of the Pilgrims even while extolling their strengths. The most of the clerical celebrants, however, repeated the arguments of Morse and Adams, shaded pro Puritan or con. Typical of the second group was the Reverend Joshua Dodge of Haverhill, who acknowledged that "the very men, who had just escaped from the iron yoke of ecclesiastical tyranny, who contended that liberty of conscience in matters of religion, was one of the most unalienable rights ever entrusted to man by his Maker, having secured the civil power in their own hands, assumed the prerogative to prescribe rules for others' faith and practice" (10). In effect, the Forefathers brought to the New World "the same exterminating spirit" that had driven them from the Old, and they persecuted "dissenters" until "the liberal system of toleration" that the Civil Wars in England brought to the "parent country" was extended to her colonies: "Thus we see, that the best of Christians are but imperfect men."

The Reverend James Sabine of Boston concurred with this view and maintained that the problem lay in the theocratic coincidence of church and state, a "blot upon the otherwise fair escutcheon of the New England churches," even unto the present day (28). Sabine's emphasis may at least in part be credited to the state constitutional convention then going on, which debated the dismissal of the old Standing Order, by which the Congregational clergy were supported by public tax money. As we have seen, the celebrants in Plymouth on December 22 devoutly wished that the "Third Article" be preserved, but others elsewhere felt differently.

The Puritans had their apologists, also, like the Reverend John Woodbridge of Hadley, Massachusetts, who noted that the persecution of the famed and revered Roger Williams was not simply for his "doctrinal errors, but for the factious spirit he manifested," and as for the Quakers, they "were far less peaceable citizens than they have been since" (19). Besides, in an age notorious for its intolerance, the Puritans were "no means remarkable" on that score. Heman Humphrey, in Pittsfield, while admitting "that in their treatment of those, who differed from them in religious opinions, they too often lost sight of the mild and tolerant spirit of the Gospel," noted that "nothing human is perfect," so that we should not be surprised to discover that the saintly Puritans "had their failings" (*Character*, 25). Observing that "the progress of mental emancipation has always been slow," Humphrey thought it "illiberal" of modern, enlightened men to "despise or condemn" a people who "lived two hundred years ago." Like so many defenders of the Puritans, Humphrey felt that their virtues far outweighed their faults, and he went on to render their accomplishments in full, including those strictly Congregational principles that Unitarians, with a "critical acumen . . . dexterously employed," had unfortunately modified (27).

Which brings us up (or back) to Orville Dewey's clever disquisition on the Puritans in 1826 as "dissenters," as dexterous a display of critical acumen as one could wish for, making the Forefathers over into promoters of reform, thence "the first successful asserters of the free and liberal principles of modern times," against which the quibble about "peculiarities" of manner and dress crumbles into a fine powder (*Claims*, 10, 12). The Puritans, Dewey observed, were the victims of British historians, most of whom were hostile critics, but in truth their best defense can be derived from "*the very histories of their enemies*" (like Hume), in which can be found sufficient evidence of their generosity. Dewey for the most part addressed himself to the "prejudices" and "principles" of the Puritans in England but remained studiously vague regarding the "trifling peculiarities" of their brethren in America. And like John Quincy Adams and Heman Humphrey, he turned the charge of "ignorance and bigotry and superstition" back once again upon their modern accusers, persons who now enjoyed the comforts of a situation made possible by the labors and sufferings of the much maligned Puritans.

Unitarians like Dewey were necessarily given pain by contemplating the faults of the Forefathers, which offended their enlightened and compassionate humanity even while reminding them of the Calvinism they had left behind. In his pacifist sermon to the Artillery Company of Boston, the Reverend Greenwood was forced to admit that those very Forefathers who were famed for "their determined resistance to oppression" were also guilty of laying "the weight of its iron hand on thought and conscience" once they had established themselves in New England (5, 8). "I would that I could . . . say, that the rights which they claimed for themselves, they had always allowed cheerfully to others; that the authority which they steadfastly denied, they had never usurped. . . . But history and truth forbid me. The persecutions of the Quakers, of the Hutchinsonians, of Roger Williams, forbid me" (11–12). In their evaluations of the Puritans as in other matters, the coincident sermons of Dewey and Greenwood testify that even Unitarians could disagree.

Where Dewey had been vague, Greenwood went on for several pages enumerating the faults of the Forefathers, including the personal stiffness and spiritual gloominess that were still, he noted, characteristic of their descendants—especially, one assumes, those with orthodox Calvinist convictions. He also rehearsed the possible "excuses" for this rigid, gloomy behavior, which did not mitigate the "fault" but included the larger "faults of the age," including a "belief in diabolic agency, witchcraft, and visions" (14–15). If, declared Greenwood, we are agreed in praising the Puritans for taking "bold and gigantic strides before their age," then we should not hesitate to blame them if "in other respects they halted with their age, and went not out from its darkness," an opinion clearly derived from the Unitarians' traditional use of Pastor Robinson's farewell advice (16). Despite this rigor of fair-mindedness, with perhaps a certain subtextual severity aimed at modern instances, Greenwood followed many other commentators on the Puritans, orthodox as well as liberal, by pronouncing the virtues of the Fathers in excess of their faults. The Forefathers, so the Trinitarian-Unitarian consensus seems to have had it, were great men for all of that, and if narrow in their tolerance were broad gauge in establishing institutions that laid the basis and foundation for the modern Republic.

Again, none of these assessments of the Forefathers emulated Jedidiah Morse in noting the difference between the founders of Plymouth and the later arrivals who laid the foundations of Salem and Boston. Even while celebrating the Landing of 1620, they confounded the Pilgrim Separatists with their Puritan brethren who followed them to America. The perspective of these commemorative sermons is definably retrospect, viewing the past from a prospect provided by the modern moment, from which events in Salem and Boston are sequential from the founding of Plymouth, when, in truth (as Morse noted) they were often separate and distinct.

It would be more than a half century before Morse's division was once again made, during which time most celebrants of early New England aspirated the Pilgrims and Puritans in one breath. This was a confusion undoubtedly reinforced by the bicentennials of 1828 and 1830, which were followed by any number of lesser anniversary commemorations during the next two decades, marking the founding of those communities that spread out from the centers established by Endicott and Winthrop. There was, after all, only one Plymouth, which tended to be outweighed by the total sum of Dorchesters, Watertowns, and Concords.

IV

The prevalence of the Puritans in the orations and addresses celebrating New England's past was aided and abetted by their popularity among fiction writers of the period as well, who likewise were faced by the contradictions in the character of the Forefathers. We recall that Rufus Choate delivered in Salem in 1833 an address that urged American authors to imitate Scott by framing romances about early New England: "Useful truths," he insisted, could be extracted from the Puritan chronicles, but there were other elements as well, best left neglected. "The persecutions of the Quakers, the controversies with Roger Williams and Mrs. Hutchinson, the perpetual synods and ecclesiastical surveillance of the old times," these were not fruitful topics to be explored: "A great deal of this is too tedious to be read, or it offends and alienates you" (30). It may be "truth," which is to say "fact," but it is also matter "about which you do not want to know, and are none the wiser for knowing" (30). In effect, the memory of the Forefathers is enhanced by exercising a certain selective amnesia.

Arguing from aesthetic grounds, Choate maintained that "he who writes the romance of history" has a license to choose from "ample but incongruous material," and though the romancer displays "the same prospect that history does," it is "from a different point of view, and through a brighter, more lustrous medium, and by a more powerful optical instrument" (30–33). While hinting at a magnifier, Choate seems to have had a Claude glass in mind, for the romancer can avoid "some things which history would show," even while displaying "the best of everything,—all that is grand and beautiful of Nature, all that is brilliant in achievement, all that is magnanimous in virtue, all that is sublime in self-sacrifice." Such selectivity is the privilege and the glory of the romancer, who "tells the truth, to be sure; but he does not tell the whole truth, for that would be sometimes misplaced and discordant."

Choate, though a protégé of Webster and a prominent Whig, never abandoned the practice of law for politics, perhaps because he was so effective as a courtroom performer. It is noticeable, moreover, that he here promotes an aesthetic that is integral to law as a profession, in which "truth" is much less important than building a case for the benefit of the plaintiff or the defendant. There is a debased Platonism detectable in Choate's emphasis on the beauties of the Ideal, but his notion of the writer as devoted to telling "the truth . . . but not the whole truth" resonates peculiarly with the ambience of the courtroom.

Yet his most revealing metaphor in discussing the creative process is commodification at its purest, without alloy: romance authors "would melt down, as it were, and stamp the bullion [of history] into a convenient, universal circulating medium. They would impress the facts, the lessons of history, more deeply, and incorporate them more intimately into the general mind and heart, and current and common knowledge of the people" (29). The notion of literature as money is certainly integral to the Whig definition of worth, to which we can add Choate's stated hope that New England as fiction would strengthen the bonds of the national Union by reminding Americans of their common "fathers": "It would reassemble, as it were, the people of America in one vast congregation" (37).

Perhaps overestimating the power of nostalgia to bind the nation—especially when the "fathers" in question were the founders of New England—Choate's unique formula for historical fiction belongs with the rhetorical strategies of his fellow Whigs, like Greenwood and Dewey, who sought by evoking the past to achieve a union between the Puritans and their lineal descendants and thereby instill a purer morality through an intense feeling of obligation to the Forefathers. There was really no room in that sanctum sanctorum for the kinds of "truth" that put obstacles in the way of filial piety.

But in point of fact a number of New England writers had already written historical romances in the manner of Scott (and Cooper) that depended upon the Puritan past for their subject, and most of them, contra Choate, used their fiction not only to confront but to emphasize the dark side of the story. True, they often followed the lead of Forefathers' Day orators by administering familiar palliatives by way of excuse, but, as Lawrence Buell has shown us, writers who looked to New England's history for materials were drawn inevitably and irresistibly to the worst aspects of the Puritan character. This was often a matter of ideology but was also an aesthetic accommodation to the demands of genre, for the formulaics of fiction then—as now—depended on melodramatic contrasts.

One exception overlooked by Buell, but noted by Dixon Wecter, was an early novel of colonial life by Harriet Vaughan Cheney, *A Peep at the Pilgrims in Sixteen Hundred Thirty Six: A Tale of Olden Times*, first published in 1824 and in 1826 and 1850 as well, suggesting some popularity over the years. As Wecter points out, Cheney portrayed the Pilgrims "as kindly, hospitable, tender-hearted, while their neighbors to the north are stern bigots," an unusual emphasis and contrast at a time when most writers usually conflated the two groups (36). Constructing a diagram exemplifying Jedidiah Morse's divided geography, Cheney mounted a plot along the lines of a Scott novel, tracing the travels through New England of a somewhat Byronic young man by means of a crowded itinerary of historical events, from the trial of Anne Hutchinson to the Pequot War.

These historical complications, occurring in a dark time for Pilgrims and Puritans alike, are strung on a plot centering about the love of the hero, Major Atherton, for Miriam Grey, a Pilgrim maid whose father intends her to marry a narrow-minded zealot. Atherton, newly arrived from England, lands first in Plymouth, his ship anchoring "beneath the very rock" that had received the Pilgrims seventeen years earlier (1:7). There he meets Miriam and is entertained by Miles Standish, portrayed as a hearty, squirelike soldier, who keeps bachelor hall. Notably, though the Pilgrims are characterized as relatively mild in their bigotries, Cheney, as her treatment of Standish suggests, seems uninformed as to the historical record—beyond the landing on the Rock by "the intrepid band of adventurers, who had forsaken the enjoyments and comforts of civilized life, braved the howlings of the wintry blast, the horrors of famine, and the terrors of an unknown wilderness, for 'conscience' sake."

By contrast, when Atherton travels to Boston, where the latter half of the novel is set, Cheney is very detailed in her handling of the controversies then raging, including a debate over the issues involved in the trial of Anne Hutchinson. Winthrop is portrayed as a wise leader, but others in his community are busy interfering with the affairs of others, and Atherton is plagued by the attentions of a constable, Master Handcuff, who seems eager to arrest him for minor infractions of Boston's complex and rigorous laws. Atherton's frequent companion and escort is Peregrine White, portrayed as a rather wild, if good-natured, young man, immune from the religious zealotry of his community. By these means, Cheney displays both sides of the early settlers of New England, and while acknowledging the Puritans' strict laws and rigorous application of them, she also attempts to strike a note of balance typical of contemporary sermon literature on the subject: "In their solicitude to establish a bond of union in their worship, they resolved that it should be done in their own way, and according to their own ideas of right and wrong; and thus, like other fallible and erring mortals, who often mistake the means in their zeal to accomplish the end, they exhibited a spirit of persecution, which has entailed a lasting reproach upon their memory" (2:22–23).

The novel ends with the inevitable union of Atherton and Miriam, rescued by the Major from captivity among the Pequots (portrayed as bestial savages), and the hero's "attachment to the primitive habits of New-England daily strengthened, and familiarized to its simple mode of worship, he became eventually a sincere, but liberal Puritan" (2:275). With her sympathetic treatment of the Pilgrims, her use of Scott's formulas, including the triumph of love over adversity, Cheney would seem to be anticipating the advice of Rufus Choate, yet like other writers of her generation, she emphasized the bigots of Boston and Salem at the cost of the friendly folks of Plymouth. There was Catharine Sedgwick's *Hope Leslie* (1827), with its depictions of intolerance and persecution, albeit attributed to the dominant spirit of the age. John Neal, operating under the radical influence of William Godwin, treated the witchcraft trials in his Jacobin novel *Rachel Dyer* (1828), but Neal ingeniously solved the problem of the Puritans' superstition by stressing the heroism of their Puritan victims and underwrote the "Americanness" of his tale by attributing the power used so ruthlessly by the witchcraft tribunal to the British system of jurisprudence.

Lydia Maria Child, in her story of a marriage between a Puritan maid and an Indian chief, *Hobomok* (1824), like Cheney did what she could to mitigate the notion of the Puritans as narrow bigots, sharing the forensic consensus that, "whatever might have been their defects, they certainly possessed excellencies, which peculiarly fitted them for a vanguard in the proud and rapid march of freedom" (6). But with her fellow novelists, Child did not avert her eyes from the "many broad, deep shadows in their characters," as Choate rather much after the fact suggested she do.

Again, it is with the Puritans of Boston and Salem that these early writers about colonial New England were chiefly concerned, though occasionally (as in the case of Sedgwick) they styled them "pilgrims." The eponymous Indian hero of Child's tale hails from the forested environs of Plymouth, but the heroine resides in Salem, where most of the action takes place. It is of some interest in this connection that *Hobomok*, as Alexander Cowie long ago pointed out, anticipates Longfellow's Pilgrim poem. For Child gave balance to her themes of miscegenation and Puritan repressiveness by a subplot containing much more realistic (and happy) domestic materials, in which a sprightly young woman instructs her lover (who comes as a representative for another suitor) that he should speak his own mind—and he does. In Child's version of the story, the outspoken girl is not Priscilla Mullins but Sally Oldham, daughter of the man who occasioned much trouble in Plymouth and Boston and whose murder precipitated the Pequot War.

Modern readers may share Cowie's regret that the author did not do more with Sally Oldham, whose independent spirit reflects her own. Child, sister of the prominent Unitarian minister and Harvard professor Convers Francis, was born into a liberal, abolition-minded family, which may help to explain the painstaking balance regarding the Puritans in her historical romance. But having married the radical reformer David Lee Childs, she abandoned the writing of fiction to join the ranks of William Lloyd Garrison's forces, with whom her career thenceforth would be identified. Notably, it was therefore left to Longfellow to celebrate the outspokenness of a Pilgrim maid, in part motivated, as we shall see, by the example of early feminists like Lydia Maria Child.

At this point, we need only to acknowledge that *Hobomok*, like other early novels about the Puritans, anticipates Hawthorne by displaying the dark side of life in Salem and Boston, for reasons that Hawthorne's instance somewhat clarifies. For whatever reasons, he is the most famous example of a New England native who used the Puritans as a basis for fiction, and by the time Choate delivered his address in Salem, the local author had already begun his experiments converting the chronicles of Massachusetts into popular coinage, though to an end that the Whig orator would not have approved.

As an active Democratic Party worker, Hawthorne had a substantive, if subversive, motive for stressing just those aspects of Puritan history that Choate assured his audience they did not really want to know about—even if the current popularity of the Gothic mode had not pointed Hawthorne's pen in that direction. Without making a case for a latent political allegory underlying his fiction, we do know that Hawthorne felt at odds with the optimistic, progressive, and reforming spirit of his own age, the emphases of the combined Whig-Unitarian political-literary platform. Hawthorne, having in "The Gentle Boy" rendered an account of the Puritan persecution of the Quakers quite in synchronization with that of Leonard Bacon, twenty years later ended his stories of the Puritans with a novel that was nothing if not subversive to the Whig attempts to sacramentalize the Puritan experience in America, and which gave only cold comfort to radicals like Child by portraying a prototype feminist as badly damaged goods. Even as his fellow Democrat and political patron George Bancroft was celebrating the Pilgrims as having launched in 1620 the essential elements of a fledgling republic, thereby reinforcing the Whig myth, Hawthorne was emphasizing the unpleasant details of a subsequent period in Massachusetts history, which all parties agreed did not coordinate well with the idea of the Puritans as apostles of political and religious freedom.

At the same time, it is possible to follow the lead of Lawrence Buell, and derive from Hawthorne's fiction a balanced account of the Puritans. As in the sermons of his contemporaries, they are shown to be men and women caught up in the spirit of their age and susceptible as well to the weaknesses flesh is heir to and subject to the dark impress of evil that in Satan takes human form. This was hardly the motive Rufus Choate sought to inspire in New England writers, but there was another oration given in Salem during a critical point in Hawthorne's period of literary apprenticeship that comes much closer to the mark. In 1828, Justice Joseph Story delivered the bicentennial oration before the Essex Historical Society, and in celebrating Salem's settlement, Story brought wide-open Democratic Republican eyes to the historical context with which Hawthorne would soon identify his career.

V

Joseph Story by 1828 had been a justice of the U.S. Supreme Court for nearly twenty years and built a reputation not as a skillful trial attorney but as a compiler of substantial legal treatises, having laid down the basis for equity law in the United States while still a young man. His opinions written while seated on the Court were notoriously wide ranging, often wandering far afield from the pertinent points or a case, and reflected a scholarly love for exploring contexts, essential to the cumulative nature of legal commentaries. In 1829 Story would assume a chair in the Harvard Law School, which gave him the opportunity to compile his many commentaries, even while continuing his duties in Washington.

His oration in 1828 is of a piece with his Supreme Court opinions and in the manner of a legal argument includes most of the precedents established by earlier celebrants of the Puritans, while exceeding any one of them in conclusive sweep. Midway, in reviewing the uses of the past, Story borrowed from John Quincy Adams by pointing to the differences in America when considering "the origin of nations": "We do not trace ourselves back to times of traditionary darkness, where truth and fiction are blended at every step, and what remains, after the closest investigation, is but conjecture, or shadowy fact" (*Discourse*, 41–42). Recorded by contemporary witnesses, the history of New England is bright as daylight on the page, removing the necessity of relying "upon the arts of the poet to give dignity to the narrative, and invest it with the colorings of his imagination. . . . We have no legends which genius may fashion into his own forms, and crowd with imaginary personages" (42).

Delivered five years before Choate gave his Salem address, Story's discourse establishes a contrary emphasis—in effect, America neither needs nor can support any Walter Scotts. Following Adams's lead, Story defined the country's history in terms that he regarded as advantageous, where Hawthorne, as well as other romantic writers of his generation, thought of them as a literary liability. History may indeed be bright upon the page in America—a light soon enough radiating from Bancroft's first volume—but the romantic spirit equated that kind of glare with the Enlightenment and thought it inimical to the needs of literature. Yet in other respects, as we shall presently see, Story's Puritans are Hawthorne's as well.

Story's oration opened with the inescapable evocation of the scene of Endicott's arrival (not a storm-blasted wilderness but a glorious New England autumn) and went on to describe the sufferings of the first settlers, their unmarked graves (best memorialized by the devotions of their descendants), the differences between the motives of the Puritans and the founders of other colonies (not including Plymouth), the complex history of dissent in England and the unfair treatment given the Puritans by "skeptic scoffers" like Hume, themes and tropes that had been long in use but seldom so eloquently expressed.

Echoing James Sabine in 1820, Story faulted the theocratic basis of Puritan governance in the New World, the "union between Church and State" that had endured in Massachusetts since its founding and, despite the efforts in 1820 of the delegates to the state constitutional convention, would prevail until 1833 (67; cf. Sabine, 28–29). The persecutions by the Puritans in America, Story explained—like others before him—was a result of their having themselves been persecuted in Europe, but it was also predictable when "civil liberty" is separated from "religious liberty" (60–61).

Story was willing to admit, with the others already cited, that the "charge against [the Forefathers] of bigotry, intolerance, and persecution" could not be summarily dismissed but must be met, so as to "gather from it instruction and admonition for our own conduct" (61). Yet in the remainder of his address, about half of the whole, Story chiefly devoted himself to explaining away the "faults" of the Puritans, taking up point by point the charges aimed against the Forefathers and refuting them or explaining the circumstances of each in turn.

To be brief where Story was lengthy, his explanations and justifications are, like those of John Quincy Adams and other defenders of the Puritans, by and large contextual: the Puritans were intolerant, but "were our forefathers singular in this respect?" (62). Obviously not, not in the early years of the seventeenth century, when there was no "single spot, however remote, in which the freedom of religious opinion was supported by prince or people." Even in modern times, "religious liberty" is more often a "matter of toleration than support," so what can one ask of the Puritans of the time of King James by way of "Christian liberality?" (64). If the Forefathers believed in witchcraft, "the same opinion then prevailed throughout all Europe. . . . We may lament . . . the errors of the times, which led to these persecutions. But surely our ancestors had no special reasons for shame in a belief, which had the universal sanction of their own and all former ages" (81–82).

Judge Story also devoted several pages to a consideration of the displacement of the Indian population—Fenimore Cooper's favorite theme, and one sensitive to the Jacksonians—but accepted it finally as a sad, even tragic, necessity that the Indian was doomed to extinction. And he went on to maintain that in their dealings with the Indians "our forefathers never attempted to displace [them] by force, upon any pretence of European right. They occupied and cultivated what was obtained by grant, or was found vacant. They constantly respected the Indians by their settlements and claims of soil" (77).

Story, in effect, was both mediational and conciliatory, admitting to the faults of the Forefathers but excusing them by setting them in their contemporary milieu, thereby putting the best possible construct on these blameworthy matters. And, on balance, with Adams and many other apologists, Story felt that the virtues of the Puritans considerably outweighed their blemishes, most especially the system of governance they established, "republican institutions" maintained by investing the "source of all power" in the people: "Thus broad, thus elevated, was the early legislation of our forefathers. If we except from it that portion, which was tinged by the bigotry and superstition of the times, we shall find it singular for its wisdom, humanity, and public spirit; and admirably adapted to the wants of a free, simple, and intelligent people" (70–71).

Story wound up his oration in the floral vein of Webster and Everett, listing the blessings bestowed on the modern generation by the Forefathers, not the least of which was the "system of public instruction, which they instituted by law, and to which New England owes more of its character, its distinction, and its prosperity than to all other causes" (72). In a minor key, which would be expanded considerably by William Sullivan the following year in Plymouth, Story emphasized the importance of national union to preserving the Republic, the necessity of avoiding the dangers that had destroyed earlier republics: "We stand, the latest, and if we fail, probably the last experiment of self government by the people" (86).

This emphasis, traceable to Washington's farewell address, brought Story's celebration of the Union in line with Democratic dogma, a closure that may explain also the odd omission of any mention of slavery as an institution. While speaking of "slavery" in its rhetorical meaning, in opposition to "liberty," a note often sounded by orators of the day with apparent blindness to the paradoxical context, Story avoided any mention of the bondage of black people. It is a silence made strange by his outspoken charge of 1819, but as with his handling of the Indian problem, it was perhaps out of deference to the sensibilities of the Jackson-Calhoun ticket.

Moreover, though he was a Democratic Republican, willing in his oration to accept the sad fate of Native Americans and avoid the problematics of slavery, Story had such strong Federalist leanings that he was distrusted by Jefferson himself and would be despised by President Jackson. His lengthy apology for the Puritans may be read in that context as well, the Federalists, as we have seen, having a decided empathy for their theocratic progenitors because of the Puritans' moral rigor, if not rigidity. Nor can we discount the familiar sectional necessity of insisting upon the primacy of the Puritans in establishing the institutions of the Republic. Whatever the reasons, by means of his reassuring message that the virtues of the Fathers outweighed their faults—by 1828 the consensus of public speakers on the subject—Story handed on a conflicted message to the next generation: the Forefathers were bigots and intolerant of other faiths and persecuted political dissenters; the Forefathers brought religious and civic freedom to America.

If Hawthorne was in Story's audience in 1829—or read the oration once it was printed in pamphlet form—he seems to have taken away what he needed from the judge's discourse, which was a catalog of the Puritans' faults without the framing contextual argument. As for Story's point about the bare beauties of colonial history in America, Hawthorne ignored that also and set to work constructing stories about the Puritans that shared romantic qualities in common with those of his contemporaries, which he styled "legends." In his fiction, that is to say, Hawthorne added in his own way to the idea of the exceptionalness of life in America, stressing the evil that the founders of New England perpetrated in the name of virtue instead of the good that they set in motion despite their faults. By his lights, the best memories are the worst.

Hawthorne did not entirely ignore the positive aspects of the Puritan presence, but in his best-known stories he stressed the tradition of zealotry and persecution, a line that if anything tended to harden as the 1850s approached and the activities of moral reformers increased in stridency. If Story struck a perfect balance between the faults of the Puritans and their virtues, then Hawthorne achieved a similar counterpoise, playing off their intolerance against the sins of those of his characters, like Hester Prynne and Arthur Dimmesdale, in whom equivalents to modern liberals could be detected.

Translated into Hawthorne's terms, Story's conflicted message read this way: the Puritans were bigoted and intolerant, but their victims were hardly innocent of the crimes for which they were punished, offenses that may well have included the actual practice of witchcraft in the woods around Salem. Hawthorne's was a Calvinist reading of the Calvinist chronicles in America, although we cannot, once again, discount a political motive, that in his dark version of Puritan life Hawthorne was providing an antidote to the Whig celebration of New England's heritage. Indeed, in *The Scarlet Letter* his contextual frame, provided by "The Custom House" introduction, is entirely contemporary and savagely partisan. Beyond this particular, the evidence of ideology is largely a matter of silence, for what is missing from Hawthorne's fiction is any hint of that defense of the Puritans we can find running through so much oratory celebrating the founding of New England.

And yet this optative stress is hardly limited to Forefathers' Day oratory, nor to Whig discourse: what New England's history told people of Webster's and Choate's generation was what it told Democratic historians like George Bancroft, that the record of the past reveals a process of perpetual improvement, of mankind moving forward and upward toward some millennial moment of social and spiritual perfection.

This was a vision pretty much shared also by Unitarians like Channing and Trinitarians like Lyman Beecher, the only difference lying in the means (and pace) by which the millennium would be attained. Channing, like most Unitarians, had a deep faith in good will and patient understanding to effect change; Beecher, in whom the Yankee pressed close to the surface, was for hurrying matters along a bit, using the occasion of revivals to urge on the future by purging society of spiritual ills—including an occasional convent.

Hawthorne was not entirely immune to this general spirit of progressiveness, and in his children's book, *The History of Grandfather's Chair* (1841), he is rather relentless in tracing the Democratic ethos from Winthrop's to Sam Adams's Boston. But in the stories by which we remember him he only pays it lip service, chiefly by way of relieving aesthetically the gloom of parables that Melville read as evidence of the author's innate Calvinism, for Hawthorne was a writer whose darkly satiric streak with few exceptions overrode his Democratic ideology. Thus the Reverend Dimmesdale, toward the end of *The Scarlet*

Letter, delivers an election sermon in the mode of a Fourth of July speech, mounting a Bancroft-like vision of a glorious future for New England, immediately following which he confesses his compound sin against God and his community and dies.

Judge Story, by contrast, ended his discourse by calling upon his auditors, whether "Fathers . . . Mothers . . . Young Men . . . Old Men," to work in unison, within their various capacities, to preserve the Republic and strive for an even more glorious future. He urged them "by the shades of your ancestors, by the dear ashes which repose in this precious soil, by all you are, and all you hope to be" to devote themselves to the cause of freedom so that "your last sun" will not "sink in the west upon a nation of slaves" (87). Again, this is the rhetorical use of that key word, but it is quite possible that some minority Federalist ears caught an encoded reference, a coupling of the idea of "Union" and "Republic" with the "tyranny" of slavery then warranted by the Constitution, the natural outgrowth of the "institutions" established by the Forefathers.

And when Story "called upon" the young men in his audience "to remember whose sons you are," that "life can never be too short, which brings nothing but disgrace and oppression," that "death never comes too soon, if necessary in defence of the liberties of your country," perhaps some of the young men within range of his voice received a message somewhat different from the one Story intended—or perhaps they did not. Certainly, the only war in defense of liberty that lay ahead was to be waged on behalf of enslaved persons of color and would require of its soldiers that they renounce bigotries equivalent to those of the Forefathers, while exercising that zeal for personal and political freedom that was undeniably the Puritans' signal virtue. On the other side of that line would be ranged those persons for whom zeal in whatever political cause was a reminder of the errors into which it propelled the Puritans, whose extremism in the name of their own liberties meant the repression of the freedoms of others, a group in which Leonard Bacon and Nathaniel Hawthorne must surely be seen as standing.

This last was the party of Compromise, which could point to the framing of the Constitution by the Founding Fathers as starting the process of toleration for opposing viewpoints and the Union as the sacred necessity for continuing it. The first was the party of Absolutes, which appealed to the Declaration of Independence as a body of truths admitting of no qualifications and would eventually appeal to a higher law that abrogated laws made by men. And the debate between these two parties, with which we shall next be concerning ourselves, may be seen as yet another contest appealing to the past in order to direct the present toward a desired future, but one in which the party of Absolutes only gradually resorted to the Pilgrims and their Rock as icons central to the principles espoused. Both parties made repeated references to the sacredness of the national memory, but the party of Absolutes increasingly invaded the memorial territory of the party of Compromise, until Plymouth Rock became identified as much with the libertarianism of the Declaration of Independence as with the consolidationism of the Constitution.

Despite Webster's summons in 1820, Plymouth Rock and the Pilgrims seemed in 1830 irrelevant to the issues of abolition, much as Leonard Bacon in 1824 insisted they illustrated the beauties of the American Colonization Society. This last was an association that surely did the Pilgrims and their Rock no favors, at least not in the eyes of the advocates of immediate emancipation. Thus where politicians and preachers for the next two decades, with a few notable exceptions, would ignore Webster's precedent and avoid the problematics of slavery in celebrating the Pilgrims, during that same period the favorite perch of abolitionists was not Plymouth Rock or the Constitution for which it so often stood, but that Enlightenment structure whose designation, like the word "election," provided a paradoxical connection with the Puritan past.

For it was the architectonics of the Declaration of Independence, a Jeffersonian structure of Palladian simplicity, that became a central icon to celebrants (and exercisers) of American freedoms. It served as an elevated platform designed to give a high profile to a distinct minority who not only used it to demand the immediate abolition of slavery but who allowed women to share that scaffolded eminence, bringing us back once again to *The Scarlet Letter* and to the end of this chapter.

CHAPTER 9

The Rock Rolled Back

Cyclopian work, this work of the Pilgrims,—with nothing below
them but the rock of ages. I will not quarrel with their rough corners
or uneven sides; above all, I will not change them for the wood, hay,
and stubble of modern builders.
—*Edward Everett*

I

Consistency, to borrow from Emerson, is the hobgoblin of thesis mongers, and it must be said at this point that the iconography of Plymouth Rock, in both its ecclesiastical and political manifestations, has a general drift rather than a consistently specific pointedness. But despite the heterogeneousness of the uses to which the Pilgrims and their Rock were put during the years following the outbreak of the Revolution—down through the jubilee decade of the 1820s—we can find a common theme and pattern throughout. Commencing with the patriotic sermons of the Revolution, then on to the rambunctious Feasts of the Federalists, and down through the orations of Webster and Everett and the embattled sermons of Unitarians and Trinitarians, we can see running a universal emphasis on Memory, a celebration not of one's own private and personal past but of communal recollection, the golden thread by which new generations can claim connections with events beyond individual recall. Though we generally associate the politics of nostalgia with conservative, even reactionary ideologies, this was not universally the case in the nineteenth century in America. As Webster was at pains to point out in 1820, the Past as a region of the mind is given point by its connection to the Future, much as the present moment hovers teeming with potential derived from the heritage of the Past that is to be delivered up to generations yet to come. We can refer again to the Reverend Kendall reading his newspaper by Plymouth Rock, for though his emphasis was on present marvels, the Past has its chronometric uses also, if only as a point from which to measure human progress.

The role and function of commemorative orators is necessarily Janus-faced, and in immersing ourselves in Forefathers' Day and like addresses we must be careful not to generalize too glibly about their relevance to contemporary matters. And yet, as we have already witnessed, speakers on those celebratory occasions habitually shaped their discourses to promote concerns of the moment, using the Pilgrims and the Rock for political or doctrinal purposes. Indeed, the emergence of such celebrations as ritual events suggests that for New Englanders of the 1820s and afterward, the Past held peculiar significance, an expression perhaps of insecurity in the face of rapid change and a concomitant drive to rival the previous generation in accomplishment, possibilities promoted by students of the period in (and at) question. Whatever the root cause or causes, orators of different and rival convictions took strength in common from associating themselves with the party of Memory and strove to make vivid historical scenes already regarded as commonplace by their auditors; paradoxically, the tenacity of convention, as we have already seen, spurred on Forefathers' Day orators to heights of forensic invention.

One result of this complex necessity was the "vision" mode employed by orators of Webster's generation, a display of theatricalness that made vivid a historic moment and did no harm to the speaker's reputation as a man of letters. Implicit in this convention was a felt need to call up by a version of necromancy the moment itself, which enabled the speaker to place his audience (and himself) in the scene. It was an intimate conjunction, close cousin to the feelings felt by persons who took advantage of proximity by standing on the Rock, an electrical shock of recollection that triggered the power of memory and enlisted the tourist in the company of the Forefathers. What made contingency with the Rock such a stimulus to memory was its status as a threshold that the Pilgrims by stepping upon set something in motion as yet incompletely enacted, so that by placing their own feet in those footsteps, living Americans could join in the common effort, becoming honorary citizens in Memory's Nation.

The contemporary vogue for historical paintings is related to this phenomenon, cued by Webster's pointed use of Sargent's depiction of the Landing, scenes that drew in the viewer as a participant witness. That theme stated by John Quincy Adams in 1802, that the United States, unlike other nations, knew the moment when its history commenced—and for New Englanders things began in 1620—was not an idle conceit. The act of memory, incorporated in orations, sermons, histories, chronicles, and works of art, was a textual umbilicus by means of which a modern generation could maintain intimate contact with and take sustenance from the Forefathers, an exercise hardly strange to a people for whom the ancient Jews were role models.

Once again, this was not the jeremiad tradition by means of which the Forefathers were held up as a pattern against which the people of New England could be measured and found wanting. The occasional use of this crabbed perspective by orthodox preachers in their bicentennial sermons in 1820 ties it to the slowly sinking barge of Congregationalism, not to the optative and majority view, which passed by under steam power and with banners flying. For it is the upbeat emphasis of most of the sermons and orations that year that defines, stressing not discontinuity but continuousness, memory being regarded as a vital electrical connection. And yet, in an era when Progress, so much praised by Whigs and Democrats alike, would be seen as a defining aspect of the American "difference," there was a companion nervousness that perhaps things were moving a bit too fast, an anxiety that valued memory as a stabilizing force, equivalent to the Constitution.

Webster might celebrate the spirit of the Enlightenment thrusting deep into the nineteenth century and bringing with it the blessings of science and its handyman, technology, but a significant number shared Lyman Beecher's worries concerning the consequences of accelerated communications. Thoreau was only one of many of his contemporaries who suspected that the news carried by the telegraph was not the most important kind of information to be read by the Rock at Plymouth. As we shall see, there were others in New England who felt that in traveling on iron rails across the country at a great rate of speed one often left something forgotten behind more important than a portmanteau sitting on a station platform. Attending celebrations of historic anniversaries with their ritual stimulation of the public memory was a way of maintaining a salutary, even salubrious contact with the stabilizing power of the Past.

In his bicentennial sermon in 1820, James Sabine observed the importance of "perpetuating a remembrance of important events and deeply to impress a recollection of them upon the minds of succeeding generations," an age-old and universal need (3). Among the "measures adopted" over the centuries and in many lands were religious holidays and feasts, the setting up of "pillars and monuments," and the building of temples and altars. Jews in observing Passover commemorate "their deliverance from Egypt"; the British celebrate the arrival of William of Orange, Americans the Fourth of July; and "the Sons of New England repair every year to the shores where their Fathers first landed, and in frugal feast upon the humblest produce of the sea, perpetuate the character of a humble race of men" (3–5). With the intention of implanting "the virtues of our Pious Fathers . . . in their children," Forefathers' Day celebrants strove to outdo themselves in re-creating by forensic necromancy the event being commemorated. For "how is the spirit of a free people to be formed, and animated, and cheered, but out of the store-house of its historic recollections?"

The question was asked by Edward Everett in 1825, on the occasion of his oration celebrating the fiftieth anniversary of the famous Battle of Lexington: "Fast, O, too fast, with all our efforts to prevent it," Everett cried out in rhetorical alarm, were the "precious memories" of the Revolution passing away, a lamentable situation symbolized by the inevitable loss of "the recollections of a few revered survivors" of the event, who were hastening toward the grave, where their precious memories would lie forever "lost and forgotten" (*Orations and Speeches*, 1:78). These sentiments were thought worthy of inclusion by George B. Cheever in his *American Common-Place Book of Prose* in 1828, along with the reflections of Andrews Norton in "The Posthumous Influence of the Wise and Good": "The dead leave behind them their memory, their example, and the effects of the actions. . . . We live and commune with them in their writings. We enjoy the benefit of their labours. Our institutions have been founded by them" (Cheever, 27). "There is," observed Norton, "a degree of insecurity and uncertainty about living worth. The stamp has not yet been put upon it, which precludes all change, and seals it up as a just object of admiration for future times."

Death is obviously both stamp and seal on the ultimate covenant, and if it thereby locks away individual memory forever—Everett's lament—then the common memory of "example," of "effects of actions," can survive by means of texts, of institutions, of the physical evidences left behind of the labors of the departed Fathers. The observances of Forefathers' Day, the celebrations of the Fourth, these emerging ceremonies were the intended means whereby a collective memory could be sustained, and generally, when the Pilgrims were cited, a conservative ritual, akin to genealogy and the arts of heraldry. It was necessary, as Everett urged, to keep on talking, lest the region, following the Forefathers, disappeared into a void of forgetfulness, a collective amnesia from which there was no return.

In 1820, Webster preferred to stand looking westward from Plymouth Rock, in the direction of progress and the future. But Webster's perspective would change, and soon enough a backward glance—the direction of memory— would seem increasingly important to him, a reversal that would signal the coincident emergence of the Pilgrims and their Rock as iconic armaments in the radical arsenal, a movement that would ironically turn upon the emergence of Webster as the Ichabod of New England, characterized as having betrayed the Pilgrim heritage. The future, which in 1820 seemed filled with the light of revealed promise, by 1850 appeared more like an opening chasm at Webster's feet, as the Rock became a most unstable perch.

Indeed, the more one talked about the Forefathers' heritage of freedom, the deeper the chasm grew, and the Rock became all the less firm a foundation. So often given shape by contemporary considerations, Memory's Nation at mid-century had become two quite distinct places, the contemplation of which was hardly reassuring to persons of a conservative turn of mind. Here again the dispute between Unitarians and Trinitarians reflects the binary, separatist tradition in New England, which by the 1830s had become associated with the abolitionist controversy, split into the defenders of the status quo and the champions of immediate emancipation, the both of whom would identify their cause with the Pilgrims and Plymouth Rock.

II

As a scholar trained in the classics, Edward Everett might be expected to revere the past, at a time when Harvard thought of English literature as ending with Pope. He was certainly an inveterate celebrant of Memory's Nation, much more given than Webster to delivering orations on the occasions of centenary and other anniversary celebrations. As a clergyman, likewise, Everett's training reinforced what was undoubtedly an inborn conservative bent, and as a Unitarian he shared the sectarian timidity in confronting radical change that inspired his devoted student, Ralph Waldo Emerson, to quit the church in disgust.

Spokesmen for the orthodox like Lyman Beecher may have voiced concern over the too-rapid pace of social change brought about by improvements in transportation—the darling issue of the Whigs—but as evangelists they ardently sought the kind of progress equated with moral reform, where their Unitarian counterparts supported issues like temperance temperately. As Beecher and Leonard Bacon demonstrated, it was likewise the orthodox who spoke out early on against slavery, although in terms of colonization, not abolition. The Compromise of 1820 may have been an alarm bell rung by Story and Webster in turn, but as we have seen it drew most of the New England clergy no farther than their study windows, hiding in fear and trembling behind a partly open curtain. By 1830, as William Sullivan testified, public men in New England tended to temporize on the problem of slavery, as testified to by the silence of William Story in 1828.

Yet at the start of the century regional spokesmen were outspoken on the subject. Horace Bushnell, in 1839, in a discourse chiefly aimed at (and against) the rhetorical excesses of abolitionist societies, maintained that New England had from the start been opposed to slavery: "Our fathers and all our statesmen of the old type were abolitionists" (24). Bushnell recalled the "feeling" in 1819, when he was a boy of seventeen in the Litchfield Hills of Connecticut, "how the spirit of the Missouri Question seized the very children of the schools. We could hardly understand the matter, but still we watched the news, as all were doing, with souls full of liberty and the Missouri Question" (25). In his *American Geography* of 1789, Jedidiah Morse was openly opposed to slavery: tracing the institution to its roots in Africa—where "savage tyrants make war upon each other for human plunder!"—Morse was "shocked" to discover that "this infernal commerce is carried on by the humane, the polished, the Christian inhabitants of Europe; nay even by Englishmen, whose ancestors bled in the cause of liberty, and whose breasts still glow with the same generous flame!" (530).

Morse's sentiment notably stops short of including Americans whose ancestors etc., and as for slavery in the South, the geographer stepped aside and allowed Jefferson to speak for his section and region. Indeed, the entire entry for "Virginia" is taken from Jefferson's *Notes*, including the passage in which the author of the Declaration of Independence stated his hope that by prohibiting the "importation" of slaves, "the increase of this great and moral evil" would be "in some measure" halted, allowing a period during which "the minds of our citizens may be ripening for a complete emancipation of human nature" (378). Jefferson's was a sentiment entirely in harmony with that policy of "gradualism" that would be espoused after 1830 by moderate and rational men in New England right down until the Civil War. And Jedidiah Morse, whose moral nature was outraged over the enormity of chattel slavery, in a sense anticipated Webster by allowing the South to have its say. That is, the more New Englanders came to "understand the matter," the more like Bushnell they opposed extreme measures and abrasive language that angered the slave power and thereby endangered the Union.

Eventually, the pressures of occasion brought William Ellery Channing out of his closet, but the Unitarian was no champion of immediate emancipation. Following, rather, the line set down by conservative politicians like William Sullivan, Unitarians hesitated to interfere in the internal affairs of Southern states. Theirs was a practical ("reasonable") point of view, anticipating that the active agitation for immediate abolition might very well defeat the purposes of the antislavery movement. Such certainly was the experience of those hardy evangels who abandoned Lyman Beecher and colonization for Oberlin and immediatism and who discovered that the closer one got to the slave states, the more violent was the reaction against the proponents of abolition. Like other champions of reform, radical abolitionists obeyed the associational impulse of the age and formed societies, the activities of which acted to arouse even further the Southern paranoia. These lessons did not escape the attention of Unitarians like Orville Dewey, who in 1825 had celebrated dissent but who by 1844 tended to favor discussion: "*Discussion* is the grand modern instrument of Reform. . . . One man like Channing, with this engine, can do more than a hundred Associations, and do it a thousand times better" (*Discourse*, 6).

It is useful in considering the implications of Unitarian and Whig tractarianism to return to the bicentennial address of William Crafts, briefly alluded to in Chapter 3. The occasion was sponsored by the New England Society of

Charleston, South Carolina, which like its counterparts across the country had been founded (in 1819) by migrating Sons of those restless Fathers who spread "Salems" ever westward as they sought pastures ever greener. The same urge to associate that caused the proliferation of societies urging reform, an outreach of Enlightenment notions of fraternity and philanthropy, inspired wandering Yankees to cohere, albeit with less earnest purpose.

Thus the Reverend Dr. C. S. Vedder characterized the founders of the Charleston society as New Englanders who had been "snowed out from under the lee side of Plymouth Rock" and who came south seeking "a warmer and more congenial climate" (Way, 3–4). They made themselves even warmer by "gathering around a cheerful fireplace" to follow the "annual and patriotic habit" of observing Forefathers' Day "in pledges of steaming punch," remembering by such wassail the "Mayflower and her hardy and God-fearing passengers, who on that dark and freezing day in December first landed on Plymouth Rock."

William Crafts in 1820 made no mention of the Rock, but in most respects his was a conventional performance, as when he summoned up a ghost of the Pilgrim past to survey with amazement the record of progress that had taken place over the intervening two centuries. Yet Craft's mood was not Webster's, and his visitor from the past reacted in the manner of Irving's Rip Van Winkle when he confronted the revolutionary changes that had occurred during his twenty years' sleep. Irving was a Federalist at the time, and Crafts seems to have been something of a southern Irving, albeit in a minor vein, in terms especially of his literary talent.

Son of a Boston-born merchant who had successfully followed his fortunes southward, and a mother native to South Carolina, Crafts was a Harvard graduate whose reputation for wit and literary promise never amounted to more than local fame. Like Irving a lawyer who did not much practice his profession, Crafts devoted his energies to the pursuit of literature and the good life, seldom a profitable combination. On his early death, just short of forty, he left behind a slim body of writings, prose and poetry that like Irving's much more substantial corpus was leavened with good humor and satire and generally avoided direct political statement.

His performance, however, on the occasion of the bicentennial celebration in Charleston was of a serious and elevated nature and observed the traditional pieties of Forefathers' Day orations. Crafts made a distinction between the Pilgrims and the settlers of other colonies in terms of motives and stressed the religious persecution of the Forefathers in the Old World. He credited that ordeal with having prepared the Pilgrims for their subsequent suffering and final triumph in the New World and along the way also praised them for their rightful and judicious dealings with the region's Indians. Finally, Crafts celebrated the deeds of the descendants of the Forefathers, the generation that during the American Revolution kept alive the tradition of heroic resistance to British tyranny.

And yet Crafts, like William Sullivan in 1829, ended his paean to progress on a note of gathering gloom, keyed by the shock of encounter experienced by his Pilgrim ghost: "Local jealousies darken the political horizon, and fill it with dismay" (15). While Webster, speaking that same day in Plymouth, was tacitly influenced by the circumstances of the Missouri Compromise, which he with other notable New Englanders had opposed both on moral and geopolitical grounds, Crafts, who supported the measure, brought the issues out into the open. The "startling question of Missouri" was "teeming with unknown and unimagined" consequences and resulted from an "evil spirit," a counterpart to his Pilgrim ghost that Crafts identified with certain parties who were interested in attacking "the early and sacred compromise of our confederacy," an action tantamount to "assailing or invalidating lawful rights" (16). If such "inquiries," as he tactfully styled them, were put forward in the name of humanity, "it is the humanity of fratricide; there is too much darkness in the color of their charity, and too much distance in the scope of its relief." Crafts hoped he was mistaken in his suspicions and ended with the carefully balanced wish that "our Statesmen, on all objects of national concern, will look to the interests of the whole and of *each other.*"

He strove to keep the terms of his discourse as general as possible, even to the point of obfuscation, and though we may not doubt the implication of his reference to "too much darkness in the color of their charity," he makes no mention of slavery or slaves. His main point, after all, and it would remain the thrust of much subsequent rhetoric in the South, was the sacred balance that needed to be maintained between the rights of states and the ideal of national union. It was a balance established by the "sacred" compromises that made the Constitution possible, hence his reference to "the interests of the whole and of *each other,*" the crux to which the matter of slavery was—in the forensic logic of the South—incidental. It is worth noting also that William Crafts did not associate the "evil spirit" of discord with New England but pointed to the "intermediate States" as fostering those kinds of "inquiry" that could lead to "fratricide." "The North and the South," he opined, "like physical extremes, have the same tendency and resemble each other," a generous and pacifying notion that the emergence of the Cotton Whigs in later years would verify.

At the same time, there is in his Charleston address an undercurrent of sectional antagonism that undermines what appear on the surface to be sentiments celebrating the Pilgrims. Thus, the persecutions the Forefathers had suffered in Europe, which he credited with forcing the "desperate and heroic enterprise" that brought the Forefathers to the New World, are defined as a historical fact illustrating "the decree of God, that . . . persecution shall avail its authors only shame and remorse, while it endows its victims with extraordinary courage, ensures them the Divine protection, and fits them for heroic suffering and achievement" (6–7). It is not difficult here to detect a contemporary analogue, an oblique allusion to the persecutory spirit that Southerners detected in the debate that attended the Missouri Compromise. Moreover, even as he celebrated the achievements of the Puritans, Crafts brought up the problem of their own persecutions, "the religious independence" of the "Pilgrims of Plymouth" having lead them "to political inquiries. How difficult it is to stay the hand that lifts but half a veil. Curiosity is like light, once give it admission and it penetrates every where." The key word here is that subtly indirect "inquiries," precisely the term Crafts later used in connection with attempts to interfere with the internal policies of Southern states, suggesting that the "inquiring" (nosy) spirit of Puritanism is still active in New England and that the lessons of the seventeenth century are still valid.

Because our emphasis here in considering the implication of the Pilgrims and their Rock to the abolition controversy will necessarily be on the New England side of the line, it is perhaps useful to note at this point that southern historiography did not make as much of Puritan heroics as did works written by northern authors. When, in 1824, Chief Justice John Marshall brought out the first volume of his life of George Washington as an independent "History of the American Colonies," he lavished considerable praise on the efforts of Captain John Smith—"one of the most extraordinary men of his age"—to secure a beachhead at Jamestown and must therefore be counted among the contributors to the mythic stature of the man who would in time be thought of as the "first cavalier" of Virginia (81). By contrast, Marshall describes the Pilgrims as "an obscure sect . . . which had rendered itself peculiarly obnoxious [in England] by the democracy of its tenets respecting church government" (78). Tracing the Pilgrims to Leyden and thence to the New World, Marshall passed over the Voyage and the Landing quickly, and giving a mere sentence to the Mayflower Compact, he credited much of the subsequent suffering of the Pilgrims to their attempt at establishing a communist society in New England, "misguided by their religious theories . . . and in imitation of the primitive Christians" (81). This, despite the fact that the "same error . . . had been committed in Virginia," until the administration of Captain Smith rectified the mistake.

Instead of celebrating the Pilgrims for their courage and piety and pointing to their institutions as the foundation of the modern Republic, Marshall emphasized their utopian zeal and quixotic idealism. Following the lead of John Quincy Adams, celebrants of the Pilgrim advent in New England occasionally remarked wryly on this mistaken and soon corrected experiment in communism, but for Marshall it is the definitive episode. Only in passing does he acknowledge that the colonists were sustained, during their many hardships, "by the hope of better times, and by that high gratification which men exasperated by persecution and oppression, derive from the enjoyment of the rights of conscience, and the full exercise of the powers of self-government" (82). But he makes no connection between "the rights of conscience" enjoyed by the Pilgrims in America or "the powers of self-government" they there established and the subsequent emergence of the Republic.

No hero like John Smith emerges from Marshall's account of the experience of the Pilgrims in America, who remain defined (pretty much as they thought of themselves) as a communal unit. Thus, where the Virginia Colony was successful in dealing with the region's Indians because of the "judgment, courage, and . . . presence of mind" of Captain Smith, who "never failed, finally, to inspire the savages he encountered with the most exalted opinion of himself and his nation," the Pilgrims succeeded in the same regard because "the natives had been so wasted by pestilence . . . that they were easily subdued, and compelled to accept a peace, on equitable terms" (39, 82). Marshall's emphasis, while warranted by the facts, certainly devalues the treaty between Massasoit and the Pilgrims, so celebrated in New England, and of Miles Standish's adventures among the Indians we hear nothing. While it can't be said that Marshall was *against* the Pilgrims, he seems not to have been very much *for* them either. Where in Captain John Smith—who was in everything he did the perfect "character of a commander"—we can detect the latent image of George Washington, Marshall's Pilgrims tend to foreshadow the people at Brook Farm.

Certainly, William Crafts in 1820 followed a similar line and, while observing the conventions of Forefathers' Day orations, managed also to carry the Pilgrims' devotion to civil liberties no further forward than 1775. Webster, though opposed to the Compromise of 1820, would in time gain notoriety for his postures of accommodation to the increasingly aggressive demands of southerners like Crafts, who perhaps thought John Smith's way of handling Indians would work with Yankees as well. Webster's espousal of compromise was made in the name of Union, but he implicitly identified the sacred fabric of the Republic with the cloth being manufactured in Massachusetts mills. Writing home to his wife from Boston, where he occupied a room commanding an "exileratin view" of the cemetery in which "Cotton Mather, the father of the Reformers . . . lies berried," Artemus Ward noted that "there is men even now who worship Cotton, and there is wimin who wear him next [to] their harts" (228).

No man was more truly named than was Daniel Webster, the prophet celebrated in his given name joined to the weaver in his last, but Webster, however much a friend to Cotton, was no admirer of the reformers associated by Artemus Ward with Mather. The unwillingness of northerners, whether politicians or preachers, to arouse the angry suspicions of southerners like Crafts that their rights were being threatened was not universally inspired by commercial considerations, but it is difficult to separate the several threads of the status quo in the banner of Business as Usual. The idea of preserving the Union "as it is" (one of Ward's favorite slogans) was the kind of patriotism that encourages quietism, and though there were religious overtones to Webster's idea of Union, the reaction of the clergymen in his audience to his call regarding slavery may be taken as a signal that Webster had overstepped a line across which he would not move again, an approximation or facsimile of the geopolitical vector surveyed by Mason and Dixon.

We can never in considering these matters discount the racist impulse, that terror of freed black people that gave the American Colonization Society such enthusiastic support even in the North, but the hesitation of the New England clergy to heed Webster's summons in 1820 was a complex and often well-meaning silence, cowardly as it might appear to some. It would soon enough be shattered by the loud protests of abolitionists who sneered at the timorous expedience of ministers and politicians and defied the efforts of colonizers by promoting the much feared idea of racial amalgamation.

We shall come to that challenge shortly, and its curious, even perverse relation to the Pilgrims and their Rock, but for the time I wish to elucidate the complexity of antislavery efforts in New England by concentrating on the career of one man, who even more than Leonard Bacon was the kind of middling person who demonstrates the intricacies of social and cultural issues more clearly than do those torchbearers who lead the parades of opposing points of view. Such persons come shedding no great shower of glory, yet like William Crafts they speak for the unelected many out of the chance publication of occasional performances, not a little resembling in this respect the mute champions celebrated by Thomas Gray. It is often worth our while to rub away the accumulated moss from the inscriptions on their tombstones in the name of a common, hence fallible, humanity.

III

On July 4, 1834, Plymouth Rock was moved for the second time, the first since 1775, sixty years previous, and as earlier the event inspired considerable ceremony. According to the Plymouth antiquarian William T. Davis, who looked back from the distance of more than seventy years, "A procession, of which Capt. Samuel Doten was marshal, preceded by the school children of the town, escorted a decorated truck bearing the Rock, then weighing 6,997 pounds, which was followed by a model of the Mayflower mounted on a car and drawn by six boys, of whom I was one" (*Memories*, 29–30). This was, of course, only the top part of the Rock, the base having remained in its surrounding wharf, but as the part associated with the Revolution, it was sacred to the Fourth and in its progress was accompanied by "the Plymouth Band and the Standish Guards."

When the Rock reached its new station, Pilgrim Hall, "an address was delivered by Dr. Chas. Cotton, and a prayer was made by Rev. Dr. James Kendall." Cotton's address has apparently not survived, but on the Forefathers' Day immediately following the removal of the Rock to its new setting—where it was surrounded by an ornamental iron fence bearing the names of the signers of the compact—the Reverend George Blagden delivered a discourse, *Great Principles Associated with Plymouth Rock*, which referred to the historic artifact to a degree not witnessed since Webster's address and which was published for general circulation.

Speaking to the audience gathered in Pilgrim Hall, at last completed with the addition (in Dr. Thacher's words) of "a handsome Doric portico in front of the edifice," which with characteristic Yankee thrift was made of wood, the Reverend Blagden erected a considerable rhetorical structure by means of the materials provided by the Rock (*History*, 256). A graduate of Yale and the Andover Seminary, he seems to have caught some of that same Trinitarian evangelical fire evinced in the fledgling oratory of his close contemporary Leonard Bacon, which, by way of Lyman Beecher, could be traced back to Timothy Dwight.

Echoing Dwight in 1800, Blagden announced at the start that "it is impossible for any one, acquainted with the history of New England, to stand on this rock, and look at these scenes, unmoved" (5). Blagden's language suggests that the inspirational perch, if only in metaphor, had become conventional, a means of magnifying the humble stone into epicentric importance: "A thing may be intrinsically small, but relatively magnificent—as the centre of a circle is but a point, while the sweep of its circumference may include the infinite of space" (5). Blagden was specifically referring to the "landing of the Pilgrim fathers," not the Rock, and echoed William Bradford in observing that "great effects frequently . . . proceed from comparatively slight causes," but it was the Rock, finally, that underlay his sermon, much as it had supposedly supported the Pilgrims.

In a characteristically American version of Alison's theory of associations, Blagden maintained that in and by itself, the Landing, when "compared with other events in the diversified history of man," amounted to not much, but "when you connect with this transaction, the principles in which it originated—the moral, intellectual and political events it has produced, and is at this hour producing;—it is when you contemplate its connection with posterity, rather than its relation to the age that gave it birth—that it swells into an importance impossible for the speaker fully to express; and of which it is difficult to form any adequate conception" (5–6). This was Webster's point, also, and like Webster Blagden called upon his audience "to stand with me on this spot, where so many influences concentrate; from which so much of light had radiated over two hemispheres of mankind; and, however feeble be our vision, look at past, present and future scenes, drawing from such a prospect whatever of practical instruction we may be able to receive" (6).

In elaborating upon the "great principles associated with the event we celebrate," Blagden managed to include in his circumferential overview most of the by then traditional points on the oratorical compass, including the "great principles of liberty" associated with the Pilgrims and the familiar balancing off of Puritan faults with Puritan virtues. If the Pilgrims were inclined to pay too much attention to "little things," such matters were in their eyes associated with God and "His government," and "like their own immortal acts on this rock, though in themselves small, they were relatively great, and in their eyes, of the utmost importance to present and future generations" (14).

Several times over Blagden returned to the Rock and the "great principles" associated with the Pilgrims who landed upon it, and which was a "memorial" of their "trials and triumphs," but eventually he came to the end of the historical part of his discourse and launched into the applicability of the example of the Pilgrims to modern times. In words echoing Webster's phrase in his debate with Hayne, Blagden pronounced "the past . . . secured" and went on to contemplate the future, urging his listeners to give themselves "anew to the duty of honoring [the Pilgrims] by our future actions, as truly as by our present words. Here, then, on this rock, from which we have been taking a survey of those great truths with which it is, and shall be forever associated, here let us pledge ourselves to be true to our fathers!" (23).

But then, with this final echo from Webster's Plymouth oration, Blagden turned, like William Sullivan in 1829, to peer into that aspect of the otherwise prosperous national scene that promoted the effects of chiaroscuro: "We have beheld the bright part of the picture; let us not be afraid to gaze on anything threatening, or dark, and to bear ourselves accordingly. Such a spirit would dishonor the descendants of the Pilgrims." Among the "discouraging" aspects of the modern moment that Blagden boldly fronted were "avowed atheists" who worked to break down "the distinctions arising from moral and intellectual attainments," radicals seeking to destroy "the necessary relations of well-ordered society," and levelers who promote "the degraded to stations for which they are not fitted, and the ignorant to the management of concerns which they cannot clearly comprehend" (24). Blagden, it is safe to assume, was no Jacksonian Democrat: "Are not many endeavoring to create a collision between the rich and poor,—between professional and working men?"

For George Washington Blagden, whose very name boasted his Federalist roots, the masses associated with the efforts of the Democrats to elevate the common man were an undifferentiated mob that included "foreigners, unacquainted, to a great degree, with the nature of our institutions," an unwholesome leaven that put the country in danger of forgetting the principles of the Forefathers, including the "worthies of our revolution . . . now nearly departed." What Lyman Beecher in Plymouth and Edward Everett in Lexington lamented in general terms of anxiety over the consequences of heedless progress, Blagden in Plymouth seized up and gave point to: it was not so much a matter of forgetfulness as ignorance, a flooding in of an alien element that had no knowledge of American history and threatened to dilute remembrance until it lost its power of recall. Thus, to Blagden's elitism we may add a large measure of bigotry, qualities that would in time become inextricably associated with both the Pilgrims and Plymouth Rock, not so much, however, on account of the activities of the Forefathers but because of the mounting anxiety of their celebrants over the next half century as the tide of immigration continued to increase.

Blagden proved prophetic also in his geopolitical pronouncements as he turned from the darkness visible in the urban, industrialized North to shadows gathering in the agrarian South. There, a "system" prevailed that promoted not only "a diversity of mercantile and agricultural interests," which was all to the good, but also "a radical difference of mind and manners, and a dangerous jealousy of feelings, which lay a foundation for constant distrust." Slavery was a system universally deplored, yet to deal with it was no simple matter, and solutions were made even more difficult by the defensive cast of the Southern character: the situation required "a comprehensive mind and benevolent heart," even while mandating a "radical" change, which is the only kind that operates for the "good of mankind" in a "permanent and progressive" way.

By "radical," Blagden meant "that the principles on which such changes proceed, shall not only be acknowledged by the head, but be seated in the heart of the people" and must emerge from "a sincere and deeply-rooted love for them" (26). Reformation of so extreme a nature necessitated an intense program of evangelical work, qualifications for which included "the fear of God," a salutary check that holds back "the passions of men," so that "the change, being radical, will be successful." In sum, truly radical change should not be brought about violently but with restraint and, one presumes, good manners.

Citing "the words of a Puritan," John Milton, Blagden urged free and open discussion of all these matters, even to the extent of allowing a hearing for "atheists and disorganizers," so that the forces of Truth and Falsehood could fight it out in an open forum, with the victory inevitably going to Truth (27). Such a context would have the added benefit of informing "ignorant foreigners" of "the principles of our fathers," making them into "useful citizens of a free republic." Finally, those who were already citizens would be awakened to a greater awareness of those ancestral principles and would recall "the price that was paid for our liberties" (27–28). In sum, the entrance to true citizenship in America was through the portals of Memory. But debate and recollection were not sufficient to solve the problem of slavery, the "dark cloud, full of lightning and storm," that cast its "portentous" shadow over the fair land, and Blagden urged his auditors to imitate Ben Franklin, who with his venturesome kite "disarmed the thunder-cloud of its terrors" and thereby "dissipated and annihilated it forever!" (28).

But Blagden wanted no kite string, no ten-foot pole for his instrument. It did no good to stand "at a distance—the distance of hundreds of miles,—and crying out, of danger and death, and crime; and upbraiding the unhappy victims who are exposed to the gathering tempest—partly, be it remembered, through our own instrumentality—as murderers, mansteaders, and pirates." No, if one wished sincerely to remove the "awful curse" of slavery from the land, then one must arouse "the fear of God in the hearts of our Southern brethren," not from the safety of Northern pulpits but by actually carrying the gospel kite of antislavery into the region that is suffering under the dark cloud of oppression. "No system of measures for the abolition of slavery can be either right or expedient, which is calculated to shut out your preachers of righteousness, and your instructors of youth, from free and welcome access to the southern section of our country" (29).

"Go then," Blagden urged his fellow clergymen, and "combine your reasonings, and feelings, and efforts with them, in the spirit of the gospel of Christ . . . and you may cherish the reasonable hope of calming the troubled elements, and dispersing the gathering clouds, ere the storm burst." But in heading southward with a Christian appeal to the hearts of slave owners, missionaries from the North should avoid self-righteousness and freely acknowledge the universality of guilt, for even the holy Forefathers, during the days of Plymouth Colony, sold "the son of King Philip and many of his warriors . . . as slaves." As brothers in sin, therefore, abolitionist missionaries should "mingle your tears in a common penitence, and encourage each other's hearts to a common reformation!" Such work for the common good needed something more powerful than the example of Ben Franklin and his magical kite; it required calling up the "spirit of the Pilgrims," not as a witness ghost but as a divinely ordained afflatus: "In the present instance, we need their influence as we contemplate what is past. . . . That rock,—that ocean,—these hills,—those graves! the graves of those that cannot die!—to him who gazes on them in the fear of the God of our fathers,—are eloquent. They speak to us of truths immutable as heaven,—precious as the happiness of earth! . . . And in the strength of that moral feeling which in the contemplation of what is old, is calculated to produce in sound minds,—let us ever venerate, and keep alive their memories and their sentiments,—let us act worthy of our sires, and the world shall yet be emancipated by the principles associated with Plymouth rock!" (30).

Blagden's was a powerful Alisonian message, advancing Webster's oath upon the Rock out of its regional sanctuary and rolling it southward, with an evangelical zeal borrowing sacred fire from the Pilgrim example. His was a resurrection that links the past to the present and points it toward the future, not like Webster's evocation of manifest destiny, which foresaw the spread of New Englanders all the way to the Pacific coast, but rather toward the glorious vision of the United States free of the dark cloud of slavery. It is the power of memory that will effect the change, remembrance of Pilgrim principles that will generate a truth overwhelming in its beauty, evident to all who attend the preachings of its witnesses. This is strong stuff surely for 1834, with no compromising postures, no appeal for support of colonizing efforts, but is in harmony with the sentiments expressed by the students even then departing from Lyman Beecher's Lane Seminary for Oberlin. It is a recruiting speech for soldiers of God to go forth not into Africa but into the darkest South, bearing the light of the Gospels to that troubled, troublesome land and thereby dispel the storm clouds of incipient war.

As the Oneida cadre of dissident students from Oberlin discovered, missionary efforts on behalf of immediate abolition often grounded lightnings in ways dangerous to one's health. Even in Cincinnati, Ohio, the pork-butchering capital located in a free state but a town separated only by a river from Kentucky, feelings against abolitionists ran high. In 1835, the Reverend Theodore Dwight Weld, the charismatic leader of the Oneida group, set out to "abolitionize Ohio" with decidedly mixed results, including showers of stones and impromptu concerts of horns, pans, and bells.

This cacaphonous parade carried him eventually into New York State, where in Troy he was greeted by a well-organized "mob" incited by fears that Weld was an advocate of slave insurrection, the memory of Nat Turner still being fresh in the public mind. Attempting to attack him bodily, the crowd showered Weld with rocks, bricks, and rotten eggs, and though he continued to hold firm to his podium and gave his sermon on behalf of abolition—and free speech—it would be his last attempt at promoting the gospel of emancipation from a public platform. Having lost his voice, Weld lost his nerve as well, and though he would continue to work for emancipation, it was generally while safely ensconced among friends to the cause.

Nor was antagonism to antislavery activities, as Weld's experience in Troy proved conclusively, limited to regions just north of the Line. In 1835, an angry mob was assembled in Boston with the intention of tar and feathering the British abolitionist orator George Thompson, who was suspected of being the cat's-paw of foreign interests seeking to promote disunion in the States—fears testifying that the South was not the only section prone to paranoia. Thompson escaped their attentions, but William Lloyd Garrison, who had organized the meeting at which the British radical was to speak, did not, and though he escaped the tar pot, Garrison was paraded through the streets of Boston with a noose around his neck (or body, depending on the source). Residents of Southern states employed implements less symbolic and processions more fierce, for as Garrison's *Liberator* regularly reported, in Dixie lynch mobs waited to act out the sneering threats of editors and politicians alike.

And what, we might wonder, was the fate of George Washington Blagden? In 1834, he was the pastor of the Salem Street Church in Boston, to whose pulpit he had been called in 1830, when that congregation was formed by Trinitarians, because of his successes in defending orthodoxy in Brighton's Congregational church. Did he, like Lyman Beecher and Theodore Weld, heed the call of the West? Or did he heed his own call and carry the gospel message of love and liberty into the South? In 1835, the sight of Garrison being posted through the Boston streets by a mob so moved a young lawyer that he became converted to the cause of abolition from a rather purposeless (if privileged) life, an entirely secular, though clearly spiritual, experience. In Wendell Phillips the Garrisonites found one of their most effective voices for immediate abolition, and Phillips was George Blagden's brother-in-law. Was Blagden likewise moved to quit his pulpit for the electrifying circuit of an abolitionist orator? Was he pushed like Phillips by his wife (Wendell's sister) into ever more radical postures?

Who, in brief, was George Washington Blagden, and what, after 1834, did he become? The answer to those questions is a short enough story, but it tells us a great deal about the kinds of choices made by New Englanders in the 1830s, especially by those who reignited the evangelical flame on Plymouth Rock, the radical character of whom is suggested by that naked quaternity providing iconic meaning to the seal affixed by the Pilgrims to their official documents. It tells as much, if not more, about those New Englanders who shunned that light but who in doing so proved to be as naked as their counterparts, not, however, in zeal but expedience. For, as we shall learn in specific detail, where the antislavery debate was concerned, George Washington Blagden was not only one of the great coat holders in history, but as the conflict between the combatants grew fiercely heated, he departed, leaving the coat hanging on a convenient peg of cautionary admonition.

IV

George Washington Blagden's given names had a sectional as well as a Federalist connotation. He was born in Washington, D.C., in 1802, to a father who had come over from England and by that time was a pioneering resident of the new capital city, where he worked as a contractor. Blagden Sr. was credited by his son's memorialist with having erected "most of the early public and private buildings in Washington," those stately Palladian structures that provided such stark contrast with the District's muddy streets, in which hogs went free but slaves were kept in pens waiting to be sold (Stoddard, 14).

The contractor's death was a martyrdom of sorts, "caused by the falling of a mass of earth upon him while he was superintending some repairs to the foundations" of the Capitol itself. The boy's maternal heritage, like his namesake's, was Virginian, and he seems to have been regarded by his contemporaries as a Southerner, though his education and career were distinctly associated with the North. It was a dual inheritance that in part explains his sectional bridgework in 1834, when he presumed to speak with some authority regarding the sensitive feelings of Southerners, even as he urged on his auditors a distinctly Northern cause.

Something about Blagden's essential character is revealed by an incident that took place while he was a student at Yale, when, during an undergraduate uprising, he "took the side of the government of the college, and by a happy union of firmness and genial influence over his fellow students, succeeded in averting the conflict" (Stoddard, 15). Thus his early history validates his subsequent stance as a peacemaker and Unionist, suggesting that Blagden had real talents as a diplomat and negotiator, just the sort of person, by birthright and natural gifts, to advance the cause of abolition in the South.

Early on, young Blagden had ambitions to become a lawyer, but the atmosphere at Yale was such that he took his peacemaking abilities to Andover, where he became a useful recruit to Congregationalism, his zeal in that regard leading to the rapid series of upward spirals that had brought him from Brighton to Boston. Then, only two years after he had enumerated the "great principles" associated with Plymouth Rock, George Blagden heeded what would be the most important call of his life, to the pulpit of the Old South Church in Boston, that bastion of orthodoxy with a lineage stretching back deep into the Puritan past.

He was a popular minister, whose sermons were occasionally published, giving him a reach beyond his immediate congregation, but unlike Leonard Bacon, whose contemporary career Blagden's closely parallels, he did not become a productive and influential scholar. Though further calls came to him, from churches in New York, Brooklyn, and Philadelphia, as well as from congregations still dark with the storm clouds of slavery, including Baltimore,

Washington, Charleston, and Savannah, Blagden was never moved to respond, believing, as he explained, "in the value of permanence in the ministerial relation as an element of usefulness" (27).

"None of these things move me," he said, quoting Saint Paul somewhat out of context, and so he did not obey his own command to preach abolition in a sympathetic and tolerant manner to his Southern compatriots in sin. Blagden was nonetheless a very useful man, but his notion of "doing good," much like that of his predecessor in the Old South's pulpit, Cotton Mather, was pretty much limited to services within the precincts of Boston. Moreover, despite his early abolitionist sentiments, he never was moved to help his brother-in-law, who was occasionally—even drastically—in need of assistance, including shelter from angry mobs.

Increasingly, to George Blagden's way of thinking, Wendell Phillips was part of the problem, not the solution. In 1835, Phillips's year of decision, Blagden had warned about the dangers of "excited states of the public mind, on great moral or political questions," especially when taken up by "highly charged, powerful imaginations, not bound down to truth by clear knowledge, nor directed in the use of that knowledge by reason regulated by the fear of God,— the only right reason. Such a power can, and sometimes has, set a whole nation in a blaze, by the irrepressible heat of its own mad workings" (*Influence*, 12).

These sentiments, introduced into a sermon titled *The Influence of the Gospel upon the Intellectual Powers*, chiefly devoted to promoting the establishment and support of Sunday schools, seem clearly inspired by the excitement stirred up by George Thompson's tour of the United States (which in May 1835 was still continuing), for the abolitionist's speeches were characterized by language regarded by advocates of the public peace as inflammatory. Wendell Phillips, though moved to outrage by the rough handling given Garrison by the Boston mob, had not yet come out publicly for abolition, but it would be difficult even now to produce a tidier capsule description of Blagden's brother-in-law as seen by his enemies once he became committed to the cause.

Still, it was undoubtedly Thompson to whom Blagden was referring in 1835, nor was his response that of a disinterested observer. It so happened that when he spoke in Plymouth on the morning of Forefathers' Day in 1834, there was in his audience the very man whose advertised appearance in Boston earlier that year had sparked the riot in which Garrison played the central (and perhaps not entirely unwilling) part. Thompson, who had been speaking in nearby Bridgewater, spoke also in Plymouth that afternoon, and according to a correspondent to the *Liberator*, "after pronouncing a high panegyric upon the orator of the morning, he proceeded to apply the principles and examples of the pilgrim fathers, as described by Mr. Blagden, to the subject of slavery in these states" (December 27, 1834).

In the next issue of Garrison's paper appeared a more specific report, a letter from a resident of Plymouth, who noted the difference between Thompson's hostile reception in Boston and the warmth with which he was received in the town where "there yet remains enough of the pilgrims' spirit, to lead them to treat a *stranger kindly*. Yes, the Old Colony has not so far departed from the faith, as to forget that its founders (our pilgrim Fathers) were pilgrims and strangers, and that they here sought an Asylum from oppression" (January 3, 1833).

According to the writer, Thompson's oratorical power was such as to engage the attention of an audience for two hours, many of whom had already sat through Blagden's performance in the morning, "whose address furnished Mr. Thompson with abundance of matter for his very powerful, eloquent and masterly production. . . . I was astonished, perfectly astonished, nor less so was the audience generally, to hear Mr. Thompson so ably *dissect, investigate,* and *apply* the remarks of the learned and able orator who had preceded him— (would that Mr. B. had heard the application to his own discourse)." Pleading lack of "time and ability," the writer hoped that "some other hand" would provide a detailed account of Thompson's remarks "and shew you how completely he 'used up' Mr. Blagden in certain topicks which were closely connected with the honor of those who have espoused the cause of the oppressed, and whose 'action,' we believe, is guided by 'principle' and 'the fear and acknowledgement of God.' "

Unfortunately, no further account of Thompson's anatomy lesson was forthcoming in the *Liberator*, nor was his address in Plymouth on December 22 included in the account of his American tour published in 1837, which recorded a number of his speeches. But its gist may be easily enough imagined by the above remarks, to which we may add a letter that appeared in the *Liberator* in 1850, when Thompson returned for his second tour of the United States. He found himself blocked once again by a mob from speaking in Boston, forcing him and his audience to adjourn and regroup in nearby Worcester, the first of a number of Massachusetts towns in which Thompson would speak, including Plymouth.

Identified only as "A DESCENDANT OF THE PILGRIMS," the writer, like the one in 1834 (perhaps the same person), noted the difference between Boston and Plymouth, "the pioneer spot in the cause of civil liberty": where Thompson could not be heard in Faneuil Hall because "the old Cradle had to be desecrated to appease the Slave Power," "here, on Forefathers' Rock, we will give him such a welcome as will cheer his heart, with the assurance that the fires he so signally aided to rekindle here fifteen years ago, are spreading with a rapidity and burning with an intensity, which will ere long do our part in consuming the last remnant of that accursed system—that 'sum of all villainies'—American Slavery" (December 27, 1850). The writer had heard Thompson in 1834 in Plymouth and testified that "the meeting house yet stands . . . from which he thundered the afterpiece for the Forefathers' celebration in 1824 [*sic*], throwing the morning celebration entirely into the shade, and contributing not a little to the present momentum which the cause has acquired among us."

The writer recalled how "vivid were his flashes," so much so "that even now, as one passes the spot, he almost fancies he can hear, 'so says Mr. Blagden.' 'There's no danger for Truth and Error to grapple in the field, says Mr. Blagden.' . . . Ay, that's all we ask—an open field and a fair fight, responded Mr. Thompson: and you know something, Mr. Garrison, of how the fight has gone here. We have never been lacking in ammunition, but the enemies' means of cutting off supplies have been great." The writer continued with an extended military metaphor with which we need not concern ourselves. The point to be made here is that Thompson used the occasion of Blagden's address in 1834 to first praise, then damn it by dissection, in effect reconstructing it by way of establishing a connection between the Pilgrims and modern reformers, precisely the point made by the Reverend Orville Dewey in 1826 but from which he and other Unitarians increasingly retreated.

George Blagden could hardly have been pleased by George Thompson's mocking use of his call for an open forum, and it is to his credit that in 1836, in accordance with his stated faith in permitting the expression of sentiments with which he did not agree, Blagden had allowed an antislavery convention, organized by Garrison and his followers, the use of his Salem Street church, at a time when many such doors were closed to the abolitionists. But the lesson of 1834 was repeated in 1837 when Blagden was accused by the *Liberator* of being a slaveholder as well as a minister who did not regard slaveholding as un-Christian.

Likewise, in 1847, in a sneering letter to Heman Humphrey that attacked the former president of Amherst College for his efforts on behalf of African colonization—the abolitionists' bête noire—Garrison took a gratuitous swipe at Blagden for having publicly and prayerfully "expressed the hope that the colony at Liberia would result as gloriously as had that of the pilgrim fathers at Plymouth, in building up a mighty empire, and bringing millions into the glorious liberty of the sons of God!" (*Letters*, 3:484). These attacks, along with the (to him) outrageous shenanigans of his brother-in-law, most certainly helped Blagden along toward his increasingly conservative, even reactionary position.

Not coincidentally it was in 1847 that Blagden chose the occasion of a fast day, declared by the governor of Massachusetts with the specific purpose of encouraging prayers that God would forward the antislavery cause, to speak out against those who would move the cause forward too quickly. Irked by what he took to be the "unchristian censoriousness" of outspoken abolitionists, who in taking advantage of free and open forums did not always speak in the conciliatory and unselfrighteous manner that was his preferred form of address, Blagden once again urged a reasonable and politic course of action.

He did not deny that slavery, as an institution, produced much that was sinful, including the breaking up of slave families and forbidding the use of the Bible to those in bondage. But he insisted that slavery, as an institution, was "appointed" by God to his chosen people in the Old Testament and had not been attacked by Christ in the New. It had even been sanctioned by that original lawyer for Christ, Saint Paul, who had specific things to say about the relations between "Master and Slave." Abolitionists who denounced the slave system as sinful were clearly denying Scripture: they should instead restrict their attacks to those specific aspects of slavery that went against biblically sustained laws. Pointing to the sin of violating the sacred bond of man and wife was one thing; declaring sinful the bondage of man or wife was another.

What Blagden was attacking in 1847 were the extremists in the cause of immediate abolition, in Boston identified with Garrison and his clique, chief among whom was Wendell Phillips. To Blagden's turn of mind, these radicals were promoting the very kind of "false ideas of political freedom" that had produced the horrors of the French Revolution, and he undoubtedly thought of his gifted brother-in-law as a latter-day Robespierre, who devoted his powers of oratory to a violent end. Blagden went on to define for his auditors the kinds of activities permissible for abolitionists, that in "condemning the sins of men, and in calling them to repentance and to Christ, we are to let the outward relations of society, as established by human law, alone, and faithfully condemn the sins committed in those relations" (25–26). This was a modern translation of Christ's injunction separating what was owed to God and what to Caesar and was the standard line promoted by establishmentarian ministers, a position equivalent to that of "Hunker" politicians who opposed radical abolition as injurious to the well-being of the state.

Blagden did not have his sermon published in 1847, but in 1854, in response to the increasing heat of the abolitionist crusade—fired up by the Compromise of 1850 and the Fugitive Slave Law—he brought it out with a prefatory introduction alluding to "the sentiments of the late and lamented Webster, so nobly expressed by him, on this subject, in 1850," that speech to the Senate of March 7 that angered many New Englanders and outraged militant abolitionists (*Remarks*, 3). Blagden spoke out also against those political zealots who entertained "the dangerous error of admitting that there is an 'inner light'—which a man may follow—brighter and clearer than that which directly emanates from the revealed rule of Heaven," a Quaker-derived spiritual impulse equivalent to "that dangerous doctrine of the 'higher law' of which so much has been said, and which Webster . . . so justly condemned in the United States Senate" (6).

It was this "light" and this "law" that were evoked by men who "would fain improve on the Scriptures themselves, in their zeal to destroy the system of slavery," a position put in a proper frame of reference by the reminder that it was in 1854 also that Thoreau wrote his "Slavery in Massachusetts" and "Life without Principle." Thus, as Wendell Phillips was pursuing his long career of emotionally charged orations on behalf of various radical reforms, his brother-in-law was heading in the opposite direction, the one toward fame, the other into the oblivion often enjoyed by understrappers of the establishment, a slow equivalent to the sudden burial of his father beneath the Capitol. Yet it must also be said that George Blagden had always remained very much the boy who had stood up for God and the college government while still a student at Yale.

Blagden's, of course, was the prevailing opinion of the day, even in Boston, and during his lifetime he was most certainly famous among his parishioners. In 1861, on the twenty-fifth anniversary of his installation in the pulpit of the Old South, the congregation staged an elaborate fete, including tributes to their beloved pastor gathered in a book published in his honor. There he was celebrated as "a conservator of our Puritan ancestors, a defender of that philanthropy and liberty which is found in the Bible, and a determined and able opponent of all other fallacious and infidel schemes for the extension of human freedom without regard to the laws of either God or man" (*Pastor's Memorial*, 55).

In his anniversary sermon, printed in the same book, Blagden once again took on "the fanaticism of technical [i.e., immediate] abolitionism," explaining that "in the beginning . . . my own sympathies and habits of thought, in common with those of most of my brethren in the ministry and members of our churches, were on the side of the most zealous reformers, and in favor of the most strenuous and uncompromising action against . . . holding any man in bondage or slavery" (76, 87). This is hardly suggested by his melioristic strategy as mapped out from Plymouth Rock in 1834, nor had Garrison and his followers encountered the kind of sympathy from the clerical establishment that Blagden suggests had existed "in the beginning"—quite the reverse.

Yet we must accord praise due as well as blame. For Blagden's argument in 1834 was not only outspoken and courageous, but it was prophetic in its anticipation of the reaction that self-righteous denunciation would engender in the South. That the minister did not obey his own exhortation is certainly not to his credit; that he was unduly optimistic concerning the efficacy of preaching mutual repentance in the South cannot be denied; but even Garrison's close associates felt that the abrasive and aggressive rhetoric favored by the editor of the *Liberator* was counterproductive, if the desired end was ending slavery without war. As Blagden pointed out in 1861, reformers who operate outside the spirit of the Gospels "become unwarrantably censorious, and necessarily irritating," and instead of promoting the desired change only drive their opponents into "the positive vindication of sins" (89).

Such an observation at that late date was validated by the war then raging, "shedding the blood of its best and bravest citizens, not for the purpose of abolishing the domestic institutions in any of the states, but for that of maintaining and enforcing the laws as they are," this before the Emancipation Proclamation was anything more than a glint in Charles Sumner's eye (90). But it is perfectly consistent with Blagden's position in 1834 and thereafter, and whatever may have been the personal factors motivating Wendell Phillips's brother-in-law, we must accord him the strength of his convictions, which were as solidly establishmentarian as the walls of his church.

In 1872, the Reverend Blagden officially retired from his pulpit, but he remained associated with his beloved congregation as minister "emeritus," and only in 1882 did he fully step down, moving to New York City, to live with his daughter and her husband. There in 1884 he died, "that perfect model of a christian gentleman," as in so much else that he had done, "peacefully," and "surrounded by children," according to his memorialist, "who are honorably and usefully settled in life" (*Pastor's Memorial*, 45–46; Stoddard, 31). He had been blessed by grandchildren, also, most notably perhaps Wendell Phillips Blagden, born in 1882, whose name was gratefully acknowledged by his childless granduncle but which may have been less welcome to his paternal grandfather. The biographies of Wendell Phillips (whose literary executor was his nephew namesake) have not had much to say about the relationships between George Blagden, the fair-haired son of Orthodoxy in Boston, and his brother-in-law, Abolition's fair-haired darling, but we may be sure that unlike the quality of mercy it was strained.

Yet their lives provide a convenient diagram of the complex ideological differences that during their lifetime divided not only Boston and New England but much of the United States north of the Mason-Dixon Line. Aside from sharing in common a family connection and the year of their deaths, both men devoted long lives to the service of what each regarded as true righteousness, the one from a religious, the other from a legal point of view. Taken together, they thereby provide, from whichever perspective each is viewed, an illustration of the mystery of iniquity, which Saint Paul detected in the difference between the the hairy and the soap-smooth brothers.

Most important for our inquiry, each man took his turn standing on Plymouth Rock, Blagden early in his career, Phillips more than twenty years later. We shall come in time to that latterly event, but it is sufficient to note here that when Wendell Phillips took his turn on the Rock, it was to declaim sentiments that still ring down the ages, while those of George Blagden, who was earnest to find in the Pilgrims substantial "principles" upon which to mount his pulpit, do not. Rather, they now gather the moss often associated with the posthumous fame of persons extolled by their contemporaries as being "firm as a rock in adherence to his convictions of truth and duty." Such persons, though often celebrants of Memory's Nation, are seldom admitted as permanent citizens there.

V

Even as George Blagden was revising his attitude toward abolition in reaction to the behavior of abolitionists, Mark Hopkins, the president of Williams College, took his turn in Plymouth on Forefathers' Day and kept alive the strong-line, antislavery tradition initiated by Webster in 1820 and reinforced by Blagden in 1834. Those citizens of Plymouth who gathered on December 22, 1846, expecting to hear the familiar story of suffering and triumph were perhaps surprised by the generic compound of divine providence and civilized progress that Hopkins doled out. Something of his unique perspective is suggested by Hopkins's initial comparison between Columbus and the Pilgrim Fathers, the both of whom came seeking one thing and found another. Columbus sought a shorter passage to India and encountered a continent; the Pilgrims sought "religious freedom" but discovered "principles" inherent in the Gospels that provided a basis for that "political and social and moral inheritance" that was the foundation of the institutions of the United States (4–5). Further, as revealed by the text, "And all ye are brethren," God according to Hopkins intended that in America there be a true "brotherhood" of the human race, "that state of equality and affection" that would realize the spirit of the Christian message. In effect, Hopkins at the start of his address voiced a meliorism not unlike Blagden's twelve years earlier. He was also willing to share the Whig vision of progress that was one of the inheritances of the Pilgrims (as the Whigs saw it), the most dramatic recent evidence of which was the railroad line that was working its way westward from Boston toward Albany and had already reached the vicinity of Williamstown, Massachusetts:

Would it not have required all the faith of our fathers to believe it, if by some magic glass, the summit of Saddle Mountain, more than two hundred miles distant, has been pointed out, and it had been revealed to them that these triumphs [of invention and the useful arts] should be so great, that in a little more than two hundred years, one should start on the morning of the shortest day in the year from beyond the base of that mountain, and the next morning be on Plymouth rock, joining in the celebration of the event of their landing? (28–29)

Here again the familiar Rip Van Winkle trope, but in Hopkins's way of think-ing a positive, not disconcerting, marvel, which certified his position that New England was a singularly blessed spot. As a region, it was a truly Christian republic, sustained by Scripture and the regular observance of the Sabbath, by the sacredness of family ties and a certainty of the future, inhabited by a people who never need fear the imposition upon them of "arbitrary power": "Such is the picture which hope paints for the future, when she looks at the capabilities of our institutions, and at the power of God through his gospel" (30).

But then like Sullivan in 1829, Hopkins near the end of his happy discourse pulled out an alternative vision, in which superstition replaces religion, the Sabbath is disregarded, and the ties of marriage and family are ignored. For there were signs and portents, not in the skies but throughout the land: "iniq-uity in high places . . . the increase of crime . . . the pertinacity of many in tempting and ruining their fellow-men for the sake of gain" (30). There was also the venting of opinions that democracy is an acceptable substitute for the Christian religion, this in the face of "the narrowness and madness of sectarian and party feeling and strife" (30–31).

Central to this dark vision was the specter that had alarmed Sullivan and Blagden also, "slavery yet wielding its lash, and extending its area in this land of professed freedom," a violation of the "great principle of brotherhood" associ-ated with the Forefathers: "Whatever is incompatible with this in the spirit and forms of our institutions, let us seek to remove. It is this which has swept slavery from the soil of the Puritans, and which we ought to labor with every energy to infuse, till it shall sweep every vestige of that dreadful curse from this land" (31). Only let the divine spirit of brotherhood prevail, promised Hop-kins, and "the chief evils connected with the necessary diversity of condition among men would cease; and everywhere, and always, men would meet each other as men, and as brethren" (32). This, said Hopkins in conclusion, "is the star of hope which we see" ahead of us, "a beautiful star" that should guide the descendants of the Puritans much as it was the navigational aid to the Pilgrims aboard the *Mayflower*, whose course was controlled by a divine hand.

It was a similar star that served to guide a host of black people, who in seeking to escape that lash of slavery used the handle of the Big Dipper as a pointer toward freedom, heralded by the North Star, the name Frederick Douglass would give his abolitionist newspaper. Douglass's autobiography had appeared in 1845, the year before Hopkins broke a long silence regarding slavery on Forefather's Day in Plymouth—ten years having gone by without any public celebration at all. The famous fugitive included in his little narrative an account of his experiences in New England following his escape from bondage, in which the region proved to be not quite the perfect insular re-public of Christian brotherhood described by Mark Hopkins.

And yet, to the abolitionists who had eventually befriended Douglass and started him on his great career, New England did resemble an island of sanctity, topped by a mountain of righteousness from which the darkness and barbaric people of the South could be very clearly observed. But New England as viewed by the abolitionists was in need of purification, also, for reasons similar to those cited by Hopkins, and it was this centripetal morality, with its essential disjunctiveness, that eventually brought the Garrisonites to Plymouth Rock, the moral omphalos of the region and section.

Garrison's was a slow progress to Plymouth, for reasons that the following chapters will reveal, but it suffices to say here that by 1850 the radical abolitionists associated with his clique had taken steps to ensure that their agenda would be represented on Forefathers' Day by taking matters into their own hands, staging their ceremonies on the day sacred to the founding of New England. As the forces suddenly let loose by the notorious compromise began to affect the collective moral compass of the nation, the Rock and the Pilgrims were co-opted by emerging radical champions, who like Webster drew their moral energies from the exceptionalism of their New England base. Memory's Nation by then was in a state of civil war.

Tabling the Rock

Richmond, Va., May —, 18&65
There is raly a great deal of Union sentiment in this city.
I see it on evry hand. . . . I met a man today . . . and sez he . . .
"Let us at once stop this effosun of Blud! The Old Flag is
good enuff for me. Sir," he added, "you air from the North!
Have you a doughnut or a piece of custard pie about you?"
I told him no, [and] he borrowed fifty cents of me, and
asked me to send him Wm. Lloyd Garrison's ambrotype
as soon as I got home.
—Artemus Ward

I

It is perhaps impossible to determine when advocates of abolition first seized upon the Fourth of July as an anniversary appropriate to their cause, but the triad of performances by Leonard Bacon in 1825 was certainly symptomatic. Efforts to extend the principles enunciated in the Declaration of Independence to all Americans had been made ever since the constitutional debates and were given further impetus by the controversy over the Missouri Compromise, especially (if not exclusively) in New England. In the "First" (perhaps the last as well) number of an antislavery bulletin published in 1820, *The Crisis*, an anonymous New Englander began his philippic against extending slavery into Missouri by citing the Declaration of Independence, asking if there were "any at this enlightened period, so hardy as to deny" its principles: "Talk even with the advocates for the extension of slavery to the new and uncultivated regions of the west, and they will acknowledge that it is a great calamity" (3).

On July 4, 1828, Heman Humphrey, who had been one of many ministers celebrating the Pilgrim bicentennial in 1820 and was now the president of

Amherst College, shoved, as it were, the usual sentiments of the day aside—
"the popular and stereotyped topics of the anniversary"—in order to take up
the theme not of independence but slavery (*Parallel*, 3–4). Humphrey would
in time be attacked by William Lloyd Garrison for his efforts on behalf of
colonization, nor would his oration of 1828 be regarded with much favor by
abolitionists: the "Slavery" the Amherst president chiefly attacked was to the
rum bottle, subjection evinced by the intemperance traditionally displayed on
anniversaries of the Declaration of Independence and, to Humphrey's mind, a
bondage much worse than that endured by black persons in the South: "If we
sit still but a little longer, and look quietly on, while this scourge is raging like a
tempest of fire on all our borders, the fourth of July will indeed come, but we
shall have no independence to celebrate. Our liberties will exist only in the
song of the drunkard" (5). Urging his students to "let total abstinence be your
own motto" and to do what they could "to purge the land of its foulest
abomination," Humphrey sought to make "a drunkard . . . as rare a monster, as
he was in the days of our Pilgrim Fathers" (40). He hoped for a future when
"posterity will look back upon the present ravages and toleration of intemperance, with emotions of astonishment, grief and horror, similar to those
which we now feel, in reading the most afflictive history of the Slave-trade."

By citing the traffic in slaves, not the continued enslavement of black people
in America, Humphrey was able to place the troublesome problem beyond the
law and into the past—as "afflictive history." But his coupling of the two kinds
of slavery was symbolic, for much as temperance reform grew out of the
Trinitarian evangelical tradition, so abolition as a moral movement grew out
of the union of evangelism and the campaign against drink. Thus Horace
Bushnell, in his 1839 attack on the perceived excesses of the antislavery associations, accused the emancipationists of having "lifted the banner of Immediate
Abolition . . . so as to make their motto sound as much like Total Abstinence as
possible" (26–27). The illustration with which later reprintings of Humphrey's
sermon were furnished, which brought together a picture of a reclining drunkard and the familiar figure of a praying black man in chains, is a suitable icon
for the genesis of reform in America. The evolution was complex and hardly
limited to New England, but for our purposes we can date it from 1829, when
William Lloyd Garrison took his turn in using the Fourth of July as an occasion for promoting reform.

Garrison, who had commenced his journalistic career as a hard-line Federalist of the Harrison Gray Otis persuasion, soon enough mingled temperance
agitation with his politics (not always successfully) and by 1828 had taken over
a newspaper that was entirely devoted to the cause of total abstinence. He was
still supporting the gradualist efforts of the American Colonization Society

and had not yet made the move to immediatism, but three years earlier, he had written an editorial concerning the need for orators on the Fourth to mitigate "ceaseless apostrophes to liberty" with some "wholesome" reflections on modern "follies," chief of which was the curse of "SLAVERY" (Garrison and Garrison, 1:66). So he was (as always) being honest to his own opinion in taking advantage of an invitation in 1829 to deliver a Fourth of July address in Boston on behalf of the Colonization Society, an oration that signaled his public commitment to the cause of abolition in general, with which his career would thenceforth be identified.

Not much, however, was heard that day in praise of colonization, for Garrison had recently come under the influence of the paramount abolitionist then operating in America, Benjamin Lundy, and it must be said that the bare-fisted logic of immediatism suited his rhetorical style. As a Federalist editor backing the reelection of John Quincy Adams against General Jackson, Garrison had depicted the hero of New Orleans as a caricature of sin incarnate, "a man whose hands are crimsoned with innocent blood, whose lips are full of profanity . . . a slaveholder, and what is more iniquitous, a buyer and seller of human flesh—a military despot, who has broken the laws of his country—and one whose only recommendations are that he has fought many duels" (106). This kind of abusive, personal attack was typical of political discourse at the time and often occasioned the kinds of duels Jackson was accused of fighting. Still, Garrison seems to have relished violent language, and his natural mode of expression was the jeremiad, a licensed philippic into which he hurled himself with such rhetorical abandon that even his close associates would come to feel he was enjoying himself at the expense of the cause he was supposed to be advancing.

"Fifty-three years ago, the Fourth of July was a proud day for our country," Garrison began in 1829, but he then moved on to recite the degenerations of that annual occasion, listing the kinds of behavior Heman Humphrey had attacked the year before, drunkenness and disorder that did no honor to the Fathers. Garrison's argument was given further heft by Jackson's recent victory, itself the cause of considerable intemperance inside the doors of the White House. For it was undoubtedly the Democratic Party the Federalist editor had in mind when he spoke of those "free" citizens "who go shackled to the polls, year after year," while those men they elect "sell our birthright for office," then make a mockery of Independence Day by extolling the ideals of the Founders (128).

Despite their differences, disenfranchised Federalists were as one in regarding with dismay the decline of the country's morality, coupled with the notion of universal suffrage: "Our politics," declared Garrison, "are rotten to the core," for what else may one conclude when "a people . . . bearing the title of freemen . . . execute the work of slaves," a couplet that brought him around to the major topic of his oration, "another evil, which, if we had to contend against nothing else, would make us quake for the issue" (127–28). So great was this enormity that the Fourth should not be a day of "boisterous merriment and idle pageantry" but one of "fasting and prayer . . . a day of great lamentation, not of congratulatory joy" (128).

Against the backdrop of Jacksonian democracy, Garrison placed the plight of "two millions of wretched, degraded beings, who are pining in hopeless bondage—over whose sufferings scarcely an eye weeps, or a heart melts, or a tongue pleads either to God or man" (129). Unlike William Sullivan later that year, Garrison did not worry about the consequences of "liberation," for though a fellow Federalist, he seems to have enjoyed the kind of freedom from establishmentarian concerns that engenders true radicalism, yet Garrison's sudden leap into the cause of abolition was a complex reaction long in preparation. In terms of ideology, his outburst of sympathy for the most marginalized group of Americans in 1829 must in part be attributed to the editor's own sense of alienation from the direction in which the United States was moving—away not only from Federalism but from New England—which was only a more extreme version of the anxiety underlying Webster's rhetorical strategies in his great orations of the 1820s.

Though the jeremiad came naturally to Garrison, its use in New England was a traditional expression of regional anxiety. It first became epidemic toward the close of the seventeenth century, as the clerisy began to lose its political heft because of expansion out of and away from towns, with an increase in material prosperity in urban areas that drew popular attention away from preparations for the millennium, conditions equivalent to the disempowerment of Federalists in the late 1820s. Guilt is ever a powerful engine of self-elevation, of the one over the many, and Garrison, like Cotton Mather, was a master of its implementation. The chief lever at his disposal, at least at the start, was the "glaring contradiction as exists between our creed," that is, the Declaration of Independence, "and [its] practice. . . . In view of it, I am ashamed of my country. I am sick of our unmeaning declamation in praise of liberty and equality; of our hypocritical cant about the unalienable rights of man" (131–32). Garrison's public expression of his shame was an early equivalent to the Bloody Shirt, waved about at every opportunity.

Two years after his epochal Fourth of July speech in Boston, during which time he had become an advocate of immediate abolition, Garrison informed "the Free People of Color" in Philadelphia and New York ("and other Cities") that he was heartily ashamed of the day sacred to American liberties: "To me it is the most unhappy day in the whole three hundred and sixty-five. The ringing of bells and the thundering of cannon are torture to my feelings. I cannot be happy when I listen to the rant of lying declaimers, or think of the daring mockery to God, in which a whole nation combines. . . . As a white citizen, I am as tall as any man in the nation; my rights are amply secured; I lack nothing. Yet . . . if there be a colored man who feels happy on the Fourth of July, he feels what I cannot" (8–9). This tactic was hardly original with Garrison: on the Fourth of July, 1825, the Reverend Nathaniel Scudder Prime took advantage of the oratorical occasion to observe that "*the Year of Jubilee*" was "*not to Africans*" (24). But Garrison undoubtedly gave the strategy of guilt wide circulation, a rhetorical trope that utilized the elemental and glaring contradiction between the principles stated in the Declaration of Independence and the presence of slavery in the United States.

This same strategy inspired Garrison's plans in 1830 to publish his abolitionist periodical, to be called the "Public Liberator," in Washington, D.C. In 1828, Garrison had been inspired by Benjamin Lundy to join others in petitioning Congress for the abolition of slavery in the District of Columbia, a symbolic cause that would occupy the antislavery forces for the next thirty years. Abolitionists of whatever pattern tended to think in iconic terms, and in one such petition, written in November 1828, Garrison vividly depicted "the manacled slave" being "driven to market by the doors of our Capitol, and sold like a beast in the very place where are assembled the representatives of a free and Christian people" (Garrison and Garrison, 1:109).

And in choosing the place where his journal was to be published, he reasoned that "the Capital of our Union is obviously the most eligible spot whereon to build this mighty enterprise," not only because it was the seat of national government but because Garrison intended it to be "the first citadel" of slavery to be taken by the forces of immediate abolition (199). In fact, the District would remain a major depot of the slave trade until the Emancipation Proclamation, but as such it was a potent symbol of hypocrisy that saw considerable service in the cause of abolition. When Garrison did establish his newspaper, it was in Boston, not Washington, but the masthead of the *Liberator* was decorated from its seventeenth number on by a cartouche depicting a slave auction and a black man being flogged within plain view of the Capitol itself.

Like the Declaration of Independence, Washington provided a ready-made symbol of the glaring difference between principles and practice, the kind of moral lapse that aroused Federalist outrage. With that tireless consistency of the absolutist temper, which views life as through a surveyor's transit, Garrison stated on the first page of the first issue of the *Liberator* the logic of publishing it in Boston, evoking "Bunker Hill" and the "birthplace of liberty," along with the inevitable Declaration of Independence. He printed also his Fourth of July oration of 1829, updated to remove his former sympathy with colonization, so as to set the record straight.

He would, declared the editor in now famous words, "BE HEARD," and he would use the strongest language possible to advance the course of truth and righteousness. These are the figures and sentiments common to much oratory on Independence Day, and it can truly be said of William Lloyd Garrison that as an abolitionist he was born on the Fourth of July. It would be almost twenty years before the Liberator found himself identifying with the Pilgrim Fathers, but the importance of that delayed conjunction was such that we need to trace the course of Garrison's slow progress toward Plymouth and its Rock.

II

Unlike its conservative counterpart, the radical temper has little regard for "deep" history, and abolitionists found sufficient historic warrant in the Declaration of Independence for it to serve repeatedly as the fulcrum on which to rest the rhetorical crowbar with which they hoped to move the world, and they sought no further for instruments of upheaval. Still, Garrison and his clique during the 1830s occasionally did drop references to the Pilgrims, to "Pilgrim soil" and the "Pilgrim spirit," generally in contexts intended to embarrass the present residents of the first by calling attention to their lack of the second.

For example, in 1837 Garrison used the annual report of the board of managers of the Massachusetts (formerly the New England) Anti-Slavery Society to attack Edward Everett, by then governor of Massachusetts, for his temporizing message to the state legislature the year before, in which he cited the constitutional guarantee of the right of Southern states to hold slaves as the grounds for a tactful silence. In Everett's words, as quoted by Garrison (who provided the highlighting as well), " 'a *conciliatory forbearance* would leave this whole *painful subject* where the Constitution leaves it, with the States where it exists, and in the hands of an all-wise Providence, who, *in his own good time*, is *able* to cause it to disappear . . . under the gradual operation of the gentle spirit of Christianity' " (*Annual Report*, 65). Huffed Garrison in response, "A descendent of the pilgrims, and the every day eulogist of our revolutionary fathers—dares to affirm, in a high official capacity, that we, the people of Massachusetts, are solemnly obligated to carry our patriotism so far as to be voiceless, tongueless, insensate, deaf and blind, though millions of our fellow-countrymen are held in galling fetters!" (67).

Everett, who increasingly served as Webster's whipping boy, suffered correspondingly at the hands of Garrison, for whom the Whig advocacy of compromise and expediency provided fat and easy targets. We can hardly fail to understand Garrison's outrage and disgust, yet the virulence of his attacks on the Whig establishment was perhaps inseparable from his general avoidance of the Pilgrims as rhetorical icons. That is, because the Landing and Forefathers' Day were essential items in the Whig iconic lexicon, they were part and parcel of Garrison's personal alienation from the Massachusetts establishment.

In the 1830s, the Whigs' smooth accommodation to things as they were was read by the abolitionists as backsliding from the principles of the Declaration of Independence, and for Garrison it could also be regarded as status quoism on the part of those who had the high social position reinforced by wealth that he lacked. That he could not claim descent from the Pilgrims was a double barrier, in terms both of social acceptability and of his rhetorical reluctance to cite the Forefathers, even though by the 1830s they were well-worn tropes connoting civil liberties in America.

Garrison's lineage, in fact, sprang from those New Englanders who in 1763 took advantage of the British expulsion of the Acadians from Nova Scotia to settle there—hardly a genealogy for a libertarian to boast about. Joseph Garrison, his grandfather, was moreover a Nova Scotian from Great Britain, and his mother (Fanny Lloyd) was the daughter of an Irish immigrant. This mixed heritage gave Garrison a somewhat displaced parentage, eventually reinforced when his father abandoned the family, leaving his wife alone with infants to care for. Working as a nurse, she was unable to maintain her family above the poverty line, which in the early nineteenth century meant starvation. Young Lloyd was finally put out with a foster family and apprenticed to a shoemaker. But he found he was unsuited to the craft and instead followed the example of Ben Franklin a century earlier, who abandoned candle making for the print shop.

Franklin himself was in his day something of a tailor's patch in the breeches of the establishment, but Garrison lacked Ben's superb tact and cosmopolitanism (to say nothing of his sense of humor and proportion). Though like Franklin he read avidly, his Baptist heritage, like his Federalism, proved a very narrow focus for his emerging political zeal, operating quite outside the Enlightenment purview—save for an emphasis on reform. Much has been made of the "class" difference that inspired Boston's Brahmins to keep their distance from such as Garrison in the emerging antislavery crusade (even Emerson regarded him with amused scorn). But perhaps not enough has been made of Garrison's own feelings of alienation from those persons of wealth and privilege who found in Webster and Everett their best spokesmen. Such people generally could trace their roots (hence their ideologies) back to Winthrop's fleet, if not the *Mayflower*, while Garrison preferred a political lineage that began with the Declaration of Independence, a document of inclusiveness, not exclusiveness, which he hoped to open still wider by fighting for emancipation.

It is useful in this regard to cite the example of the Reverend Samuel Joseph May, a Unitarian minister and reformer and one of those who, along with his brother-in-law, Bronson Alcott, had gone in 1830 to hear Garrison lecture in Boston and come away converts to immediate abolitionism. May became a founding member of the New England Anti-Slavery Society and would remain a member of Garrison's clique for many years, despite reservations concerning the other man's intemperate tactics. May, unlike Garrison, could claim membership in Boston's elite, having origins deep in the Puritan chronicles of Massachusetts—his mother was descended from that aboriginal abolitionist Judge Samuel Sewall—and his education at Harvard made him an integral member of the Brahmin elite. A sweet-natured and generous man, Sam May was everything that Lloyd Garrison was not.

At about the time he was plunging into activism on behalf of abolition, May contributed to the ongoing debate between the orthodox and liberal wings of the Congregational Church, taking a stand that not only defined his difference as a Unitarian minister but placed him squarely in the center of our ongoing concern. The occasion was the publication in 1830 of *A Tribute to the Memory of the Pilgrims, and a Vindication of the Congregational Churches of New England*, by Joel Hawes, "D.D., pastor of the First Church in Hartford." Hawes, driving his pen under the influence of Lyman Beecher, was chiefly concerned with promoting the Trinitarian notion that the Forefathers shared with the primitive Christian church an abiding faith in the motions of Grace, that this was what brought them to America, and that a belief in salvation through Grace was the true way of Congregationalism, as opposed to the Socinian heresy regarding the efficacy of works. Following Beecher's lead but without his agility, Hawes used his "lectures" to attack the Unitarian churches, which because of their fealty to Socinianism "have renounced the truth, and gone over to the side of heresy" (150–51). Taking offense, the Reverend May also took the offensive and in a series of "Letters" demolished Hawes's argument point by point, using his own sources against him.

With careful scholarship and an outspoken frankness, May proved that the Congregational loyalty to the Calvinist notion of Grace neither was validated by the teachings of the primitive Christian church nor served as the main reason the Pilgrims left Europe for the New World—one of Hawes's main points by way of hitching the orthodox dinghy to the *Mayflower*. Moreover, May made it clear that it was the aggressive posture of Trinitarians like Hawes— who placed "the supposed sentiments of Unitarians . . . in a most disparaging contrast, with the supposed sentiments of the Pilgrims"—that made it necessary for Unitarians to speak out "in defense of that great principle for which our Pilgrim Fathers endured so much—that which was the *fundamental* doctrine of the Reformation—that 'Liberty, wherewith Christ has made us free' " (*Letters*, 53, 54). Along the way, May referred at length to John Robinson's parting charge to the Pilgrims, throwing those liberal sentiments regarding "more light" into his adversary's face. May was perfectly willing to acknowl-edge that the Pilgrims came to America believing in the " 'doctrine of grace,' " but so also, he noted wryly, "they came in the belief of witches, ghosts, and supernatural interpositions," all quite incidental to their "fundamental" faith in religious and civil freedom (19).

Toward the end of his argument, May in one magnificent sweep of refer-ences asserted the primacy of the Unitarians in celebrating the Pilgrims, along the way attesting to the validity of Lawrence Buell's assertions regarding the interlock between that progressive faith and the emerging Whig Party: "No men have delighted, more than Unitarians, to do the Pilgrims honour. None have paid a higher tribute to their memories. Let me remind you of Hon. J. Q. Adams', Daniel Webster's, Edward Everett's, William Sullivan's discourses at Plymouth—to Rev. Orville Dewey's Election Sermon, F. W. P. Greenwood's discourse, from which several extracts may be found in some of our school books—to Judge Story's centennial address at Salem, Hon. Edward Everett's at Charleston, and President Quincy's at Boston. Where else will you find the memories of our Forefathers eulogized, with so much *discriminating* justice, and impressive eloquence?" (37). May's italicized emphasis on "discrimina-tion" referred to the necessity dictated by truth to acknowledge the faults of the Forefathers, once again made necessary by the orthodox insistence on cele-brating doctrinal rigidity as the "genesis," as Leonard Bacon would put it, of the true churches of New England.

Most of the orators listed by May would in time be anathematized by Garrison's clique for their compromising and equivocating positions on slav-ery, the very qualities for which Unitarians were taken to task by defenders of the orthodox faith. Sam May, obviously, was an exception in this regard, and we can find a definitive jointure in his attack on Hawes and orthodoxy with his subsequent commitment to the logic of immediatism: in asserting that the reason the Pilgrims came to America was not because of their "attachment to the 'doctrines of grace' or the doctrines of Calvinism," May substituted as "the main spring of their enterprize . . . a determination not to acknowledge the authority of man in religion," thereby celebrating a distinctly libertarian—not to say Antinomian—spirit in the Forefathers (38).

According to May, the Pilgrims coupled with this antiauthoritarian impulse a deep dismay over "symptoms of decay in the public *virtue*," which also contributed to their decision to flee the Old World, corruption occasioned by "the rise and spread of zeal for the maintenance of *Systems of Faith*. The Pope was not the only Anti-Christ. *All human authority in religion is Anti-Christian.* And the desolating influence it has had in New England proves it to be so" (49). Though specifically attacking the doctrinal legalism of the orthodox, May throughout his response to Hawes was promoting his own historical and

Unitarian continuity, which sought to enlist the Pilgrims on the side of Christian liberalism, that progressive force for change often evinced as "zeal for good works," which did not exclude the overthrow of ecclesiastical power held "over the consciences of men, which should be subject to God and Christ alone!" (51, 49).

In May's version of Unitarianism, there is a celebration of that natural (even Emersonian) inclination in humankind that seeks to break down stone walls and shatter chains of repression, whether in terms of doctrinal rigidity or chattel slavery. His faith in progress, which was the driving force behind contemporary movements for reform, inspired May to work not only for abolition but also for the causes of universal peace, temperance, rights for women, and the improvement of schools. He was assuredly an exceptional Unitarian clergyman, unapologetic in his Socinianism, and even while William Ellery Channing was still celebrating his cloistered virtue, Sam May was at work in the fields of the Lord.

Yet May remains rather a minor figure in the history of abolition, if a ubiquitous and always positive presence, very much as he stood in Louisa May Alcott's memory, as an escapee from a novel by Dickens, forever appearing in the doorway at just the right moment with cash or groceries to save the starving workers in Bronson's dream factory from making the ultimate sacrifice to domestic solidarity. It is indicative of his character that it was May who, having done his share in setting free the slaves, "Freed from Toil and Care the Declining Years of William Lloyd Garrison" and is credited with such on the dedication page of the life of Garrison assembled by his children. May was the very image of the Christian gentleman, charitable to the last, and as such was an avatar of what he saw as the Pilgrim zeal for good works. He was, once again, all that Garrison was not, with whose own aggressive assertion of "the exercise of power over the consciences of men" May found frequent occasion to disagree.

It is helpful in defining the difference between the two men to cite the words of George Frisbie Hoar, who in 1895 took his oratorical turn in Plymouth on Forefathers' Day, the 275th anniversary of the Landing. Senator Hoar's address has already been cited for its celebration of John Robinson as a proponent of political reform, and we will return to it subsequently as an anthology of liberal attitudes of the day. Hoar had been an abolitionist from early on, but one who preferred to work through political mechanisms, and was instrumental as a young man in helping form the Republican Party. He of course knew both Garrison and May, and in attempting to make for his audience a distinction between the Pilgrims of Plymouth and the Puritans of Salem and Boston, he compared the two colonies with hypothetical utopias alternatively founded by "Waldo Emerson or Samuel May," on the one hand, and "Garrison or Parker

Pillsbury or Stephen Foster" on the other, a division that placed Emerson and May on the side of liberal and open-minded Pilgrims like William Bradford, while Garrison—along with the two others in his clique—was aligned with such as John Endicott (*Proceedings*, 15). Hoar's was not only a wise and a useful distinction, but it acts to further cement the connection between Sam May and the Pilgrims, even while holding Garrison at the distance he seems to have preferred from Plymouth.

All of which brings us back to the report of the January meeting in 1837 of the board of managers of the Massachusetts Anti-Slavery Society. Samuel May, who had recently left his Connecticut parish for a pulpit in South Scituate, near Plymouth, rose in his turn to rejoice concerning his new proximity to the society's headquarters in Boston, then moved on to the main point he wished to make: "Mr. President, I am now, you know, a resident in the Old Colony—not many miles from Plymouth rock. My thoughts have often, of late, reverted to the memorials of those high-souled men, who first came there seeking an asylum from civil and ecclesiastical tyranny—and I have been impelled onward in the enterprise, which has brought us here today, by the perception I have clearly had, that the abolition of slavery is but another and a broader phase of the same great and holy cause, for which our Pilgrim fathers and mothers cheerfully sacrificed all the comforts of life in civilized England—encountered the perils of a voyage across the broad Atlantic—and the hardships and dangers of living in this then howling wilderness" (*Report*, xxix).

The Reverend May, according to the note that appears at this place, "went on at some length to trace the resemblance, and show the identity of their purposes and ours," a lack of details in the transcription that we may here regret. Like the failure of the *Liberator* to report George Thompson's response to the Reverend Blagden's sermon in 1834, this lacuna testifies to Garrison's lack of interest at the time in the relevance to abolition of the Pilgrim priority, he of course having the final editorial hand. But what is most pertinent to our concerns was May's subsequent point, not only that the efforts of "our puritan forefathers" to preserve "the sacred principles of civil and religious liberty" should be emulated by their descendants, in remedying "the far grosser violation of those same principles, which we see at this day in our country," but that the connection between the abolitionists and the Pilgrims was closer than was popularly imagined:

> I shall be told by some, that the resemblance I have endeavored to point out is not real—for the Puritans were molested in their *own* rights, persecuted in their *own* persons—whereas we abolitionists, they say, are meddling in other folks' matters. . . . Sir, I am ashamed that there are men and women, ay professed christians and christian ministers, too, in our country, who

would have it thought, that a man must suffer injury in his own person, or his own rights before he can reasonably complain—that it is therefore no grievance, no concern of mine, that there are millions of my fellow beings, my countrymen, who are trodden down into the dust. . . . I am sincerely grieved that there are such men and women . . . among the lineal descendants of the Pilgrims. To such, therefore, it is necessary to show . . . that we are ourselves most seriously molested, by the system of slavery and its abettors, in the exercise of our civil and religious liberties. (xxix)

What May was chiefly referring to, in his allusion to "molestation," was not the mobs that increasingly gathered outside places where abolitionists intended to speak but the increasing difficulty Garrison's people were having in finding a place *to* speak: "Here, Sir, the birthplace of the American Revolution, the cause of impartial liberty is shut out from all the churches and halls, that are under control of the citizens" (xxxi). May pointed out the obvious irony that "although Faneuil Hall is still standing, the friends of liberty 'once sacred, now trampled upon,' the friends of true liberty, can find no shelter than *this*," a reference to "the loft of the stable attached to the Marlboro' House," the only place the society could find in which to meet. May was speaking to the necessity of constructing their own meeting place, but his incidental desire that the abolition movement be more firmly linked to the Pilgrims by experiencing persecution was about to be granted.

"The main object," observed the editor of the *Liberator*, early in 1837, "is to keep the subject before the public eye, and by every innocent expedient to promote perpetual discussion. We wish to bring Truth and Falsehood in continual *juxtaposition*, for we know full well that 'truth never came off the worse in a fair and open encounter'" (January 2). This delayed echo of George Thompson's mockery of the Reverend George Blagden's agenda was in reference to the Anti-Slavery Fair held in Boston on December 22 past, a "choice" of date that the editor declared was "accidental," but a coincidence that provided "a pleasant and appropriate manner of celebrating the Anniversary of the Pilgrims."

The dual occasion was observed by a motto placed "in large letters . . . around the Hall . . . 'On this day did our FATHERS *land* on the Rock of Freedom; let us *stand* firmly on this Rock,'" but the editor's attention was equally taken up by the various commodities on display for sale, including politically correct cakes "made of sugar not manufactured by slaves," near which "was placed the motto, FREE LABOR," and other articles, including pen wipers and needle books, stamped with inspirational mottoes rivaling the one decorating the hall. These were the means of "keeping the subject before the public eye" of antislavery, for as the editor pointed out, "the ladies" in charge of the fair "have ever regarded the pecuniary benefit derived from these sales as but *one* of the several reasons in their favor."

The Garrisonites, in keeping with the propensity of an age that produced the Raven, the Whale, and the Scarlet Letter, thought always in terms of symbolic, allegorical, and iconic displays, which would convey messages moral in meaning and as reminders perpetual, if in the present instances frangible—even edible—in substance. It was a very flexible kind of visual rhetoric and could be expanded to frame the significant as well as the ephemeral occasion. Soon enough Garrison would be provided with a magnificent opportunity to give the fullest exercise to his iconic imagination, and he would do his best to fulfill it. And as things turned out, that "accidental choice of day" proved to be one of those coincidences of a prophetic kind, for when next the members of the Massachusetts Anti-Slavery Society were given an opportunity "of celebrating the Anniversary of the Pilgrims," it was no accident and would point the way forward to a sequence of like celebrations that would mark a major revision of Garrison's rhetorical vocabulary.

By January 1837, the chain of events was already in the process of formation that would certify the violent consequences of the literature circulated by the American Anti-Slavery Society, which had in 1834 inspired from Dr. David M. Reese of New York a dire prediction. Denouncing the society as "both Anti-American and Anti-Christian," and its proposals "wild, visionary, and Utopian" and "treasonable" as well, "because at war with the laws of the land," Reese foresaw that "the means they employ are calculated to engender civil strife, servile war, insurrection, and bloodshed" (42–43). In New Hampshire, New York, and Pennsylvania, mobs led by "responsible" citizens hooted and hollered outside meeting places where antislavery speakers were scheduled to appear; buildings were burned and presses were destroyed. But it was the martyrdom of the Reverend Elijah Lovejoy, in Alton, Illinois, that provided the murderous climax to these outbursts of public outrage, fulfilling the Reverend May's desire and Dr. Reese's threat in a way that neither man could have foreseen.

The circumstances of Lovejoy's death were not entirely helpful to the abolitionist cause and contributed to an increasing lack of unity in the movement. But the abolitionist's martyrdom did indeed provide the occasion for "keeping the subject before the public eye" by an iconic display far more dramatic than those assembled by the "ladies" of the Anti-Slavery Society, being an "expedient to promote perpetual discussion" that was perhaps more manipulative than "innocent." Most important for our concern, the promotion of Lovejoy's martyrdom took a wide stride forward from that motto displayed at the Anti-Slavery Fair in 1836, and established a vital connection between the abolitionists of Massachusetts and the Pilgrim Fathers. For the occasion of Lovejoy's death moved Garrison and his clique inevitably toward Sam May's neighboring proximity to Plymouth Rock, though less perhaps in the spirit of Bradford than in the footsteps of John Endicott, who early on had left Boston to conduct some business in the vicinity of the Pilgrims regarding festivities that had taken a wrong direction.

III

"The past year," observed the editor of the sixth annual report of the board of managers of the Massachusetts Anti-Slavery Society, presented at the annual meeting in January 1838, "has exhibited the American people covering themselves afresh with pollution and blood, and audaciously defying the God of justice in the language of blasphemy" (*Report*, 3). The editor—Garrison surely—delivered up a catalog of sins, ranging from the callous treatment of Indian tribes by the perfidious Andrew Jackson to threats by Southern representatives to drag John Quincy Adams bodily from the Hall of Representatives because of his uncompromising opposition to the nation's capital remaining "THE CITADEL OF AMERICAN SLAVERY" (22). This, despite the "strength and glory of the anti-slavery cause, that its principles are so simple and elementary," "self-evident truths," like those of the Declaration of Independence, "fixed stars in the moral firmament."

Increasingly, however, Garrison's associates in New York and Massachusetts tended to navigate by other beacons, either because he insisted on including numerous reforms with abolition or because he persisted in his attacks on the clerisy, thereby offending ministers otherwise sympathetic to antislavery. Garrison's reaction was typical: clad in the whole armor of self-righteousness, he renewed his pledge to "speak the truth of God in its simplicity and power . . . regardless whom it may please or offend among men" and compared his struggle to the American Revolution, while temporizers and caviling clerics were modern equivalents to "Tories—traitors to their country—the enemies of Liberty" (24). In effect, Garrison attempted to cover over confusion in the ranks of abolition by upping the rhetorical ante and sought to instill loyalty among the remaining members of the Massachusetts Anti-Slavery Society by reminding them of the acts of courage displayed during the Revolution, when "paving stones in the streets were taken up and hurled at the heads of the myrmidons of tyranny—human blood was poured out like water—and the dead bodies of the friends and foes of liberty were piled up in hecatombs round about" (32–33).

Wading through these torrents of rhetorical gore, Garrison arrived at the penultimate item in his catalog of injustices, the death of Lovejoy at Alton, where "the abolition cause, which had passed through many an ordeal of violence, received A BAPTISM OF BLOOD" (33). Garrison listed the many sufferings of the abolitionists over the years, but hitherto "the cause had not found a martyr—it had not been baptized with innocent blood—not a life, of the multitudes threatened and endangered, had been lost!" (34). Though himself an exponent of nonviolence, Garrison exulted in the violence of others when it forwarded the good work of abolition, and Lovejoy's was a very useful martyrdom, having an effect on public opinion—and the agents of that opinion—that the death of another abolitionist under similar circumstances would not have had. It considerably widened the arena from that formerly occupied by emancipation, by women's rights, by universal peace, and the other reforms with which Garrison had identified himself, and he intended to remain in the center, the cynosure of the newly sympathetic public gaze. In sum, he, as much as his cause, needed Lovejoy.

Elijah Lovejoy was certainly an amalgam of the conflicted causes that characterized the marriage of revivalism and reform in the 1830s, but the fame of his martyrdom was ironically incidental to the causes to which he devoted himself. Born in Albion, Maine, in 1802, educated at Waterville (Colby) College, Lovejoy after a brief experience as the editor in St. Louis of a Whig newspaper returned to the East and enrolled in the Princeton seminary. Licensed in 1833 as a Presbyterian minister, Lovejoy returned to St. Louis, but now as the editor of a religious paper, and soon began to promote a triangular program of reforms not much different from that preached by Lyman Beecher, a mixture of abolition, temperance, and anti-Catholicism. But St. Louis was not Boston, and none of the three causes were very popular there.

So in the face of mounting public hostility Lovejoy fled with his press and his principles up and across river to Alton, Illinois, a village settled by enlightened New Englanders like himself that had up until then enjoyed considerable prosperity, thanks to a booming market in lead. Lovejoy's readers had no quarrel with his antislavery sentiments, so long as he championed gradual, not immediate, abolition. But the editor soon became impatient with the slow course that emancipation was taking in the West, and his position hardened into immediatism, with a concomitant hardening of feelings in Alton toward Lovejoy. It was a mood given added depth by the town's having fallen on lean times because of a drop in land prices and a glut in lead, a long-distance effect of the Panic of 1837.

These changes in editorial position and public temper took place over several months' time, but a turning point occurred when Lovejoy chose July 4, 1837, as the date on which to print an editorial calling for the formation of an Illinois chapter of the by then notorious American Anti-Slavery Society, an organization regarded locally with much the same emotions as was the Illuminati in Federalist Boston. Lovejoy's first printing press had been destroyed the evening of the day he had arrived in Alton, but the destruction was attributed to brigands from St. Louis, and the town took up a collection to replace it. After his call on the Fourth of July for the organization of a state auxiliary to the American Anti-Slavery Society was eventually heeded, in October, Lovejoy had two more presses destroyed with regularity and openness by the outraged citizens of enlightened Alton. A fourth (and last) press arrived on November 7, and Lovejoy with some friends put it under armed guard in a riverside warehouse. With the coming of darkness, the committee of local rearrangements duly arrived, carrying arms of their own, and in the ensuing gun battle a member of the mob and Lovejoy were shot and killed.

It was not so much that an abolitionist had been murdered that aroused clergymen and newspaper editors to outrage, but that a minister had been killed defending his right to publish his opinions, and as Garrison observed in the Annual Report of 1838, "pulpits, which had never found a voice to denounce the enslavement of millions of coloured men, were now wrought up to speak out boldly against this bloody atrocity" (36). Even Southern newspapers spoke out against the crime, their sympathy for a brother editor strongly seasoned by their realization that in gaining such a martyr the abolitionist cause had obtained a terrific (and unearned) moral edge. By way of assuring that such would be the case, the board of managers had met in Boston soon after the murder took place and issued a series of resolutions, including one in defense of Lovejoy's use of arms (a tender issue among champions of nonviolence), that "he was amply justified by the principles set forth in the Declaration of Independence [and] by the example of our revolutionary fathers" in arming himself against "the implacable, seditious, and desperate enemies of public order, liberty and humanity" (37).

That the red-hot iron of public opinion be struck into the desired shape before it cooled, the board also urged its "Parent," the American Anti-Slavery Society, to name a day "not too far distant" on which public meetings would be held "simultaneously throughout the free States by Abolitionists and the people generally . . . to commemorate the tragical death of Elijah P. Lovejoy, and thus give a mighty impulse to the cause of liberty throughout the land and the world" (38). In response, the parent society in New York appointed a date that Garrison in his report deemed "singularly appropriate, being in itself full of thrilling associations," but which may have come as something of a surprise when the summons first arrived (39).

Perhaps because the New York society was made up largely of staunch Congregationalists, who had perhaps grown tired of Garrison's repeated attacks on their brethren, the date chosen "was the *twenty-second of December*—the anniversary of the landing of the Pilgrim Fathers upon the rock at Plymouth," famous already in New England—as Garrison noted—"but how much more heart-stirring in connection with so strange an event!" It is not difficult to detect Garrison's discomfort with this choice of date for that particular "event," nor is there much enthusiasm in his remark that "the day was extensively observed by abolitionists, and greatly to the furtherance of their holy cause" (39).

Thus though Sam May got his wish in triplicate, the martyrdom of Lovejoy certifying the connection between abolitionists and the Pilgrims beyond his fondest dreams, the evidence suggests that Garrison was never more than a half-hearted celebrant of the connection. Moreover, the proceedings of the meetings in Boston and elsewhere on December 22, 1837, somehow dropped from that horizon that the passage of time establishes as History. This disappearance was not entirely, we must assume, because of Garrison's subsequent neglect of the event, but certainly it began there.

Of the several speakers in Boston on that occasion, two were quoted in brief by Garrison in his 1838 report: the first was Edmund Quincy, son of Josiah Sr., "a descendant of one of the Pilgrims," who thought it "a sublime idea, that, throughout the vast extent of the free portion of this continent, the sons and daughters of New England are gathered together on this, the birthday of their common mother, to pay due honors to the memory of a brother, who has willingly laid down his life in defence of those principles of liberty, to which she owed her birth" (*Annual Report*, 39). Notably, the idea of the Pilgrims and their Rock does not loom large in the quotation given, their association with "those principles of liberty" remaining tacit, not explicit. The other speaker cited was Wendell Phillips, who in the words quoted by Garrison made no mention of the Pilgrims either but instead wrapped the martyred Lovejoy in the national flag: "He took refuge under the banner of Liberty—amid its folds; and when he fell, its glorious stars and stripes, the emblems of free institutions, around which cluster so many heart-stirring memories, were blotted out in the martyr's blood."

Nor did Phillips mention Plymouth but instead expressed sorrow at the knowledge that the mob in Alton "were heard encouraging each other by reference to old Boston! Alas, my native city! art thou indeed so fallen? To be praised by praiseworthy men was once pronounced the highest honor. To what depth of degredation must she have fallen, whose time-honored name has become the motto and war-cry of a mob!" These emphases by Phillips (and Garrison) will shortly be explained by examining the rhetorical context from which they emerged—which was not the Landing in 1620. But we need to note here that Garrison's decision to quote only Quincy and Phillips in his report was strategic, the two young men being very recent recruits to his cause, for both were prized acquisitions, members of Boston's educated and wealthy elite. Small wonder that Garrison decided to decorate Lovejoy's rhetorical bier with these lustrous and newly lighted beacons of freedom! All three young men, as it were, would contribute greatly to the movement.

Wendell Phillips, in particular, would become Garrison's most articulate champion, sharing with him an interest in reforms in general—including women's rights—a latitudinarianism that had already caused the Massachusetts Anti-Slavery Society to drop the *Liberator* as its official organ. Again, the death of Lovejoy was most definitely a triumph and a turning point in the history of abolition as a movement, but if it gained strength from its new association with freedom of the press, it almost instantly thereafter fell apart into factions—or, more appropriately, sects—each with a different agenda.

Yet Phillips as a radical was cut from different fabric than was Garrison, having been first drawn into antislavery activities not because of his concern for the suffering black people in the South but because of the (to him) larger issue of civil rights. Trained as a lawyer, Phillips had been shocked by the sight of Garrison being dragged through the streets of Boston, a stark violation of due process. More recently he had been outraged by the gag rule enacted in Congress—a measure aimed specifically at John Quincy Adams and his efforts to rid the District of slavery—and in March 1837, before Lovejoy's murder, Phillips had spoken out at a meeting against this repression of the people's right to petition their representatives.

But it was on the evening of December 8 that Phillips came out publically for Garrison's cause, at a meeting called by the Liberator "to express . . . alarm and horror" over Lovejoy's death, which dramatically illustrated "the prostration of civil liberty," being "the murder of a christian minister for daring to maintain his inalienable and constitutional rights" (*Report*, 40). Garrison was too impatient to await the 22d, and with typical precipitousness and a desire to capitalize on Lovejoy's death before the body was cold in the public memory—"The all-animating voice of God is still saying—'Speak unto the friends of holy and impartial liberty, that they GO FORWARD!'"—he set about to arrange an earlier commemoration of abolition's first martyr. He may also have sought to anticipate the formal occasion and thereby steal some of its thunder, and in this last he was certainly successful beyond his dreams.

Garrison wanted to use Faneuil Hall for his meeting, but a petition signed by nearly one hundred "respectable citizens and legal voters," headed by the name of William Ellery Channing, did not convince the mayor and aldermen to open the doors of "the old Cradle of Liberty" to cradle rockers like Garrison. What worked the required magic, as Garrison saw it, was the forthcoming city election, which, along with a set of resolutions presented by him to the mayor and board, changed their collective mind, and Garrison's clique was allowed the use of Faneuil Hall. The result was precisely the "scene of confusion, which would be disreputable to the city, and injurious to the glory of that consecrated Hall" that had been feared and anticipated by the mayor and aldermen.

It was not the activities sponsored by Garrison, however, that caused the uproar and scandal but the presence at the meeting of persons hostile to abolition. The mob, instead of being outside the building, as before, was now mingled with those who had come to praise Lovejoy, whom the protesters sought to bury with raucous ridicule. The spokesman of this group was James Trecothick Austin, the state attorney general, who rose up in his private capacity to denounce the proceedings and was wildly cheered by his supporters. Speaking uninvited from the floor, Austin delivered a sneering attack on Lovejoy, who in his opinion had died "the death of a fool," and defended the action of the Alton mob by appealing to the most ancient of laws, "the original and immutable law of self-preservation, and necessary self-defense."

By Austin's lights, "the people of Missouri had as much reason to be afraid of their slaves, as we should of the wild beasts" in a zoo, and it was Lovejoy's vaunted purpose to set them free. Not coincidentally, it had been the law of self-preservation that Garrison had earlier cited as having justified Lovejoy's use of arms. Then too, the attorney general compared the display of force by the Alton mob to the actions of the Patriots of 1773—one of the Garrisonites' favorite similitudes for themselves—who took "their protection under the security of their own arms, and marching down from this Hall—*an orderly mob*—poured the disgusting instrument of their degradation into the Sea" (*Report*, 49; Garrison's italics).

Wendell Phillips struggled toward the platform through the consequent confusion like a swimmer from a heavy surf, carried by one current while resisted by another, and despite hostile cries from Austin's supporters, he gained the attention of the crowd. Until that moment he had been a young lawyer with no particular commitment save to his semi-invalid bride, the lovely Ann Greene, whose own zeal for abolition and like reforms would subsequently be deflected through her husband. True, Phillips had been shocked by the spectacle of Garrison's near lynching, and, as already noted, he had spoken out earlier against the notorious gag rule.

But his appearance on the platform on the night of December 8, 1837, was generally regarded by himself, hence his biographers, as a moment as liminal in his personal life as Paul's conversion at Tarsus. We are talking, admittedly, about mythic iconography, for what Phillips actually said on December 8 was mostly a reprise of his speech nine months earlier, a period of gestation that produced a birth the momentousness of which was largely a matter of circumstances. On both occasions he spoke as a professional man about matters of law, but the highly charged emotions of the later meeting gave particular energy and fire to his argument.

Speaking necessarily extempore, Phillips began by expressing the outrage felt by many in the hall over the presumptuousness of the state attorney general, not only in tacitly lending the weight of his authority to the actions of the Boston mob in Faneuil Hall but specifically in throwing "the glorious mantle of Revolutionary precedent" over the murder of Lovejoy in Alton (*Report*, 48). In a brilliant display of legal logic, Phillips accused Austin of having read "our Revolutionary history upside down," a phrase that drew upon the public memory of the circumstances of Cornwallis's surrender and thereby associated Austin with the Tory side of the struggle (49). The Patriots of 1773, as Phillips explained, were resisting taxes unconstitutionally thrust upon them by Great Britain, while the mob at Alton were resisting "laws we ourselves have enacted," and for Austin to maintain otherwise, drawing "the conduct of our ancestors into a precedent for mobs . . . is an insult to their memory. . . . Sir, for the sentiments he has uttered, on soil consecrated by the prayers of Puritans and the blood of Patriots, the earth should have yawned and swallowed him up!"

Phillips went on for much longer, but the remainder of what he said was not included by the editor of the report of 1838, perhaps because it had been given in full in the *Liberator*, or perhaps because of considerations of space. Certainly its importance gained proportionately as Phillips's career as a reformer grew, and the excerpt in effect conveyed the emphasis of his remarks, which were aligned with the stated purpose of the meeting—to protest the violation of Lovejoy's civil rights and declare the illegality of the mob action that took his life.

That Phillips did not once mention slavery can be excused by the requirement insisted upon by the mayor and aldermen that the "inflammatory subject" not be brought up in Faneuil Hall, a restriction that the attorney general obviously ignored even as it was honored by the abolitionists present. But subsequent events do suggest that the door through which Phillips entered the abolitionist movement was the same one that opened onto the platform that night, for his concern was not so much with the plight of African Americans as with the threat to the traditional liberties of Anglo-Americans that the murder of Lovejoy seemed to pose.

A man gifted with a trial lawyer's theatricality, Phillips was an extraordinarily effective speaker and generated considerable controversy during his long and active career as an agitator for reform. Drawing deep strength from his social standing, Phillips is best characterized by that slight smile seen in his portraits and photographs, his elegant orations usually leavened with humor, giving agitation for emancipation a degree of charm and literary expressiveness it had hitherto lacked. He was Garrison's counterpart, even in his oratory providing an antidote to the other man's fiery and abrasive language, but beneath the brilliance and versatility of his forensic performances we can find a consistent focus on matters of law. Wendell Phillips not only brought grace and wit to the abolitionist movement, but by opening the discourse to include matters beyond the simple standard of the Declaration of Independence, namely the rights given to American citizens by the first ten amendments to the Constitution, he considerably widened the arena.

Handsome, gifted, and wealthy enough to devote himself entirely (and purely) to reform, Phillips was after Channing the most welcome addition to the cause of abolition and in the long run would prove to be the most valuable by far. Once again, though Phillips had already spoken out in defense of American liberties in connection with the abolitionist debate, it would always be that impromptu oration on the evening of December 8 with which his crossing over would be associated. It was a sparkling performance given particular drama by the circumstances that inspired it, recalling Patrick Henry's noble words before the House of Burgesses.

But much as Henry's often quoted phrase is of dubious historicity, we have only to compare the relatively brief excerpt quoted by the editor of the *Report* with the version published in Phillips's collected speeches (where it appears with an extended account of the context from which it emerged) to realize that considerable revision took place over the interval, insertions of witticisms and elaborations—the sparkle—that make his argument all the more effective but historically suspect. Hardly as apocryphal as the iconic version of the Landing, Phillips's December 8 speech belongs pretty much in that same category of myth.

IV

The absence of any mention of the formal commemorative gathering on December 22 from most, if not all, histories of the abolitionist movement can at least in part be attributed to the much more famous meeting that preceded it. Other reasons for that omission can only be conjectured, but we can easily determine why Phillips's remarks on the later occasion were not included in his collected speeches, for the best parts were simply transferred to his "impromptu" remarks on the 8th. Phillips apparently anticipated the opinion of his posterity that the circumstances of that night in Faneuil Hall outmatched the historical frame provided by Forefathers' Day—and did what he could to ensure its priority. Fortunately for scholars of revision (and revisionary scholars), Phillips's original speech of December 8, as I have already noted, was recorded in full in the *Liberator* (December 15, 1837), as are the orations delivered on December 22 following (January 5, 1838). Of the two events, the last has the greater interest here, and we will be concerned with it thenceforth.

Notably, of the several speakers on the Forefathers' Day set aside for a memorial to Lovejoy, only Edmund Quincy evoked the spirit of the Pilgrims.

The reason may be found in the number of the *Liberator* published (coincidentally) on December 22, which contained a busy and exultant listing of commemorations being held all over the country that day in memory of both the Pilgrims' wintry arrival and Lovejoy's violent departure. There were also printed a lengthy open letter "TO ABOLITIONISTS" from the Reverend Dr. Channing and private correspondence from young Quincy to Garrison, the both signaling glorious acquisitions to the cause.

Channing's Areopagitican emergence from his closeted musings on Milton was certainly good news for the cause of abolition, but it was the enlistment in Garrison's clique of young men of high place like Quincy that set the Liberator's stock high. Quincy's letter testified to his earnest resolve to come out for immediate abolition, with a check enclosed for a lifetime membership in the Massachusetts Anti-Slavery Society and a subscription to the *Liberator* with like terms. Notably, the letter was a month old and had obviously been held back for this especially auspicious and appropriate occasion.

Once again, these were high times for Garrison, and he fairly vibrates off the page with excitement, devoting an item entitled "Most Honorable" to Quincy's conversion: "Mr. Quincy," crowed Garrison, "is a son of President Quincy of Harvard University, and a member of the bar in this city. He is a regular descendant of one of the Pilgrim Fathers, whose name he bears. Never should a Quincy be found among the apologists or defenders of slavery. How glowed the fire of liberty in the bosom of Josiah Quincy [Edmund's grandfather], of deathless revolutionary memory! In thus enrolling his name among the advocates of our enslaved countrymen, at such a crisis, in a city like this, and surrounded as he is by hostile influences, Mr. Quincy displays great integrity of mind and moral independence."

Garrison also took the opportunity to remind his readers that Quincy would be among the speakers at the memorial for Lovejoy that evening. Because of the anniversary occasion appointed by the "Parent Society," Garrison obviously took especial pains to point out Edmund's genealogical connections, in effect something by way of a shove to propel the young man onto the platform as a reminder of his intended function there. Quincy's coming-out speech was hardly as brilliant or memorable as Phillips's earlier performance, but it was certainly serviceable, if only because he made the necessary connections mandated by the occasion, while other speakers, including Garrison, did not.

Instead, the Liberator chose the moment—brief and late in the evening—to "rejoice" that the meeting had *not* been held in Faneuil Hall, where, on December 8, "a padlock" had been placed on their lips regarding any mention of slavery, a subject not denied them in Marlborough Chapel, the place of the present meeting. Garrison took the opportunity also to certify further Channing's emergence in the cause by quoting from his work on slavery, published two years earlier, in which that very careful Unitarian had wryly observed that "'one kidnapped, *murdered* Abolitionist would do more for the violent destruction of slavery than a thousand societies. His name would be sainted. *The day of his death would be set apart for solemn, heart-stirring commemoration.* His blood would cry through the land with a thrilling voice, would pierce every dwelling, and find a response in every heart'" (Garrison's italics).

As always unwilling to let a good thing lie, Garrison with his characteristic love of symbolic tableaux seized up Channing's prophesied martyr and made him grotesquely Lovejoy. He wished that the dead body of the slain abolitionist "could be brought into this Chapel, followed by a train of manacled and sorrow-stricken slaves, supporting the living though insensible form of his agonized wife,—such a spectacle would plead with a voice, that has not been heard here this evening, and excite emotions wholly unutterable," which last reservation never occurred to the characteristically tone-deaf Garrison. That the much more delicately nuanced Channing may have objected to his words having been given such literal and theatrical form is suggested by his subsequent reneging on his participation in the first memorial for Lovejoy, on the grounds that the dead man's use of violent means was unjustified.

As I have noted, Quincy did what he could to Pilgrimize the occasion, first by noting the appropriateness of the date, "this holy anniversary, for the unanimous celebration" throughout the country "of the obsequies of our martyred brother.... It is a sublime idea, that throughout the vast extent of the free portion of this continent, the sons and daughters of New-England are gathered together on this, the birthday of their common mother, to pay dire honors to the memory of a brother, who has willingly laid down his life in defence of those principles of liberty, to which she owed her birth" (January 5). Quincy also was proud of those (obviously few) surviving descendants of the Pilgrims "who can look back to the Rock of Plymouth without shame; who can contemplate the example of the Fathers, and not blush to think that they are their sons." Adapting to the occasion a traditional strategy of Forefathers' Day orations and sermons, Quincy placed against the light shed by these sterling heirs of the Pilgrims the general decline in virtue and vision to be found in New England, lamenting in words familiar to the jeremiad "how low and base are the ideas of liberty which now prevail, compared with those which the Mayflower wafted to these shores."

Quincy conjured up not a Pilgrim ghost but a present-day lover of democracy, an "enthusiast from one of the old despotisms of Europe—his mind filled and warmed with the noble sentiments of liberty." The visitor would be taken to the nation's capital and would have "his admiring gaze" directed to the "eternal truths of the Declaration of Independence and the Constitution of the

United States," but then he would "descend the steps of the Capitol" to the "marketplace," rather in the manner of Dante being led into Hell by Virgil, where he would hear "the clank of chains, the resounding lash of the whip, the wail of miserable captives . . . men and women, and children, sold under the hammer beneath the broad folds of the star-spangled banner." What the foreign visitor would confront, in effect, would be the masthead of the *Liberator*, a quick segue from the *Mayflower* that must have gladdened the heart of the editor.

The allusion provided a transition to Quincy's next point, which joined Garrison himself in tandem to Lovejoy, not mentioning the Liberator by name but picturing him as another martyr, being "dragged through the streets [of Boston] with a halter about his neck." This humiliation enlisted Garrison in the company of that other "generous son of New England," whose "heart's best blood . . . has steeped . . . the banks of a distant river. This is their crime; that they dared obey the paramount laws of their country!"

Can such things happen, wondered Quincy aloud, "in New England? Is this the faith we have received from the Fathers? Are these the deeds of the sons of the Pilgrims? Can it be possible, that such an atrocious tyranny can have usurped the rightful supremacy of those principles of liberty which our Fathers loved more than their lives? . . . Alas! Sir, let the streets of the city reply; let the temples of our God, which have been violated by the enemies of freedom, in almost every village in New England, answer!" It must be said that Quincy's evocation of the Forefathers was not his dominant emphasis; moreover, his use of the Pilgrims was traditional to the abolitionist strategy: they were a standard, like the Declaration of Independence, against which the present generation was to be measured—and inevitably found wanting. Again, this is the strategy also of the jeremiad, a genre genetically engineered into Garrison's consciousness, and Quincy, given his own lineage and assignment, did not vary much from the model. In effect, by choosing the moment to glorify Garrison even as he memorialized Lovejoy, Quincy managed to place the Pilgrims in the margins of his text.

For his part, once again, Wendell Phillips largely ignored the Forefathers, mounting an argument anchored in the same grounds as his earlier, impromptu performance, addressing himself to the violation of Lovejoy's rights, as an American citizen, to freedom of speech and the press. Only toward the end of his address did he get around to the subject to which the 22d was sacred, noting that "freedom of thought was our fathers' guiding star over the ocean," which put the *Mayflower* in a posterior position to that ship of state, the Constitution. Nor did he elaborate on the idea, choosing instead to attack at length the "rioters at Alton" for "encouraging each other by reference to old Boston," the passage singled out by the editor for quotation in the *Report* of

1838. And his most effective symbolic image, likewise, was that flag-wrapped Lovejoy also quoted in the report, which may be found among the figures translated into his speech of December 8.

Furthermore, it should be noted that even though the "padlock" had, as Garrison observed, been removed from the subject of slavery, Phillips on December 22 never got around to that topic. He even made it clear that Lovejoy had not been defended by his friends at Alton "as an abolitionist" but as an advocate of the freedom of the press—precisely the "martyrdom" that had inspired such an outpouring of sympathy and indignation throughout the land. This was the issue Garrison himself sought to emphasize, but not to the exclusion of immediate abolitionism, and though Phillips would in the future be an extremely effective spokesman for the cause of emancipation, on the evening of December 22 as on the 8th, that was not his subject nor his concern. In good time, Phillips more than made up for his omission, and in a context that took Lovejoy from where he had been "planted on his constitutional rights" and placed him on Plymouth Rock.

But in 1837, indeed for the succeeding decade, only a minority of the abolitionists in New England sought to establish parallels between the Pilgrims and themselves, using the Forefathers repeatedly as grace notes but not in an extended figure. It comes, therefore, as something of a surprise to read in the *Liberator* on December 28, 1849, that Garrison and his clique, in conjunction with the Old Colony Anti-Slavery Society, had celebrated in Plymouth "in a very appropriate manner . . . the 229th anniversary of the landing of the Pilgrim Fathers." In effect, this was a return to the strategy suggested by the parent society in New York in 1837 regarding the fitness of Forefathers' Day for abolitionist events, but given Garrison's imperfect sympathy with that suggestion, his turnabout in 1849 deserves some study.

The main purpose of the meeting was to announce George Thompson's return to America the following year and to extend to him an invitation to assist in the celebration of the 230th anniversary of the Landing. Perhaps Thompson's earlier performance in Plymouth in part inspired the decisive move, and Garrison's clique could anticipate that, as in 1834, doors would be closed to the British agitator in Boston. In the number of the *Liberator* for December 27, 1850, which contained a report of the anniversary meeting in Plymouth, there appeared a letter dated November 19 in which a correspondent from that town noted that if Thompson "could not be heard in Faneuil Hall, the old Cradle [having been] desecrated to appease the Slave Power," that "our friend" was always welcome in "old Plymouth—the pioneer spot in the cause of civil liberty; and here, on Forefathers' Rock, we will give him such a welcome as will cheer his heart." This is the same letter, signed "A DESCENDANT

OF THE PILGRIMS," that contained the reminiscence of Thompson's appearance in Plymouth in 1834, thereby making the connection hard and fast. But there were other possible considerations, as well, including Garrison's need to add new armaments to his rhetorical arsenal, the lamented Fourth having perhaps lost its pop and flare.

Hints as to the ideological drift that brought Garrison and Phillips to Plymouth may be found in the prefatory material supplied by the two men to Frederick Douglass's autobiography, first published in 1845, a book that was—along with the author—another important recruit to the cause of immediate abolition. Where Phillips and Quincy had been welcomed a decade earlier for their wealth and social position, Douglass was greeted with open arms as a powerful speaker and an effective writer who was of African descent and had experienced slavery firsthand. But where the other two men had indisputable credentials, Douglass was such a gifted orator that his background was questioned, making it necessary that he write his autobiography, and the material contributed by Garrison and Phillips was intended to attest the genuineness of both Douglass and his book.

Thus Garrison retold the story of the abolitionist meeting on Nantucket in 1841, when Douglass had been prevailed upon to address the audience, at first haltingly but then with increasing facility as he warmed to his subject. Garrison had at the time compared the young speaker to Patrick Henry, the both having been "so eloquent in the cause of liberty" (35). But then Garrison had advised the Nantucket audience that an escaped ("self-emancipated") slave was not safe—"even in Massachusetts, on the soil of the Pilgrim Fathers, among the descendants of revolutionary sires." For his part, Wendell Phillips took an opposite tack, emphasizing the positive aspect of New England by characterizing the Deep South as the perpetually bad place, "that (for the colored man) Valley of the Shadow of Death, where the Mississippi sweeps along" (45). Phillips's geography was framed to reinforce the movement of Garrison and his clique toward an open declaration of Northern secession or dis-Unionism, as the editor repeatedly separated the "Old Bay State," as he called it, from that "noon of night," as Phillips called it—the region south of the Mason-Dixon line.

Phillips therefore ended his introduction by looking forward to the time when "New England, cutting loose from a blood-stained Union, shall glory in being the house of refuge for the oppressed" (46). Such a schism would "consecrate anew the soil of the Pilgrims as an asylum for the oppressed [and] proclaim our welcome to the slave so loudly, that the tones shall reach every hut in the Carolinas, and make the broken-hearted bondman leap up at the thought of old Massachusetts." Given the Unionist sympathies of both the

Whigs and Democrats in "old Massachusetts," this hoped-for realization of a new Separatism was a futile, if theatrical, gesture, which put off a large number of antislavery sympathizers because of its obvious quixotism.

Even Douglass soon declared his independence from Garrison, whose arbitrary and authoritarian ways made "old Massachusetts" sound mighty like "Old Massa" to the former slave. But in 1849, he was still numbered among the Garrisonites and was included on the platform when they gathered in Plymouth, in preparation for the subsequent meeting in which the ground sacred to the memory of the Pilgrims would be dedicated to the renewed ideal of Separatism. Increasingly, Garrison and his clique gave expression to the old Puritan impulse of which the Liberator was so clearly the reincarnation, if not always in ways he was willing to acknowledge.

V

Wendell Phillips at the meeting in Plymouth in 1849 presented a resolution from the Business Committee that identified "the Puritan" as "emphatically the radical reformer of his day," a notion that had been available ever since Orville Dewey made a similar point in 1825 but had seldom been acknowledged by Garrison or his associates (*Liberator*, December 28, 1849). The Puritan, as Phillips defined him, "was in favor of the largest liberty and the widest toleration of which his age had conceived, his whole course an individual protest against the civil and religious institutions of his time; and hence we proclaim the Anti-Slavery enterprise his lineal and only representative, and this the first real celebration of his landing, the first true to his spirit and worthy of his memory." These last two clauses provide the strongest clue to Garrison's reasons for having suddenly discovered Forefathers' Day, and that was to take it away from the Pilgrim Society, which had made no plans for a celebration in 1849—or, as it turned out, for the year following—for reasons that shall be discussed in Chapter 11.

In 1846, Mark Hopkins had spoken out on Forefathers' Day in Plymouth against slavery, but it was in placating terms offensive to immediate abolitionists. What was needed to honor the Pilgrims truly, as Phillips's resolution stated, was the "speedy abolition of slavery," forwarded by "a spirit of determination, enterprise, self-sacrifice, courage, and absolute reliance on God for success, such as was sublimely exhibited to the world by the Pilgrims of Plymouth Rock—the adventurous exiles of the Mayflower—in their efforts to find a land in which they could enjoy civil and religious liberty." Obviously, there was no need to go to Plymouth in order to make that point, but Garrison not only loved symbolic occasions and settings, but he thrived on opposition and notoriety, which inspired in him the fierce glee attributed to old warhorses and Puritans of the John Endicott stamp.

By all reports (in the *Liberator*), the meeting in Plymouth in 1849 was a great success and boded well for the celebration to come the following year. Parker Pillsbury—a member of the clique and the agent for the Plymouth County Anti-Slavery Society—wrote the editor that "it was a good idea to put 'Plymouth Rock' under the corner of the Temple of Liberty we are erecting, as you so truly did on 'Forefathers' Day.' . . . Your celebration here was worth everything in the cause" (January 11, 1850). Pillsbury testified that the event had sparked a general enthusiasm for reform in Plymouth, inspiring in him the certainty that "our prosperous days may be dawning. May we bear them as well as we have the days of adversity." But neither Pillsbury or Garrison could have foreseen the great gift that would be handed the cause of abolition by the Compromise of 1850 and the consequent passage of the Fugitive Slave Law, which, more than any abolitionist resolution, speaker, or society—or combinations of speakers and societies—brought the sympathy of New England over to antislavery reform. Equally important, by making his infamous speech of March 7 in support of the compromise, Webster may have made more concrete his connection with the Union and the Constitution, but in the minds of many New Englanders he had abdicated his place on the Rock.

The space did not remian vacant long: when Garrison and his friends gathered in Plymouth on Forefathers' Day in 1850 for the 230th anniversary of the Landing, the affair was, according to the *Boston Republican*, especially noteworthy for its "popular thrusts" at Webster, who was no longer "a tower of strength in Plymouth County" (quoted in *Liberator*, January 3, 1851). Sojourner Truth was foremost in assailing Webster as the "confounder of the Constitution," for as a black woman and a former slave—as well as a speaker rivaling Douglass in power—she took especial warrant from her color and personal history. As in 1849, a resolution was forthcoming from the Business Committee, which once again cited the Pilgrims as radicals, adding this time that they had "asserted the supremacy of the higher law of God over the inferior law of man." This was a new note in abolitionist rhetoric that had been introduced into the debate by Senator William H. Seward, in his outraged response on March 11 to Webster's speech four days earlier supporting Clay's compromise measures and the Fugitive Slave Law.

In promoting the anniversary meeting, Garrison employed his usual genius, boosting the "GRAND CELEBRATION AT PLYMOUTH" and encouraging his readers to "let the attendance and spirit give proof, that we regard the right of conscience and free speech as did our Pilgrim ancestors, worthy of sacrifice" (December 20, 1850). Garrison also informed Pilgrim-minded persons that tickets for what amounted to an excursion train were available at bargain rates, and provided the scheduled times of departure, thereby fitting a Yankee blade to his Puritan handle. These particulars are less important than the sudden, if not finally surprising, phenomenon of Garrison and his cohort taking over the Pilgrims and the Rock for their own ideological purposes.

Thus the correspondent from Plymouth reported in the *Liberator* on January 3, 1851, that "we have had many anti-slavery meetings in Plymouth, but never such a gathering as this. . . . If a slave hunt could be attempted at Plymouth . . . it would take a strong force to remove a fugitive slave from this town, even if his defence should be left to the women alone. . . . 'The Pilgrims' spirit has not fled.'" A year later, the *Liberator* reprinted a review in the *New York Christian Inquirer* of George Hillard's address before the New England Society in New York, in which Webster's memorialist had steadfastly defended the Whig position on the Fugitive Slave Law. The reviewer declared that "an oration on Plymouth rock on the obligation to return fugitive slaves, seems to us a desecration of the holy spot whence American liberty took her departure" (January 23, 1852).

In the following chapter we will be considering a collateral track, by means of which a number of abolitionist writers not directly affiliated with Garrison anticipated and reinforced his attempts to radicalize the Pilgrims (and Pilgrimize his radicals). It was an evolution that would have at its far end one of Wendell Phillips's finest rhetorical moments, when in 1855 he seized the anniversary day in Plymouth from the hands of the Pilgrim Society for the cause of abolition. This was a speech that, unlike his famous "coming-over" performance in 1837, was less a spontaneous than a well-rehearsed bit of forensic theater, preparations for which may be seen in the sequence of antislavery celebrations of Forefathers' Day, commencing in 1849. Played against Webster's notorious reneging on his position on slavery in 1820, the emergence of Wendell Phillips in 1855 was the culmination of a process that began by inviting, then honoring George Thompson by "standing on the Rock." In making that gesture, in taking that stance, Phillips was hardly innocent of the subversive implication of what he was doing, nor was he, we may imagine, ignorant of George Blagden's earlier assumption of the same position on the Rock—and what came of it in the afternoon.

Whatever the reasons, explicit and tacit, behind the decision by Garrison and his clique to take over Forefathers' Day for their own purposes, it meant displacing the usual Whig display of platitudes. It was therefore equivalent to the moment, seventy years earlier, when the Liberty Boys attempted to co-opt the Old Colony Club's plans for the anniversary of the Landing. Though perhaps a marginal event in the history of the abolition movement, it assuredly meant a major shift of emphasis in the uses to which the Pilgrims and their Rock had hitherto been put. And what Garrison was attempting to do in 1849 (and, more pointedly, in 1850) was what George Thompson's tour de force had accomplished in 1834, a turnabout that would capture for abolition the anniversary sacred to the Whig establishment, much as Garrison had earlier taken over the Fourth of July. Once again, by casting themselves in the image of the Pilgrims, they thereby realized Orville Dewey's notion, expressed a quarter century earlier, that the Forefathers were "the first successful asserters of the free and liberal principles of modern times." At last, as Thoreau observed of John Brown's capture of rifles stored at the Harpers Ferry armory, the tools of revolution were in the right hands once again.

CHAPTER II

Written on the Rock

Give it only the fulcrum of Plymouth Rock,
an idea will upheave the continent.
—Wendell Phillips

I

When Daniel Webster in 1820 took charge of the Rock, it was as an icon already sacred to civil and religious liberty, which he opposed to the notorious traffic in slaves. George Blagden, likewise, evoked Plymouth Rock in association with his scheme for evangelizing the South into emancipation. Thus, when Garrison finally "discovered" the Pilgrims and their Rock in 1849 and began to associate immediatism with the Forefathers, it was not that the Rock had moved into the neighborhood of radicalism but rather that it had remained where it was then standing, which was where the Liberty Boys had moved it at the start of the Revolution.

Essential to the radical impulse is a reactionary primitivism, and like the orthodox celebrants of the Pilgrims, Garrison's attempts to seize the day and place sacred to the Landing were intended to return the occasion to its original purity—whether associated with the newly arrived Pilgrims, the Patriots of 1775, or a Webster capable of speaking out against the traffic in slaves. As a symbolic gesture, it was part and parcel of Garrison's oft stated desire to purify a degenerate New England, the old orthodox errand but with a definably Arminian burden, and it provided warrant for his subsequent secessionist argument. But other voices of protest, who lacked Garrison's deep social wounds, had already picked up Orville Dewey's theme of 1825 and like Sam May were associating, for better and for worse, the Pilgrims with the spirit of reform.

In Dover, New Hampshire, in 1836, the Reverend David Root of that town read a sermon to the Haverhill Anti-Slavery Society in which he not only defended the use of harsh language by the abolitionists but compared them in "steadfast integrity of character" both to the "patriots of the revolution" and "the Pilgrim Fathers of our own New England" (10, 14–15). What recommends these sentiments to us is not only that they promoted an association that Garrison—already under fire for his abrasive and violent language—would eventually foster but that the secretary of the Haverhill Anti-Slavery Society in 1836 was John Greenleaf Whittier, who was also one of the committee of three who requested from Root a copy of his sermon for publication. For Whittier would soon enough emerge as the poet laureate of the abolition movement, whose poems of protest were not only deeply informed by American history but celebrated the Pilgrims as nascent abolitionists.

And yet, because of his own origins, Whittier was never in total agreement with Garrison and his clique, and his personal and political background presents an amalgam that suggests strong affinities with the Liberator's nemesis, Daniel Webster. Where Garrison was a city boy who had grown up a virtual orphan, Whittier, like Webster, was raised on a New Hampshire farm in which family ties were firm and affectionate. Unlike Squire Webster, Whittier's father could not afford to send his talented son to college, but the boy hired himself out as a shoemaker in order to cover his tuition in the local academy. It was the only advanced schooling Whittier would receive, no barrier at the time to his chosen career as a journalist and a step beyond Garrison's education, whose experience as a cobbler was hardly voluntary.

Whittier's most famous and beloved poem, *Snow-Bound* (1866), celebrated the domestic harmony of his boyhood with a view toward fostering a mood of reconciliation that the poet hoped would follow the Union victory in the Civil War, and a similar spirit pervades much of his public life in the years before the war became inevitable. The support from the network of societies that Garrison built through his abolitionist activities Whittier received from his loving mother and sisters, so intimate a context that he seems never (unlike Garrison, a dedicated family man) to have felt the need for marriage and children of his own. It is a connection that validates the mediational basis of his ideology, for Whittier was from the start of his public career a Whig, sympathetic to Webster's fervent championship of Union, with an outspoken loyalty to that larger, national family against which Garrison was in permanent revolt.

Whittier's early years as a journalist, like Garrison's, were associated with reform-oriented newspapers, but where Garrison was a remnant Federalist, Whittier championed Henry Clay's perpetual candidacy for the presidency until it crumbled under the pressure of the increasing intransigency of the South. Whittier then switched his allegiance first to the Liberty and then the Free-Soil Party, always searching for a peaceful, political settlement to the slavery question. If Webster's Unionism was underwritten by his Unitarian faith, Garrison's separatism by the dual inheritance of a secessionist Federalism and a Baptist evangelism, so Whittier's pacific inclinations were warranted, even dictated, by his Quaker faith, a religion that, like that of the Unitarians, pre-fereth a soft word always, as opposed to the Garrisonian exhortative and abrasive heritage.

Yet Whittier was early on associated with Garrison and the Massachusetts Anti-Slavery Society. In the 1820s, before either man had become identified with abolition, Garrison had published Whittier's first stumbling efforts in verse, the kind of favor that poets seldom forget. But on important points of ideology, Whittier differed from Garrison, especially regarding the justifiable use of violence, which for the Quaker was an oxymoron. Thus, bucking the tidal wave of sympathy for Elijah Lovejoy, Whittier stubbornly tried to intro-duce a resolution at a meeting of the American Anti-Slavery Society that condemned the martyr's use of arms at Alton. It was both a logical extension of his pacifist faith and a stark contrast to Garrison's willingness to compromise his own pacifist principles for the sake of ideological advantage. And where Garrison drifted inexorably toward rhetorical extremes that ended with his burning a copy of the Constitution, Whittier remained steadfast in his hope of attaining reconciliation with the South and eventually parted company with the abolitionist movement.

Even in his poems written to forward the cause of abolition, he called out for the slave states to join the "union" of free states, and though there is an implicit separatism in that rhetorical distinction, Whittier put the division to work for an end antithetical to Garrison's hoped-for disunion. He sought, that is, to mend, not widen, the breech between North and South, to heal and not to wound. Significantly, where Garrison perpetually waved the national shame about like a battle flag, addressing himself to present crises ever new, Whittier tended from the very start to regard New England's past as a foundation for the modern tradition of civil liberties. And rather than point out glaring contra-dictions between the ideal and the real, he worked to bring the nation back on the course set by the Forefathers. His was a perspective that puts him with Samuel May and Emerson in that division between "Pilgrims" and "Puritans" framed by George Frisbie Hoar, and, as we shall see, Whittier himself in his poetry and prose writings often made the same distinction.

Likewise, Whittier's conciliatory and scholarly disposition places him with Webster and Everett as Whig celebrants of national memory. He also shared with Rufus Choate a faith in the power of literature to effect a more per-fect union, and about the time that Choate delivered his Salem address that pointed to Scott as a model for American writers, Whittier was planning "a work of fiction, which shall have for its object the reconciliation of the North and the South,—being simply an endeavor to do away with some of the preju-dices of the Southron and the Yankee" (Pickard, 1:101). According to his biog-rapher and nephew, Whittier planned to mingle elements of Sterne "and the smooth gracefulness of W. Irving," a curious and ironical note given Irving's own at least fictional hostility toward the Yankee as well as his considerable contribution to the plantation house myth by way of his influence on John Pendleton Kennedy. The novel was never written, or rather it had already appeared in a reasonable facsimile as *Northwood: A Tale of New England* by Sarah Josepha Hale in 1827, a Webster-friendly novel resolutely Unionist in sympathies and sharing Whittier's faith in the domestic bond as salvational to both the individual and the nation.

But by 1850, shocked into a rude awakening by Webster's March 7 speech, Whittier finally abandoned his faith in the Whig Party, signaling his departure with his devastatingly effective "Ichabod," the last (and highly allusive) fragment also of his earlier admiration for Irving. And yet Whittier continued to seek a political solution to the problem of slavery, where Garrison and Wendell Phillips preferred to remain pure and (in the eyes of many) ineffective in their unbending moral postures. And, once again, Whittier in his poetry and prose continued to inform the modern instance by means of historical analogues. But in his hands, the progressive view of history had an iron edge, thanks also to his Quaker heritage, which gave him a perspective on the Puritans shared by few other prominent Whig writers, his ancestors having felt the bite of that lash whose use the liberal celebrants of colonial Massachusetts either lamented or ignored.

II

Whittier was perpetually, even constitutionally fair minded and had stated the positive side of the Puritan equation in his first pamphlet promoting abolition, *Justice and Expediency* (1833). There he examined the roots of the anti-slavery movement in New England, tracing it to laws against slavery framed in colonial Massachusetts. "It was," he declared, "the Puritan's recognition of the brotherhood of man in sin, suffering, and redemption, his estimate of the awful responsibilities and eternal destinies of humanity, his hatred of wrong and tyranny, and his stern sense of justice, which led him to impose upon the African slave-trader the terrible penalty of the Mosaic code" (*Writings*, 7:124).

By Whittier's accounting in 1833, New England was perpetually the good example, minor flaws aside, and its particular star of virtue was Massachusetts: "At this time, there is no state more thorough in its practical adoption of . . . democratic principles. No property qualifications or religious tests prevail; all distinctions of sect, birth, or color, are repudiated, and suffrage is universal. The [spirit of] democracy, which in the South has only been held in a state of gaseous abstraction, hardened into concrete reality in the cold air of the North," a geo(ideo)logical perspective that allied him not only with Garrison but with Federalist celebrants of New England's virtue like Josiah Quincy.

With Everett and other memorialists of the Pilgrims, Whittier credited the New England difference to the rockiness of its soil and the rigor of its winters. It was an environment that encouraged the development of hardihood and hard work, a "system of economy and industry" that, if shared by Virginia, would have given that region "Freemen in the place of slaves, industry, reputable economy, a virtue, dissipation despised, emigration unnecessary" (84). Much as New England's heritage of freedom and prosperity may be traced to the principles established by the Forefathers, so it is the "very reputation of our fathers, the honor of our land, every principle of liberty, humanity, expediency" that mandate antislavery reform on the part of their descendants: "Short of liberty and equality we cannot stop without doing injustice to their memories" (28). Though his conclusions were similar to Garrison's, Whittier's was a reasoned argument with a Whiggish respect for precedent and the authority of history; and while the other man was still using the Declaration of Independence as a universal unit of measure, Whittier established a line originating with the Forefathers of New England that provided a mandate for the future conduct of its people.

Implicit in Whittier's historical perspective was the strategy of the jeremiad, Garrison's favorite implement, yet his use of the past was hortatory, not punitive. And when in his poetry Whittier went on the attack, he generally employed ridicule, not self-righteous sermonizing, and yet, as early as 1837, was quite capable of reversing his emphasis where the Puritans were concerned in order to make a satiric point. In that year the Congregational clerisy had published a "Pastoral Letter" that mandated the closing of their pulpits to itinerant evangelists and other promoters of unrest. It was a measure with a clearly political agenda, and among the main targets were women who sought to address congregations on radical issues. The stated goal was to remove their churches as settings for "perplexed and agitating subjects" that promoted "alienation and division," language that provided a target so huge and palpating that Whittier could not but reach for his sharpest pen. In his poetic response, "The Pastoral Letter," Whittier recalled for the Congregationalists those "glorious days, when Church and State / Were wedded by your spiritual fathers," a painful subject for ministers who had so recently lost their status as the "Standing Order."

But that was the poet's intention throughout, to make the clergy as uncomfortable as possible, playing upon the assertion of the orthodox that they were the true apostles of the Good Old Way. Whittier reminded them sarcastically of the glory days of Cotton Mather, when "no vile 'it'nerant' then could mar / The beauty of your tranquil Zion, / But at his peril of the scar / Of hangman's whip and branding-iron." This too was part of the Good Old Way, inseparable from the maintenance of virtue and the establishment of universal education, which last was not exclusive of flogging. Whittier next played upon the commitment of the modern orthodoxy to reasonable and moderate discourse on the subject of abolition, but in drawing the following distinctions between modern Congregationalism and old Puritanism he mostly emphasized the similarities:

> Your fathers dealt not as ye deal
> With "non-professing" frantic teachers;
> They bored the tongue with red-hot steel,
> And flayed the backs of "female preachers."
> Old Hampton, had her fields a tongue,
> And Salem's streets could tell their story,
> Of fainting woman dragged along,
> Gashed by the whip accursed and gory! (51)

Whittier's allusion to "female preachers" being flogged by the Puritans was intended to perform double duty, serving as a reminder of how Quaker women who invaded the pulpit in the Good Old Days were punished, but striking out as well at the orthodox animadversions in their pastoral letter against women speaking in public. This last was in obvious reference to the abolitionist lectures of the Grimké sisters, highly effective allies of Garrison and the wife and sister-in-law of Theodore Weld. The effect of Whittier's devastating analogue aside, the clerisy's attempt at repression was self-destructive: a young woman who viewed the Congregational conference at North Brookfield that authorized the pastoral letter was so infuriated by the sight of "the Reverend Doctor Blagden walking up and down the aisle, turning his head from side to side and looking up at the women in the gallery with an air that seemed to say, 'Now! Now we have silenced you!' " that she resolved on the spot to become a public lecturer (Blackwell, 25). The woman was Lucy Stone, who became one of abolition's most outspoken and popular advocates and an ardent champion of female suffrage and whose testimony bears witness that the Reverend Dr. Blagden's notion of conciliatory and tolerant postures and an open forum did not extend to women, who should be kept in the gallery, where they belonged.

In this particular, Blagden and his Congregational colleagues were fiercely opposed by Whittier, despite his own opposition to weakening the abolition movement by concurrently agitating for women's rights—another matter on which he disagreed with Garrison. In his "Pastoral Letter" he converted the atrocities of the Puritan past, whether "manhood to the scaffold led" or "suffering and heroic woman," to a lecture on repression in general: he was motivated, Whittier claimed, to turn "The pages of intolerance over, / That in their spirit, dark and stern, / Ye haply may your own discover!" This was hardly the heritage of the Puritans that modern Congregationalists wished to acknowledge, but it was certainly in line with Samuel May's response to Joel Hawes.

Moreover, by holding up the embossed mirror of the past to the faces of the present, Whittier reinforced Leonard Bacon's demonstration that same year that to whatever use you put New England's history, those dark chapters of bigotry and persecution could not be erased but were interlocked with the positive aspects of the Puritan legacy. Thus, if modern democratic institutions could be traced back to the first generation, so also could the modern version of repression expressed in the pastoral letter: "Alas! in hoof and horns and features, / How different is your Brookfield bull / From him who bellows from St. Peter's!" (50–51). And in shaming the ministers by evoking the pope (Roman Catholicism being at that time under savage attack by Congregational stalwarts), Whittier's image of "hoof and horns" also suggests the traditional features of the Devil. "The Pope," observed Sam May wryly in 1830, "was not the only Anti-Christ."

Notably, the thrust of Whittier's "Pastoral Letter," by stressing the negative side of the Puritan heritage, reversed the emphasis of his early pamphlet, *Justice and Expediency*. Perhaps because of the increasing intransigency of the orthodox toward the activities of abolitionists, which made Whittier's balanced view of the Puritans less and less tenable, when he finally wrote his only extended work of fiction, in 1849, it was not along the lines projected in the early 1830s but was very much in the spirit of Hawthorne.

Margaret Smith's Journal is framed as an autobiographical narrative written by a young English woman touring the province of Massachusetts in 1678–79, and the story moves back and forth between lyrical descriptions of New England scenery and depictions of the people who live there as superstitious bigots and pompously self-righteous persecutors of Quakers and helpless old women charged with witchcraft. In effect, Whittier's novel provides a tour through Memory's Nation, not, however, the heroic period of New England's past but that later time associated with those episodes that Rufus Choate would have had neglected by writers and hence removed from memory's landscape.

In contrast to his obvious delight in recalling the crimes against dissenters by the Puritans of Salem and Boston, Whittier generally credited only favorable attributes to the Pilgrims, this at a time when most commentators conflated the two groups. Throughout his antislavery poems we find repeated evocations of the "Pilgrim spirit," "Pilgrim blood," "Pilgrim pulse," "Pilgrim's banner," and the like, always in a positive, exhortative context. In his "Stanzas for the Times" (1835), Whittier spoke out against the repression of free speech in Boston, inspired by objections made by a proslavery meeting in Faneuil Hall that the activities of abolitionists were "endangering the foundation of commercial society" (35). In attacking these encroachments on civil rights, Whittier reminded New England of its heritage, not Puritan repression and censorship but the legacy of "Plymouth's rock, and Bunker's mound . . . each spot of haunted ground / Where Freedom weeps her children's fall" (35). As we have seen, Garrison often seasoned his discourse with ready, if superficial, references to the Pilgrim heritage, but Whittier made much more substantial use of it, in the manner of a Forefathers' Day orator summoning up the ghost of the Pilgrim past to haunt the present degeneracy of New England: "What faces frown upon ye, dark," he wrote in "Moloch in State Street," "With shame and pain? / Come these from Plymouth's Pilgrim bark?" (166).

This is the same jeremiad strategy that Garrison used by referring to the heroes of the Revolution, but in line with his mediational politics Whittier's was an alternative vein of invective, in which the rhetoric of blame and shame played a relatively minor role. Much more typical of his muse was a poetic epistle supposedly written from Kansas by an Episcopalian priest (a sect associated with the South), who was apprehensive about "The Yankee abolitionists [who] are coming / Upon us like a flood—grim, stalwart men, / Each face set like a flint of Plymouth Rock / Against our institutions" (180). And in 1854 Whittier put in the mouths of "Kansas Emigrants" similar sentiments: "We cross the prairie as of old / The pilgrims crossed the sea, / To make the West, as they the East, / The homestead of the free!" (176).

This evangelical burden is epitomized in one of Whittier's most complex and effective abolitionist poems, "The Panorama," written late in his antislavery career, 1856, a time when deep lines of division were being drawn in the national dispute in terms of both ideology and geopolitics. Breaking with his former mediational posture, Whittier adopted Garrison's rhetoric of division at last. The title refers to that now forgotten aspect of showmanship in mid-nineteenth-century America where a lengthy canvas displaying a changing scene—as, for example, life along the length of the Mississippi River—would be unrolled on a stage with informative commentary by the showman in charge.

These were impressive displays, the very dimensions of the huge canvas scrolls (advertised as being "a mile long") adding an element of promotional awe, and were enjoyed by Americans as diverse in their tastes as Longfellow and Thoreau. But Whittier's was a panorama with a difference, for his showman unrolls a scroll with considerable more propagandistic bite than the usual travelogue sequence: it displays the alternative cultures of slavery and freedom, projected in turn upon the backdrop of a western Eden, a "mystic West," "the new Canaan of our Israel," a prospect (and a metaphor) historically associated with both the "swarming hive" of the North and the "poor Southron on his worn-out soil, / Scathed by the curses of unnatural toil" (3:195).

Informed by the ongoing debate as to whether slavery will be permitted in the Kansas and Nebraska Territories, Whittier's poem looks back to the distinction he drew in *Justice and Expediency* between North and South, in which he pointed out that if Virginia had shared a heritage of adversity and industry with New England, it would have had no need of slaves but would have developed a "reputable economy" and found "emigration unnecessary." By 1856, the South still needs to find fresh fields to cultivate, and New England is being encouraged to send out emigrants for quite a different reason, namely to extend its institutions into the West, which will either become a bustling scene of peaceful productiveness or "Fate's reverse," a region cursed by slavery, which brings with it a tolerance of dissipation and a general lack of moral fiber.

Whittier's showman is not merely content to display the alternative futures for the West but lectures in pointed terms, reserving his fiercest comments not for the "Southron" but for those Northerners who temporize, "Who watch and wait, and from the wrong's control / Keep white and pure their chastity of soul" (201). By 1856, Whittier saw the worst enemies of abolition as belonging to the party of Expedience, whose timorousness in the face of injustice compared unfavorably with the outspoken language of "the braggart Southron," who was at least "open in his aim," direct and destructive as a cannonball (202). By contrast, there was "the mean traitor, breathing northern air" without inhaling virtue, a veritable caricature of Yankee smugness, "With nasal speech and puritanic hair, / Whose cant the loss of principle survives, / As the mud-turtle e'en his head outlives" (202). These latter-day "Puritans," to be identified generally with those orthodox ministers still counseling moderation, may be distinguished from the modern "Pilgrims," whose covered wagons are *Mayflowers* in miniature.

By contrast to his pacifist, Unionist ideology, Whittier in this late poem against slavery is the master of a ferocious invective, who approaches the extremes that Leonard Bacon associated with the Quakers of the seventeenth century, so unlike the quiet, mild-mannered demeanor of their modern descendants. While it is a mistake to identify a poetic voice—especially when the vehicle is satire—with the personality of the poet, there remains a puzzling contradiction between Whittier's deeply reconciliatory nature and the violence of his muse in "The Panorama." And yet we can see in poems like "Ichabod" and earlier efforts occasional flashes of equivalent outrage, which suggests that in Whittier's view poetry could serve as a conduit channeling anger into a useful and presumably harmless artifact, under the assumption that no one ever died from a poem.

But if this was the case, then Whittier seems eventually to have realized that violence in whatever form begets violence, for his poems most certainly made the way straight for an episode that put Lovejoy's use of arms in the shade of an apocalyptic darkness. Soon enough one of those personified Plymouth Rocks rolling through Kansas would turn into something of a juggernaut, a destructive engine of self-righteousness that would not only put Whittier's pacifist faith once more to the test but would contribute to his decision to depart the abolitionist movement—and his violent muse—for good and all.

III

Of a similar order and effect to Whittier's use of the Pilgrims as avatars of virtue in verse forwarding the cause of abolition were the radical writings of James Russell Lowell, whose poems of protest during the 1840s were powerful celebrations of the Puritan spirit, without Whittier's saving grace of Quaker principles or Garrison's problematic attitude toward New England's past. Less prolific than Whittier in the production of protest verse, and the master of a fine anger that was as a rapier to Garrison's knobby rhetorical club, Lowell wrote some very memorable lines while under the influence of reform. Yet beneath his reforming zeal, he concealed a deeply conservative core. Indeed, Lowell provides a lively demonstration that abolition had many faces, for he wore quite a few.

Born into a wealthy family with a tradition of antislavery sentiments, raised in a home decorated by a portrait of Wilberforce, Lowell while at Harvard kicked over that as well as other traces, taking the opportunity of his "College Poem" to ridicule abolitionists and reform in general. Planning on a genteel and privileged life dedicated to literature, Lowell, like Wendell Phillips, fell in love with a reformer, hence with reform, and married both and for the next decade devoted his literary skills to abolition. But with the death of Maria White, Lowell abandoned ultra-abolitionism and became a Unionist, thereby reversing the evolution of Whittier's radicalism. Where Whittier's Unionism was integral to his Quaker religion, Lowell's was a political faith touched with a mysticism perhaps absorbed from Carlyle but which was certainly akin to Emersonian transcendentalism. Yet in terms of style and attitude, Lowell was closer to Carlyle than was Emerson himself.

Carlyle may be said to have worn his transcendental philosophy like a thick German cloak over an angular Calvinism, but of Lowell we may observe that the disguise was never very effective, and in time the corners wore through the fabric and became the main items of display. For the outbreak of the Civil War awoke in Lowell a fierce nationalism, always a conservative impulse, which swept away the rags and tatters of his vestigial radicalism, leaving the Calvinist in full view. Upon war's end he wrote a defense of Puritanism that advanced Judge Story's apologia of 1828 into a hard-edged *tractatus* on the necessary limits of liberty, in effect translating John Winthrop into the latter half of the nineteenth century. Eventually, his early, radical poems were cut into snippets suitable as decoration for the speeches of an emerging class of postwar Republicans who were largely responsible for the reactionary reconstruction of the Puritan idea. By both intention and accident, Lowell became an apologist for the Protestant ethic, with its emphasis on the beauties of hard work that is essential to Carlyle but only tacit in Emerson's writings.

Where Phillips, like Garrison, continued to promote radical agendas until his death, Lowell even more than Whittier (who after the war wrote poems on behalf of the labor movement) became disenchanted with politicized reform. Had Maria not died, his reversion might have been delayed, but it was perhaps inevitable, if only because of Lowell's boisterous sense of humor, a dubious gift for anyone thinking of a career in reform. Lowell stands, that is, at the extreme end of the spectrum from Garrison, and between them we can place Phillips of the wry smile and Whittier with his often savage (but hardly comedic) satire. There is an element of playfulness in Lowell's advocacy for reform that may have been derived from Carlyle's cosmic laughter but which also suggests a certain lack of commitment to the cause of abolition. That is, he often employed in his writings for reform a raillery equivalent to that by which the man from Ecclefechan kept himself at an ironic distance from his materials but which in Lowell suggests a lack of absolute commitment, validated by his consequent retreat into conservatism.

I V

Lowell's best-known contribution to abolition (and perhaps to literature as well) was *The Biglow Papers* (1848), a Carlylean gallimaufry that is part learned interlocution, part dialect poetry (counterpoint familiar to the minstrel show), the chief target of which was not slavery so much as the Mexican War and the tergiversations of Whig politicians. It is also a comic celebration of the Yankee character by a man who was most definitely not one of them, the origins of which are traced in an introductory essay by the "editor," a Unitarian minister, Homer Wilbur, "A.M.," all the way back to "our Plymouth rock, where a handful of men, women, and children not merely faced, but vanquished, winter, famine, the wilderness" (*Writings*, 10:49). To this familiar, if facetious, note, the "editor" adds an evolutionary account that mocks the conventional pieties of orations celebrating the anniversary of the Landing.

Thus by Lowell's account the Pilgrims were able to conquer the wilderness and its adversities because they were "a hard-faced, atrabilious, earnest-eyed race, stiff from long wrestling with the Lord in prayer, and who had taught Satan to dread the new Puritan hug. Add two hundred years' influence of soil, climate, and exposure, with its necessary result of idiosyncrasies, and we have the present Yankee" (48). Any number of the Forefathers' celebrants, from Edward Everett to Whittier, credited the New England character to the effects of soil and climate, but Lowell, unlike Whittier, seems to be conflating the

Pilgrims with the Puritan bluenoses, a mixture expressed by Lowell's own phrase, the "strange hybrid" derived from "the old Puritan" (49). Put the modern Yankee on a desert island, poses Lowell, "and he would make a spelling-book first, and a salt-pan afterward."

In a later chapter, we will be considering the genesis of the Yankee as it relates to New England's sensibilities regarding its revised place in the world. But its relevance to Lowell's poem is slight, for the chief "Yankee" in question, Hosea Biglow, is a collateral cousin to Seba Smith's Major Jack Downing, which is to say he is a distinctly literary creation, intended to represent the animadversions of the "common man" toward the politicians who claim to represent his interests. Lowell is generally thought to have been faultless in his use of Yankee dialect, but in his hands it is not an instrument of local color but a weapon turned against the Mexican War, conceived as a Southern attempt to extend its power (and slavery) westward at the cost of the lives of young Americans inspired to enlist by having their vainglorious ambitions aroused. Along the way, Lowell parodied the postures of political candidates who, after being elected, change their "convictions" with the alacrity of the vicar of Bray and whose speeches are filled with noble but meaningless phrases, including hackneyed references to "The American eagle,—the Pilgrims thet landed,— / Till on ole Plymouth Rock they git finally stranded" (103). That is, they end up back where the process first began, the threshold now a rhetorical desert island.

The Biglow Papers, with its humorous version of the Pilgrims and their celebrants, needs to be put into the perspective of other poems by Lowell written in the service of reform, serious verse in the high Victorian—but detectably Carlylean—mode. In "Freedom," one of the poems Lowell contributed during his years as corresponding editor (1848–51) of the *National Anti-Slavery Standard*—the most literate of the abolitionist journals—he threw back into their faces the Whig orators' customary Forefathers' Day boast about the Pilgrim heritage of liberty: "We are not free," the poet announced, for freedom is not a permanent or secure situation but must constantly be sought (9:275). Freedom is not a matter of the past but of the future and can only be glimpsed as from a mountaintop, a distant and boundless prospect: it is ours only "if we be strong,"

> Or if we shrink, better remount our ships
> And fleeing God's express design, trace back
> The hero-freighted Mayflower's prophet-track
> To Europe entering her blood-red eclipse. (276)

"Hail to thee, poor little ship Mayflower, of Delft-Haven," wrote Carlyle in *Chartism* in 1839, "poor common-looking ship . . . yet what ship Argo, or miraculous epic ship built by the Sea-Gods, was other than a foolish bumbarge in comparison? Golden fleeces or the like these sailed for . . . [but] thou little Mayflower hadst in thee a veritable Promethean spark; the life-spark of the largest Nation on our Earth,—so we may already name the Transatlantic Saxon Nation. They went seeking leave to hear sermon in their own method, these Mayflower Puritans; a most honest, indispensable search; . . . seeking a small thing, they found this unexpected great thing! Honour to the brave and true; they verily, we say, carry fire from Heaven, and have a power that themselves dream not of. Let all men honor Puritanism, since God has so honored it" (29:179). The Carlylean resonances in Lowell's celebration of the *Mayflower* are unmistakable and may be found also in his most famous evocation of the Pilgrim ark as a vessel of radical change, which occurs in his great and often quoted "The Present Crisis."

This is a poem written in 1845 whose refrain translates John Robinson's farewell to the departing Pilgrims into terms evoking the nineteenth-century faith in progressive change: "New occasions teach new duties; Time makes ancient good uncouth; / They must upward still, and onward, who would keep abreast of Truth" (191). A stirring anthem, with a detectably Carlylean emphasis in both its sentiments and its language, and with an emphasis on the need for heroic and positive actions celebrated in common by contemporary British poets as unlike as Browning and Tennyson, Lowell's poem reveals the essential religiosity of reform, whether or not actually connected to a sect. Assuming the elevated stance of Victorian seriousness, Lowell looks back to the voyage of 1620: "Was the Mayflower launched by cowards, steered by men behind their time? / Turn those tracks toward Past or Future, that make Plymouth rock sublime?" (190).

Though the poet himself is looking backward, it is clear that the Pilgrims did not, Lowell's being that characteristic American use of the associationist aesthetic, which starting with Webster in 1820 calculates the importance of historic events in terms of their impact on the future. It is the Pilgrims' prophetic "track" that gives Plymouth Rock its sublimity, his Pilgrims being "men of present valor, stalwart old iconoclasts," whose "truth" is turned into the "falsehood" of "history": "Hoarding it in mouldy parchments, while our tender spirits flee / The rude grasp of the great Impulse which drove them across the sea" (190).

This is again that activist theme associated with Carlyle's handling of Past and Present, reading history as a register of a transcendental "great Impulse." And it is in terms recalling Sam May's ungentle handling of Joel Hawes's orthodox "defense" of the Pilgrims, for Lowell labels "traitors to our sires," those men who make "their creed our jailer." Once again, as the May connection attests, this is the reading of Robinson's farewell that is associated with Unitarian celebrations of the Pilgrims, which regard change as progressive, desirable, and inevitable. It is in harmony also with Emerson's antipathy toward the "dead hand" of the past, even with Longfellow's beamish "Excelsior," to say nothing of Tennyson's "Ulysses": "We ourselves must Pilgrims be," Lowell mandates, "Launch our Mayflower, and steer boldly through the desperate winter sea, / Nor attempt the Future's portal with the Past's blood-rusted key" (191).

Published in the *Boston Courier* on December 11, 1845, Lowell's poem is yet another anticipatory hint of Garrison's identification of the Pilgrims with the cause of abolition. The date is close up against Forefathers' Day, indeed was the actual day (Old Style) of the original Landing, and it thereby challenges the usual celebration by Whigs anxious to invoke the Pilgrim spirit in a manner that reinforces the status quo. As if to reinforce this emphasis, in another poem published in the *Courier* later that same month, "An Interview with Miles Standish," Lowell became much more specific about the failings of modern commemorations of the Landing. Imitating the oratorical convention of summoning up a Pilgrim ghost, he turned the trope to quite a different end from the usual purpose of convivial necromancy.

Seated by his evening fire, the poet finds a ghostly presence materializing in his "antique high-backed Spanish chair. . . . A figure grim and rusty, / Whose doublet plain and plainer hose / Were something worn and dusty" (9:223). Because of a "buccaneerish air" about this unearthly visitor in "garb outlandish," the poet hopes he will learn of a treasure buried behind the wall, but the visitor's message is otherwise: "Just then the ghost drew up his chair / And said, 'My name is Standish.' "

> "I come from Plymouth, deadly bored
> With toasts, and songs, and speeches,
> As long and flat as my old sword,
> As threadbare as my breeches:
> They understand us Pilgrims! they
> Smooth men with rosy faces,
> Strength's knots and gnarls all pared away,
> And varnish in their places. . . .
> *They* talk about their Pilgrim blood,
> Their birthright high and holy!
> A mountain stream that ends in mud
> Methinks is melancholy." (224)

Where Jeffersonian editors forty years earlier had ridiculed the Federalists for insulting the memories of the abstemious Pilgrims with a vast consumption of liquor, Lowell pillories their descendants the festive Whigs for worshiping "the sacred compromises" sanctioned by the Constitution. The result is an irony somewhat outside Lowell's frame, given that the compromises were made to pacify the modern (Democratic) descendants of Jeffersonian Republicans:

> "Those loud ancestral boasts of yours,
>   How can they else than vex us?
> Where were your dinner orators
>   When Slavery grasped at Texas?"

In opposition to the supple motions of the Whigs, Lowell places the "stiff knees" of Standish, who half draws out his sword in a threatening gesture, refusing to play "forefather to such a rout," men who so willingly bow their noses "to the stone / When Slavery feels like grinding" (225). Instead, the old soldier delivers a prophecy, reading in the coming of dawn a "forewarning" of some new, messianic hero soon to arrive:

> "Child of our travail and our woe,
>   Light in our day of sorrow,
> Through my rapt spirit I foreknow
>   The glory of thy morrow;
> I hear great steps, that through the shade,
>   Draw nigher still and nigher,
> And voices call like that which bade
>   The prophet come up higher." (226)

This idea of a Savior shaped by the forces of the age is not the same thing as the Whig notion of the Great Man but is Carlylean and apocalyptic. Earlier that year, Lowell had published another poem in the *Courier*—whose editor, Joseph T. Buckingham, was credited with having in him "some Pilgrim-stuff that hates all sham"—"The Capture of Fugitive Slaves near Washington," in which Lowell himself delivered up prophecy. Crediting to the Pilgrims' Landing "on the Bay State's iron shore" a forecast "that slavery should one day be no more," he expressed a certainty that, as in ancient times,

> Out from the land of bondage, 'tis decreed our slaves shall go,
> And signs to us are offered, as erst to Pharaoh,
> If we are blind, their exodus, like Israel's of yore,
> Through a Red Sea is doomed to be, whose surges are
>   Of gore. (299)

Once again, despite Lowell's evocation of the Pilgrims, in spirit as well as birthright he seems himself much closer to the Puritans, with their gemlike morality and penchant for apocalyptic prophecy. His Miles Standish certainly looks forward to Longfellow's gruff *Gloriosus*, but he has something of Endicott's grim feistiness also. Despite the high Victorianism of Lowell's "The

Present Crisis," it too resonates with the militant zeal Carlyle celebrated in Cromwell, being urgent with a sense of destiny identified with necessary, if bloody, reforms. There is likewise an undeniable Puritan dimension to his satiric attack on the plump descendants of the Pilgrims observing the anniversary of the Landing by loading themselves with food and drink. It is not unlike the opposition of Uncle Toby and Malvolio, if we can imagine Malvolio the hero of the play. There is, that is to say, an element of Garrisonianism in Lowell, despite deep differences in background. With Whittier, he contributed to the progress by means of which the Pilgrims standing on Plymouth Rock would by 1850 take on the likeness of the Liberator, which is to say a lean and Puritanic look, while the Rock itself became a symbol of adamantine (Garrisonian) resolve in the face of continued and often violent opposition.

V

I do not wish to insist on more than the evidence warrants, but there are any number of indications during the decade of the 1840s that abolitionist literature was casting itself into a mold that would have a definitive impress on subsequent events, much as Whittier's violent muse outran his pacifist ideology. Like that torrent of pamphlets published by the American Anti-Slavery Society, the volume of which gave the impression in the South of abolitionist unanimity in the North, we are talking about effects that are undeniable, because cumulative, though chimerical at the start, much as *Uncle Tom's Cabin* is made up of materials derived from the same abolitionist propaganda. Even *Moby-Dick*, that Carlylean anti-Carlyle anatomy, contributes to even as it derives from these contexts, for though Captain Ahab was obviously inspired by Shakespeare's Lear, he has something about him of the the Liberator as well, being outspoken in his opposition to a perceived evil.

Consider the *Liberty Bell*, the annual sold at that yearly Anti-Slavery Fair in Boston, which was published for twenty years, between 1839 and 1859, and whose title and embossed covers evoked the traditional Garrisonite connection with 1776. This famous abolitionist anthology was edited by Maria Weston Chapman, the chief force behind the Boston Female Anti-Slavery Society and one of Garrison's most ardent champions and loyal co-workers. Hers was a gift book with an edge to it, replacing the usual bland miscellany of poems, essays, stories, and steel-plate engravings with similar materials entirely devoted to arousing abolitionist sentiments. It was integral in form and function to those various handicrafts offered for sale at the fair, which merged artifacts of middle-class life with radical slogans. Intended as much for display as consumption, the *Liberty Bell* was meant for the parlor, which given its incendiary contents was like decorating the home with detonator caps. It was a subversive use of commodification that looked forward to *Uncle Tom's Cabin*, which likewise employed all the literary conventions of a sentimental age toward a radical end.

If the *Bell* differed in contents from the usual gift book, it was its general avoidance of historical material, in keeping with Garrison's own bias. Though Chapman herself could claim descent from Pilgrims, unlike Sam May she seems not to have evoked the Landing in connection with antislavery sentiments. Instead, her readers were given literature stressing ideological argument and anecdotes illustrating the harsh treatment suffered by slaves, logging in the kinds of lumber from which *Uncle Tom's Cabin* would be built. Snippets from speeches by Garrison and Phillips were a regular feature, as were Garrison's own impassioned abolitionist sonnets, but as in those speeches and sonnets, little was heard of the Pilgrims and their Rock.

One early exception was a poem in 1840 by John Pierpont, the Unitarian minister and author of the popular *Airs of Palestine* (1816) and the aforementioned editor of school readers featuring occasional literature celebrating the Pilgrims, including his own. As well known in its day as Hemans's anthem was Pierpont's own Forefathers' Day ode, written for the celebration in Plymouth in 1824, "The Pilgrim Fathers,—Where Are They?" By 1840, Pierpont had a good idea where the Pilgrim Fathers could be found, and in a poem entitled "Plymouth Rock," he located them on the north side of the Mason-Dixon Line. Pierpont placed them in a prayerful position on the Rock, asking that their blood "Shall westward flow, till Mississippi's flood / Gives to our children's children his broad plains, / Ne'er let them wear, O God, or forge a bondman's chains!"

More in this freedom-loving-Pilgrim vein would be heard in the years to come, but in 1840 Pierpont's ten brief lines were something of an anomaly in the *Liberty Bell*. This was in keeping with the Garrisonite emphasis at the time, though a foreshadowing of the Liberator's future strategy is suggested by the illustration accompanying the poem, which reproduced the vignette decorating the membership certificate of the Pilgrim Society. And then, in 1848, as Garrison began laying his plans for usurping Plymouth Rock, there appeared "The Runaway Slave at Pilgrim's Point," a long and angry poem that was given even more novelty by its authorship. For the poem was an original contribution solicited by the editor from Elizabeth Barrett Browning, not yet famous for her *Sonnets from the Portuguese* but a rising literary light in Europe nonetheless, who could count among her American fans both Poe and James Russell Lowell.

Browning had thought her longish narrative rather strong stuff, "too ferocious, perhaps, for the Americans to publish," suggesting that she did not sufficiently appreciate the appetite of the Garrisonites for ferocity (*Poetical Works*, 191). That Browning was somewhat nearsighted regarding American matters in general (a common British impairment) is conveyed by the first three stanzas of her poem:

> I stand on the mark beside the shore
>   Of the first white pilgrim's bended knee,
> Where exile turned to ancestor,
>   And God was thanked for liberty.
> I have run through the night, my skin is dark,
> I bend my knee down on this mark:
>   I look on the sky and the sea.
>
> O pilgrim-souls, I speak to you!
>   I see you come proud and slow
> From the land of spirits pale as dew
>   And round me and round me ye go.
> O pilgrims, I have gasped and run
> All night long from the whips of one
>   Who in your names works sin and woe!
>
> And thus I thought that I would come
>   And kneel here where ye knelt before,
> And feel your souls around me hum
>   In undertone to the ocean's roar;
> And lift my black face, my black hand,
> Here in your names, to curse this land,
>   Ye blessed in freedom, evermore. (192)

The line placed in the fugitive's mouth, "Where exile turned to ancestor," is a very effective encapsulation of the liminal process as captured by any number of depictions of the Landing, in a few words evoking the long transition from exile (radical) to ancestor (reactionary) that the Pilgrims experienced in the hands of their posterity. But Browning seems to have had only the most general idea of the circumstances of the Landing, a vacuity challenging Felicia Hemans's former ascendancy in these matters, much as the younger woman replaced the older (now dead) poet in the affections of the reading public—and Wordsworth.

Not only had Browning created something called "Pilgrim's Point" (which is in the title only), but the "mark" on which she places her fugitive's knee lacks the specificity of Plymouth Rock. And in a later stanza the escaped slave speaks of the place "where the pilgrims' ships first anchored lay," suggesting perhaps some confusion with Winthrop's fleet. Poetic license always allows for compression as well as conflation, but what can we make of the extent of ground covered by the slave's flight? In the course of one night her feet take her from a place where "mangos" grow in forests (perhaps "mangroves" were meant) and slaves are driven in gangs between rows of "canes"—presumably sugar of the kind deemed politically incorrect by Maria Chapman and the Female Anti-Slavery Society. Somehow the fugitive has run from Louisiana to Massachusetts in twelve hours' time.

These howlers mitigate the poem's effect but do not gainsay its depth of seriousness, that "ferocity" to which Barrett Browning alluded. The fugitive slave woman is a victim of the miscegenetic curse of bondage, having been forced to submit to the lust of her white master. The child that results from this rape is in her eyes a monster, being "far too white, too white for me," so white that she could not "look into its face" (193). Smothering her baby, the slave mother buries the body in a grave "scooped beneath the moon," deep in the mango forest. Hunted down, she is whipped and still bears the visible scars on the wrists of the ropes that tied her "to the flogging place," badges of dishonor that she displays to her auditors—"Ye . . . born of the Washington-race"—as evidence of the terrible discrepancy slavery brings to "this land . . . the free America." The poem ends with the fugitive slave on Pilgrim's Point, hoping to die so that she may join "the white child waiting for me / In the death-dark where we may kiss and agree." It is a final image with strong Christian suggestivity, the poet's piety underscoring the obvious irony derived from the dark side of "amalgamation" as realized in the South.

Miscegenation is traditionally a tragic theme in America, and it would supply a number of incidents in Stowe's compendium of abolitionist tales of horror. But most such fables hit well below the Mason-Dixon belt, while Barrett Browning through ignorance perhaps but most certainly through design locates her enormities within a day's journey by foot from the landing place of the Pilgrims. She thereby enables a grim confrontation with that ghostly crew so often summoned up by Forefathers' Day orators but with a far different purpose: exile confronts exiles, but with no hope of becoming anybody's "ancestor."

Browning actually composed her poem of protest in 1846, a year after the *Narrative of the Life of Frederick Douglass* was published, which tells of the author's own mixed parentage and ends with his flight to Massachusetts, the details of which were abbreviated to protect his accomplices, thereby accelerating his passage, and perhaps inspiring Browning's truncated geography. Douglass soon discovered that because of "the strength of prejudice against color" among his fellow workers in the celebrated land of the Pilgrims, he was unable to find work as a ship caulker (150). And though eventually welcomed into the ranks of the abolition movement as living proof that African Americans were capable of great literary expressiveness, the author was at risk of capture once he published his book: Douglass sailed for Great Britain, where he was given a hero's reception, and felt for the first time that his color was neither a racist barrier nor an abolitionist's barricade. Between 1845 and 1847 he delivered a series of lectures that not only won many friends for emancipation but earned Douglass the money with which he could buy his liberty.

The experience of the most famous fugitive slave of the day provided a disjunctive picture of New England, at once an asylum and a possible trap, putting a shadow across the region's self-esteem regarding its reputation for moral rectitude and the championship of civil rights. Douglass's plight thereby warranted that moment in Browning's poem when the "proud and slow" spirits of the departed Pilgrims circle the praying slave woman but do not extend a helpful hand. The poem was sent off to the *Liberty Bell* on December 21, 1846, hardly a coincidental date, and Browning's abolitionist verse narrative may be taken as a response, twenty years later, to Hemans's lines about the Landing that emphasized the difference between the freedom-loving Pilgrims and other settlers in the New World.

By 1852 Plymouth Rock was firmly installed in Garrison's iconographic temple. The Massachusetts Anti-Slavery Society did not meet that year in Plymouth, though Phillips and Quincy spoke at the Forefathers' Day festivities sponsored there by the Old Colony Anti-Slavery Society. But at their regular August celebration of West Indian emancipation, Garrison read aloud an "original" poem by John Pierpont, "The Slave Catcher," which updated the poet's earlier tributes to the Pilgrims. In 1852, Pierpont placed the Landing on the near side of the Fugitive Slave Law, and once again he posed a critical question: Supposing at the moment of the Forefathers' arrival a cry had come from a nearby "wigwam's shade" that an Indian slave had escaped—would the Pilgrim Fathers have joined in the chase after the fugitive? (*Liberator*, August 6, 1852). "To catch a fleeing slave" is Pierpont's exact phrase, an echo (perhaps unconscious) of Donne's famous line regarding falling stars and mandrake roots and certainly in the abolitionist phrase book equally associated with impossible (because intolerable) acts. The poem is also, if incidentally, interesting as attesting to the fact that Native Americans kept slaves, information generally elided from romantic (and revisionist) accounts of noble savagery.

A firmer connection between Garrison's activities and Barrett Browning's "Pilgrim's Point" is provided by "The Fugitive," another poem published in the *Liberator* later in 1852, on December 24, obviously timed to coincide with Forefathers' Day. As in "Pilgrim's Point," an escaped slave comes to Plymouth Rock "to bathe me in this consecrated sea—Receive its baptism in the holy name / Of Liberty" (208). Kneeling with head upon the "sacred rock," the fugitive bids the ocean "come and dash your spray / Ye white waves, o'er me!" But this ceremony of self-immersion is interrupted when the fugitive hears "the dreaded voice of my old master near" and is threatened with a flogging. This, despite the slave's reminder that "We're treading on consecrated ground. / These are the very waves which proudly bore / The Pilgrim Fathers to this distant shore; / This sacred rock received their wandering feet." The scornful master reminds the fugitive that the law of property overrides all other considerations: the slave is his, "to scourge, to torture, and to kill."

There follows a sequence of stanzas in which the fugitive calls in turn for help to the "Sons of the Pilgrims," "the Genius of Liberty," and finally on "God in Heaven," but each appeal is ridiculed by the master as he continues to menace his slave with the punishing rod. The Pilgrims' descendants, he points out, are too busy building churches, making money, and "decking old graves" to help him; the spirit of Liberty "vanished long ago" from New England, and although God is still in his Heaven, his commands are "no longer regarded in the land." The fugitive in the madness of desperation plunges from Plymouth Rock into the sea, disappearing beneath the waves as all Nature responds with shrieks and moans. From this Gothic finale, the poet suddenly awakens, for what was a horrible reality for the slave has been only a nightmare, suggesting that hope yet remains for New England. It is a conclusion that recalls not only a similar suicide in *Uncle Tom's Cabin* but the upbeat end of Stowe's romance, with the son of Tom's former master swearing allegiance to abolition in the presence of the dying slave-hero.

Signed obscurely "S***** Holmes," "The Fugitive at Plymouth" makes up in drama what it may lack in poetic skill and testifies not only to the influence of Mrs. Browning's earlier work but to the increasing inclination of the *Liberator* to associate the Pilgrims and the Rock with contemporary crises. That the poet seems never to have actually visited Plymouth, but was apparently operating under the influence of Hemans's misconception about the setting of the Landing, introduces an unintentionally humorous dimension: a dive into the water from the seaside base of Plymouth Rock would in 1852 have required a standing broad jump of Olympic length. So we must lump the "Fugitive" with "Pilgrim's Point," and any number of depictions of the Landing, as reflecting piety uninformed by geological and geographical fact.

Still, in terms of metaphor, the juxtaposition of Fugitive, Pursuing Master, and a New England deaf to the appeals of escaped slaves provides an effective alternative to the sacred trinity of Embarkation, Compact, and Landing. Moreover, its melodrama reflects the reaction of a growing number of Massachusetts citizens toward the sight of fugitives being escorted through the streets of Boston by federal marshals. The poem and its contemporary context likewise suggest that the smug sanctity of Forefathers' Day as celebrated by the Whigs was in need of strategic revision, the tacit point made by Lowell in 1845 and Garrison and his clique in 1849 and 1850.

VI

The contents of the *Liberty Bell*, along with the poems of Whittier and Lowell, also serve as a reminder that contextuality is an organic phenomenon and as such can develop a life of its own, if occasionally of the kind generated by Dr. Frankenstein. And so the book assembled from the *Bell*'s component parts by Harriet Beecher Stowe, who depended even more on Theodore Weld's anatomy of atrocities, *American Slavery as It Is* (1839), took on a terrible energy and was destructive of the peculiar institution far beyond the author's intentions. At some point in the abolitionist campaign a line had been crossed that was liminal in its power to transform, of which *Uncle Tom's Cabin* was one very significant product, a work of fiction that claimed to be a compilation of facts but was given added life by drawing upon a myth already in motion.

In attacking the system of slavery, Stowe attempted to achieve a balanced fairness, not too much different from the sort of thing recommended by the Reverend Blagden and projected as a novel by Whittier early in the 1830s. Perhaps also borrowing from Sarah Hale's *Northwood*, which as William R. Taylor has demonstrated is concerned with the effects of southern climate and culture on virtuous sons of the Puritans, Stowe tactfully gave New England origins to her cast of "Southerners." This includes not only the prototypical and lassitudinous cavalier St. Clare but that monster of bigoted redneck violence Simon Legree, a regional linchpin that implies a shared guilt where the dreadful system of slavery was concerned.

Nor by 1852 had the daughter of Lyman Beecher abandoned her faith in the efficacy of colonization as the "solution" to the problem of freed blacks, but much as southern readers were not at all mollified by her attempts at maintaining balance, so northern champions of abolition like Garrison who cheered on the success of *Uncle Tom's Cabin* paid no attention to her terminal solution. Instead they continued to promote the cause of immediate emancipation, using Stowe's book to energize further a campaign in which she had no interest. The outrage felt by her readers over the martyrdom of Uncle Tom called out for retribution from the Northern side, while the departure of her alternate hero, George Harris (modeled after Douglass), for Liberia was ignored. "Do what you feel is right," counseled Stowe in her afterword, an appeal to the New England conscience that became a terrible swift sword.

It is worth noting here that in 1852 Sarah Josepha Hale's *Northwood* was republished with a revised subtitle, *Life North and South*, with the intention of providing literary balance to *Uncle Tom's Cabin*. Hale added material that echoed Stowe's advocacy of colonization, but gave her novel a thoroughly happy ending, in which transsectional familial union was emphasized in the hope of saving the Union, resulting ironically in a reinforcement of the plantation myth. By 1859, it can be safely said, the line between fact and fiction had become hopelessly blurred, Stowe and Hale giving melodramatic and sentimental form to the ongoing debate over slavery, while abolitionists summoned up the ghosts of Pilgrims and Puritans past in order to validate their cause, forcing them into postures they had never before assumed.

Senator Charles Sumner, carried along by an onrush of self-righteousness and literary inspiration, conflated Don Quixote with a live "Southron" and thereby triggered an explosion of offended honor that the code of knighthood absorbed from Walter Scott had instilled in southern readers. This in turn offended an equivalent sense of chivalric idealism on the part of northern radicals like Lowell. Scott was not, contra Mark Twain, responsible for the Civil War, nor was the publication of *Uncle Tom's Cabin* the event that launched the Rebellion, despite Lincoln's fabled remark. And yet in a certain sense fiction was responsible for setting in motion the War between the States, lending its imaginative coloration to the complex ideologies that engendered the conflict.

We may doubt the efficacy of the Garrisonian emphasis on the sufferings of African American slaves when set against the negative economic consequences for the North of secession, yet his late discovery of the Pilgrim/Puritan evoked a response in the New England sensibility and may well have accelerated the split in the Whig Party between those persons of Conscience and of Cotton. But the greatest literary event of the 1850s, another compound of abolitionist facts and fictions, appeared late in the decade and gave human and dramatic shape to a combination of myths that proved to be an overwhelmingly powerful attraction for writers of considerable stature in New England who had been slow, even reluctant, to identify themselves with the Garrisonite cause, chief of whom was Ralph Waldo Emerson.

Moncure Conway, the Virginia-born Methodist minister converted to Unitarianism by exposure to the Harvard Divinity School and to transcendentalism and abolitionism because of Emerson's influence, was, like so many persons sympathetic to emancipation, outraged over John Brown's use of arms in 1859 at Harpers Ferry. And looking back from the vantage point of a half century, Conway by the end of the century saw the New England connection clearly: "It appears to me now that there had remained in nearly every Northern breast, however liberal, some unconscious chord which Brown had touched, inherited from the old Puritan spirit and faith in the God of War" (1:303).

No one could ever accuse this disciple of Emerson of a foolish consistency: Conway was the man who first thought of *Uncle Tom's Cabin* as a serial romance with no bearing on the institution of slavery as it was maintained in Virginia, but once his attitude toward "the slavery question" changed, he was able to regard Stowe's book as "a photographic representation of things going on in States farther south" (192). And in the end, after Conway learned that "Brown had secured money for his violent purpose by concealing that purpose . . . and also had led some of his small band to their death by similar concealment," he once again revised his incarnation of "the old Puritan spirit," this time into a scheming and duplicitous Yankee, a long-lived southern stereotype (302).

But we should perhaps keep in mind Conway's observation that Captain John Brown's advent did resonate in harmony with the "old Northern myth" embodied in Garrison and celebrated by Lowell and Whittier. It was Oliver Wendell Holmes for whom, in 1855, abolition was abomination, disunion anathema, and his cousin Wendell Phillips an apostate from the Brahmin caste, who put the best frame finally around the figure of Captain John Brown. The attack on Sumner (and Sumter), the enlistment of his namesake son and near death from battle wounds, eventually converted Holmes to the god of war, but the occasion for his definitive sentiments came long after hostilities had ceased. It was a dinner honoring Harriet Beecher Stowe on her seventieth birthday in 1882, and Holmes, who himself was getting on in years, was still capable of exercising a certain skeptic wit. His contribution to the celebration was one of his famous after-dinner poems, which contained these critical lines:

> All through the conflict, up and down
> Marched Uncle Tom and Old John Brown,
>   One ghost, one form ideal;
> And which was false and which was true,
> And which was mightier of the two
> The wisest sibyl never knew
>   For both alike were real. (*Works*, 13:277)

It has been observed that the Civil War produced very little contemporary fiction inspired by events. But then it can also be said that there was a considerable body of imaginative literature that had already fought that war, not the least of which was Stowe's misconstrued novel and Captain John Brown as forecast by the abolitionist muse.

CHAPTER 12

Setting Free the Rock

Resolved, that while a fragment of Plymouth rock remains, it
will rebuke the pharisaical devotee, the trimming demagogue, the
facile conformist, the cowardly persecutor, the effeminate self-seeker,
and justify unlimited contumacy, division, strife, and secession for
righteousness' sake.
—*William Lloyd Garrison*

I

For two years, 1849 and 1850, as I have noted, there were no Forefathers' Day celebrations at Plymouth sponsored by the Pilgrim Society. These
omissions may be attributed not to ideological conflicts but to the conclusions of a committee established to determine the correct date of the Landing,
which were published in 1850 in a slim but for traditionalists a burdensome
pamphlet. In it, the committee announced that the young men of the Old
Colony Club in their attempt to translate the Old Style calender into the New
had miscalculated by one day that sacred anniversary. After a lengthy and
mock-pedantic explanation of sidereal and other mysteries, the committee
announced the "true" date as December 21 and attempted to offset objections
to the revision by noting, "It is not the gathering crowds of 22d December,
1769, the earliest public observance, that we would exemplify; but only show
our admiration for the landing upon Plymouth rock of the blessed few, at the
Winter solstice of 1620" (*Report*, 6).

As the exclusivist agenda might suggest, the committee in its rigor of definitive zeal also determined that the Landing as celebrated thereafter would
honor the first exploratory party—the "blessed few"—under Captain Standish,
rather than the entire passenger list of the *Mayflower*, an argument that emphasizes the point that in its sere historicity the committee was decidedly icon-
unfriendly: "Reverence for progenitors, as well as self-respect, forbids us to
permit any mixture of fiction with the great truths of their story." No longer

would "a false assumption of a day . . . for the consecrations . . . of these glorious mile-stones of memory" be permitted (9).

Given that the spirit of such celebratory occasions had been hitherto politically conservative, it is hardly surprising to find that there were many residents of Plymouth who were not swayed by the facts and maintained their lawyerlike loyalty to a higher authority, namely the precedent of the Whiggish succession of John Quincy Adams, Webster, Everett, and Rufus Choate. The controversy seems to have continued for a time, with the usual consequence of temporary inaction, and where the delay caused by the deliberations of the committee provided a window of opportunity through which Garrison and his clique climbed into the anniversary occasion, the continued contretemps opened that window to a doorway.

The mood in Plymouth was facetiously expressed by the retrospective view of "D.Y.," correspondent of the *Anti-Slavery Standard*, in 1856, namely that "the Pilgrim Society having let the day drop, the Abolitionists, with that mettlesomeness which is the badge of their tribe, picked it up, and perverted it from its proper ends to their own base ones. Instead of making it a good comfortable occasion of magnifying the Fathers, for the purpose of inferring [*sic*] how much more enlightened, wise, and intelligent the Sons are, they have . . . used it as an opportunity of venting their spleen against our most cherished institutions, as well as against our First Men" (quoted in *Liberator*, January 4, 1856).

The Pilgrim Society did celebrate Forefathers' Day in 1851, on the traditional day of December 22, but the chief contribution was not an oration but a poem by Allen C. Spooner. Read in response to the toast "The Faith of the Pilgrims," Spooner's opus was a tongue-in-cheek performance that celebrated the faith of that "hard, flint-visaged race," not only in "God and Christ," but most especially in the Devil:

> This made the axis of the Pilgrim mind—
> This made them stubborn in their good old way—
> This made New England what even now we find—
> This made us all what'er we are to-day. (8)

Written in the spirit of the essay on the Yankee genesis in *The Biglow Papers*, Spooner's spoof suggests a loosening of the clerical halter in Plymouth, and it was certainly acceptable to Garrison, who printed it in full in the *Liberator* on his poetry page (January 16, 1852).

Plymouth seems to have found this newfound friendliness on Garrison's part less than welcome: rather than take a chance on having their proceedings co-opted by the abolitionists, the society, unlike the Old Colony Club when similarly threatened by the Liberty Boys, simply abandoned Forefathers' Day in 1852 to the Old Colony Anti-Slavery Society. This surrender, if it was that, became abject in the year following, when the descendants of the Pilgrims elected to celebrate not the Landing but the Embarkation from Delft Haven, on August 1. But other reasons may be found for this midcentury revision of emphasis from the Arrival to the Departure, which have to do with a much larger, national frame of reference and not local antiquarian and political wrangles.

The popular and effervescent New York journalist N. P. Willis wrote of attending a dinner in Plymouth in August 1849 celebrating the "Pilgrim Embarcation," at which he "*saw and heard Webster*," for whose convenience the affair seems to have been held: "The real object, probably, was to meet Mr. Webster over the pilgrim theme—his Congressional duties preventing him from attendance here in the winter" (*Hurry-Graphs*, 12). In Willis's summary account of his remarks, Webster in addressing an audience of congenial spirits, including "other eminent New Englanders in Congress," conjoined his usual outline of "the progress of the principles of the pilgrims" to expressions of "his feeling as to liberal usage and prompt equalization of rights to all who are once covered with our banner" (a reference to creating states from the territories acquired by the Mexican War), and, casting a look across the sea to Hungary, "he expressed a confidence that the liberty, panted for abroad, could not long be kept under" (15). In his "impassioned conclusion," Webster stressed "the probable and possible future of our own country, and the needful extension of the pilgrim principles through its remotest limit of space and time," not including, we may be sure, any account of those persons "covered with our banner" who as yet "panted for liberty."

We need not doubt Willis's account of the reasoning behind the celebration of the Embarkation in 1849 to open up the subject further. In her discussion of the historical paintings in the rotunda of the Capitol, which included Robert Weir's depiction of the Pilgrim Embarkation, Ann Uhry Abrams notes the common emphases joining the eight versions of the American past, scenes of discovery, of military victories, and of religious signification: "Illustrating that fragile balance between the imperfect past and the glorious future, the . . . rotunda paintings depict historical points or events about to happen. Columbus journeys between the old world and the new, the Pilgrims are similarly poised between Europe and America, Pocahontas moves from her aboriginal background into a Europeanized culture, and De Soto opens the untamed West for European settlers" (77–78). But as Webster pointed out in 1820, what makes a historical event important are its consequences, an evaluation that is invariably dependent on the contemporary moment. Thus a contemporary witness, quoted by Abrams, observed that *The Baptism of Pocahontas*, John

Gadsby Chapman's contribution to the "National Hall," was in terms of American history a nonevent, for Christianity did not make significant inroads into paganism.

Commenting on the religious signification of the rotunda paintings, Abrams notes that "during the antebellum years, Christian values and national purpose were believed to be inseparable," and she points out the Protestant emphasis of the scenes in question (78). But much as the conversion of Pocahontas by Chapman gains meaning from its tragic, miscegenetic frame, so Weir's emphasis on the Embarkation, not the Landing (which was the original subject announced and which would have met all the criteria of the rotunda paintings), parallels the emerging emphasis of John Robinson during the 1830s and 1840s. Notably, the pamphlet describing the painting included Robinson's letter given to the Pilgrims at the moment of their departure.

Moreover, even as Weir's tableau dodges the question of whose Landing Forefathers' Day was supposed to celebrate, it displaces the statist, militaristic stress of Sargent's rendition of that problematic scene. Drawing strength from authenticity (the conversion of Pocahontas, like the Landing, was apocryphal), Weir's painting also reverberates with piety during a period characterized by considerable evangelical activity in America, perhaps inspiring not only Charles Lucy's own version of the Departure (see fig. 4) but his pietistic depiction of the Landing (see fig. 1).

And yet Webster in 1849 did not touch on these themes, if we may credit N. P. Willis with accuracy, but focused on the troublesome problem of national expansion, which New England had always regarded with uneasiness, not only because it diminished the region's representative power in Washington and drained the available labor pool but because of the old Federalist fear that a republic cannot be extended beyond a certain periphery or it would come apart at the seams. And certainly in 1849 the United States seemed to be doing exactly that.

This underlines the chief irony of the increased emphasis on the Embarkation, which is an intensely secessionist moment, being a celebration of the Separatist spirit essential to the ideology of American Puritanism. It is not an arrival but, as Abrams suggests, a departure, a breaking away from the corruptions of the Old World in order to preserve the purity of what the Pilgrims regarded as a correct observance of gospel ideals. In his own note on the meaning of his work, not cited by Abrams, Weir stated in 1843 that he wished to include in the rotunda a painting "whose subject should commemorate an event connected with the history of our eastern states; since they were the first to grapple in that struggle for liberty, the achievement of which, is our glory and boast" (*Picture*, 3). To this hegemonic emphasis we can add Weir's declara-

FIGURE 14. Robert Weir's *Embarkation of the Pilgrims* (1843). Weir's depiction of this pious moment, in which Robinson is placed in a prominent but not dominant position in a semicircle of his departing parishioners, carries democratic connotations. It may be compared with the handling a decade later of the same subject by Charles Lucy (see fig. 4), in which Robinson is given an exhortative posture dominating the composition, a romantic scene that, like Rothermel's *Landing*, emphasizes emotions rather than the calm determination of Weir's Pilgrims and puts the minister in a position of towering authority.

This is in stark contrast to Lucy's handling of the Landing (see fig. 1), which conveys a mood similar to that of Weir's version of the Embarkation, the wrenching drama of departure replaced by heroic resolve in facing the future. The pyramidal composition holds, with Governor Carver now given the central position, a convention of historical painting (as in Leutze's depiction of Washington crossing the Delaware) but one that validates authoritarian social structures. Weir's painting, intended for the rotunda gallery in the Capitol, seems much more in keeping with the egalitarian spirit not only of Congregationalism but republicanism. Note the arms and armor on the deck, exemplifying the idea that these prayerful people will not hesitate to fight for their convictions, a convention found also in White's depiction of the signing of the Compact (see fig. 3). (Courtesy Pilgrim Society)

tion that he was "influenced by the high moral character of the scene," which he saw as the first step toward "that separation from the dominion of the old world which made us an independent people."

By 1849, it was not only the South that was threatening to solidify its hegemony by setting up as an independent republic: William Lloyd Garrison and Wendell Phillips used the occasion of the publication of Frederick Douglass's autobiography to insist on the moral purity of New England and would continue to press for separation of free from slave states, an ideology likewise implicit in the Free-Soil movement. Thus, whatever the reasons given at the time for the new emphasis on the Embarkation, it was an event that in terms of the times had a dis-Unionist signification. It was therefore far more suitable to the purposes of Garrison and southern fire-eaters than to those of Webster and his fellow Whigs, and it would be toward that end, finally, that its celebration would be turned.

Along with the use of August as a date making straight and unimpeded the path for Webster, Willis included among the reasons for celebrating the Embarkation in Plymouth "easier access to the place . . . and the chance of finding agreeable guests among the distinguished strangers from the South in the travelling season . . . and indeed this celebration seems likely to become the more important of the two." Here he must be accounted something of a prophet, as we shall see. For in the words of those in charge of the celebration of the Embarkation in 1853, the summer seemed a more genial time "for taking measures to erect a monument in the town, in or near 'Forefathers' Rock,'" which was the main purpose of the event (*Account*, 3). As a banner (one of many hung for the occasion) announced, it was "Forefathers' Day Thawed Out" (11). It was both a fine and a great day for Plymouth, with a grand procession, several marching bands, and the aforementioned banners and symbolic mottoes, as well as arches over the street made of evergreen boughs, a traditional feature of celebrations in New England ever since President Washington came calling many years earlier.

The catalog of decorations covers several pages of the official account of the celebration, but among the most notable was an obelisk "bearing the likeness of President Pierce," with the motto "Our Pilgrim Fathers," while at the base was displayed the sentiment "Plymouth Rock—first stepping-stone to the Temple of Liberty" (14). That Pierce was a Democrat did not dampen the patriotism of Plymouth citizens, who were after all trying to encourage as much participation in their fund-raising effort as possible, and the Pilgrim Society had sent an invitation to President Pierce, among many other "First Men" of the day, the most of whom, including Pierce, had declined. By way of pointing out its purpose, the town had erected an elaborate arch over the wharf-side base of the Rock itself, supported by twin pillars bearing the mottoes "No New Englander could be willing to have that Rock buried or forgotten" and "This Rock has become an object of veneration in the United States," thereby conjoining the sentiments of Timothy Dwight and Tocqueville (16).

Webster had the year before been buried but was hardly forgotten, and that he was still an object of veneration in Plymouth was attested by the displays of bronze busts of the Great Man with accompanying mottoes. A Masonic signal of sorts was provided by the motto "John Robinson, the Keystone of the Pilgrim Arch," mounted on a "splendid" structure erected between the homes of Abraham Jackson and "Mrs. Barnes," whose doorway was further decorated by the esoteric sentiment "The Moral Electricity of the Pilgrims. May the Matrons of the Earth take a Shock from the Leyden Jar"—at least as reported in the *Account*, though the copy at hand has "Matrons" deleted in ink and "Nations" substituted in its place, suggesting sentiments more conformable with the mysteries of Freemasonry and certainly more comfortable for Mrs. Barnes.

The Pilgrim Society had also done its best to increase interest in the proposed monument (as well as avoid controversy) by assembling speakers with a geographical and ideological representativeness, including (as N. P. Willis had put it) a "distinguished stranger from the South." As the society's president, Richard Warren, observed, "We have come up from the north, the south, the east and the west, irrespective of party, abandoning for the time all political distinction, having no particular opinions, knowing only that we are brethren and sisters of our dear America, descendants from a noble ancestry of the good and truly great" (35–36). Not having "particular opinions" was Artemus Ward's style, a politic flexibility for the sake of expedience that expressed the compromising spirit of the age, and present on the dais was Edward (now Senator) Everett, elegant evasiveness personified. Moreover, balance and proportion were provided by surrounding Everett with a generous menu of opinions, represented by Everett's radical counterpart in the U.S. Senate, Charles Sumner; by John P. Hale, the ardent Liberty Party and Free-Soil man from New Hampshire; and by Charles Wentworth Upham, Unitarian minister and historian.

It would be difficult to imagine a more carefully selected panel, who were intended to reflect the complex political crosscurrents in New England in 1853. Moreover, to add Democratic and demographic balance there was Mr. Richard Yeadon, not a politician but a member of the press from Charleston, South Carolina. And it would be this last gentleman who would in cavalier fashion rend the delicate fabric woven by President Warren's committee, providing an apt demonstration of Whittier's observation that with "Southrons" (as with Garrisonians), soft words did not turn away but inspired wrath. If the panel of speakers was intended to effect the kind of inclusive representativeness for which Unitarianism is famous, then and now, Mr. Yeadon demonstrated that southern chivalry enters panel discussions with horsewhip in hand.

II

As expected, Edward Everett, in responding to the sentiments "*The Embarkation of 1620,—and its results*," provided an extended demonstration of how to avoid offending anyone at a time when offense was easily taken, yet at the last, Everett managed to let fly a discordant note or two. His chosen topic was the always troublesome but in 1853 hardly controversial subject of the Native American, whose tenancy had been displaced by the wave of progress attending the westward course of empire. The presence of God being omnipresent in this process as in all things, it was plainly decreed that the Indian was "doomed by a mysterious Providence to pass away" (*Account*, 69). We may here again make reference to the implications of Chapman's rotunda painting and note that by 1853, Fenimore Cooper and a legion of lesser talents had worn the features on Everett's chosen theme so smooth by handling that Longfellow would feel perfectly safe in using it in his Algonquin epic two years later. It would seem to have been ideologically neutered, but it will never do to underestimate Everett's subtlety, so silken in its weave as to be often invisible.

That the orator's subtext was indeed political is suggested by the presence of a detectable ideological strand in his tapestry, a kind of code keyed by his definition of the "problem" of the Indian as one of the self-solving kind. We can detect, therefore, a secondary meaning in Everett's having expressed in regard to the disappearing Native American sentiments typical of a certain Whig/Unitarian turn of mind, which tended to credit all such "solutions" to the workings of Providence (i.e., Progress), adding by way of polite regret a regular infusion of Alases! For the "problem" of the Native American was implicitly, even tacitly, an oblique extension of the "problem" of the African American, which persons of a conservative turn of mind were certain that God would solve in his own time without any help from radical abolitionists.

Again, in such a view, all things worked toward a Panglossian end, a process that for Whig celebrants of American history began with Columbus, cited by Everett as the first of many "Discoverers," whose heroic voyage brought civilization to a continent hitherto uninhabited save by that providentially displaced people who were obliging History, God, New England, and the United States, by removing themselves at a convenient rate proportionate to the advancing waves of civilized persons. "The discoverer has come; but the settler, the colonist, the conqueror, alas that I must add! too often the oppressor and destroyer, are to follow in his train. By these various agencies, joyous and sorrowful, through these paths of triumph and woe, the culture of the Old World, in the lapse of successive generations, reformed of its abuses, enriched with new arts, animated by a higher spirit of humanity, transferred from the privileged few to the mass of the community, is to be reproduced and perfected in the West" (69–70).

In this transcendent display of Progress, the Native American, like the African American, tended to get lost in the iconographic van. Everett had earlier cited two "solitary Indians" who had recently been sighted in Boston harbor in birch-bark canoes, "gazing in silent wonder at the city of the triple hills," who provided a mute but effectively symbolic and prophetic tableau. They had "paddled their frail barks," ghosts summoned from a distant past, "through this strange, busy, and to them, no doubt, bewildering scene; and having made the circuit of East Boston, the navy yard, the city itself, and South Boston, dropped down with the current, and disappeared among the islands," much in the manner of Thoreau's mystical "Red Face of man," evoked at about this same time, also (64).

The summoning up of ghosts to witness the marvels of modern progress was by 1853 a well-worn Forefathers' Day trope, and Everett's tangential Indians would be followed by necromancy more appropriate to the occasion. Included on the platform was Mr. H. A. Scudder of the newly formed Cape Cod Association, yet another person invited by way of achieving balance, for Provincetown increasingly thought of itself as a friendly rival to Plymouth, being the place where the Pilgrims first landed. "Why, Sir," said Scudder, echoing Emerson, "here is Plymouth rock, and there is old Cape Cod—there too, is Cape Cod Harbor. What places [are] so memorable among the records of the past?" (*Account*, 50–51).

Scudder went on to "take along" with him on a tour of modern America a group of Pilgrims summoned up for the occasion. "Embarking on board one of our noble steamers," they would be carried around the bay, then to the "city of the Pilgrims," not Plymouth but Boston, to view the evidence there of prosperity (58). Next, they would climb aboard "the iron steed of this nineteenth century" and be taken through the "six republics" of New England, and from there across the entire United States, all populated by descendants of Pilgrims and Puritans. They would visit "the great capital of our nation, and there behold her noblest institutions based upon the principles of that compact originally signed by them in the cabin of the Mayflower, in the harbor of Cape Cod,—would they not hold up their hands in wonder and amazement?" (58–59).

What Scudder's ghostly tourists were definitely not treated to was that sight familiar to the readers of the *Liberator*, the plain evidence in "the great capital of our nation" of the traffic in slaves, at which in beholding the Pilgrims might well "hold up their hands," though hardly in admiration. But that was not on Scudder's agenda, who did what he was invited to do, celebrate the inheritance common to Provincetown and Plymouth, not drag in the problematic matter of slavery, which, unlike the matter of the Indian, was showing no signs of solving itself. His, like Everett's, was a Whig view and progressive, which cited examples of material growth and technological invention as proof that things were always getting better. "The work, the work must go on," intoned Everett in dismissing the Native American with appropriate Virgilian sadness, and it was therefore incumbent upon New Englanders to carry on the errand first "undertaken by the Pilgrim Fathers of New England, on the spot where we are now gathered" (238).

What the Pilgrims introduced to this continent, according to Everett's safe because traditional thesis, were the two "Master Ideas" of the Western world, "GOD and LIBERTY," and while tacitly refusing to extend the last of these two blessings to four million Americans still laboring in chains, Everett did close with a thinly veiled allusion to those who would like to do so (72). The sentiments of the former Unitarian minister regarding radical reformers were very close to those of the orthodox Reverend Blagden (present on the occasion to deliver appropriate passages from Scripture, while his Unitarian counterpart, the Reverend Kendall, gave the prayer), indicating how much in sympathy were the Protestant clergy of whatever denomination in this particular.

But the former Reverend Everett, in castigating those who would destroy the good work the Pilgrims had first set in motion, chose a figure integral to the Whig faith in internal improvements, a railroad train, but not the one on which Mr. Scudder had put his visiting delegation of Forefathers: "In a word . . . [the Pilgrims'] political code united religion and liberty, morals and law, and it differed from the wild license which breaks away from these restraints, as the well-guided railway engine, instinct with mechanical life, conducted by a bold, but skilful and prudent hand, and propelled in safety towards its destination, with glowing axle, along its iron grooves, differs from the same engine when its speed is rashly urged beyond the point of safety, or when, driven by criminal recklessness or murderous neglect, it leaps madly from the track, and plunges with its crushed and shrieking train into the jaws of destruction" (77). Undoubtedly, to Everett's turn of mind, one such Casey Jones was Charles Sumner, his radical colleague in the Senate. Though sharing Everett's aversion to slavery (both men would oppose the Kansas-Nebraska Bill in 1854), Sumner did so in such outspoken terms as to bring the concentrated wrath of the South down quite literally upon his head in 1855, while Everett, under increasing fire from Conscience Whigs like Sumner because of his Unionist advocacy of moderation, simply resigned his office.

Perhaps in keeping with the purpose of the occasion, Sumner's own tone that day was restrained. In his brief remarks, in response to the toast "*The Senate of the United States,—the concentrated light of the stars of the Union,*"

Sumner resisted the bait tossed to him and wasted little time saluting that glorious banner. Instead, with a reminder that "it is the Pilgrims that we commemorate today, not the Senate," Sumner trod under his foot if not the banner of Union then "all pride of empire, all exultation in our manifold triumphs of industry, of science, of literature, with all the crowding anticipations of the vast untold Future"—the themes celebrated in Everett's oration— "that we may reverently bow before the forefathers" (*Account*, 81). Even the title of his remarks, when published as *A Finger Point from Plymouth Rock*, conveys this emphasis. Like Everett, but toward a far different end, Sumner tended to talk in codes, as when, just above, he swept away the concerns of the Whig Party, under the pretext of focusing his attention on the Forefathers.

Likewise, in urging his auditors to follow "those primal principles of duty, which, from the landing at Plymouth Rock, have been the life of Massachusetts," Sumner chose to emphasize the great Pilgrim tradition of Separatism, which as we have seen was the ideological emphasis of the Embarkation: "I like this word, sir. It has a meaning" (81–82). And its meaning to many of his auditors was secession, not that logical extension of nullification repeatedly threatened by those "Southrons" but the geopolitical version of come-outerism proposed by Garrison and Phillips. Flattering also to the Garrisonians was Sumner's emphasis on the persecution suffered by the Pilgrim Separatists: "Against them, the whole fury of the law was directed. Some were imprisoned; all were impoverished, while their name became a byword of reproach" (83). Sumner did not make explicit the connection with modern-day abolitionists, no more than Everett had put specific hands on the throttle of his locomotive, but then by 1853 neither man needed to.

In his closing words, Sumner used the rhetoric of dismissiveness with which he had opened, honoring the Pilgrims "not for any triumph of discovery, science, learning, or eloquence," those items familiar to Whig discourse, but for that "divine virtue which made them, amidst the reproach, the obloquy, and the hardness of the world, hold fast to Freedom and Truth!" (85). Placing himself and his auditors with the Pilgrims on Plymouth Rock, Sumner declared, "We cannot fail to be elevated by their example. . . . No pusilanimous soul here to-day will declare their self-sacrifice, their deviation from received opinions, their unquenchable thirst for liberty, an error or illusion. . . . Conformity or compromise might, perhaps, have purchased for them a profitable peace, but not peace of mind; it might have secured place and power, but not repose. . . . Better be the despised Pilgrim, a fugitive for freedom, than the halting politician, forgetful of principle, 'with a Senate at his heels' " (85). That, concluded Sumner, "is the voice from Plymouth Rock, as it salutes my ears. Others may not hear it. But to me it comes in tones which I cannot mistake."

Encoded for those with the right kind of ears by words like "compromise" and "fugitive for freedom," the message could hardly be misunderstood.

Sumner closed his implicit link between the Pilgrims and abolition by ending with "words of noble cheer," the final lines of Lowell's celebrated hymn, that identified the wave of western progress with which the Pilgrims were invariably associated, with the abolitionist crusade: "We ourselves must Pilgrims be, / Launch our Mayflower, and steer boldly through the desperate winter sea." They were words most certainly appropriate to the occasion, if one viewed the Embarkation as the first step toward universal emancipation. But they seem to have been lost on at least one person in attendance that August day, a Whiggish reporter from the *New York Courier and Enquirer*, whose remarks were appended to the official account of the celebration.

The reporter concurred with the wisdom of staging the celebration of the Pilgrim Landing on the day of their Departure, which rendered "due attention to our creature comforts" and shed a properly nostalgic tear over the departed Webster, even while acknowledging Edward Everett's place in the "illustrious chain" of (Whig) orators in Massachusetts: "To such thorough sentences it has seldom been my good fate to listen" (*Account*, 174–72, 179). He was much less pleased by Sumner's performance, however, which he judged in elocutionary terms but with an undoubtedly political bias. Thus, instead of "pouring out" his words like Everett's "grateful utterances," in a "full, rich voice," Sumner's manner of speaking seemed carefully calculated and self-conscious: "Sumner either hesitated and was forced to think out in advance that which he desired to say, or else . . . he weighed very carefully the full import and meaning of his opinions." Despite the subjectivity of the reporter's assessment, this is probably a fair assessment of Sumner's manner, given the care with which he encoded his message.

If only because of the decorums of the Plymouth celebration, which like those early commemorations of the Landing by the Old Colony Club attempted to rise above politics, discretion was the order of the day. But as in those years that immediately preceded the War for Independence, certain opinions were (in a phrase made current by William H. Seward) "irrepressible." Thus John P. Hale, late the Liberty Party candidate for the presidency, was carefully circumspect for the most part, delivering up a traditional celebration of the Pilgrims as avatars of "spiritual freedom," who in pursuit of that ideal evinced "an unshrinking courage, an unshaking faith, and reverence for the Divine law" (*Account*, 114). But when he summed up "the elements of their success,—faith, courage and reverence for the Divine law," he self-consciously risked "offending delicate ears" by associating the Pilgrims' victory with their principled adherence to "the *higher law*" (114). In 1853, merely to mention

Seward's other famous phrase served to identify the speaker, whatever the context, with the Conscience side of the dying Whig Party.

Hale was not alone among those on the platform who violated the decorums of the day. Thus John Henry Clifford, governor of Massachusetts and a Whig, chose to rail against the proponents of "Manifest Destiny," in 1853 a slogan identified with the geopolitics of the Democratic Party, lately reaching out toward Cuba, with some tacit help from Senator (then Secretary of State) Everett. But the greatest offender was a member of "the great estate of the realm," journalist Richard Yeadon from the Old Palmetto State, who gave a most effective demonstration of "the power of the press," the terms of which suggested that South Carolina was already a State of War.

In response to what he conceived to have been salvos from "Bunker Hill," Yeadon manned "the Palmetto Fort," and pausing only to pay tribute to "your Pilgrim fathers and Pilgrim mothers" (with what he obviously felt was a courtly bow to "the lovely daughters of the Pilgrim mothers"), along with an apostrophe to Plymouth Rock as "the rock of truth," Yeadon plunged on "like the gallant and lamented [Pierce Mason] Butler, the commander of the ever-glorious Palmetto regiment" slain in the recent war with Mexico and a champion of nullification in 1832: "I must not, and will not, shun a place in the picture, though it be near the flashing of guns" (*Account*, 88–89).

Elaborately apologetic for his place on the platform—"I almost sink appalled from the task"—Yeadon stuck to his guns. He began by claiming ancestry equivalent to that of the sons of the Pilgrims, being of Huguenot lineage and thereby descended from people "who fled from even greater persecutions than did your Puritan fathers and encountered equal perils and made equal sacrifices with them for religion and liberty." Having presented his credentials in a way that marginalized the event being celebrated, Yeadon went on to perform a service not on the day's agenda.

All the speakers who had preceded Yeadon, as we have seen, addressed themselves in muffled terms to the contemporary problem of slavery. But the South Carolinian, for his part, mounted a clear-throated tribute to Webster, Clay, and Calhoun, each of whom was associated with the preservation of slavery and all of whom were now dead, leaving a great space behind: "They all alike towered above the men of their country and of their time, moral and intellectual pyramids in the midst of an intellectual and enlightened generation" (90). But the location mandated an extended tribute to Webster, and Yeadon made him the central figure in his triptych of heroic complicity, credited with having saved the Union by "giving the full benefit" of the Constitution "to the cotton States of the South and West" (93–94). Though the displays mounted in Plymouth that day indicated that considerable sympathy for Webster yet remained in Massachusetts, newspaper accounts of the ceremonies attest that Yeadon's remarks inspired a sibilant response from some persons in the audience.

Yeadon next took Everett himself up into the coils of his Laocoön-like configuration, honoring him as "Webster's worthy successor . . . the great speaker of the day, the gifted, the glorious Everett" (94). Yeadon thanked that son of Massachusetts from the bottom of his deep and perfervid "Southron" heart for "the declaration and sentiment uttered by him in Congress, many years ago, but still indelibly impressed on my memory: 'There is no cause in which I would more readily shoulder a musket, than to put down a servile insurrection in the South'" (94). Everett's had been an impulsive testimonial born out of his desire to demonstrate Whig solidarity with the South, but torn from the contextual fasces of Union ideology, the remark served as a rod in the hands of Everett's radical adversaries for many years thereafter, and he could not have much appreciated it being waved about by Yeadon.

Indifferent to the effect of his remarks, the man from South Carolina urged Everett to "cherish and imitate" Calhoun's expansionist spirit by helping the Union toward "the loftiest and happiest destiny for itself, with the two oceans for its longitudinal, and the North Pole and the Isthmus of Darien for its latitudinal boundaries,—civilizing, Christianizing, and peopling the American continent, and by their glorious example and influence regenerating the human race" (95). Since this process, as viewed from the Palmetto State, involved extending the bondage of a considerable number of representatives of "the human race," as well as reaching as far as the Monroe Doctrine permitted, it was something more by way of progress than Everett wished to celebrate and flew directly in the face of Governor Clifford's animadversions against Manifest Destiny. But it was certainly a forthright, if buncombish, blast of southern grapeshot from the "Palmetto Fort" and a violent contrast to the carefully chosen indirections of the day.

Yeadon was not yet done, however, and wound up his extravaganza of praise for the dead and the living (who at that moment perhaps wished that he was indeed with Webster, Calhoun, and Clay) by bringing up the subject that was supposed to be the main order of the day but which all the speakers before him and after had ignored, the matter of monuments, in specific the one to be raised in Plymouth to the Forefathers. But Yeadon blithely disregarded the intended agenda and instead proposed that there be raised "a common memorial in the shape of a work of art, so perfect in design and creation as to perpetuate the memory, worth, and services," not of the Pilgrim Fathers, but of the "illustrious trio" whose praises he had been singing, "CLAY, WEBSTER, CALHOUN,—Let a group of statuary, chiselled in Parian marble, perpetuate their memory at the national capital; or let Kentucky, Massachusetts, and South Carolina pile a common monument to the illustrious three at Ashland,

Marshfield, or Fort Hill, to awaken the admiration and kindle the emulation of posterity, 'till suns shall set and rise no more'" (95–96).

Again, there were people in Massachusetts who shared the gist, if not the violence, of Yeadon's sentiments, and monuments to the man who remained still godlike in the hearts and minds of die-hard Whigs had been proposed in Boston and elsewhere—but not without controversy. This was just the sort of thing that the organizers of the celebration in Plymouth had hoped to forestall, and the ever genial and affable John Hale—who followed Yeadon in the order of speakers, being next to the last on the program—did what he could to mitigate the fiery journalist's performance by humorously twitting him for his Crockett-like grandioseness: "Today, in the most eloquent language, we have had the Genius of the country taking her seat at the center of magnetic attraction, swallowing Chimborazo for supper, and kissing the sunset with an affectionate embrace"—but the cat, or to some noses, the polecat, was out of the bag (109).

For whatever reason, the Whiggish reporter from the *New York Courier and Enquirer* did not use the power of the press to give Yeadon's sentiments further circulation, nor did the other newspaper version of the celebration included in the official *Account* mention Charleston's contribution. But it was published in full by the *Boston Courier*, with the notation that the "speech was complimented by hisses from certain crazy and rabid abolitionists," while Garrison used the *Liberator* as a pillar of self-righteousness on which to display the South Carolinian in a manner not too much different from the slave being flogged on his masthead.

Declaring his "admiration" for Yeadon's "impudence" in "eulogizing" the Whig triumvirate "as the conservators of the 'peculiar institution,'" Garrison made reference to "his intended compliment to Mr. Everett, as a gentleman who had volunteered 'to shoulder his musket and march to the South, to put down an insurrection of slaves,'" which he reckoned was received by Everett "with a very peculiar gratification" (August 5, 1853, 122; for the *Boston Courier*, Matthews, 391). Garrison declared himself "comforted" by Yeadon's having been "handsomely hissed," which was hardly the point of the *Courier*'s account, a difference that suggests the deep division even in Massachusetts regarding the fugitive slave controversy.

So much, in other words, for the efforts of the Pilgrim Society to rise above the ideological fray and maintain a high-minded, transcendent tone of celebration. As the members of the Old Colony Club discovered, there are times when apolitical discourse is not in order: much as the Liberty Boys had attempted to take over Forefathers' Day for their own purposes, so their self-styled modern equivalents were about to rectify the Whig monopoly by converting Embarkation Day to the same uses to which they had already put the anniversary traditionally devoted in Plymouth to the Landing.

III

Speaking in 1854 at the annual meeting of the American Anti-Slavery Society, Garrison expanded upon his account of the celebration in Plymouth on August 1 the year before. He wasted few words on Everett's performance, "an eloquent speech, for he never makes any other, but it was full of poison and death to this nation . . . playing into the hands of those who talk about 'manifest destiny'—the annexation of one country after another, until we swallow up all creation 'and the rest of mankind.' (Laughter.) It was his bid for the Presidency" (*Proceedings*, 131).

Instead, Garrison gave indignant emphasis to the speech of Sumner, who in effect had betrayed the righteous cause with which he was identified by not speaking out openly in support of the "Anti-Slavery struggle" but instead had chosen words that could give "offence" to no one: Sumner had "stood upon the 'proprieties' of the place, and did not deem it judicious to make any allusion to the existence of Slavery in our country, lest it should mar the harmony of the occasion!" Remarks like these provide an apt demonstration of the difference between the Baptist and the Brahmin notions of comportment, but they also reinforce Whittier's objection to the failure of northern politicians to respond in kind to southern fire-eaters, an accusation that could hardly be laid to William Lloyd Garrison.

It was not that Garrison had not deciphered Sumner's encoded celebration of the Pilgrims, which bore "inferentially on our own times (if any one chose to see it) in regard to the question of Slavery." It was, as his parentheses indicate, that Sumner's inferential language did discredit not only to the senator but to the Forefathers: "Something more obvious and more direct than an inference was imperatively demanded by the Pilgrim spirit; for who among the most time-serving, ever thinks of taking umbrage at the most extravagant panegyrics that can be bestowed upon the memories of time-honored saints or heroes, or imagines that they are applicable to the 'heretics' and 'fanatics' of our own day?" Garrison insisted that there was no more "appropriate" an occasion for "a fearless rebuke of our great national sin than the celebration of Forefathers' Day at Plymouth Rock," an objection that confused the traditional celebration with the one in question (*Proceedings*, 131).

Garrison's language and strategy suggest how far he had gone since 1849 in identifying the cause of abolition with the Pilgrims. In 1853 the Old Colony Anti-Slavery Society had once again celebrated the Landing of the Forefathers in Plymouth, and Garrison had read a resolution that, among other things, observed that the "living presence" of the "Pilgrim spirit" was "throughout this nation . . . regarded as disorganizing, schismatical, revolutionizing and infidel as it was at the time of the embarkation of the Pilgrim Fathers at Delft Haven, and [was] treated accordingly" by establishmentarian authorities (*Liberator*, December 30, 1853). Once again Garrison conflated the two events but here acknowledged the secessionist implication of departure, which he had somehow missed in decoding Sumner's performance in August.

Garrison's frequent conflating of the Landing with the Embarkation was typical of his careless way with fact when promoting the Truth as he saw it. Equally generous to a fault with condemnation, Garrison in 1854 had castigated Senator Hale for being "careful to make no allusion to American Slavery," though the Liberator reserved his purest scorn for Yeadon, "a man . . . of a different stamp" than the other speakers: the South Carolinian, though far from home and surrounded by the descendants of the Pilgrims, had the brass "to stand up before that vast assembly, and eulogize Slavery, the Fugitive Slave Law—and Webster, Clay and Calhoun as demi-gods, because they had given their colossal strength to the support of them both! Yes, he had the assurance to compliment Edward Everett to his face, for having said, in his place in Congress, that, in case of a slave insurrection, he would be ready to buckle on his knapsack, shoulder his musket, and march to the assistance of the slaveholders! That was on Forefathers' Day [*sic*], at old Plymouth Rock!" (132).

It is noteworthy that Garrison made some subtle adjustments to Everett's actual words as quoted by Yeadon—his account in the *Liberator* having already substituted the dread "S" word for "servile"—here adding the gratuitous "march to the assistance of the slaveholders!" But when Garrison had a point to make, he did so without regard to fine distinctions, and in this he was but Yeadon's journalistic counterpart, his Puritan profile neatly dovetailing with that of the Cavalier. In attacking Sumner and Hale and misquoting Everett by way of Yeadon, Garrison's only thought was to emphasize the need for the North to speak out against slavery in the strongest kind of language, evincing "a spirit as daring and as vigilant as that which defends it; as willing in one section of the country as another to speak its own thoughts, and to defy consequences."

Garrison noted wryly that the date observed in Plymouth in 1853, August 1, was coincidentally "the anniversary of British West Indian Emancipation," which the abolitionists had celebrated that August, as for the twenty years previous. What, he wondered aloud, would the "fair-weather devotees" of the Pilgrims do, if the radicals decided to take over Plymouth in August as well as in December? (130). But his remarks had the effect of inserting the abolitionist presence into those other "proceedings" and were preceded and abetted by the address by the Reverend Theodore Parker during the abolitionist celebration in August that had gone on concurrently with the festivities in Plymouth. Parker had taken the opportunity provided by the duality of the date to mount a complex analogy between the emancipation of the West Indies and the embarkation of the Pilgrims, and as it happened there was a difference in one day in the scheduling, enabling the abolitionist minister to witness the goings-on in Plymouth, so that his remarks were informed by what he had seen there.

"At first sight," said Parker, there would seem to be no connection but a coincidental date in common "between the embarkation of the Pilgrims at Holland and the emancipation of the black man in the West Indies" (*Liberator*, August 12, 1853). But when one realized that the Pilgrims had carried with them "two great ideas . . . God first and Liberty second," then there appeared "a connection, not accidental, but substantial, essential." The echo of Everett's speech was hardly accidental either but was in the spirit of George Thompson's use of the Reverend Blagden's discourse nearly twenty years earlier.

Parker certified the connection by making explicit mention of his presence in Plymouth the day before, when, standing "with the rock of Plymouth under his feet," in the midst of scenes that inevitably brought back "the time when those men, few in numbers, strong in principles" had come ashore, "he could not help thinking how powerful the idea of right, and how powerful the sentiment of trust in God had shown themselves to be." Parker then made up for the omission committed by Senator Sumner and pointed out how "the religion of those Pilgrims revolutionized a large part of the Christian world."

Yet Parker was also reminded, by the presence of the rich and powerful persons up on the speakers' platform, of the sharp contrast between the modern moment and the time when Puritans had been kept from such places of honor: "The platform of the scaffold, with the headsman's block for its central point," was the only kind of public eminence those Puritans were familiar with. It was a juxtaposition that reflected badly on Everett's failure to speak one word "in favor of the liberty which was denied to every seventh man in this blessed land." Parker also wondered aloud about the presence on the platform of a "South Carolinian," a man whose "talk was military" and who had complimented Everett for being willing to shoulder a musket and march South "to put down an insurrection of slaves." This turn of events was accounted by Parker an unlikely spectacle to take place near "Plymouth rock, associated with the memory of Robinson, and Winslow, and Carver, and Miles Standish," and "a strange speech to be made on the anniversary of Old England's emancipation, and in the heart and centre of New England Puritanism itself."

Having begun his discourse by borrowing a phrase from Everett to use as the text of an address intended to rectify Everett's omissions, Parker next employed the time-honored Whig tradition of summoning up the ghosts of the Pilgrim past, "the spirits of Robinson, and Standish, and Carver, and the rest of that noble company," who seem to say " 'Be strong, for you are right with God; the might of God is on your side, and you shall surely triumph.' " And he ended his speech with a phrase ineradicably associated with yet another great Whig oration in praise of the Pilgrims, that of Rufus Choate, words delivered in 1843 before the New England Society in New York and made more memorable by having been used in a popular song of the day, "A Church without a Bishop, and a State without a King."

We will be considering that oration and equivalent Whig performances in the chapter following, but I cite it here to emphasize the extent to which Parker was emulating George Thompson's strategy, which had become essential to the mocking tenor of Garrisonite performances when addressing the matter of the Pilgrims. Once again, the net effect of Parker's performance in August 1853 was to anchor the abolitionists firmly to Plymouth Rock, not by again taking over Forefathers' Day (despite Garrison's confusion of dates) but by setting up a reminder that in fleeing to August 1 the Whig celebrants of the Pilgrims would not be able to escape the Truth, which would pursue them wherever they went and would flog them with their own words in following after.

Parker's performance was not as forceful as Garrison's denunciation of the Pilgrim celebration of the Embarkation, which appeared in the same issue of the *Liberator*, but then it was Parker's way always to avoid a harsh, adversarial tone and to blur his attacks with oblique, quietly mocking praise, a manner essential to the Brahmin (and Unitarian) cast of discourse. We can say of his remarks what Parker said of Sumner's speech of the day before: "He spoke as they would expect Mr. Sumner to speak; not as they would expect his friend Garrison or Wendell Phillips to speak, but he spoke as Charles Sumner would speak, and he [Parker] . . . believed that he always spoke as Charles Sumner thought. . . . He spoke earnestly, bravely, and well." Friend Garrison had been much less charitable, but then he had written as Garrison would speak, much as Phillips, when given the opportunity to address the matter of the Pilgrims, would speak in quite a different manner from all these others.

The occasion was the attempt in 1855 of the Pilgrim Society to reclaim Forefathers' Day, accepting at last the committee's decision that the 21st was the authentic date. The orator of the day was William H. Seward, whose connection with the Pilgrims was remote, he being from New York and having no New England antecedents. What Seward was in 1855 was a Republican, a hybrid recently born of the union of Conscience Whigs, Free-Soilers, and other factions opposed to Southern expansion and the extension of slavery into territories about to become western states. Starting in the 1830s, Seward's career had been under the care of Thurlow Weed, the resident ghost in the Albany Whig machine, who oversaw his rise up through the state legislature to the governorship and on to the Senate of the United States. Both men had come around with the winds of change and crossed over into the Republican camp, and because Seward had bravely opposed the Compromise of 1850, and because his career had been consistently devoted to emancipation—a devotion to civil rights balanced by an ardent interest in internal improvements of the civil engineering kind—he could advertise himself in Massachusetts as an acceptable substitute for the dishonored and now defunct Webster.

In sum, Seward was a Whig with a conscience and a Republican with a portfolio, but he was also an advocate of gradual abolition through orderly and constitutional means, and though he had introduced the idea of the "Higher Law" into the antislavery debate, he was careful not to make much use of that phrase afterward. By 1855, Weed was grooming him for the presidential campaign the following year, and Seward, in order to further his reputation not only as a seasoned politician but as a man for all seasons, had become increasingly cautious in his public statements. The proceedings on Forefathers' Day in 1855 were not published by the Pilgrim Society, but hardly because of Seward's oration, which was so politically correct (in terms of caution) that it was printed in Albany the following year, then later issued as one of the "Documents published by the Republican Association of Washington City" (Matthews, 390).

Thus Seward's speech may not have been what Garrison claimed for Everett's address in 1853—his "bid for the Presidency"—but it was certainly an appeal for the support of New England should his candidacy become real. That is to say, Forefathers' Day served ambitious politicians, including Adams, Webster, and Everett, among others, as an event equivalent to the New Hampshire primary today, an opportunity to draw national attention and earn the votes of New England citizens. And because the decorums of the day mandated a discourse that took the highest ground, it was an occasion that incidentally provided the greatest tactical advantage where controversial subjects were concerned.

Seward therefore carefully observed just those "proprieties" that Garrison in 1853 had attacked Sumner and Hale for heeding. On the other hand, in celebrating "The Pilgrims and Liberty," Seward jettisoned the usual furniture of commemoration, calling up no elaborate images of a tearful Embarkation, a solemn Signing, or a prayerful Landing. His was instead a very carefully reasoned discourse on "the Puritan principle," which he summarized in this well-considered and balanced (if complexly compound) sentence:

The Puritan principle tends to the pure republic, by virtue of its conservative protection of the individual member of the state against its corporate oppression; by virtue, also, of its elevation of individual conscience, thus bringing down the importance of the aggregate mass, and raising the personal importance and dignity of the subject or citizen; by virtue of the importance it attaches to personal rights, exalting them above material interests, and so *making those rights, and not property*, the primary object of the care of government, and by virtue, still further, of the openness, directness, and frankness of conduct which it requires. (*Works*, 4:196; emphasis added)

I have italicized the one phrase that aligns this otherwise unexceptional statement with the argument of the abolitionists, but hardly in a style that would give Garrison much comfort, Seward having taken the long way around the burning barn.

He likewise tended to give the by then problematic Pilgrims a wide berth, and while careful to define them as opposed to compromise, Seward refrained from associating them with modern radicalism. Moreover, in maintaining that "civil liberty is an object of universal and intense desire," and in observing that "the abolition of African slavery by all of the European nations, and, with few exceptions, also by all of the American states," had already taken place and that the same "great principle" would be universally adopted "at some period not far distant," Seward did not name a date (198, 195). He was in fact careful to emphasize that "Truth is not aggressive, but, like the Christian religion, is first pure, then peaceable," and that the "courageous reformer" need not "shrink from controversy" but should not "make nor seek occasions for activity" and always remain "unpassioned." Seward's position was perfectly in harmony with both the decorums of the occasion and Republican politics in Massachusetts in 1855.

The usual dinner followed Seward's oration, followed by the usual toasts, but what occurred during the toasts was not usual, at least not in occasions sponsored by the Pilgrim Society. Rising to respond to the sentiment "*The Pilgrim Fathers,*—Their fidelity amid hardships and perils, to truth and duty, has secured to their descendants prosperity and peace," Wendell Phillips carried the spirit of the Pilgrims as defined during previous celebrations of Forefathers' Day by the Old Colony Anti-Slavery Society into the midst of the gathering assembled by a far different auspice. We may wonder what such a person was doing at such a function in such a place and why he had been scheduled to speak at all. Surely, given the record of Phillips's previous performances, his sentiments could been have predicted to have much to do with the Pilgrims' "fidelity amid hardships and perils, to truth and duty," and not much to do with the rest.

Equally anomalous was the wild applause that greeted Phillips's remarks, as recorded in his collected speeches, but that can be explained by the fact that the Old Colony Anti-Slavery Society was scheduled to meet in Plymouth the next morning, the traditional date of Forefathers' Day, and the enthusiastic response may indicate that a considerable number of abolitionists were there with him. The alternative and less likely explanation is that the temper of the community had indeed been influenced, as Parker Pillsbury suggested, by the earlier visits of the Garrisonians. Whatever the reasons for his inclusion and friendly reception, Phillips certainly did not speak in cypher, for allowing him into the establishment tent in no way shifted the direction or violence of his rhetorical discharge.

He began with a humorous citation of a witticism by his cousin Oliver Wendell Holmes, and then, having made the obligatory compliment to the day's orator, he seized upon one of Seward's phrases and, following the strategy established by George Thompson, went to work making improvements to it. Seward, in playing down the Pilgrims' potential as revolutionaries, had argued that the Forefathers were products of the Reformation and as such had "neither disclosed nor discovered any new truths of morals or of government . . . nor was it their mission to institute a new progress of mankind" (4:185). "How true it is," observed Phillips ironically, "that it is not truth which agitates the world!" (*First Series*, 229). What the Pilgrims "gave the world was not thought, but ACTION. . . . Men, who called themselves thinkers, had been creeping along the Mediterranean, from headland to headland, in their timidity; the Pilgrims launched boldly out into the Atlantic, and trusted God," a phrase that echoes Lowell's great hymn, and which was followed, in the stenographer's record, by the notation "Loud applause."

The Pilgrims are misunderstood, according to Phillips, because they are regarded chiefly in terms of their prophetic potential—the Webster tradition— and "not in what poor human bodies actually produced at that time." Thus when orators conjure up the spirits of Carver and Bradford, imagining them alive once again, they clothe them "in the same garments" they wore in their time and picture them "walking in the same identical manner and round that they did in 1620. It is a mistake. The Pilgrims would be, in 1855, not in Plymouth but in Kansas. [Loud cheers]" (230). Rather than calling up the ghosts of the Forefathers and having them bless the evidences of modern progress, Phillips was resurrecting them as active participants in forwarding radical change, not throwing up their arms in amazed admiration but shouldering arms for Kansas. "We should bear in mind development when we criticise the Pilgrims,—where they would be today. Indeed, to be as good as our fathers, we must be better. Imitation is not discipleship" (231).

Having radicalized the Pilgrims in terms similar to those resolutions read by himself and Garrison at the meetings of the Old Colony Anti-Slavery Society, Phillips next tore the Forefathers bodily out of Seward's ornate and carefully qualified context and placed them on a revisionary Rock:

Neither do I acknowledge, Sir, the right of Plymouth to the whole rock. No, the rock underlies all America; it only crops out here. [Cheers.] It has cropped out a great many times in our history. You may recognize it always. Old Putnam stood upon it at Bunker Hill, when he said to the Yankee boys, "Don't fire till you see the whites of their eyes." . . . Jefferson had it for a writing-desk when he drafted the Declaration of Independence and the "Statute of Religious Liberty" for Virginia. Lovejoy rested his musket upon it when they would not let him print at Alton, and he said "Death or free speech!" I recognized the clink of it today, when the apostle of the "Higher Law" came to lay his garland of everlasting—none better right than he— upon the monument of the Pilgrims. [Enthusiastic cheering.]

. . . Ay, Sir, the rock cropped out again. Garrison had it for an imposing-stone when he looked in the faces of seventeen millions of angry men and printed his sublime pledge, "I will not retreat a single inch, and I will be heard." [Great Cheering]. (231–32)

We may not doubt Seward's reaction to having had his "Higher Law" tossed to him as he was first placed in company with Lovejoy and Garrison on Plymouth Rock, then shipped aboard the *Mayflower* with boxes of Beecher's breech-loading Bibles bound for Kansas: "He knows so much about the Mayflower, that, as they say in the West, I know he was 'thar.' [Laughter and applause]." Phillips went on to give pointed emphasis to most of Seward's carefully cir-cumspect remarks, in rapid, declarative, forthright, witty sentences, peppered with anecdotes, a lively and entertaining tribute yet hardly humorous in terms of radical purpose.

What Phillips intended to accomplish was serious enough, to claim the Pilgrims and Plymouth Rock once and for all for abolition and thereby realize the truth of what Orville Dewey had said thirty years earlier, though in a way that Dewey could hardly have found gratifying. Converting the Forefathers from sacred relics to holy terrors, he likewise gave the Rock a subterranean and subversive quality of immanence, along with a volcanic propensity to suddenly "crop up" as the pedestal of radicalism, the very antithesis of that stable thresh-old of empire conventionally evoked by Whig celebrants of the Pilgrims. As a work of literature, Phillips's speech was an extension of Whittier's abolitionist poems and Lowell's sonorous anthem, the period to which he gave in his closing words: "They say, Sir, I am a fanatic, and so I am. But, Sir, none of us have yet risen high enough. Afar off, I see Carver and Bradford, and I mean to get up to them," which last was greeted by "loud cheers" and should remind us that Thoreau, early on, was an admirer of Phillips's style of public address.

As Webster in 1820 had nationalized Plymouth Rock, making it over into an icon of perpetual material progress, Phillips in 1855 claimed it for radical reform, prying up that Federalist symbol of statist stability from where it had rested for so long. "Plymouth Rock," Edward Everett had intoned in his eulogy for Daniel Webster, "all but moved at his approach" in 1820; but in 1855, it did move, released like the Pilgrims themselves from the weight of conservative tradition (*Orations and Speeches*, 3:159). And then it began to move faster and faster, until it was a juggernaut rolling toward an apocalyptic conclusion. In setting free the Rock, Phillips may be said to have released forces that had been held back for more than a quarter century, and few that day who applauded the act, even those who led the cheers, could have been fully aware of the consequences, though it is worthy of note that fifteen years went by before the Pilgrim Society ventured to celebrate Forefathers' Day again.

For there was also set in motion in 1855 an as yet unknown, even shadowy shape, a man born in the Litchfield Hills in Connecticut but raised on an Ohio farm, who had spent much of his earlier career pursuing the dream of prosperity held out by the Whig faith in material progress but who was never successful in anything save failure—and siring children. Though a Yankee in heritage and outlines, he was virtually a travesty of the type, his hard-bitten shrewdness and perpetual calculation of advantage masking a dreamy idealism, in effect putting into action the two faces of Ralph Waldo Emerson.

Abandoning speculative ventures, this Yankee Quixote had recently associated himself with farming once again, tilling the rocky, adversarial soil of the Catskills, labor like that which, according to Everett and Whittier, was virtue itself, and he would soon enough gain a measure of immortality by joining Lovejoy as a martyr in the cause of abolition. As much as Lovejoy became a product of abolitionist rhetoric of the 1830s, so it was the escalating mood of militancy among champions of emancipation during the 1840s and 1850s from which John Brown drew strength, inspiration, and resolve, becoming in symbolic terms the westering Pilgrim and iron-hard Puritan evoked by Phillips, by Garrison, by Whittier and Lowell, among many others. When Plymouth Rock next cropped up, it would support John Brown at Harpers Ferry.

IV

The cohesion of rhetoric into the person of John Brown will be the concern of a subsequent chapter, but this is the proper place in which to consider that part of Wendell Phillips's contribution that provides an interface with his rock-moving speech of 1855. During the period of Brown's trial and execution, Phillips delivered two lectures celebrating the martyr hero, the first and perhaps most important of which was read in Henry Ward Beecher's Plymouth Church in Brooklyn and was entitled "The Lesson of the Hour." Phillips turned the occasion into a display of forensic dynamite, beginning with his definition of the lesson of the hour as "insurrection," which on November 1,

1859, would have certainly sent a ripple of reaction through the audience, an aftershock from the explosion at Harpers Ferry less than two weeks previous. At this point, it should be remembered, public opinion was running high against John Brown, deemed a madman at best, at worst a bloody fanatic.

Having caught the attention of his audience, Phillips then reassured them: what he meant, he explained, was "insurrection of thought," which always precedes the "insurrection of arms" (*First Series*, 263). He continued on in the same vein, noting that "we have been carrying on this insurrection of thought for thirty years," an epoch Phillips dated from the first number of the *Liberator*. But then, with another sudden twist, the sort of thing that made his speeches a rhetorical theater in which one is never sure which way the plot will turn, Phillips announced that "John Brown of Osawatomie" was *not* an insurgent, there being no real government in Virginia against which to raise a revolt—"only a chronic insurrection" (272). "You see," continued Phillips, who had been received about evenly with cheers and hisses until that moment, "I am talking of that absolute essence of things which lives in the sight of the Eternal and the Infinite; not as men judge it in the rotten morals of the nineteenth century, among a herd of States that calls itself an empire, because it raises cotton and sells slaves" (272–73). This was the turning point, after which his reception became unanimously enthusiastic.

Phillips regarded the hero of Osawatomie as "the natural result of antislavery teaching" and as a resurrection also of the spirit of "Puritan Presbyterianism . . . a regular Cromwellian dug up from two centuries" ago (273, 276). But even as he graced John Brown with the dual identity of an abolitionist and a Puritan, Phillips made one of his characteristic digs in the ribs of the orthodoxy, listing Brown's "five points" of theology as "the fist, the bowie-knife, fire, poison, and the pistol," in effect a Calvinist creed of violent retribution: "God makes him the text, and all he asks of our comparatively cowardly lips is to preach the sermon" (276).

Captain John Brown, Phillips declared, had introduced a new element into American politics: before, the South had evinced an unimpeded power to corrupt, buying up "Webster with a little or a promise, and Everett with nothing. [Great laughter and applause.] John Brown has given her something else to think of. . . . He has taught her that there has been created a new element in this Northern mind; that it is not merely the thinker, that it is not merely the editor, that it is not merely the moral reformer, but the idea has pervaded all classes of society" (277–78). What John Brown brought about was "not an insurrection"; it was "the penetration of a different element" into the South, "an element . . . in the Yankee blood which obeys ideas . . . an impulsive, enthusiastic aspiration, something left to us from the old Puritan stock; that which made New England what she was two centuries ago; that which is fated to give the closest grapple with the Slave Power today" (282).

Brown as a remnant Puritan was also to Phillips's way of thinking an active forwarder of Progress, and Harpers Ferry one stage in a continuing sequence, one scene in an unrolling panorama. Like the colonies planted by Raleigh and Gosnold, it would "be swept away" but "by and by will come the immortal one hundred," the passengers of the *Mayflower* who landed on "Plymouth Rock, with 'MANIFEST DESTINY' written by God's hand on their banner, and the right of unlimited 'ANNEXATION' granted by Heaven itself." It should perhaps be pointed out that these slogans were turned by Phillips to uses quite different from those of Democratic expansionists and refer to the extension of radical ideology, not slave territory: "It is the lesson of the age. The first cropping out of it is in such a man as John Brown" (282). In the rapid flow of Phillips's discourse one can be carried right by that outcrop without noticing it; its implication can only be understood by reference to his speech of 1855, for by its agency Brown now joins those other heroes of Liberty who stood fast on Plymouth Rock.

In his subsequent address celebrating John Brown, delivered shortly after the martyr had been hanged, Phillips expanded considerably on "the Puritan Principle." In his opening line he "thanked God for John Calvin," hardly sentiments to be expected from the nemesis of orthodoxy, but Phillips provided little comfort for Congregationalists, for he went on to celebrate the man sacred to Trinitarians for having originated the democratic impulse, "the triumphs of the people against priestcraft and power," and, more important, the Puritan love of action: "The Puritan was not a man of speculation" (*Second Series*, 294–95). We may remember here Lowell's activist notion of the Puritan, swordlike in militant utility.

Puritanism is not pluralism, and as evinced in John Brown, it "is impersonating ideas; it is distrusting and being willing to shake off what are called institutions" (297). This was the main point Phillips made in his Plymouth speech in 1855, now given specific shape in and by John Brown: "Insurrection is epidemic in the State; treason is our inheritance. The Puritans planted it in the very structure of the State. . . . I thank God for that Massachusetts. . . . They do not know how to be servile within forty miles of Plymouth. They have not learned the part; with all their wish, they play it awkwardly. It is the old stiff Puritan trying to bend, and they do it with a marvellous lack of grace" (305). So also Lowell's stiff-kneed Standish, railing at the craven suppleness of Whig celebrants of Forefathers' Day.

As a different Yankee, moreover, Brown was also an improved Puritan, being "braver than Carver or Winthrop, more disinterested than Bradford, broader than Hancock or Washington, pure as the brightest names on our catalogue, nearer God's heart. . . . John Brown is the impersonation of God's order and God's law, moulding a better future, and setting it for an example. . . . This is the lesson of Puritanism, as it is read to us today" (307–8). It is also a lesson that Wendell Phillips took thirty years to learn, for his orations celebrating John Brown as a Puritan hero provide a considerable contrast to his memorial address for Lovejoy on Forefathers' Day in 1837, in which hardly a word about the Pilgrims or the Puritans was mentioned. Yet Phillips remained consistent in one respect, for as his reference to Virginia as a state of permanent insurrection suggests, Phillips's emphasis was always on matters of law.

"Connecticut has sent out many a schoolmaster to the other thirty States," he had informed the audience gathered in Beecher's Brooklyn church, "but never before so grand a teacher as the Litchfield-born schoolmaster at Harper's Ferry, writing as it were upon the Natural Bridge, in the face of nations, his simple copy,—'Resistance to tyrants is obedience to God.' [Loud cheers]" (*First Series*, 271). Scrawling Jefferson's favorite motto (associated with the Cromwellian regicides) on a Virginia landmark famously celebrated by the sage of Monticello is a graffito with a vengeance. But in the act of writing it on the Natural Bridge, Phillips's Brown in effect is placed not only in Jefferson's company on Plymouth Rock but in Elijah Lovejoy's as well, who had taken his stand not against slavery but for the freedom of the press.

In being given a place by Phillips on the Rock, John Brown is immortalized less as a champion of the slave than of rebellion against the tyrannical authority of the state: "John Brown sails the sea a Lord High Admiral of the Almighty, with his commission to sink every pirate he meets on God's ocean of the nineteenth century" (272). The law imprisoned Brown in Virginia, but Brown correctly beheld *was* the law in Virginia, the Higher Law, which is an expression of "that absolute essence of things which lives in the sight of the Eternal and the Infinite; not as men judge it in the rotten morals of the nineteenth century." As always with Wendell Phillips it is the law finally that is the central issue, around which coheres the critical mass of his argument.

This is not to say that Phillips was insincere in his abolitionism. But it does suggest that he had a single-minded consistency that can be traced back through so much that he did and said, back to that moment when he forced his way through the crowd at Faneuil Hall and stood up for Lovejoy's—and his own, and everyone's—civil rights. That was his cause, his long legal brief, and with dreadful and consistent logic it placed John Brown on Plymouth Rock in 1859, not because he attempted to start a slave insurrection but because he had revived in him a Puritanism that was virtually indistinguishable from the Spirit of Laws.

And that John Brown is virtually indistinguishable also from John Adams and his *Dissertation upon Canon and Feudal Law*, much as Wendell Phillips and William Lloyd Garrison and Edmund Quincy are difficult to distinguish when standing in a very bright light from those Federalists who dragged Forefathers' Rock into the nineteenth century. For the radical spirit in New England stems from a deep-rooted conviction that the law not only underlies but overarches America, a principle as different in its circumstantial application as were John Winthrop and John Endicott, or John Adams and John Quincy Adams, but consistent in holding fast against political expediency and moral drift: it was not for nothing that the younger Adams was known in Massachusetts in his elder years as "Plymouth Rock."

CHAPTER 13

Rock Ballast for the Ship of State

Now, if you were to see a great fleet, spreading all their canvass,
throwing over their ballast and committing themselves to the wildest
winds, you would see in visibles the invisible spirit of our times. We
cannot entirely prevent it. But we may counteract it by a spirit of
moral conservation. Let us lay the injunction on our youth; let us
teach it to our children, that old principles tried by experience, are
not lightly to be shaken. We have something to keep as well as to gain.
—The Puritan

I

In tracking the ongoing debate in Plymouth between the Garrisonites and the Whiggish constituency of the Pilgrim Society, we have neglected
the parallel series of celebrations hosted by the New England Society in the
City of New York. Much as it had served as a venue for hard-line Trinitarians in
the 1820s, so the annual observation of Forefathers' Day in New York maintained a conservative political consistency regarding reform between 1837,
when Leonard Bacon gave the Quakers a radical profile, and 1855, when, finally
breaking with its own tradition, the society in New York, like its Plymouth
counterpart, yielded to the spirit of the times. The program on December 22
(New York persisted in observing the traditional date) featured two speakers,
the one a committed ultra-abolitionist poet, the other a conservative orator
who turned out to be more reactionary than many in the audience were willing
to tolerate. Moreover, detectable echoes of Wendell Phillips's remarks may be
heard in the oration, in effect reversing what might be called the Thompson
effect and giving the advantage, if it was that, to New York.

Before confronting this ideological playoff, we need to consider briefly the
sequence of orations that preceded it, if only because the best of these, famous

in their day, help to reinforce the context of the climactic celebration, which was in all ways at odds with what had gone before. Equally important, the sentiments expressed over the intervening years help fill in the blanks caused by the failure of the Pilgrim Society to celebrate Forefathers' Day between 1836 and 1846, as well as compensate for those intervals associated with the committee's report in 1850. The New York society met regularly, without equivalent gaps between celebrations, and seems to have been subject to no ideological conflicts, for most of the speakers at the anniversary dinners were Whig in politics and often from Massachusetts, which meant that they were gradualists and compromisers and after 1850 were increasingly on the defensive.

We start with 1839, when the speaker was Robert C. Winthrop, descendant of the first governor of Massachusetts, a Harvard graduate and like Everett a protégé of Webster, having begun his practice of law under the Great Man's tutelage. Winthrop had gone on to serve for five years as a popular representative to the General Court and decided in 1839 to advance his career by announcing his candidacy for the U.S. House of Representatives. Like Webster in 1820 and Everett in 1824, Winthrop demonstrated his ambition for high office by delivering an oration on the most elevated, disinterested plane. He would follow in the great Whig tradition thenceforth, his address in New York being but the first of many such he would give during a long career of public service, following his election to Congress in 1840.

Statesmanlike in bearing and address, Winthrop was in less visible respects a politician, with a talent for spreading his sails to catch the prevailing breeze. And in New England in 1839, following the martyrdom of Lovejoy and the expressions of public outrage, the wind was definitely blowing from the North and in favor of antislavery sentiments. Having therefore devoted a large part of his oration to the providential character of the Pilgrim experience, a properly pious emphasis, Winthrop came to the point where he added the power of "Conscience" to the equation, "inspiring a courage, confirming a resolution, and accomplishing an enterprise, of which the records of the world will be searched in vain to find a parallel" (*New England Society Orations*, hereafter "*NESO*," 1:246).

For the sake of comparison, Winthrop cited the example of Jamestown, and though, as a Whig in the model of Webster and Everett, Winthrop was no enemy of the South, he noted that differences did remain between the two colonies and were there from the start. Thus the Jamestown Charter "contained not a single element of popular liberty," as compared with the Mayflower Compact, and it was symptomatic of the Virginia settlers also—in contrast to the familial basis of the Pilgrim settlement—that they had imported a shipload of women "to be sold to the planters for wives," a gesture heavy with dark prophecy: "Would to God, that all the traffic in human flesh on the Virginian Coast even at this early period had been as innocent in itself and as beneficial in its results!" (253).

This cargo and auction of women, as Winthrop's aside suggests, was preludic to a subsequent and fatal shipment of human beings, which Winthrop worked up as the rhetorical high point of his oration and which yielded a starkly iconic contrast between the purposes and destinies of the colonies centered by Jamestown and Plymouth. For even as the *Mayflower* was approaching the New England coast in 1620, bearing its liberty-loving passengers, a Dutch man-of-war was heading for Chesapeake Bay, with a cargo of "twenty slaves," who would provide "the foundations of domestic slavery in North America."

George Bancroft had noted these coincidental voyages in the first volume of his monumental history of the United States, published in 1834, but Winthrop elevated the twin events to cosmic significance, keying the essential, even tragic difference between the two colonies: "I see those two fate-freighted vessels, laboring under the divided destinies of the same Nation, and striving against the billows of the same sea, like the principles of good and evil advancing side by side on the same great ocean of human life. I hear from the one the sighs of wretchedness, the groans of despair, the curses and clankings of struggling captivity, sounding and swelling on the same gale, which hears only from the other the pleasant voices of prayer and praise, the cheerful melody of contentment and happiness, the glad, the glorious 'anthem of the free.' . . . Freedom and Slavery in one and the same year, have landed on these American shores" (256–57). Winthrop's description of the two quite different ships is in the "vision" mode by which Webster and Everett "saw" the *Mayflower* as it approached the New England coast, but by adding the unnamed Dutch slaver, he called up a terrible twin that was essential to the emerging division between North and South. He thereby added yet another rhetorical trope to the conventions of Forefathers' Day orations, tracing "the bright and shining wake" of the Pilgrims to their "bleak and storm-beaten Rock," while lowering a curtain of shame over the arrival of that other, fatal ship (228, 224).

Like Webster's stirring words in 1820, Winthrop's remarks were focused on the slave trade, not the institution itself. And his emphasis on Providence, brought forward from his discussion of the Pilgrims' errand, gives a certain bias to his diptych as well, expressed in his "hope" that the figure of Liberty in America will not "for ever" be doomed to the iconic companionship of a slave. This hopefulness is integral to the gradualist view, that God in his own time would solve the problem of slavery. Like Everett, Winthrop was opposed to the extension of slavery, and having assumed Webster's senatorial desk in 1850 when Webster was appointed secretary of state by Fillmore, he was unhappy also with the chief consequence of the Compromise of 1850. He opposed the Fugitive Slave Bill, but without the stern display of conscience for the sake of Liberty he celebrated in his Pilgrims, and he consequently lost the election in 1851 to Charles Sumner, a man for whom "outspoken" is too mild a word for his opposition to the slave interests.

Yet Winthrop remained an attractive possibility for proponents of mediation and compromise. As late as 1854, writing to Emerson on July 3, Whittier anticipated the 4th by calling for a new antislavery coalition, made up of Conscience Whigs, Free-Soilers, and anti–Kansas-Nebraska Democrats: "The Whigs especially only wait for the movement of the men to whom they have been accustomed to look for direction. I may be mistaken, but I fully believe that Robert C. Winthrop holds in his hands the destiny of the North. By throwing himself on the side of this movement he could carry with him the Whig strength of New England" (Pickard, 1:374). Whittier was prescient in foretelling the birth of the Republican Party, but Winthrop was not a man inclined to hurl himself in any direction, and he remained loyal to the Whig Party long after it had been laid to rest with Daniel Webster.

As Emerson had noted in his journal that year, "One would say, if ability & position availed, Mr. Winthrop, of all men, would be justified in a manly independence. But such saying betrays a beautiful ignorance of the habits & exigencies of our happy land. . . . Mr. Winthrop is a strong example of the insufficiency of any & all outward advantages to resist public opinion in this country" (*Journals*, 13:71). To Emerson's way of thinking, Winthrop was typical of the "great men of today," like Webster and Everett, who could be of no help in solving contemporary problems, "they deriving entirely from the old dead things" (83). As if to bear out Emerson's connection between the Whigs and the dead past, Winthrop withdrew from politics into the study of history and the regular production of orations that permitted the display of those "blameless morals, elegant tastes, [and] popular manners" that Emerson had allowed him while withholding a final measure of approval. Even so, Winthrop's remonstrance against slavery in 1839 was singular in the orations delivered to the New England Society, and he must be given credit for his courage, whatever his subsequent course of inaction.

The *Mayflower*, moreover, continued to dominate figurative discourse in New York, perhaps because it dominated the seal of the society, and in 1843, Rufus Choate, another rising star of the Whig Party, celebrated the "heroic" age of the Pilgrims by alluding four times to the signing of the compact on board the Pilgrim ark. He gave the Rock only a passing mention, as a point from which to view the heroism of the past, "from whose personages, and from whose actions, the orator may bring away an incident or a thought that shall kindle a fire in ten thousand hearts, as on altars to their country's glory"

(*NESO*, 1:330). From that vantage point, Choate demonstrated the truth of his proposition by striking oratorical sparks, in his invocation of "a state without king or nobles; a church without a bishop," inspiring the song to which Theodore Parker would refer twelve years later.

Ironically, the reference was not to the Pilgrims, with whom it would thenceforth be associated, but to the Swiss Republic, where English Puritans had found refuge during the reign of Queen Mary, resulting in "an influence which has changed the history of the world" (334). From this interlude "in a valley which might seemed hollowed out to enclose the last home of liberty," there came both "a new theology" and a "new politics," inspiring "the great civil war of England; the Republican Constitution framed in the cabin of The Mayflower; the divinity of Jonathan Edwards; the battle of Bunker Hill; the Independence of America," rather much a lump sum in which the Pilgrims figure but do not dominate (336, 334).

Webster was present at the New England Society dinner in 1843 and provided a "response" to Choate's oration, which in its coupling of Compact and Constitution had provided an opening that Webster chose not to seize. Instead, he addressed himself to "the commerce of the United States," which pointedly included all of the states, none of which, properly considered, had a commerce of its own: "There is . . . nothing that makes us more cohesive, nothing that more repels all tendencies to separation and dismemberment, that this great, this common, I may say this overwhelming interest of one commerce" (*NESO*, 1:357).

Webster thereby placed a solid cargo in the *Mayflower*, giving Choate's "spirit of liberty" a little Yankee cargo, from which, to certain sensitive ears in Newburyport, perhaps the clinking of chains might have been heard. But Webster's audience in New York heard what they wished to hear, summarized by the Great Man's toast, to "*the mercantile interest of the United States,*" which was received with "loud and repeated applause." We may take this enthusiasm as a demonstration that, for most Whigs in 1843, all glorious generalities about the genesis of the Constitution were ballasted by an abiding faith in the sacredness of property, whatever form it might take.

II

When Forefathers' Day was celebrated in New York in 1850, the custom of featuring a main speaker was set aside, and the dinner held in the Astor House was the main event, which even more than usual opened the festivities to spontaneous effusions, the responses to toasts that provide a kind of graffiti revealing the complex sentiments felt on those occasions. The guests assembled included such literary luminaries from Great Britain as G. P. R. James and Sir Henry Bulwer—then also minister to the United States—clerics representing several Protestant denominations, as well as the presidents of the St. Nicholas, German Charitable, St. Andrew's, and St. George's Societies, a general of the army, and the president of Columbia College.

But perhaps the most prominent guest was Daniel Webster, in whose honor the dinner seems to have been held. In observing the traditional date of December 22 (though to avoid the Sabbath the dinner was actually given on the 23d), the New York society seems to have pointedly violated the findings of the committee appointed by the Pilgrim Society regarding the true date of the Landing. More to the immediate point was the fact that it was chiefly celebrating not the Forefathers but the orator famous for his celebration of them, which was the sort of thing the committee had remonstrated against.

Webster by December 1850 needed all the support he could get. His speech in the Senate on March 7, for "the Constitution and the Union," had been widely received as supporting Clay's advocacy of compromise regarding slavery in the states that would emerge from the new territories acquired as a consequence of the Mexican War. Webster had opposed that war in 1848, as having consequences that would "disfigure" the Constitution, turning it into "a deformed monster . . . not founded on equality, but on the grossest inequality," a "process" moreover that would continue "until this Union shall fall to pieces" (*Writings*, 10:32). He was speaking, of course, as a New England man, against that notorious provision in the Constitution giving slave states three-fifths of a vote for every slave, as well as the disproportionate representation between the Senate and the House that the admission of thinly populated states would produce.

Though Webster referred to the Constitution, it was the further disempowerment of his region that was his main concern, for both geopolitical factors would diminish New England's shrinking hegemony. But in 1850 he pointedly declared that he spoke "not as a Massachusetts man, nor as a Northern man, but as an American," a notion aptly borrowed from Thomas Jefferson, nor was this the only praise he heaped on Virginia (57). He spoke as always for Union, and against discord and secession, denouncing the notion of "peaceable secession" as "an utter impossibility," equivalent to "the breaking up of the fountains of the great deep without ruffling the surface. . . . There can be no such thing as a peaceable secession" (93).

The avowed purpose of his March 7 speech, long in preparation and eagerly awaited by his colleagues, was to spread oil upon the waters of dissension, north and south, and by a scholarly reprise of the history of the dispute over the extension of slavery, to bring some rational and enlightened understanding to "things as they are," an acknowledgment that "Slavery does exist in the United States," and if not specifically protected by the Constitution, tacitly so (65). It has been said that it was this speech by Webster that gave the notion of compromise, so essential to the framing of the Constitution, a bad reputation, but nowhere does Webster actually mention compromise. His defining word was "conciliation."

He talked about a number of things and lamented the intemperate, even violent language that had lately characterized journalistic discussion and congressional debate on the matter of slavery, of which both the North and South were guilty. He declared himself in this relation opposed to abolition societies as not "useful," having over the past twenty years "produced nothing good or valuable," only "mischiefs" by their "interference with the South," which made rational discussion in Southern states about the matter of slavery tantamount to impossible (89).

It was not Webster's purpose to give comfort to William Lloyd Garrison and his clique, who seldom gave comfort to him, but if he thought that his abrupt dismissal of Garrison's efforts for emancipation would promote understanding, he was mistaken. Indeed, as we have seen, his speech turned out to be his greatest gift to the abolition movement since his famous words against the traffic in slavery in 1820. Because although Webster did not speak out for compromise but against disunion and secession, he also spoke forcibly in favor of the return of fugitive slaves to their owners and for the use of federal authorities to facilitate that return, in accordance with the law of the land. If the burden of his speech was consistent with his habitual championship of the Union, so his argument for enforcing the law of 1793 was consistent with his speaking out against the illegal traffic in slaves in 1820 but was read by antislavery proponents as a betrayal of his earlier position.

Webster also gave his support to efforts "for the transportation of free colored people to any colony or any place in the world," in effect championing the forlorn hope still associated with the American Colonization Society (96). Of any other "mode" of "extinguishing or meliorating" slavery, Webster as he acknowledged "expressed no opinion." Though he dedicated his speech on "the Constitution and the Union" to "the People of Massachusetts," there were a number of persons in that state who by the time it was published were not at all interested in receiving the honor so bestowed and who like Whittier had decided that Webster was no longer their representative man.

As a reward for his loyalty to Union over section, Webster was made secretary of state by Millard Fillmore, a post traditionally regarded as a steppingstool to the presidency, which only reinforced his image as opportunism personified, earning the loathing of former worshipers like Emerson and the savage glee of Garrison. On December 23, 1850, however, Webster was surrounded by his proper element and was celebrated by the New England Society in New York, not reviled, for his March 7 speech: "On my right hand," announced the president of the society, "behold the illustrious defender of the

Constitution, whose name will be cherished throughout all time by every true American" (*Dinner*, 38). And the sentiments offered in toasts uniformly supported Webster as well, not because he favored compromise but because he had ardently supported the Union: "Talk of disunion! No man dares to breath the thought in the lowest whisper. No! No! No!" cried Simon Draper, vice president of the society. "When I think of the Constitution of the United States, and of the Union which is secured by it, I would speak of them as holy things; I would say 'touch not,' 'handle not.'"

It should be said also that if Webster in March had spoken not in favor of compromise but against secession, he made no mention of the Pilgrims or Plymouth Rock, but in December that omission was more than made up for. As befitted the occasion, allusions to the Rock and invariably to the *Mayflower* were frequent, but as in Webster's March speech, it was to the Union that most of the speakers returned. Thus the Reverend George Washington Bethune, a Dutch Reform minister, spoke at length on the beneficial influence on the Pilgrims of their stay in Holland, whence they derived their devotion to "Constitutional freedom" (34). Even while quoting Rufus Choate's by then famous "Church without a Bishop," Bethune in effect relocated that utopian republic from Switzerland to the Netherlands. But he ended by crediting to the Dutch "cradle" of republican principles the discovery by the Pilgrims of "the necessity and advantage of Union," which brought him easily back from "the men and women of Plymouth rock" to Webster, and to dis-Unionism, which was tantamount to "treason."

Webster himself rose to respond to the sentiments "The Constitution and the Union, and their Chief defender," and as he did so was greeted by "the most prolonged and tumultuous cheers," a demonstration of Whig solidarity. It is perhaps useful to remember that the parallel celebration in Plymouth that year was the one honoring George Thompson, this at a time when the Garrisonites were entertaining resolutions calling for "the immediate abolition of the Constitution" unless the Fugitive Slave Law was repealed as "an instrument for the extinction of our liberties" (*Liberator*, December 27, 1850).

And for their part, the abolitionists were as loud in expressing their enthusiastic approval of George Thompson in Plymouth as the celebrants in New York were in their applause for Webster: as the *Liberator* reported, "cheers, 'three times three,' were repeatedly given for him in the most rapturous manner. . . . He could not have had a more intelligent, discriminating, moral and philanthropic body to address" (December 27, 1850). Nor could Webster for his part have found a more congenial audience, made up of men for whom commerce was the lifeblood of the country and the Union and Constitution the auricle and ventricle of its heart, hence the chief source of the wealth that made the conviviality of the celebration possible.

The honored guest enhanced the intensity of that mood by an extended reference to the wind and rain audible to the celebrants in the dining room of the Astor House, which he compared to the wintry scene the Pilgrims encountered in 1620, the present comfort and good cheer providing dramatic contrast and inspiring gratitude for the difference. After remarking on the virtues of the Fathers and the changes in social attitudes that had taken place since their arrival, including the wholesome spread of tolerance for religious differences, Webster noted that the present chief justice of the United States was a Roman Catholic, yet "no man . . . imagines that the judicature of the country is less safe" because of it (17). In 1850, and for some time thereafter, the chief justice was Roger B. Taney, who in the minds of some Americans would seem to be less "safe" than sorry, most especially after the Dred Scott decision in 1857.

In good time Webster got around to the set piece expected of him, the Landing of the Pilgrims, and began by evoking "the 'Constitution' which was adopted on board the Mayflower in November, 1620, while that bark of immortal memory was riding at anchor in the harbor of Cape Cod" (18). Mindful perhaps of objections to his statist emphasis in 1820, Webster insisted on the connection made between church and state in the Compact, "which invokes a *religious* sanction and the authority of God on their *civil* obligations." Then, playing on the "vision" convention with which he and Everett had made the arrival of the Pilgrims so vivid, Webster declared, "There is the May-flower," but then jokingly pointed to the "small figure of a ship, in the form of confectionary, that stood before him."

The sugar in this model, unlike the sweetening banned from the cakes sold at the antislavery fairs in Boston, was presumably not politically correct, which means it had probably been refined from cane cut by southern slaves. A ship model made from such material might to some minds suggest a slave ship, but that was hardly Webster's intention. He went on to convert the *Mayflower* to a nosegay of sorts, by developing an extended analogy to the New England flower of that name: "Yes, brethren of New England, yes! that Mayflower was a flower destined to be of perpetual bloom! [Cheers.] . . . It will defy winter; it will defy all climate, and all time, and will continue to spread its petals to the world, and to exhale an ever living odor and fragrance 'to the last syllable of recorded time' [Cheers.]" (19).

Next in his tour de force of Forefathers' Day conventions, Webster conjured up the ghost of Elder William Brewster and brought him to the feast, "entering the door at the further end of this hall . . . a tall and erect figure, of plain dress, of no elegance of manner beyond a respectful bow, mild and cheerful, but of no merriment that reaches beyond a smile." This was not, however, a censorious figure but, as the convention demanded, a Whig-friendly spirit, and with that ventriloquist skill that had made his tribute to John Adams in 1826 a forensic legend, Webster gave voice to Brewster, who praised the dinner guests for having built so well on the meager foundations the Pilgrims had provided: " 'Is this magnificent city, the like of which we never saw nor heard of on either continent, is this but an offshoot from Plymouth rock . . . ? Does this scene of refinement, of elegance, of riches, of luxury, does all this come from our labors?' "

Perhaps mindful of the corrections made by the Reverend Whelpley on a similar occasion a quarter century earlier, Webster had his Brewster observe that material prosperity was not sufficient in itself to honor the Forefathers, whose " 'hopes were on another life.' " As the living generation of Americans " 'spread yourselves and your children over the continent,' " thus realizing the territorial imperatives of " 'your great destiny,' " they should " 'carry Puritan hearts' " with them and " 'cherish an undying love of civil and religious liberty,' " being willing to " 'shed your heart's blood to transmit them to your posterity' " (20).

Such piety combined with action—including warfare—was necessary to make the diners " 'worthy descendants of CARVER and ALLERTON and BRAD-FORD, and the rest of those who landed from stormy seas on the rock of Plymouth.' [Loud and prolonged cheers.]" Given the expansionist context of 1850, Brewster's remarks most likely were intended to reinforce Webster's speech in Plymouth in 1849, in which he expressed the hope that Pilgrim principles would prevail in the territories newly acquired by the Mexican War, a conflict that not incidentally realized Webster's geopolitical prophecy in 1820, even though he was by 1848 fearful of the consequences of so vastly extended an empire.

Along with his performance on March 7 that year, Webster's display of forensic necromancy on December 23 was an apt demonstration that his wizard powers had not left him, though he had less than two years of life remaining. Again, the frequent applause given his remarks was undoubtedly inspired in part by his earlier speech on behalf of the Union, much as the event itself was intended as testimony compensating Webster for the obloquy he had suffered at the hands of liberal Whigs. Encouraged, perhaps, by the warm response, Webster went on to a further demonstration of his rhetorical magic: with the storm outside beating upon the windows of the Astor House, he suggested that the Pilgrim ship "be considered this night as an emblem of New England, as New England now is," for like the nation itself the region was "a ship, staunch, strong, well-built, and particularly well-manned. She may be occasionally thrown into the trough of the sea, by the violence of winds and waves, and may *wallow* there for a time; but, depend upon it she will right herself. She will, ere long, *come round to the wind, and will obey her helm.* [Cheers and applause.]" (21). This was not Lowell's *Mayflower*, packed to the gunwales with radical gunpowder, but its Whig counterpart, no less pointed in the direction of the future.

By means of his nautical metaphor Webster asserted the power of the Constitution and the Union to survive the "local agitations" that had lately characterized the sections of the nation: "I am one of those who believe that our system of government is not to be destroyed by *localisms*, North or South! [Cheers.] No; we have our private opinions, State prejudices, local ideas; but over all, submerging all, *drowning* all, is that great sentiment, that always, and nevertheless, *we are all Americans*" (22). This transcendent spirit of nationalism, which Webster had been championing since 1830, he identified with the Compromise of 1850, which guaranteed there was "no longer imminent danger of dissolution in these United States. [Loud and repeated cheers.] We shall live, and not die. We shall live as united Americans. . . . No, gentlemen; the time for mediated secession is past. Americans, North and South, will be hereafter more and more united. . . . And who doubts it? If we give up [the] Constitution, what are we?"

These sentiments were a reprise of a high emotional moment in his March 7 speech, in which Webster cried out against secession as an impossibility, which would violate not only the Constitution but the natural geography of the nation, which provided no geological barrier between North and South and whose central feature was the great Mississippi Valley, which unified those cardinal directions: "Why, what would be the result? Where is the line to be drawn? What States are to secede? What is to remain American? What am I to be? An American no longer? Am I to become a sectional man, a local man, a separatist, with no country in common with the gentlemen who sit around me here, or who fill the other house of congress? Heaven forbid!" (*Writings*, 10:93).

Once again, Webster did not mention the Pilgrims in his speech of March 7, and this passage suggests why: not only were the Pilgrims separatists, but they were, in large part thanks to Webster, essential to New England's high opinion of itself as a section especially virtuous because of the institutions set in motion by the Forefathers. And Webster himself surely knew of the long-lived connection between himself and the Federalist movement toward secession as a reaction to the War of 1812: "Heaven forbid!" that such associations be brought forward in 1850, as the nation and Webster's political career teetered on the brink of dissolution. "You are a Manhattan man; I am a Boston man," he declared toward the end of his remarks in New York, by way of asserting consensus, but this last in terms of a national constituency for Webster meant literally nothing, and as for his sectional base, that was crumbling beneath his feet.

The currents against which Webster himself was struggling are suggested by the sermon read that Forefathers' Day in 1850 by the Reverend William Deloss Love, of the Howe Street Church in New Haven, *Obedience to Rulers.—The*

Duty and its Limitations. We have hitherto limited our discussion of the transmutation of Pilgrims into abolitionists by considering the models provided by Garrison and his clique, but the Reverend Love's anniversary sermon suggests that the idea by midcentury was gathering considerable force. His primary text was William Seward's "Higher Law," which was first cited by the senator from New York in objecting to Webster's appeal to the Constitution in his March 7 speech—and seldom thereafter. But Love quoted many authorities, biblical and modern, who sustained a learned discourse by means of which Love carried his auditors toward that tableau so familiar to celebrants of Forefathers' Day:

> What more shall I say, than to remind you of the reasons that impelled [the Pilgrim Fathers] to this wilderness land, and remind you also that *this day is the Anniversary of the landing of the Pilgrims on Plymouth Rock*, to gain your assent to the doctrine, that, *disobedience to tyrants over the conscience is the hallowed service of God.* . . . Descendants of the Pilgrims, children of the Puritans, while today the blood of your fathers courses your veins, are their spirit and principles enthroned in your hearts and governing your lives? There is a subject now at issue with this American people, which may test us on this important question. Do you believe that all men are created free and equal, that they are endowed with inalienable rights, among which are life, liberty, and the pursuit of happiness? How can you have ever heard of the Pilgrims, and not believe it? (10–12)

Clearly, Love subscribed to Garrison's opinions, if not to the *Liberator*, and whatever the history of his own commitment to abolition, his sermon reflects the increased urgency felt in New England because of the Fugitive Slave Law, the consequences of which he went on to address.

Throughout the region, local antislavery societies were producing resolutions to the effect that the signers would not obey the law and if given the chance would take in escaped slaves and hide them from the authorities, whatever the risk to themselves. And where Webster on Monday would call up the spirit of Elder Brewster, Love on Sunday had conjured that dark familiar who might appear at the door "at midnight," a sudden, if not unexpected, guest "begging for shelter and bread," appealing for the charity of "the good Samaritan" (13). But the Christian is forbidden by the law "to act toward him . . . with any hope of saving him from slavery" and must choose therefore between the law and the dictates of Conscience: "*Can* you deliver a fellow mortal into slavery? Will your conscience suffer the enormity? No! Be worthy of your Pilgrim sires. Peaceably bear the penalty of a law that commands sin, as *they* did. Go to prison as they did. Go to prison as the apostles did. Die rather than do wrong" (14). But what, Love rhetorically demanded, about the Constitution, "the national compact?" His response was unequivocal: "I have made no compact to return the fugitive. I never will. If I had, I would forswear it today. Compacts and laws that require me to sin, may take care of themselves; and God will then take care of me and my country and my country's laws" (14–15).

This was precisely the kind of discourse the Reverend Bethune of New York had in mind as traitorous, nor was opinion unanimous in New England regarding the authority of the higher law over man-made compacts and laws. Love's radical views were countered that same day in New Haven in a sermon by the Reverend W. S. Dutton, pastor of the North Church, who used as his text not Seward's phrase but Webster's remark in 1820 that honored the Forefathers for their religious principles. Religion, to Dutton's mind, was "the cause of the emigration of the colonists," contrary to the opinion of "some orators, who . . . are accustomed to eulogize our fathers as the special apostles of civil liberty or republicanism, as though that was their first and chief object" (3–4). There is some irony here, because the quotation taken by Dutton from Webster's Plymouth speech was hardly representative of that discourse. But then like Love, Dutton was pulpit-high in political ideology, for in citing Webster's Plymouth oration, he was not only plucking out the single coal that best served to light his own lamp, but he was also taking issue with the emphasis of those public persons for whom "civil liberty" was an encoded reference to abolition.

The following evening the Reverend Bethune ended his remarks with "the words of that one true Book, which your Fathers brought with them in the Mayflower, as their best treasure;—'Out of the South cometh the whirlwind';— 'FAIR WEATHER COMETH OUT OF THE NORTH,' " Scripture that reminds us once again of the storm that raged that night outside the Astor House (*Dinner*, 36). It was a place bearing a name sacred to the idea of western empire and commerce in the Empire City and the Empire State, the both of which were threatened by the ideological storms then raging through the country in reaction to the Compromise of 1850 and the Fugitive Slave Law. "Take away the bond of our Union, and the wars which must inevitably follow will be fratricidal," insisted Bethune, holding out before the members of the New England Society the horrible specter of disunion: "But this cannot, shall not be. The God of our fathers will not suffer it to be," a reference to deity that curiously parallels Love's otherwise quite different point.

"Things have changed," Webster observed in his remarks that same stormy night in New York, speaking of the Pilgrims' "stern and unbending virtues," which had been replaced by modern toleration and sectarian latitude. But removed from context, his words could have served Webster as an epitaph, for as things change, they also come around again. Sweet reasonableness and the spirit of conciliation may have characterized the modern Unitarian faith, but the old Puritan spirit would soon enough resurrect itself, less in the shape of the gentle Elder Brewster of Webster's imagination than the armor-clad, unyielding form of Miles Standish as summoned up by Lowell.

Webster closed with lines of poetry that evoked " 'the meteors of a troubled heaven, / All of one nature, of one substance bred,' " the which, having been lately opposed " 'in th' intestine shock of civil discord,' " would now march " 'in mutual, well-beseeming ranks.' " Lending the sanction of the Elizabethan world picture to contemporary broils, with another nod to the frightful weather outside, the quotation was cleverly applied to the contemporary "agitation" and the hoped-for resolution without open conflict (24). But with the advent of that resurrected Puritan, as with the boasted birth of Owen Glendower, meteors would again be indicators of a "troubled heaven," large with portents of war.

III

In 1851, George Hillard delivered the Forefathers' Day address before the New England Society in New York in which he reinforced Webster's position regarding the Fugitive Slave Law. His was a performance that was in large part a conventional rehash of Whig positions relevant to the Pilgrims, including that parlous matter of narrow-minded repressiveness on the part of men who were credited with having brought civil and religious liberty to America: "It is easy to praise the Puritan Fathers of New England; it is not difficult to blame them" (NESO, 2:142). But Hillard worked his careful way from the Pilgrims' "reverence for authority" and "stern sense of order" to the modern instance, which seemed ripe for a little Puritan repressiveness: "Law is too often written and spoken of, as if it were the arbitrary decree of some superior and irresponsible power, and not the national reason and conscience, prescribing rules of conduct to the national will" (142, 156–57). In effect, the Pilgrim heritage of liberty had become licentiousness, aided and abetted by the "wolves and polecats of the press," which "directs the currents of popular prejudice and popular passion against the judiciary . . . so that it may neither smite the guilty nor protect the innocent" (157).

This observation brought Hillard to his main and controversial point, that "if there be any descendant of the Pilgrims who gives his hand in aid of popular violence, directed against the law, whether it be to destroy an abolition press . . . or to . . . rescue a fugitive slave from the hands of justice . . . he dishonors the blood which flows in his veins" (158). Hillard was an equilibrist, who managed to be both the law partner and friend of Charles Sumner and Hawthorne's friend as well, and he would be (in 1852) Webster's official memorialist. He attempted to achieve a similar balance in his lament on modern lawlessness and ended his address with the hope that "the stately march of our laws and speech, which began at the rock of Plymouth, will ever move in the paths of honor and of peace" (162). Hillard had also observed of Plymouth Rock, "which was a shelter to our fathers in the piercing storm of trial," that it "must spread for us its healing shadow, in the feverish blaze of prosperity," but it was the shadow of Daniel Webster that continued to loom over the Forefathers' Day festivities in New York, with repeated appeals to the sanctity of the Union in the face of attacks from abolitionists and Southern secessionists (156).

By 1854, that shadow had merged with cosmic thunder clouds darkening in the West, but William Evarts, a trial lawyer and until recently the assistant U.S. district attorney for the southern district of New York, took in a wide and hopeful prospect, celebrating those sons of the Puritans not only "in this central metropolis" but those "in the fair cities of the South, and in the wide valley of the West" (239). In 1850, Evarts had defended the Fugitive Slave Law but thenceforth had drifted toward the party of Conscience, which became in 1855 the Republican Party, and a determined balance can be detected in his Forefathers' Day oration. Evarts's was primarily a conventional celebration of the Pilgrims as "the germ and nucleus of an independent political state," but it carried a suggestive and original subtext (253).

Thus, in Evarts's view, the people who landed "on the Rock of Plymouth" in effect transplanted to America "the stone, which the builders of English liberty, and English law, and English power, rejected," making it "the head of the corner of our constituted state" (252–53). Adepts may recognize here the architectonics of Freemasonry, detectable also in Evarts's observation that "the tie which bound" the Pilgrims together "was that of brotherhood," of "mutual support and aid" (250). These fraternal factors contributed to the permanence of the union that was the Pilgrims' community in America, and Evarts quoted John Cushman's sermon of 1621 that had exhorted a loving bond of community among the Pilgrims. But it was applicable also to the common ties that bound together the far-flung "sons of the Pilgrims," yet another brotherhood, witnessed by the New England Societies spread throughout the land (250).

The reciprocity between the precepts of Freemasonry and the founding principles of the United States is familiar enough, here traced back not to the ancient Egyptians but to the Pilgrim Fathers. It was national union, however, that was Evarts's main subject, which, having been based on Pilgrim principles and reinforced by persons of New England ancestry now residing throughout the land, would long endure: "Doubt not their influences will soon penetrate and pervade the whole general mass of society throughout the nation; fear not but that *equality of right, community of interest, reciprocity of duty* will bind this whole people together in a perfect, a perpetual union" (266). Clearly the spirit of the late and lamented Daniel Webster was still in attendance at the annual dinners of the New England Society in the City of New York.

In contrast to its often defiant Unionism, and inspired perhaps by Evarts's confraternal emphasis, the society determined in 1855 to mount a balanced program, coincidental with the same decision made by the Pilgrim Society in Plymouth. The occasion in New York, moreover, marked not only the 235th anniversary of the Landing but the "Semi-Centennial" of the society itself, a special occasion mandating an enhanced program. Not one but two speakers were invited to address the society on Forefathers' Day, the first a minister better known as a poet, John Pierpont, the second a poet better known as a physician, Oliver Wendell Holmes. The last named had already earned a reputation for wit and humorous occasional verses, but his lasting fame as the Autocrat had yet to eclipse his fame as a lecturer at Harvard in anatomy. Earlier that year, when in the course of laying pipes from a newly constructed water works in Plymouth, laborers had uncovered some bones on Cole's Hill—the site of the first Pilgrim burial ground—Dr. Holmes was called in to authenticate the remains as certifiably those of "the earliest settlers of Plymouth" (Russell, *Pilgrim Memorials*, 84).

Where in 1826 Pierpont had asked his poetic question regarding the present location of the Pilgrim Fathers, Holmes in 1846 had written an ode, "The Pilgrim's Vision," for the Forefathers' Day celebration in Plymouth. Holmes comforted a frostbitten Forefather by treating him to a panoramic display of the triumphs that would follow his sufferings on the American strand, cleverly reversing the strategy of the conventional necromantic exercise, bringing, as it were, the Future to the Pilgrim, not the Pilgrim to the Future. A final and somber note was achieved by ending the poem with the visionary colonist in his grave, perhaps awaiting exhumation and identification by Dr. Holmes but until then kept alive by "memory."

Helpful in this memorializing effort was the "hoary rock" celebrated in the last stanza of the poem, described as yet standing "in the waste of ocean. . . . Be this his latest legend,—HERE WAS THE PILGRIM'S LAND!" (*Works*, 12:64). This same stanza was subsequently used to decorate the title page to William S. Russell's *Pilgrim Memorials, and Guide to Plymouth* (1855), in which was also published the news about Holmes's identification of the Pilgrim bones, a contingency that may have inspired the New England Society to invite the penultimate Brahmin to New York, but Holmes recommended himself to those merry gentlemen in other ways as well.

Given the convivial nature of the society's celebrations, perhaps it was Holmes's lighthearted jeu d'esprit "On Lending a Punch Bowl" that served to open the door of the Astor House to him. Written at about the same time as Lowell's "Interview" with the ghost of an angry Standish, it calls up a Miles with a rather Falstaffian profile, quite different from Lowell's stiff-kneed soldier. Holmes's Standish is anything but a self-righteous old Puritan, being a jolly good fellow who would be right at home among Webster and his friends and glad to join in their bibulous festivities.

In fact, Holmes's poem was an indirect protest against the current agitation for temperance reform—that root of the branch of radicalism that was abolition—though it was framed as an imaginative history of an ornate "caudle" or loving cup, designed with two handles so as to be passed from guest to guest, and it has likewise been passed down through the ages from owner to owner, until it ends up in Leyden, and

> With those that in the Mayflower came—a hundred
>   souls and more,—
> Along with all the furniture, to fill their new
>   abodes,—
> To judge by what is still on hand, at least a hundred
>   loads. (12:70)

This last is a palpable hit regarding the claims to ownership of genuine "Pilgrim" artifacts handed down from the passengers on the *Mayflower*. It set the tone for what followed, for Holmes's poem was definably not like his "Pilgrim's Vision" in the filiopietistic vein. Working from the well-known fact that the military man hired by the Pilgrims was not himself a Puritan, Holmes makes of Standish a soldier who takes in his courage with a draft of "the fiery Hollands," sharing none of the Pilgrims' fabled aversion to liquor harder than beer. Downing this berserker beverage before heading out to deal with the Indians, Standish and his men teach a salutary lesson to the Pequots: "Run from the white man when you find he smells of Hollands gin!" (71). This was not what the Reverend Bethune meant when referring to the influence of the Netherlands on the Pilgrims, but such sentiments were certainly in accord with much that went on during (and especially after) Forefathers' Day dinners in New York, and in claiming the present ownership of the convivial bowl, Holmes most certainly recommended himself for inclusion in that annual collection of choice spirits.

Finally, Holmes was qualified as well by being no more a champion of abolition than he was a friend to temperance: in a letter to Lowell in 1845 he had stated his conservative position in firm detail. Until the events in Kansas and Nebraska and the brutal attack on Sumner (a fellow Brahmin and friend) on the floor of the Senate, Holmes remained a staunch Unionist and an advocate of compromise, and in 1855 he was still in harmony with the conservative tenor of New England Society celebrations—or so it would have seemed to the committee who invited him to share the honors with and provide balance to John Pierpont. As it turned out, Holmes somewhat exceeded expectations, and as so often was the case in matters in which the metrical doctor was involved, the effect was one of surprise, even for Holmes himself. One could not expect less from him, even if one did not know what to expect, and generally one did not. In that one respect, at least, he was truly kin to his cousin Wendell Phillips.

Indeed, the 1855 celebration in New York of Forefathers' Day was an evening of many surprises, to which Pierpont contributed his share. Though one could hardly expect the elegant old Unitarian to go back on his many years of commitment to the abolitionist cause, still, at the age of seventy, Pierpont might have been expected to turn in a short poem. There was encouraging precedent in the verses he had contributed to the *Liberty Bell* in 1840 or had provided Garrison to read at the Anti-Slavery Society meeting in 1852. But, perhaps animated by the opportunity to address such a large and influential auditory, Pierpont turned out an ode of considerable length that reworked both previous efforts and then added much more.

Inspired to mount a bold challenge to the New York celebrants of Fore-fathers' Day, he demanded they not "become the vassals of slave-hunting knaves" (*NESO*, 2:323). As in his poem of 1852, he asked if the Forefathers who had knelt on Plymouth Rock would have countenanced "Slavery's galling chain" or joined in the pursuit of a "thrall" escaping from bondage in an Indian village. And what of his present audience—"Shall we play the hound?" If the law should demand a slave's return, "Shall we seize and drag him back / Fainting, bleeding, bound?"

> Ay!—when we're in love with chains;
> Ay!—when in our bastard veins,
> No drop of the blood remains
>   Of those pilgrim men!
> Ay,—when our own backs we strip,
> That what blood we have may drip
> For the lordlings of the whip,—
>   Then,—and not till then! (324)

Declamatory, written to be read aloud, like the earlier, shorter works the ode absorbed, Pierpont's poem is one with the whole body of forensic perfor-mances that identified the Pilgrims with the cause of reform and associated them with the recent agitation against the Fugitive Slave Law.

Holmes by contrast provided for the occasion something quite out of the ordinary, both in form and in content. It was not, like Seward's oration deliv-ered in Plymouth on Forefathers' Day that same year, a carefully reasoned dis-course that evaded controversy while attempting to sound substantial (Holmes was not running for office), nor, like Phillips's response, was it a display of verbal pyrotechnics (that was not his style). Holmes's performance was not strictly an oration at all but was a casual, at times rambling, even conversational display that wanders discursively with a number of digressions, the randomness of which is misleading. Because the wily physician from Boston most definitely knew where he was going and where he hoped to take his audience, and began with an effective image of community, by means of which he presumably meant to form a common bond with his auditors.

They occupied, he pointed out, "the inner circle of a triple cordon which surrounds us with his harmonious parallels: the Republic, the City of New York, and 'the innermost ring,'" namely the social occasion that had brought together "children of a common descent . . . a whole family-Bible full of cousinships and brotherhoods" (*NESO*, 2:271). We can here again recall William Evarts's fraternal message, but instead of relying on Freemasonic terms, Holmes conceived of the people assembled before him that evening as a reasonable facsimile of Brahmin Boston, privileged persons bonded by family connections. Yet he also celebrated the "affinities" of the larger blood tie, which were witnessed by the formation of New England Societies "at the South, and in the West, as well as in the East," the very existence of which illustrated the unity even in separation of common facets, "like the invisible seams which run through the different planes of a crystal" (272–73). It was Dr. Holmes's pleasure never to let his audience forget that it was listening to a man of science, for whom arcane, even esoteric figures were as familiar as they were novel to his auditors.

But he could also descend to common pathways and moved on from crystallography to a lyric description of the New England landscape, with an emphasis on those rocky hills and rivers suitable for millstreams, not waterways, an environmental signal that this is a place where the only alternatives are "work or starve." Such a landscape had produced a type recognizable to all who are native to the region, being uniform in their "sturdy love of liberty, in thrifty ways of life, in habits of methodical industry, in reverence for religion and education, and in respect for law" (274). This was familiar stuff, a genealogy celebrated by persons as different as Everett, Lowell, and Whittier. But Holmes was heading not toward Lowell's Yankee but to his much more tightly wound counterpart, the Brahmin, who was, after all, a creature of Holmes's own invention, like that other gift to parlor conversation, the stereoscope.

Yet like Lowell's Yankee, Holmes's native New Englander uniformly "claims his descent from the Pilgrims of Plymouth, lineally it may be, virtually at any rate, and no man need ask more than once why we have entered that third circle of intimate communion, which is narrower than the common citizenship that belongs to most of us, and falls far within the broad zone of republican Americanism which includes us all" (275). What Holmes was referring to by the "third circle" was not a place in Dante's *Inferno* but a kind of inner sanctum in Paradise, equivalent to the Athenaeum in Boston. Himself a clubman in the loosest sense, for whom associations like the Saturday Club provided a comfortably relaxed but securely tight society, an intellectual, not a philanthropic, brotherhood, Holmes was here promoting a note of exclusiveness that was rarely heard on such occasions in New York. It was an element of elitism brought down from Beacon Hill, a vestal light with which he intended to bring illumination to the benighted regions outside New England's bounds.

But there is something else also detectable here, which extends beyond mere snobbery and reaches toward the exclusionary politics of the Know-Nothing Party, then gathering considerable force. Even Holmes's figure of the "inner circle," while borrowing sanctity from a purely American lineage traceable to the Pilgrims of the *Mayflower*, has another connotation. For the Know-Nothing Party was a secret society that in its publications not only promoted the sanctity of native birth but was fond of citing an intimate connection with the Pilgrims and the Rock, as well as with Webster, Washington (George), and the sacred Union.

But Holmes had no specific quarrel to pick with Romanism, nor did the problem of the Irish apply: his focus was on an issue more deeply threatening to the Republic and its tidy concentricity of circles. But first he took the obligatory step of repeating and celebrating the familiar story of the Pilgrims, a sacred image that whether only "sketched, or finished, shall always be held up," if only for a moment: "We will lift it as the Host is lifted in Romanist processions, and reverently uncover it" (278).

At times Holmes's conceits are metaphysical in their unlikeliness, here comparing the Pilgrims as a sacred icon to the transubstantiated Host of Roman Catholicism and the rituals that celebrated it, anathema to the people he was supposed to be honoring. But it was just this kind of unlikely figure that added so much interest to Holmes's orations as to his conversation—between which, once again, there was not much difference, in terms of duration as well as structure. Thus he attempted to explain the Pilgrims' decision to leave Holland for America by suggesting that if they had stayed in Leyden, they would have come to resemble "the boors that sat for their portraits to the Dutch and Flemish painters," a "process of degradation" by which the progeny of Carver and Bradford would have been transformed into "ruffed and shovel-hatted burgomasters," and the heirs of Standish enrolled in the ranks of "that glorious train-band, the breathing miracle of Vander-Heist" (289). Such comparisons certainly are true to the concern of the Pilgrims regarding the long-range effects of their residence in Leyden, but given the predictable presence of bona fide descendants of the original settlers of Manhattan in his audience, Holmes might have used a more sympathetic touch.

Holland, as it were, would be heard from. The anniversary dinner was as usual followed by the traditional lighthearted festivities, which in 1855 tended toward the heavy-handed end of jocularity. Perhaps the mood was darkened by the problems in Kansas, and it was in addition burdened by an interminable disquisition in response to "*The Clergy of New England*" by "the Reverend Dr. Lothrop, of Boston." For the minister shared Holmes's random prolixity but without an iota of his wit, being a master of stultifying language that worked the opposite effect intended—"Aye, sir, Plymouth Rock! There are stupendous facts, grand and weighty truths, and instructive history, worthy of the profoundest study, indissolubly connected with that rock" (*Report of the Semi-Centennial Dinner*, 90). Taking his turn in this sequence of dampeners, the president of the St. Nicholas Society, James De Peyster Ogden, felt obliged to correct Holmes's thinking regarding the Dutch by reminding him of the history lesson delivered in 1850 by the Reverend Bethune: "You will be pleased to recollect, sir, that your Puritan fathers enjoyed the advantage of nine years' residence in tolerant and Republican Holland before they landed on Plymouth Rock. . . . I smile at the idea . . . that their morals were in danger . . . by contact with the Dutch" (103).

The following year, there appeared J. L. Motley's *Rise of the Dutch Republic*, which would certify at length this connection, about which Holmes, as one of the historian's good friends and testing grounds, was presumably well aware. His remark anent the character of Netherlanders was apparently meant to be humorous, a sly allusion to the "degraded" Dutch of the New Netherlands lampooned in Irving's burlesque *Knickerbocker History*, but if that was indeed the case, New Yorkers of Dutch descent were not amused. Nor was this the only instance that evening in which Holmes's point miscarried, as we shall see. But let us return to the orator, who by means of ornate classical allusions and further scientific touches at length got himself and his audience on board the *Mayflower*—"O, the dreadful Atlantic!"—and at last to the American strand (*NESO*, 282).

He continued on in his digressive patter, which included a pastoral interlude in celebration of a New England boyhood, describing the pleasures and joys of the countryside, nostalgically conceived and idyllic in setting: "This is the privilege of the young man of New England birth; nature, nor wholly rough and uncultivated . . . but nature subdued and humanized" (290). Derived from Wordsworth's Hesiodic landscape, Holmes's New England reinforces an essential exclusiveness, providing by means of memory "an inward sanctuary of peace and repose" preserved even after the boy becomes a man immured in some city countinghouse.

But, asked Holmes, are we "worthy of the past which we inherit and the land which we love?" In answer, he pointed to the map of the Union with New England covered over and asked his audience to add up the names of famous persons from that one region and then those from the rest of the United States and compare the lengths of the two parallel columns, a form of double book-keeping with only one, predictable, quietus: "We are almost ashamed to think how large a part of all the best thinking and writing that is done in the country either comes from her soil directly, or at least has passed through her intellectual alembic. . . . Are there any that think the heart of New England is asleep?" (292). Certainly not the most of the hearts there present, which beat in unanimous syncopation with that regional aorta, whose "proverbial ingenuity is as active in opening new channels for benevolence as in the invention of labor-saving machinery."

This was the kind of wisdom that to the Whig way of thinking was conventional, but Holmes anticipated that to some in his audience New England's lead in the nation's moral progress might appear at times to be taking a dangerously accelerated course. While speaking out in praise of fanatics—"Wo to the land that has no enthusiasts, no fanatics, no madmen!"—in Holmes's view such tolerance was a mechanic notion akin to bloodletting and purging, those standard tools in the doctor's little bag, or like draining a swamp, allowing the free vent of noxious waters lest they prove mephitic (293). It was a philosophy and a psychology inherited from the Enlightenment, and he likewise shared the Enlightenment reservation regarding enthusiasm when it came to specific agitations for reform: "The extreme temperance movement is of New England origin. The anti-slavery passion burns most fiercely in New England bosoms" (294).

The problem with these two movements is that they demand specific legislation by way of solution and thereby harden the emotions of the moment into the "crowding Judaism" of laws passed to mend perceived social ills. To Dr. Holmes's turn of mind, the most monstrous example of Levitical particularism in recent times was the notorious "Maine Law" enforcing total abstinence, which, "for all the wretches it may save," creates many more "hypocrites, and rebels, and law-haters." As for the "present moral aspect of New England" regarding slavery, he was equally earnest in opposition and considered at length "the great question" of the day in terms of its effect on "the destinies of the whole country" (295). Holmes may have had narrow-gauge views on progress when it took the shape of moral reform, but he was careful to switch over to a broad-gauge perspective in order to make his point.

"No sin of our own, not even intemperance, is so perpetually before the conscience of New England as this detested social arrangement of our neighbors," declared Holmes, who was quick to concede that no one would want further extension of that arrangement within the western territories of the United States. He expressed the ardent hope of saving "every inch of American soil we fairly can for freedom." But, given New England's legal ties to a number of other "confederate sovereignties," what can it do but exercise considerable tact in urging reform, a position entirely in harmony with William Sullivan's sentiments in 1829. There may be, he admitted, a certain "manly logic" under-writing extreme postures of antislavery zeal, like tearing up the Constitution, insulting southern slaveholders, and standing tall in the face of the conse-quences. But the proponents of such logic must be allowed not only its prem-ises but its conclusion: "They must either annul the contract made by their fathers, or keep it."

Like Webster in 1850, Holmes argued that the Constitution is a sum of parts, none of which can be negotiated separately and none removed without doing irreparable damage to the whole. He also echoed Webster in noting that if utility is the final goal of political action, then for all the extremism on the part of the abolitionists nothing has happened to reduce the extent of slave terri-tory: "Slavery, then, is amongst us exactly like any physical fact" (297). What, then, should we do? Should we continue in this moral offensive until it breaks out in open war, or should we "feel and act to these Southern men as equals and brothers . . . always in the spirit of Christian love?" This was not really a question, and along with the rest of Holmes's discussion of the problem, it recalls the sweet reasoning of the Reverend Blagden in 1834 as well as Webster's emphasis on conciliation.

But then Holmes moved on to a subject rarely, if ever, raised in discourse under such auspices, the tricky and dangerous ground of race, which contains questions seldom settled "according to the abstract principles of justice" (298). Descending therefore to particulars, Holmes in effect cast himself down from a relatively high place of principle into a brier patch with an attendant slough, the usual consequence of attempt to talk openly and sensibly about a matter that was a facsimile tar baby. Like Br'er Everett two years earlier, Holmes began by deflecting the discussion through the Native American, who comes off, however, as something less like one of Cooper's noble statues than a pesky redskin as viewed through the pages of a Crockett almanac.

Holmes's Indian is a "half-filled outline of humanity," a "sketch in red crayons of a rudimental manhood," whose proclivity for acts of barbarism inevitably results in his extermination by the white man, "and so the red-crayon sketch is rubbed out, and the canvas is ready for a picture of manhood a little more like God's own image" (298). This figure is completely in accord with Everett's providential view, but instead of mounting a nostalgic, senti-mental tableau, like those anachronistic Indians paddling around Boston be-fore obligingly disappearing into the horizon, Holmes in effect drew a chalk caricature on a blackboard and then wiped it away with a rag.

Holmes's genocidal dismissal of the "red man" was only a prelude to an extended discourse on a problem so difficult and complex that it was seldom open for discussion save by persons of extreme views, either romantic apologists or bigots, and Holmes (unlike Everett or Longfellow) was certainly not of the first class. By his account the erasing of the red-crayon savage was not only inevitable but could serve as historical proof that the Black Face of Man (as after some minstrel show) would likewise be wiped away leaving only the White Face behind. Holmes's hope was not for "the perpetual continuance of the present relationship between . . . the white and the black races," but he saw "no apparent solution of it except in the indefinite."

"Here, as in the case of the Indians, or any other inferior tribe of men, our sympathies will go with our own color first. . . . The creator has hung out the colors that form the two rallying points, so that they shall be unmistakable, eternal; nay, there is hardly a single sense that does not bear witness to the ineffaceable distinction of blood, only prevented from producing open opposition by the unchallenged supremacy of the higher of the two races. The white man must be the master in effect, whatever he is in name; and the only way to make him do right by the Indian, the African, the Chinese, is to make him better by example and loving counsel" (298–99).

Not even the conservative precincts of the New England Society of New York were quite ready for this kind of thing, and about halfway through Holmes's highly articulate and vividly illustrated outburst of unmitigated racism there was heard, in the words of the official account of the celebration, "an audible hiss." Nor was it a run-of-the-mill kind of hiss, the sort that greeted Mr. Yeadon in Plymouth, for it was, as it proved to be, the hiss heard round not only Manhattan but all the way to the far reaches of Boston as well.

A little bit of Beacon Hill fell from heaven that day and lay writhing in the mire that was churned up by the wheels of journalism, which, while often self-righteous to a fault in their workings, turn much more quickly than do the mills of God. Greeley's *Tribune* rushed Holmes to judgment as yet another meddling Yankee, a "Boston joker" who presumed to teach New Yorkers "how to preserve the Union": Manhattan had plenty of available talent on hand without needing "a Boston doughface to come here to teach us. . . . The Doctor thinks that Cuffee ought to know his place and be kept in it. We think the same of the small jokers" (December 24, 1855).

The *Liberator* rushed into its columns editorial outcries from other newspapers concerning the Holmes debacle but uncharacteristically refrained from comment. Garrison apparently for once had decided that discretion was the better part of the bargain where a beloved local celebrity was involved. Typically, he reserved his editorial venom for the *Boston Post*, which had attacked the *New York Tribune* for its rough treatment of Holmes, "because the doctor doubted the wisdom of rapid abolition": "Dr. Holmes," noted Garrison, "is welcome to such a backer as that venal, parasitical, purchased tool of the Slave oligarchy," a discharge of spittle that not accidentally managed to spray the doctor even while aimed in another direction (January 11, 1856, 5).

But the leading lights of reform who shared Holmes's status, like Theodore Parker and Wendell Phillips, made public their regrets, and Sumner sent Holmes a pamphlet in an attempt to correct his thinking. Even Emerson confided his displeasure in a way that was certain to reach Holmes's burning ear, for New England—at least the liberal part of New England—was not pleased, no more than New York was amused. Holmes's New York oration was, on a small scale, equivalent to Webster's speech of March 7, which it echoed, being a betrayal of New England's cherished sanctity, and resulted predictably in a blast of sanctimoniousness. In liberal, latitudinarian, and by 1855 largely abolitionist Boston, this sort of thing would not do.

Given the doctor's breezy self-assurance in his Kiplingesque assumption of the white man's burden ten years before Kipling was born, he was probably only saying that which had often been thought but was thought best not expressed on Beacon Hill, save perhaps discreetly behind the veil of window curtains. Emerson himself had confided in his journal equivalent notions—"How long before the Indians will be extinct? then the negro? Then we shall say, what a gracious interval . . . between man & beast!"—but this meditation on missing "links" did not find its way into his published essays (*Journals*, 13:54).

It was expected of rabid opponents of amalgamation like Dr. Reese of New York to spew his venom in public, but even an aroused James Trecothick Austin had the good sense to speak of such matters in terms of precedent and law. Proper Bostonians by contrast wished freed blacks Godspeed on their way to Liberia or waved fond farewells to Fred Douglass as he wisely took ship for Great Britain. But here now was Dr. Holmes, the sprightly, witty soul of Boston Brahma, saying the thing that was not said, calling a spade a spade, then playing it for a winning hand.

Yet, finally, not much came from this tempest in the Autocrat's teapot. Everett's reputation among the liberals of the Whig Party never quite recovered from his toeing the Mason-Dixon Line; Webster's was demolished by his March 7 speech; Robert Winthrop was turned out of office for his failure to speak up loud and clear against the Fugitive Slave Bill; Richard Yeadon was ridden out of town on Garrison's raillery; but Oliver Wendell Holmes survived entirely intact, indeed would shortly emerge in the pages of the *Atlantic* as a master of the personal essay and beloved savant to all (if mostly white) America.

But for a time he was the victim of the kinds of people he called "moral bullies," most of whom were identified with reform, surely a painful position for a man who had so publicly laughed reformers to scorn. While ignoring the trouser-tearing attacks of Horace Greeley, he wrote ornate clarifications of his true intentions to Parker and Sumner: he always, he swore under the cover of private correspondence, preferred Right of whatever hue over Wrong of whatever shade. Color there may have been in his geopolitics, but in his psychic geography there was only the Up of the good and the Down of the bad. "I may be wrong," he wrote to Emerson, "but I wish to be right more than ever" (Tilton, 228). How can you continue to kick a dog with a wagging tail?

The moral bullies soon enough ran on down the road to carry their bloodied champion Sumner out of the Senate chamber, and Holmes turned to explaining in public less troublesome issues, like "The Lyrical Passion." But then, in 1857, in the very first issue of the magazine he had named, and which was edited by a Lowell recently reclaimed from the radicalism he had opposed, the Autocrat burst back through the curtain with that table, chair, and teacup rescued from his literary attic, to perform the role by which the nation came to know best the genial presence always welcome as the best of Holmes.

IV

Nor should we leave Dr. Holmes standing before the New England Society naked as Phryne before her judges, if only because he did not end his oration with that racist rhapsody. Holmes rolled on, slipping easily from distinctions of color to sectional strife, the kind of anarchy that will bring babies "into the world, ring-streaked, speckled and spotted with the birthmarks of local or national jealousies that will make them unworthy of the name of American," suggesting that there was an intimate connection deep somewhere in Holmes's psychic basement between civil disputes and miscegenation (300). He cited the "solemn words of warning left us by one whose wisdom and virtue an incredulous generation still confesses," namely Daniel Webster, thereby openly aligning himself with the geopolitics of compromise and accommodation, should anyone have some doubts remaining. With considerable figurative complexity he set up an elaborate analogy, depicting New England as symbolically connected by an umbilical "isthmus" to the rest of the nation: "the great confederacy" was his phrase, an important card in the Nullifier's slim pack, reinforcing as it did the notion of state sovereignty and independence.

As with the greater isthmus in Nicaragua, a favorite locus for geopoliticians and filibusters with expansive views, hands were essaying to dig that vital link away, to create the monster disunion. These destructive efforts must be met by fighting secession as on a moral battlefield and by cultivating toward the South "that good-will, that spirit of charity and forbearance, without which the name of Union is . . . a sad jest." Where five years earlier Webster had summoned up the benign ghost of Elder Brewster to urge morality on his festive crew, now Holmes called up Black Dan himself, smoking from the Pit, to urge his auditors to fight the good fight: "Sacrificing no right, yielding nothing to menaces or flattery, making new battle-fields, if necessary, wherever the sacred privileges of freemen are invaded." For at all costs the Constitution must be saved, the Union preserved.

Somewhat singed in some eyes from keeping such close company with Webster, Holmes moved on to his closing benediction, the terms of which bear a curious resemblance to the ornate toast raised by Wendell Phillips during the Plymouth celebration that same year. Having opened by describing the New England Society as a circle within a circle, Holmes ended by evoking "the password of our New England Eleusinia—the pivot of our local patriotism— the centre where our recollections of the past must ever rally—the eternal 'Monument to the Forefathers'—the rock hallowed by the feet of the Pilgrims. . . . God grant that it may prove always a true symbol of the character of the men of New England!" (301). Phillips had read the Rock as a great, subterranean, subcontinental shelf, a subversive force that had suddenly cropped out here and there across the land from Plymouth to Alton, Illinois, the type and symbol of the irresistible and unpredictable force associated with the spread of liberty. By contrast, Holmes regarded the Rock with no more accuracy from a geologist's point of view but as the iconic bedrock of union, a monolithic presence not unlike the equally granitic Webster:

> As every flake that has been splintered from it as a memento carries its elements and character, unchanged wherever it is borne, so let the sons of her soil be true to their origin wherever they may wander; as the rock is not a loose fragment or a rounded boulder, but a part of the solid core of earth itself, to which it will hold until the planet is rent asunder; running under the soil that hides it, under the mountains that are piled upon it, under the rivers that flow over it, under the craters that have spouted fire above it, and so is one with the heart of the great sphere forever; thus, let New England forever hold with heart, and soul, and strength, to the sacred confederacy which looks on the continent as its destined heritage. (301–2)

At first glance, this might be taken as another reverse instance of the Thompson effect, Holmes having self-consciously framed a figurative response to Phillips's apostrophe to the Rock. The possibility becomes more likely when we realize that the New England Society still celebrated the traditional date of the 22d, despite the committee's report of 1850. Because Plymouth observed the new and corrected anniversary, a sufficient lapse would seem to have occurred for Holmes to have made a last-minute addition to his remarks. As we will see, in a later chapter, he was quite capable of such revisions when given cause. But the likelihood diminishes when we discover that although the anniversary dinner in New York was held on the 22d, the performances by Pierpont and Holmes took place the night before, on Friday the 21st. So as to open the event to a larger audience, the poet and the pundit spoke in the Church of the

Puritans, not the Astor House, an event advertised as being free to the public. In effect, the cousins spoke in different places to different ends at one and the same time.

This circumstance also provides a somewhat different context for that hissing incident, the audience being mixed and not exclusively limited to members of the society. In the same issue of the *Tribune* in which Greeley's outraged editorial appeared, a contrasting opinion was published under "City Items" entitled "Balancing the Account," which suggests that Holmes was not alone in drawing an adverse reaction, nor was he without his champions. For it was reported that his "proslavery passages" were "lustily cheered," suggesting that "the audience was almost exclusively composed of Boohoos," an impression that was corrected by "the still more rapturous applause which greeted" Pierpont when he read lines that "poured wrath upon the Fugitive Slave Law and its supporters."

It was now the turn of the "Boohoos" to "hiss like serpents," but the applause for Pierpont was so loud that it drowned out their sibilant objections: "The friends of Freedom retired with the feeling that their account current with the Union-savers for *that* evening was effectively balanced." Certainly, during the after-dinner remarks at the Astor House the following day—closed to the general public—only a good-natured allusion was made about the incident, John Pierpont turning out two couplets comparing Holmes's hostile reception to the "harmless hiss" of geese and snakes (85).

The conclusion of Holmes's speech, whatever its context, may be usefully compared to Wendell Phillips's extended figure and, because it worked toward an antithetical end, may be taken as its counterpart. Where Phillips's conceit threatens anarchy and removes the Rock from the regional monopoly repeatedly insisted upon by a prior sequence of mighty Whig voices, Holmes anchored the Rock in place as a symbol of stability and thereby reinforced the Whig tradition by once again centering and locating its one outcropping in Massachusetts. Even while following the country west, in fulfillment of Webster's prophecy, the peregrinating sons of New England's rocky soil by carrying specimen splinters of the sacred stone can retain vital contact with the Pilgrim Mecca. Thus if Wendell Phillips may be credited with setting free the Rock, then Oliver Wendell Holmes can be said to have enlisted it as ballast for the ship of state, even as he defined the terms—racist and statist—for the war that was yet to come.

CHAPTER **14**

Wherein the Rock Becomes a Rolling Stone

The rock, by its rounded edges, bears evidence of its rolled
character, as well as of the attempts to break specimens from it;
which fortunately its extreme hardness renders seldom successful.
—*William Russell*

I

As Unitarians displaced orthodox Trinitarians into Second and
Third Churches of Christ across New England, in effect replacing the Puritan
continuity with a kinder, gentler version of Congregationalism, there appeared
a new threat to the Northeast's sense of its exclusive corner on virtue. This was
the Yankee, a manifestation of duplicit dealings and sly manipulation that may
be dated from 1820, a year associated with both Fenimore Cooper's heroic
version, Harvey Birch of *The Spy*, and Washington Irving's comic alternative,
Ichabod Crane in "The Legend of Sleepy Hollow."

William R. Taylor, and more recently, Cameron Nickels, have delineated the
origins and efflorescence of the literary Yankee, Taylor stressing the heroic—or
"transcendental"—aspect, Nickels the humorous. But over the years a third,
dark side of the comic Yankee also emerged, eventually supervening over the
other two types. It is a transformation that may be keyed to the rise and fall of
Daniel Webster, by Taylor's definition the most transcendental Yankee of them
all. Notably, "Ichabod," a Hebrew word signifying "the glory (of New England,
vice Israel) has departed," served Irving at the start of the process and Whittier
at the end, giving scriptural point to his scathing dismissal of the once Great
Man, "so fallen! so lost!"

The stage Yankee retained a quality of comic innocence throughout the
period, and Seba Smith's Major Jack Downing and James Russell Lowell's
Hosea Biglow served as ironic commentators on the Jackson administration
and the Mexican War. But Downing succumbs to Potomac fever, and Biglow's
idealism is balanced off by the rampant patriotism and finally the chauvinistic
and self-seeking ambition of Birdofredom Sawin, who ends up a resident of

the Confederate South and a perverſid racist of the Pap Finn breed. The implication seems clear: for all his associations with rural New England, the Yankee type contains within him an evil seed. He is in effect a type and symbol of lost pastoral innocence conceived as a fall from grace. If as defined by Lowell the Puritans were men with empire in their brains, then the latter-day saints seem similarly obsessed by the cash nexus.

Irving in his comic *History of New York* provides the necessary genesis by conflating the Yankee with the original settlers "of Connecticut and thereabouts." Thus the Puritans are characterized as "a certain shrewd race of men, being very much given to indulge their own opinions," especially regarding "the liberty of conscience . . . and speech," which they enforced "line upon line, precept upon precept, lash upon lash" (*Irving*, 493). "The zeal of these good people . . . did for a while betray them into errors, which it is easier to pardon than defend. Having served a regular apprenticeship in the school of persecution, it behoved them to shew that they had become proficients in the art. They accordingly employed their leisure hours in banishing, scourging, or hanging, divers heretical papists, quakers and anabaptists, for daring to abuse the liberty of conscience; which they now clearly proved to imply nothing more, than that every man should think as he pleased in matters of religion—providing he thought right; for otherwise it would be giving a latitude to damnable heresies" (494–95). This is the familiar charge that defenders of the Puritans would seek to refute and from which Irving moves easily to the hypocritical Yankee custom of "bundling," to which he "chiefly attributes the unparalleled increase of the . . . tribe" (497).

The consequent overpopulation of the region, in turn, necessitates "a certain rambling propensity, with which, like the sons of Ismael, they seem to have been gifted by heaven, and which continually goads them on, to shift their residence from place to place, so that a Yankey [*sic*] farmer is in a constant state of migration," a roving habit that made them "exceedingly obnoxious to our ever honoured dutch ancestors" (498). Having shouldered "like a true pedlar . . . a heavy knapsack," and with his family following after in a covered wagon, the emigrant sets out with ax and staff, whistling "yankee doodle" and "as confident of the protection of providence . . . as a patriarch of yore, when he journeyed into a strange country of the Gentiles" (498).

The "Gentiles" in question were the original settlers of neighboring New York, and "what chiefly operated to embroil our ancestors with these strange folk, was an unwarrantable liberty . . . of entering in hordes into the territories of the New Netherlands, and settling themselves down, without leave or licence, to *improve* the land" (501). It is this Yankee propensity for supplantation that provides the chief tension of Irving's "legend" of Sleepy Hollow, for though employed as a schoolmaster, Ichabod Crane has the usual regional obsession: his love of Katrina Van Tassel is conflated with his lust for her family farm, which he plans to convert to cash that he will invest in western lands. If, as William Taylor suggests, the chivalric South was in large part an invention of New York writers, then Irving must be given his due where the Yankee is concerned as well: Ichabod Crane casts a long, lean, and rapacious shadow southward, an extension of the interloping, "improving" Yankee as defined in Irving's *Knickerbocker History*.

It is, however, in the figure of the Yankee peddler that the negative associations of the regional type tend to be concentrated. Thus Cooper's Harvey Birch manifests as part of his disguise a rapacious greed for money and is reputed to possess magic powers presumably derived from the Devil. More true to the type is the bred-in-the-bone greed of Virgil Hoskins, who figures in a little-known southern novella, *Memoirs of a Nullifier*, first published in 1832. Hoskins, who dies and is sent to Hell, is forced to confess to all manner of swindles, including passing counterfeit money to his father at the age of six, along with the usual tricks, selling "in the course of one peddling expedition, 497,368 wooden nutmegs, 281,532 Spanish cigars made of oak leaves, and 647 wooden clocks," a charge that Hoskins is hardly ashamed of, claiming "that was counted in our place about the greatest peddlin trip that ever was made over the Potomac" (43).

There is very little that emerges over the first fifty years of the nineteenth century regarding Jedidiah Morse's region that cannot be found in the sections on New England in the *American Geography*. As early as 1789, we find him complaining that people get the wrong impression of the way New Englanders talk because of a minority of uneducated natives who use exaggerated neologisms and a "drawling manner"—an essential component in the comic Yankee. And worse, because of an equivalent few crooked itinerant peddlers, residents of other states entertain the erroneous idea that New Englanders are "a knavish, artful, and dishonest people" (147). But as with the "characteristic" drawl, only a minority of Yankees "have recourse to knavery for subsistence. . . . In New England, there is as great a proportion of honest and industrious citizens, as in any of the United States."

This was the same argument from proportion that was used in defense of the Puritans, that if they were guilty of small-minded bigotries, they were also capable of the largest kind of views. But much as the dark dimension of Puritanism survived the apologists, thriving in fiction by New England writers, so in Morse's coda is found the stereotype that will endure, a sly counterpart to the canting, hypocritical Puritan, who preaches charity on Sunday and spends the rest of the week persecuting Quakers. In the bell-crowned hat traditionally worn by the comic Yankee can be found the remnant reminder of the steeple-shaped hat of the Puritan.

Further complexity was added to the formula by the antislavery crusade, chiefly identified with New England. By the mid-1850s, writers in the South were creating antitypes to the self-righteous images of heroic crusaders for freedom promulgated by abolitionist presses. This activity had become accelerated with the sensational reception of *Uncle Tom's Cabin*, and none of it was intended to give a favorable report of New England character. The type, after the publication of Stowe's novel, was gender neutral, and in Joseph G. Baldwin's *Flush Times of Alabama and Mississippi* (1853), there is a fictional episode involving an aging spinster schoolmistress, "a new importation from Yankeedom" into Alabama, which beneath its Irvingesque frame seethes with sectional hostility, given particular point by the phenomenon of women assuming positions of prominence in the abolitionist movement: Miss Charity Woodey "was one of those 'strong-minded women of New England,' who exchange all the tenderness of the feminine for an impotent attempt to attain the efficiency of the masculine nature; one of that fussy, obtrusive, meddling class, who in trying to *double-sex* themselves, *unsex* themselves, losing all that is lovable in woman, and getting most of what is odious in man" (213).

The very antithesis of the southern feminine ideal, "engaged in the police business of life, rather than the heart and the affections," Miss Woodey is all too representative of her region, "the starched, strait-laced community" identified with "the interior villages of Connecticut," at the heart of which was a "little coterie of masculine women and female men—with its senate of sewing societies, cent societies, and general congress of missionary and tract societies" (212–13). Armed with a stiff-necked notion of "duty" and "conscience," Miss Woodey "had come out as a missionary of light to the children of the South" and had used her schoolroom authority to impose a moral "strait-jacket" on her students: In her self-righteous eyes, "everything was wrong. Everything must be put right" (213–14). By "right," Miss Woodey had more in mind than comportment and penmanship and attempted to indoctrinate her students with her "enlightened sentiments . . . on the subject of slavery in particular; [for] her sentiments on this subject were those of the enlightened coterie from which she came. . . . She was as blue as an indigo bag."

Baldwin's sketch is concrete testimony of the extent to which the traditional tension between Yorkers and Yankees as dramatized by Knickerbocker writers would be transferred to the sectional hostilities between North and South, exacerbated by the nullification controversy and the much hotter matter of abolition. As early as 1820, William Crafts had expressed himself politely but firmly concerning the impropriety of northern interference in southern affairs. And though abolition was the immediate target of Baldwin's story, it is fairly easy to detect the outline of the interloping Ichabod Crane in the features of the meddling schoolteacher. The community's solution is similar, if less violent, for having determined that Miss Woodey must go, the townspeople set upon the reform-minded spinster a local lawyer of forthright, if rough-hewn, manners, who in conversation feeds her disinformation about the South.

This includes not only (fictitious) atrocities inflicted on slaves, thus validating her erroneous ideas, but the fate that awaits meddling Northerners who question the system. There was, for example, another "Yankee schoolmistress," who as the lawyer informs Miss Woodey, was " 'mobbed for saying something against slavery; but I believe they only tarred and feathered her, and rode her on a rail' " (221). Quick to take the hint, the schoolmistress departs, leaving behind in her haste "a letter, addressed to Mrs. Harriet S— . . . containing some interesting memoranda and statistics on the subject of slavery and its practical workings, which I should never have thought of again had I not seen something like them in a very popular fiction, or rather book of fictions, in which the slaveholders are handled with something less than feminine delicacy and something more than masculine unfairness" (221–22).

Later in the decade, Artemus Ward told of a "Thrilling Scene in Dixie," the Showman having been seized by "Seceshers" on the mere suspicion of entertaining incorrect "principles" and "rid on a rale the next day, a bunch of blazin fire crackers bein tied to my coat tales. It was a fine spetycal in a dramatic pint of view, but I didn't enjoy it" (157). As we have already seen, the Showman had no particular sympathy for "Cuffee," but in other regards he was a quintessential Yankee as seen by southern eyes. Ward, with his traveling menagerie, waxworks, and other attractions, was inspired at least in part by P. T. Barnum, whose autobiography, first published in 1855, boasted of the author's Connecticut origins as well as the "humbugs" by which he had bilked thousands of Americans, in the North and South, claiming that philanthropy was his chief motivation.

Barnum's was a version of Yankee dealings not smiled upon in either place, but it certainly reinforced the southern notion of the New England character. As a hostile reviewer of Barnum's book noted in the *Christian Examiner* for March 1855, the author was the kind of "low-minded, money-making, vulgar and shallow 'Yankee' . . . of wooden-nutmeg notoriety, in whom 'the chivalry of the South' find the type of Northern character, and upon whom they look with an intensity of contempt which none but a Southerner can fully measure, and which makes the word 'Yankee' the most opprobrious epithet that Southern lips can frame" (256–57).

Barnum's may have been a profile hard to fit to the caricature of the Abolitionist, with gleaming eye and intrusive nose, absolute morality personified, yet this double image was a kind of Siamese twin, the swindling and the reforming Yankee joined by a common Puritan bond. Thus the same reviewer in the *Christian Examiner* noted that there was "another side to New England life, a side which has its imperfections, doubtless, and its incongruities, yet bright, very bright, with a redeeming and inspiring glory" (258). The reviewer placed Barnum's book next to James Parton's 1855 *Life of Horace Greeley*, finding "by the side of cant and cunning and charlatanism, honor and earnestness and gallantry, and indomitable noblest humanities." Yet both men had sprung up "out of this tough old puritan soil . . . and from the same stratum of New England society" (258–59). The " 'chivalric Southerner' " might "hate" a Horace Greeley, but the New Hampshire–born reformer could never inspire the "contempt" aroused by the Yankee from Connecticut. The reviewer, Charleston-born William Henry Hurlbert, a southerner but a Harvard-educated Unitarian and antislavery writer, was certainly well qualified for this balanced appraisal, though he was perhaps overly optimistic in his view of the southern reception of "manly" abolitionists like Greeley, whose "bright glory" often inspired the kind of blazing reception given Artemus Ward.

In a piece entitled "Town and Rural Humbugs," a reviewer for *Knickerbocker Magazine* (March 1855) drew a similar contrast to Hurlbert's, this time between Barnum's *Life* and *Walden*, finding in Thoreau's book a much needed "antidote" to the other, though it was the Concord hermit's opposition to the "idolatrous worship of the almighty dollar" that the reviewer found salubrious, not his opinions regarding slavery: "In the New-England philosophy of life, which so extensively prevails where the moral or intellectual character of a man is more or less determined by his habits of thrift, such a book as 'Walden' was needed. Extravagant as it is in the notions it promulgates, we think it is nevertheless calculated to do a good deal of good. . . . Where it exerts a bad influence upon one person, Barnum's auto-biography will upon a hundred" (241).

Again, New York was seldom friendly to the Yankee idea, the *Knickerbocker Magazine* perhaps less so than other journals, but the reaction to Barnum's chicanery was such that Thoreau (like Greeley) seemed to shine like the lamp of Diogenes by comparison, a New England Hyperion to a satyr. These pairings recall the differences between the Yankees created by Seba Smith and Lowell—who share certain positive qualities with Greeley and Thoreau—and those wrought in the pattern provided by Washington Irving, brought up to date in the sly, grasping person of Barnum. Yet as Hurlbert observed, both types had common origins, and that once again and always was the problem: where apologists for the Puritan had difficulty reconciling the good that the founders of New England left after them with the bad they committed while alive, so satirists had no trouble attacking the Yankee on both fronts, as hypocritical opportunist and canting reformer, terrible twins who were but logical extensions of the Puritan character, that dark plant deep rooted near Plymouth Rock.

Among the unintended results of George Washington Blagden's sermon in Plymouth entitled "Great Principles Associated with Plymouth Rock" was a letter that appeared in the Episcopalian journal the *Churchman* in 1835 that used for its own ends Blagden's address in a way not dissimilar to George Thompson's. The letter was written by the Reverend Thomas Winthrop Coit, a descendant of Puritans and a convert in 1826 from Congregationalism who, until 1835, had been a resident Episcopalian clergyman in Salem and Cambridge, Massachusetts. Taking Blagden's sermon for "a sort of Pilgrim manifesto," Coit attacked the Congregational minister for his promotion of "the celebrity of Plymouth-rock heroes," a fame falsely warranted by their persecution in the Old World and their sufferings in the New (429, 15–16). Blagden was hardly alone among the celebrants of the Pilgrims to call attention to their sufferings in Europe and America, but he was near at hand, and Coit seized him up for a cudgel with which to belabor the long-standing tradition.

It was Coit's argument that not only was suffering not a Pilgrim monopoly—it was shared by the Forefathers with Greenland whalers, among many others—but the matter of persecution was factitious, since the Pilgrims had come to America from Holland, where they had enjoyed tolerance and had prospered. The Pilgrims' motives for coming to the New World were hardly pure in origin, if Puritanic in spirit, for to "the invaluable privilege of free thought" must be added the powerful lure of "making money a little faster" than they had been able to do in Holland. By the Pilgrims' own admission, they came in pursuit of " 'the then profitable trade of furs and skins' " (17). Which is to say they were embryonic Yankees.

This attempt at desacramentalizing "Plymouth-rock heroes" was obviously sectarian at base, for unlike Robert Winthrop, who shared a common ancestor with the Episcopalian priest as well as his faith, Thomas Winthrop Coit was clearly tired of the ritual abuse dealt out to the Anglican Church by Forefathers' Day celebrants. The Reverend Coit was interrupted in his discourse for a time, but by 1845, now rector of Trinity Church in New Rochelle and a member of the New-York Historical Society, he decided to pick up the thread of his argument and weave it into something more substantial.

In a book of some five hundred thickly packed pages, *Puritanism: or, A Churchman's Defence Against its Aspersions, by an Appeal to its own History*, Coit exposed to his satisfaction the materialistic basis of the Pilgrim adventure, with learned references to Cotton Mather, William Hubbard, and Nathaniel Morton, among other Puritan historians. He made reference as well to Judge Story's bicentennial address in Salem (which Coit had heard delivered) as well as other modern authorities, including Rufus Hawes, Leonard Bacon, and

George Bancroft, the most of whom were used against themselves as Coit set about to deconstruct the mountain of pieties built up over the years about the Puritans, right down to that bedrock boulder.

The result is a still readable and often amusing exercise and provides a salutary antidote to the tiresome diet of self-gratulation served up regularly on anniversaries of the Landing in New England and points west: "Does not history cry, 'Shame upon such misrepresentation! by the solemn testimony of facts, and their own lips?'" (129). Dismissing the claims to the contrary that rose yearly "from New England Societies, orations, songs, and dinner tables," Coit cited Governor Carver himself as testifying that "the Puritan could voluntarily forsake his native land, and an adopted land of sweet church-liberty, and live in a wilderness, if . . . he could follow his trade roundly" (112–13). Coit also observed of the "*exuviae Puritanicae*," piously exhibited in New England museums, along with the chips reverently knocked from the "'Sanctified Rock,'" that they were equivalents to the sacred "relics" associated with Roman Catholicism, idolatrous items deemed abominations by the Puritans and their descendants (483).

But the burden of Coit's book is a massive proof of Puritan intolerance, along with a running argument emphasizing the present disarray found in New England churches, which perhaps explains his own personal defection and retreat to the Mother of all Protestant denominations. His letter of 1835 served as prolegomenon and preface to the whole, being a preliminary attempt to desanctify Plymouth Rock by regarding that celebrated landing place as having no greater significance than "some spot of clay, or sand, in Virginia, or Maryland, or Pennsylvania" (14–15). By pluralizing these liminal zones, Coit was obviously chopping away with an ax at the main stem of the vine celebrated by Cotton Mather. Remove the claim of the Pilgrim celebrants that they were a special and exceptional instance, inspired by only the purest motives of piety, and they become no better than their counterparts as colonists elsewhere.

An anatomy lesson of the heft and Yankeephobic drift of *The Knickerbocker History* but without Irving's broad sense of humor—Coit's wit tended toward the scalpel in pointedness and edge—*Puritanism* must be accounted a weighty attempt to demystify the Pilgrims. But in his letter of 1835 Coit had already started the process, assigning to the Forefathers motives that were associated with the emerging Yankee stereotype: "They wanted a little more notoriety—a little more power—a little more money" than was to be found in England or Holland, "so nothing remained but to . . . steer for a land where they might be unrivalled and supreme. Verily this is the plain case, and the whole of it" (18). In 1835, Coit's was a lonely voice in Cambridge, Massachusetts, but a brave one, and yet it must be said that even some celebrants of the Pilgrims were willing to trace a line of descent between the Forefathers and the present-day Yankee, if in somewhat more positive terms, along the lines eventually made famous by Lowell in his *Biglow Papers.*

When in 1834 Samuel Breck read his Forefathers' Day discourse in Philadelphia, a city associated with a primal instance of Yankee initiative, he followed a conventional line by observing that wherever a descendant of the Pilgrims went, he carried with him "a spirit of enterprise, tempered by prudence, intelligence and system." The Yankee, by Breck's account, is happiest when "*employed. Action* is really the *life, business,* and rest of his mind" (42). Breck celebrated what Coit would the next year condemn, that aggressive version of the Protestant ethic—"We must keep moving, in search of a port, with profitable employment in it"—and boasted that it was the parent stock, the peregrinating Puritans, that contained "the *germ* of *Yankeeism,* now developed in their descendants."

But he also insisted that part of the whole was an element of idealism— "order and piety are . . . co-operative influences in all his occupations." For if the Yankee seems chiefly motivated by "the love of money," which "exercises his ingenuity, and fills the patent office," and carries him "from the Hyperborean regions of both poles, through all the circles of the earth, and . . . every latitude," such industry often results in "princely gifts" to benevolent institutions (43). But then Breck was able to defend the Puritans from the charge of severity and gloom by finding abundant "merriment" in the *Magnalia.* His argument was the familiar one that had been used to extenuate the Puritans' narrowness and bigotry by pointing to the piety and virtue that inspired them. But the main point to be considered here was his willingness to concede (even anticipate) Coit's point that the generic Yankee could be traced to a Puritan (Pilgrim) root.

Breck was taken one step further by Peleg Sprague in 1835, who delivered the Forefathers' Day address in Plymouth and who maintained that the characteristic restlessness of New England natives did not owe its ultimate origin to the Pilgrims but could be traced even further back, to the "indominable, severe Saxon blood . . . most remarkable for endurance, perseverance, and tenacity of purpose" (7). Inheriting this élan vital, the Puritan added an element of idealism, a "religious principle," and a "religious enthusiasm, deep, ardent," and, because of Saxon tenacity, "unyielding" (8). Like Jedidiah Morse, Sprague admitted that "some unworthy sons of New England who have gone forth from us, have been false to their ancestry," but that did not mean that New Englanders in general were prone to "cupidity and fraud" (13). The very appearance of the region evinced "the purity of our character," especially "the villages and farm-houses of . . . the Old Colony," a district "least contaminated by foreign intermixture" and like Pilgrim Hall therefore a kind of museum, less of artifacts than race memory, the omphalos of which was Plymouth Rock.

In his sermon the year before, which as at the start of a game of billiards had sent balls scattering in all directions, the Reverend Blagden had pointed to the amnesiac effect of foreign immigration on the national memory, and Sprague was reinforcing that point, adding to the traditional notion of exceptionalness the ideal of exclusion. Like Blagden's sermon entire, the effect of this emphasis would have a long reach into the years following the Civil War, a time when the theory of Saxon "blood" would likewise gain greater circulation. But, in 1835, the most of Sprague's argument was familiar stuff, a defensive counterattack on "those who are willing to impute to us a narrow and illiberal spirit," by pointing to "our internal improvements, not to our canals and railroads, the fruits of private enterprize, but that admirable system, sustained for ages by the annual self-taxation of the whole people, by which free public roads are every-where maintained, in a degree of convenience and excellence nowhere rivaled by a society of equal numbers or equal means" (17).

To these material blessings, Sprague added the pious spirit brought by the Pilgrims, who established their colony "not only on the rock of Plymouth, but the Rock of Ages." Their government was not rule by force but was rule by laws, certified by the Mayflower Compact, legal channels directing the inherited Saxon energy. The Forefathers "struck the rock in the wilderness, from whence have flowed the waters of life," closely identified with the "Puritan blood," that high-octane fluid that now "flows everywhere, swelling every vein of this great republic, diluted perhaps by intermixture, enfeebled perhaps, but still imparting something of its pristine strength and ardor" (12, 11). Throughout the nation, New Englanders "have taken the lead in energy and activity, and wherever there have been the greatest advances, there you may be sure to find the sons of New England."

It is the dual inheritance of Saxon energy and Puritan piety and jurisprudence that has resulted in "this pervading zeal and ardor and energy . . . which has studded our iron-bound coast with cities and villages, and clothed our barren fields with verdure—which has subdued the forest and spread far and wide the beams and blessings of civilization." But by 1835, despite the Reverend Blagden's warnings, the notion of "pervading zeal and ardor and energy" associated with New England had been given the lean and humorless features of William Lloyd Garrison, whose eyeglasses gleamed with overabundant zeal. Moreover, the great debate with Hayne over nullification that had brought Webster so much fame and glory in New England had caused only trouble for native sons resident below the Line.

Even as Samuel Breck was speaking in Philadelphia, a more anxious voice was heard in Charleston, for when Dr. Joshua Barker Whitridge rose to deliver his Forefathers' Day address before the New England Society, it was with a deep sense of grievance. In fact, it was the specifics of *The Memoirs of a Nullifier* with its noxious satire of Yankees that had aroused the ire of the speaker, who strove to set the record straight. Dr. Whitridge, of the College of Medicine in Charleston, moved quickly through the familiar tropes of the Pilgrim story and rather hastily disembarked the Forefathers: "From their shallop they landed men, women, and children upon a rock—aye—upon the rock which has been the foundation not of New England alone, but of the greatest Republic of which the world could ever boast" (14).

The burden of Dr. Whitridge's address was taken up with the implications of the difference between the Pilgrims and the "early settlers of Virginia and New York," precisely the "invidious comparison" he claimed he did not wish to draw and about which Blagden had cautioned in 1834 and to which Coit had objected in 1835. If the future of the country had depended on "the character of the first settlers of Virginia and New-York, we should never have existed as an independent nation" (15). It was the "sterling stuff as constituted the Puritans" from which the national character was formed and which had come to be associated more recently with "the honorable appellation of YANKEES" (21).

By associating Yankees with the Puritans, Whitridge hoped to lay to rest the continuing propensity to use the regional designation as a term of sarcastic contempt. He was addressing himself through his auditors to those persons who believe New Englanders are "mean and selfish in their disposition, sly, cunning, apt to overreach—in short, dishonest whenever they can get anything by it—and that their motto virtually is, if not the avowed principle of action, 'Every man for himself and God for us all'" (23). With Jedidiah Morse and Samuel Breck, Whitridge admitted that there were bad apples in the basket, but he objected to the rotten few spoiling the rest. He reckoned that it was "the rascality of one renegade Yankee" that was behind all "the stories of the wooden clocks and wooden nutmegs" then in circulation (24).

Whitridge also followed the line of argument that the negative image of New England was contradicted by the evidences of progress within its borders, the many institutions of learning, religion, and charity that belied the myth of penurious brigandage. And along with pointing to its many bustling and prosperous industries, he listed the names of its great men, from Bradford and Winthrop to Webster and Channing, the main stars in "a galaxy of others. . . . A more brave, generous, high-minded, self-sacrificing people is not to be found on the face of the earth, than the noble race who settled the New-England colonies, and who may thus be said to have founded the Western Empire. Their descendants are now scattered broad-cast over the face of our whole country, exercising their skill and industry, for their own and others' benefit—

disseminating their influence for the good of their fellow-citizens, and for the general welfare of society" (27).

Dr. Whitridge at once filled in Webster's geopolitics of 1820 and anticipated the argument of Dr. Holmes in 1855 in figuring New England as the grand source of talent and center of industry in America, and his argument was sectional as well as regional in spirit. If Yankees were attacked elsewhere, it was "the result of sheer envy and jealousy, and if rightly apprehended would be regarded as a compliment." For they have become the models for emulation throughout the United States, to the extent that "whatever of national character we possess, it is admitted by British and all other travellers, is derived from New England." Therefore, "ridicule and abuse . . . of the character of Yankees . . . by some of the inhabitants of other States" should be worn as a badge of honor: "Is there a Yankee among us who does not rejoice to regard New England as the place of his nativity?" (26). It may be needless to add that it was precisely this kind of self-righteous assertiveness that violated the southern decorum of self-effacing courtesy and drove ever wider the gap between the cavalier and his northern counterpart.

III

Whitridge's Puritan-to-Yankee genesis was celebrated in other regions as well, if not always with that obnoxious New England whine of self-justification. In Detroit, in 1846, Alexander Buel delivered a Forefathers' Day address before the New England Society of Michigan and took the celebratory tack conventional in such performances, perhaps even more so than most. For he compared New Englanders who traveled into western regions to those citizens of the Roman Empire, who carried with them wherever they went "the fame and power of the Imperial City" (5). "The American citizen, as he traverses every land and sea, feels himself invested with the power and insignia of popular freedom, and now the adventurous pioneer of the West is bold to exclaim, 'I am a Son of New England.'" What began with "the Pilgrims' landing upon Plymouth rock" has become the seamless whole of a splendid republic, whose "influence upon the civilization of a world no human intellect can measure. . . . Today, from Plymouth Rock . . . New England . . . looks out proudly upon her child[ren] of the West . . . whom she has sent forth as the embodiment of her spirit and genius, the emissaries of her civilization. Today she extends her maternal hand and claims us still. NEW ENGLAND HAS NO EXILES" (6–7).

After thirty pages devoted to hyperbolic praise of New England culture, Buel returned to the Landing, a "blessed, glorious view" elevated by "moral grandeur," irradiated by "the splendors of heaven," and given sublimity by "the magnificence of terrestrial scenery!" (35). Revealing the Western spirit that identified itself with the grandiloquent spaces in which (and to which) it grew, Buel's address also suggests the dangers of reading Carlyle in the rarified atmosphere of Michigan. For he characterizes the Pilgrim as a child of "the spirit-form of the Reformation," figured as "an aged and giant mother, bearing aloft the sacred oracles of God and Nature's scroll of freedom [as] she steps upon the ice-bound coast [and] points her mighty child to a new home" (36). Exceptionalism has seldom had a more colossal form, requiring less the "pencil" of a Benjamin West (inadequate as Buel saw it to the occasion of the Landing) than the tools of those wood engravers who supplied illustrations for the Crockett almanacs.

Buel's Carlylean "spirit-child" has a heroic, even godlike outline, maturing as "a stout, athletic, manly form, moving his magic wand o'er the shores of the Atlantic; peopling them with a new race, and adorning them with the fruits and flowers of civil and religious freedom." His "New England pioneer; himself a Pilgrim son of a Pilgrim father," resembles the transcendent version of Daniel Boone, as "from the tops of the Alleghenies he looks out upon the great Western Valley, with a comprehensive vision not satisfied, until it rests upon the distant mountains of the Pacific" (35–36). Buel's is a Whitmanesque Yankee, who yearns to "repose on the sands of the Western ocean, breathing in the swift-coming future the fragrance of oriental climes."

Whatever the realities behind it, Buel's steam-driven prose expresses a manifest expansionism, and like the Davy Crockett his Yankee "spirit" evokes, it has in its very gargantuanism a comic dimension. Buel's is both a variety of the transcendent Yankee as defined by William Taylor and a manifestation of the mythic version abstracted by Constance Rourke from the comic almanacs of the day. There is, moreover, none of that defensive element that characterized orations celebrating the Puritan genesis in Massachusetts, Pennsylvania, and South Carolina, suggesting that in Michigan the idea of the Yankee was not only favorably received but that western eyes were fixed in a western direction only.

We have by contrast a Forefathers' Day address delivered in 1848 by the Reverend Charles Brandon Boynton before the New England Society of Cincinnati, a town in which proslavery feelings could run high, as Theodore Weld had learned more than twenty years earlier, when he tried to preach abolition to the mob. And since, by 1848, the idea of emancipation was invariably (if not exclusively) associated with New England, the Reverend Boynton had not much to say about magic Pacific sands but devoted a number of pages to defending the Yankee character, in terms that gave his discourse a reformist curve.

Boynton had come to the ministry by an indirect route, having first practiced law and then assumed the presidency of the first railroad built through the Berkshires, a line intended to connect Boston with the Erie Canal, hence with the western regions. Apparently the Whig notion of internal improvements, essential to the idea of union, was not sufficient to his idealism, for Boynton took Presbyterian orders in 1840, then filled pulpits in western Massachusetts and eastern New York, a track that paralleled the one running from Boston to Albany and which pointed Boynton toward the farther West. He arrived in Cincinnati in 1846, where he assumed the pulpit of the Vine Street Church, remaining there for thirty years with occasional interruptions.

Boynton was precisely the kind of enterprising New Englander praised in the sermons and speeches of others, combining as he did the skills and energies of a man of business and the piety of a man of God. He was active, moreover, in the antislavery cause and would set out in the fall of 1854 to explore the possibilities and advantages of the Kansas Territory, presumably with an eye to luring Free-Soil settlers to the region. His report was published as a book, and henceforth Boynton developed a second career as a writer, with a broadening interest in international affairs. Between 1865 and 1869, he served as chaplain to the House of Representatives, using his leisure to compile a history of the U.S. Navy during the Civil War.

I cite these facts in order to establish that Boynton was a man with wide and expanding views, far in excess of the usual range of a Presbyterian minister. He took great pride in his New England heritage, which he seems to have regarded as being under fire along the northern banks of the Ohio River in 1848, suggesting that not much had changed since Weld's noisy visit. The setting therefore gave particular resonance to Boynton's otherwise traditional observation that the Pilgrim Fathers were chiefly honored by their posterity because they, "first among all men, embodied the great principles of liberty in the institutions of a permanent state, and gave them a practical bearing upon the interests of humanity" (7).

His, in effect, were Lowell's Pilgrims, much as Boynton had literally prepared the way for Whittier's Pilgrims in Kansas: they did more than "talk of human freedom and the rights of men" but set in motion the "Spirit of Liberty," in the form of "institutions" that provided "a medium through which it can act upon the world. . . . Let those who are disposed to sneer at Yankee ingenuity, remember that they claim among other notions, the crowning invention of all time, a machine for the destruction of despotism and the elevation of man: free institutions founded on the principles of the gospel." Here was a Yankee notion that had changed the world.

In rehearsing the familiar scenes associated with the Pilgrim story, Boynton passed rather quickly by the voyage of the *Mayflower*, the Compact, and the Landing, although he did allow that the Pilgrim adventure formed an "epic poem of the highest order," "a poetry of hardship and suffering" (14). But Boynton had an ax to grind other than Buel's Bunyanesque implement, and rather than inflate the myth, he chose to defend the character of the Pilgrims and their modern descendants in terms of specifics, beginning with the old and by 1848 familiar charge that the Puritans had persecuted the Quakers and hanged people accused of witchcraft.

In putting on his clerical collar, Boynton had not left his lawyer's briefs behind: he pointed out that the Quakers were punished "on account of their transgression of the civil law" and noted that to ridicule the Puritans for hanging witches meant "sneering" at the Bible itself, which acknowledges both the Devil and his human subjects (22). As for the "narrowness of mind" attributed to the Puritans, Boynton followed the traditional line of pointing to the "common school system," the origins of which were in New England (25). His was in general a conventional argument, reminding us that the champions of abolition included any number of the orthodox, but Boynton's immediate occasion was not the slavery issue, however much it provided the background.

His was another defense of New Englanders against the reputation for having "a mean, penurious spirit," being "in love with a cent," and even looking upon "a half cent" as worthy of fond regard (27). This, he maintained, put a sour construction on "the saving, thrift-loving spirit of the Puritans," and while admitting with Morse, Breck, and Whitridge that "individual examples of Yankee meanness can be found," Boynton denied outright that "frugality" equates with "a sordid soul." As with the matter of witches, New England's thrifty character is sanctioned by Scripture, and "if she has demanded the half cent with one hand, with the other she has freely distributed her millions" to charitable causes (27). And then, putting on his railroading cap, Boynton noted that New England's "laborious industry and strict economy" had provided the necessary capital for the many internal improvements from which the West had benefited, constructing railroads and canals and "aiding every western town in its weakness" (27–28).

This was, once again, the familiar compensatory argument used in the 1820s to defend the Puritans against charges of bigotry. Yes, Boynton was quick to admit, "Yankee ingenuity" had its dark side, having produced "excellent wooden nutmegs and horn gunflints, to say nothing of cast-iron axes, and other similar notions." But that same genius, honestly applied, had "also built a Lowell [the factory town, not the poet], and filled all New England with those fair white villages which are the admiration of the world, the brilliant gems that adorn her homespun robe" (29). Moreover, if one were to remove from the land "the products of Yankee ingenuity" and "put a sudden stop to the workings of Northern industry," the worst nightmare of southern chivalry would be realized: "Every slave must of necessity then be dismissed, so soon as the present set of implements should fail; for chivalry has not learned to make its own hoe-handle or axe-handle, much less can it shape the axe or hoe itself, but sits in gentlemanly helplessness, sneering at the ingenuity upon which it depends for its daily bread" (29).

This, then, was the point toward which Boynton had been heading, determined by his resolve to argue down the stereotype of the greedy, swindling Yankee by appealing to his transcendent Puritan origins, thereby reinforcing the antitype of the languid cavalier: "Puritanism with its stern and heightened orthodoxy was placed on the snow covered northern rocks; its opposite and rival, enjoyed the productive lands and balmy skies of Virginia. The practical workings of these two systems in their development, is more instructive than all the theories that have ever been broached." In a display of what can only be called muscular Christianity, Boynton went to work on those contemporary particulars to which the Puritan genesis gave meaning:

> How happened it, that [Virginia's] Northern neighbor became the prolific germ of the nation, the mother of American liberties, of commerce and manufactures, and the whole educational system of the country? How has it occurred, that New England and her Northern sisters have filled this west with a free civilization, making it a wonder on earth, and planting the valley over with the churches of Jesus?—How is it that New England has thus gone on from strength to strength, and from one notable achievement to a higher still; showing an expansive life unequalled in the world's history for its power and steadiness, and has become the very centre of vitality? While Virginia and her sisters are neither the centres of commerce, nor manufacture, nor education, nor internal improvements, nor of religious influence [and] are already in their dotage, while Puritanism among the snows, is in the full tide of successful experiment and vigorous growth? (30)

Celebrants of the Pilgrims as different as Everett and Whittier had cited the climate and rock-ribbed soil of New England as contributing to the strength and vitality of its residents, with an occasional pitying nod toward Virginia, but Boynton here asks one of those long and loaded kinds of questions that would increasingly characterize the rhetorical armament race between North and South. His argument has none of Garrison's pious fury over the plight of African Americans, for Boynton, once again, was a Free-Soiler, which placed him outside the circling campfires of the ultra-abolitionists. While acknowledging that slavery is "the withering pestilence of the South," he insists that there is "a mightier cause lying back of it all," which has less to do with the failings of the South than the virtues of the North, the key to which is Puritanism: "Puritanism was the soul of New England, and the South from the first has been animated by another spirit" (29).

Boynton acknowledged that a minority of "noble Puritans," like Washington and Patrick Henry, had been raised on southern soil, but these were exceptions, for the region has been under "the power of a different spell," the opiate called chivalry that allowed and was even sustained by human bondage: "Had the South been Puritan, she would have hurled slavery from her long ago, even as the North has done": "Puritanism is a quickening spirit; wherever it dwells, it breathes everything into life, and bestows the boon of freedom. Where it is not, liberty, industry, and prosperity will wither and die. Puritanism stood on Plymouth rock, and she scattered the darkness and rubbish of ages with one stroke of her wand; she leveled the forests about her, she breathed young empires into life, and consecrated them to Liberty and God. Puritanism in its broad sense, is the only Spirit of Life, Freedom, and Power on the wide globe: is the only truly living thing" (30–31). By contrast, the South and its "moving [and antique] spirit," chivalry, are both "perishing away."

Boynton's antislavery argument is basically a hard-line utilitarianism based on commonsense reasoning: slavery and its counterpart, chivalry, are already dying and soon enough will be dead, while vital life signs are to be found in New England and in those regions influenced by New England culture. In Boynton's view there will be no apocalyptic confrontation between North and South because the war is already over, and New England has won. For what kind of threat was secession if it meant cutting the South off from implements manufactured in the North? And even if things continue as they had in the past, the "peculiar" institutions of the South, including chivalry, were doomed, having been disconnected from the vital flow and sources of modern American life.

And yet, at a later point in his oration, Boynton admits that the northern spirit of enterprise, improvement, and manufactures has had a down side, that Yankee energy and ingenuity brought much gain but also loss. This admission comes out of his nostalgic depiction of an earlier New England, a veritable utopia of "true christian, social intercourse. . . . Nowhere else on earth has there been a more notable and joyous exhibition of the family relation . . . ; nowhere have the dignity, sanctity, and purity of home been better preserved" (24). Recalling "the sleigh rides and apple pairings [sic], the pumpkin cuttings, the corn huskings, the spinning bees, the evening party" of his youth, Boynton sighs for the amusements of a lost rural paradise, which expressed the "true social feeling, for which modern amusements are, in many respects, a very meager substitute. . . . The march of the commercial and manufacturing spirit has withered up the freshness of rural joys, and in the feverish race for wealth, men have forgotten how to be happy" (24–25).

The result by Boynton's account is a reversal and contradiction of his earlier emphasis on Yankee get-up-and-go, as opposed to the slavery-induced lassitude of the chivalric South. A price has been paid, the disappearance of New England's innocence, "a pure, free, healthy and joyous social intercourse" that "is not discoverable in the country now." This is the same pastoral asylum that Whittier would nostalgically re-create after the war, for the popularity of *Snow-Bound* undoubtedly resulted from the further increase of not only the spirit of enterprise and productivity that Boynton celebrated in the first part of his sermon but the accelerated loss of rural virtue. Somehow or other, in giving full exercise to the Puritan virtues, New England had lost its soul, a conclusion William Bradford had reluctantly arrived at in making his quietus two centuries earlier and to which Henry David Thoreau was likewise coming at Walden Pond.

IV

A virtual validation of Boynton's lament, Webster by 1850 seemed to many of his contemporaries living proof of New England's moral decline, much as his move from rural New Hampshire to Boston signified the region's abandonment of its pastoral tradition. Likewise, the transition from godlike Daniel to Black Dan could be read as a coefficient of the emergence of the dark side of the Yankee character, in the North identified not with abolitionist agitators but with their expedient counterparts, who had compromised principle for the sake of maintaining commercial ties with the South. Always a "transcendent Yankee," even after his fall, Webster after 1850 was no longer the Transcendentalist's Yankee, a decline that may be charted in the musings of Ralph Waldo Emerson. At the start of his career—which coincided with Webster in the fullness of his own—Emerson regarded the Great Man as having been "cast in the heroic mould" of the Forefathers: he was the "conscience of the country," standing "sure" on the ground of "common sense and common good" (*Works*, 9:398–99).

He was a man-mountain, like Monadnoc grounded in the granite of New Hampshire. Webster's "counsel" came from his heart, in him "eloquence" was "truth," for he was a man entirely "self-centered," so that when he spoke, "It shook or captivated all who heard, ran from his mouth to mountains and the sea, / And burned in noble hearts proverb and prophecy." These lines were written in 1831, following Webster's magnificent response to Hayne, celebrating in poetry the idea that the orator's face was a "beacon" from which Americans "might gather omens" for a brighter future. But then, Webster's flame having become in Emerson's eyes smoky with a stench of corruption, in 1854 he wrote that "Nature's grandest brow" bore the graffito "*For Sale.*"

Where earlier Emerson had coupled Webster with the moral integrity of the Forefathers and the strength of natural forces, in 1851 he made a distinction: "The ocean & the elements are at the back of the brave old puritans of the world when all the Websters are putrid. . . . Tell him that he who was their pride in the woods & mountains of New England is now their mortification; that they never name him; they have taken his picture form the wall & torn it—dropped the pieces in the gutter" (*Journals*, 11:346, 351). In 1852, on the occasion of Webster's death, he looked back at the Great Man of former days, who "was there for cause: the reality; the final person, who had to answer the questions of all the faineants, & who had an answer. But alas! he was the victim of his ambition; to please the South betrayed the North and was thrown out by both" (3:111–12).

For what had elevated Webster in the eyes of his New England countrymen in time brought about his fall: his steadfast defense of the Constitution, to give it the best construction, resulted in his March 7 speech in 1850. It was, of course, susceptible of other constructions, for Webster by 1850 was propped up by a stickwork of personal compromises, the result of his need for financial support to feed his expensive tastes—the greatest of which, ironically, was the model farm he maintained at Marshfield. His consequent willingness to bend to the wishes of the industrialists who filled his pockets was the kind of moral pliability identified with the dark side of the Yankee character.

The sense of loss confided by Emerson to his journals was perhaps best expressed in public by Theodore Parker, who in a long memorial sermon performed a moral autopsy, pronouncing Webster a great man who was greatly flawed. Where other abolitionists like Garrison and Phillips were ferocious in their glee, virtually dancing on Webster's grave, Parker mitigated and softened his outrage with a pervasive sadness, ever and again measuring the Webster of 1850 against the orator of 1820, 1825, and 1826: "At Plymouth Rock . . . at Bunker Hill . . . and at Faneuil Hall . . . each of these orations was a great and noble effort. . . . I was a boy ten years old when he stood at Plymouth Rock, and never shall I forget how his clarion words rang in my boyish heart. . . . I was helped to hate slavery from the lips of that great intellect, and now that he takes back his words, and comes himself to be slavery's slave, I hate it ten-fold harder than before, because it made a bondman out of that proud, powerful nature" (*Centenary Edition*, 7:346). Notably, this was one of the rare occasions in Parker's works where he alludes to Plymouth Rock, cited in connection with Webster's great speech a total of seven times throughout, choric repetition intended to diminish the Webster of 1850.

Webster dead was chiefly mourned by surviving Whigs, as the lost Champion of the Union and Defender of the Constitution, roles for which he was celebrated while alive. When the New England Society in New York met in December 1852 to celebrate the Landing, the members forwent the annual dinner, hushing "the voice of festivity" in memory of the man who had so often graced the dining room with his presence. And the speaker for that occasion, the Reverend William Adams, ended his lengthy address on the admirable aspects of the Puritan character with some necessary words: "New

England's greatest son has gone . . . to rest in that Pilgrim dust which he so much loved and honored. . . . He has gone! We have laid him down in the spot which he had himself chosen, by the side of our forefathers, and within sight of the Rock which their feet first touched" (*NESO*, 2:201–2).

Recalling how that "sonorous voice had so eloquently celebrated this day of our forefathers in words which will ever adorn our national literature," Adams went on to celebrate Webster as "the genuine growth of our own soil, and the peculiar product of our own institutions. . . . Springing from the bosom of the people, working his way upward by his own spontaneous and irrepressible force, he could not have been what he was but for the peculiar influences of his New England home."

In the House of Representatives, William Preston of Kentucky likewise associated Webster with the power of place when he intoned, "The winds of autumn have swept the stern New England shores—the shores of Plymouth, where the Pilgrim Fathers landed—and caught up the expiring breath of DANIEL WEBSTER as he terminated his life of honorable service" (*Obituary Addresses*, 50). "The surges of the wintry ocean, as they beat upon the shores of Marshfield, are a fitting requiem," observed Preston, for the man who " 'like a solid rock by seas enclosed, / To raging winds and roaring waves exposed.' " Again and again his memorialists reached for some aspect of the landscape with which to express their sense of so great a man, the idea that like Plymouth Rock he was from the native granite of New England hewn. These natural analogies operated beyond commonplaces and seem to have been a universal reaction to the sheer massiveness of Webster the man, with its attendant specific gravity, inertia contained yet radiating great power from a field of force.

" 'How lonesome the world seems!' " exclaimed one of the "plain neighbors" after the Squire of Marshfield had been laid to rest, and many another, far greater man felt likewise (Choate, *Addresses and Orations*, 310). We should not perhaps make too much of what Rufus Choate derived from the words of that graveside mourner, the one being Webster's friend and fellow Whig, the other his neighbor, but surely we can acknowledge the likelihood of a universal sense of loss. Something very big had dropped from view, leaving an immense vacuity behind, and if Webster alive could evoke by his sheer presence a sense of the sublime, then the chasm left by his death must have inspired among many Americans a psychic vertigo and pervasive anxiety.

Until his own death, in 1859, Choate remained faithful to the Whig Party and to the memory of Daniel Webster, and of the Great Man's many eulogists, he said it best: "The hunter beyond Superior; the fisherman on the deck of the night-foundered skiff; the sailor on the uttermost sea—will feel, as he hears these tidings, that the protection of a sleepless, all-embracing, parental care is withdrawn from him for a space, and that his pathway henceforward is more solitary and less safe than before" (240). At the moment of his death, at the nadir of his decline and fall, Webster was still the greatest public man of his day.

What chiefly emerges from Choate's eulogy is a sense of Webster as a natural monument, one of those features of the landscape rich with historical associations of which Alison wrote: "There is nothing which does not bring him by some tie to the memory of America," and, as with matters of place, it is this that lends such sublimity to his memory: "We seem to see his form and hear his deep, grave speech everywhere. By some felicity of his personal life; by some wise, deep, or beautiful word, spoken or written; by some service of his own, or some commemoration of the services of others, it has come to pass that 'our granite hills, our inland seas, and prairies, and fresh unbounded magnificent wilderness,' our encircling ocean, the Rock of the Pilgrims, our new-born sister of the Pacific, our popular assemblies, our free schools, all our cherished doctrines of education, and of the influence of religion, and material policy, and the law, and the constitution, give us back his name. What American landscape will you look on, what subject of American interest will you study, what source of hope or anxiety, as an American, will you acknowledge, that does not recall him!" (232).

Throughout, Choate stresses Webster's American "difference," associating the Great Man not only with the American landscape but the blessings of a modern nation-state. His career, starting from a point that in 1820 had signified the slow, if inexorable, growth of republican institutions from their primitive origins in the Puritan past, was associated with the continued growth and expansion of those institutions, the fabric of which is identified with the public consciousness. If the United States is Memory's Nation, then Webster is the National Man, being a creation of the collective recollection of a grateful people, from whose "bosom," as the Reverend Adams put it, he had sprung.

Even after 1850, Emerson could recall sadly that Webster had been "the one eminent American of our time, whom we could produce as a finished work of Nature" (*Works*, 11:202). Webster's had been such a magnetic presence "that his arrival in any place was an event which drew crowds of people, who went to satisfy their eyes, and could not see him enough. I think they looked at him as the representative of the American Continent . . . a fit figure in the landscape" (221). Webster now fallen and gone, what Emerson needed was a new hero, made great by having "Christ in the heart," an entirely self-reliant man, for "to make good the cause of Freedom, you must draw off from all foolish trust in others. You must be citadels and warriors yourselves, declarations of Independence, the charter, the battle and the victory" (234–35).

George Washington was one such, whose "Athenaeum" portrait by Gilbert Stuart Emerson had hung in his dining room. Washington put forth a "certain

Apalachian strength" that "expressed the country" in its infancy, a "noble, aristocratic head, with all kinds of elevation in it, that come out by turns. Such majestical ironies, as he hears the day's politics, at table. We imagine him hearing the letter of General Cass, the letter of Gen. Scott, the letter of Mr Pierce, read to him" (*Journals*, 13:63; cf. 369). As Emerson's observations anent the presidential race in 1852 make clear, there was no paragon equivalent to either Washington or Webster presently on the scene, and Webster himself had radically diminished himself by his "effrontries" before he died. Franklin Pierce, characterized by Emerson as "a toad in amber," would soon be elevated to the White House, and all was not right with the world.

This anxiety of absence is effectively expressed by a lengthy poem, *Nebraska*, that appeared anonymously in 1854 from the press of John P. Jewett, a Boston publisher notable for having issued *Uncle Tom's Cabin*, Margaret Fuller's *Woman in the Nineteenth Century*, and Maria Cummins's *The Lamplighter* during that troubled decade. Despite this liberal, even radical aegis, the author expressed an ardent desire for the return not only of Webster but of Clay and Calhoun, even while extolling the virtues of Whittier, Wendell Phillips, and Garrison—who had published promotional excerpts from the poem in the *Liberator*. Filling out the forms prepared by Whittier and Lowell, the poet laments the hypocrisy of New England, which promises the fugitive slave asylum and then hunts him "through Boston's classic streets / Until the stones beneath his feet cried 'Shame!' " (25–27).

> Descendants of the Pilgrim stock,
>   By all the free blood in your veins,
> By all the prayers at Plymouth Rock,
>   Strike off the boundsman's galling chains!
> By all the blood your fathers shed,
>   By all the laurels they have won,
> Stand up for freedom as they did
>   At Concord and at Lexington. (18–19)

These were the kinds of sentiments that would have recommended the poem to Garrison, but *Nebraska* espouses the kind of antislavery solution that he opposed, one that was identified with political action and would be the program of the emerging Republican Party.

Yet the poem is pervaded by an evangelical, messianic fervor and expresses a deep-felt desire for some Emersonian Man to emerge as a charismatic leader of sterling virtue and undaunted courage. Reciting a litany of those emerging politicians from Seward to Sumner, any of whom, largely on the basis of their shining newness, might prove a potential savior, the poet dismisses them all as lacking sufficient size for the crisis at hand. What is needed is a champion cast in the mold of the "granite giant" called up in the poem's opening lines, "whose imperial brow"

> Shone like the moon amid his night of hair,
> And whose magnetic eyes pierced through the veil
> Which hides the future from the vulgar gaze, [who now]
> Sleeps on the borders of the broad, deep sea,
> Where winds and waves his requiem sing for aye!
> O that the deep unto the deep could call
> In tones of startling thunder, and awake
> The mighty man who slumbers softly there,
> That he might rise, and in the nations' ear
> Unsay the words in which his heart beat not—
> Words stereotyped to yokes upon the necks
> Of slaves beneath the flag of stripes and stars—
> And then, with his surpassing power of speech,
> Rebuke ambitious traitors, who would sell
> Their country as they sell their countrymen! (3)

Lending suitable elevation to the subject by utilizing blank verse in the Miltonic model, the poet engages in an exercise of posthumous regeneration, redeeming Webster by having him recant his speech of March 7, thereby enabling him to turn against the men who had betrayed him in 1852 by refusing him the nomination and who by 1854 were betraying the compromise itself. This would be a "Daniel to translate the fire / Which burns upon the walls at Washington," a prophet-hero triply distilled from obloquy, not only cleansed of the mortal part but repentant of his pact with the Devil that had hurled him into the purgatory of political nil.

Having in the opening lines given a godlike outline to Webster, the poet maintains an apocalyptic vein throughout, and having created an Eden out of Nebraska (anticipating Whittier's "The Panorama"), the poet calls for a "Watchful angel armed / With sword of flame at Eden's guarded gate," a Gabriel to "Protect this pleasant garden of the west," perhaps an obvious image but one ominous with militant posturing (10). Though its call to the Pilgrim Fathers on Plymouth Rock was by 1854 a ritual abolitionist invocation, the poem's conclusion reinforces its chiliastic, which is to say Puritan, spirit. What is needed is some divinely appointed "Herculean arm" to shake "the temple of our Capitol."

It would be the tall and lanky Abraham Lincoln who would eventually fill the space made available by the absence of Webster, but he was at best a reluctant avenging angel, and he came from the wrong cardinal direction. For the poet looks chiefly to New England for help (suggesting the regional origin of the work), where the "pulpit speaks" in "trumpet tones" but without effect, alas! (14–15). As for Edward Everett, "the Apollo of the sacred desk," that "polished, ministerial man" devotes himself to meekly apologizing for the New England abolitionists "and their reckless course!" (16). Though gifted with a mouth "sweet as Hybla's ancient hive" and words "as musical as golden bees," Everett plainly lacked sufficient "GRIT" for the Herculean task ahead.

Ironically, it was the sectarian and factional wrangling among the antislavery advocates that produced the splinter parties whose only effect was to allow vacillating mediocrities like Pierce and Buchanan to clamber blandly into the White House, inspiring a nostalgia for the days of the great Triumvirate, who for all their faults maintained a heroic faith in the sanctity of the Union. They had brought to the national government a solidity of purpose and a monolithic institutionalism that was reassuring even if contrary to a literal interpretation of the Declaration of Independence and the Bill of Rights. Something substantial had indeed disappeared from view, and midges were left quarreling for the tenancy of the empty air.

In 1854 there was, however, another candidate in the field, brooding in the solitude of North Elba in the Adirondack Mountains, a man born in New England who unlike Webster put forth the characteristic lean and hungry Yankee shape and who was not a lawyer-politician but a farmer. Equally important, in the eyes of Emerson and Thoreau, among other New Englanders radicalized by the Fugitive Slave Law, the man who had been born in Torrington, Connecticut, was the right kind of peddler, carrying westward in his wagon tools to be placed in the right hands at last. He was, to borrow once again William Taylor's epithet for Webster, a "transcendent Yankee," and the transcendentalists claimed him for their own, although, as Taylor maintains, John Brown was for the South the worst kind of Yankee, abolitionist and peddler combined.

In celebrating the martyred abolitionist in 1859, Wendell Phillips had seen this connection: "It is a libel on the Yankee to think that it includes the whole race, when you say that if you put a dollar on the other side of hell, the Yankee will spring for it at any risk," for John Brown was the kind of native-born New Englander whose blood contains an element "which obeys ideas . . . an impulsive, enthusiastic aspiration, something left to us from the old Puritan stock" (*Second Series*, 281). In these sentences, Phillips melted down sixty years of New England defensiveness regarding the Yankee and then poured it flaming hot into the mold provided by John Brown.

CHAPTER **15**

Carving a Face on the Rock

Picter of a Arsenel is represented. Sojers cum & fire at it. Old Brown
cums out & permits hisself to be shot. He is tride and sentenced to be
hung on the gallus. Tabloo—Old Brown on a platform pintin upards, the
staige lited up with red fire. Goddiss of Liberty also on platform, pintin
upards. A dutchman in the orkestry warbles on a base drum. Curtin falls.
Moosic by the Band.
—Artemus Ward

I

For Herman Melville, John Brown was a portent: a "meteor of the war" that followed his death, but if Brown's advent was portentous, he did not drop from a clear, nighttime sky—save in Pottawatomie. No modern biographer has more completely defined the threads in the fabric of contemporary events with which Brown was either intimately or indirectly involved than Richard Boyer. By Boyer's accounting Brown's life was part and parcel of his age, expressive, however, of the dark, subterranean side, even in his many financial reverses having experienced failures that gainsaid the Whig vision of steady and irreversible progress. John Brown in other ways was virtually the thin shadow of Daniel Webster, with his New England birth and his rural associations, a continuity, moreover, that lacked the other man's fatal entrance into the urban zone, as well as the temptations that a career in politics engender.

As we have seen, Captain John Brown had been prepared for by nearly a decade of abolitionist rhetoric, and after 1855 he was given terrific power by his association with events in Kansas, from which he emerged as a champion of the oppressed and an apostle of freedom. By 1859, as he courageously faced the consequences of his stand at Harpers Ferry, Brown seemed to many reform-minded New Englanders as having more than filled the space left open by the defection and death of the Great Man. If Webster was traditionally pictured as standing on Plymouth Rock, then John Brown came to be thought of as the

330

Rock personified, as a presence equivalent to that field of force Wendell Phillips set in motion in 1855, by which time Brown was moving remorselessly toward an inevitably apocalyptic conclusion.

Intrinsic to this process were literary influences tangential to the propaganda engendered by abolitionist presses, for the New England intelligentsia who emerged as his champions had been conditioned by a long exposure to Carlyle. *Heroes and Hero Worship* promoted the idea of culturally determined champions, and its celebration of Cromwell gave new vigor and militancy to New England's Puritan heritage, further validating the connection between the Pilgrims and the abolitionist cause. Emerson and Thoreau, notably, who would become ardent celebrants of John Brown, were both well read in Carlyle, and Emerson may be accounted his disciple, being in both senses Carlyle's American Correspondent. Melville also read Carlyle, if with a much more skeptical eye, which in part accounts for his prophetic manifestation of Captain Brown in Captain Ahab, with a conclusion that Emerson and Thoreau might well have heeded. But if to such as Melville John Brown was a meteor, a sign in the sky that things were not well in the Republic, then for those who read Carlyle's text with Christian spectacles, Brown was an Angel of Light.

Brown's first biographer, James Redpath, who had emigrated from Scotland at seventeen to America and who because of his religious training and journalistic instincts was almost immediately drawn into the abolitionist crusade, established the hagiographic outlines of the martyred insurrectionist that still pretty much obtain. If Boyer has mapped the contextual terrain for modern readers, Redpath's biography provided the symbolic geography for his contemporaries. As a historian he was detectably under the spell of Carlyle and, with some additional help from Sir Walter Scott, undoubtedly saw in Brown something of the Border Chieftain mingled with the fierce Covenanter. But Redpath stressed his hero's New England origins, antecedents, and character and sought to present him in distinctly American terms.

John Brown's paternal grandfather and namesake had fought and died in the Revolution, providing a proper patriotic connection, but Redpath traced his lineage back well past the earlier Captain John Brown. Relying on family tradition presented as fact, he gave him a genealogy as exclusive as it was pure: "Among the group of godly exiles who knelt at Plymouth Rock, on the 22nd of December, 1620, and returned thanks to the Almighty for His goodness to them in preserving them from the dangers of the Deep, was an unmarried English Puritan, a carpenter by trade, of whose personal history all that now can be known is, that his name was Peter Brown" (14).

Though Redpath knew nothing about Peter Brown, the Pilgrim myth already in place provided a sufficient profile, somewhat reshaped to meet the needs of the present occasion: "That he came over in the Mayflower, is evidence enough that he feared his God, respected himself, and strove prayerfully to obey the divine commands; choosing rather to sacrifice the comforts of English civilization, and enjoy in the wilderness his inherent rights, than calmly contemplate the perpetration of wrong by sinners in high places, or to rest satisfied with the sophistical belief, that, by the philosophy of an enlightened selfishness, or the diffusion of correct principles of political economy, all the evils of the age would peacefully be rectified—in a century or two!"

Clearly, the traditional circumstances usually cited for the Pilgrims' departure for the New World have been clipped and edited to coincide with the ideological conflicts of the 1850s, a bias that is as traditional as the ritual citation of persecution and flight from British tyranny that gave point to the earliest use of the Pilgrim example. These presumptions, founded on generalities and placed with the ur-Brown on Plymouth Rock, are gainsaid by the fact that the Peter in question died without siring a son. But such a hard object as a fact would hardly ripple the waters here, for even without that genealogical connection, Redpath could have come to similar conclusions about Brown's Puritan lineage, for we are talking about the deep, subterranean needs of myth. If the foregoing chapters accomplish nothing else, they lay down a baseline of ideologically inspired rhetoric that starts at Plymouth Rock and culminates in Captain John Brown.

Certainly Redpath's abolitionism was of the most militant, Garrisonian stamp, and like Garrison he was interested in revolutionary precedent, which in Brown's case was a matter of record. Redpath noted that a monument in Canton, Connecticut, erected in memory of the earlier (and regularly commissioned) Captain John Brown, recorded that he was of "the fourth generation, in regular descent, from Peter Brown, one of the Pilgrim Fathers." But Redpath's emphasis in what followed was clearly on the heritage of the Revolution, not the Separatist experiment:

> Why did Captain John Brown, "of the fourth generation, in regular descent," risk his life—"throw it away," as our politicians phrase it—by opposing it to the hitherto resistless strength of a mighty empire? Why not wait until, by the aid of a "constitutional republican party," the evils then endured should have been peacefully abolished. What was he to Massachusetts, or Massachusetts to him that he should leave his family and fight her battles? Personal liberty he had; his house was his castle; no power on earth dared molest his property, or wife, or children. It was only a petty question of taxation that called him to the field, but in it there lay embodied a political right; and, rather than submit to an infringement of it, he resolved to "throw his life away," if need be. We now honor him for it; for we see in it the spirit of the first Peter Brown, who would not wait for the convenient

season of corrupt and heartless demagogues, but chose rather to abandon his native land, and enjoy his liberty at once. (16–17)

Redpath demonstrates a clear line of virtuous and courageous action, coupling the Revolutionary War hero's unwillingness to wait for some political (i.e., Republican) party to solve the country's problems with the Pilgrim's refusal to imitate modern politicians by counseling patience as the best solution to religious persecution.

But to Redpath's way of thinking the conduct of the first Captain John Brown was "far nobler" than that of Peter Brown, "for it is not solely for himself, as in the Puritan's case, that he abandons home and friends. It is for a neighboring colony, and the rights of his race, rather than for his personal immunities." Redpath's argument shadows Wendell Phillips's lawyerlike distinction between the Liberty Boys and Elijah Lovejoy, or Sam May's distinction between the Pilgrims and the abolitionists: "Only one step further was possible on the ladder of disinterested benevolence—to fight for a race, poor, despised, friendless, and inferior; and this crowning glory to the family of Peter Brown, the Puritan, was reserved for the grandson of the revolutionary captain" (17). Much as Whig orators saw the sequence from Puritan to Patriot as a progressive series, a purifying process by means of which the perceived flaws of the Puritans were refined away, so Redpath read the Brown family tree as lifting heavenward toward moral superiority in ever more transcendent and disinterested sacrifice for a greater good. Of the faults of the Puritans we hear nothing, only of a consistent striving toward social perfection. The utopian view does not accommodate the Fall, no more than the Unitarians countenanced Calvin.

By such a genesis was Redpath able to find in the penultimate Captain John Brown a virtual resurrection of both the old Puritan and the Patriot officer who had died in the service of his country. The emphasis is on the martial element, with frequent allusions to the martyr hero of Bunker Hill, General Joseph Warren, and to George Washington himself. Though Redpath credits John Brown with combining the humble piety of Christ with the heroism of Old Testament warriors, it is the latter to which he makes the most frequent reference: "He was the last of the old Puritan type of Christian. Gideon, to him, and Joshua, and Moses, were . . . but holy examples set before us, by Deity himself, for our imitation and our guidance. . . . If the Bible is the true Word, it follows that it is right to slay God's enemies, if it be necessary thus to deliver God's persecuted people" (39). Which is tantamount to saying that in Brown's eyes the New Testament was never written, a form of illiteracy of which the "old Puritan" was often guilty as well.

We should not expect propagandists to make fine theological distinctions, but Redpath's easy blend of New and Old Dispensations was a calculated response to those abolitionists whose pacifist principles turned them against John Brown. Garrison was among that number, but only for a faltering moment before declaring that a higher truth prevailed. Whittier, who had earlier distanced himself from Lovejoy, regarded Brown's advocacy of slave insurrection as a rash, even insane policy that "injures the cause he sought to serve" (Pickard, 2:425). In his poetry, Whittier was willing to send the Pilgrims off to Kansas, but he left out instructions as to how they were to comport themselves once they arrived, and pacifists the Separatists (old and new) never were. Redpath, in an account of a visit to John Brown in his armed camp in Kansas, noted the proximity of a nearby town "named Plymouth, in honour of the Puritans,—who had crossed the sea for the same purpose that they were now crossing the prairie: 'To make the West as they had the East, / The Homestead of the Free,'" in effect quoting Whittier's lines back at him in a context that validated the use of force in effecting the cause of freedom (114).

It was during this same visit that Redpath declared of Brown and his men, "I had seen for the first time, the spirit of the Ironsides armed and encamped. And I said, also, and thought, that I had seen the predestined leader of the second and the holier American Revolution." Conflating Cromwell with the American Puritans overlooks a few historical discrepancies, but it does reinforce the Carlylean contingency: John Brown, we are told, "was a great admirer of Oliver Cromwell," and Redpath quotes a letter styling him "the Cromwell of our Border Wars" (45–46; 225). But, once again, it is the American Revolution, not the English Civil War, that is Redpath's favorite analogy, and in defining Brown's political creed, he calls him "an abolitionist of the Bunker Hill school," in a passage designed to elevate his hero to transcendent status by establishing some distance from the activities of contemporary agitators:

> He followed neither Garrison nor Seward, Gerrit Smith nor Wendell Phillips: but the Golden Rule, and the Declaration of Independence, in the spirit of the Hebrew warriors, and in the God-applaused mode that they adopted. "The Bible story of Gideon," records a man who betrayed him [Redpath frequently quotes Brown's enemies to his credit], "had manifestly a great influence on his actions." He believed in human brotherhood and in the God of Battles; he admired Nat Turner, the negro Patriot, equally with George Washington, the white American deliverer. He could not see that it was heroic to fight against a petty tax on tea, and war seven long years for a political principle, yet wrong to restore, by force of arms, to an outraged race, the rights which their Maker had endowed them, but of which the South, for two centuries, had robbed them. (105)

It is in his opening chapters, in laying the foundation of his tribute to John Brown, that Redpath chiefly emphasizes the Puritan elements of his hero's character: "That stern old English sense of justice; that grand Puritan spirit of inflexible integrity" (42). But ever and again, as in this same passage, Redpath sees also in Brown the spirit of George Washington, "Virginia's greatest chief," whose sword the Captain had carried during his defense of the engine house at Harpers Ferry. He had appropriated it from Lewis Washington, son of Bushrod, who was the general's nephew and heir and, incidentally, founder of the American Colonization Society. Captain Brown was "slaughtered by Washington's native State, for attempting to carry out to their legitimate results [the] sayings and achievements" of Virginia's greatest man. The most memorable of Washington's "sayings," however, could hardly be read as lending sanction to insurrection—that was Jefferson's part—and his acceptance of the leadership of the army of the War for Independence rested on the authority of a provisional government of more substance than Brown's scrap of paper.

Once again, Redpath was not a historian but a hagiographer, in haste to pull together precedent and precept that would validate John Brown as a hero in the great American tradition, thereby discounting the notion (early promoted by liberals seeking to save him from the gallows) that he was simply a lunatic in arms. Thus Redpath could see in the second "Captain" John Brown "that same spirit of resistance to wrong" evinced by his namesake, "which recently,—nay, at this very hour,—men are branding as insane!" Important to this assemblage was the simple rural home in the Adirondacks, where the Brown family lived in primitive but loving circumstances: "The Puritan idea,—here it was outlived; nowhere else was the grandest thing brought over in the Mayflower so sacredly preserved. Some descendants of the passengers in that classic ship have chairs, and tables, and other material evidences of her voyage to America; but this great family had the Idea that she personifies, not pompously displayed in parlors or museums, but modestly, unconsciously, in their daily lives" (46–47). Redpath notes that the "daily life in the household of John Brown" also "exhibited . . . the sayings of Franklin . . . and the Declaration of Independence." Part Puritan, part revolutionary, part Franklin, part Washington, inspirited with the principles of the Declaration of Independence and the Mayflower Compact, Redpath's Brown is a kind of pocket compendium of historical analogies, a moving pantheon of patriotic virtues, Memory's Nation given human shape.

Along with his own impressions and recollections, Redpath pieced out his biography with a number of letters by persons who had known John Brown, a quilt of testimonials that reinforce his argument concerning the man's heroic qualities. Among them is a narrative by Thomas Wentworth Higginson, who, in 1859, while Brown was awaiting trial in Charlestown, paid a visit to his home in North Elba, so as to comfort his wife and family. Himself of Puritan descent, Higginson was both a Unitarian minister and a militant abolitionist, who led raids to rescue fugitive slaves held by federal marshals in Boston. He shared with Garrison his dis-Unionist sentiments and had joined the secret cabal that financed Brown's ill-fated expedition, which is to say that he was something less than a disinterested visitor.

At the conclusion of his narrative, Higginson declared of the insurrectionist that he was "almost the only radical abolitionist I have ever known who was not more or less radical in religious matters also. His theology was Puritan, like his practice; and accustomed as we now are to see Puritan doctrines and Puritan virtues separately exhibited"—a palpable hit against the Congregationalist establishment—"it seems quite strange to behold them combined in one person again" (69). It is toward this conclusion that Higginson's narrative makes its single-minded way, providing a suitable landscape as a backdrop for a man who was that admirable anachronism, a Puritan in principle and an abolitionist in action.

Higginson's account of his trip to North Elba is shaped from the beginning by aesthetic considerations so as to enhance the reader's impressions of John Brown, associating the heroic Captain with a sublime landscape. His is the reverse Alisonianism that characterizes the emerging romantic sensibility, in which the scenery serves to enhance events and persons, rather than being informed and elevated by them. "The traveler into the enchanted land of the Adirondack," notes Higginson, "has his choice of two routes. . . . The one least frequented and most difficult should be selected, for it has the grandest mountain pass that the Northern States can show" (60).

For a man on an errand of mercy, Higginson's motive is curiously akin to that of a tourist, yet his choice seems to have had a rhetorical bias, permitting the description of a landscape reminiscent of that associated also with Webster's New Hampshire: "On your left the giant wall now appears nearer—now retreats again; on your right foams the merry stream, breaking into graceful cascades—and across it the great mountain Whiteface, seamed with slides. Now the woods upon your left are displaced by the iron wall, almost touching the road-side; against its steep abruptness scarcely a shrub can cling, scarcely a fern flutter, it takes your breath away; but five miles of perilous driving conduct you through it; and beyond this stern passway, this cave of iron, lie the lovely lakes and mountains of the Adirondack, and the homestead of JOHN BROWN" (60–61). Higginson's interest in the landscape is obviously not that of a mere aesthete, for the sublime passageway through the mountains is a suitable threshold to the little house in the wildwood.

Webster's strengths were invariably associated with his wilderness origins and georgic boyhood, and like qualities are associated with the Brown homestead as described by Higginson, "a little frame house, unpainted, set in a girdle of black stumps, and with all heaven about it for a wider girdle." Like the Reverend Adams's evocation of Webster's childhood home, Higginson's is a landscape of rural virtue, an apparently simple description that manages to convey both the unpretentious and pious domestic life of the hero and associate it (and him) with the spartan life of the frontier.

Placed on a "high hill-side," surrounded by forests and "the glorious line of the Adironidacks on the east," the farmhouse is also a blockhouse of sorts, commanding to the south a view of "the one slender road leading off to Westport, a road so straight that you could sight a United States marshall for five miles" (61). This paramilitary site has "no ornament nor relief about it" but takes its character from "the setting of mountain and horizon," yet there is one "decoration which at once takes the eye, and which, stern and misplaced as it would seem elsewhere, seems appropriate here. . . . It is an old, mossy, time worn *tombstone*—not marking any grave, not set in the ground—but resting against the house as if its time were either past or not yet come. Both are true—it has a past duty and a future one."

The stone bore the name of the first Captain John Brown and, having been removed to make way for the more impressive memorial in Canton, had been "brought hither by his grandson bearing the same name and title." Brown had chiseled upon it the name of his son, Frederick, with the inscription " 'murdered at Osawatomie for his adherence to the cause of freedom' . . . and he himself has said . . . that no other tombstone should mark his [own] grave." For Higginson that tombstone has a mystical significance, as an omphalos centering the farm and the girdling tree stumps and sky: "Its silent appeal has perpetually strengthened and sanctified that home" (62). The implication of this self-consciously selected symbol—chosen first by Brown, then emphasized by Higginson—is in keeping with the abolitionist emphasis on the insurrectionist's Revolutionary War antecedents. Like the mountain pass and the "iron wall," it signifies as well John Brown's adamantine character, and the setting also evokes (though Higginson does not mention it) the "iron-bound coast" associated by Edward Everett with the stern, unyielding character of the Pilgrims.

Landscape, tombstone, fixed fortitude, all add up to an aggregate portrait of undaunted courage, of linear action as straight in purpose as Redpath's road leading the way from the farm, down which Brown and his sons had set out for Kansas—and beyond. By Redpath's account the Captain is a man of "fixed principles": even his manner of walking, turning neither "to the right nor left" but moving "straight on," "with a solemn, earnest countenance . . . and every one he met made way for him. So in his ideas" (188). It is all of a piece, like the great boulder by the house—next to which John Brown desired to be buried after his execution—so in keeping with his character as all witnesses testified: "'his iron will and unbending purpose were equal to that of any man, living or dead.'" All of which goes to suggest that Daniel Webster now had a successor and Plymouth Rock a human face, or, as Wendell Phillips put it, in a phrase quoted in the *Boston Atlas and Daily Bee* on November 21, 1859: "He was . . . Plymouth Rock grown into a grand personality."

II

Captain John Brown, it must be said, felt little piety for the Pilgrims or their Rock. He had visited New England in 1857, hoping to raise the money whereby he could realize his insurrectionist scheme, but although he favorably impressed Thoreau and Emerson with his natural nobility, not much financial support was immediately forthcoming, and that which was eventually produced had been raised in great secrecy. Departing once again for the Kansas to whose bloodiness he had contributed (knowledge of which he chose not to promote), the disappointed descendant of Puritans wrote a ferocious jeremiad entitled "OLD BROWNS FAREWELL to the Plymouth Rocks, Bunker Hill Monuments, Charter Oaks, and Uncle Thoms Cabbins," in which he berated the "Heaven exalted people" of New England for having denied him and his cause "even the necessary supplies of the common soldier," while, sneered Brown, they continued to live "amidst . . . wealth, luxury, and extravagance" (Ruchames, 106).

In spirit, if not orthography, Brown's denunciation of luxury-loving descendants of the Pilgrims resembles Lowell's poetic interview with Miles Standish, when the old veteran half draws his sword in anger over the cowardice of the men filling their faces in honor of the Forefathers while backing down before Southern aggression. The broadsword was incidentally Brown's weapon of choice in Pottawatomie, being not only silent but perhaps a self-conscious evocation of Gideon's divinely empowered weapon. Unlike Brown, Lowell's soldier replaces his sword in its scabbard, refusing to stain the hem of Freedom's "white vesture" with blood, a gesture and a sentiment suggesting that Lowell shared the nonviolent ideology of Garrison and Whittier, whatever the painful qualities of his pen.

By 1859, moreover, Lowell had, as it were, sheathed his own weapon: after the death of his reform-minded Maria, he had left publications like the *Anti-Slavery Standard* and after a sojourn in Europe had become the editor of the newly created *Atlantic Monthly*, a liberal but not a radical journal. When in late October of that year—following the abortive raid on Harpers Ferry—Higginson had proposed an article about John Brown for the *Atlantic*, Lowell begged off, declaring himself "a little afraid of Brown" and anticipating that his publisher "would be more so" (*Letters*, 1:298). Once Brown's doom had been sealed, the *Atlantic*, like a number of formerly cautious journals, celebrated the Captain as a misguided but sincere hero, a martyr to his cause, but Lowell himself would remain silent concerning the martyr hero, even as New England was brought to a rhetorical boil.

In the last of the *Biglow Papers*, written at the end of the Civil War, Lowell called up another figment of the Puritan past, "a Pilgrim Father" who appears to Hosea as he sits slumbering on a Sabbath day in the old schoolhouse of his childhood. It is an ancestral apparition not unlike the Captain Miles Standish who appeared in Lowell's abolitionist poem twenty years earlier: "He wore a steeple-hat, tall boots, an' spurs / With rowels to 'em big ez ches'nut burrs, / An' his gret sword behind him sloped away / Long 'z a man's speech thet dunno wut to say" (*Writings*, 11:216). This last is not the old Puritan's problem, who, in response to the farmer's doubts about the best course for the victorious Union to take in dealing with the defeated but defiant South, rips out a Puritanical, violence-prone solution: " 'Smite 'em hip an' thigh! . . . / And let every man-child die! / Oh fer three weeks o' Crommle an' the Lord! / Up, Isr'el, to your tents an' grind the sword!' "

This was the bellicose attitude that Lowell had once prized in Miles Standish and that Redpath celebrated in Captain John Brown, but in Hosea Biglow's opinion, backed by that of the Reverend Wilbur, " 'Thet kind o' thing worked wal in ole Judee, / But you fergit how long it's ben A.D.' " His ancestor still holds for sudden and decisive action, stomping out the idea of slavery along with the fact, illustrating his point with his boot and awakening Biglow from his dream. With this the poem ends and with it the second, wartime series of the *Papers*, a final note of inconclusiveness that perfectly illustrates Lowell's own·slow swing toward conservatism: " 'The moral question's ollus plain enough— / It's jes' the human-natur side thet's tough.' "

Among the literati of New England, Brown's greatest defenders were Emerson and Thoreau, to whom we can add Wendell Phillips, whose eloquence on Brown's behalf we have already sampled. These were, not coincidentally, the three to whom Redpath dedicated his biography of the martyr hero, as being "Defenders of the Faithful, who, when the Mob Shouted 'Madman!' said, 'Saint!' " Not coincidentally, because if these three prominent New Englanders were aroused to take courageous stands in defense of Captain John Brown, their writings in that regard bear testimony to an early acquaintance with Redpath's own hagiographic portrait. Though his biography was not published until 1860, the chief points of Redpath's tribute first appeared in the *Boston Atlas and Daily Bee* in a series of articles that began running on October 21, 1859, a scant three days after the news broke in New England about the raid on Harpers Ferry. Drawing on his encounter with John Brown several years earlier in Kansas, Redpath pronounced the "Insurrectionist" a "Puritan in the Cromwellian sense of the word," an "American Moses," who enlists only men who put "principle" before self-interest.

That is, if Brown's insurrection took shape from the angry language and appeals to the Puritan spirit of poets like Lowell and Whittier—but in terms they both would renounce—then it was Redpath's Brown that inspired Emerson and Thoreau to enlist as ardent defenders of the Captain's violent acts. In his famous plea for John Brown, first delivered a week after Redpath's series began, Thoreau noted that he had read "all the newspapers I could get, the week of this event, and I do not remember a single expression of sympathy for these men. I have since seen one noble statement, not editorial, in the *Atlas and Bee*," a statement quoted from Thoreau's speech by the newspaper cited (November 2, 1859; cf. *Writings*, 4:421). Again, the charge of madness was brought by persons who had hoped to save Brown from the gallows, a ploy opposed by the strategy of those (including Brown himself) who regarded the insurrectionist as more valuable dead than alive. Emerson, Thoreau, and Phillips, whether intentionally or not, contributed their share to this strategy of martyrdom, rendering opinions bent to Redpath's statement, on October 21, that the notion that the insurrection had been the "insane attempt of a madman" was an "utter falsehood."

Of these three, the last two were already predisposed to favorable views of action in the name of a higher law and needed no swaying by Redpath. Emerson is a different case, having emerged from the troubled 1830s and 1840s as something of a Hamlet—at least in his journal soliloquys. As there are two Hamlets in the play, the one no less active though buried, so there are two Emersons detectable by 1850, much as photographs of his face have been seen to reveal a definitive binarism, the dreamy idealist and the shrewd Yankee. Only in this instance we discover in the alternative Emerson an integrated whole, the Yankee merged with the idealist, resulting in a reasonable approximation to the old Puritan, in whom, traditionally, both qualities were to be found, thereby making by Perry Miller's account the road straight from Cotton's Boston to Emerson's Concord.

It was the Yankee part of Emerson that had been drawn to John Brown upon first encounter, in March 1857, when "Captain John Brown gave a good account of himself in the Town Hall, last night" (*Journals*, 14:125). By that date, Brown had already gained a reputation in the East for acts of bravery in Kansas, and he spoke out boldly in Concord for the use of force in righting wrongs. Emerson was impressed by Brown's self-advertised talent as a shepherd and horseman, pastoral skills always valued by romantic lovers of the primitive. But he was also mightily taken by Brown's display of that strong self-determination and centeredness he had celebrated in his essays. Brown declared his faith, warranted as he had stated by his experience, that "one good, believing, strong-minded man is worth a hundred, nay, twenty thousand, men without character, for a settler in a new country, and that the right men will give a permanent direction in the fortunes of a State," an opinion that struck Emerson as a truth essential to the man who expressed it. And in his subsequent essay entitled "Courage," Brown would provide an active example of what Emerson meant by the word.

In the original version of that essay, read in Boston early in November 1859, as John Brown sat in Charlestown with his fate as yet not decided, Emerson portrayed the insurrectionist as a "new saint, than whom none purer or more brave was ever lead by love of man into conflict and death." Emerson's Brown was in effect a semblance of the Savior, "waiting yet his martyrdom; and who, if he shall suffer, will make the gallows glorious like a cross" (*Atlas and Daily Bee*, November 9, 1859). These were the words that Redpath echoed in his dedicatory praise of Emerson, but the Concord sage apparently had second thoughts about deification, and in the published version of his essay Emerson emphasized instead Brown's commonsense courage, which is what had attracted him to the man in the first place. He would also celebrate Brown as combining in his person "that perfect Puritan faith which brought his fifth ancestor to Plymouth Rock with his grandfather's ardor in the Revolution," but by the time Emerson wrote those lines, first delivered at a meeting called to raise money for John Brown's family, indeed by the time he read his lecture on courage two weeks earlier, Captain John Brown was in the hands not only of the authorities in Virginia but of the journalist from New York (*Works*, 11:268; cf. *Atlas and Daily Bee*, November 21, 1859).

Emerson's conversion to espousing violent acts against slaveholders was in sharp contrast to his earlier reservations regarding not only abolition but reform in general. From his transcendent height of Olympian indifference he tended to regard the antics and excesses of zeal displayed by reformers as amusingly eccentric—"Picturesque" was his aestheticized response to the Chardon Street Convention in 1842. Yet, with many other high-minded New Englanders he had been shocked and appalled by the death of Lovejoy, which inspired a revealing entry in his journal for 1837, a virtual diagram of Emerson's problematics of reform:

When [someone] comes to me & represents the importance of this Temperance Reform my hands drop—I have no excuse—I honor him with shame at my own inaction.

Then a friend of the slave shows me the horrors of Southern slavery—I cry guilty guilty! Then a philanthropist tells me the shameful neglect of the Schools by the Citizens. I feel guilty again.

Then I hear . . . of a brave man [Lovejoy] who resists a wrong to the death and I sacrifice anew.

I cannot do all these things but my shames are illustrious tokens that I have strict relations to them all. None of these causes are foreigners to me. My Universal Nature is thus marked. These accusations are parts of me too. They are not for nothing. (5:437; cf. "The Heart," *Lectures* 2:287)

Emerson's former mentor William Ellery Channing had by then declared himself for abolition and was moved, as we have seen, by Lovejoy's death to take an active role in protesting the action of the Alton mob. Not so Emerson, for whom feelings of guilt, assuring him of his common humanity with drunkards and slaves, are to his way of thinking adequate contribution to the causes he cannot bring himself to support openly, tortured logic that makes a virtue out of indecision and inaction, as if adapting Milton's famous sonnet on his blindness to his own situation: "They also serve who feel bad about doing nothing." It was this attitude that enraged John Brown twenty years later in the bland face of New England's refusal to grant him more than extended periods of polite attentiveness. Here also, it must be said, is the root and branch of modern liberalism, distilled like so much of Emerson's thought from his earlier Unitarianism, which, as in the instance of Orville Dewey's praise of Channing, forever confuses discussion with decisive action.

On the same page of the 1837 journal, again in obvious reference to Lovejoy, Emerson wrote, "I sternly rejoice, that one was found to die for humanity & the rights of free speech & opinion." His main point was to make a distinction between the false chivalry of the South, where "there are always men enough ready to die for the silliest punctillo; to die like dogs who fall down under each other's teeth," and the true chivalry of the North, but his "stern rejoicing" remained confined to his journal. Moreover, a few pages later Emerson noted, "I do not like to see a sword at man's side. If it threaten Man, it threatens me," pacifist sentiments in line with the thinking of Whittier (439).

And yet, by 1859, Emerson, unlike Whittier, was quick to jump to John Brown's defense for his use of violence against the slaveholding South, championing as a martyr a man who, like Lovejoy, had died in the service of a highminded cause but who could hardly plead the use of arms in self-defense. Clearly, the Compromise of 1850 and the Fugitive Slave Law acted to bring Emerson out of his own closet and write against slavery, but there was something about Captain John Brown's theatrical stand at Harpers Ferry that, unlike Lovejoy's martyrdom, caught his conscience and drew him at last to take a public position in favor of armed insurrection.

In fact, John Brown filled a long-vacant place in Emerson's psyche, an equivalent space to that felt by the poet of *Nebraska*, who also was aroused to apocalyptic pronouncements. Emerson's journal entries reveal a sequence that provides a kind of tunnel paralleling the stridently public highway taken by

Garrison and Phillips and heading toward the same destination. Though we generally regard Emerson as a champion of the future, with a radical faith in spiritual progress that matches the Whig celebration of technological change, there can be found in his journals a contrasting nostalgia for the past. Most important here, there was something about the archaic Puritan character he found attractive, and long before 1857 he was eager to find evidence that the old Pilgrim spirit was still active in the world.

"I have been to Plymouth," wrote Emerson in his journal in 1834, "& stood on the Rock & felt that it was grown more important by the growth of this nation in the minutes that I stood there" (4:261). This visit took place at an important moment of liminal transition in Emerson's life, after he had resigned his pulpit and more recently returned from Europe, where he met and conversed with Coleridge, Wordsworth, and, most important, Carlyle. In 1834, also, he moved to Concord, beginning his life anew, and a year later would marry his second wife, Lydia Jackson, herself a native of Plymouth whom he had met while lecturing there. But these life changes are usually identified with his emerging career as the transcendental sage of New England and seem hard to reconcile with his taking his turn on Plymouth Rock in the succession established by Timothy Dwight and Daniel Webster. Still, Emerson's thoughts were much more in line with Webster's progressive vision than with Dwight's filiopietism, an emphasis that provides an essential key between the Whig and the transcendental view, and are of a piece with his early worship of the godlike Daniel.

Emerson's awareness of the meaning of the Pilgrim Landing can be definitively dated from the day ten years earlier when he recorded his reading of Everett's "rich strains at Plymouth" and his youthful objections to the orator's emphasis on "fortune" instead of "Providence" in accounting for the Pilgrims' success (*Journals*, 2:318–19). Emerson certainly preferred Everett's Unitarian optimism—"this consenting declamation . . . on the auspicious promise of the times"—to "that ill omened cry of warning & fear that in the Middle age [of New England] bemoaned an enormous degeneracy and the destruction of the world growing nigh at hand." But in dismissing the dismalism of Cotton Mather and the Puritan tradition of the jeremiad, Emerson also in 1824 celebrated the strengths of "the great men of our first age," like Bradford, Standish, Cotton, and Winthrop: "The adventurous spirit which distinguished the settlers was begotten by the fanaticism of the Reformation—a spirit which confides in its own strength for the accomplishment of its ends & disdains to calculate the chance of failure" (2:227).

Earlier that year Emerson had celebrated "the theory of the strong Impulse" evidenced by the Puritans: "A few stern leaders of that stern sect nourished in their bosoms settled designs of reform & gave to the design such shape &

impulse, that when they slept in the earth, the hope failed not. It was the nursling of an iron race. . . . Whatever . . . of vigorous sense, or practical genius, this country shews, are the issue of Puritan stock" (2:197). This is not our familiar Emerson, radiating benignity from the center of Concord, but his notion of "the strong Impulse," which in his reflections on Everett's 1824 oration became "Eloquence is best inspired by an Infinite Cause," surely has a familiar ring.

Later that same year, in harmony with other clergy of his generation, Emerson (in words already quoted) defended the Pilgrims against the charge of fanaticism: "The Puritans of 1620 had not a rash or visionary thought about them," and if they "erred after as bigots," they also "erred on virtue's side" (2:211). But as time went on, in accord with the changing attitude of his contemporaries toward the Puritans, Emerson's balanced view of 1824 became somewhat more complex. Thus, in 1842 he noted in his journal that "in the days of the Pilgrims & the Puritans, the preachers were the victims of the same faith with which they whipped & persecuted other men, and their sermons are strong, imaginative, fervid, & every word a cube of stone" (8:231). This sentiment curiously grants to the Puritan preachers a measure of the suffering they were causing Quakers and dissenters, not in terms of punishment but performance: as "victims" they suffered no pain but attested to the power of their (obviously erroneous, hence self-victimizing) convictions by the strength of their sermons.

We may wonder what Whittier's response to this paradox might have been, the preacher in his pulpit equated with his victim on the scaffold (or suffocated under a "cube of stone"), but Emerson was less concerned with the sufferings of the persecuted than with the strength of faith witnessed in the persecutors. The passage in Emerson's journal occurs right after a disparaging remark about modern preachers being more "cunning" than "intelligent," so that the "whole institution sounds hollow," and even "the ablest of the . . . unitarian clergy spread popular traps," a criticism that oddly coincides with the charges so often aimed at Unitarians by orthodox ministers, that they preached by insinuation, not openly, fearing to admit their heretical beliefs (231). Their Puritan predecessors may have been the "victims" of their Calvinist faith, but their sermons were open and forthright, built on and from bedrock convictions.

The year before, 1841, Emerson had cast another fond backward glance toward the Puritans, who, despite their decline into "ritualists" in their later days, had "solemnized the heyday of their strength by the planting and the liberating of America. Great, grim, earnest men, I belong by natural affinity to other thoughts and schools than yours, but my affection hovers respectfully about your retiring footprints, your unpainted churches, strict platforms, & sad offices, the iron-gray deacon & the wearisome prayer rich with the diction of ages" (8:53). The occasion for these journal reflections was the death of the Reverend Ezra Ripley, pastor of the Concord church since 1778 and long a resident in the Old Manse. Though a Unitarian, not an orthodox Calvinist, Ripley was hardly a liberal cleric like Channing, and for Emerson he still trailed clouds of the old Puritan glory.

"The fall of this oak of ninety years," Emerson noted in his journal, "makes some sensation in the forest, old and doomed as it was. He has identified himself with the forms at least of the old church of the New England Puritans; his nature was eminently loyal, not in the least adventurous or democratical & his whole being leaned backward on the departed so that he seemed one of the rear-guard of this great camp and army which have filled the world with fame and with him passes out of sight almost the last banner and guide's flag of a mighty epoch." It is typical of Emerson that he placed himself, as it were, on the sidelines watching the last banners of the great parade passing into oblivion, yet his metaphor associates the Puritan spirit with arms and the man, hardly a far-fetched figure. A similar spirit prevails in the memorial tribute to Ripley that Emerson spun out of these observations, an essay that is often neglected though it is identified with his most creative period. In it, Emerson associated Ripley "with the ideas and forms of the New England Church, which expired about the same time with him," a careful revision of his journal passage that emphasizes the minister's transitional character, with a like emphasis on the ephemerality of doctrine (*Works*, 10:383).

What Emerson left out of his memorial essay is a journal passage that in effect resurrected the "old church of the New England Puritans" by means of a complexly organic metaphor: "Well the new is only the seed of the old. What is this abolition and non-resistance and temperance but the continuation of Puritanism tho' it operate inevitably to the destruction of the church in which it grew, as the new is always making the old superfluous." By "seed of the old" Emerson obviously meant seeds cast by the old, though given his nostalgic frame, it certainly reflects anxiety in the face of change and if taken literally would imply a reverse genesis by which the Puritans would be brought back by the activities of their modern counterparts.

But what Emerson seems to imply was something quite different, which was that as Unitarianism had emerged from the husks of a dessicated Calvinism, so the reforms of the day had emerged from the liberal urge of Unitarianism and in reifying that spirit would ultimately destroy it, to be replaced presumably by something else in turn. Again, Emerson had no great tolerance for reforms—as led by reformers—but his identification of the reforming impulse as being in a direct line of descent from Puritanism (which he by 1841 was hardly unique in observing) is pivotal to his attitude toward the value of the Pilgrim Fathers when placed against the decline of the Puritan spirit in their descendants.

By 1851, following the Compromise of 1850 and the decline of Webster and his fellow Whigs into empty postures and slogans, Emerson extended his contempt of Unitarian clergy to their political counterparts, especially Everett, who was both a clergyman and politician. He regretted the "derelictions" of his former mentor, whose "fame . . . is dear to me, & to all his scholars," who were left to wonder "whether there was no sincerity in all those apostrophes to freedom . . . was it all claptrap? And as to the name of New England Societies, which Mr. Choate Mr. Webster, & . . . Mr. Everett address, & are responded to with enthusiasm, it is all a disgusting obsequiousness" (*Journals*, 11:346). By now, Emerson's attitude toward Forefathers' Day celebrations matches that of Lowell in his Miles Standish poem: "This affectation of using sacred days & names,—Washington's birthday forsooth, & the Pilgrims' day, for the effusion of all this rancid oil of eloquence on compromises" was all show and sham, resembling the fraudulent displays of spiritualists who for their own ends maintained contact with the dead (357).

What was missing from modern statesmen was "the iron Calvinism which . . . steeled their fathers seventy five years ago," a quality present only in the elderly Josiah Quincy, "who has renewed the hereditary honour of his name" while "the others are all lapped in after dinner dreams and are as obsequious to Mr Webster as he is to the gentlemen of Richmond & Charleston" (353). Compared with the "stern old fathers of Massachusetts," men like Rufus Choate are mere phrase-mongers, "whose talent consists in a fine choice of words which he can hang . . . indiscriminately on any offender" (347). But even as Emerson was preparing to speak out against the Fugitive Slave Law and was railing against Webster, Everett, and Choate for their weasling defense of compromise, he could celebrate "Webster's Plymouth Speech," a contrast that anticipates the strategy of Theodore Parker's memorial sermon a year later.

Having been for thirty years "declaimed" by schoolboys, that oration had created "in their nature . . . sentiments conscious of and hostile to" the language and spirit of the abominable law for whose passage Webster was responsible (*Journals*, 11:357, 356). Likewise, in listing Webster's "great speeches" in that same journal of 1851, Emerson began with "his discourse at Plymouth denouncing Slavery" but then ended the list by comparing Webster's earlier sentiments to his recent, which when run together had the same effect as " *Hail Columbia*, when sung at a slave-auction" (11:345).

Where, then, was one to find the "brave old puritans of the world," men still in harmony with the natural elements? "The word liberty in the mouth of Mr. Webster" now reminded him of "the word love in the mouth of a courtesan," but where were the mouths in which it could resonate honestly, modern equivalents to the celebrants of "that old religion . . . which taught privation, self denial, & sorrow," yet which "dwelt like a Sabbath peace in the country population of New England" (11:346; 7:444)? In the old Puritan view, "a man was born not for prosperity, but to suffer for the benefits of others," like the region's maple trees, "which all around the villages bleed for the service of man." Where and who were the men who qualified to match the old Puritans in power of conviction and willingness to serve without praise?

There was Garrison, who by 1851 had identified himself and abolition with the Puritan spirit, but in Emerson's opinion Garrison was something of stick, who with his "logic & routine" had forgone "all juice and animal spirits & elemental force" (8:523). He had become "venerable in his plan, like the tart Luther, but he cannot understand anything you say, and neighs like a horse when you suggest a new consideration" (11:231). Here, Emerson was echoing the Unitarian criticism of the orthodox, warranted by Robinson's farewell advice to the Pilgrims, an ironic context given the treatment Garrison had received from Congregational clergy.

Emerson was put off as well by Garrison's reliance on "numbers," on "societies," always a fatal flaw for the champion of self-reliance: "Himself is not enough for him" (7:281). This fault was shared by Wendell Phillips: "Take away the party & they shrivel & vanish" (13:282). Both men by Emerson's accounting were empty vessels, given a shadow substance by their own rhetoric: "I have always the feeling that they may wake up some morning & find they have a capital mistake, & are not the persons they took themselves for" (281). As for the *Liberator*, it was a common "scold," quite distinct from a "sibyl." No one would mistake Xantippe for Cassandra.

"O bring back then the age when valour was virtue," Emerson lamented in 1851, "since what is called morality [today] means nothing but pudding" (11:351). His immediate target was ministers of God who used the Bible to justify returning slaves to their masters: "If this be Christianity, it is a religion of dead dogs." What was chiefly lacking was that "stern & high religious training, like the iron Calvinism which . . . steeled their fathers seventy five years ago" (11:353). As for the once admired then regretted Everett, Emerson now mocked him in his own voice as a pompous ass so proud of the "great many fine sentences I have turned" that in surrendering to a federal marshal "a black man of my own age," he gives the fugitive slave "a copy of my Concord & Lexington & Plymouth & Bunker Hill address to beguile [his] journey from Boston to the plantation whipping post" (11:359–60). Perhaps motivated in part by disgust, Emerson that same year was at last inspired to take action, at least in terms of speaking out, though less against slavery than the law mandating the return of fugitives to their owners.

In 1851 he read his first address that confronted the "filthy law," a "statute which enacts the crime of kidnapping" and was such an effront to the higher law as to virtually guarantee "natural retribution" against its proponents (*Works*, 11:201, 186–87). The loathed Webster of Emerson's journals was likewise now hauled up for the public gaze, his picture torn down "from the wall" and "his speeches thrust into the chimney," for he is "a man of the past, not a man of faith or of hope" (202–3). And yet when it came to answering his own question, "What shall we do?" his response was curiously in line with the Free-Soiler position, which was to "confine slavery to slave states, and help them effectually to make an end of it" (207). Emerson in 1851 was as certain as George Bladgen had been in 1834 that "everything invites Emancipation" and was sure as well that the American public would gladly come up with the money necessary to buy the freedom of four million slaves (209).

But by 1854, the inertia of the American people had worn Emerson's patience thin, so that when he next addressed the enormities of the Fugitive Slave Law, on the anniversary date of Webster's March 7 speech, his mood was less optative. He began with a lament for the Great Man's fall along the lines of Parker's memorial sermon: "If his moral sensibility had been proportioned to the force of his understanding, what limits could have been set to his genius and beneficent power?"—precisely Parker's point two years earlier (*Works*, 11:223). He remembered Webster standing before the Bunker Hill Monument in 1843, speaking words betrayed by the Compromise of 1850: in contrast to the granite obelisk, "this eternal monument of his fame and of the Union is rotten in four years," for as a "covenant" it sanctions a crime, and if "slavery is good," so is every felony in the book, "all good and to be maintained by Union societies" (235).

Emerson grouped the Unionists with the abolitionists as people who put their faith in useless associations: "To make good the cause of Freedom, you must draw off from all foolish trust in others. You must be citadels and warriors yourselves, Declarations of Independence, the charter, the battle and the victory. Cromwell said, 'We can only resist the superior training of the King's soldiers by enlisting godly men.'" How handily this notion meshes with the idea Emerson brought home with him from hearing John Brown in Concord in 1857: "The right men will give a permanent direction in the fortunes of a State" (*Journals*, 14:125).

This Carlylean appeal to the single hero, the godly, great-hearted champion, is essential to Emerson's notions of self-reliance and true representativeness and receives constant reinforcement in all of the maxims that surface like sounding whales in his address on March 7: "Self-reliance, the height and perfection of man, is reliance on God," a sentiment that presents a Yankee face as well as a Puritan one: "Liberty is aggressive, Liberty is the Crusade of all brave and conscientious men, the Epic Poetry, the new religion, the chivalry of all gentlemen. This is the oppressed Lady whom true knights on their oath and honor must rescue and save" (*Works*, 11:244).

By 1856, as the violence in Bloody Kansas turned Emerson's head toward the West, he compared "Massachusetts in its heroic day," which "had no government—was an anarchy," with every man being "his own governor; and there was no breach of peace from Cape Cod to Mount Hoosac," to the California of the gold rush, when "every man throughout the country was armed with knife and revolver, and it was known that instant justice would be administered to each offence, and perfect peace reigned" (*Works*, 11:252). No longer put off by men who carried swords, Emerson by 1856 was at last ready for Osawatomie Brown, who would prove to him "the folly of the peace party in Kansas," which had put great faith in the power of their wrongs to bring about the right, a passive position that only made certain their defeat (*Journals*, 14:125). What Brown proposed was militant action, the way of the West—and the East when it had been "West." Liberty was not to be rescued by pamphleteers and peace parties.

Captain John Brown was a "solitary nullifier" who threw himself on his "reserved rights," fulfilling Emerson's expectation, in 1844, that "every project in [the] history of reform, no matter how violent and surprising, is good when it is the dictate of a man's genius and constitution" (*Lectures*, 2:338; *Works*, 3:255, 254). "He was a man very easy to read, for his whole life & conversation was consistent & transparent," wrote Emerson in his journal of the late Ezra Ripley, and of John Brown: "The man is so transparent that all can see him through, that he had no second thought, but was the rarest of heroes, a pure idealist, with no by-ends of his own" (*Journals*, 8:57; 14:334). John Brown, Emerson would conclude when dedicating the memorial to Concord soldiers killed in the Civil War, was "a Puritan," with an "integrity incorruptible, and an ability that always rose to the need" (*Works*, 11:360).

Where Webster had been a man of mighty words, John Brown was one for great deeds: "He believed in his ideas to that extent that he existed to put them all into action; he said 'he did not believe in moral suasion, he believed in putting the thing through.' He saw how deceptive the forms are." Brown was the redemption of a fallen New England, being "a fair specimen of the best stock" of that region, "a religious and manly person" who had "that force of thought and that sense of right which are the warp and woof of greatness." He had sprung from "Orthodox Calvinism" and like all New England farmers was "mighty in the Scriptures; had learned that life was a preparation, a 'probation,' to use their word, for a higher world, and was to be spent in loving and serving mankind" (279). Unitarianism having long since failed him, disappointed by the empty posturing and obdurate positionings of the abolitionists, Emerson was ready and willing to embrace a hero from an older yet light-filled age, and what may have been lacking in the John Brown he had met in Concord was made up for by Redpath's journalistic improvements.

Brown was to Emerson's view close to a literary creation, "a romantic character absolutely without any vulgar text," so naturally refined that "all gentlemen, of course, are on his side," as are all women, "drawn to him by the predominance of sentiment" (280). The Brahmin who had found Garrison tunnel visioned and boring, Phillips a self-creating man of the theater, found in this simple, taciturn farmer the hero he had been waiting for, a Saint George for America, displaying the qualities of true heroism, "courage, and disinterestedness, and the love that casts out fear." Captain John Brown belongs in the company of those chivalric knights, men who, "like the dying Sidney, pass the cup of cold water to the dying soldier who needs it more. For what is the oath of gentle blood and knighthood? What but to protect the weak and lowly against the strong oppressor?" (281). This is a very rapid promotion, elevating Brown in the field to a brevet knighthood, under the assumption that arms make the gentleman, providing the cause is right.

Thus it was the advent of John Brown, sucked into Emerson's soul to fill the vacuum left by Daniel Webster, that occasioned the first public expression of his long-concealed admiration for the Puritan, as well as a sense perhaps of some inadequacy in himself, so often disguised in his attacks on Edward Everett for moral cowardice. "In an age of trade and material prosperity," Emerson noted toward the end of "Boston," an address read in that town in 1861, "we have stood a little stupified by the elevation of our ancestors. *We praised the Puritans because we did not find in ourselves the spirit to do the like*" (210; emphasis added). And what of Emerson's praise of John Brown? Did Brown, in personifying the virtues of the past, in putting principles into action, in sacrificing self, family, material comforts, and ease, in uniting "old Puritan" with "old Patriot," not only demonstrate the psychic vacuum in the heart of New England but in Waldo Emerson as well?

This is not a question.

III

Thoreau was famously Emerson's disciple, who put into action the teachings of his master, the sort of thing that can dismay the instructor. In 1848, while Thoreau was acting out at Walden Pond the precepts of *Nature*, Emerson grumbled in his journal that Henry "is like the woodgod who solicits the wandering poet & draws him into antres vast & desarts idle, and bereaves him of his wits. . . . Very seductive are the first steps from the town to the woods, but the End is want & madness" (*Journals*, 10:344). Emerson's favored view of the wildwood was from his study window, and he likewise found the Concord Pan somewhat stiff in conversation at the dinner table, in manner abrupt and lacking in human warmth. He was, in fact, a modern approximation of those old Puritans Emerson doted upon in his journal.

At heart an anarchist, at root a true radical, Thoreau was much closer to the Puritan ideal than he seems himself to have realized, his experiment at Walden Pond a secessionist or separatist gesture, his cooking fire a small candle of the kind Governor Winthrop thought to make a beacon for the world to see, his cry of "Simplify!" the demand of the Protestant reformer. He was drawn to the drama and paradox of captivity narratives, wrote his most famous book in the mode of spiritual autobiography, and in his public pronouncements tended to prefer the jeremiad. He was certainly well read in the chronicles of colonial New England but seems to have confused the earliest settlers with their Yankee descendants, dull clods, as he saw them, driving oxen to market at sunrise but failing to notice the dawn. Thus he faulted John Winthrop for grumbling about the hospitality extended him during a winter night spent with Indians, noting that the single fish offered for dinner was all that the Indians had for themselves, a fact that held a truth to which the governor was blind.

Between 1849 and 1855, Thoreau took three pedestrian trips along the length of Cape Cod, the journal record of which was incorporated in the posthumously published book of that title. He used *Mourt's Relation* as his guide in retracing the footsteps of the Pilgrims, an account that he regarded with a skeptic's eye. At Provincetown, he noted the contrast between what the Pilgrims saw—or said they saw—and the present condition of the landscape: "The Pilgrims say, 'There was the greatest store of fowl that ever we saw.' We saw not fowl there, except gulls of various kinds" (*Writings*, 4:253). Given Thoreau's love of puns, this stress on "gulls" suggests that the Pilgrims either were mistaken or were attempting to mislead others, and he was likewise skeptical about their enthusiastic description of the great varieties of trees they found on the Cape—a sign of the soil's fertility—where now there were none. Thoreau preferred Captain John Smith's observation, made six years previous to the advent of the Pilgrims, which dismissed the future site of Provincetown as a place of sand dunes, "overgrown with shrubby pines . . . and such trash" (255).

Despite claims made for them by their festive celebrants, the Pilgrims "possessed but few of the qualities of the modern pioneer. They were not the ancestors of the American backwoodsmen. They did not go at once into the woods with their axes. They were a family and church, and were more anxious to keep together, though it were on the sand, than to explore and colonize a New World" (256). That we may agree with Thoreau in this instance in no way should detract from his distinct lack of enthusiasm for the Forefathers, whose domestic proclivities were in the eyes of their celebrants a signal difference between the settlers of Plymouth and those of Jamestown, while Thoreau identified them with the stay-at-homes of modern Concord. Thoreau's backwoodsman, a solitary male with ax in hand, is a mirror image cast upon the water of Walden Pond, that world of his own making. Backwoodsmen also brought families with them "and were anxious to keep together." Memory's Nation, ever and again, is subject to petition and recall.

Thoreau had been taught by Emerson to be wary of history, as a collection of errors with little relevance to the present moment, but where his mentor remained a closet worshiper of the Puritans, from whom he could claim descent, Thoreau, like Garrison, had no vital connection with that exclusive past. He declared himself grateful that New England, unlike Rome, had not been built on the ruins of an earlier civilization, a sentiment quoted approvingly by Emerson. Like the Liberator, moreover, he did have a very sharp eye regarding the contradictions of the modern day between the ideal and the real.

In 1851, he had traveled by boat and foot down the coast from Boston to Plymouth and passed by Webster's luxurious farm at Marshfield en route. Learning from a neighbor that the Great Man "would eat only the produce of his farm during the few weeks he was at home," Thoreau noted sourly: "Ate only what grew on his farm, but drank more than ran on his farm" (*Writings*, 2:351). He put ashore on Clark's Island on Sunday, enabling him to share the Pilgrim experience of spending the Sabbath there, and on Tuesday followed the Forefathers over to Plymouth, but any possibility of empathy was blocked by the weather, the month being July and a drizzly rain falling. Thoreau only later learned "that I had landed where the Pilgrims did and passed over the Rock at Hedge's Wharf" (356–57).

He dutifully performed the function of a tourist, interesting himself in elderly residents who remembered the man who could remember Peregrine White and like antiquarian matters, but he was equally devoted to informing himself in data pomological and floral, Plymouth being famous for its pears, dating from a tree planted by the aforementioned White. Thoreau also visited Pilgrim Hall, before which the other half of Forefathers' Rock resided and of which he noted dryly, "They used to crack off pieces . . . for visitors with a cold chisel, till the town forbade it. The stone remaining at [the] wharf is about seven feet square" (365). Thoreau's penchant for mensuration is intrinsic to his surveyor's sensibility, and both are clues to the Enlightenment bones that sustained his romantic spirit. With careful deliberation he took inventory of the humble and domestic items on exhibit in Pilgrim Hall, including furniture brought over on the *Mayflower*, the kind of systematic activity that is not particularly friendly to mythmaking. In a similar spirit, he sounded the bottom of the "bottomless" Walden Pond.

Which is to say that Thoreau's piety for the past had its limits. "Plymouth end of world" he noted in his journal—"fifty miles thither [i.e., from Boston] by railroad. Old Colony road poor property. Nothing saves Plymouth but the Rock" (366). Having passed by the foundation of the Republic in the rain,

Thoreau did not bother to retrace his and the Pilgrims' steps, and if he had, he would hardly have, like Emerson, sensed the nation growing even as he stood there. He did not identify Plymouth with the future, save as it could be sustained economically by its past. Even as Garrison and Wendell Phillips were reclaiming the Pilgrims for abolition, Thoreau was shunning such rhetorical business for action. In October of the year he had visited Plymouth, he put a fugitive slave on a train for Canada.

Unlike his mentor, Emerson, Thoreau admired Phillips, but it is notable that when he sent a letter to the *Liberator* in 1845 praising Phillips as a public speaker, Thoreau emphasized "the freedom and steady wisdom, so rare in the reformer, with which he declared that he was not born to abolish slavery, but to do right" (*Writings*, 4:313). As we have had opportunity to observe, "doing right" in Phillips's frame of reference had a legalistic bias, but for Thoreau it was the root of his own kind of Puritanism, which appealed not to Scripture or the Constitution but to the higher law. It is worth noting, moreover, than in his journal in 1853 he dismissed both Phillips and Garrison as being no better than "the overseers and faculty of Harvard College. They require a man who will train well under them. Consequently they have not in their employ any but small men,—trainers" (11:365).

Thoreau's ire had been aroused by the abolitionists' refusal to hire Bronson Alcott as a lecturer, but his opinion echoes Emerson's regarding the diminishing effect of associations as well as Frederick Douglass's reason for leaving "Garrison and Phillips, etc." And as for Douglass, in that same letter to the *Liberator*, Thoreau repeated Phillips's story about the reaction to the announcement made in New Bedford by the fugitive slave that he would write his autobiography, that "the murmur ran round the room, and was anxiously whispered by the sons of the Pilgrims, 'He had better not!'" (4:313). In sum, whatever his reservations about Garrison "etc.," their rhetorical tropes came easily to Henry David Thoreau.

We may therefore think of Thoreau as occupying a middle ground (as he does in Redpath's dedication), standing between Emerson and Phillips regarding Captain John Brown. For if Emerson saw Brown as the old Puritan resurrected, who preferred action to words, if Phillips defined him as less an outlaw than were those Virginians who dragged him still bleeding to the scaffold, Thoreau saw in Brown the Man of Principle undefiled, a Puritan in essence but essentially disconnected from history. Moreover, though Thoreau shared with Emerson a deep distrust of associations, being as he said an Odd Fellow in truth, and was hardly the kind of man to put himself under the instruction of Garrison and Phillips—having his eye on a North Star far beyond their powers of vision—Thoreau shared the abolitionists' penchant for outspoken and abrasive denunciations of his fellow Americans.

It is notable that the occasion of his coming out for abolition, his lecture "Slavery in Massachusetts," was an Anti-Slavery Convention held in 1854 on the traditional Fourth of July, the same holiday on which nine years earlier Thoreau had set up housekeeping at Walden Pond. In this jeremiad, which would be published in the *Liberator*, Thoreau declared, "The majority of the men of the North, and of the South and East and West, are not men of principle," a sentiment perfectly in accord with his notion of Wendell Phillips's chief virtue, that he was "born to do right" (4:400). But men like Phillips were by Thoreau's accounting a minority in New England, and in defining the moral vacuity at the heart of the American public, Thoreau in effect opened up a very large place for John Brown to fill.

In his Fourth of July oration, a speech that is regarded as a foundation stone of American radicalism, Thoreau in effect joined that long line of Garrisonite speakers who had declared themselves reluctant to celebrate the day sacred to Liberty in a land where slavery was tolerated: "Every humane and intelligent inhabitant of Concord, when he or she heard those bells and those cannons, thought not with pride of the events of the 19th of April, 1775, but with shame of the events of the 12th of April, 1851" (4:392–93). When he spoke of "slavery in Massachusetts," it was not merely in reference to the invasion of that sacred ground by the instruments of that abominable institution but to the "servility" of politicians who permitted such unprincipled acts to be carried out, an observation that was a well-worn truth in the rhetoric of the Garrisonians.

Thoreau shared likewise the outrage of Wendell Phillips when he spoke out in defense of John Brown in 1859, and we would be hard pressed to judge between the two men in terms of their rhetorical effectiveness in standing up for insurrection. It is worth noting that between his oration of 1851 and his address of 1859 Thoreau had looked into Bradford's *History of Plimoth Plantation*, apparently for the first time. This was in December 1856, and he quoted in full in his journal Bradford's famous description of the "weather-beaten face" that New England turned toward the Pilgrims when they arrived, a climate that had not changed over the interval: "It required," noted Thoreau, "no little courage to found a colony here at that season of the year," a sentiment that was a commonplace of Forefathers' Day addresses but which suggests that the climate of Thoreau's own opinion toward the Pilgrims was warming (15:169). "Nature" may not have "changed one iota," but Thoreau seems to have come around considerably. He was now ready, as it were, for Captain John Brown, of the sixth generation, "in regular descent, from Peter Brown, one of the Pilgrim Fathers."

Yet Thoreau's John Brown was hardly Emerson's reconstituted Puritan but was very much a projection of the advocate of civil disobedience: "No man in America," he would declared in his "Defense of John Brown," in October 1859, "has ever stood up so persistently and effectively for the dignity of human nature, knowing himself for a man, and the equal of any and all governments. In that sense he was the most American of us all" (4:425). But as Thoreau had set up his camp at Walden Pond within rifle shot of Lexington, so as the "most American," Brown was also "like the best of those who stood at Concord Bridge, on Lexington Common, and on Bunker Hill, only he was firmer and higher principled than any that I have chanced to hear of as there. It was no abolition lecturer that converted him. Ethan Allen and [John] Stark, with whom he may in some respects be compared, were rangers in a lower and less important field. They could bravely face their country's foes, but he had the courage to face his country herself when she was in the wrong" (411).

As we have seen, it was in his series in the *Atlas and Daily Bee* that Redpath first called Brown an "Abolitionist of the Bunker Hill School," a man who "*despised* the Republican Party," who had acted independently as well of the Garrisonians, and who "admired Nat Turner as well as George Washington." Thoreau was careful to follow Redpath's lead, not only distancing Brown from the abolition movement but elevating him above the heroes of the Revolution to which Garrison habitually referred. It was an emphasis that ironically forced him into the terms of radical logic, which traced the flower to its root, bringing Thoreau (again after Garrison) back to the Rock at Plymouth:

> He was one of that class of whom we hear a great deal, but, for the most part, see nothing at all,—the Puritans. It would be in vain to kill him. He died lately in the time of Cromwell, but he reappeared here. Why should he not? Some of the Puritan stock are said to have come over and settled in New England. They were a class that did something else than celebrate their forefathers' day, and eat parched corn in remembrance of that time. They were neither Democrats nor Republicans, but men of simple habits, straight-forward, prayerful; not thinking much of rulers who did not fear God, not making many compromises, nor seeking after available candidates. (412)

This passage resonates with Lowell's and Emerson's contempt for Forefathers' Day dinners. And in a style reminiscent of Wendell Phillips's pointed simplicity it echoes Redpath's early celebration of Brown as a Puritan and anticipates Redpath's subsequent apostrophe to Peter Brown the Pilgrim. Moreover, there immediately follows a quotation from Redpath's newspaper account of his visit with Brown in Kansas in which the hero of Osawatomie called for "men of good principles" to aid him: " 'God-fearing men,—men who respect themselves, and with a dozen of them I will oppose any hundred such men as these Buford ruffians' " (412; cf. *Atlas and Daily Bee*, October 21, 1859).

Thoreau does not refer constantly to Brown as "the old Puritan" in the manner of Redpath no more than he had Emerson's deep psychic need to reify New England's heroic past. His Brown had chiefly what he early defined as "the Qualities of the Recruit," being like himself "a man of Spartan habits," even to eating "sparingly . . . as became a soldier, or one who was fitting himself for difficult enterprises" (413). But the echo image always is Old Ironsides, not the fabled man-of-war but Cromwell's army for which the USS *Constitution* was familiarly named. Thus, when recalling the forthrightness of Brown's speech in Concord in 1857, Thoreau observed that in simplicity of truth it "was like the speeches of Cromwell compared with those of an ordinary king" (414). Clearly, Brown's actions caused Thoreau to revise his notion of the Puritan, much as the insurrectionist put a cutting edge on his idea of the farmer, but it was in the terms of Redpath's revisionist myth, itself a product of Garrisonian rhetoric.

When Thoreau came to describe Brown's courageous response to his death sentence and his calm words of defiance—" 'you may dispose of me very easily . . . but this question is still to be settled,—this negro question, I mean; the end of that is not yet' "—he went on to predict that the time will come "when the painter will paint that scene, no longer going to Rome for a subject; the poet will sing it; the historian record it; and, with the Landing of the Pilgrims and the Declaration of Independence, it will be the ornament of some future national gallery, when at last the present form of slavery shall be no more here" (440). Thoreau was only partly right, because it was not the Old Man's defiant confrontation with his captors that provided the most enduring image. But the important thing here is that Thoreau was willing at the last to include his light-filled hero in the company of the Forefathers, both early and late, like Emerson bringing his account in line with Redpath's assessment.

IV

In Thoreau's evaluation, Brown was endowed with a peculiar aura of grace, for everything that happened during the Captain's final days "redounded to his infinite advantage,—that is to the advantage of his cause" (448). Was there not, Thoreau wondered aloud, some providential agent, some divine "theatrical manager" who "arranged things so wisely to give effect to his behavior and words. And who, think you, was the manager? Who placed the slave woman and her child, whom he stopped to kiss for a symbol, between his prison and the gallows?" This was the Christlike gesture that had melted Whittier's Quaker heart, so at the last he was able to forgive Brown his use of violence, even immortalizing that kiss in a poem of absolution, which moved the insurrectionist from the Old to the New Testament at the final moment of his drama:

> The shadows of his stormy life that moment fell apart;
> And they who blamed the bloody hand forgave the loving heart.

That kiss from all its guilty means redeemed the good intent.
And round the grisly fighter's hair the martyr's aureole bent. (4:106–7)

The story of Brown and the slave child first appeared in the *Tribune's* account of Brown's execution, the episode having occurred as the insurrectionist was being led from the Charlestown jail to the wagon that would carry him to the gallows. Redpath likewise made much of the scene, including the newspaper account verbatim but without quotation marks, suggesting that he may have been its author:

> As he stepped out of the door, a black woman, with a little child in her arms, stood near his way. The twain were of the despised race for whose emancipation and elevation to the dignity of children of God he was about to lay down his life. His thought at that moment none can know except as his acts interpret them. He stopped for a moment in his course, stooped over, and with the tenderness of one whose love is as broad as the brotherhood of man kissed it affectionately. That mother will be proud of that mark of distinction of her offspring; and some day, when over the ashes of John Brown the temple of Virginia liberty is reared, she may join in the joyful song of praise which on that soil will be justice to his memory. (397; cf. *New York Daily Tribune*, December 5, 1859; reported also in the *Atlas and Daily Bee*, December 6, 1859)

Wendell Phillips had also been touched by the power of this iconic display of divine love, and in his graveside eulogy for John Brown in North Elba, he ended a description of the Old Man's last days, during which he had "unfolded trait after trait of earnest, brave, tender, Christian life," with a Webster-like "vision" of immediacy: "We see him walking with radiant, serene face to the scaffold, and think what an iron heart, what devoted faith! . . . —see him stoop on his way to the scaffold and kiss that negro child—and this iron heart seems all tenderness. Marvellous old man!" (*First Series*, 289). In effect, Phillips was already at work ensuring that Brown's final act would be (as Thoreau predicted of the earlier scene in which Brown confronted his accusers) added to "the Landing of the Pilgrims and the Declaration of Independence" by employing the rhetorical "vision" with which Webster had increased the pitch of those great moments.

In 1867, by which time Captain John Brown was no longer being vilified as a madman and a fanatic but as a saint whose sacrifice had been validated by the Civil War, the martyr's final moment with the slave mother and child was painted by T. S. Noble. This icon was rendered as a print made even more popular by a version marketed by Currier and Ives, and then, in 1884, the Irish American artist Thomas Hovendon rendered his own and much more famous

FIGURE 15. Thomas Hovendon's mythic configuration *The Last Moments of John Brown* (1884), which validates Redpath's revisionary version of the insurrectionist's death. The Gideon-like agent of Old Testament vengeance is converted to a Christlike figure, thereby casting the fable (and Whittier's poem) in concrete visual form. (Courtesy Metropolitan Museum of Art; gift of Mr. and Mrs. Carl Stoeckel, 1897 [97.5])

version of the event, a work that is now indeed hung in "some national gallery" (the Metropolitan). Although the picture was painted well "after the fact" (as a modern critic has put it), it was rendered with a photographic verisimilitude attesting to the skill of the artist as well as to the sanitizing and sacramentaliz-ing effects of time. In sum, the painting so vividly captures the moment that the viewer feels like a contemporary witness, and it thereby acts to further validate that theatrical event.

Hovendon's painting virtually illustrated Redpath's text, fixing the post-humous image of John Brown not as a soldier in Ironsides armor, not as the martyr in the Charlestown courtroom confronting his persecutors with ringing words of defiance, or, posing with Washington's sword as he defended the engine house at Harpers Ferry, but as a kind and gentle man of principle whose thoughts, unto the last, were of others. Until William Steuart Curry created a John Brown for the twentieth century, reviving the Old Testament image of a prophet with arms upraised, his beard blowing in the winds of terrific change, standing on the verge of madness divinely induced, Hovendon's Christlike martyr was the dominant icon, equivalent in power to "the Landing of the Pilgrims and the Declaration of Independence."

But like the circumstances of the Landing, Brown's pious gesture was an event central to Memory's Nation, a mythic moment testifying to the fallibility of recall, even within what we are pleased to call modern times. Thus if Hovendon's tableau redeemed Brown to Christianity, much as Charles Lucy's piety-laden depiction of the Landing displaced Sargent's militant icon, it was a product of contemporary sensibility in the service of propaganda: in sum, it is a fiction. The revisionary process may be dated from 1910, when Oswald Garrison Villard firmly removed the essential icon from the picture: "No little slave-child was held up for the benison of his lips, for none but soldiery was near and the street was full of marching men," nor has more recent scholarship much altered that fact (554–55).

The myth was in part generated by an item published in the *Liberator* on December 12, 1859, in which Brown was reported to have told his jailer he did not want to be accompanied to the gallows by a minister but by "a family of little negro children, headed by a pious slave mother," a tableau in all ways reminiscent of Garrison's scenario involving Negro pallbearers and the grieving widow attending Lovejoy's coffin into Faneuil Hall (Finkelman, 52). But this would have been a fairly dignified display when compared with the abolitionists' "Barnum-like" proposals and plans for Brown's remains after the event: packed in ice, Brown's corpse was to be exhibited throughout the Northeast, before being " 'taken to the Church of the Puritans and there amid imposing and solemn ceremonies given opportunity for the natural & heartfelt expression which every live man here felt burning within him' " (49).

But for the abolitionists to perform their *Pietà*-like drama, they needed John Brown's body, which the dead man's widow steadfastly refused to provide, much as she had earlier declined Lydia Maria Child's offer to tend her husband's wounds. Our sympathies are surely with Mary Anne Brown, for to the modern sensibility, such theatrical gestures seem grotesque. But what the abolitionists sought to effect, having celebrated Brown alive as an Old Testament agent of divine vengeance, was to shift their hero over into the New Dispensation and celebrate him dead as a Christlike martyr.

Which is to say they sought, as did Whittier in his poem, to sentimentalize him, and though we may not doubt Child's sincerity, at the same time we can see that her gesture, if allowed to take place, would have provided an icon evoking the traditional picture of those sorrowful women bathing Christ's wounds after his deposition from the Cross. Not incidentally, it would also have displayed Lydia Maria Child in a posture perfectly illustrating True Womanhood, thereby displaying Abolition as having a female as well as a Christian heart. Again, given the evidence in Mrs. Stowe's book of the efficacy of sentimentalism as an abolitionist weapon, we could hardly have expected otherwise from the Garrisonians, but the wonder of it is that Thoreau, generally so skeptical in his view of his contemporaries, could have fallen in line with this as with so much that was essential to the emerging rhetoric of the radical abolitionists.

Yet such complicity by 1859 seems to have been inevitable. When he printed Whittier's poem of absolution regarding John Brown in the *Liberator*, Garrison noted wryly and at length the extent to which the Quaker poet's earlier poetry celebrating the heroes of the Revolution might have served as inspiration for the attack on Harpers Ferry, and though Whittier wrote a rebuttal, Garrison (as always) had the last word, as well he might. Because if John Brown can be read as a creation of Whittier's patriotic poetry, so also as a popular icon the insurrectionist was in large part the work of James Redpath, who by 1859 was clearly operating under the influence of the fiery rhetoric of Garrison and Wendell Phillips. Redpath may have distilled and refined that rhetoric, but his Brown—and Emerson's and Thoreau's—was a creation of the Liberator, to whom we here give the last word. Writing to an unknown person in Concord on December 18, 1859, Garrison observed that "John Brown executed will do more for our good cause, incomparably, than John Brown pardoned" (*Letters*, 4:665). The Higher Logic forever operates in the shadow of the Higher Law.

CHAPTER 16

Feminizing the Rock

> *"O whot—whot!" screamed the femaile, swingin her*
> *umbreller in the air. "O, whot is the price that woman pays*
> *for her expeeriunce!"*
>
> *"I don't know," sez I; "the price to my show is 15 cents pur*
> *individuooal."*
>
> —*Artemus Ward*

I

In Felicia Hemans's celebration of the Landing of the Forefathers, the Pilgrims are depicted as making "the sounding aisles of the dim woods ring" with "the anthem of the free," but this particular trope was largely neglected over the next twenty years, the preference being for prayerful, not hymn-singing, Separatists. Then, in 1845, Seargent Prentiss read before the New England Society in New Orleans a Forefathers' Day address that followed Mrs. Hemans's precedent by describing the Pilgrims with voices raised in song, not prayer: having with their "footsteps pressed the famous rock which has ever since remained sacred to their venerated memory," they sang "a hymn of cheerful thanksgiving to the Good God, who had conducted them safely across the mighty deep, and permitted them to land upon the sterile shore" (11).

Prentiss followed the lead of Everett and Whittier, among others, by accounting the barrenness of New England a blessing, but the bleakness of the scene was mitigated by the speaker's easy conflation of the Landing with the First Thanksgiving, a "cheerful" celebration of plenty just then beginning to emerge as an alternative Pilgrim icon. Born and educated in Maine, Prentiss had plenty of opportunity to experience the blessings of bleakness, but his subsequent departure for southern climes suggests that he preferred happier advantages, a paradox implicit in his singing Pilgrims on their Rock.

Yet these melodious Puritans, like the evocation of Thanksgiving, are in tune with cultural chords of the day, for as the United States entered what has

been called the "Feminine Fifties," there emerged not only a remarkable number of women writers but a marked increase in popular songs. These included
hymns with an evangelical fervor, like the one that provided the tune for Mrs.
Howe's extrapolation from "John Brown's Body," yet another translation of the
old insurrectionist into an equivalent, if militant, Christ. It was entirely fitting,
therefore, that the received image of the Pilgrims' stern piety be somewhat
mitigated even while maintaining (and refining) the spiritual aspect of their
errand. Nor was the emergence of Thanksgiving as a secular ritual incidental to
the feminization process, given the iconic centrality of women to that feast, an
intensely domestic occasion.

In 1802, Joseph Croswell had given significant parts to "Mrs. Carver, Mrs.
Brewster, Mrs. Standish," among the Pilgrim wives, though less as individuals
than a dramatic chorus, a group that chiefly functions, as Mrs. Brewster puts it,
as an avatar of "virtue," which "shines most in our resignation" (12). The
celebrants during the Federalist Feasts of Shells routinely hoisted bumpers to
the "Fore-Mothers" as well as the Forefathers, nor were the women of the
Mayflower neglected by orators, who regularly inserted some mention of their
courage in adversity by way of grace notes: "We listen," intoned Webster in
calling up his vision of the Landing, "to the chiefs in council; we see the
unexampled exhibition of female fortitude and resignation; we hear the whis-
perings of youthful impatience, and we see . . . chilled and shivering childhood,
houseless, but for a mother's arms, couchless, but for a mother's breast" (*Writings*, 1:184).

In calling up this vision, Webster was assisted by the presence of Sargent's
painting, and any number of depictions of the Landing included women and
children among the Pilgrims gathered on Plymouth Rock. In the cartouche
decorating the certificate of membership in the Pilgrim Society, designed
in 1820, we have the figure foregrounded of a Pilgrim woman rummaging
through a Pilgrim trunk, an image in keeping, as we have seen, with Edward
Everett's depiction in 1839 of Cape Cod's maternal and protective arm. But the
male hegemony for the most part held for the first half of the nineteenth
century, much as the speakers themselves were invariably men.

By 1850, however, the sentimental spirit began to overtake the collective
image of the Landing, and in Charles Lucy's depiction the idea of suffering
womanhood is given compositional prominence, much as the martial note of
Sargent's painting is displaced by a pacifist emphasis (see figs. 1 and 2). Virtually contemporary with Lucy's depiction of the Landing was William Rothermel's stormy, Gothicized scene, at the center of which we see Rose Standish
being handed ashore by a solicitous Miles, a tempestuous moment that takes
its meaning from Rose's early death, suggesting the fragility of womanhood as
well as her strength. These are themes essential to the sentimental mode engen-

FIGURE 16. The 1869 engraved version of Rothermel's *Landing* (*top*) contains certain significant differences from the painting (see fig. 13). Here, Rose is given a highlight emphasizing her saintliness, and by having her face turned toward the viewer, the engraving gives an impression of childlike delicacy, in keeping with the feminization of the Pilgrims. The same emphasis, once again, may be found in Lucy's depictions of both the Landing and the Embarkation (see figs. 1 and 4). Ironically, there is some evidence that Rothermel had as his model for Rose Standish a winsome youth who as Captain Alfred Thayer Mahan would become an articulate advocate of the uses of sea power. Ironic, not only because of the feminized scene, but because the setting violates a basic rule of navigation for dramatic effect, a concept that would gain added currency in a treasury bill (*bottom*) designed to conjoin the Columbian and Pilgrim centennials. (Rothermel engraving courtesy Pilgrim Society)

dered in America by the example of Dickens, Tennyson, and Charlotte Brontë in Great Britain, literature in which suffering women are given central place.

In Croswell's play, Rose Standish tells of a terrible nightmare she had the night before the Landing, in which a secret religious service led by a suspended minister back home in England was suddenly interrupted by British soldiers: fleeing up the back stairs, Mrs. Standish was overtaken by "a huge grenadier, with glit'ring arms," and she awoke screaming, hoping "it might prove a dream" (12). Mrs. Brewster reads the nightmare as a hopeful sign that persecution in England will inspire many more to leave for America, but Rose's subsequent fate puts a darker frame on the dream, her death giving the Pilgrim experience a tragic dimension.

In 1855, the Reverend John Pierpont's abolition-friendly poem read before the New England Society in New York brought together the image of singing as well as feminized Pilgrims, lifting their voices upon departure from the Old World, however, not when landing in the New. Well known for his *Airs of Palestine*, a history in verse of sacred music, Pierpont had good reason for stressing song, but by limiting music to the outset of the Pilgrim voyage, he further emphasized the subsequent suffering in America of the Foremothers, a focus as in Rothermel's painting centered on the figure of Rose Standish and her gallant, stalwart husband.

In Pierpont's poem, Miles Standish stands watch on the deck of the *Mayflower* as it sits at anchor at night off Cape Cod, thinking of the human "treasure" stowed beneath his feet. This cargo is far more valuable than the gold and jewels carried by a Spanish galleon, being of the transcendent, unworldly—and feminine—kind: "For, here, firm faith, unsullied honor rest, / Woman's true heart, and beauty's spotless breast; / In all, the spirit to endure and dare" (*NESO*, 2:309–10). Not that Pierpont neglects the men of the *Mayflower*, "All men of valor, and all men of prayer . . . Who want no bishop, and will have no pope," for in lines evoking Rufus Choate's famous slogan (and the song it inspired), Pierpont once again celebrates the heroic, even revolutionary aspect of the Pilgrims, in keeping with his abolitionist bias.

Yet in Pierpont's Unitarian version the male Pilgrims are "full of grace, faith, charity and hope," distinctly New Testament virtues, suggesting a gentler, kinder Puritan, thereby displacing the harsh outlines of the earlier Old Testament profile, yet another testimony to what Ann Douglas has called the "Feminization of America." Pierpont, like Garrison, joined abolition agitation to promoting the cause of women's rights, a movement gathering great headway by 1855, and the poet gives the female half of the passenger list a profile inspired by the notion of True Womanhood. The Pilgrim Mothers not only define the gentle edge of the heroic enterprise but are essential to the vision given Miles Standish by an angel that same night, that "an embryo empire sleeps beneath thy feet." Thus the *Mayflower* becomes pregnant with a new nation, but it is a genesis that will be impossible without the presence of Pilgrim women, in whom the heroic seeds will be planted.

The idea of seeds and seed time dominates the opening stanzas of Pierpont's poem, as when he assures his auditors (thereby correcting Mrs. Hemans's error) that "no craggy barriers, beetling o'er the strand" confronted the Pilgrims as they approached the mainland. The shoreline shows only "sandy slopes, with granite boulders strown," including fields where Indians had once raised corn, now providing ground in which "the seeds of faith and liberty shall grow . . . to be planted by an exiled few, / On this cold, barren border of the New" (310–11).

Refusing to describe the Landing itself, song-struck or otherwise, as a scene beyond the capacity of the human hand to convey, Pierpont provides instead a touching description of the death of Rose: "One little month,—and on that icy shore, / Death's cold hand touched her, and she bloomed no more!" With the Victorian (and abolitionist) penchant for the funereal that would inspire Garrison's notion of pageantry, Pierpont calls up a vision of Rose's final rites, her grave surrounded by "her famished sisters," who offer up a "Requiem," yet another inset song, but one stressing suffering, not hope: "We have heard thy prayer, that God would make thy husband strong, / To bear the burden, that his heart would have to bear ere long" (315).

Pierpont, until 1855 associated with his question regarding the whereabouts of the Pilgrim Fathers, now rose to the occasion and the times and created an equivalent hymn that celebrated the Pilgrim Mothers, whose presence, as comforters and consorts, was essential to the success of the enterprise:

> Look at those women, on that dreary shore!
> You know what they could bear, by what they bore.
> O, with what faith and love they met their lot!
> What should a woman be, that they were not?
> Rendering, in every sphere, the tribute due,
> All true to God, all to their husbands true. (316)

In contrast to Croswell's "resigned" Pilgrim women, Pierpont's are heroic in their suffering. They are pioneer wives, leaving "home, country, ease," to brave "wild beasts, that through the forest prowl," the "stealthy savage, aiming at their life," and even worse, the rigors of "a New England winter!" All these perils "Pilgrim women met . . . like men!" But they also evince their essential gender by serving as nurses for their sick husbands, "soothing [their] pains as none but women can." True partners in adversity (in sickness, as it were, as in health), "Were they not helps meet for these Pilgrim men? / Oh, yes! 'When shall we look upon their like again?' "

As with his famous question of 1824, Pierpont hastens to answer his own inquiry: such women are still with us, "in Labor's cottage, or in Pleasure's halls," ready always to lend a helping or a healing hand: "Standing, thoughtful, by the maniac's cage, / Watching a sister on her dying bed, / Or dressing her for burial when she's dead" (317). This is the Nursing Woman, a maternal presence epitomized in real life by England's Florence Nightingale during the Crimean War and Louisa May Alcott and Walt Whitman during the War between the States. Lydia Maria Child, we will recall, was anxious to bathe the wounds of Captain John Brown, thereby validating the caring side of Abolition.

In literature, Oliver Twist is nursed back to health on several occasions by kindly women, Brontë's Jane attends the injured Rochester, and the heroines of both *Evangeline* and *The Scarlet Letter* tend the sick and dying. Like Long-fellow's and Hawthorne's otherwise quite different heroines, Pierpont's Pil-grim women are sisters not under but in folding back (or winding) the sheets, yet even while associated with illness and death, these heroines are seen as essential to the propagation of an empire of men: " 'Tis well our Pilgrim fathers to revere; / But let us hold our Pilgrim mothers dear; / For, but for them, which, of us, had been here?" (317).

At the last, Pierpont must have his chuckle—this was, after all, a poem written to be read at a festive, not funereal, occasion—but the poet's is finally a serious purpose, in keeping with the Garrisonian program of elevating women even as the cause of emancipation was being advanced. Once again, Pierpont's Pilgrim Mothers are shaped to the image of True Womanhood that Lawrence Friedman has abstracted from the antebellum period in America and Ann Douglas has associated with the Unitarian Church, being women who are not so much heroines in their own right as devoted attendants upon their heroic husbands and male compeers. Rather than posing a challenge to their hus-bands, Pierpont's Pilgrim women supplement and complement them. This arrangement is validated by Pierpont's image of the Pilgrims singing on their decks of gold: "Man's organ tone, and woman's silvery note, / Blending in one" suggests gendered harmony, if not perfect equality before the Lord (304).

In line with Jane Tompkins's theory of sentimental empowerment, the sub-ordinate, complementary role played by Pierpont's Pilgrim women is en-hanced by the martyrdom of Rose Standish, who is important to the Pilgrim story because she died, a fate essential to her gender: notably, the far more significant death of Governor Carver is given no space in Pierpont's poem. We should note here that Rothermel was not the only painter of the period who gave specific space to Rose Standish, who is seen with her hand on Miles's shoulder in the far right foreground of Robert Weir's *Embarkation* (see fig. 14), and in Charles Lucy's depiction of the Departure, she is seen in the same compositional corner being clasped by Standish's strong arm (see fig. 4). These postures suggest opposing but complementary roles: in Weir's painting she lends support to her husband, in Lucy's she is supported by him, both positions in keeping with Pierpont's point of view. For in dying, Rose is sanctified by and sanctifies the Separatist errand, and though her husband assumes the traditional male posture of protectiveness and hardihood, it takes meaning from his wife's sacrifice and death. Once again, this image of the suffering woman is hardly original with Pierpont, but is essential to the sentimental (and feminizing) spirit, endemic to the reforming impulse of the age.

If from their marriage beds American mothers sent forth a stream of pioneers, their deathbeds served (at least in pious and sentimental literature) as bully pulpits, from which they issued edicts and provided models of courageous death, icons of often literal conspicuous consumption. That image in Pierpont's poem of Standish's "Lovely Rose" already "fading" away below the deck the captain is pacing—in effect a premature burial—is surely reflective of an influence other than Poe's. Nor is it an example, so frequently illustrated by dying flowers, of carpe diem, which is a pagan, not a Christian, theme.

To her dying day, as her sisters acknowledge in their hymn, Rose continued to sustain and support her husband, who drew his strength from her devotion to him. Theirs is a synergetic relationship by means of which True Womanhood merges with the Passion of Christ. Something similar happens to the long-suffering Evangeline of Longfellow's poem, but in Hawthorne's Hester Prynne, as we shall see, an antithetical evolution occurs, thanks in large part to the emergence between 1847 and 1850 of an alternative heroic model to quiescent suffering and noble sacrifice as regnant tropes for literary women in America.

II

By 1850, the issue of women's rights was gaining strength in the Northeast, having been given considerable momentum by the Seneca Falls Convention of 1848, and the pliable ideal of "True Womanhood" was slowly being displaced by the "Strong-minded Woman" as satirized by Mortimer Thomson in his popular parody of Longfellow's *Hiawatha*:

> She was one who "spoke in public"
> At the Woman Rights Conventions;
> One who wore the Bloomer costume,
> Half-way petticoats, half breeches,
> This the masculine co-partner,
> This the woman just imported
> From the distant He-Bride Islands,
> Whom our youthful hero married,
> And brought home to rule his mansion. (204–5)

The reference to the "He-Bride" Islands is a pointed jibe at Fanny Wright, the Scottish-born freethinker, abolitionist, and founder of a utopian community who was dead by 1856 but whose long career of public speaking on behalf of reform both provided a role model for American feminists and inspired ribald male conjectures as to her true sex.

Without impugning the security of Thomson's grasp of his own gender, it can be said that the male American identity had been challenged by Amelia Bloomer's having stolen the "breeches" of her fellow journalists by means of the garment given her name. Bloomer's periodical, the *Lily*, was founded in 1849 in connection with the Seneca Falls Convention, and in 1853, reporting the proceedings of the women's rights meeting in Worcester that year, it recorded the remark by a Mrs. Mehitable Haskell that whatever women's rights might be, they were certainly an improvement over their wrongs. In like spirit were the words credited to "a San Francisco lady": " 'The Pilgrim Fathers, forsooth! What had they to endure in comparison with the Pilgrim Mothers? It is true that they had hunger and cold and sickness and danger—foes without and foes within—but the unfortunate Pilgrim Mothers! They had not only these to endure, but they had the Pilgrim Fathers!' " (Mott, 2:51). Clearly, the notion of True Womanhood was in trouble.

The shift of emphasis is registered in an essay by Elizabeth Oakes Smith, "The Women of the Mayflower," which first appeared in a gift book in 1848 and got further circulation by being anthologized also in a Know-Nothing annual for 1855. This last and dubious venue was no indication of Smith's own politics, for the American Party was generous in its literary inclusiveness, however narrow in its nativist doctrines. It packed the annual with all matter of patriotic effusions, including celebrations of the Pilgrim priority and precedence— an essential plank in the American Party's exclusionist platform. We may doubt that the anonymous editor paid close attention to Smith's essay in any event, for under a superficial layer of conventional sentimentality we can detect a subversive core of steel, suggesting that Pierpont's notion of the patiently suffering and sustaining Puritan woman was by 1855 already out of date.

In 1851, there appeared Smith's *Woman and Her Needs*, which decidedly reversed Pierpont's emphasis and marked a change of course for the author as well. Born in Maine in 1806, Elizabeth Oakes Prince had at the age of seventeen been forced by her mother to abandon her intended career as a teacher of young women and marry a man nearly twice her age. Elizabeth's husband was Seba Smith, creator of Major Jack Downing, the vernacular Yankee chronicler of the misdeeds of the Jackson administration, but the crotchety and prematurely bald journalist seems to have confined his sense of humor to his writing. Thus Elizabeth Smith certainly knew what women's wrongs were, having for many years submitted herself to the ideal of True Womanhood, meaning the unquestioned rule of her husband, even to the extent, so she claimed, of giving him five sons and no daughters because he was partial to boys.

It is a remark, moreover, that suggests a quietly subversive sense of humor helped her to survive a union with a man fourteen years her senior but even older in terms of appearance and temper. She was both intelligent and resourceful and, after her husband suffered financial losses during the Panic of 1837, became an author herself in an effort to supplement the family income. At first signing herself "Mrs. Seba Smith," she also used a male pseudonym, the pixyish "Ernest Helfenstein," but finally settled on Elizabeth Oakes Smith, turning out prose and poetry for literary magazines and annuals, along with plays and book-length fiction, including dime novels.

Oakes Smith, as she later came to style herself, published in 1843 "The Sinless Child," a popular expression of romantic pantheism with a heavily Christian subtext, written in the ballad stanza of Coleridge's *Ancient Mariner*. The poet, who even as a girl was convinced of her own "sinlessness," hence of the essential fallacy of her parents' strict Calvinism—with its doctrine of infant damnation—granted her marvelous child a transcendental sense of harmony with a salvational Nature. Her sermons to her mother and her given name—Eva—no doubt contributed to the complex creation of the most sinless child in American fiction.

By 1850, Smith had become an advocate of woman's rights, and her Eva by necessity grew up into a strong-minded woman named "Bertha," the heroine of *Bertha and Lily* (1854), who, in the words of Ann Douglas, is "brilliant, beautiful, and radical" and whose relationship with a liberal young minister ends in marriage and a virtual turnabout in gender roles (Douglas, 108). This was precisely the arrangement ridiculed by Mortimer Thomson, with the husband becoming important chiefly through association with his wife. For it is Bertha who directs Earnest's ministry, and in his eyes she is a female incarnation of Christ.

Both the "strong-minded" Bertha and her submissive husband, Douglas tells us, are autobiographical projections, reflecting Smith's admiration for the handsome Reverend Ichabod Nichols of Portland, Maine, whose liberal doctrines and charming presence must have provided a stark contrast to the withered yet rigid stick she had married. Given Smith's abiding sense of sinlessness, adultery may never have been a possibility, yet in her novel she seems to have worked out a vicarious union that echoes the relationship between Hester Prynne and Dimmesdale, much as the triangle in *The Scarlet Letter* bears obvious similarities to Smith's unhappy domestic situation. Thus if Hawthorne gave fictional shape to gossip in Portland, Maine, then Smith got her revenge by imposing on Hawthorne's novel a feminist closure.

There are, moreover, specific connections to be made between Elizabeth

Oakes Smith's emerging notions of womanhood and Hawthorne's Hester, which center on the authors' contrasting use of the Puritan heritage. As the fatal flaws in his heroine and her lover and husband suggest, Hawthorne was drawn to the Puritans not only because of his much advertised genealogy (and the imperatives of historical romance) but because the Calvinist certainty of man's essential depravity appealed to his own abiding sense of human imperfection. By contrast, Smith's identification with the Puritans (from whom she was also descended) was strongly influenced by her feminism, inspiring in her essay on the *Mayflower* women subjective and highly imaginary "portraits" of long-suffering victims of male callousness and indifference, "Hesters" whose legitimacy as wives and mothers in no way diminished their sense of isolation.

Smith's essay begins with a lengthy childhood reminiscence of the "May Flower" that she had gathered with her schoolgirl friends on May Day, a beautiful and fragile bloom that seemed "the link that binds us to the angels" (*Wide-Awake*, 265). The flower also provided a tie to the Pilgrim women, credited by Smith with having named it after the "frail bark" that carried them to the New World, for it was likely the first blossom to greet "the eye of woman, when the bleak winter abated its rigors; and the sunshine, in revealing its beauty, whispered, all is not utterly barren and desolate in this 'howling wilderness' " (266). In the portraits that followed, Smith would go on to develop this contrast between frail and sensitive flowers and the barrenness and desolation of the New England scene that seems much more an abstraction from her own marriage than an informed discussion of Old Colony days.

That she would insist that the name "May Flower" reminded the Pilgrim women not only of their ship but the beloved Maypole, "bedecked with blossoms in 'fatherland,' " suggests that the author either was not familiar with the actual writings of the Pilgrims or was in covert sympathy with their archrival, Thomas Morton. Certainly, in her account of the battle between gloom and gaiety for empire in the New World, there is a decided balance in favor of the defeated party, identified not with the Merrymount crew but the "Women of the Mayflower." For Smith the May Flower provided a feminist continuity, a daisy chain of sympathy "binding the sex of the present day to the suffering, struggling, devoted, and unrecorded matrons of that day of hardy toil, and self-sacrificing love and duty."

Smith's sympathy for the Pilgrim wives and daughters anticipates John Pierpont's characterization in 1855, for hers too are suffering women, "who stifled the weakness of the sex, smothered the heart's yearnings, and nobly and patiently died, while their stern husbands and fathers laid the corner-stone of empire" (266). But if Smith's Pilgrim women seem therefore exemplars, like Rose Standish, of True Womanhood, in whom the gentle and martyred version of Christ is centered, Smith perceives their husbands less as protectors than oppressors, rather Hebraic in outlines. For the martial and ascetic version of Puritanism is invested in the male side of the Pilgrim ledger, the weight of which contributes to the suffering and deaths of their wives.

Thus if the May Flower is the "one blossom decking the hoary crown of winter" and is thereby "the pitying gift of spring," so the Pilgrim wives "with their hardy graces must have served somewhat to abate the savageness of virtue in those hard principled, hard thinking men" (267). This is a complementariness not found in Pierpont's celebration of Pilgrim harmony and introduces a patently subversive element, for even as she begs not to be thought "irreverent," Smith goes on to describe the marital relationships of the Pilgrims in terms easily decoded by her contemporary feminists: "They were Cromwellmen, Milton-men, full of the arrogance of manly prerogative, little careful for the gentleness suited to the lady's bower, and rarely disposed to turn aside to the 'delectable fields' of merely domestic enjoyment" (267).

What male writers, even those sympathetic to the cause of women's rights, found admirable in the Puritans and prognostic of Captain John Brown, Smith regarded with a pre-Freudian perspective as repressive, an "ascetic renunciation of the natural tendencies of the human heart, that reflection of human sympathy, a rooting out as it were of human sensibilities." Although coming from quite a different direction and dictated by her own circumstances (it is easy enough to detect Seba Smith's sere features here), Oakes Smith's image of the Puritan male corresponds to (and may have been influenced by) Hawthorne's Endicott. On the other hand, *The Scarlet Letter* proposes a consequence that Smith stops well short of suggesting, even as she creates an equivalent setting of female longing surrounded by a "monkish" wall of male dedication to duty at the cost of the domestic affections.

Certainly, Smith resembles Hawthorne in her use of doublespeak, for in praising the Forefathers she manages to condemn them. They were "men of severe duty, often of high thought, men jealous of freedom, tenacious of principle," but they were "not men full of the charities of life," being constructed for "reverence, not for love." As builders of empire, whose cornerstone they laid at Plymouth, the Pilgrim men are justly famous, while their wives remain unfairly "unrecorded," laid to rest under that cornerstone: "So far as our sex is concerned, the records of those times are barren indeed" (269). But Smith assumes that "where woman is . . . there must have been griefs, bitter and heart-breaking. There must have been crushed affections, yearnings for tenderness and sympathy, too great for womanly endurance, sobbings stifled in the sternness of duty and a weariness of life hard to be borne."

In effect, what Smith's "must-have-beens" give us is an explanation equivalent to Hawthorne's for Hester's moral lapse, that the strict mores of the Puritans fostered the very impulses they sought to repress. But where Hawthorne gives rebellion an openly sexual dimension, Smith sublimates it into a feminist politics, based on her assumption that there "must have arisen a desire to cope with these lords of creation" that took the form of looking "for new combinations for affection—a new form of the altar, since the old is destroyed, upon which she [the Pilgrim wife] may hang the sweet garlands of her love." Smith's reference is not to some pagan and wildwood shrine but the one sanctified by marriage: whatever her own daydreams may have been, her Pilgrim wives did not entertain erotic, adulterous fantasies about young ministers.

But if they did not follow Hester's route, Smith's Pilgrim women ended up in the same place. Hester in the lonely cottage to which she has been exiled undergoes a transformation, losing the "essential attribute" of a woman, the capacity for "Affection" that got her there in the first place: "Such is frequently the fate, and such the stern development, of the feminine character and person, when the woman has encountered, and lived through, an experience of peculiar severity" (*Works*, 5:198). But adversity not only "crushes" Hester's capacity for love, it turns her "from passion and feeling, to thought," a transformation parallel to that of Smith's Puritan women. For by taking advantage of their isolation from domestic affections, they began "to think," to develop their minds by considering "the principles, whether in politics or religion, of those we love, not blindly, but with searchingness and patient thought," and began to come to their own conclusions, "to cavil" with the severe theology of their men: "Hence the restless action of the female mind throughout New England and that preponderance of intellectual development, so remarkable, and becoming effective, not only in point of duty, but moral harmony" (Smith, 270).

By Smith's account the wives of Plymouth became prototypes and progenitors of their modern feminist counterparts, strong-minded and independent women. So also Hester "in her lonesome cottage, by the sea-shore," where, "standing alone in the world . . . she assumed a freedom of speculation . . . which our forefathers, had they known of it, would have held to be a deadlier crime than that stigmatized by the scarlet letter. . . . The world's law was no law for her mind." (199). This passage is introductory to that digression crucial to the psychological burden of Hawthorne's novel, which ends with the definitive and revelatory sentence "The scarlet letter had not done its office," thereby discounting the effectiveness of penitence based on notions of ostracism as a salutary antidote to antisocial behavior.

Hester's stoic acceptance of her punishment, regarded by the Puritan community as evidence of her repentance, is but a mask, and her isolation promotes a "tendancy to speculation," the conclusions of which not coincidentally parallel the most extreme assumptions of radical feminists. For if "the dark question" of women's rights is to be answered, "the whole system of society is to be torn down, and built up anew . . . [and] the very nature of the opposite sex . . . is to be essentially modified, before woman can be allowed to assume what seems a fair and suitable position" (200).

But Hawthorne was careful to emphasize the moral deviance essential to Hester's enlightenment, which essentially discounts her vision as a realizable program for change. "Stained with sin," she cannot become "the destined prophetess," for her "love" is the profane, not the "sacred," kind (311). Smith, by contrast, emphasizes marital faithfuless and, using for her fulcrum and lever the Puritan reputation for repressiveness, characterizes her Pilgrim women as rebels only by necessity, not choice, and nowhere suggests that a sexual revolution is in sight. Something further of the differences between Hawthorne and Smith can be seen by comparing their portraits of Anne Hutchinson, with whom Hester is implicitly associated and who emerges as the strongest profile in Smith's slim gallery of "Pilgrim" portraits.

In his stories of the Puritans, Hawthorne took full advantage of the license permitted by historical romance, but they were also based in part on his research in the ample record available of colonial life in the mid-seventeenth century. By contrast, Smith in her essay was hampered by the dearth of information about the wives of the Pilgrims, and she seems not to have been aware of what little was known. As a result, her resurrection of three heroines from the meager annals of women in the early days of colonial Massachusetts required her to repair to Boston for two of them, the Lady Arbella Johnson and Anne Hutchinson. The only bona fide Pilgrim to figure in Smith's pantheon of American Minervas is "the mother of Peregrine White," about whom nothing is known save that she gave birth to the first child born to the Puritans in America. Thus White's very identity is subsumed, even absorbed by her male child.

This blank is filled in by Smith with the features of a wife and mother "who must have been a cheerful, active, beautiful woman, able to cope in an off-hand practical manner with the worst hardships of a new world life." And when to this admirable, if entirely imaginative, "portrait" Smith adds the assumption that "she must have had a certain audacious affectionateness, by which she disarmed the ferocity of polemic discussion," we are given yet another baseless assumption about the home life of the Pilgrims that tells us much more about Elizabeth Oakes Smith than about the nameless mother of Peregrine White.

About Rose Standish we hear nothing, suggesting once again a certain vacuity in Smith's knowledge of the Pilgrim venture, because she gives us instead the Boston version of Standish's wife, the "lady Arabella [sic] Jonson [sic], whose brief history is far more touchingly effective than any embellishment of fancy." Despite this demurrer, Smith goes on to render an extensive demonstration of her imaginative reach, for by her account both the Lady Arbella and her husband (unnamed) were a version of American Quixote, having "sadly mistaken their vocation, when, in the excess of religious and political zeal they tempted the hardships of the wilderness" and died shortly after landing at Shawmut.

From this "slight glimpse," Smith creates a lovely, tender, refined lady, "a creature the imagination delights to contemplate, whose moral greatness made her forget her disabilities of physical power; whose intellect seemed only second to her delicacy and tenderness, and these again subordinate to her resolute devotedness. She is the embodied poetry of the Pilgrim race" (271). At this late point, we can fault no one for conflating the Puritans with the Pilgrims, such being endemic to any number of Forefathers' Day and Fourth of July orations. At the same time, we must concede that persons who promote political agendas seldom worry over particulars and often assume, if not openly claim, the same license given to poets and writers of fiction. This brings us to the contrasting portraits of Anne Hutchinson drawn by Hawthorne and Smith, both based on the available record yet each serving quite a different ideology.

In his biographical sketch of Hutchinson, Hawthorne's agenda was that of a conservative Democrat, for whom the Puritan rebel was prophetic of a modern problem, which he often identified with Margaret Fuller. While ostensibly "not looking for a living resemblance of Mrs. Hutchinson," he noted "portentous . . . changes gradually taking place in the habits and feelings of the gentle sex, which seem to threaten our posterity with many of these public women, whereof one was a burden too grievous for our fathers." He anticipated with dread the day when "fair orators shall be as numerous as the fair authors of our own day. . . . The evil is likely to be a growing one" (*Works*, 12:217–18).

Hawthorne used the occasion chiefly to rail against "fair authors" (like Fuller), but there can be found in his portrait overtones of his hostility toward abolition and disunion. For Hutchinson is accused of "promulgating strange and dangerous opinions, tending, in the peculiar situation of the colony, and from the principles which were its basis and indispensable for its temporary support, to eat into its very existence. . . . Unity of faith was the star that had guided these people over the deep; and a diversity of sects would . . . have excited a diminutive civil war among those who had come so far to worship together" (219, 222). We can likewise derive from Hawthorne's picture of Anne at her trial not only the outlines of Margaret Fuller and the Grimké sisters but a forecast of Hester Prynne: "In the midst, and in the centre of all eyes, we see the woman . . . standing loftily before her judges with a determined brow," as Corinne-like, "she bursts forth into eloquence" (224). We are not very far from Hester posed silently but eloquently on her scaffold.

Smith's portrait of Anne Hutchinson resembles Hawthorne's in being a prototype of the modern feminist, but with a contrary emphasis, for she is characterized as "a woman so remarkable as to throw the whole colony into a ferment by the vigor of her understanding, and the force and boldness with which she advocated her opinions." Smith's Hutchinson is a prototypical strong-minded woman, whose quality of courage is defined as not characteristically "feminine"—that is, passive and long suffering—but "equal to those of the other sex with whom she had to compete," suggesting that the Boston rebel was an early Bloomer. She set an example for "the women of the day," who were inspired by her precedent to question the doctrines and hence the authority of the male leaders of the community—in short, "to cavil." Indeed, it was Hutchinson's subversive influence among Boston women that brought about her trial, during which she defended herself in a "clear and vigorous [i.e., masculine] manner."

Hawthorne devoted a detailed page to Hutchinson's forced exile and death, and following the brief observation that under "the Dutch jurisdiction" in New York "she became herself the virtual head, civil and ecclesiastical, of a little colony," he hastens on to her murder at the hands of Indians, a "last scene . . . as difficult to be described as a shipwreck, where the shrieks of the victims die unheard, along a desolate sea, and a shapeless mass of agony is all that can be brought home to the imagination"—precisely the fate suffered by Margaret Fuller (225). For her part, Smith refrained from discussing in detail her heroine's "subsequent banishment and her many misfortunes" and brought her essay to a close with a paragraph that bears comparison to Hawthorne's ruminations concerning the consequences of Hester's penitential isolation:

Anne Hutchinson, with her affluence of thought, and her clear, vigorous understanding, her searching and courageous power of combination, so beyond the age in which she lived, stands out as the type of intellectual [i.e., strong-minded] woman, and is the base of that large class of thinkers in that section of the country [e.g., New England], who command the respect of the other sex, and sometimes provoke their fears; and who, if not loyal to themselves, and single in their search for truth, may be used hereafter by those who dare not hope to suppress them (since "banishment" now would little obviate the difficulty), as were their lively sisters, on the other side of the water, when they were enrolled by the Illuminee into lodges, and made subservient to the progress of revolution. (272)

Notably, Smith brings her essay to closure by placing herself in a submissive posture as a woman ready and willing to be "used," to be made "subservient to the progress" of reform. But in that word "subservient" "subversive" can be found, which was Hawthorne's reading surely of the pose, carefully delineated in both his biographical sketch of Anne Hutchinson and his explanation of how the scarlet letter failed in the exercise of its office.

Smith ends with a prayer "that the restless power of thought, so characteristic of a New England woman, may keep even pace with the developed harmonies of what is truly womanly, and that the religion which has so much to do with the head, may never retire from the citadel of the heart" (272–73). As with Hawthorne's frequent expostulations of similar sentiments, we need to probe past the first little layer. For her final note of piety does not at all detract from Smith's emphasis on the necessity for "pertinacious questionings" by women when male doctrines are shoved into their purview, even when that domain is limited to the hearthside and home. Such questions could include a challenge to what Hawthorne called the "long hereditary habit, which has become like nature," namely the unquestioned superiority of "the opposite sex" (200).

And finally, it is not difficult to read Smith's account of these three "Pilgrim" women as a kind of allegory of her own life: she began as a dreamy young woman who thought of founding a school for girls but was forced to set aside such visions when pushed into marriage and motherhood, rather much as if Lady Arbella had become the mother of Peregrine White. But in time Smith learned to define her own identity by engaging in competitive discourse with her intellectual husband, even as she displaced him as the creative center of the home, becoming at last her own person. She became in effect another Anne Hutchinson, that strong-minded woman who through the exercise of her reasons triumphs over the male hegemony of Massachusetts, even while holding fast to her duties as wife and mother, those "developed harmonies of what is truly womanly."

Though she came too late to the platform as an advocate of women's rights to have provided a model for Hester in that particular, Smith was certainly part of the continuity that occasioned Hawthorne so much discomfort, with Anne Hutchinson at one end of the sequence of strong-minded women and Margaret Fuller at the other. Hester without her "A," Smith was a reasonable equivalent to Hawthorne's description of those "persons who speculate the most boldly [yet] often conform with the most perfect quietude to the external regulations of society."

Hers is a kind of chrysalis of self-protective camouflage from which one day will emerge "the angel and apostle of the coming revelation . . . a woman, indeed, but lofty, pure, and beautiful; and wise, moreover, not through dusky grief, but the ethereal medium of joy; and showing how sacred love should make us happy, by the truest test of a life successful to such an end!" (311). Once again, Hawthorne's recipe for his angelic apostle is an impossible combination of virtues, virtually free of human faults, ensuring that the male hegemony will continue to hold sway, while Oakes Smith by means of her parabolic Puritan women suggests that it is male exclusionism like Hawthorne's that will provide the fulcrum for the lever that will elevate women to true and entirely human equality.

When Seba Smith died, in 1868, his wife's feminist principles caused her to change her name to Oakesmith, and her pulpit envy was finally consummated in 1877, when she became pastor of an independent church in Canastota, New York. This was the final stage in a metamorphosis that eerily bore out Hawthorne's prophecy of what Hester might have become had she not been "a woman stained with sin," that is, "the destined prophetess" of "a new truth" regarding "the whole relation between man and woman on a surer ground of mutual happiness" (311). Mercifully for Hawthorne, for whom such a consummation was not devoutly to be desired and who was careful to predicate what he assumed was an impossible level of purity for "the angel and apostle of the coming revelation"—but which Smith's sense of her own sinlessness gainsaid—he was not around to witness this ascension.

Hawthorne would never concern himself in his fiction with the Pilgrim story, perhaps because the saga of the Separatists at Plymouth contained nothing of the Gothic element that recommended to contemporary sensibilities the goings-on in Salem and Boston that Rufus Choate had dismissed as irrelevant to American literature. Typically, we find Hawthorne in 1842 consoling himself on his snowbound seclusion at Brook Farm with the recollection "that the Plymouth pilgrims arrived in the midst of storm, and stepped ashore upon mountainous snow-drifts; and, nevertheless, they prospered, and became a great people,—and doubtless it will be the same with us" (*Works*, 9:226–27). Hawthorne's easy facetiousness reinforces the certainty that there was nothing in the story of a people who carved a kingdom from a snowdrift that appealed to his sensibility. Again, Harriet Cheney's *Peep at the Pilgrims* is a minority of one, even among novels by women about the early Puritan presence, and it was set sixteen years after the Landing.

This problematic matrix makes Longfellow's *The Courtship of Miles Standish* (1858) all the more remarkable as an idiosyncratic production, being the only significant work of literature produced in America during the nineteenth century that uses the first year of the Pilgrim presence in New England as its backdrop. Invariably drawn to scenes of domesticity with a sentimental, pious aura, Longfellow, as in *Evangeline*, gave his poem a heroine very much in the contemporary model of True Womanhood, yet with a distinctly encoded advance toward liberation, in keeping with the changing temper of the times. As we shall see, Longfellow's Pilgrim poem is as much a response to *The Scarlet Letter* as Hawthorne's Hester was a perverse rearrangement of Oakes Smith's Anne Hutchinson, both works being inextricably tied to the emerging issue of woman's rights.

It needs to be said at the start that Longfellow was well aware of the dark side of the Puritan presence in America, for the persecution of Quakers and the witchcraft trials provided the material for his "John Endicott" and "Giles Corey of the Salem Farms," poetic dramas published together as *The New England Tragedies* in 1868. But those Hawthornesque tragedies were for Longfellow atypical exercises and did not share the popularity of *The Courtship of Miles Standish*, which Longfellow framed as a love story with a pastoral setting, leaving the dark aspects of Puritan life for his two closet dramas. By so doing, Longfellow, like Harriet Cheney in 1824, observed that definitive line of demarcation early mapped by Jedidiah Morse between the Plymouth and the Massachusetts colonies.

But unlike Cheney's novel, Longfellow's poem with its focus on the first two years of the Plymouth colony did not (indeed, could not) permit his gaze to stray toward Salem or Boston, and his poem therefore must be accounted a separatist exercise in every way. Thus where his tragedies were preceded and to a large measure co-opted by the fiction of Catharine Sedgwick, John Neal, Lydia Maria Child, Hawthorne, and even Whittier, Longfellow's Pilgrim story is not only singular in its chronological setting but is unique in the annals of American literature as a happy version of Puritan life in the New World.

There is, of course, that long line of optative Forefathers' Day orations and sermons, which when taken together amount to a considerable volume—a continuity that is nothing if not literary. As we have seen, the story of the Pilgrims' first year in its simple heroism most certainly provided a useful rhetorical device, whether celebrating the Separatists as founders of the Republic or as ur-radicals pledging their lives to the service of Liberty. Yet not only did it lack the melodramatic oppositions that were the stock in trade of writers of romantic fiction, but by honoring the Pilgrims' own sense of themselves as a communal, collective body, it also lacked the element of human interest. It is to Pierpont's credit that he hit upon the sentimental device of celebrating the contrast between the stalwart Standish and his dying, delicate Rose, but Longfellow's emphasis in what was essentially a chronological sequel to Pierpont's ode would be anything but funereal.

We can hardly doubt that Longfellow was familiar with Forefathers' Day orations and the occasions that inspired them, yet in most respects his poem not only operated outside that tradition but resulted in significant and long-lasting modifications to it. Pierpont's poem certainly opposed the Whig tradition of Unionist celebration by introducing the Garrisonite notion of the Pilgrim-as-abolitionist, but that was hardly Longfellow's desire, nor was he interested in promoting the idea of the suffering woman further than he had already done in *Evangeline*. His was above all else a celebration of the positive side of life among the Separatists, with less emphasis, however, on the heroic than on the domestic element, and he characteristically, if perversely, posited the prevalence of romantic love against a backdrop so often portrayed as lacking even the bare essentials of civilized existence.

And yet like the Puritans of Oakes Smith and Hawthorne, Longfellow's Pilgrims are shaped along lines dictated by ideological matters current in the 1850s, and his poem is a thoroughly contextual work. Where *Evangeline* indirectly reflected Longfellow's nostalgia for the Old World, his *Courtship* openly stresses what can be called American themes, and where the brunette heroine of his French Canadian epic is a figment of European romanticism, the blonde, blue-eyed maid at the center of his Pilgrim romance is very much an American girl cut to what was then a modern pattern. Moreover, the notion of exile becoming ancestor that originates with Elizabeth Barrett Browning's antislavery poem is the operating principle of Longfellow's effort, more than has hitherto been realized, and gives considerable heft to the signal role Longfellow gave to Plymouth Rock.

Of equal importance, as with Hawthorne, was Longfellow's genealogy: on his mother's side Longfellow was a descendant of John Alden—his great grandfather was Plymouth's Peleg Wadsworth, who had contributed an ode to the Old Colony Club's celebration of Forefathers' Day in 1769. Not only did this give him a vested interest in the Pilgrim story, but it validates the likelihood of his awareness of the oratorical tradition that stressed the element of adversity, the wintry Landing and the year of suffering and death that followed. Yet where Smith exploited that backdrop to emphasize the grim life of Pilgrim women, Longfellow managed to derive from the same circumstances a rustic pastorale, largely by ignoring some unhappy facts.

In 1858, we should note, Sarah Josepha Hale was using her *Godey's Lady's Book* to promote the annual observation of the First Thanksgiving as a national anniversary that would help preserve the Union, and her eventual success in gaining the sympathetic ear of President Lincoln, though too late to prevent the war, would establish that familial feast as a rival to Forefathers' Day. In time, Thanksgiving would supplant the anniversary of the Landing even in New England, especially after the region began to celebrate that other festive occasion, Christmas.

Similarly, in *The Courtship of Miles Standish*, Longfellow managed to displace the oratorical tradition of hardship and suffering that dated from revolutionary days, and provided instead what became for subsequent generations the dominant and largely domestic image, not a wretched group of Pilgrims huddled together against the cold and sharing a few last grains of parched corn, but a healthy young couple finding love in an American Eden. The poem ends, moreover, on a celebratory note equivalent to the First Thanksgiving, with the reconciliatory emphasis sought by Sarah Hale, lacking only the ab-original presence.

Setting up in the New England wilderness a pastoral equivalent to his Acadian idyll, but without the tragic expulsion, Longfellow replaced the praying group on Plymouth Rock with a much more fructive icon. Most significant, perhaps, his drama does not include the familiar trinity—Departure, Compact, Landing—but stresses instead the refusal by all of the Pilgrims to return with the *Mayflower* when it set sail for England after that first terrible winter, a gesture confirming that New England was now their home. This not only would be a signal shift of emphasis but, as with Longfellow's cast of characters and his erotic fable, would be highly influential on subsequent accounts of the Pilgrims.

The artist George Henry Boughton would within a decade exploit the notion of the Pilgrims as exiles, posing a couple resembling John and Priscilla as they stood sadly watching the *Mayflower* depart, one of a number of similar compositions by Boughton that were highly popular in their day. Much as Longfellow's other famous poems flowed through murmuring schoolrooms immemorial, giving generations of Americans their sense of what poetry was supposed to be, so his became America's Pilgrims, and their names were the hitherto uncelebrated Priscilla and John Alden.

A photograph that had much popular circulation late in the nineteenth century provides a key to Longfellow's iconic revisionism. It shows Priscilla at her spinning wheel, attended by her adoring John, as through a tiny, many-paned window we catch a distant glimpse, a framed hint only, of Plymouth Rock. The reversal of emphasis is central to Longfellow's version, the sacred Rock being relegated to the equivalent of a picture on the wall. As any number of Pilgrim celebrants insisted, Plymouth was a "colony of families," and this emphasis on domesticity would be given mass circulation by Longfellow's poem, in which a felicitous union is certified by an image so enduring that it remains even now central to the continuity of American myths. Like Irving's Hudson River "legends," the story of the Plymouth triangle has become part and parcel of what we are pleased to call our "folklore."

Once again, Longfellow's *Courtship* takes up where Pierpont's ode of 1855 ended, centering as it does upon the captain's maladroit efforts to replace his beloved Rose, selecting a girl whose Christian name (Mullins) suggests a somewhat hardier plant (mullein) than the delicate blossom destroyed by the New England winter: "What I thought was a flower," muses a bitter Standish after his rejection, "is only a weed," but a weed by another name is a flower still (331). And in Priscilla Mullins (or Mullens, the spelling varies, and Longfellow, for poetic reasons, calls his heroine simply "Priscilla"), we find the conventional notion of True Womanhood strategically revised, effecting a compromise with

FIGURE 17. Engraving after George Henry Boughton, *The Return of the Mayflower* (ca. 1870), one of a number of depictions by the artist of the Pilgrims as exiles, inspired by Longfellow's poem and perhaps by the increasing immigrant presence in the United States. Rather than emphasizing the triumph of escape from the religious repression of the Old World, Boughton's paintings portray the pathos of a people voluntarily cut off from their homeland. That this couple is intended to represent John and Priscilla seems obvious, but it is typical of Boughton that he places the Pilgrims in small, isolated groups, in contrast to the massed body of the *Mayflower* passengers used in most depictions of the Landing, thereby enhancing the idea of exile, emphasizing separation rather than Separatism. (Courtesy Plimoth Plantation)

the contrary ideal of the Strong-Minded Woman. Priscilla, well after the fact, is just such a "woman of the *Mayflower*" as Oakes Smith would have recognized, nor should we neglect the priority of Lydia Maria Child, who in *Hobomok*, as we have seen in chapter 7, told a very similar story, thereby giving it a feminist seal of approval.

Though Longfellow's journal reflects his awareness and concern with contemporary matters, they are seldom reflected save obliquely in his verse, and for the most part his poetry during the troubled 1850s reflects like a calm body of water the heavenly blue of an unclouded sky. But along with detectable signs in *The Courtship of Miles Standish* of the contemporary feminist agenda, Long-

FIGURE 18. We have in this turn-of-the-century photographic tableau a host of anachronisms, from the wool on Priscilla's spinning wheel to the bricks in the fireplace and the glass in the window, through which Plymouth Rock and the stern and rock-bound coast may be seen. This is but one of many depictions of John and Priscilla shown at the critical moment in Longfellow's poem, matched by numerous pictures of Priscilla alone, stereotyped as "the Pilgrim Maid," intended for parlors all over the United States. (Courtesy Plimoth Plantation)

fellow's poem about the Pilgrims' first year in America may be seen to contain reflections of the most important ideological conflict of his day. It is notable, given the positive aura of the poem, that Longfellow's love story was written during same the period in which he was working on his two Hawthornesque dramas that focused on John Endicott's persecution of the Quakers and the Salem witchcraft trials, which the poet seems to have regarded as relevant to his own turbulent decade, in which intolerance characterized both sides of the antislavery debate. Notably, in 1868 he sent manuscript copies of the finished plays to his friend Charles Sumner, with the observation that they were "Pleas for Toleration," still a pertinent issue though within a somewhat different context than ten years before (Tucker, xxxvi).

This was material, however, that was hardly congenial to Longfellow's talents, and in the midst of the difficulties he experienced in working out his tragedies, the poet suddenly hit upon the idea for what he called his "Puritan idyll." It was an apparent contradiction in terms that was so suitable to his genius that the process of creation went smoothly, while his *New England Tragedies* would not be published for another ten years. Because of this interval, the three works are seldom thought of as a unit, yet at the start the Plymouth story seems to have been conceived by Longfellow as a comic counterpart to the tragedies with Boston and Salem settings—hence "Puritan idyll"—and the first, uncompleted version of *Courtship* was written as a drama as well.

The manuscript of the play still exists, and though some critical revisions in the plot sequence were made, the story remains pretty much the familiar fable that retains, for persons of a certain age, a vague odor of schoolroom chalk. As always, what is most interesting in the process of revision is what is left out, and early on in the drama, the following conversation takes place between Standish and his young friend John Alden:

> Standish (*filling a pipe*). Alden, have you and Mary Chilton ever settled your dispute as to who landed first on Plimouth rock?
> Alden. No, the question still remains unsettled.
> Standish (*sitting down opposite to Alden*). Well, I will settle it for you. You were the first man, and she the first woman.
> Alden. Adam and Eve.
> Standish. In this new Garden of Eden. If you should marry her, Alden, you would have all the honors in the family. (*Strikes fire with flint and steel.*)
> Alden. I never thought of that.
> Standish. Well, think of it now. (*Smokes and meditates. Alden continues writing.*) (295–96)

Alden, however, does not give the possibility a second thought, and nothing further comes of this conversation, which is a cunning feint by Standish that will allow him to bring up his interest in Priscilla Mullins. As in the later version, he asks Alden to propose for him, "a handsome young woman" being "a kind of breast-work that I am afraid of"—another line that did not survive the transition from play to poem. But the "question" regarding the priority of Mary Chilton and John Alden remains something of a subtext, nor was it a trivial matter for Longfellow, who as a descendant of Alden considered he had a vested interest in the contest, which over the years had generated considerable antiquarian interest and some heat—at least in Plymouth.

IV

The first published account of the Chilton/Alden rivalry appeared in an early history of Plymouth written in the form of "Notes" by Samuel Davis, that living relic of the Pilgrim past who so impressed young George Ticknor with his anecdotal recollections. Appearing in *The Collections of the Massachusetts Historical Society* in 1815, Davis's antiquarian memorandums included the following item under the heading "Forefather's Rock": "There is a tradition, as to the first person who first leaped upon this rock, when the families came to shore, Dec. 11, 1820: it is said to have been a young woman, Mary Chilton" (174).

While noting that the story came from an impeccable source and opining that it was true to the circumstances of the occasion, a "young person" being eager "after a long confinement on ship-board to reach the land," Davis was content to leave it "in the hands of history and the fine arts." The editor of the *Collections* seems, however, to have been of a more skeptical turn of mind, for under this anecdote there appears a footnote that stressed the unreliability of oral traditions, the authenticity of which becomes very weak as the distance increases from the event. Yet whatever his reservations regarding the facts, the editor was content to leave the story in "the hands of the fine arts," if not history, "for the purposes of [which] a female figure, typical of faith, hope, and charity, is well adapted."

Despite its suitability for the arts, Mary Chilton's priority did not go unchallenged, and by 1815 a competitor was already in the field, backed by descendants of John Alden. The first published mention of Alden's candidacy appeared in a collection of epitaphs edited by one of his many descendants, the Reverend Timothy Alden, and published in 1814. In the third of five volumes, Alden gathered together a number of inscriptions garnered in Plymouth and Duxbury, and in the entry for John Alden, quoting "a certain communication" from "president [John] Adams," like himself descended from the Pilgrim cooper, he claimed for his ancestor that "he was *the stripling, who first leaped upon the rock*" (3:264). This claim got further validation in 1820, when one of the toasts proposed in Plymouth that Forefathers' Day was to "the venerable President ADAMS; a distinguished descendant of that vigorous youth who first sprang on Plymouth Rock" (*Columbian Centinal*, December 27).

On the other hand, there were those who maintained a skepticism less generous than that of the editor of the *Collections* of the Massachusetts Historical Society: in 1830, Francis Baylies published a history of Plymouth in which he covered the main points of the cohering saga, including the Compact and the Landing, and alluded to the Rock, "which now bears a consecrated character, to which pilgrimages are made, and to which the posterity of the pilgrims delight to throng, to call up the sublime associations with which its history is connected, and to view the spot which received their forefathers" (1:59). But Baylies felt that the order in which the Pilgrims arrived was a trivial matter, detracting from the sublimity of the Landing: "The honor . . . has been pertinaciously claimed for John Alden and Mary Chilton. It is now impossible to settle this question of precedence—neither is of any importance for the illustration of human character to know which it was—for such a purpose it is far more important to ascertain who it was that first embarked in the ship that was to bear the pilgrims forever from the civilized world."

Like many another plain dealer, Baylies was ignored. After all, if the Pilgrims were essential to the American idea of exceptionalism, implicit in this notion was the concept of exclusionism, which nourished the importance of determining just who among the Separatists was first ashore. In 1832, Dr. James Thacher brought out his long-awaited *History of the Town of Plymouth*, and as the physician who as a young man in 1776 had received such a patriotic jolt from standing on Forefathers' Rock, he gave it two pages in his book. Arguing that it was indeed the magic threshold of subsequent empire, by that late date a commonplace, Thacher was less sure regarding the rival claims made by "the descendants of John Alden and Mary Chilton" for priority of arrival, "since the closest investigation discloses no authority nor a shadow of evidence in favor of any individual as being the first who landed" (30).

And Dr. Thacher introduced another bone of contention, namely the question as to what was meant by "first ashore," since neither of the two contenders had been among the party of explorers who had first put in at Plymouth. Thus the event in question must have happened—if it did happen—after the *Mayflower* had "arrived in the harbor from Cape Cod." That problem solved, Thacher went on to repeat the "traditional anecdote" long regarded as correct "among the Chilton descendents," one of whom, as it turned out, was his wife, a tacit display of uxoriousness that left John Alden out of the picture.

When in 1834 Samuel Breck defended the character of Yankees before the Society of the Sons of New England in Philadelphia, he hewed to Dr. Thacher's line but elaborated somewhat upon it, Mary Chilton now becoming "a brave woman, one of the passengers on the Mayflower," and who, having made known her determination "to be the first to step upon the Rock," was courteously deferred to by the others in the shallop, they being "willing to indulge her," and thereby enabling Mary "to establish her claim" (15). In 1839, Robert Winthrop lent his authority to the story, but rather than repeat Breck's chivalric emphasis, he informed the New England Society in New York that the idea of a woman being the first ashore gave meaning to the Pilgrims' "pledge that there would be no retreating."

For Winthrop the presence of women among the passengers provided emphatic "assurance" that they had come "to their *home*," a key difference between the first colonists of New England and those of cavalier Virginia (*NESO*, 1:254). And in Charles Lucy's *Departure of the Pilgrim Fathers*, Mary Chilton was given a place of honor, posed thoughtfully under John Robinson's upraised right arm, with John Alden nowhere in view (see fig. 4). The tradition honoring Mary Chilton's precedence would have a long life, culminating in Jennie Brownscombe's contribution to the tercentenary event (see fig. 6), with its Botticellian figure dominating the composition, an American version of Mariolatry. For it would appear to be Mary, not Providence, to whom the kneeling figure of John Alden (identifiable by his carpenter's leather jerkin) is making his devotions, though Priscilla in her Pilgrim cap may be seen interposing herself between the two, sly touches suggesting that Brownscombe was quite familiar with the dispute. But the claims of Alden's descendants were not discountenanced by the claims of the arts, of chivalric gallantry, or of the need to establish the domestic nature of the Pilgrim errand.

When William S. Russell, who had succeeded Thacher as the resident historian-antiquarian in Plymouth, published in 1846 his *Guide to Plymouth, and Recollections of the Pilgrims*, he attempted to achieve one of those compromises that were much in the air at the time, incorporating Breck's chivalry with Thacher's authority: "It is not improbable that some rivalship occurred between Mary Chilton and John Alden as to which should first land on the Rock: and the young gallant doubtless yielded his claim to the lady—as might be expected of the modest youth, who afterwards became the favored choice of Priscilla Mullins" (181).

There then follows the local legend that would provide one of the most familiar stories in our popular literature, displacing the contest between the claims of the descendants of Mary Chilton and John Alden with a much more complex but not entirely unrelated rivalry, relegated by Russell to a footnote: "Tradition states, that Captain Standish, after the death of his wife, proposed a matrimonial alliance with Miss Mullins, the daughter of William Mullins, and that John Alden was engaged as the messenger to announce his wishes. But the lady, it seemed, was not so much enamored with the military renown of Standish as by the engaging address of the youthful advocate, dextrously hinted her opinion to that effect, by which course an end was put to all hope on the part of the distinguished military leader of the pilgrims."

This, then, is the bifold seed of Longfellow's play and poem, John Alden serving both as the gallant, Sir Walter Raleigh–inspired escort of Mary Chilton

FIGURE 19. Henry Bacon's *The Landing of the Pilgrims* (1877) (*top*), with a chivalrous John Alden handing a dainty Mary Chilton onto the Rock. By this time, Rose Standish had been displaced as the prominent female presence in the tableau of the Landing, a revision emphasizing not the pathos but the prevalence of the Pilgrims, which was essential to Longfellow's poem as well. The change culminated in Jennie Brownscombe's pyramid of the 1920s (see fig. 6) and reflected the burden of the many sermons and orations that emphasized the domestic "difference" of the Pilgrims.

Bacon's placing another boat in the background suggests that this is the "second" landing, following the first beachhead by Miles Standish and his exploring party. Used also by Brownscombe, the backgrounded vignette is remarkably similar to William F. Halsall's well-known painting, *The Mayflower in Plymouth Harbor* (1882), that hangs in Pilgrim Hall, represented here (*bottom*) by the artist's ink sketch of the composition, one of the very few that render a realistic profile of the low-lying, sandy beach. (Bacon painting courtesy Pilgrim Society) and the shy suitor of Priscilla Mullins. Russell's notion of this polite arrangement was sufficiently long lived to inspire the painter Henry Bacon, twenty-five years later, to portray an elegantly attired, rather delicate seeming John handing a petite Mary onto the Rock, an Edwardian treatment of the Landing whose genteel aspects were undoubtedly inspired by Longfellow's *Courtship*, even though, unlike the play, the poem contains no mention of Mary Chilton.

Longfellow, however, did not have to resort to Russell's guidebook for the story on which his poem was based. Timothy Alden, so instrumental in forwarding the candidacy of his ancestor (and Longfellow's) for the honor of being the first person upon the Rock, also rendered the first published account of the alternative legend, "which has been carefully handed down by tradition." His rendition of the story was cued by his mention of the death of "Rose Standish, consort of captain Standish . . . on the 29 of January, 1621":

> In a very short time after the decease of mrs. Standish, the captain was led to
> think, that, if he could obtain miss Priscilla Mullins, a daughter of mr.
> William Mullins, the breach in his family would be happily repaired. He,
> therefore, according to the custom of those times, sent to ask mr. Mullins'
> permission to visit his daughter. John Alden, the messenger, went and
> faithfully communicated the wishes of the captain. The old gentleman did
> not object, as he might have done, on account of the recency of captain
> Standish's bereavement. He said it was perfectly agreeable to him, but the
> young lady must also be consulted. The damsel was then called into the
> room, and John Alden, who is said to have been a man of most excellent
> form with a fair and ruddy complexion, arose, and in a very courteous and
> prepossessing manner, delivered his errand. Miss Mullins listened with respectful attention, and at last, after a considerable pause, fixing her eyes
> upon him, with an open and pleasant countenance, said, *prithee, John, why
> do you not speak for yourself?* He blushed, and bowed, and took his leave, but
> with a look, which indicated more than his diffidence would permit him
> otherwise to express. However, he soon renewed his visit, and it was not
> long before their nuptials were celebrated in ample form. (3:265–66)

Alden's account is more substantial and detailed than Russell's and may well have provided the source for Lydia Maria Child's version, in which fictional characters act out the story. It contains as well the observation that "it is said, how true the writer knows not, that the captain never forgave" his self-interested messenger "to the day of his death," a tradition that Longfellow revised for his own purposes.

What is clearly missing from Longfellow's poem, moreover, is the elaborate rigamarole involving Priscilla's father, which was included in the earlier dramatic version. This revision may have followed a hint dropped by William

Russell in his revised and updated guidebook, which appeared in 1855 as *Pilgrim Memorials, and Guide to Plymouth* and which attempted to keep its head above the waves of continued controversy. For one thing, in 1850 the same committee of antiquarians and horologists who had met to certify the correct date of the Landing felt it was necessary as well to clarify the matter of who landed first.

In effect echoing (without credit) Francis Baylies, they solved the question of priority by dismissing it: "When paying our ancestors the debt of gratitude, we should rather exclude, than encourage . . . doubtful traditions, as the ignorant are wont to heap on important events. Who first landed on the rock? was once an idle inquiry, thought to be met by the claims of Mary Chilton, till an equal competitor was found in John Alden;—as if each pretence were not childish;—as if we did not know, that Alden was not one of the twelve that first came in the shallop, that no woman was within many miles of this spot for several days, and that Mary Chilton, especially, was occupied in attendance on her dying father, who lived but two days after the little expedition left Cape Cod harbor" (4).

This no-nonsense opinion conveniently ignored the distinction established by Thacher between "two" Landings, the committee being made up of men for whom any compromise was impossible: "First" was "First," and no other need apply. But the committee's historically minded exclusiveness, like the sere decision regarding the correct date of the Landing, not only ran counter to the felt need to determine whose was the very first foot ashore but as a consequence led to more controversy, the details of which need not concern us here. They are in any event thoroughly covered by William Russell in his revised and updated guidebook, who held out for the priority of Mary Chilton, based on the authority not only of Samuel Davis but James Thacher. That the doctor's wife was a descendant of the bumptious young woman was a connection interpreted by Russell as not resulting in a conflict of interest but lending further authority to Thacher's account.

Of more relevance to the genesis of Longfellow's poem were some second thoughts Russell had entertained about the likelihood of Miles Standish's rush to matrimony so soon after the death of his beloved Rose. He also took into consideration the early death of Mr. Mullins, alluded to in the committee's report of 1850, which discounted that part of the story in which Alden asked Priscilla's father for her hand on behalf of Miles Standish. Russell's observations were put forward in the name of compromise, for the point he wished to make was not that the tradition was factitious but that the courtship had actually taken place at a later time than the one traditionally cited, which not only relieved Standish of the charge of unseemly haste but removed the problematic Mr. Mullins from the action.

Moreover, there being any number of Standishes then living in Massachu-setts, not a few named "Miles," Russell also sought to eradicate any suggestion that the captain was unsuitable material for courtship and marriage, and his final pronouncement is a marvel of circumlocutory prose: "We are justified in assuming that a 'flirtation' actually occurred at the commencement of 'good old colony times,' and that Cupid and Mars were in open conflict—that Miss Mullens was irresistibly attractive in person, manners, and character, since a military hero was fairly conquered, never before known to surrender, being severely but not mortally wounded; as a certain skillful lady, who came over in the ship Ann, in the year 1623, and became his second wife, was able to effect a perfect cure" (22–23).

Longfellow, perhaps following Russell's genteel remonstrances, moved the story well forward when he revised his play into the poem, so that everyone's thoughts of love take place in the spring of 1621, several months after both Rose Standish and Mr. Mullins were in their graves. Following the same logic, Longfellow also postponed the actual wedding for another suitable interval, so as to avoid offending contemporary sensibilities while ignoring the happy but artistically untidy fact that Standish was successful in finding a second wife shortly thereafter. That the friends are reunited even as the wedding is taking place is yet another revision of Alden's version, in keeping with the conciliatory mood of the poem, which is very much in the compromising spirit of Russell's account of these controversial matters. However it is also clear that Longfellow attempted through the power of his muse to displace the priority of Mary Chilton, who does not figure in the poem.

Yet the spirit of the lively maiden pervades his Puritan idyll, albeit transposed to the equally spunky Priscilla, a subtextual matter that reinforces the feminist emphasis. Again following Ann Douglas's lead, we can read Longfellow's poem as having been thoroughly feminized: not only is Priscilla, like Mary Chilton, made of courageous stuff, being an entirely self-directed young woman, but John Alden is by contrast a rather passive, even Hamlet-like young man. He is a thoroughly Unitarianized swain and quite different from that prickly cooper who was occasionally given to violent actions when the interests of his colony were affected, which is the John Alden that history hands down to us. In effect, it was Oakes Smith's Bertha and Earnest all over again, and, as we shall soon see, it was Longfellow's response to *The Scarlet Letter*, in which another strong-minded woman demands that her lover take action but to no avail.

V

Because of the popular emphasis on John and Priscilla, it is easy to forget how much of Longfellow's poem is devoted to Miles Standish's adventures among the Wampanoags. This includes the fiery captain's bold turning of

Pecksuot's knife against him, which at the time earned the mild reproof of John Robinson back in Leyden, who wished for a more tolerant handling of the native population. In this part of his "idyll," Longfellow depended on Edward Winslow's account of the first several years of the colony, available in Young's *Chronicles*.

But the record being scant in this early period regarding the character and activities of John Alden, Longfellow apparently felt justified in making him over into something he never was, not only a sensitive, even poetic youth, but a man of pen and paper, not hoops and staves, a scribe and hence literally a man of letters. The result is a picturesque and certainly intentionally comic contrast between the two suitors, the blustering, boastful soldier and the quiet, if mockingly polite, man with the pen, who responds to all of Standish's boasts with a smiling assent that sends to the reader signals of his superiority.

Longfellow increases this underlying difference by emphasizing the strain put on the friendship between the soldier and the poet when Standish's courtship goes awry, which figures in Timothy Alden's account. Where in Alden's version Standish retains his enmity life-long, in the poem the two men reassume their friendship, but not before the sensitive scribe, suffering from guilt for having "betrayed" his friend, thinks seriously of leaving America for England on the departing *Mayflower*. This provides a major turning point in the story and is an element that is entirely Longfellow's invention, central to his emphasis on reconciliation.

Like the realists of a later generation, the poet refuses his hero the privilege of a sentimental sacrifice dictated by a misguided chivalric notion, but he gives Alden's reasoning a basis derived from the Puritan propensity for "reading" events as signals from God. That is, John Alden sees all signs as telling him that his feelings for Priscilla are self-indulgent, that he has strayed from his duty, and that he must return to England as a gesture of self-abnegation, there to live a life of penitential remorse. But at the last minute, Longfellow has his young hero obey the impulse of his heart, not the stern dictates of Calvinist logic—has him become, as it were, a Unitarian—even as he stands poised on Plymouth Rock for departure.

We can detect in this an echo of Shakespeare's romantic comedies, which inevitably involve a misunderstanding and temporary separation of the lovers, and for her part Priscilla is a Pilgrim version of Rosalind, being an outspoken, plucky, self-determined young woman. This is the defining hint of the "strong-minded" feminists of the fifties, keyed by the most famous episode in the poem, in which she tells John Alden to speak for himself, not for Standish. Less well known is Priscilla's long speech about the failure of men to understand women that follows, which begins with an apology for having spoken out so boldly:

"It was wrong, I acknowledge; for it is the fate of a woman
Long to be patient and silent, to wait like a ghost that is speechless,
Til some questioning voice dissolves the spell of its silence.
Hence is the inner life of so many suffering women
Sunless and silent and deep, like subterranean rivers
Running through caverns of darkness, unheard, unseen, and unfruitful,
Chafing their channels of stone, with endless and profitless murmurs."
(*Works*, 2:325–26)

An epitome of silent suffering is Alice Archer in Longfellow's novel *Kava-
nagh* (1849), who represses her love for the hero even as her best friend becomes his bride, and who is conveniently disposed of by an early death from
consumption. This is the New England Nun, that familiar to sentimental
fiction to whom Emily Dickinson would give a revolutionary identity, suggesting that underground rivers have powerful currents. But Priscilla is cut to a
different pattern, and when Alden responds to her apology with some reassuring poetic hyperbole about woman being a paradisiac river flowing through an
oriental garden, she impatiently interrupts him:

"Ah, by these words I can see . . .
How very little you prize me, or care for what I am saying.
When from the depths of my heart, in pain and with secret misgiving,
Frankly I speak to you, asking for sympathy only and kindness,
Straightway you take up my words, that are plain and direct and in earnest,
Turn them away from their meaning, and answer with flattering phrases.
This is not right, is not just, is not true to the best that is in you;
For I know and esteem you, and feel that your nature is noble,
Lifting me up to a higher, a more ethereal level." (326–27)

Just who is lifting whom is problematic here. Certainly in her directness of
address Priscilla is in nineteenth-century terms a "modern" woman, nor is she
much lacking in twentieth-century forthrightness: "Let us, then, be what we
are, and speak what we think, and in all things / Keep ourselves loyal to truth,
and the sacred professions of friendship" (327).

Struck virtually dumb by these frank declarations, Alden has no choice but
to agree to their terms, and when next seen with Priscilla, some months later,
he is placed by her in a position symbolic of equality: "Show yourself worthy of
being the model of husbands. / Hold this skein on your hands, while I wind it,
ready for knitting" (340). As Alden soon learns, equality has its returns, for as
Priscilla disengages the yarn, she touches his hands again and again, each time
"sending electrical thrills through every nerve in his body." Longfellow is

seldom thought of as an erotic poet, but even Standish is to a degree given a sexual impetus, not so much in his attraction to the young Priscilla but, as Lawrence Buel has suggested, in his reaction to her refusal, when he rushes out and stabs his two Indians, a sublimated act of frustration.

Still, Longfellow makes it clear that Standish's violence is an expression of his fury over having been "betrayed" by his friend, a clear violation of the chivalric male bond. Alden, for his part, impulsively rushes down to the seaside with the intention of returning with the *Mayflower*: but then Alden catches a glimpse of Priscilla, "standing dejected" among the other Pilgrims gathered to bid Captain Jones goodbye, and "With a sudden revulsion his heart recoiled from its purpose, / As from the verge of a crag, where one step more is destructive" (320). Longfellow's figure magnifies the Rock by association, but Alden is rescued by history as much as by a change of heart, for as Rufus Choate had reminded his New York audience in 1843, "When in April The Mayflower sailed for England, not one Pilgrim was found to go" (*NESO*, 1:346). In any event, the Rock cannot serve as a point of departure for the Old World, for by Longfellow's account it is already a threshold to the future, "a doorstep / Into a world unknown—the corner-stone of a nation!" (319). And John and Priscilla will be the inheritors and progenitors of that future, much as their wedding procession is a "picture . . . of the primitive, pastoral ages," yet "fresh with the youth of the world," a pageant of promise suitable to an American Eden (348).

"Strange is the heart of man," Longfellow declares in considering Alden's impulsive resolve to remain with Priscilla, "with its quick, mysterious instincts!" (320). But the poet's own motive is something of an open book, for Alden, in declaring his decision to stay in America, goes on to assert, "As my foot was the first that stepped on this rock at the landing, / So with the blessing of God, shall it be the last at the leaving!" Neatly affirming his ancestor's priority with Alden's own words, even as he has him turn away from the Old World back toward the New, Longfellow uses this episode of his own invention as the dramatic high point in the poem. "Forefathers' Day," Longfellow would note in his diary on December 22, 1858, "the day when John Alden stepped ashore on Plymouth Rock" (Longfellow, *Life*, 2:329, 326). The poet was serene in the certainty that his Puritan idyll, twenty thousand copies of which had already been published, would certify the ancestral priority.

He was overly optimistic in this particular, but certainly his personal investment served to give added force to historical fact by concentering the Pilgrims' resolve in one man. And by giving Alden's decision a romantic aura, the hero's act evinces a triumph of the power of love that begins the process of reconciliation essential to the poem's resolution. As their ship sets sail for the Old World, the two lovers merge themselves with the unanimous decision of "strong hearts and true! Not one went back in the Mayflower! No, not one looked back, who had set his hand to this ploughing!"

In effect, the decisive moment further validates the Separatist impulse, but in a way quite different from the Departure and the Landing. For in John Alden's decision to stay in New England and marry Priscilla, he opts to preserve the unity of the little colony, the sanctity of which will be symbolically reinforced by their marriage. That is, beyond the personal equation, Longfellow's poem can be read as a quiet equivalent to the Whig celebration of national union, much as the wedding of John and Priscilla with which the poem ends is in the communal spirit Sarah Hale thought to promote by institutionalizing Thanksgiving.

Something more of the implication of Alden's decision can be derived from a comparison of the relevant sections of Longfellow's poem and Choate's oration. For Choate, choosing the return of the *Mayflower* in lieu of its arrival may have been dictated by the need to find a new trope with which to celebrate the Pilgrims, but because of the deadly effects of the intervening winter, the sacred Rock by his account is something of a gravestone. An icon not of pious triumph but pathos, it took its meaning from the Pilgrims who were buried on Cole's Hill behind it, a "symbol of what life had been to them . . . symbol also of the Rock of Ages on which the dying had rested in the final hour. . . . You might stand on that bank [above Plymouth Rock] and hear the restless waters chafe and melt against that steadfast base; the unquiet of the world composing itself at the portals of the grave" (345).

The imagery here suggests John Alden's reflections as he stands on Plymouth Rock, which dwell on thoughts of the "narrow chamber" in which he can lie with his secret shame, "in the chambers of silence and darkness." Choate's emphasis is not on self-indulgent sentimentality, however, but on the great losses suffered by the Pilgrims during the first year—which Longfellow bypasses—and he goes on to describe yet one more burial, in sight of the *Mayflower* as it lies at anchor ready to sail for England, a loss made even more graphic by the prospect of the ship's departure.

In the manner of Daniel Webster, Choate summons up a vision of that funeral, presided over by Elder Brewster, whose tones "were full of cheerful trust, and they went to hearts as noble as his own. 'This spot,' he might say, 'this line of shore, yea this whole land, grows dearer daily, were it only for the precious dust which we have committed to its bosom" (350–51). Thus even the dead contribute to the weal of the community, and as the dreary winter fades into the promise of spring, so " 'Our night of sorrow is nigh ended, and the joy of our morning is at hand. The breath of the pleasant south-west is here, and the singing of birds.' "

Much like Brewster in Croswell's play, Choate's Elder foresees that a mighty nation will spring from "our loins" and that "centuries hereafter" the populations of great cities "'shall come together, the good, the eminent, the beautiful, to remember our dark day of small things; aye, generations shall call us blessed!'" Their resolve strengthened by the Elder's words, Choate's Pilgrims are able to remain behind as their ship sets sail: "Without a sigh, calmly, with triumph, they sent The Mayflower away, and went back, these stern, strong men, all, all to their imperial labors" (353).

In Longfellow's version of the Departure, Elder Brewster is the central figure also, the traditional Old Man of popular prints and poetry—"Covered with snow, but erect . . . the hill that was nearest to heaven"—when in truth Brewster was only in his fifties and would live until 1644 (312). But instead of delivering prophecy, Longfellow's Brewster simply bares his "hoary head" and bids his people pray: "and they prayed, and thanked the Lord and took courage." There then follows a passage that bears a close comparison to Choate's evocation of Plymouth Rock, that memorial stone with an unmarked graveyard behind it:

Mournfully sobbed the waves at the base of the rock and above them.
Bowed and whispered the wheat on the hill of death, and their kindred
Seemed to awake in their graves, and to join in the prayer that they uttered.
Sun-illumined and white, on the eastern verge of the ocean
Gleamed the departing sail, like a marble slab in a graveyard;
Buried beneath it lay forever all hope of escaping. (322–23)

But the fatal grimness of the scene, with its marble slab of finality, which seems to echo the funereal emphasis of Choate's evocation, is somewhat alleviated after Brewster, "wrapt in a vision prophetic" that he keeps to himself, has led the Pilgrims back to the village. Left alone, John Alden stands musing "on the shore, and watching the wash of the billows / Around the base of the rock, and the sparkle and flash of the sunshine / Like the spirit of God, moving visibly over the waters" (323). In effect, Longfellow gives Alden the prophetic glimpse Choate grants Brewster, not of any specific future, but of a hope paired with the creation of the world, in America to be played over again. Once again, the poem's emphasis is on courtship and marriage, themes hardly in accord with the oratorical tradition but certainly in keeping with the domestic and Unionist emphasis of the Feminine Fifties, as well as an expression of the poet's intention to create a "Puritan idyll."

Under the Rock—Something for Bowdoin

In a word, old Roger Chillingworth was a striking evidence
of man's faculty of transforming himself into a devil, if he will
only, for a reasonable space of time, undertake a devil's office.
—*Nathaniel Hawthorne*

I

As I have already suggested, the central figure in Longfellow's *Evangeline* is a pluperfect example of the ideal celebrated in Pierpont's poem, less the childbearing necessity. A flawless vessel of maidenhood, Evangeline was the quintessential heroine of the day, sinless and tireless in her suffering as she wanders in search of her missing lover, Gabriel, the two having been separated during the diaspora of the Acadians. Her search ends when, an aged woman acting as a nurse in Philadelphia, Evangeline is reunited with Gabriel on his deathbed. Like Pierpont's Rose Standish, she is a heroine who exemplifies the ideal of True Womanhood, a thoroughly Christlike figure, whose deathbed reunion with her betrothed is a devout and not only sinless but sexless consummation.

We have seen how in Priscilla Longfellow provided Evangeline's counterpart, influenced by both the source of his story and changing attitudes toward women. Equally significant for our purposes, in Hester Prynne Hawthorne created a heroine who like Evangeline is a nurse and a woman separated from first her husband and then her lover, but with defining differences. Hawthorne had himself been inspired by contemporary sentimental literature and agitation for reform but with literally contrary results. Where Longfellow's chaste and unbelievably faithful heroine is a model of True Womanhood, Hawthorne's passionate and adulterous counterpart suggests that emerging antitype, the Strong-Minded Woman given to platform demonstrations of outspokenness, as well as bearing before her a badge of nonconformity to community mores.

Though like Evangeline Hester serves her community as a nurse, her pose of humble contrition is a mask beneath which she maintains a subversive defiance to the Puritan notion of penitence, declaring herself ready to flee with her lover if only he would bring himself to act. On the other hand, even as she appears to be a prototype feminist inspired by the example of Anne Hutchinson, with overtones of Stael's Corinne, Hester is a woman whose personal salvation comes through the agency of her motherhood, a conflicting emphasis that reminds us how much Hawthorne detested female reformers. Notably, unlike the Pilgrim women celebrated by Whig orators, Hester gives birth to a child who will not contribute to building a New World order but will marry into the Old World aristocracy. Hawthorne in this as in other ways anticipates the stories of Henry James, but in terms of his contemporaries he certainly seems to be working consciously against the specifics of the sentimental tradition as utilized by Longfellow.

We know that Longfellow got the story of the exiled Acadian from an anecdote first told to Hawthorne, who in private expressed resentment over the expropriation, but in his polite response to Longfellow's anxious inquiry, Hawthorne observed that had he told the story himself, it would have been quite a different tale. Thus it is possible that a condign motive lies behind the points of resemblance shared by *The Scarlet Letter* and *Evangeline*, but the matter did not end there, for there seems to have been a subtle genre warfare going on in the works by these very different graduates of Bowdoin. For if *The Scarlet Letter* may be read as a dark parody of *Evangeline*, in which the romantic convention of separated lovers is given a sardonic twist or two before the twain are finally united (as in Longfellow's poem) by death—"one tombstone serving for both"—so Longfellow seems in his *Courtship of Miles Standish* to be responding to his friend's dark romance, as if posing a corrective alternative to that Boston-based story by means of a tale derived from a Plymouth tradition.

For example, Longfellow has been faulted by strictly constructed antiquarians for having placed Priscilla's cottage at a distance from Plymouth at a time when the settlement was a fortified village, an anachronism abetted by having her spin wool gathered from sheep yet to arrive in the colony. As we have seen, Priscilla at her spinning wheel provides an element essential to the domestic and feminist dialectic of the poem, but her remove from the village as well as her characteristic activity may be read as analogous to the location of the cottage where Hester Prynne sits sewing clothes for her persecutors. Placed by the seashore at a distance from Boston, and with a view opening to the West, Hester's is a setting symbolic of both her penitential isolation and her personal independence. By contrast, placing Priscilla's cottage at a remove provides intensification of the idyllic element.

Thus John Alden, instead of simply stepping across Leyden Street on his reluctant embassy for Standish, must make his painful way through "the tran-

quil woods" where "bluebirds and robins were building / Towns in the populous trees, with hanging gardens of verdure, / Peaceful, aerial cities of joy and
affection," a wildwood scene of loving domesticity that mocks his thwarted
hopes and inner "commotion and conflict" (296). But it also serves to give a
pastoral threshold to his encounter with the virtuous heroine, who is in so
many ways Hester's counterpart. As John pauses outside her door, he hears "the
musical voice of Priscilla" raised in song—the familiar strains of a Thanksgiving hymn—an icon that evokes the singing as well as the essentially feminine
Pilgrim, as well as a happy alternative to the picture of Hester sitting alone and
forlorn at her needle.

Yet Priscilla's grateful song is her way of dispelling thoughts of home, the
same kind of memories that haunt Hester on her scaffold, of "the hedgerows of
England" that would be "in blossom . . . and the country . . . all a garden" (299,
301). This is the theme of exile preceding ancestordom that is central to the
meaning and resolution of Longfellow's poem, and it is quite different from
Hester's isolation, which is never resolved. To the contrary, it results in her
daughter finding a future in the Old World, not the New.

Though finally accepted, if not forgiven, by the Boston Puritans, Hester
returns after spending much of her life abroad to a solitary and celibate life in
the cottage by the seaside, while Priscilla becomes the fructive womb of American empire. Priscilla, like all of the Pilgrims, has sacrificed the comforts of
civilization in order to plant a new nation, while Hester's is a subversive errand.
Much as her sewing will feed the vanity of Boston heirarchs, in effect subverting
their faith, so as a nurse she tends their corporeal, not spiritual, needs, leaving
their souls to the care of the Devil, toward whom their earthly pride is inevitably carrying them, resplendent in the clothes she has made.

Alone in her cottage, Hester is visited by those thoughts that the Puritan
authorities would have regarded "as perilous as demons to their entertainer,
could they have been seen so much as knocking at her door." But in Longfellow's version it is John Alden who comes knocking at the door, the first step
of several that give Priscilla's isolation a happy and fulfilling conclusion, a
fairytale ending. Hester, on the other hand, continues on her lonely way, her
hope of effecting a glorious future made impossible by her sinful state, and
when in desperation she urges her lover to declare himself by fleeing with her, a
bold act matched by Priscilla's famous demand to John Alden, his resolve is
momentary and ends in a Hamlet-like and fatal irresolution, while Alden's
confusion is short lived.

This pattern of reciprocative response is reinforced by the historically incorrect but all-important wedding procession through the woods to Duxbury
with which Longfellow's poem ends. That John Alden eventually acquired a
bull as his portion of stock imported from England is a matter of record, but it

occurred some time after his nuptials, so that Priscilla's milk-white mount is yet another anachronism. It is also borrowed like the quest in *Evangeline* but to a far different end from Keats: in his wedding procession Longfellow combines the lovers pursuing and pursued on one side of the Grecian urn with the sacrificial progress on the other, resulting in a "picture" of the "primitive, pastoral age" that is at once suited to a New World landscape and has something of a pagan, pre-Christian look. Longfellow thereby linked the Pilgrim couple to their counterparts in Hawthorne's story about Endicott and the Maypole, for Longfellow's pair are central figures in a setting that translates to the New World the pagan customs of the Old. We can have no doubt as to what Endicott's reaction would have been had he encountered that procession making its way through the Plymouth woods, but he is kept out of the picture, allowing jollity, not gloom, to reign at least in that part of the empire staked out by the Pilgrims.

Endicottism has its representative in Miles Standish, not, however, the adversary of Maypoles but the Puritan captain who settled the hash of Pecksuot. Solidly anchored in the Pilgrim chronicles, Standish's bloody business among the Wampanoags, coupled with the jealous rage reported in Timothy Alden's anecdote, gives the soldier who was never a member of the Separatist Church a definably Puritan profile. Moreover, though the captain repents of his anger, having sublimated it by means of warfare, and returns from one of his campaigns against the Indians in time for the wedding, the circumstances of his appearance suggest the essential difference between Longfellow and Hawthorne in their portrayals of the Puritans. Rumors of Standish's death have preceded him, so that when he appears in the midst of the ceremony, "clad in armor of steel, a sombre and sorrowful figure," he is taken for a ghost, like Banquo at the banquet: "Is it a phantom of air,—a bodiless, spectral illusion?" (344). He is no ghost, but his silent presence at the wedding of John and Priscilla is less a fatal hand on the union than a signal that Standish is indeed "dead," being a relic of the old British ways that will be renounced in the brave new world.

The captain represents the "old-fashioned gentry in England," having "something of camp and court, of town and country conmingled"—he is in short (and he was) a squire, and perhaps a bit of a cavalier. Given the temper of the times we can even read in Standish a hint of the fire-eating spirit of the South—that spirit of "camp and court[house]"—while the gentle Elder Brewster in voicing John Robinson's remonstrance regarding Standish's un-Christian handling of the Indians provides a generally bland, even melioristic (shall we say Unitarian?) position, the pacific and reasonable New England policy toward the South. We may here recall Longfellow's "plea for toleration" in his *New England Tragedies*.

Brewster's is the sole "voice for peace" heard among the Pilgrims before the hotheaded soldier is unleashed against the native population, but we are intended to sympathize with it (313). Again, in his grim advent at the wedding Standish is not unlike Endicott appearing on Merrymount, but the pageant continues with his blessing, even as it makes him irrelevant to the American Eden. In Longfellow's version, once again, it is not pagan jollity but pastoral bliss that wins the battle for empire, yet Calvinist gloom is the loser, surely, much as the martial spirit gives way to the marital fact, with that Whiggish assertion of union at the end.

These intertextual patterns may simply be matters of coincidence, but they help to define two very distinct sensibilities as well as reinforce the Plymouth "difference" from Boston. Thus Longfellow was a celebrant of rural and domestic virtues as embodied in his progenitors the Pilgrims, while his Bowdoin classmate derived satisfaction from exposing the hypocrisies and morbid cruelties of his own Puritan ancestors. In Whig orations the dark side of New England's history was read as a sign of the progress made over the past two centuries, but Hawthorne gave the notion his own peculiar twist: "Let us thank God," he wrote in "Main Street," "for having given us such ancestors; and let each successive generation thank Him, not less fervently, for being one step further from them in the march of ages" (*Works*, 2:460). Again, where Hawthorne's Democratic politics show themselves is in his relentless deconstruction of the Whig tradition that the Puritans were the champions of religious and civil freedom, insisting that their notion of Liberty resembled "an iron cage" (449).

Hawthorne was hardly alone in savaging the Puritans, having before him the examples of Sedgwick, Child, Neal, and Whittier, for whom the Boston theocracy served as a bad example of persecutory zeal. But this does not discount Hawthorne's efforts to hinder the Whig campaign to rescue the Puritans (hence New England) from obloquy and glorify them as founders of the Republic. Then too, given his dislike for reform and reformers, Hawthorne could not have been moved to applause by the appropriation of the Puritans by Garrison and his crew, and in his campaign biography of Franklin Pierce, another Bowdoin classmate, he peddled the official Democratic line regarding slavery, which was the gradualist doctrine of allowing matters to take their own course.

"The good time is coming," promised Hawthorne's Democratic patron, the historian George Bancroft, in 1854, "when humanity will recognize all members of its family as alike entitled to its care . . . when man will dwell with man as with his brother; when political institutions will rest on the basis of equality and freedom. But this result must flow from internal activity, developed by universal culture; it cannot be created by the force of exterior philanthropy, and still less by the reckless violence of men whose desperate audacity would employ terror as a means to ride on the whirlwind of civil war" (*Miscellanies*, 514–15). Yes, Brothers (as Bancroft called his fellow members of the New-York Historical Society), a good time is coming—in its own good time.

Franklin Pierce spent his four years in office doing what little he could to speed "the Progress of Mankind" along—and it was predictably very little, for as a Democrat who shared the Whig fealty to union he temporized while Kansas burned. Pierce did reward his college chum with a consulship, which removed Hawthorne from the American scene for a critical period, spent in Great Britain and Italy, as John Brown rode the whirlwind of civil war into Harpers Ferry. The fruit of this sojourn was *The Marble Faun*, which reinforced Hawthorne's absence by establishing the tradition of expatriate fiction, a romance about which we shall be hearing more in the proper place below. But in the meantime we can further fill out the diagrammatic use of the Pilgrims during the critical period of the 1850s by reference to yet another Bowdoin graduate, Seargent Prentiss. One of those peregrinating New Englanders who found their way deep into the Southland, Prentiss stayed there, in his case undergoing a rather remarkable transformation, from a characteristic Yankee to a prototypical cavalier. Nor, as we shall see, is his example irrelevant to a consideration of the south side of Plymouth Rock.

We have already referred in chapter 15 to Prentiss's Forefathers' Day oration delivered in New Orleans in 1845, with its idiosyncratic use of Felicia Hemans's singing Pilgrims. But this was not the most important revisionary element in that address, which bore complex testimony to the contortions increasingly required of New England natives transplanted to the South. Though slight as a literary performance, Prentiss's oration was much praised and circulated in its day and provides a convenient third in a trinity of artifacts produced by graduates of Bowdoin.

This is not to single out Bowdoin College for special consideration as a progenitor of ideological conflict in antebellum America. But it is certainly worthy of note that such a small institution in Maine turned out in the 1820s an impressive array of talents, including not only Longfellow, Hawthorne, Pierce, and Prentiss but Calvin Stowe, a stalwart of orthodoxy but better known as the husband of the woman who wrote the book that started the great war. Coincidental surely, these biographical contingencies provide one of those paradigms in American life that illuminate, suggesting the multiform tensions among persons who shared origins in common yet went very disparate ways.

II

No one surely went further geographically or ideologically than did Seargent Prentiss. Born in Portland, Maine, in 1808, he escaped a family background of poverty by heading for Natchez soon after graduation from Bowdoin, where he was shortly admitted to the Mississippi bar, and by 1832 was practicing law in Vicksburg, then enjoying boom times because of its central place in the cotton economy. Prentiss quickly accumulated a considerable fortune, becoming well known as a trial lawyer not only in Mississippi but nationwide, and having entered politics, he as rapidly rose from the state legislature to the U.S. House of Representatives, where he virtually overnight gained a reputation as a fiery and highly effective orator. Prentiss remained an ardent Unionist and continued to campaign for Whig candidates after leaving Congress in 1839, his departure occasioned by his defeat in a run for the Senate.

It is perhaps useful to remind ourselves that in 1839 his fellow students at Bowdoin, Hawthorne and Longfellow, were only just beginning to attract national notice as authors, Hawthorne emerging from a decade of obscurity and hackwork with *Twice-Told Tales* (1837), Longfellow from the restrictiveness of an academic career with *Voices of the Night* (1839). Franklin Pierce had been elected to Congress about the same time as Prentiss but distinguished himself chiefly by a dual devotion to committee work and the social life of the capital, from which he was recalled in 1842 by his wife, to engage in a lucrative but exclusively local practice of the law in Maine, and seemed destined for a relatively obscure career.

But when Prentiss returned to Natchez in 1839, he had already enjoyed national prominence and had behind him a career that would have taken other men a lifetime to accomplish, suggesting that there was something about the South that caused a forced efflorescence on the part of New Englanders who settled there. From one point of view, Prentiss seems living proof of Sarah Josepha Hale's thesis in *Northwood*, as outlined by William R. Taylor, that Yankees with rural origins could make the transition to southern aristocracy so long as they did not succumb to indolence but maintained their Puritanic rigor and kept busy. But what happened to Prentiss over the next decade suggested quite a different fate, permitting a tragic reading of his meteoric rise.

According to Richard Boyer, Prentiss emerged during the late 1830s as a prototypical fire-eater and became the very incarnation of the proud, self-dramatizing southerner. Given his northern origins and the short time it took to bring him to chivalric flower, there must have been an element of theater in Prentiss's makeup, backed perhaps by an element of anxiety lest he be tarred with the Yankee brush (and feathered likewise). So deep dyed a "Southron" had Prentiss become that he was given a eulogistic chapter in Joseph G. Baldwin's *The Flush Times of Alabama and Mississippi* (1853), which was set during the period of Prentiss's sudden rise to fame and fortune. Even discounting a certain amount of help provided by Baldwin, it is clear that Prentiss was an example of a self-constructed personality that provides an important alternative to those far-flung "sons" of the Pilgrims who were celebrated by his contemporaries as carrying the spirit of New England into the South and West. And what he became in large part informs his oration, which provides an alternative version of the meaning of the Pilgrim advent.

Baldwin's sketches impose on his subjects, fictional or otherwise, a number of literary touches, and many references to Byron appear in his portrait of Prentiss, inspired not only by the lawyer's chronic limp, the result of a child-hood illness, but by his "classic features" and a "fiery and restive nature" (157). Byron's example inspired many memorable literary characters in American literature, from Cooper's tragic buccaneer in *The Red Rover* to Stowe's heroic mulatto, George Harris, in *Uncle Tom's Cabin*, but Baldwin shared the major-ity consensus in regarding Byron's influence as problematic.

Animated by "moral and personal daring," Prentiss was equally reckless with a hand of cards and a dueling pistol. He was gifted with an "imaginative and poetical temperament" that seasoned his courtroom performances, and Prentiss likewise evinced "scorn and deep passion" when attacking accused criminals in the dock. To these Byronic qualities Baldwin added Prentiss's "satiric wit" and a perpetual "craving for excitement," as well as his occasional "air of melancholy." Prentiss had a great love of literature, especially Scott and Shakespeare, the twins of genius who drew him into "the scenes of medieval chivalry," an "ideal world" and "mystic dream-land" that was inhabited by "crusaders and knights-templars" (156).

Prentiss, by Baldwin's account, absorbed the letter of chivalry like a dry blotter, yet underlying his fine qualities of personal loyalty, generosity, and boisterous good nature was an "intense bitterness," traceable to "imagined slights put upon him in his unfriended youth," as well as "angry passions," which were as much a part of him "as any other sentiments or qualities" (145, 156–57). Part Manfred, part Don Juan, part Ivanhoe, part Prince Hal (with a fiery dash of Hotspur), and drawing on his wealth of reading by way of informing his oratory and courtroom performances, Baldwin's Prentiss is a literary amalgam, as well as "a type of his times, a representative of the qualities of the people, or rather of the better qualities of the wilder and more impet-uous part of them" (144).

Prentiss's characteristic Yankee restlessness and ambition were mitigated for Baldwin by his impetuous good nature and underlying melancholy, but these combined qualities prompted the recklessness that was his fatal flaw. Like Byron's, his was essentially a self-destructive personality, his brilliance lacking the necessary fiber and backbone of a "*presiding spirit of Duty*" (159). That is, to the extent that Seargent Prentiss became a prototypical southerner, he lapsed from the high moral standard associated with the New England character by Sarah Josepha Hale and lacked just that quality exhibited to excess in Baldwin's other characteristic New Englander, the abolitionist schoolteacher Charity

Woodey. In sum, by making the transition from Yankee to cavalier, Prentiss had lost the mettle essential to the Yankee's stiff spine.

Baldwin's recollections of 1853 were rounded by the fact of Prentiss's death in 1850, at the age of forty-two: "What he *might have been*, after a mature age and a riper wisdom, we cannot tell" (161). Baldwin hinted that Prentiss had the potential to "command the loftiest heights of fame" had he lived, but the facts suggest otherwise. In 1845, his fortunes had taken a sudden downward turn, when a Supreme Court decision stripped him of his property, real estate held by a challenged title. It was this setback that mandated his move downriver to New Orleans, which promised advantages lacking in Vicksburg. Prentiss once again established a law practice, once again made money, but heavy drinking along with a chronic propensity for gambling reduced both his health and his fortune. It was not long before Prentiss exemplified that other kind of popular literature, the pious tracts citing the evil consequences of drink and addiction to the "green cloth" of the gaming table, a downward slide that ended with his early death.

It was shortly after arriving in the Crescent City that Prentiss delivered his Forefathers' Day address before the New England Society of New Orleans, obviously at a critical juncture in his career. Its importance to him is suggested by the fact that it was read from a manuscript, in contrast to the extempore orations that had given him his reputation for fire and brilliance. However, diligence in this instance proved counterproductive, for the address was not regarded as one of his best efforts, but it was much trumpeted, not only in New Orleans—where it was printed entire in a local newspaper—but in New England as well, where the address was excerpted in the public prints as essentially a local product, which in terms of conventions it was.

For in celebrating the "day dear to the sons of New England," who, wherever they may be, "gather in spirit around the Rock of Plymouth," Prentiss hit all the familiar stops of the genre, with an initial stress on the importance of a well-furnished past, that attic region we have identified as Memory's Nation: "The human mind cannot be contented with the present. It is ever journeying through the trodden regions of the past, or making adventurous excursions into the mysterious realms of the future. He who lives only in the present, is but a brute and has not attained the human dignity" (7). But as for the future, that glorious, if dim, prospect dear to Whig orators, Prentiss shrunk back as from some weird midregion, cloudy and dark and haunted by specters that flee at our approach: "We wander in its dim precincts till reason becomes confused, and at last start back in fear, like mariners who have entered an unknown ocean. . . . Then it is we turn for relief to the past, that mighty reservoir of men and things. There we have something tangible to which our sympathies can attach; upon which we can lean for support; from whence we can gather knowledge and learn wisdom."

Prentiss's anxiety may have been merely rhetorical, or it may have reflected his recent tumble from fortune with a concomitant uneasiness about his own future. For whatever reason, he insisted that "men cannot live without a past; it is as essential to them as a future. Into its vast confines we still journey today, and converse with our Pilgrim Fathers. We will speak to them and they shall answer us" (7–8). This is the traditional refrain of celebrants of Memory's Nation, yet Prentiss did not linger long among the Pilgrim Fathers but moved on to a recital of Forefatherly accomplishments that enriched the present moment, from the Compact to the establishment of free public schools. These are familiar Whig themes, as was Prentiss's "proud" comparison of the Pilgrims' conduct "with that of the adventurers of other nations who preceded them," especially the Spanish, whose cry was ever for "Gold!" (9).

The Pilgrims, instead of heading for a tropic zone, just such an "Arcadian bower" as Raleigh claimed to have found in Guiana, set out instead for a region that "would hold out no temptation to cupidity" (11). Given Prentiss's own history, this seems a strange emphasis, praising the Pilgrims for having settled on a "sterile shore" instead of heading as he did for more fertile ground, but it was traditional wisdom, as we have seen. And save for having their voices raised in song, Prentiss likewise rendered a conventional picture of the Pilgrims posed on "the famous rock which has ever since remained sacred to their venerated memory," their faces "glowing with a pious confidence which the sharp winter winds cannot chill, nor the gloomy forest shadows darken." It is an icon "full of moral grandeur," for "nothing can be more beautiful, more pathetic, or more sublime," a conventional Alisonian note.

Prentiss likewise accorded conventional praise to the industriousness of modern New Englanders, who with the "indefatigable enterprise" of their ancestors have "wrestled with nature till they have prevailed against her, and compelled her reluctantly to reverse her own laws. . . . Upon the banks of every river they build temples to industry and stop the squanderings of the spendthrift waters. They bind the naiades of the brawling stream, and compel them, like the sad daughters of Danaus, to pour unceasingly from their glittering urns the sparkling treasures of their crystal fountains" (13). Despite the familiar subject matter, Prentiss's perfervid diction and classical allusions betray his southern conversion, and when he wound up his celebration of the accomplishments of New England, he brought them all home to New Orleans, by means of a startling image that broke with the well-worn sentiments that made up the burden of his oration.

His final emphasis was intended to reinforce the Unionism of his auditors, who shared with Prentiss his New England origins and shared as well an abiding loyalty to the United States: "Here floats the same banner which rustled over our boyish heads, except that its mighty folds are wider and its glittering stars increased in number. . . . Accursed, then, be the hand put forth to loosen the golden cord of Union; thrice accursed the traitorous lips, whether of Northern fanatic or Southern demagogue, which shall propose its severance" (14). He went on to assure his listeners that any such possibility of disunion was only a figment of fear, for "the Union cannot be dissolved; its fortunes are too brilliant to be marred; its destinies too powerful to be resisted." He assured them also that in New Orleans would the Union find its "greatest triumph," its "most mighty development." This expression of local pride brought him to his final vision, not of the Landing of the Pilgrims but the arrival of their sons in New Orleans a century hence.

"Still wandering from the bleak hills of the North," these Pilgrim sons would find themselves on "the banks of the Great River." Then will they exclaim "with mingled pride and wonder, Lo! this is our country: when did the world ever witness so rich and magnificent a City—so great and glorious a Republic!" This bright vision of the future that Prentiss had earlier regarded as dark and uncertain was, like Webster's in 1820, given a century mark, and like Webster's Prentiss's was a Whig prospect of shining promise with foundations deep in New England's past. Yet the millennial vision was moved from Plymouth to New Orleans, a metaphorical shift of geopolitics that relocated the sons of the Pilgrims to just the kind of semitropical region Prentiss had praised the Fathers for having avoided. Plymouth Rock was thereby displaced by the banks of the Great River, the Mississippi, on which that "raw Yankee boy," according to Judge Baldwin, had experienced his southern epiphany.

Prentiss's oration was published posthumously, in 1851, both as a tribute to the speaker and perhaps by way of reassuring the citizens of New Orleans that the Yankee sons resident there did not share the outrage expressed by their northern cousins over the Compromise of 1850 but remained solidly in support of the Union. Had Prentiss lived and prospered (to answer Baldwin's conundrum), we may not doubt the direction the orations of that perfect pattern of a southern fire-eater would have taken during the next decade, nor is it likely that the sanctity of the Union would have continued to be his theme.

Some hint is given by the parallel career of Benjamin Faneuil Dunkin, who in 1819 had anticipated Webster by giving a spirited tribute to Plymouth Rock in Charleston, South Carolina, on the occasion of the founding of that city's New England Society. Despite Dr. Holmes's assurance in 1855 that the annual meetings of those far-flung societies "send a glow through the hearts of [New England's] distant children, and call their names and images fresh and warm into the memories of those whom they have left behind," other, more local associations tended to override childhood loyalties, at least in the South (301). Thus Dunkin, who by 1855 had become the chief justice of the Supreme Court of South Carolina, would go on to become one of the signers of the Declaration of Independence for the Confederate States.

As for Prentiss's prophetic displacement of the Universal Yankee Nation to New Orleans, his adopted city did not have to wait out a century for that event. On May 1, 1862, New Hampshire–born General Benjamin Franklin Butler entered the city under the guns of the Union fleet and set in motion a regimen not unlike the improvements made to Philadelphia by his namesake, albeit in much shorter order and with far greater severity. Butler's military presence was so heavy handed on southern gentlemen and ungallant to their ladies that it earned him the sobriquet "Beast Butler" and the Union army a reputation for arbitrariness and rapacity unmatched until Sherman set out from Atlanta to the sea. This was not what Prentiss had meant by the Union's "greatest triumph," but it was undeniably a massive assertion of Yankee initiative, giving New Orleans an improved system of sanitation even as it strung up one of its citizens for having hauled down the same star-spangled banner that Prentiss had celebrated as an abiding and transcendent symbol of nationalism. But then Butler was a graduate (like Elijah Lovejoy) of Colby, not Bowdoin, College.

III

It was, coincidentally, in 1862 that Hawthorne himself headed south, when he was privileged to travel into a zone that as everyone knew at the time was history in the making, the battle line of the Civil War, then located only a short distance outside the nation's capital. Though hardly a participant, he was nonetheless a witness, and what he saw and his ruminations about the scenes and people he encountered provide a curious and complex guide to a mind so oblique that it never seemed more than half made up. It was, moreover, this tour that would bring Hawthorne at last to the Pilgrims posed on Plymouth Rock, placing them in the context of events even as they unfolded, and the account of his trip provides an iconic as well as a narrative frame that is essential to an understanding of Hawthorne's idiosyncratic use of the Landing.

Hawthorne had returned from his sojourn abroad in 1860, the year in which *The Marble Faun* was published, and the major work undertaken after his return was *Our Old Home*, his collection of travel sketches set in England, which would be published in 1863, the year before his death. It is to that same nonfiction genre that "Chiefly about War Matters" belongs, yet as a narrative of events it is highly literary in form, for Hawthorne played the roles of both narrator and "editor" of his own work, this latter a censorious presence who removed objectionable material deemed "unpatriotic" and likewise supplied footnotes critical of the "author's" attitude toward the government and the war effort.

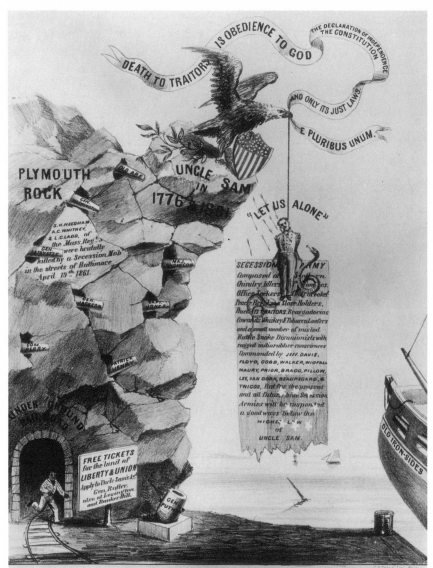

FIGURE 20. Plymouth Rock fights the Civil War, ca. 1862, a patriotic lithograph that, among many other themes, lends sanction to General Butler's hard way with rebels in New Orleans. (Courtesy American Antiquarian Society)

Styling himself "A Peaceable Man," Hawthorne thought by these means to effect a strategy that would enable him to be critical of the Washington scene and get away with it, even as he engaged in self-censorship while placing the blame on the "editor," whose interference reflected the kind of tacit repression of dissent that is characteristic of modern warfare. Though a product of Hawthorne's last and discouraged years, it is a small masterpiece of indirection, which reveals throughout his imperfect sympathies with the Union cause.

The occasion for the trip southward was an invitation from Horatio Bridge, another prominent Bowdoin friend, to visit him in Washington, an opportunity that the author welcomed, because, as he explained in the article in the *Atlantic Monthly* that resulted from the journey, there is "a kind of treason in insulating oneself from the universal fear and sorrow, and thinking idle thoughts in the dread time of civil war" (12:300). Hawthorne's journey took place as General George B. McClellan and the Army of the Potomac were making their slow way toward "the mysterious and terrible Manassas," but most of what he witnessed was well behind the advancing line, much as most of what he wrote was chiefly between the lines in terms of what he was really saying, which placed an ironic construct on his stated reason for leaving home.

Hawthorne's tone in "Chiefly about War Matters" was often openly facetious, like his early observation that one anticipated horror of the war was the "terrible idea" that it would fill the country with men bearing military titles into civilian life. Hawthorne glumly predicted that "one bullet-headed general will succeed another in the Presidential chair; and veterans will hold the offices at home and abroad" (393). He was right in this prophecy, for though the presidential process stopped with Grant, postwar society was studded with brevets galore. Still, in 1862 that would not have seemed to most Americans the most serious threat to the Republic posed by the war, nor given the seriousness of the conflict was such facetiousness called for, yet this air of mild ridicule characterizes many of his remarks throughout.

Of a similar sort was Hawthorne's tendency to aestheticize events, which promoted a certain distance, as when McClellan's effortless (if illusory) victory in driving the Confederate forces from Manassas reminded him of "old romances, where great armies are long kept at bay by the arts of necromancers, who build airy towers and battlements . . . and thus feign a defence of seeming impregnability, until some bolder champion of the besiegers dashes forward to try an encounter with the foremost foeman, and finds him melted away in the death-grapple" (304). Hawthorne could even find a comic element in McClellan's effortless victory, which, though "connected with the destinies of a nation, takes inevitably a tinge of the ludicrous," all that mighty preparation, followed by a plunge into "nothing at all!"

Before visiting the war zone, Hawthorne headed for the Capitol building, again with his equivalent Claude glass in hand, noting that "in its outward aspect, the world has not many statelier or more beautiful edifices, nor any, I should suppose, more skillfully adapted to legislative purposes, and to all accompanying needs. But, etc., etc." (305). These etceteras mark the first of the "editorial" excisions, credited here with removing the author's unkind characterizations of "some prominent Members of Congress," but not removed was the clear implication that whatever was removed provided a glaring contradiction to the stately and beautiful design of the Capitol building, with its Palladian outline an icon of Union incarnate.

Moreover, what Hawthorne as his own "editor" allowed himself to report on during his tour of the Capitol was a problematic sequence of encounters, which began with his meeting Emanuel Leutze, who was painting his great fresco that depicted the westward course of empire. The mural was an expression of imperial expansiveness inspired by the conclusion of the Mexican War and celebrated by the Democratic Party as fulfilling the Manifest Destiny of the United States. But that tremendous acquisition of western territory had contributed largely to the causes of the present conflict, a connection that Hawthorne did not comment upon. Instead, with a certain relentless cheeriness, he took consolation from the mural's celebration of "energy, hope, progress, [and] irrepressible movement onward," which gave hope "at this dismal time, when our country might seem to have arrived at such a deadly stand-still" (308).

Hawthorne also derived consolation from Leutze's own activity, "so calmly elaborating his design, while other men doubted and feared, or hoped treacherously, and whispered to one another that the nation would exist only a little longer" (307). But he also placed against the "cheerful augury" of Leutze hard at work "a sinister omen," noting that "the freestone walls of the central edifice are pervaded with great cracks, and threaten to come thundering down, under the immense weight of the iron dome,—an appropriate catastrophe enough, if it should occur on the day when we drop the Southern stars out of our flag." Once again, Hawthorne displays his readiness with allegory (here with a Poesque turn), but one wonders about the suitableness of the observation and the figure to the times and the occasion. And that phrase "appropriate catastrophe" seems once again to hold up an aesthetic frame—or lorgnette—between the viewer and the scene.

A similar frame is placed around President Lincoln himself, with whom Hawthorne met and conversed, who appeared to him "about the homeliest man I ever saw, yet by no means repulsive or disagreeable." Lincoln was deemed acceptable by Hawthorne because, though a "Western man," the lanky president seemed in appearance "the essential representative" of the classic Yankee type (309). Yet he could not rest entirely easy in the notion that this man, "out of so many millions, unlooked for, unselected by any intelligible process that could be based upon his genuine qualities, unknown to those who chose him, and unsuspected of what endowments may adapt him for his tremendous responsibility, should have found the way open for him to fling his lank personality into the chair of state,—where, I presume, it was his first impulse to throw his legs on the council-table, and tell the Cabinet a story. . . . It is the strangest and yet the fittest thing in the jumble of human vicissitudes."

Hawthorne's struggle to come to terms with Lincoln further confirms the suspicion that he was at heart a Jeffersonian, not a Jacksonian, Democrat, with imperfect sympathies toward those common men he was supposed to celebrate, especially when they were enabled through an inexplicable series of unexpected circumstances to move upward into places traditionally occupied by Great Men. Hawthorne might acknowledge Lincoln's progress from a "backwoods humorist" to "as good a statesman (to speak moderately) as his prime-minister," namely William H. Seward. But he could not shake his conviction that at base the president was unworthy of his post, lacking "cultivation" and "refinement." Though "honest at heart," Lincoln seemed to betray a certain Yankee slyness, having "a sort of tact and wisdom that are akin to craft." In sum, because Lincoln "looked" like a stereotyped Yankee, he was at best a transcendent version of Sam Slick, a "backwoods humorist" (says Artemus Ward) sudden hurled into high office. Hawthorne might have admired Lincoln as a quintessential American type, but in the end he was much more comfortable with Frank Pierce, who, if he was chiefly famous for having done nothing, did it handsomely and with style.

With the landscape of war as with President Lincoln, Hawthorne continued to view things in terms of aesthetic values, from the *Monitor*—"ugly, questionable, suspicious, evidently mischievous,—nay, I will allow myself to call it devilish"—to the newly heaped earthworks of Fort Ellsworth, the chief advantage of which was that they provided "a beautiful view of the Potomac" but whose "bare, precipitous sides" were an affront to the sensibilities. In time, Hawthorne consoled himself, the fort would become a "historic monument, grass-grown and picturesque," and as a memorial "of an epoch of terror and suffering," it would serve "to make our country dearer and more interesting to us, and afford fit soil for poetry to root itself in; for this is a plant which thrives best in spots where blood has been spilt long ago" (317). This is an observation that hastens to historicize and aestheticize a structure yet to fulfill its intended function, along the lines laid down by Archibald Alison.

Hawthorne got as close to the actual facts of combat as he would get when he visited the old engine house at Harpers Ferry, where he found his "Yankee heart stirred triumphantly" by the discovery that "John Brown's fortress and prison-house" had been made over into a prison for Rebel soldiers. Before entering the building, Hawthorne reflected on the character of the martyred insurrectionist who would forever be associated with that place, the "sturdy old man" who had "dealt a good deal of deadly mischief among his assailants, until they broke down the door." He admitted readily he was not "an admirer of old Brown, any farther than sympathy with Whittier's excellent ballad about him may go," a reference to the poem inspired by Redpath's account of Brown's Christlike kiss (327).

As the Whittier reference suggests, Hawthorne's feelings about Brown as with so many other matters in his narrative were deflected through literature. Thus he objected with orotund indirectness to the "apophthegm of a sage," the unnamed Emerson, "whose happy lips have uttered a hundred golden sentences," a reference to "that saying (perhaps falsely attributed to so honored a source), that the death of this blood-stained fanatic has 'made the Gallows as venerable as the Cross!' " This was the very phrase celebrated by Redpath and later excised by Emerson from his address in 1859 on "courage," perhaps at Hawthorne's heavy hint.

"Nobody," Hawthorne declared of John Brown, "was ever more justly hanged," an opinion that hardly placed him in the company of Emerson, Thoreau, and Phillips. Hawthorne was willing to concede that Brown "won his martyrdom fairly, and took it firmly," but he rounded off his judgment by stating his belief that "any common-sensible man, looking at the matter unsentimentally, must have felt a certain intellectual satisfaction in seeing him hanged, if it were only in requital of his preposterous miscalculation of possibilities." In his address on Progress in 1854, George Bancroft had likewise celebrated "reason" and "common sense," which he had opposed to the rash fanaticism regarding slavery that hoped to employ terrorism as an agent generating "the whirl-wind of civil war."

But in echoing Bancroft's language, Hawthorne's pronouncement on John Brown resonates as well with the logic of James Trecothick Austin, who had dismissed the martyrdom of Elijah Lovejoy as "the death of a fool." In obvious anticipation of the kinds of reaction predictable in Boston to such an opinion, the "editor" here observed in a footnote: "Can it be a son of old Massachusetts who utters this abominable sentiment? For shame" (327–28). As a conservative Democrat, Hawthorne could hardly have brought himself to glorify John Brown, and beyond mere political considerations, fanaticism offended his Enlightenment sensibilities, which valued reason and balance, just those intellectual qualities that found "satisfaction" in Brown's fate.

Inside the engine house, Hawthorne encountered a specter that was Brown's counterpart, a Rebel prisoner whose physical appearance sent Hawthorne into aesthetic shock: "This fellow's face was horribly ugly. . . . He spoke not a word, and met nobody's eye, but kept staring upward into the smoky vacancy towards the ceiling. . . . He was a wild-beast . . . —an unsophisticated wild-beast,—while the rest of us are partially tamed, though still the scent of blood excites some of the savage instincts of our nature" (330). This "wild beast of a man" had not only spurned the cries of a wounded Union soldier for help but had stomped him to death "as he lay writhing beneath his feet" (330).

It was a nakedly brutal act with not even a shred of the fabled southern gallantry to clothe it, a demonstration of a purely animal nature, that lowest common denominator in us all from which the power of reason keeps us free, the perpetrator a yahoo entirely lacking an iota of the "moral and intellectual development as we have received." This representative of humankind is difficult to reconcile with Bancroft's Democratic philosophy, having been endowed by Andrew Jackson with the power of a vote and having been handed by Jefferson Davis a uniform and a musket but remaining otherwise untouched by political progress in the South, that utopia of Jeffersonian and Jacksonian democracy.

Hawthorne solaced his readers, if not himself, with the assurance that one benefit of the war would be the liberation of "this class of Southern whites from thralldom," hence opening them to the kind of influences that would make them "capable of the degree of mercy and benevolence that exists in us"—meaning New Englanders—a transformation that would guarantee that the war had been waged for at least one good purpose, even if it was not one generally cited by champions of the conflict. Such a transformation would finish the process always central to the Democratic platform, elevating the common man to his proper place in society.

As for those people for whose sake the war was thought by some to have been fought, Hawthorne encountered a specimen handful, creatures of an even lower order than the uncouth prisoner in the engine house, "contrabands escaping out of the mysterious depths of Secessia," "pregnant token of a social system thoroughly disturbed" (318). He was favorably disposed toward these escaping slaves, to the extent that he found them "far more agreeable" as "specimens of their race" than their northern counterparts, but again his judgment was conditioned by aesthetic considerations: "So rudely were they attired,—as if their garb had grown upon them spontaneously,—so picturesquely natural in manners, and wearing such a crust of primeval simplicity (which is quite polished away from the northern black man), that they seemed a kind of creature by themselves, not altogether human, but perhaps quite as good, and akin to the fauns and rustic deities of olden times" (319).

This is not the primitivism that led Thoreau back again and again into the woods or thrilled Garrison when he discovered that Frederick Douglass actually sounded like Theodore Parker in blackface. Hawthorne's was a purer aestheticism, valuing those homeless ragamuffins for the same reason that Murillo painted their Spanish equivalents, finding their rags and poverty aspects of the picturesque. These tattered contrabands were much more attractive objects for purposes of literature than was Frederick Douglass in top hat and tails, suggesting that jolly rout that rescued Una in the wildwood or the maskers dancing with the young bride and groom around the Maypole.

Yet Hawthorne did voice concern for the wild folk passing him like some raggedy cloud driven in a northward direction by the winds of war. Unlike their poor-white equivalents, they could not expect to benefit from the conflict, and he was tempted to discourage them from advancing farther toward the North, where these escapees from the soft Southland would have to "fight a hard battle with the world, on very unequal terms. On behalf of my own race, I am glad and can only hope that an inscrutable Providence means good to both parties." This is that same great "Mediator," as Bancroft called him, on whom the Democrats had relied to solve eventually the problem of slavery. But John Brown had elected to speed the process along, and here was the dark fruit of his rash and fanatic gesture, hurrying northward to an unpromising but even now divinely determined destiny.

There is nothing here that is inconsistent with Hawthorne's political or artistic philosophy, cold as it might seem to modern readers, and we must grant him the accuracy of his prediction, however much Olympian in terms of disinterestedness. But what are we to make of the curious passage that follows? an anomalous digression that occurs about a fourth of the way into his narrative, and toward which we have been making our own slow way in following Hawthorne's track:

> There is an historical circumstance, known to few, that connects the children of the Puritans with these Africans of Virginia in a very singular way. They are our brethren, as being lineal descendants from the Mayflower, the fated womb of which, in her first voyage, sent forth a brood of Pilgrims on Plymouth Rock, and, in a subsequent one, spawned slaves upon the Southern soil,—a monstrous birth, but with which we have an instinctive sense of kindred, and so are stirred by an irresistible impulse to attempt their rescue, even at the cost of blood and ruin. The character of our sacred ship, I fear, may suffer a little by this revelation, but we must let her white progeny offset her dark one,—and such portents never sprang from an identical source before. (319)

This is the kind of fatal, patterned coincidence that is typical of Hawthorne's fictions, the husband of Hester Prynne being redeemed from captivity the very day that his wife is exposed on a scaffold for an adultress, or the pastor and the woman he took in adultery meeting by chance in the woods. Who cannot but admire the neatness of the arrangement here, which crowds into intimacy the sainted passengers of the *Mayflower* with the cursed race that they, had the

Pilgrims been allowed to return to the nineteenth century, would—in the view of Whittier, Garrison, Phillips, and Lowell—have dedicated their resurrected lives to free. Those are the "we" of which Hawthorne is speaking, a first person plural and editorial voice that in speaking for New England (and the readers of the *Atlantic*) surely did not mean to include such as the author himself and his very good friend Franklin Pierce.

Hawthorne's anecdote in effect conflates those two voyages of 1620 noted by George Bancroft in his history of the United States and elevated into such stirring prose by Robert Winthrop in 1839 with the intention of drawing a very deep line of demarcation between the purposes and consequences of the Plymouth and Jamestown colonies. But here the two ships have become one, and it is the *Mayflower* that serves as the vessel both of freedom and of servitude, that ark so sacred to the memory of the Pilgrims now converted to a dark slaver with its human cargo enduring the horrid middle passage made so graphic by Judge Story in 1819 and grandly denounced by Daniel Webster the following year. Had Hawthorne somehow confused the two ships? Or did he pick up this information in those tireless researches of his in which in imaginatively retracing one scholar has claimed to find so many clues to his mysterious parables? Or was this "historical circumstance" found, like a much more famous one, in a bundle of manuscript rescued from the attic of the Custom House or perhaps the Old Manse?

The answer is not hard to find. We need look no further than in Hawthorne's journals, where he recorded on September 22, 1854, a dinner party in Liverpool, at which he and Sophia met Monckton Milnes, Lord Houghton, who reminded Hawthorne of Longfellow in appearance and manner and who "is considered one of the best conversationalists at present in society." Among the gems bestowed upon Hawthorne that evening was this multifaceted jewel: "Mr. Milnes told me that he owns the land in Yorkshire, whence some of the pilgrims of the Mayflower emigrated to Plymouth, and that Elder Brewster was the Postmaster of the village. . . . He also said that in the next voyage of the Mayflower, after she carried the Pilgrims, she was employed in transporting a cargo of slaves from Africa—to the West Indies, I suppose. This is a queer fact, and would be nuts for the Southerners" (*Works*, 7:537). Nuts, indeed, and undeniably a very queer fact, made even queerer by Hawthorne's use of it in his narrative of encounter with the backside of the Civil War, where he elevated it to a metaphor of the power of sympathy to effect reform, which Sacvan Bercovitch has read as a miscegenetic, even incestuous figure, indeed as a summation of virtually all that Hawthorne ever wrote.

Well it may be that, and even more, but the bit of antiquarian gossip Hawthorne recorded in his journal is not a matter of fact but fiction. We know, and have known for almost a century, that there were a dozen merchant ships with the name *Mayflower* operating out of English ports in the early years of the seventeenth century, and one may indeed have served as a slaver, but it wasn't the one that carried the Pilgrims to the New World. That particular vessel—whose captain and owner, the redoubtable Christopher Jones, died upon his return from New to Old England—was eventually refitted by his widow for the Norwegian trade. Milnes was mistaken in his ship, and Hawthorne in his man, too easily accepting as historical fact this bit of impossible lore, even as he thought how pleasing the story would be "for the Virginians," for as a makeweight it would help equalize that balance of virtue claimed by the descendants of the Pilgrims. Toward that same end, in his revision of the journal entry for his narrative of 1862, Hawthorne changed the destination of that ghost ship from the Indies to "southern soil," which we may imagine (at least in the 1620s) meant Virginia itself.

"The character of our sacred ship, I fear, may suffer a little by this revelation," observes Hawthorne with a sadly resigned shake of his head, a clue surely to the intention of this passage, which has very little do do with the elective affinity between white people and black in New England but is essential to his use of the Puritan example through much of his fiction, which was to discount the Whig myth of New England's precedent and priority in promoting civil rights. That is, by purporting to explain the "irresistible" tie between the radical reformers of New England and the African slaves of Virginia, Hawthorne was actually and intentionally desacramentalizing the *Mayflower* by constructing a metaphor of amalgamation that he knew would come as a terrible shock to the celebrants and descendants of the Pilgrims, whose sympathies with black people were, like Hawthorne's own, imperfect.

But the facts were otherwise, not that they change Hawthorne's fiction, but since the fiction was validated, even warranted by the presumed fact, then we must look elsewhere for the source of that "irresistible impulse" to effect by war the abolition of slavery, "even at the cost of blood and ruin." His notion of a terrible Gemini, a Chang and Eng held by a fleshly bond, tells us much more about Hawthorne than about the abolitionists, and, once again, it tells us a great deal in retrospect about his own "irresistible impulse" where his treatment of the Puritans was concerned. Hawthorne was forever drawn to the notion of secret sins infecting subsequent generations, and May Flowers of hope were not his kind of blooms. He preferred those poisonous growths from Rappacini's garden, emblematic of misbegotten inquiry, yet another testament of man's fallen state.

So the anecdote pleased him, even beyond its political implication, the emphasis on the blood bond being yet another mysterious elixir with profound, even fatal effects, that situation central to his last, unfinished fiction. Indeed, what is this but one of those fables, complete in itself, and with tremendous implications for New England's sense of its own sanctity? There is in Hawthorne's version of the New World no New Eden, no New Promised Land, and certainly no Puritan idyll. There is only man, fallen man, relying on his God-given reason to make the best of a sinful world.

"No human effort, on a grand scale," declared Hawthorne in "Chiefly about War Matters," "has ever yet resulted according to the purpose of its projectors. The advantages are always incidental. Man's accidents are God's purposes. We miss the good we sought and do the good we little cared for" (332). It is this fatalistic view of divine design that permeates Hawthorne's writing, from "The Gentle Boy" to his notion of the benefits the Civil War would bring to the poor whites of the South, who were hardly the intended beneficiaries. It is a tragic but also a comic vision, finally, depending upon the context, and it hardly comports with the progressive Democratic dogma as explicated by George Bancroft, save in resigning all action to the dictates of the Divine Being as the grand Mediator of man's fate.

Here, once again, Hawthorne from beneath the shade of his editor's visor provides a contradictory footnote, insisting that "the counsels of wise and good men are often coincident with the purposes of Providence," surely Bancroft's point, "and the present war promises to illustrate our remark," certainly Lincoln's hope. But the "Peaceable Man" has already planted seeds of doubt, as he earlier traced the abolitionist enthusiasm back to the "fated womb" of the *Mayflower*, thereby discrediting it as a holy vessel sacred to the idea of New England's separation from the corruptions of the Old World and their perpetration in the New.

Toward the end of his war narrative, Hawthorne paused to express his pity for those persons, still to be found in Washington, who "have a conscientious, though mistaken belief, that the South was driven out of the Union by intolerable wrong on our part, and that we are responsible for having compelled true patriots to love only half their country instead of the whole." What is this but further evidence of the author's love of reason and balance that characteristically inspired him to express that Enlightenment spirit of fair play that is the positive side of the skeptic attitude? And in the penultimate paragraph of "War Matters" he pauses to express his pity for such "mistaken" persons, then resigns himself to the necessity of the conflict having to continue until peace "and a truer union" are established.

For war is a courtship of a rough kind, but perhaps a truer affection "and a quiet household may come of it at last. Or, if we stop short of that blessed consummation, heaven was heaven still, as Milton sings, after Lucifer and a third part of the angels had seceded from the golden palaces,—and perhaps all the more heavenly, because so many gloomy brows, and soured, vindictive hearts, had gone to plot ineffectual schemes of mischief elsewhere" (344–45).

At the last, then, with that willingness to put the best construct on all dark matters, Hawthorne, as with the pulling of a cord and the lifting of a curtain, becomes at one with William Lloyd Garrison and Wendell Phillips, evoking that old Pilgrim dream of separation, by means of which the North may remain pure with the undiluted light of Heaven, leaving the South to descend to a deeper Hell.

But here again the author steps in as his ubiquitous, officious "editor" and insists that this folly of accepting a divided Union—hence no union at all—is a sentiment equivalent to defining John Brown's execution as a logical, commonsensical act: "We should be sorry to cast a doubt on the Peaceable Man's loyalty." But isn't that just what the Peaceable Man has been saying, that one may number him among those "residents and visitors" in Washington who have deep reservations concerning the cause and outcome of the great war for the Union and who secretly feel that a well-adjusted scheme of secession might prove a better, less costly, and commonsensical solution? And wasn't that the purport of Franklin Pierce's notorious letter to Jeff Davis? And don't we find passage after passage to the same end in Hawthorne's own letters during the war years?

As late as July 1863, he wrote to his radical sister-in-law, Elizabeth Peabody, that "the best thing possible, as far as I can see, would be to effect a separation of the Union, giving us the West bank of the Mississipi [*sic*], and a boundary line affording as much Southern soil as we can hope to digest into freedom in another century. . . . You cannot possibly conceive (looking through spectacles of the tint which yours have acquired) how little the North really cares for the negro-question, and how eagerly it would grasp at peace if recommended by a delusive show of victory. . . . If the Southern statesmen manage their matters sagaciously, there may come a revulsion of feeling that would give them more than they ever asked" (*Centenary Edition*, 18:591). By 1864, Hawthorne himself was dead, fittingly, perhaps even justly while in the company of his beloved friend Franklin Pierce.

In that year there appeared in the *North Atlantic Review* an essay that was ostensibly a review of Hawthorne's collected works but which in effect provided a contemporary assessment of the man himself. Written by George William Curtis, a writer, editor, and agitator for reform who was, to put it briefly, everything that Hawthorne was not, the essay is a studied attempt to be fair to a man who, in 1864, was seen as standing on the wrong side of things as they were, if only because, by Curtis's account, he attempted that straddling act associated with the temporizers regarding abolition. Despite Curtis's attempts to do justice to the dead author, we find him expressing amazement that Hawthorne in 1860 could write in *The Marble Faun* (a book that Curtis regarded as "one of the most perfect works of art in literature") that there was in his native land " 'no picturesque and gloomy wrong, nor anything but a commonplace prosperity, in broad and simple daylight' " (346, 350–51).

Had not, wondered Curtis, *Uncle Tom's Cabin* already proved otherwise, or was "crime never romantic . . . until distance ennobles it? Or were the tragedies of Puritan life so terrible that the imagination could not help kindling, while the pangs of the plantation are superficial and commonplace?" (351). Asked Curtis of his readers, "What other man of equal power, who was not intellectually constituted precisely as Hawthorne was, could have stood merely perplexed and bewildered, harassed by the inability of positive sympathy, in the vast conflict which tosses us all in its terrible vortex?" That remains even today a very good question.

Curtis attempted to solve the enigma of Hawthorne's blindness to the tragedy of modern events by quoting from the reminiscence of a man who had accompanied the author on his southern tour in 1862 and who defined Hawthorne as having (in Curtis's words) a "mental constitution" that rendered him incapable of "moral condemnation": " 'Of two lines of action, he was perpetually in doubt which was the best; and so, between the two, he always inclined to letting things remain as they are' " (353). Thus, although " 'nobody disliked slavery more cordially than he did . . . yet the difficulty of what was to be done with the slaves weighed constantly upon his mind. . . . This ingrained and inherent doubt incapacitated him from following any course vigorously. He thought, on the whole, that Wendell Phillips and Lloyd Garrison and the abolitionists were in the right, but then he was never certain that they were not in the wrong, after all; so that his advocacy of their cause was of a very uncertain character. . . . In politics he was always halting between two opinions; or, rather, holding one opinion, he could never summon up his courage to adhere to it and it only' " (353–54). Here again is our Hamlet-Hawthorne, given credit for a tragic perplexity, that noble melancholy his contemporaries saw as essential to the man. But Hawthorne's literary response was characteristically to take refuge in irony, as demonstrated by the Manippean editorial frame within which he placed the record of his southern tour.

The testimony of Hawthorne's friend, to Curtis's way of thinking, provided the explanation of why "it was that the tragedy of an old Italian garden, or the sin of a lonely Puritan parish, or the crime of a provincial judge, should so stimulate his imagination with romantic appeals and harrowing allegories, while either it did not see a Carolina slave-pen, or found in it only a tame prosperity. . . . His genius obeyed its law" (354). Thus when Hawthorne "wrote like a disembodied intelligence of events with which his neighbors' hearts were quivering—when the same half smile flutters upon his lips in the essay 'About War Matters,' sketched as it were upon the battle-field, as in that upon 'Fire-Worship,' written in the rural seclusion of the mossy Manse," Curtis could equate this disinterestedness with "Donatello in his tower of Monte Beni, contemplating with doubtful interest the field upon which the flower of men are dying for an idea." Yet as a reformer and a man perpetually aroused to action by the wrongs suffered by humanity, Curtis was forced to admit that "as you see him and hear him . . . your heart, bewildered, asks and asks again, 'is he human? Is he a man?'" Here we have another very good because eternal question.

Why was it, Curtis went on to wonder aloud, that "while the Puritans were of all men pious, it was the instinct of Hawthorne's genius to search out and trace with terrible tenacity the dark and devious thread of sin in their lives?" (344). Thus in *The Scarlet Letter* there is "wanting a deep, complete, sympathetic appreciation of the fine moral heroism, the spiritual grandeur, which overhung [the] gloomy life" of the Puritans, resulting in "an imperfect picture" of early New England life (344). Why, Curtis asked, does Hawthorne render such a one-sided account of Puritan life? That is a question that can be answered, and it has been one purpose of the foregoing two chapters to do so.

That is, when in 1862 Hawthorne made his long-delayed excursion into Pilgrim territory, he brought with him the ideological burden that is sustained by so much of his fiction inspired by the Puritan example. If the colonists celebrated by Pierpont and Longfellow as a pluperfect instance of the domestic ideal could not be accused of the sins of their Puritan counterparts in Salem and Boston, neither could they be allowed to stand as stainless exemplars of the radical impulse in America. With that sly indirection that characteristically blurs moral judgments in his fiction, Hawthorne sought to discredit the Pilgrims by association with slavery.

He placed the Landing not only within the context of that story relayed by Lord Houghton but up against the modern instance of agitation for emancipation compounded by the problem exemplified in the ragged band of former slaves headed north. And this complex amalgam was located at a critical juncture in a narrative of travels that reveals throughout Hawthorne's imperfect sympathy with the Northern cause, expressing a covert readiness to recognize the Confederacy, indeed suggesting that such may be the inevitable outcome of what must be acknowledged an unnecessary because futile conflict.

Hawthorne in effect positioned himself between his Bowdoin schoolmates Longfellow and Prentiss. The first was a celebrant of the Pilgrims as the domestic spirit incarnate, bringing his cast to a happy resolution of their differences by a marriage that can be read as a validation of the larger, geopolitical Union, much as Whig orators celebrated the Compact as a draft of the Constitution and Plymouth Colony as a fledgling Republic. The second, while sounding all the typical themes of those Whig orations, ended by bringing the sons of the

Pilgrims to the banks of the Mississippi, suggesting that the future of the United States was, like his own, south of the Mason-Dixon Line.

As for Hawthorne, with his hints of miscegenation and even incest, he not only discountenanced the domestic purity celebrated by Longfellow but obliterated the exceptionalism essential to the Whig ideology. And he did this in a narrative that may end in a Washington riven with dis-Unionist sympathies and symbols—the cracks under the Capitol dome—but which definably carried the narrator and his covert ideology in a southward direction. In other words, like Seargent Prentiss, Hawthorne gave his version of the Landing a detectably southern accent, where Longfellow sought to reinforce the sanctity of the Pilgrims by celebrating their unanimity in staying put.

CHAPTER **18**

Cutting a Colossus from the Rock

They speak of monuments!
—*Rufus Choate*

I

In 1853, the Whiggish correspondent from the *New York Courier and Enquirer* who reported so favorably on the Plymouth celebration of August 1 took advantage of the occasion to record his impressions of the town itself. He found the streets of Plymouth "picturesque" in their crookedness, with a "wandering-about cast of character," suitable to the purposes of the Pilgrims who had laid them out, "without thought of future city mappings" (*Account*, 172). To a New Yorker, for whom the gridiron plan was the modern form of "city mapping," such haphazardness was quaint but hopelessly inefficient. Only Leyden Street was "somewhat straight," symbolic of Holland itself, "where everything is fixed and certain." Plymouth likewise contained a mixture of buildings that were elegant and those that shared the randomness of the streets, "quaint structures, shingled in all directions, as if that species of lumber in the time of our forefathers had been ridiculously cheap."

Overall, the effect was pleasing: "It is pleasant to see them thus mingled" (173). But finding one's way through such a haphazard maze was frustrating, for like many visitors before him, the reporter attempted to visit the Rock, a site equivalent in his mind to St. Peter's in Rome but one not as easy to find. The popular imagination, according to the reporter, thought of Plymouth as "a small and very old settlement, with a bold bluff point projecting out into the sea, and the Rock the most conspicuous feature of the scene" (175). But that was the "Plymouth of the mind," and instead of being a prominent feature of the landscape, the Rock had to be sought among crowded warehouses and narrow streets, pointed to not by "letters of iron or carvings of granite" but a sign chalked on a door.

The reporter found this not at all quaint but sacrilegious: "Before the citizens of New York would allow a memorial so precious to be buried up, obscured amidst wooden warehouses . . . 'our people' would sell the Battery and mortgage the Park." The chief purpose of the celebration of 1853, the reporter noted, was "to begin the noble enterprise of the erection of a monument, to be raised, they say, on the very Rock . . . where those noble-hearted men first felt the presence of that land which they . . . shaped into the land of order and law and religion" (176). And in the reporter's opinion, this "good work" would go a long way toward rectifying the present situation, at once calling attention to the Rock and instructing the sea "that thus far, and no farther, shall its proud waves go."

The reporter was, of course, referring to the bottom part of the Rock, which remained embedded in the earthen wharf that had been built in 1742 over the protests of Elder Faunce. That wharf, and the wooden structures surrounding it, were by 1853 in sad shape, Plymouth having long since declined as an active port. Most visitors were tourists, their pilgrimages facilitated, as the reporter noted, by "the construction of the Old Colony Railroad," before which the town "must have been a locality to find which a visitor must have been in earnest." If, as Thoreau pointed out, all that modern Plymouth had to offer was its Rock, by 1853 the town fathers had decided to do what they could to call attention to that fact. Out of this flurry of antiquarianism for the sake of the tourist dollar came the guidebooks of William Russell and the proposal to erect a monument over the Rock.

Thus the decline of the spirit of commerce that had built the wharves and warehouses necessitated the arousal of an equivalent spirit of boosterism, raising funds to tear down the buildings nearest the Rock and constructing in concrete form a celebratory gesture drawing attention to the site and the Pilgrims who landed upon it. There were other considerations involved in the building of the monument, as we shall see, but that tension between commerce classically considered and artifacts commemorating the past—early epitomized by Elder Faunce's remonstrance—was an essential part of the American scene in the nineteenth century and was eventually reconciled by conceiving of monuments as having commercial value in themselves as a lure that would draw tourists and their dollars.

At the start, as advocates of Alisonian associationism lamented, the United States had very little of historical interest to offer; what the country did have was a glorious future, which would be realized by constructing roads, bridges, and canals. These architectonic features, while evoking the great public works of the Roman Empire, were associated less with accomplishments of the Past than with future potential, the realization of which would prove to be the country's most promising field for expression, leaving the Past to Europe and its ruins. To this last class belonged monuments, the very outlines of which were reminiscent of European convention and were therefore anomalous in a country that, as Terence Martin has shown us, defined itself chiefly by its differences from the Old World. But by 1850, at least in New England, this attitude was beginning to change, and not only because villages like Plymouth began to think of commodifying Memory's Nation by means of souvenirs.

There appears among Timothy Dwight Alden's collection of epitaphs and related curiosa an account of a monument erected after the Revolution on Beacon Hill, which by its function and fate exemplifies the first phase of this American dilemma. Described by Alden as "a plain column of the Dorick order . . . substantially built of brick and stone" stuccoed over, this structure was erected in 1790, and placed on its top was a "large eagle of wood, gilt," to a total height of sixty feet (1:52). The column was square in shape, and on each of the four sides were "inscriptions, adapted to render it of use in commemorating the leading events of the American revolution, as well as an ornament to the hill, and a useful landmark" for purposes of navigation.

Of the inscriptions, the one on the east side is perhaps most to the point here: "Americans, while from this eminence, scenes of luxuriant fertility, of flourishing commerce, and the abodes of social happiness, meet your view, forget not those, who, by their exertions, have secured to you those blessings" (53–54). Among the earliest monuments commemorating the Revolution, this column was put up less than twenty years after Yorktown and in the year that, as one of the inscriptions recorded, Washington was first inaugurated president and the "Public debt funded," which last attested to the Federalist inspiration behind the erection.

But in 1811, as Alden recorded, "this column was taken down . . . and a great part of the lofty and beautiful eminence, on which it stood, has already been removed into the Mill Pond," a twin gesture of sacrilege and desecration to which Alden, as an antiquarian, should have objected but which he regarded as further evidence of "that enterprising spirit, which has ever characterized the Bostonians," and which would make possible the construction of "handsome accommodations for the increasing population of the metropolis of New-England" (52). Clearly, even in Alden's eyes, monuments were a sometime thing, being commemorations of a past that forever yields to the demands of the present as determined by the perceived needs of the future. During the first fifty years of the Republic, Boston was obviously conflicted regarding the sacredness of beautiful views enhanced by historical events, and dumping the top of Beacon Hill into a mill pond in order to facilitate real estate speculation is as concrete a symbol as one could find of Yankee priorities.

But by 1817, New England, host in 1814 to the Hartford Convention and unfriendly to President Madison's war, felt a need to assure the rest of the country that it was still very much a part of the Union. Boston greeted President Monroe with an enthusiasm matched only by that with which it later celebrated the return of Lafayette, and out of this renewed spirit of patriotism arose the Era of Good Feelings and the proposed but indefinite outline of a monument to be placed on Bunker Hill. In psychic terms, this structure would replace the missing masonry pillar on Beacon Hill much as it would replace in actuality a wooden column that had earlier been erected on Bunker Hill to the memory of General Joseph Warren by the Freemasonic brotherhood.

The building of the Bunker Hill Monument reinforced another, related phenomenon, for during the 1820s Boston became the spiritual capital of Memory's Nation, as the sequence of centennial observations associated with that decade testifies. Over the succeeding years, the city would be the scene of monument and memorial building equaled only by equivalent activities in the capital of the United States. That phenomenon would eventually have its effect on neighboring Plymouth, and we therefore need to review the history of the obelisk raised on Bunker Hill as a prelude to a consideration of the complex rationale behind the monument associated with Plymouth Rock. As with the emergence of the Rock as a regional icon, the Bunker Hill Monument was associated with Daniel Webster, who may be said to have risen in national prominence as the obelisk he twice celebrated was being built, much as his New England base was forever identified with the Pilgrim threshold to America.

II

The choice of Webster as the orator of the day at the laying of the cornerstone to the monument in 1825 was virtually without a competitor, given his success at Plymouth five years earlier and his increasing identification with Massachusetts. And he magnificently seized the day on behalf of Boston, for the stress of Webster's oration was on the special character of that city as the moral center not only of the United States but of the world. His speech was an ornate gloss on the most significant meaning of the monument, which was to certify the importance of New England as a region, despite its shrinking influence on the future course of the nation, an impotence that had been given new and shocking significance by the Missouri Compromise of 1820.

It was intended to serve as a concrete signifier of New England's importance in furthering the cause of the Revolution, raising a shape identified by Horatio Greenough as a pointer (or exclamation mark) declaring "Here!" By Webster's account, the monument on Bunker Hill was an omphalos that permanently located the genius of Liberty (hence the moral force of the nation) within the precincts of Boston. The implicit point was that Plymouth Rock was no longer sufficient for that purpose, a conclusion to which the leading citizens of Plymouth would themselves eventually come, a decision in part forced upon them by the fact of the competing monument in Boston.

We can find something by way of a rationale for building the great obelisk in the opinions then current regarding the function of national memorials, beginning with an essay on the subject by the son and namesake of Archibald Alison. The father's associationist theory of the Sublime would seem to have been abrogated in Boston by the destruction of both Beacon Hill and its monument, but it was reified by the subsequent erection on a hill determined as having more value as sacred soil than as potential real estate—perhaps because it was then located well outside the expanding precincts of Boston. And the younger Archibald—eventually Sir Archibald—provided the proper rationale for erecting the obelisk, his "National Monuments" having appeared in *Blackwood's* in July 1819 as the movement for the memorial on Bunker Hill was gathering momentum. The idea, once again as expressed by Horatio Greenough, was to enhance the historical associations of a particular scene by installing a permanent pointer, and the argument advanced by the junior Alison was certainly in keeping with this purpose.

A barrister and a purblind Tory, for whom the French Revolution was a disastrous mistake and its consequences proof of the corruptions humankind are heir to, Alison would in later years write a popular history of modern Europe that gave literary form to his conservative lack of vision. He was, that is to say, an equivalent Federalist, and his essay may be translated into terms relevant to the psychic condition of New England at the end of the War of 1812. It was general in its terms but specific in aim and was addressed to the proposal then current to erect a monument in London celebrating Britain's final victory over Napoleon. Alison's chief purpose was to promote the construction of another monument in Edinburgh, a counterbalancing memorial and a permanent reminder of the contribution of Scotland's armies to the great victory.

Beyond the immediate occasion, Alison's essay drew urgency from the Scotch patriot's fear that his native country would lose its historical identity by being amalgamated into a greater Britain: "There are few examples in the history of mankind, of an independent kingdom being incorporated with another of greater magnitude, without losing, in process of time, the national eminence, whether in arts or arms, to which it had formerly arrived" (74). Alison sought to "arrest this lamentable progress, and fix down, in a permanent manner, the genius of Scotland to its own shores." Where New England writers had difficulty implementing Alison Senior's associationist aesthetic because of the thinness of their own chronicles, the region's political champions could certainly translate Alison Junior's warning concerning the importance of monuments into terms relevant to the continuing expansion of the United States.

That is, what Scotland feared as a former nation-state New England feared as a region, and though Alison's discourse contained elements extraneous to the situation in America, it could be read for its central emphasis on the importance of monuments to reinforcing memory. Alison's thesis was contingent with his father's associationist aesthetic, and he began by evoking the power of monuments to assist "the influence of . . . national recollections," thereby preserving "the most valuable inheritance" of the "forefathers," a patristic patriotism with a definable resonance in Massachusetts: "The erection of a national monument, on a scale suited to the greatness of the events it is intended to commemorate, seems better calculated than any other measure to perpetuate the spirit which the events of our times have awakened in this country. It will force itself on the observation of the most thoughtless, and recall the recollection of danger and glory, during the slumber of peaceful life. . . . While it will testify the gratitude of the nation to departed worth, it will serve at the same time to mark the distinction which similar victories may win. Like the Roman capitol, it will stand at once the monument of former greatness, and the pledge of future glory" (76). Such logic certainly had force in New England in the 1820s, as the surviving statesmen and veterans of the Revolution dwindled away, a loss to which the coincident deaths of Adams and Jefferson in 1826 gave particular point.

But assertions of sectional integrity had problematic associations in the United States, as Washington's farewell address insisted. In reaching for architectonic terms in his stress on national unity—"it is a main pillar in the edifice of your real independence, the support of your tranquility at home, your peace abroad, of your prosperity, of that very liberty which you so highly prize"— Washington hinted at a function for monuments in America antithetical to what Alison would propose for Great Britain. Washington's farewell provided the main prop for an emerging Whig discourse, in which the sacredness of the Union was asserted repeatedly in the hope of preserving the country from the threatening specter of secession. This program was exacerbated by the increasing tension between the policies of the central government and the desires of the southern states, but which was as much sectional as it was a matter of state sovereignty.

That is, in promoting the idea of the Union as a "main pillar" supporting the nation's prosperity, New England politicians tended to locate the base of that central column near Boston, in the ground made sacred by the first battles of the Revolution. But these arguments, Federalist in origin, necessarily contradicted Washington's emphasis on the importance of sectional submission to the ideal of national union. In effect, in seeking to assert New England's hegemony, its champions worked against the very ideal of sectional subordination they also championed. Though built of granite, the Bunker Hill Monument was erected on an ideological fault line.

Coincident with Alison's essay was William Tudor's *Letters on the Eastern States*, published also in 1819. Tudor, a pioneer in New England's ice trade, the founding editor of the *North American Review*, and a die-hard Federalist, opined that "the erection of public monuments, the keeping alive the remembrance of great services, by the aid of the arts, is the reward most ardently desired by genius and heroic virtue" (182). The written record of history, Tudor declared, is not sufficient for the adequate celebration of great men, who "must be represented in visible memorials in our temples and public edifices; there they are recognized by every citizen, and not reserved for the observation of the student" (183).

Tudor was an exponent of associationism in the appreciation of scenery ("The total absence of ruins, deprives us of what is an abundant source of associations in Europe"), and his argument in 1819 concerning monuments was a logical extension of the senior Alison's aesthetic theory (322). In 1816, Tudor had ruminated in his *Review* concerning the proper form for a monument to George Washington—a national need that was about to be fulfilled in Baltimore—and during the same period had argued for building a substantial memorial on Bunker Hill, having purchased the site of the earthen redoubt as a show of good faith.

An Episcopalian, Tudor was no unqualified admirer of the Puritans, noting "the cruel character and appalling ferocity of [their] religious creed," but he celebrated without reservation the triumphs of the Revolution that filled the landscape around Boston with the kind of "associations that occupy the mind": "Here first began, in words and writing, resistance to oppression, and here that resistance was first sealed in blood. Every hill, every point of land around the town, is still crowned with the first breast-works of the Revolution. Lexington and Bunker-hill are parts of the landscape. It is the classic ground of American patriotism and valour, and the interest it excites, must increase with all succeeding ages" (76–77; 357–58). That phrase "classic ground," an epithet first made current by Joseph Addison's ruminations on the Italian landscape, would become a byword, even a cliché, in celebrations of Boston sites associated with the Revolution. It implicitly connected them with the Roman republic and thereby promoted the need for modern equivalents to ancient architectural erections—something more impressive than the mounds remaining from former earthworks.

Still, there were those New Englanders who felt that place alone was sufficient to evoke patriotism, that without public memory monuments were equivalents to the giant effigy in Shelley's poem, bearing a name whose meaninglessness was accentuated by untenanted desert sands. Despite the regional chauvinism that dictated the terms of his oration at the dedication of the Bunker Hill Monument in 1825, Daniel Webster held this latter view and rather brashly chose the celebratory occasion to air his opinion: "The record of illustrious actions is most safely deposited in the universal remembrance of mankind," Webster declared, a continuity of spirit of which stone structures are merely tokens and not the thing itself (*Writings*, 1:237).

Monuments, like eulogies, "belong to the dead," and for himself, Webster much preferred to honor the living, in terms that suggested that the memory of General Joseph Warren and his men is best preserved by means of oratory, not granite. Their names would continue to live in the hearts of patriots long after "this monument" had crumbled away, a point reinforced by the empty space before which the speaker stood, the structure in question having not yet risen above its foundation. It is quite possible that Webster felt that any such erection was a competitive kind of discourse, that silent stone was to be forcibly assigned a place secondary to oratory as the way in which to keep the Alisonian associations of place alive.

Moreover, much as Boston in 1811 had preferred real estate futures to stuccoed memorials and historic heights, so Webster in 1825 declined to rehearse the events that had generated the Revolution or to describe the historic battle the monument was intended to commemorate. Having praised the surviving veterans of the Revolution there present, and made specific mention of General Lafayette, the honored guest of the nation and the occasion, Webster chose to emphasize his favorite theme during those years, the "great changes which have happened in the fifty years since the battle . . . was fought." This was an emphasis on progress similar to that of his oration in 1820, and though it may have been influenced by the renewed cordiality with Great Britain during the Era of Good Feelings—which perhaps necessitated a tactful silence regarding the signal causes and events of the Revolution—Webster's stress on national progress was in harmony with an emerging Whig ideology.

Where in 1820 Webster's theme was localism with a national reach, in 1825 it opened to include an international perspective, and he pointed to the recent revolutions in Europe and South America as the heritage of 1776: "The last hopes of mankind . . . rest with us . . . and there is opened to us . . . a noble pursuit, to which the spirit of the times strongly invites us. Our proper business is improvement. Let our age be the age of improvement. . . . And, by the blessing of God, may [our] country itself become a vast and splendid monument, not of oppression and terror, but of Wisdom, of Peace, and of Liberty, upon which the world may gaze with admiration for ever!" (253–54). Webster's emphasis on progress, once again, put him in the ironic position of using the occasion to diminish the monument over whose dedication he presided, yet the oration of 1825 was (and still is) generally regarded as his finest forensic effort and was widely reprinted and excerpted in textbooks, including John Pierpont's reader.

In his subsequent address at Bunker Hill, delivered in 1843 at the completion of the monument, Webster would revise his attitude toward monuments, and not only because the massive presence of the finished obelisk made it impossible to ignore: "It is itself the orator of this occasion," he asserted; "the powerful speaker stands motionless before us" (*Writings*, 11:262). Yet his chosen figure not only emphasized once again the primacy of oratory but placed Webster between the obelisk and his audience. Though Webster declared himself moved by the monument's "silent, but awful utterance," he went on to impose upon it his own meaning, to use it in another of his ventriloquist acts.

"This column," declared Webster, with an obvious bid for analogous thinking, "stands on Union. . . . I know not that it would totter and fall to the earth, and mingle its fragments with the fragments of Liberty and Constitution, when State should be separated from State" (265–66). Neglecting the heroism of General Warren, Webster drew comparisons between the great obelisk and George Washington, for it shared the general's "uprightness . . . solidity . . . durability," the greatness of which stands out "in the relief of history, most pure, most respectable, most sublime" (281).

Webster's neglect of Warren was no slip of the memory but signaled his slide from a regional to a national emphasis, which was not only in the service of his presidential ambitions but for the sake of preserving the Union, by bringing Virginia through the agency of Washington into close proximity to Massachusetts. The easy confidence of 1825 was no longer available, for if the United States was the last, best hope of mankind, it was increasingly threatened by secessionist forces in the North as well as the South. The times necessitated a reminder that sectional divisions were anathema to George Washington, a stress on national union, not revolution and independence. We can never dismiss Webster's ambition as a determining factor, but his revision of emphases was not entirely subjective and self-serving: conservative sentiment regarding monuments in general would begin to shift for reasons other than those stated by Sir Archibald and William Tudor.

Webster's performance in 1843 drew the ready admiration of Ralph Waldo Emerson, who willingly bought the orator's strategic coupling of himself and the monument as symbols of Union—"There was the Monument, and here was Webster" (*Works*, 11:221). But the oration, like the completion of the monument itself, was made possible by Sarah Josepha Hale, who likewise regarded the great obelisk as a means of holding the country together, part and parcel of her Unionist novel, *Northwood*, and her subsequent efforts on behalf of Thanksgiving as a national holiday. Funds for the project were notoriously slow in coming, and it became something of a joke; the Panic of 1837 brought a halt to construction entirely, having wiped out the fortunes of many prominent New Englanders—including Daniel Webster. But the influential editor of *Godey's Lady's Book* devoted her personal energies and magazine to raise the money that brought the obelisk to its final height, taking care all the while not to tread on male egos—a way of walking that was second nature to Mrs. Hale.

Politically conservative, Hale in her steadfast nationalism was the female counterpart to Webster, and William R. Taylor has diagrammed the points of correspondence between the two Whig champions. But she remained in the Great Man's shadow, a subordinate place in keeping with her notion of True Womanhood, and Webster, for his part, did not step aside, a display of ego that was at least gender neutral: if he did not mention Mrs. Hale in 1843, neither did he allude in either of his Bunker Hill orations to Solomon Willard, the model maker and carver of figureheads who had designed and supervised the construction of the monument.

Chosen over other more lustrous competitors, Willard certainly deserved acknowledgment, not only for his pioneering use of granite as a building material but for having constructed the first railroad in the United States, used to haul stone for the monument from the Quincy quarry to dockside. In all respects he should have been celebrated by the celebrant of American progress, but Webster was obviously not interested in encouraging competition as New England's representative man and tended as in 1825 and 1843 to elevate persons already safely dead or nearly so.

III

By 1850, Mrs. Hale was hard at work promoting Thanksgiving as a national holiday, and perhaps for that reason she did not take up the cause of the much larger obelisk then rising in Washington, D.C. Its design was the creation of Robert Mills, a Jeffersonian Republican who shared his mentor's love of Palladianism but who made the transition to Jacksonian Democracy with ease, executing a number of projects during the 1830s that left his often heavy footprints all over L'Enfant's great plan.

Earlier, in 1815, Mills had designed for Baltimore a monument to Washington, a Doric column rising 160 feet as a pedestal for a marble facsimile of the general, just such a structure as William Tudor had thought best. Mills had also submitted a columnar design to the competition for the Bunker Hill Monument, as well as (he later claimed) a sketch of an obelisk as an alternative possibility. Willard admitted to having seen Mills's drawing, but only "in passing," and the matter is clouded by Horatio Greenough's claim that he too sent in an obelisk design to the committee, this at the age of twenty.

Mills's claim to priority does suggest that his design for the far more ambitious monument in Washington was intended at least in part as revenge for having been passed over in Boston. But then there is a detectable quality of envy traceable in the complex history of monument building in nineteenth-century America, inspiring men to mount erections ever higher, expressions of self as well as of regional and national pride. Nor was the design for which Mills received his commission in 1836 the simple and expressive tower now in place: the proposed Egyptian obelisk of 600 feet in height was to have a neoclassical portico around its base—a testament to Mills's lingering fealty to Jefferson—a platform sustaining a triumphant figure of Washington in a chariot pulled by galloping horses, which might be seen as expressing something more of Andrew Jackson's military style than that of General Washington.

This glaring anachronism was equivalent to Greenough's portrayal of a half-naked Washington in a toga, and it likewise shared considerable ridicule for its unlikeness, inspiring Mortimer Thomson's satiric epithet, "hideous in whole and in detail" (230). Matters of taste aside, the cost of the proposed design was the final determining factor, and by the time Mills died (in 1855), the portico and chariot had been sacrificed to economy. With structural revisions the obelisk eventually rose (long after Mills' death) to 555 feet only, sufficient, it was generally agreed by Congress, for the occasion. It was certainly high enough to dwarf the Bunker Hill Monument— which peaked at 221 feet— and towered like Washington himself in Webster's words "high above the column which our hands have builded."

The speaker at the laying of the cornerstone to the Washington Monument in 1848 had been Robert C. Winthrop, who in his address borrowed heavily from Webster's Bunker Hill orations, resulting in the kind of doublespeak for which Winthrop would become increasingly notorious: "Think not," he instructed in his closing words, "to transfer to a tablet or a column the tribute which is due from yourselves. Just honor to Washington can only be rendered by observing his precepts and imitating his example. . . . He has built his own monument. . . . This wide-spread Republic is the true monument to Washington" (*Addresses*, 1852 ed., 88–89). On the other hand, Winthrop had but a minute before insisted on the importance of the monument as an expression of "the gratitude of the whole American people to the illustrious Father of his country!" (88).

If, like Webster in 1825, Winthrop regarded any monument as inadequate to the occasion—"Build it to the skies; you cannot outreach the loftiness of his principles!"—like Webster in 1843 he regarded monuments as essential to the survival of the nation: "Let the column which we are about to construct, be at once a pledge and an emblem of perpetual union! Let the foundations be laid, let the superstructure be built up and cemented, let each stone be raised and riveted, in a spirit of national brotherhood!" (88). In sum, Washington might not need a monument (though he deserves one), but the United States does, which will serve as a reminder that "the Union, *the Union in any event*, was . . .

the sentiment of Washington," so that "the Union, *the Union in any event,* [will] be our sentiment this day!"

On July 4, 1851, in what would be his last public address, Daniel Webster spoke at the laying of the cornerstone to the expanded Capitol, an occasion that called for yet another revision in his attitude toward monuments. In effect, he recycled the themes Winthrop had borrowed from him, except we hear no more about the relative unimportance of stone. Union was the dominant theme—"Today we are Americans all; and all nothing but Americans"— and the occasion demanded yet another extended tribute to the greatest celebrant of the Union, George Washington, who by laying the cornerstone to the original Capitol had "laid his hand on the foundation" not only of the building but the nation, assisting in the "perpetuation of the Union and the Constitution" (*Writings*, 4:314). Webster was here in agreement with Sir Archibald Alison, who had noted in 1819 that a capital city gives strength to a nation by its very presence, by "its public squares and magnificent edifices," and the capital of the United States gains even more cohesion, in Webster's view, by the "immortal name" it bears (Alison, 414–15).

Webster pointed to the as yet uncompleted Washington Monument as a fit symbol of national unity and summoned up the Marble Man himself in the shape of Houdon's statue, through whose mouth Webster asserted the sanctity of "the union of the States," the theme of the general's farewell address and the senator's oratorical career (317). Webster still considered himself a likely candidate for the presidency, and the identification of himself with Washington was framed much to the same end as his use of the Bunker Hill Monument as a ventriloquist dummy in 1843. But the emphasis of this oration suggests that monuments were now essential to the preservation of mankind's last and best hope. Webster pointed also to the bridge over the Potomac designed (by Mills) and built by the order of Andrew Jackson, a structure of "ever-enduring granite, symbolical of the firmly cemented union of the North and South" (315). Clearly Webster had come a long way from Bunker Hill and 1825 and like Solomon Willard had come to put a great faith in granite.

Quite a different stress distinguished radical rhetoric during this same troubled period. Thus we find James Russell Lowell echoing Webster's earlier sentiments by insisting that "whatever man or event needs a pile of stones for memory does not deserve one, and whatever or whoever is worthy of such costly lapidary does not want it. Great men and great deeds live in history and song. The hero, the wise man, the artist, all build their own monuments, broad-based as continents, lasting as love and reverence" (*Anti-Slavery Papers,* 1:222–23). This pungent observation was written in 1848 and takes an added measure of meaning from the occasion, which was Lowell's objection to building the Washington Monument in the District of Columbia, still notorious among abolitionists as a center for the slave trade. While acknowledging that the Father of His Country had been "a slave-holder," Lowell took solace from the fact that Washington had never trafficked in slaves: "Let no shaft raise for so great and good a man in a market place for human flesh! . . . Let no man, abolitionist or not, contribute to rear an obelisk within hearing of the man-seller's hammer, and in front of which the wretched slave-coffle shall be driven to the hopeless South!" (222–23).

Politics aside, Lowell's main point was the one made by Webster in 1825, though he asserted it in terms less orotund than blunt: "The age which builds monuments is that which has seen heroism fairly underground," a mortuary moment when the "only duty left is to put up the gravestone and pay for the Latin" (217). In language evocative of Emerson, not Webster, Lowell observed that "the living heroic does not borrow of the quarry, nor hire the sculptor. It builds religions and states, not tombs. It commemorates the great actions by greater. When greatness has become traditional, then men make up the loss in stone and bronze." Lowell claimed that "Emerson's ode, simple and grand," would long outlast the memorial stone that had displaced the "sacred privacy of Concord field" (217).

But his greatest objections to monuments had the characteristic Yankee ring, being founded on the principle of utility: no monument is "truly beautiful" because all monuments are "useless," and are not in keeping with the character of the "Anglo-Saxon race," which has never "shown much aptitude for any architecture except that of colonies and states." Anglo-Saxons are practical and pragmatic, excelling in carpentry and constitutions but not the finer arts: "Our rivers swarm with the monuments of Fulton" (216). And the prototype of the Anglo-Saxon spirit set loose in America was the Pilgrim/Puritans, who upon landing began to build "a state and a commerce. . . . They made a religion hard, square, and unyielding, and then constructed square boxes to hold it where they might be sure to find it once a week. . . . From such a race architecture for architecture's sake was not to be looked for. They have built best what was useful and practical, as ships, railroads, and aqueducts. In all the United States there is not a beautiful church. . . . But we have handsome shops enough" (220–21).

There is something Thoreauvian in this perverse celebration of utility, but it also echoes the aesthetic principle for which Horatio Greenough is now best known and which comports oddly with the sculptor's often overwrought fealty to the neoclassical tradition. In celebrating a Greenough-like utility, Lowell attacked Greenough's Washington, on the grounds of both proportion—"Great men do not require to be represented as giants"—and Roman costume: "The clothes that were good enough for the man are good enough for the marble"

(219). But then Lowell felt that all "present statues of Washington are poor," for the same reasons that Columbus's achievement beggars the greatest of monuments, the Pyramids: "Columbus has a hemisphere for commemoration . . . yet who shall tell us what mighty conqueror pitched those huge granite tents upon the desert's edge. He has stone enough, but is forgotten" (216–17).

By 1851, the consequences of the Mexican War, including the Compromise of 1850 and the Fugitive Slave Law, made the building of monuments of whatever sort a futile exercise in the eyes of many conscientious Americans. Ralph Waldo Emerson called for a moratorium on monuments altogether, proposing that the money be used instead to buy the freedom of slaves: "Here is a right social or public function, which one man cannot do, which all men must do. . . . Was there ever any contribution that was so enthusiastically paid as this will be?" (*Works*, 11:208–9).

Emerson proposed a tax on chimneys and suggested that citizens give up their "coaches, and wine, and watches" and that churches melt down their silver communion vessels for the abolitionist cause: "The father of his country shall wait, well pleased, a little longer for his monument; Franklin for his, the Pilgrim Fathers for theirs, and the patient Columbus for his." Emerson had other suggestions, completely in syncopation with the generous beat of his heart, but perhaps not in coordination with the national pulse. If Webster's flaw was that he was too much in the world, Emerson's fault was that he was not.

In 1859, well ahead of the great men in Emerson's list, Webster himself got his memorial statue, placed on the State House grounds in Boston. Executed in bronze by Hiram Powers, it depicts the senator in modern dress, pointing with a scroll to a bound bundle of fasces that he holds in his left hand in the manner of a cane, deftly suggesting that even as Webster defended the idea of the Union as maintained by the Constitution, so he was as a political figure supported by it. If Powers's effort was one more attempt to affirm national union by means of statuary, it must be said to have had far less effect than did his *Greek Slave* on the course of events. By that late date, celebrants of union were becoming desperate, and on the Fourth of July, 1858, the orator of the day in Boston had expressed sentiments diametrically opposed to Emerson's.

"Where are the memorials of the great past?" demanded John S. Holmes. "Where is the tomb of the elder Adams, the Nestor of the Revolution. . . ? The grave of the great Jefferson lies still and unfrequented. . . . Monroe till this hour lingered in a borrowed tomb. The 'old man eloquent,' the Spartan son of this State [John Quincy Adams], slumbers beside his father, and shares the common forgetfulness of his greatness" (16). Of the power of national memory Holmes said nothing but stressed instead the public amnesia as he ran down the roll call of the great neglected: Sam Adams, Benjamin Franklin, William Wirt. "How think you the spirit of the past is to be preserved among us?" (17).

Holmes cited the examples of Greece and Rome, which maintained "perpetual tribute to the greatness of the dead" and accorded "lofty honors . . . to the living," but in the United States, "the very tomb of the Father of his Country is a thing of bargain and sale," thanks to "the miserly descendent of a great name," who dared set a price on Mount Vernon (17, 16).

Holmes quoted Sir Archibald Alison on the loyalty of the Swiss to the memory of " 'those who had died for their country's freedom' " and noted that the French had Napoleon's tomb, that Arabs devoutly visited the tomb of the Prophet, and England boasted that communal sarcophagus, Westminster Abbey, but as for Americans, "where are our memorials of the of the great Past? There is Faneuil Hall—there is Bunker Hill with its monument—*but where are all the rest?*" Holmes saw this national neglect, this "careless indifference to the associations and memory of the past," as a clear and present threat to the Union, "a painful illustration of the decay of patriotism among us" (15). The "commercial standard" had become the common unit of measure, putting a "market value" on men and principles, so that some states were now willing to reckon "the cost of maintaining the mother of us all—the Union of the American States" (14).

This last was in reference to certain secessionist grumblings from the Southland, the residence also of that niggardly descendant of George Washington, but Holmes's attack on the commercial spirit was clearly aimed at a target closer at home and is at least in sentiments at one with philippics mounted by a broad spectrum of radical pundits, mostly located in Concord. Holmes's objections came from a deeply conservative consciousness, as evidenced by his association of monuments with a reverence for the past: "The Present rests upon the Past—the Future rises out of it." This was a thought in harmony with Seargent Prentiss's emphasis in 1845 and with Webster's insistence late in his life that the Past, like Property, is the foundation and warrant of social stability.

Holmes reminded his auditors that during the Revolution patriotic Americans had sold their most precious possessions, "the old silver—the household treasure," donating them to the great cause, identified now with the building of monuments (14–15). But he stopped short of actually calling for such a drastic levy to fund public statuary, apparently not sharing Emerson's optimism regarding the spontaneous generosity of his fellow Americans. And where Emerson had called for a moratorium on monuments, Holmes demanded their erection as the first line of defense against disunion: "We must raise statues and monuments and celebrate the birthdays of the great men and great events of that [earlier] time, and fill the land with constant reverence for their greatness."

Beside Holmes on the platform sat Edward Everett, who had resigned from the Senate in 1854, worn out from ill health and the personal attacks on his integrity during the debate over the extension of slavery into Kansas and Nebraska. He devoted himself thenceforth to helping the "Southern Matron" (Miss Anne Pamela Cunningham) raise the funds necessary to purchase Mount Vernon from the "miser" referred to by Holmes, John Augustine Washington, so as to preserve it as a perpetual memorial to the Great Man. This was a project favored also by Sarah Josepha Hale, whose *Lady's Book* in combination with the *Southern Literary Messenger* had joined forces in 1855 in yet another scheme to save the Union, this time by saving Washington's home. Toward that end, Everett traveled about the country repeatedly delivering an oration he had originally composed in 1856 for the anniversary of Washington's first visit to Boston. He likewise took advantage of Boston's celebration of the Fourth of July in 1858 to urge that Independence Hall in Philadelphia be preserved: "Let every stone and every brick and every plank and every bolt, from the foundation to the pinnacle be sacred. . . . Let it stand to the end of time, second only to Mount Vernon, as the sanctuary of American patriotism" (*Eighty-Second Anniversary*, 93).

Whatever his failings in the eyes of Emerson, in 1858 Edward Everett was a one-man national trust, who thought in terms not of raising new monuments but of saving old buildings. Preserving these artifacts was essential to preserving the national memory, and before them posterity would "kneel in gratitude to the Providence which guided and inspired the men who assembled therein, to call its wall salvation and its gates praise!" And all these efforts to prolong remembrance in the United States were inspired by a unanimous sense on the part of conservative Americans that something solid was needed by way of a linchpin to hold the states together, that oratory could go only so far in saving the country from falling apart.

Everett, with Webster, had begun his career as a tireless champion of change in the name of Progress, but as the future grew dark with the threat of disunion and war, Everett, like Webster, turned increasingly to the past as a refuge and a bulwark. Like an exhausted swimmer hoping to find the means by which he could at least keep his head above a rising tide, he began to grope with his feet for something firm, a past made reassuringly solid by the continuity provided by monuments and relics. This was just the kind of public furniture associated with the Old World, valued in the New, however, not for the sake of its aesthetic potential but, in a sense not meant by Lowell, its utility.

IV

As in so many other matters, whether the agitation for revolution or abolition or the debate between Trinitarians and Unitarians, Plymouth was a microcosm of opinion in New England regarding the importance and necessity of monuments. In 1800, in his Forefathers' Day oration—included in part in Jedidiah Morse's history of New England—Judge John Davis of Plymouth noted that if no tombstones decorated the graves on Cole's Hill of the Pilgrim Fathers, originally left unmarked to conceal the number of deaths from the Indians, it was an absence not to be regretted: "They may be hidden from your view, lest reverence for your ancestors should generate to useless or debasing superstitions" (Morse and Parish, 378). This was hardly the argument of either Webster or Lowell in their protests against the need for monuments, but it does suggest that deep in the collective unconsciousness of New England there lingered echoes of the old Puritan stricture against idolatrous forms, to which Davis added the positive Puritan emphasis on education: "Having few visible memorials of men, so illustrious, in the indulgence of your grateful emotions, you are prompted to a study of their characters, and from that study you cannot fail of instruction." For such a study, Judge Davis pointed out, libraries were filled with "their writings," and the Forefathers likewise still lived "in their institutions," where those who wished to seek might find them.

In 1829, even as he celebrated Plymouth Rock as a visible memorial and the fit object of "homage" due the Pilgrim Fathers, William Sullivan felt that the regular celebration of Forefathers' Day should suffice for a monument to the founders of Plymouth: "Let the granite obelisk tower over blood-drenched hills; sublime in its elevation, sublime in its simple grandeur; fit emblem of that sublimity of character which it rises to commemorate," and likewise let a "noble column" rise (in Baltimore) bearing "the marble image of the SAVIOUR of his COUNTRY," but where the memory of the Pilgrim Fathers was concerned, "Let your anniversaries be the hallowed conservators of those works of gratitude" (42). Like Webster during this same period, Sullivan felt that monuments were a kind of noble irrelevancy in the United States, where public memory is the best memorial, periodically refreshed by celebratory occasions that keep alive the great names and deeds of the past.

In 1843, while on a European tour with his bride, Horace Mann visited Leyden, sacred as the place of the Pilgrims' departure for America, and found that "no monument marked the spot whence they departed. . . . Even in Plymouth, art has obliterated all vestiges of their footsteps; for the spot on which they first trod is now ten feet below the surface of the wharf, where commerce plies its occupation. But what need have such men of monuments? A monument to their names is but an object placed near the eye to intercept the real vision of their greatness. Not the gates of Leyden city, whence they departed from the Old World, not the Rock of Plymouth, where they entered the New, are monuments of their glory; but the free institutions of America, the career and the capacities of human improvement opened throughout that boundless Western World, are the monuments and testimonials of their worth" (Mary Mann, 214–15). Mann recalled his many visits to Plymouth, where, seeking to recover the spirit of the Pilgrims, he stood looking out "from the shore eastward, as it were to see them coming, for freedom's sake, to a strange and inhospitable shore," following "their desolate course" from Leyden, "a path which was illuminated only by the light of duty, and in which they were upheld only by the love of truth."

This open, seaward vista, uncrowded by man-made structures, seemed fit memorial to that lustrous journey and that shining band of brethren, but by 1850, the people now residing in Plymouth felt otherwise. With the reporter from New York, they had come to the conclusion that if the Pilgrims had been lighted to the Rock by duty, tourists seemed to need a more concrete form of illumination. Despite the growing pile of orations and histories and compilations of documents certifying the importance to the nation of the Landing, Plymouth at midcentury sensed a need for something more solid and substantial by way of a paperweight than the Rock, whose sacred associations seemed to grow less, not more, impressive with repetition, much as the stone itself had shrunk over the years, thanks to the efforts of tourists to obtain a specimen piece. There was, of course, the question of national union, which in Boston had inspired in conservative citizens a felt need for monumental structures, but in Plymouth it seemed more a matter of the town's own survival, threatened not by the rise of John S. Holmes's bogeyman, the commercial spirit, but its departure.

The idea of a monument to the Pilgrims dated in Plymouth from 1821, when the Pilgrim Society deemed that any surplus funds left over from the cost of constructing Pilgrim Hall be used for that purpose, an impulse clearly in sync with the ongoing discussions concerning Bunker Hill. But since the available money proved inadequate for the first project—it lacked a portico until 1834— the society had to let the one structure do double duty, and the Rock was hauled in front of the building that same year to emphasize the fact. In 1824, the gift of a guinea had been bestowed on the society by the will of a Boston gentleman to serve as the "nucleus" of a monument fund, but the adventures of that particular coin were limited to the society's coffers, and William Sullivan's comments in 1829 regarding the inadvisability of building a monument to the Pilgrims may have been a polite gesture excusing the inability of Plymouth to do so. In the mid-1840s, things began again to move slowly forward, the town of Plymouth voting a gift of land to permit the relocation of a store, which, according to William Russell in 1846, would leave "room to erect a suitable monument near the Rock, and to enclose the same with an iron railing" (*Guide*, 180). The purpose of the fence was to allow pious visits without facilitating equally pious "depredations," which were continuing to reduce the Rock, filiopietism having the effect of diminishing the object of worship in an exponential ratio to its veneration.

It should perhaps be pointed out once again that the "Rock" in question was the part left sticking out of a wharf, not the top half, which had been placed in front of Pilgrim Hall and was already protected by cast-iron pickets decorated with the names of the Forefathers. Russell, who was ardent in his attempts to further the fame of his town, noted in 1846 that "it has long been a subject of regret, that this memorial of the Landing has remained in its present situation, and there can be no doubt, that New England will cheerfully bestow the moderate sum required for an appropriate monument" (180). This is the kind of optimistic shove that is necessary to start things moving, but it was not until 1850 that the Pilgrim Society took formal steps in the right direction, empowering its trustees to raise the necessary funds.

The trustees required several reminders of the duty before them, but by 1853, in connection with the celebration on August 1 of the Departure from Leyden, they were able to report some very modest progress, including the celebration itself, designed to call attention to their fund-raising efforts. Yet it is notable that only one of the speakers that day made any mention of the putative purpose for the occasion, and the journalist from South Carolina notoriously diverted attention to his own proposal for a memorial to the dead Whig Triumvirate. Not even Sumner's "Finger Point from Plymouth Rock" was given an obelisk shape.

Perhaps because they were stung by this forensic indifference to their project, to which we can add the insulting remarks of the reporter from New York concerning Plymouth's neglect of its Rock, the trustees of the society set about to establish an orderly system of subscriptions with which to solicit contributions, and in 1854 a committee was appointed to "secure plans and to communicate with architects concerning a monument" (*Proceedings . . . Monument*, 11). A competition was announced with three hundred dollars as the prize for the best design, and by the end of 1855 an architect had finally been chosen. Both Seward and Wendell Phillips mentioned the plans for the proposed monument during their speeches on Forefathers' Day in Plymouth that year, in contrast to what must be called the stony silence of the speakers on Departure Day two years previous.

Seward "cheerfully" cast his own wreath "upon the tomb of the Pilgrims" and loaned his voice "to aid your noble purpose of erecting here a . . . monument to the memory of the Pilgrims" (4:184–85). Even while insisting that such a memorial was "quite unnecessary to their fame," Seward acknowledged that something concrete was "alas, only too necessary to correct the basis of the world's judgment of heroic worth" and then set about erecting an ornate rhetorical structure, which could serve for the observant as an apt demonstration of the cheapness of words when compared with granite blocks:

> Make its foundations broad as the domain which the adventurers of the Mayflower peacefully, and without injustice, rescued from . . . savage tribes! Let its material be of the imperishable substance of these everlasting hills! Let its devices and inscriptions be colossal, as becomes the emblems and tributes which commemorate a world's ever-upheaving deliverance from civil and religious despotism! Let its shaft rise so high that it shall cast its alternative shadows, changing with the progress of the sun in its journey, across the Atlantic and over the intervening mountains to the Pacific coast! It must, even then, borrow majesty from the rock which was the first foothold of the Pilgrims on these desolate shores, instead of imparting to it sublimity. (184–85)

This was an intricate dance typical of Seward, by means of which the purpose of the Pilgrim Society was forwarded while preserving the traditional notion that Plymouth Rock was sufficiently sublime unto itself, indeed would continue to serve as the source of the projected monument's power.

The remarks of Wendell Phillips later that evening were necessarily brief but hardly less grandiloquent and, as we have already observed in connection with his celebration of Plymouth Rock, were intended as gentle ridicule of Seward's pompous hyperbole even while observing the necessity of honoring the purpose of his hosts. Once again, Phillips brought to the occasion some seven years of rehearsal, by means of which the Garrisonians had sought to co-opt the Pilgrims for their own purposes, a priority that clearly dictated Phillips's strategy throughout his remarks. Where the orator of the day had called for a monument whose foundations would be as broad as "the domain" taken from the region Indians, Phillips proposed placing "one cornerstone on the rock, and the other on that level spot where fifty of the one hundred were buried before the winter was over," surely an architectural challenge, which he would on a subsequent occasion increase considerably by way of further radicalizing the monument, proposing "to put one corner at Harpers Ferry, and another at Alton" (*First Series*, 232; cf. *Boston Atlas and Daily Bee*, November 21, 1859).

But in 1855 Phillips's political purpose was revealed when he proposed writing two mottoes on the monument to the Pilgrims: "one, 'The Right is more than our country!' and over the graves of the fifty, 'Death, rather than Compromise!' " The first of these gave a purposeful spin to Seward's notion of the higher law, which Seward did not mention in his own address, and the second adapted Patrick Henry's famous (if apocryphal) alternatives to a repudiation of Webster's speech of 1850. As Lowell's essay of 1848 suggests, the radical temper is seldom inclined to the building up but rather the tearing down of monuments, and, as his subsequent modification in 1859 bears out, Phillips's proposal was chiefly intended as a rhetorical scaffold to which he could nail his slogans.

And yet in New York that same evening, John Pierpont, who shared Phillips's radicalism, was all in favor of a monument to the Pilgrims, lamenting in his ode that not even a "simple head-stone" reveals to the passing stranger the "resting place" of the Forefathers:

> Is not their place of rest
> Worth being noted,—consecrated, blest?
> O'er their neglected graves sea breezes pass;—
> We hear them sighing through the tall, dead grass;—
> Say—in that sighing, does the thoughtful ear
> No tone reproachful from these sleepers hear? (*NESO*, 2:317–18)

Citing "monumental piles" ancient and modern that provided precedent, Pierpont went on to call for memorial stones that would "tell the world" where the "sacred treasure of their garnered dust" was buried (318–19, 329). But as with Phillips, Pierpont was undoubtedly motivated by the current campaign by the abolitionists to co-opt the Pilgrims for their own purposes, which was the burden of his poem, and his stress on the neglect of the Forefathers in terms of monuments was but one more goad to the present generation to revive their radical spirit.

As if to prove that exceptions define the rule, Oliver Wendell Holmes that same evening disagreed with Pierpont and sided with Lowell, with whom he differed radically on radical matters. Lowell in 1848 had felt that "a pyramid heaped upon Plymouth Rock, holy with the footsteps of those who unlocked the future of mankind," would be both "trivial and obtrusive" (*Anti-Slavery Papers*, 1:217). And in 1855 Holmes insisted that "it is not by displays of art . . . that we can best honor the soil of Plymouth, and the memory of its colonists. The sea is their eternal monument so long as its blue tablet shall glisten in the light of morning" (*NESO*, 284).

This was in substance Horace Mann's sentiment, for where Nature so effectively honors the Pilgrims, there was no need for "Art to come, with her elaborate conceptions, to lead away the hearts of living pilgrims from the memory of those plain and rudely clad men and women." This opinion was clearly out of phase with the conservative wisdom of the day, and recalling the sensation Holmes would cause that day by his outburst regarding slavery, we can only acknowledge the extent to which the Boston physician and wit was at odds with those of his contemporaries with whom he was either personally or ideologically connected, which resulted in his taking contrary positions that he was later forced to revise or retract.

Thus, having disagreed with Pierpont, never mind Seward and Phillips, and evoked the deity in forbidding the scattering of the Pilgrims' "precious dust . . . in digging foundations for some ambitious Valhalla that is to make Plymouth the Mecca of *dilettanti*," Holmes performed a sudden about-face. He had, as he confessed, "seen the proposed plan . . . since these words were written" and now declared himself reassured, indeed struck with "admiration" over the artist's design (286). But he stuck to his argument that Plymouth was the wrong place for any such monument, not only because it would "intrude its academic graces between us and the one single, sad, glorious memory that hallows the bay and the hill" but because the town was "a plain village" that could not sustain such an effort. It should therefore "content itself with the plainest and most durable records to mark all its chief places of interest."

In 1848, Lowell had similarly ridiculed the District as the place to put the Washington Monument, not only because it was a center of the slave trade but because it was "such an out of the way place. . . . New York would be a more appropriate spot" (222). But the setting Holmes had in mind for "this jewel of art" was "the very heart of the great city of the Puritans"—Boston. "Ambitious ornaments" most properly belong in "the great centres of art and wealth, where the world can see them, and where they are in keeping with the surrounding objects." After all, he reasoned, Plymouth was "rich enough" with natural monuments.

The Pilgrim Society remained oblivious to the logic of Holmes's proposal—which was made after all (as Horace Greeley ungratefully noted) in New York—and were quite willing, as Holmes put it, "to spend half a million and have the result called the 'Plymouth Folly,'" rather than once again surrender their fame to Boston. Yet history bore out Holmes's prophecy, and as the recent study of the Monument to the Forefathers by James O'Gorman bears witness, both the work and its architect-artist share an oblivion made even greater by the ambitious scope of the project. Moreover, though it was colossal in concept and execution, the monument was to a degree ephemeral, being a creation dictated by the troubled mood of the 1850s, the iconography of which was a kind of frozen rhetoric tying the structure to contemporary terms of discourse.

As the sentiments of Seward, Phillips, and Pierpont attest, radicals of the day joined conservatives like Webster and John S. Holmes in calling for monuments, not however as symbols and certifiers of national union but as part of the program by which the Pilgrims were being converted to abolitionists. Thus the impulse motivating the Pilgrim Society may have been essentially conservative, even commercial, but the result at least in part expressed by its iconography a radical and hence a temporal agenda.

In effect that ideological fault line that underlay the Bunker Hill Monument had its equivalent disjunction in Plymouth, a deep division reflected in the contrary views of the cousins Wendell Phillips and Oliver Wendell Holmes, who thought of the monument in opposing terms, in accordance with their radical and conservative agendas. Theirs was hardly the only house divided over the dominant issue of the day, but their contrasting views toward the proposed monument in Plymouth certainly demonstrated the different directions that Federalism under different names could take.

v

Certainly the "artist" alluded to by Holmes was well qualified to give concrete shape to both the conservative impulse and its radical counterpart, yet because of this complex, even conflicted motive, the resulting design can hardly be said to carry out Holmes's insistence that such a memorial should "have for its two leading qualities simplicity and durability" (285). For in attempting "to rival the moral grandeur of the scene with the ideal beauty" of his conception, the architect of the monument realized Holmes's fear, that his creation would be the kind of "success which will be a misfortune."

The man in question was Hammatt Billings, who by 1855 had warranted Holmes's confidence by having in partnership with his brother designed or made improvements to a number of important buildings in Boston, including that Brahmin temple the Athenaeum. A classicist by training, as James O'Gorman informs us, Billings had yielded to the contemporary fashion for the exuberant Italianate style in architecture, even as he remained loyal to the axial line of the restrained Greco-Roman heritage. Much like Mills's lifelong advocacy of Jeffersonian Palladianism—but without the jarring consequences evinced in the original design for the Washington Monument (to which Billings with many of his fellow architects objected)—this skeletal neoclassicism does suggest a residual conservatism, at least in matters of art.

And yet, as O'Gorman also points out, Billings accepted a number of assignments that aligned him with radical causes, in 1850 designing a new masthead for the *Liberator*—preserving the iconic protest against the slave trade in the nation's capital while adding a millennial final panel that prophesied emancipation—and in 1852 he drew the illustrations for the American edition of *Uncle Tom's Cabin*. Billings did other work also for Stowe's publisher, John P. Jewett, who brought out a line of abolitionist and reform works, and the artist contributed illustrations for books advocating temperance as well. At the same time, Billings had proposed a gigantic memorial statue of Daniel Webster for the Boston Public Garden, suggesting balance and proportion in his politics as well as his public works. Yet over all he presents himself as a man sympathetic toward reform during a period when a large number of his fellow Bostonians were moving in a similar direction, and the design he proposed for the Monument to the Forefathers reflects that tendency, even as it retains an essentially conservative outline.

It was, moreover, an outline of considerable size, recalling the colossal Webster that was Billings's earlier conception, as well as anticipating a gigantic Minuteman he proposed for Lexington in 1859. Billings actually designed two monuments, the one a relatively modest canopy to be erected over the dock-side base of Plymouth Rock, but it is the other that was the most noteworthy, conceived not as a single shaft or column but as a human figure towering 150 feet above the spectator. O'Gorman certifies Billings's awareness of ancient example, but there was at least one American precedent—at least in terms of a proposed design.

In 1839, Henry A. S. Dearborn, a Federalist recently turned Whig, an enthusiast for internal improvements and a supporter of the idea for the Bunker Hill Monument, published a pamphlet calling for an imperial system of canals and rail lines that would unite the country. And in tribute to the man who had made the Erie Canal possible, Dearborn proposed the erection of "a colossal bronze statue of the illustrious DE WITT CLINTON" at the entrance to the canal at Buffalo, towering "a hundred feet high" and "holding aloft in one hand, a flambeau, as a beacon light, to designate, in the night, the entrance, and pointing with the other, in the direction of the route of the Erie Canal" (22–23). Dearborn was in all ways prophetic in his time, if not entirely in tune with practicality. That is, engineering skills were certainly in place in 1839 permitting rail lines and canals, but funding was not easily come by for a project of such a vast magnitude, and neither technology nor funds were available for the construction of a bronze figure of the size intended.

Billings, for his part, preferred to use granite, a material associated with the Bunker Hill Monument and (as Seward pointed out) the hills of New England, but more pertinently with Plymouth Rock itself. This last connection was expressed by the design of his monument, which placed the colossal figure of "Faith" on a towering pedestal with one great foot resting on a representation of the sacred stone. As originally conceived, the base was to be large enough to house a small museum, from which stairs would ascend to a platform at the feet of Faith, 80 feet above the ground, permitting a view of the major land (and sea) marks of Plymouth.

For the monument was not to be situated next to Plymouth Rock, which would be honored and protected by the granite canopy also designed by Billings, but was to be erected on a hill to the north of Plymouth village, which would serve as a vantage point in terms of both the view available and the visibility of the towering figure of Faith. With her foot on the replicated Rock, Faith was depicted as cradling a large Bible in one arm as the other was

FIGURE 21. Original design by Hammatt Billings for his Plymouth colossus (1855), with Faith standing on a stylized Rock. This engraving, as well as miniature, bronzed metal versions of the statue, were given to persons donating money to the ambitious project. As the lowest priced of the premiums, the engraving had a relatively large distribution, and the picture was likewise displayed in literature promoting the Forefathers monument. (Courtesy American Antiquarian Society)

extended upward as if pointing to heaven, a rhetorical gesture that bade the viewer "to trust in a higher power," a simple enough allegory and one that would have been powerfully effective had Billings been content to leave well enough alone.

But with that love for elaboration and eclecticism inherent to the age, the architect reinforced the central figure with four subsidiary abstractions seated against each side of the pedestal, depicting Morality, Education, Law, and Liberty, Puritan graces surely, but which rather much overloaded the effect of the monument. Moreover, there were to be entablatures depicting the hallowed scenes of the Pilgrims' progress: the Departure, the Signing, the Landing, and the Treaty with Massasoit—which last had recently emerged as a testament to the Pilgrims' pacifist inclinations, while Thanksgiving, as O'Gorman notes, had to wait for the Civil War.

Matters of taste aside, Billings's design considered as an iconoplastic exercise must be said to have expressed a number of themes and subjects voiced by the celebrants of the Pilgrims over the years, and as a very large woman standing on Plymouth Rock, the colossus gave massive validation to Samuel Davis's judgment in 1815 concerning the symbolic fitness of having Mary Chilton be the first Pilgrim to set foot on that sacred stone—women, as Davis noted, traditionally serving as personifications of the Christian virtues, Faith, Hope, and Charity. Two of the four supporting allegorical figures (Morality and Education) were also women, a gendered balance that resists ideological interpretation.

In iconic language the ancillary figures in Billings's design were likewise conventional save in one revealing respect: his conception of Liberty departs radically from the standard female figure with pole and liberty cap. Billings used a sitting male, wearing a Roman helmet and breastplate, with the added touch of a lion's pelt thrown over his shoulder, a traditional emblem of popular (i.e., Republican) power. With drawn sword and wearing manacles, from which dangle segments of a broken chain, the figure suggests Spartacus, the slave who led a revolt in ancient Rome. The hero of Robert Montgomery Bird's immensely popular play *The Gladiator* (1831), which as Curtis Dahl has suggested resonates with Nat Turner's rebellion, Spartacus was both a familiar and a provocative figure by 1855.

The sculptor Thomas Crawford was engaged at the time in a dispute with the secretary of war, Jefferson Davis, over the design of the headgear worn by the bronze statue intended to grace the Capitol dome. Crawford had given his "Armed Liberty" the traditional liberty (or Phrygian) cap, worn by freed Roman slaves as a badge of their emancipation, but the secretary objected that the symbol was irrelevant to freeborn Americans. His was a standpoint that conveniently ignored an entire class of "Americans" for whom the idea of liberty was

FIGURE 22. The monument as completed (*left*), considerably reduced from the original design and with a correspondingly diminished Rock, barely visible as a footrest. Billings's unique depiction of Liberty (*right*) has a definably Spartacus look, and the epauletlike object on his right shoulder is the paw of a lion's pelt, ancient symbol of republicanism. (Photographs by Alice H. Seelye)

(as Davis presumably thought) at best irrelevant and at worse a cause of discontent, even rebellion. Crawford capitulated and gave Liberty a helmet decorated with an eagle's head and feathers, inspiring interpretive confusion ever since, the final version having from the ground a distinctly Indian look, suggesting Pocahontas or the Indian Queen, icons perhaps not incidentally sacred to southern origins.

On August 2, 1859, celebrants gathered in Plymouth to lay the cornerstones to Billings's two monuments, an occasion that as in 1853 honored the Departure from Leyden and an anniversary that, as N. P. Willis had predicted, would increasingly be associated with festivities honoring the Pilgrims. Both local newspapers, the *Old Colony Memorial* (Whig/Republican) and the *Plymouth Rock* (Democrat), set aside their political differences to promote the affair and put out jointly a special issue describing the parades and decorations and a description of Billings's proposed monument. Public opinion was clearly in favor of the project—to the extent that it was reflected in the two newspapers—

the *Memorial* in particular remarking on the necessity of promoting Plymouth as a tourist center, an end that the colossus would surely forward. The speakers invited for the occasion were necessarily enthusiasts for the monument idea and as in 1853 seem to have been chosen to represent a fair range of geopolitical locations as well as a generally liberal cast of mind.

This happy uniformity was perhaps best expressed by Governor Salmon P. Chase of Ohio, who was thought of at the time as a potential Republican candidate for the presidency. Chase revealed his Whig roots by speaking in generous, Unionist terms and proposed the erection of a matching monument in Jamestown, which would assure the world "we are all brethren of a common Union, and mean to maintain 'Liberty and Union,' one and inseparable, now and forever," a self-conscious echo of Webster's speech against nullification in 1830 that drew "prolonged and enthusiastic applause" (*Illustrated Pilgrim Memorial*, 37). Only John P. Hale—the former Democrat, Free-Soiler, and Liberty Party man, now the Republican senator of New Hampshire—sounded a radical note, perhaps to rectify what Garrison had regarded as his sin of omission when he had spoken in Plymouth in 1853 with no open reference to the burning issue of the day.

"Why," he wanted to know, "have we met here to build a monument to the Pilgrims?" Wasn't Plymouth monument enough? Wasn't Massachusetts? Was not "all of New England a great living, breathing, speaking monument to the Pilgrims?" These, of course, were leading questions, which Hale used as a springboard for a daring display of verbal acrobatics:

> I do not know what is in the hearts of the rest of you, but I will tell you what is in my own. I want the monument, notwithstanding; and if we had more such living monuments, I should say of this monumental stone, let it rise! And why? I want it raised as a monument to the memory of the past, a monument to the present, and an eternal provocative to the future. (Loud applause.) I know there are some men who think that this agitation, which was introduced by the great principles of the Pilgrim Fathers of New England, has gone far enough. There are some timid conservative friends, worried to death by the agitation which had been kept up by the proclamation of those eternal principles which that monument is built to commemorate. (Applause.) But, sir, I am not of the number. (Great cheering.) I want the war to go on. (37)

It needs to be said here that the "war" Hale was referring to was not the abolitionist struggle but the ongoing battle for the reunification of Italy led by Garibaldi, a great favorite and a former resident in the United States. As such, the senator's remarks were in keeping with Webster's sentiments in 1825 concerning the role of the United States in encouraging the spread of liberty abroad. But Hale's remarks bore an audible subtext, keyed by the word "agitation," which blessed the antislavery forces as well, and at times he sounded very much like Wendell Phillips in 1855: "Now, sir, I do not believe that we have done with those great truths which the Pilgrims proclaimed. I do not believe that the revolution which here commenced when our fathers stepped on Plymouth Rock, and Faith and Hope and Prophecy shook hands together, and history commenced—I do not believe that revolution is finished. No sir; it is only the beginning that is finished; and I hope, as has been suggested, there will be another monument erected. . . . I hope that . . . our posterity will engage in laying the corner-stone of another monument, and that monument shall be one to commemorate the full fruition of all the Pilgrims prayed for, and patriots fought for, and that it shall be in the possession of ourselves or our children. (Applause.)"

Despite the obvious nod to Governor Chase, it is doubtful if the other monument Hale had in mind would correspond to the one proposed for Jamestown, but with the one in Plymouth and the "monument on Bunker Hill" it would provide points for a vector of revolutionary, not consolidationist, implication and would bring about "the consummation of that which was prayed and fought for [for] so long." Hale did not list the particulars of that "consummation" of the "spirit of liberty," but what he and perhaps a large part of his audience had in mind was "a nobler and a higher monument to the memory of New England, and that is, the vindication of New England principles, in whatever theatre, on every proper occasion." Hale's sentiments were met with "prolonged cheering," and from our perspective they shadow forth the outlines of John Brown's stand at Harpers Ferry, news of which would soon break upon the land.

Though the connection may have been purely coincidental, John Brown and his men set out along a route to which they had been pointed by Senator Hale, toward a "theatre" and an "occasion" that would surely in some minds "vindicate New England principles" to the world, a drama enacted against newspaper headlines chronicling Garibaldi's equivalent exploits in Europe. We may wonder if the Reverend Dr. Blagden would have allowed his name to be enlisted as one of the prominent sponsors of the Forefathers monument, with a quotation from a letter urging that "no reasonable expense be spared in rearing a memorial of the Pilgrims at Plymouth," had he known the direction in which the ceremonies in 1859 were going to take (*Illustrated Pilgrim Memorial*, 27).

Likewise, there is some irony in the inclusion of Governor Henry A. Wise of Virginia among the names on a circular describing the monument published in that same year of insurrection, to whom were attributed the sentiments that the Pilgrims had "helped to found empires of freedom for all time" (*National Monument*, verso). Ironic, because Wise had responded in harsh terms to

Sarah Josepha Hale's appeal to Virginia in 1856 to join in a national observation of Thanksgiving as a holiday promoting union, which the governor read as yet another abolitionist gambit: "This theatrical national claptrap of Thanksgiving has aided other causes in setting thousands of pulpits to preaching 'Christian politics' instead of humbly letting the carnal Kingdom alone and preaching singly Christ crucified" (Appelbaum, 133).

Wise was foolish enough in his hostile response to Hale's sincere appeal, but what he was correspondingly blind to in Billings's design soon enough gave shape to his paranoia regarding Yankee schemes. The governor of Virginia would be confronted with a single face of the Pilgrim spirit, who put into action, broadsword and all, the implications of Freedom on Billings's statue long before it had actually been built. Wise would get Christ crucified, moreover, in a sufficiency well beyond his desire and in a form unconformable to his own statist faith. That fault line between section and union was about to yawn wide, for, by 1859, monuments, like the Pilgrims and Plymouth Rock, were at last in the right hands, serving to sanctify a revolution inspired by an earlier American example that was not what Webster in 1825 had in mind.

CHAPTER **19**

The Rock's Red Glare

The nineteenth century lit up its lives with the glare
from Plymouth Rock.
—The Fugs

I

The evolving standpoint of James Russell Lowell regarding the Puritans reveals how a former agitator for reform could fall back on an increasingly conservative position. To the removal of the influence of his wife, Maria, we can add the outbreak of the Civil War as a factor permitting, even encouraging Lowell's innate conservatism, much as the advent of John Brown had accelerated his departure from radical abolition. Notably, the second series of the *Biglow Papers*, more or less turned out by Lowell under protest in support of the war effort, is far more cautious in its opinions than the first.

Thus we hear the Reverend Homer Wilbur observing that while the Puritan Forefathers of Massachusetts "showed remarkable practical sagacity as statesmen and founders . . . such phenomena as Puritanism are the results rather of great religious than of merely social convulsions, and do not long survive them. So soon as an earnest conviction has cooled into a phrase, its work is over, and the best that can be done with it is to bury it" (*Writings*, 11:208). This opinion synchronizes with Lowell's earlier animadversions against the decline of moral rigor in Massachusetts, but it is offered in tandem with the notion "that we cannot settle the great political questions which are now presenting themselves to the nation by the opinions of Jeremiah or Ezekiel as to the wants and duties of the Jews in their time." And the whole is prefatory to Hosea Biglow's meditation not on the war itself but on the problems of the uneasy peace that followed, "Su'thin' in the Pastoral Line."

Wartime is not generally a period during which great social reforms are introduced, although the same may be a consequence (as Hawthorne intimated) of such conflicts. An important waymark in Lowell's evolution appeared in 1864, being a visit, as it were, not to the field of battle but to "New England Two Centuries Ago," the period he had earlier defined as the seed time of American radicalism. Inclined as before to sneer at the superficial "exhalations" that emerged from "a Pilgrim Society Dinner," Lowell assured the readers of the *North American Review* that "Puritan thought and Puritan self-devotion" were at work wherever "there is piety, culture and free thought" (*Writings*, 4:5, 4).

Yet Lowell was not willing to support the notion that Puritanism was a primitive form of democracy and instead celebrated the Trinitarian faith that supported "the little shipload of outcasts who landed at Plymouth" and which was "destined to influence the future of the world. . . . Faith in God, faith in man, faith in work" (4). The greatest of these, apparently, was work, for if "New England history is dry and unpicturesque," it is because the region's chronicles are filled with "the noise of axe and hammer . . . an apotheosis of dogged work, where, reversing the fairy-tale, nothing is left to luck" (5).

This is the same emphasis on utility that characterized Lowell's objection to monuments in 1848, but there is detectable here a shift toward the emerging ideology of the postwar period, identified with what is now called the Protestant ethic. Where in 1848 Lowell celebrated the Anglo-Saxon penchant for building empire, not monuments, in America, he now portrayed the Puritans as "business men, men of facts and figures no less than of religious earnestness. . . . The liberty of praying when and how they would must be balanced with an ability of paying when and as they ought" (12). History in this view is rendered in terms of profit and loss, accounts payable and receivable, bound in the uniform and universally recognizable calfskin not of chronicles but ledger books.

The sprightly, Thoreauvian impudence that characterizes Lowell's radical writings is missing from his 1864 essay, much as his earlier celebrations of the Pilgrims that made them over into abolitionists manqué are overwritten here by his attempt to present them as commonsensical men of practical affairs. If they were intolerant of other sects, that was because the colony was "the private property of the Massachusetts Company," whose success was dependent on corporate "unity," which was threatened by the "chaos" that results from liberty being entrusted to "feeble-minded and unreasoning persons" (13).

If the Puritans were intolerant, reasoned Lowell, that is because "toleration . . . is something which is won, not granted. . . . The Puritans had no notion of tolerating mischief" (23). Like those Forefathers' Day orators he loved to ridicule, Lowell by 1864 is quick to turn Puritan vices into virtues, and in declaring that Puritanism as a faith "had nothing whatever to do" with the witchcraft hysteria, he notes that the "delusion" was worldwide in its prevalence, the old contextual argument that Lowell would work up into a learned treatise four years later (14).

Lowell's Puritan as the "apotheosis of dogged work" is Governor John

Winthrop, pictured as a wise and good administrator. Though he was a man of business, the kind of business Winthrop undertook was imperial in nature and continental in implication: "The figure of Winthrop should be as venerable in history as that of Romulus is barbarously grand in legend" (17). Clearly, the old Anglo-Saxon drive, "unpicturesque" and "devoid of sentiment," remains operative, but empires are not built by the sword alone (7). In sum, if Weber was able to attribute the Protestant ethic to the heritage of the Puritans, it was Lowell who provided the defining warp to the weave.

Lowell was still under the influence of Carlyle, an advocate of work transcendentally perceived, and his style remains more graphic and picturesque than the platitudinous terms of Plymouth orators, but his sentiments are surely theirs. Thus he identifies the Puritans with "certain creatures whose whole being seems occupied with an egg-laying errand they are sent upon. . . . Puritanism, believing itself quick with the seed of religious liberty, laid, without knowing it, the egg of democracy . . . [and] however visionary some of their religious tenets may have been, their political ideas savored of the reality. . . . If what they did was done in a corner, the results of it were to be felt to the ends of the earth" (16–17). This brings to mind Carlyle's second apostrophe to the Pilgrims of the *Mayflower*, in *Heroes and Hero Worship*, in which he points to the difference between Puritanism in 1620—"despicable and laughable"—and Puritanism as a modern, American phenomenon: "Puritanism has got weapons and sinews; it has fire-arms, war-navies; it has cunning in its ten fingers, strength in its right arm; it can steer ships, fell forests, remove mountains;—it is one of the strongest things under this sun at present!" (5:145).

With earlier celebrants of the Puritans, Lowell emphasized their positive accomplishments, especially the New England system of universal education: "The first row of trammels and pothooks which the little Shearjashubs and Elkanahs blotted and blubbered across their copy-books, was the preamble to the Declaration of Independence" (22). In 1848, Lowell had the Puritans building boxes to serve as weekly repositories of their piety, but in 1864 the prototype was not the church but the schoolhouse, that "small square one-story building" from whose windows could be heard "whole platoons of high-pitched voices discharging words of two or three syllables with wonderful precision and unanimity" (19).

In a metaphor inspired by the contemporary occasion, Lowell's schoolchildren become a "small infantry" and his schoolhouse an "original kind of fortification . . . the martello-towers that protect our coast. . . . The opening of the first grammar-school was the opening of the first trench against monopoly in church and state" (22). Notably, it is to the schoolhouse, not the church, that Hosea Biglow repairs for his Sabbath-day reflections about the problems of Reconstruction, the hard realities that the glorious Union victory had produced. The war was over but the struggle yet availed, and what was needed were leaders cast in the Winthrop, not the Endicott, mold.

Again and again in his 1864 essay Lowell returns to his Yankeefied Puritans, being "shrewd, practical men, busy about the affairs of this world, and earnest to build their New Jerusalem on something more solid than cloud. . . . It was far less the enthusiasm than the common sense of the Puritans which made them what they were in politics and religion" (83). Busy as they were "founding here a commonwealth on those eternal bases of Faith and Work," the Puritans had no leisure to entertain "revolutionary ideas of universal liberty," and their libertarianism can be traced not to political thought but to their "abiding faith in the brotherhood of man and the fatherhood of God" (87). The Pilgrim Fathers were not the visionaries, the "men of grand conceptions and superhuman foresight" so often celebrated in Forefathers' Day orations: "An entire ship's company of Columbuses is what the world never saw" (86–87).

Lowell's refashioning of the Puritan into a hardheaded, strong-armed man of business is part and parcel of the emerging Republican ideology given acceleration by the war, which produced in its officers (as Hawthorne wryly anticipated) the men who would become the leaders of the new industrial age. We are not far from the posthumous Emerson, who would be mistakenly regarded as a champion of the work ethic because of his emphasis on self-reliance and who was celebrated by Theodore Roosevelt at century's end as having helped "to create the atmosphere of enthusiasm and practical endeavor" that was "The Strenuous Life" (*Works*, 13:351). As early as 1865, Lowell contributed to this perverse metamorphosis, defining Emerson as a "new avatar" of Puritanism, whose "teaching tended . . . to self-culture and the independent development of the individual man" (*Writings*, 2:135, 138).

It was during this same period that Hosea Biglow overhears a debate between the Bunker Hill Monument and Concord Bridge that generated lines with a considerable postwar trajectory, celebrating the Puritans as "stern men with empires in their brains," who raised up the "strange New World," a "brown foundlin' o' the woods . . . who grew'st strong thru shifts an' wants an' pains" (*Writings*, 11:140). Lowell's figure here recalls Alexander Buel's mythic Yankee colossus standing astride the Rocky Mountains, for his visionary "young Ishmel" holds "With each hard hand a vassal ocean's mane" and is "skilled by Freedom an' by gret events / To pitch new States ez Old-World men pitch tents."

Biglow's vision is framed as a backward glance, but it looks forward also to the idea of American empire that emerges late in the nineteenth century. Like his Puritan, Lowell was more prophetic than he knew, and the idea of embattled virtue that is essential to his hardworking, hardhanded Separatist would in time take shape as that muscular Christian identified by the end of the century

FIGURE 23. Photoengraving of Saint-Gaudens's *Puritan* (1885), a statue that gave iconic shape to Lowell's idea of a grim but dynamic set of hard-jawed, hardworking men. (From Storrs, *The Puritan Spirit*)

with "the highest and most earnest thinking of the time" (*Writings*, 4:87). It is an image made concrete in Saint-Gaudens's Puritan of 1885, the bronze figure in cloak, steeple-crown hat, Bible and staff, who comes striding toward us out of the past, his heavy shoes making solid contact with the earth, the embodiment of an idea "hastening toward its own fulfilment" as it sought out Carlylean coefficients of the strenuous life into which to pour itself with all the kinesis of an avatar.

Saint-Gaudens's Puritan carries no broadsword but a very large book, presumably a Bible but suggesting also a ledger, accounts receivable perhaps, a suitable symbol for an age in which the Land of Promise sought by the Forefathers became a matter of promissory notes about to be called in. It was during this same period that Uncle Sam, still characterized as a Yankee Jonathan, began to sport the kind of beard called an "imperial," as he eyed certain islands in those "vassal oceans" that were still the property of Spain, cradles of a sort for a whole nursery of little brown foundlings. Much as Lowell derived from the Puritan heritage the ideological rationale for the Civil War, so he provided the essential elements for the dialectic of empire that spawned the Spanish-American War.

II

Although the militant edge of Lowell's Puritan can be detected in his sword-carrying Captain Standish, it would be Longfellow's version of the Pilgrims' soldier that would survive the Civil War, a figure whose popularity overrode the poet's mild ridicule of the vainglorious Miles. Again, the patriotism engendered by the war had a defining effect. By contrast, Longfellow's "other" Puritan work, *The New England Tragedies*, never had the vogue of his Pilgrim idyll. By the time they were published, the two closet dramas were anachronistic, for with their grim portrait of Endicott as a persecutor of Quakers and an equally dark rendering of the Salem trials, they belong with the fiction of Hawthorne and other literature critical of the Puritan's persecutory and superstitious character that appeared during the thirty years before the war. Longfellow's guilt-riven Endicott, a tragic victim of his own bigotry, has nothing in common with Lowell's revisionist version of the Puritan as an early avatar of the business spirit. By contrast, the no-nonsense, can-do spirit expressed by Longfellow's chain-mail captain, whatever the poet's intention, seemed cut to the necessary pattern.

What a new age would demand of the Puritans is suggested by two orations inspired in 1870 by the 250th anniversary of the Landing—if "inspired" is the best word for those performances. The orator of the day in Plymouth, Robert C. Winthrop, elegant and orotund as ever, was openly self-conscious of the precedent and priority of great speakers like Webster, Everett, and Choate: as if

to compensate, he added to the weight of convention a review of recent scholarship concerning the Pilgrims' sojourn in Leyden. In New York, Ralph Waldo
Emerson spoke before the New England Society, and if Winthrop brought with
him an account of recent research on the Pilgrims, Emerson toted along a
collage of his own previous efforts—chiefly his "Boston" of 1861—self-reliance
of the kind exemplified by his predecessors in the Old Manse, who regularly
recirculated their sermons. Yet, as with Lowell's use of the Puritans in 1864, we
can detect in both performances in 1870 certain alterations that mark the
transition enforced by the war.

Anticipating Lowell, Emerson in his "Boston" address of 1861 had observed
that "the power of labor which belongs to the English race fell here into a
climate which befriended it. . . . Nature is a frugal mother and never gives
without measure. . . . In Massachusetts she did not want epic poems and
dramas yet, but first, planters of towns, fellers of the forest, builders of mills
and forges, builders of roads, and farmers to till and harvest corn for the
world" (*Works*, 2:204). Yet again, this was the gist of what Lowell had to say
about the Anglo-Saxon spirit in 1848, suggesting the uniformity of thinking as
the Brahmins made straight the way for the Protestant ethic and its coefficient
the muscular Christian, ushering in an age that still favored building an empire
to writing (or reading) epic poems.

Because of his reliance on "Boston," Emerson's celebration of the founding
of Plymouth chiefly commemorated the latter-day city, and because he borrowed also from his centennial discourse in Concord, in which he lovingly
recounted the spirit of independence and cooperation he had discovered in
studying the town records of his place of residence, the "very early Pilgrim"
from which he claimed descent turned out to be a joking reference to the
"pilgrims" of his birthplace, as they were also called in his discourse of 1835
(*NESO*, 2:395; cf. *Works*, 11:32–37).

He did make a theological distinction between the founders of Plymouth
"as Brownists and Separatists" and the "Puritans" of Boston and noted "the
honorable distinction of that first colony of Plymouth . . . that they did not
persecute; that those same persons who were driven out of Massachusetts were
then received in Plymouth" (376, 388). But these distinctions are minor points
in his address, and in his own way Emerson (like Hawthorne in 1862) seems to
have been desacramentalizing the Landing, characterized as an "immense mistake." In 1870 he attributed the error to the terms of the Pilgrims' charter,
which extended the "little patch of territory by the sea" all the way to the
Pacific Ocean (373).

The import of this remark is elucidated by the full text of his Boston address
of 1861, in which Emerson had wondered aloud why, with the future site of the
metropolis of New England then unoccupied, "Governor Carver had not bet-

ter eyes than to stop on the Plymouth sands," a beachhead distinction that not only gave Boston the preference but eliminated the role, even the presence of the Rock, substituting for an icon of adversity one of sterility (*Works*, 12:191). In 1870, Emerson had sense enough not to bring this observation forward, but he did renew his insistence that Boston, unlike Plymouth, was "not an accident" but a town purposely planted by "men of principle," whose impulse was inherently "national" and was an important part of "the history of political liberty" (380; cf. "Boston," 188).

In 1870 as in 1861 it was Boston, "the capital of the Fathers, which . . . commands attention as the town which was appointed in the destiny of nations to lead the civilization of North America." Emerson noted that "Boston is sometimes pushed into an attitude of theatrical virtue to which she is not entitled, and which she cannot keep," but most of that oration seems to have been devoted to just such a claim, as in the phrase immediately following Emerson's demurrer: "The genius of the place is seen in her real independence, the productive power, and Northern acuteness of mind which is in nature hostile to oppression" (388). As sundry tablets and statues memorial testify, in Boston's mind Boston had won the war, and virtue remained triumphant in the metropolis of Massachusetts.

It must be said that by 1870 Emerson had lost some of his own productive power and acuteness of mind, and his self-plagiarisms were symptomatic of decline. By contrast, Robert Winthrop, though only six years younger than Emerson, was in the prime of middle age and would deliver one of his most famous public addresses—on the centennial of Cornwallis's surrender—before both houses of Congress in 1881. Yet his performance in Plymouth was also uneven, his consciousness of precedent inspiring what amounts to a lengthy rehash of same. Opening his oration by remarking "on the influence which has flowed, and is still flowing, in ever fresh and ceaseless streams, from yonder Rock, which two centuries and half ago was struck for the first time by the foot of civilized, Christian man"—a metaphor dating from the Reverend James Flint's sermon of 1816—Winthrop went on to wade up a veritable river of conventions, carrying with him a weight of recent scholarship that acted to slow his ponderous advance against the current (*Proceedings* [1870], 24).

Since his forced retirement from the Senate in 1851, Winthrop had increasingly devoted himself to scholarly pursuits, an avocation that explains his emphasis in 1870. He devoted a portion of his oration to his own researches, which took him to Scrooby Parish and Leyden but also to the library of the bishop of London, where he was privileged to touch the manuscript containing the recently discovered history of Plymouth Plantation penned by William Bradford, the worth of which far exceeded "all the treasures of art, or of antiquity, or of literature, which that palace contained" (58).

By digressing on his own pilgrimage, Winthrop took a full thirty pages before he got the actual Pilgrims aboard the *Mayflower* and under way. Nothing was said of that coterminous Dutch man-of-war with its human cargo that had inspired such fire and brilliance from Winthrop in 1839, though in a footnote he remarked that "there is not a particle of evidence to authorize or justify the loose statement, sometimes made [as by Hawthorne], that [the *Mayflower*] was engaged in the slave trade after her return to England" (203). Winthrop had never abandoned his Whig principles, and in the spirit of amity and Reconstruction he gave full credit to "the prior settlement of Jamestown," insisting that Virginia "must always be remembered by the old Colony with the respect and affection due to an elder sister"—if not "a better" (83).

If there was something new in Winthrop's oration, it was his digressive discourse on Anglicanism and Separatism, justified by both historical circumstances and the speaker's own Episcopalianism. In his Concord oration, Emerson had noted that "the best friend the Massachusetts colony had, though much against his will, was Archbishop Laud," a dialectical paradox on which Winthrop elaborated, without acknowledging Emerson's priority or echoing his irony, even while preserving the essential note of transcendental discourse (*Works*, 11:31). "Almost all great movements," Winthrop declared, "are but the resultants of opposing forces" (62–63). It is passages like this that remind us of the proximity of the Whigs to the transcendentalists when it came to a mystic appreciation of unity, although the former generally attended to the roots of the tree while the latter could most often be found swaying in its upper branches. Of like contingency was Winthrop's celebration of Plymouth Rock, which occurred fully halfway into his oration.

"They have landed," he finally announced: "They have landed at last," tidings that must have been received with considerable satisfaction by his auditors (73). As if to make up for his procrastination, Winthrop dilated upon the poetics of the event, commencing with the singularness of "that one grand Rock,—even then without its fellow along the shore, and destined to be without its fellow on any shore throughout the world,—Nature had laid it,—the Architect of the Universe had laid it,—'When the morning stars sang together and all the sons of God shouted for joy'" (74).

The notion of the Rock being "laid," given its egglike shape, recalls Lowell's grotesque comparison of the Puritans with "certain creatures whose whole being seems occupied with an egg-laying errand." But as his biblical quotation indicates, it was the traditional notion of the Rock as foundation stone or threshold that Winthrop had in mind: "There it had reposed, unseen of human eye, the storms and floods of centuries beating and breaking upon it. There it had reposed, awaiting the slow-coming feet, which, guided and guarded by no mere human power, were now to make it famous for ever."

Traditional also was Winthrop's defense of the Puritans against the charge of intolerance, and while admitting that the Pilgrim leaders "were perhaps of a somewhat more lenient and liberal temper than those who settled elsewhere," he refused "to pander to the prurient malignity of those who are never weary of prying into the petty faults and follies of our Fathers, and who seem to gloat and exult in holding them up to the ridicule and reproach of their children" (85–87). Winthrop deferred for his authority to Josiah Quincy's bicentennial address of 1830, which explained the attitude of the founders of Boston as " 'a measure of self-defense' " necessary for their preservation against " 'a certain introduction of anarchy' " that would have resulted from placing " 'their government on the basis of liberty for all sorts of consciences' " (88). In this apologia for Puritan intolerance, Winthrop may have been drawing on tradition, but he was also laying down the parameters for subsequent celebrants of the Forefathers, as the notion of "anarchy" began to assume new forms, emerging not from the problematics of agitation for abolition but associated with activities challenging the basis for social order in the entire United States.

Revisionary also was Winthrop's use of the convention associated with so many prewar celebrations of the Pilgrims, the summoning up of the ghosts of the Forefathers and confronting them with the modern moment, wondering aloud "What would they think, what would they say?" (98). Where earlier speakers had amazed the resurrected Pilgrims with the railroad and telegraph, Winthrop emphasized more recent inventions, including the Atlantic cable, the marvels of modern photography, the mercifulness of anesthetics, and all the other signs of material progress and prosperity evident throughout the land: "What more could they possibly wish to complete and crown the vision of glory vouchsafed to them?" (101). Well, plenty, by Winthrop's accounting.

Where earlier celebrants of progress, from Webster in 1820 to the Reverend Kendall in 1850, had been content to bedazzle their auditors with an account of modern marvels, Winthrop was less sure that material progress had been accompanied by moral improvement. Instead of marveling over the accomplishments of their "sons," Winthrop's necromantic Pilgrims asked a series of leading questions regarding the ratio between "the moral welfare of the country" and "its material progress," a sequence that ends with inquiries concerning the spread of a "cankering and debasing luxury," the "sovereignty of the market-place," and the ubiquitous presence of "vice and crime" in the nation: " 'Is there purity and principle and honor in your public servants? Or are corruption and intrigue threatening to make havoc of your free institutions, rendering all things venal, and almost all things, except mere party disloyalty, venial, in your State and National Capitals?' " (101–3).

The jeremiad as we have seen is occasionally an aspect of Forefathers' Day performances, but the instances are usually those in which an orthodox man of the cloth is the speaker. The great Unitarian/Whig tradition, with few exceptions, is celebratory, not condemnatory, so it must be said that although he employed the time-honored tropes of the genre, Winthrop was radically departing from Whig precedent. Even as the Concord Sage was raising his glass at the New York celebration, lending sanction to Lowell's notion that the business of Americans was business, Robert Winthrop was expressing concern about the negative effects of the prosperity that northern states were enjoying as a direct result of the industrial and commercial growth promoted by the recent war. As a remnant Whig, Winthrop in 1870 was in the position of that superannuated Federalist William Sullivan forty years earlier, who had feared for the health of the Republic in the face of Jacksonian Democracy.

He was, moreover, backed in his forebodings by his former political champion, John Greenleaf Whittier, who was not able to attend the festivities but sent a letter in which, having like Winthrop distinguished between the Pilgrims and the founders of Boston and Salem, he went on like Winthrop to acknowledge a present need for a little Puritan starch in the moral fiber of the country. "Our age," noted Whittier, "is tolerant of creed and dogma, broader in its sympathies, more keenly sensitive to temporal need; and, practically recognizing the brotherhood of the race, wherever a cry of suffering is heard its response is quick and generous" (*Proceedings*, 187). This was presumably the end toward which Whittier and other reformers had been working in the years before the war, but by 1870 the Quaker poet felt that perhaps matters had gone too far, and while still seeking "the reform and well-being of the criminal," society should pay equal attention "to the safety of the community" (188). The modern sensibility was "amiably tender," but it needed "the counterpoise of a strong sense of justice," a qualification not too much different from Lowell's call six years earlier for a judicial tempering of the libertarian spirit. "With our sympathy for the wrong-doer," Whittier suggested, "we need the old Puritan and Quaker hatred of wrong doing; with our just tolerance of man and opinions, a righteous abhorrence of sin."

Considering the revisionary tendencies observed in the performances of Winthrop and Whittier, one of the most interesting contributions to the Plymouth festivities in 1870 was the after-dinner response to a toast made by Senator Henry Wilson, who had risen like one of Horatio Alger's avatars of the Protestant ethic from plowboy to president of a large shoe manufactory. During the turbulent 1850s, Wilson had entered politics as an ardent abolitionist and Free-Soiler and had been elected to replace Edward Everett after his resignation from the Senate. Thenceforth, Wilson had aligned himself with the most radical of the Republicans. He had urged Lincoln to declare emancipation as a tactical as well as a humanitarian step and during the early years of Reconstruction took a hard line toward the South.

It is not surprising, therefore, that in responding to the toast "The Compact of the Mayflower," he used the opportunity to echo Wendell Phillips's sentiments of 1855, transferring from Plymouth Rock to the Compact that long line of radical champions who had stood for "equal law for the general good" down through the years:

> It inspired the burning eloquence of James Otis, and the pen of the organizer of the American Revolution, that grand old Puritan, Samuel Adams. It inspired the majestic eloquence of Daniel Webster, when he stood here half a century ago, and denounced the slave-trade as the crime of his century. It inspired John Quincy Adams in his grand struggle, in the hall of Congress, to maintain the sacred right of petition; and the martyred Lovejoy to vindicate, on the banks of the Mississippi, the freedom of the press. It inspired William Lloyd Garrison when he proclaimed immediate emancipation and his firm resolve to be heard by the American people. It inspired Abraham Lincoln in his immortal Proclamation of Emancipation, which smote the fetters from the limbs of three and a half millions of men. (131)

Wilson went on to declare that the Compact would continue to inspire the descendants of the Pilgrims and other "brave men in the advancing future to hope on and struggle on to make equal and just laws for the general good, the vital, animating, and living spirit of American institutions." In effect, he espoused a living, even rampant tradition of radical reform, the most active avatar of which in 1870 was Wendell Phillips himself, who had first hit upon that catalog device used by Wilson but who was also conspicuously absent from the list. The reasons for his exclusion are not difficult to determine.

While Garrison, though remaining ardent in his radicalism, had been forced to the sidelines by the illness of his wife, Phillips—whose invalided Ann would survive him—remained active in the ongoing battle for reform. Garrison had continued, while he was still able, to work for women's rights and temperance, and against prostitution and the neglect of Native Americans, all causes acceptable to the Massachusetts establishment, but Phillips had by 1870 taken up the cause of American labor. He had, moreover, allowed himself to be nominated by both the Labor Reform and Prohibition Parties for governor of Massachusetts.

Phillips had no desire for public office but hoped that he could obtain sufficient leverage to unseat Senator Wilson, who despite his own earlier radicalism had as a Republican become increasingly identified with exploitive capitalism, accompanied by a softening of his attitude toward southern aristocrats. As a shoe manufacturer he was the target of attacks by American workers who objected to his employing cheap labor in the form of Chinese imported for that purpose. However, Phillips's enlistment in the cause of Labor did his

FIGURE 24. Engraving of Tompkins H. Matteson's *Signing the Compact on Board the Mayflower* (1853). Matteson's tableau, a commissioned painting, was intended to emphasize the corporate and civil rather than the pious basis of the Pilgrim advent. Again note the armor on the deck, borrowed almost literally from Weir's *Embarkation* (see fig. 14). (Courtesy Pilgrim Society)

reputation considerable harm, for if workers regarded him as something of a snob and were further put off by his support of prohibition, his fellow Brahmins as in the 1830s thought of him as a traitor to his class.

Wilson handily retained his Senate seat and ran as vice president with the incumbent Grant two years later, thereby lending the Republican ticket a much needed element of personal probity but with no perceptible effect on Grant's second administration. Wilson died in office in 1875, while Phillips continued his radical career, fighting vested interests until the end, and though he most certainly deserved a place in Wilson's apostolic list of champions motivated by the principles of the Mayflower Compact, it is easy enough to understand why he did not make the cut. "New occasions," Lowell had famously written, "teach new duties," a slogan that like a rifle can be turned in more than one direction.

The examples of Lowell and Wilson are symbolic registers of the tendency during the post–Civil War years of formerly radical Republicans to enlist their energies in the service of business interests. Slowly but inexorably, the figure of the Pilgrim/Puritan began to take on a new meaning, as an embryonic capitalist difficult to enlist on the side of Labor but highly suitable to the ideology of

Work for whatever wage the market will allow. Emerson, in "Boston," in reviewing the utopian experiments of his own day, so ephemeral in their effects, regarded "with new increased respect the solid, well-calculated scheme of these emigrants, sitting down hard and fast where they came, and building their empire by due degrees," another sentiment in which he anticipates not only Lowell but his own Gilded Age celebrants (*Works*, 12:199).

The modifications and adjustments to the idea of the Puritan that Lowell set in motion after the Civil War may be illustrated by Tompkins H. Matteson's *Signing the Compact on Board the Mayflower*. Painted in 1853, it is a picture that could have been read at the time as sanctioning the radical image of the Pilgrims, and lacks that hand raised by Elder Brewster toward the providential light flooding the cabin that gives center and meaning to Edwin White's tableau (see fig. 3). Instead, Brewster's hand holds out a pen to a thoughtful Governor Carver, emphasizing the importance of the written word to the Puritans, an iconic display equivalent to John Trumbull's depiction of the signing of the Declaration of Independence. But by 1870, Matteson's painting could have served, with Emerson's description attached, as an affirmation of contractual stability, akin to a boardroom drama and hardly utopian in implication. The paper in question was after all a document empowering a corporate as well as a separatist structure.

III

Lest we receive the impression that a monolithic uniformity regarding the Pilgrim/Puritan characterized the Forefathers' Day performances of the 1870s, we should make passing reference to the labors of John A. Goodwin, a native of Plymouth and an amateur historian. Having been invited by his fellow aldermen of Lowell to deliver "an historical address on the Pilgrims" on the carefully correct date of December 21, 1876, Goodwin was constrained by circumstances to speak on the traditional day, but this did not prevent him from laying about with Standish-like vigor in an attempt to lay a number of other mistaken myths to rest.

Goodwin attacked "a cloud of popular errors," chief of which was "to speak of the Pilgrims as Puritans," which they were not either in matters of doctrine or persecutory tendencies. He also certified the wisdom of the report of 1850 regarding not only the proper date but the number of persons who came ashore the day of the Landing, corrected thinking that once again discountenanced the debate concerning the priority of Mary Chilton and John Alden (*Pilgrim Fathers*, 25–26). While he was at it, Goodwin dismissed Longfellow's anachronistic white bull, as well as the wedding journey in which it played such a central part, for "a bridal trip of a half an hour's duration, would have placed the tourists in the unbroken wilderness" (30).

But in his attempts to rescue the Pilgrims from popular error, including their reputation for belief in witchcraft—"The sable clouds of superstition might still cover the heavens [in the seventeenth century], but in the pall there was a little rift, through which a single ray of light stole down and formed a halo around Plymouth Rock"—Goodwin turned the heavy weight of his research to certifying the hoariest myth of all, that on that haloed stone "Freedom's ark had found its Ararat!" (38, 26). He also helped set in motion yet another myth, that the homes first reared by the Pilgrims "were built in log-cabin style," certifying their connection to modern pioneers (26).

Goodwin's point about the theological and statist difference between the Separatists of Plymouth and the Puritans of Salem and Boston was hardly original with him: we will recall the distinction made by Jedidiah Morse in his *Geography* and Harriet Cheney's definitive "peep" in 1824. Moreover, as Albert Matthews has recorded, Goodwin's was but one voice in a debate that had been raging in a scholarly war since 1866, chiefly focused on the issue of Separatism (Matthews, 375–82). In 1870, as we have seen, both Emerson and Winthrop noted the distinction, Winthrop observing in his orotund way that "there were some shades of difference in the religious sentiment and in the civil administration" of the two colonies and that "the charges of intolerance, bigotry, superstition, and persecution, which there seems to have been a special delight, in some quarters, of late years, in arraying against our New England Fathers and founders, apply without doubt more directly to other Colonies, than to that whose landing we this day commemorate" (*Proceedings*, 86–87).

Still, Goodwin must be given the advantage on the score of weight, his argument having been expanded in a hefty volume published in 1886, which added to the emerging popular image of the Pilgrims that was, with all its errors, the work of Longfellow and which had gathered further headway with the nationalization of Thanksgiving during the Civil War. "This is a larger Thanksgiving Day," announced Senator George Frisbie Hoar on the occasion of the 275th anniversary of the Landing in Plymouth, and he would devote much of his address—in which he portrayed John Robinson as a prophet of political liberalism—to the defining differences between the Pilgrims and the Puritans of Boston, with an outspoken bias in favor of the former (*Proceedings* [1896], 45). And yet it must be said that the dominant discourse of the Gilded Age followed the conservative line laid down not in but by Lowell.

Consider the postwar career of Charles Sumner. Attacked in 1853 for his meliorism by Garrison and in 1855 for his offenses to southern honor by Preston Brooks, Sumner would emerge during Reconstruction as a Republican of the deepest and most unyielding convictions. We can recall how Longfellow in 1868 sent a manuscript of *The New England Tragedies* to Charles Sumner in advance of publication, defining the work as a "plea for Tolerance." But we may doubt its effect on the senator's determination to force civil rights for African Americans on the defeated South, which Sumner would have had difficulty equating with Endicott's persecution of Quakers. Indeed, the effect of Longfellow's plea for tolerance may be said to have had the effect on Sumner of cold water on hot steel, tempering his Puritanic mettle in a way not intended by the poet.

On the other hand, Sumner had none of Wendell Phillips's sympathy for American (white) labor, nor was he ever accused of betraying his own class, quite the reverse, for he derived great strength from his aristocratic base. It provided a privileged height from which he could look down on lesser, error-prone mortals, a prospect like that promised in heaven for Puritan saints. The furious contempt he had let loose on Southrons before the war he released on Andrew Johnson afterward, anger fueled by a volatile self-righteousness that his near martyrdom had intensified. Nor was General Grant's elevation to the White House regarded with favor by the Boston Brahmin, who regarded the squat, cigar-smoking, whiskey-drinking former General of Armies with distaste bordering on disdain.

Predictably, it was not long before President Grant offended Sumner in matters more serious than taste, and the campaign began with Sumner firing the first shot. He opposed Grant's choice for secretary of the treasury, A. T. Stewart, the newly rich department store magnate from New York City, like Henry Wilson an example of Emersonian self-reliance wrongly construed but widely celebrated by Horatio Alger Jr. Sumner took his stand on the constitutional grounds that a businessman should not be appointed to the post, which would provide opportunities for profiteering, but Grant's appointment went through over his objections.

That Sumner's opposition was valid on other grounds—the fabulously successful merchant proved incompetent in office, suggesting that self-made men were not entirely without structural flaws—did not alleviate tensions between the senator and the White House. They became bow-string tight in 1869, when Sumner, as chair of the Senate Committee on Foreign Relations, opposed Grant's favorite project, the annexation of Santo Domingo, which offended Sumner because it was a perceived threat to the integrity of an embryonic black republic.

Sumner won this particular fight, but at a considerable cost to himself, for Grant's allies in the Senate forced him out of his cherished chairmanship of Foreign Relations. In retaliation, Sumner played a prominent role in heading the liberal Republican opposition to Grant's reelection in 1872, promoting the candidacy of Horace Greeley with his characteristic outspokenness, aiming all his eloquence and learning at a man he defined as corruption epitomized. Undiscouraged by Greeley's loss to Grant, Sumner seems to have gained a large measure of self-esteem from defeat, as having ennobled him because of his righteous cause. When he was invited in 1873 to be one of the speakers at the annual Forefathers' Day celebration hosted by the New England Society in New York, he turned the occasion to what he perceived to be political advantage.

During the twenty years since he had appeared at Plymouth to celebrate the Embarkation, Sumner had not spoken much about the Puritans. In his *Prophetic Voices Concerning America* (1874), he had assembled a chorus of seers who spoke "concerning the future of America and the vast unfolding of our continent," and had resurrected John Adams's story about the prophetic lines that had been " 'inscribed . . . into a rock on the shore of Monument Bay in our old Colony of Plymouth,' " but Sumner's emphasis was on George Berkeley's poem, not the apocryphal doggerel (5, 24). The only bona fide Puritan cited for his prophetic voice was Samuel Sewall, who in 1723 saw New England as having fulfilled the biblical promise of a "New Heaven" in a "New Earth," but then Sewall recommended himself also as "the first of our Abolitionists" in point of time, if not rank (27–28).

This last distinction Sumner seems to have thought to claim for himself, which is the general drift of his address in New York in 1873. He rose to respond to the toast "The Senate of the United States"—the same as in 1853—by mounting a celebration of the Puritan character that not a little resembled Sumner as viewed by his warmest champions. His opinion of his colleagues had not improved over the years, and he began by suggesting (as in 1853) that "the most prudent" response possible would be to say nothing regarding the U.S. Senate. The tactful void that followed was filled by Sumner with a high-minded moral discourse that presented the Pilgrims in conventional terms, celebrating "that inborn virtue" brought to America by the "humble company that landed on Plymouth Rock," and which was tacitly embodied in the man who stood before the assembled members of the New England Society in New York (*Works*, 20:297).

Sumner also stressed the importance of the Compact and quoted John Robinson's parting words to the Pilgrims, not in its theological context but as "a plain recognition of the law of Human Progress, little discerned at the time, which teaches the sure advance of the Human Family, and opens the vista of the ever-broadening, never ending future on earth," an observation entirely in keeping with the radicalization of the Pilgrims by the abolitionists during the antislavery crusade as well as with the premise of his recent book. By 1873 Sumner's celebration of the "sure advance of the Human Family" could now include civil rights for African Americans, and even closer to home was his notion that the Pilgrims provided "an illustration of the supremacy which belongs to the triumphs of the moral nature," hardly an objectionable sentiment but one that pointedly called attention to the speaker's private aura. Nor can we doubt the issues Sumner had in mind when he, like Lowell and Whittier but toward a different end, called for tempering the freedoms guaranteed by the Constitution by means of justice, which last he defined as "nothing but Right applied to human affairs. Do not forget, I entreat you, that with the highest morality is the highest liberty," yet another push forward for civil rights (298).

Sumner gave closure to his remarks with an insistence that the Pilgrims provided a "universal lesson" for modern times: "The conscience which directed them should be the guide for our public councils; the just and equal laws which they required should be ordained by us; and the hospitality to Truth which was their rule should be ours. Nor would I forget their courage and steadfastness. Had they turned back or wavered, I know not what would have been the record of this continent, but I see clearly that a great example would have been lost. (Applause.)" (299). It is not difficult to distinguish (at least in Sumner's eyes) between the Pilgrims gathered in council and the U.S. Senate in 1873, nor is it difficult to detect the similarities (in Sumner's eyes) shared by the speaker and those persons of immaculate virtue he celebrated.

Greeted enthusiastically when he rose to speak, Sumner was rewarded by frequent applause during his address, and when he finished, the audience rose to give "cheer upon cheer," as the stenographer recorded parenthetically. Surely those present were not so much moved by the speech itself, loaded as it was with familiar sentiments, as they were by the speaker, frail and worn from fighting the good fight on behalf of black Americans and already suffering from the illness that would soon result in his death. Nor could they have failed to notice the speaker's own outline in his profile of the Pilgrims, not only their reliance on conscience and their exercise of virtue but their "courage and steadfastness" in working for what they took to be "the Right in human affairs."

In his speeches in the Senate promoting civil rights, Sumner's consciousness of his own virtue often broke into the open as he cited his past record of efforts on behalf of persons of color in the United States. In 1873, similarly, he was casting himself in the role of a modern-day Puritan, pointing a finger not only at Plymouth Rock but at that amalgam of sterling qualities that was Charles Sumner. And opposed to this avatar of virtue was the Grant administration, not only in terms of corruption and venality but in its willful vindictiveness toward Sumner, whose very frailness was a register of the cost he had paid for his principled steadfastness. It was an opposition that the speaker did not elucidate, leaving it for his auditors to make the connection, but it hardly took a sensitive ear to detect.

Sumner's Puritan qualities were remarked upon by his fellow liberal Republican George William Curtis when in 1883 he spoke before the New England Society in New York on the occasion of Forefathers' Day. In his celebration of "Puritan Principle and Puritan Pluck," Curtis eulogized the by then late Senator Sumner as the "distinctive Puritan statesman of our time, the worthy political descendent of John Winthrop and Samuel Adams . . . whose lofty character and unstained life was a perpetual rebuke of mercenary politics and mean ambitions," which in effect was Sumner's implication in 1873 (*Orations and Addresses*, 1:256).

Curtis then went on to tell an illustrative anecdote, recalling a discussion with Sumner "upon some public question, and as our conversation warmed I said to him, 'Yes, but you forget the other side.' He brought his clinched hand down upon the table till it rang again, and his voice shook the room as he thundered in reply, 'There is no other side!' There spoke the Puritan," declared Curtis: "There flamed the unconquerable spirit which swept the Stuarts out of England, liberalized the British Constitution, planted the Republic in America, freed the slaves upon this soil, and made the Union a national bond of equal liberty," a pronouncement that drew applause and in effect placed Sumner on Plymouth Rock. But Curtis's story also emphasized his colleague's stubborn, not to say arrogant, intransigence, his refusal to yield an inch in any argument, suggesting that he was of the Endicott and Garrison cast of mind.

That Sumner, like Endicott and Garrison, could be his own worst enemy is suggested by another anecdote, the implication of which is that the arrogant, stiff-necked senator had been forced to listen to, if not acknowledge, "the other side." It was a moment, moreover, that occurred that very same evening of December 22, 1873, when his remarks drew not only a standing ovation from the members of the New England Society in New York but a rebuttal from General William Tecumseh Sherman, like Grant a rather splintery hero of the war.

What aroused Sherman's ire was a humorous digression in Sumner's speech, demonstrating the abject poverty of the Pilgrims during their first years in America, illustrated by the hapless efforts of Captain Miles Standish to raise money in England. Standish "succeeded in borrowing (how much do you suppose?) £150 sterling. [Laughter.] Something in the way of help . . . 'though at fifty per cent.' So much for a valiant soldier on a financial expedition" (294–95). To the casual eye this would seem a harmless enough joke, but given Sumner's previous record of insult and abuse aimed at President Grant, Sherman detected in the anecdote an insulting reference to the administration of his former commanding general. Sherman may have, as the record notes, "joined" the rest of the company in "laughter," when Sumner concluded his story, but it may also have had a hard, metallic sound.

According to Chauncey Depew, who witnessed the event, Sherman was quick to respond to Sumner's implicit coupling of Grant and Standish as military men incompetent in matters of civilian government. Though he was a "stranger to a New York audience" and not known as a public speaker, he rose up and, in the very face of Sumner's reputation as a "world-famed orator," defended not only his beloved general but his own "pride in his profession of a soldier" (Depew, *Orations, Addresses, and Speeches*, 1:131; hereafter cited as *Orations*). Avoiding abuse, and with "impressive eloquence," Sherman expressed in "direct and simple" terms "his faith in his friend, and . . . the merits and mission of the soldier," a response that brought to mind "the brilliant dash and resistless momentum of a charge of cavalry. . . . It was a speech Captain Miles Standish might have made after two hundred and fifty years of American opportunity, and the mighty soul of the Puritan captain seemed inspiring the voice and the presence of his advocate."

The occasion for Depew's reminiscence was a memorial service for General Sherman in March 1892, almost twenty years after the death of Sumner. Depew's address, like Curtis's eulogy for Sumner, celebrated its subject as a Puritan, in this instance a man who spoke "the language of the Puritan soldier." For "the intensity of his passion for the Nation would in other times and surroundings have made him a general in the Parliamentary army or the leader of a New England colony" (131). If we pair Depew's recollection with Curtis's, then on that evening of December 22, 1873, Puritan faced Puritan across the festive board, soldier confronting statesman, the victor in a war that had been waged to prove Sumner right now rising to show where he was wrong.

It is a very small moment in the 1870s, that decade of tumultuous change and reversions of the social and economic order, but for our purposes it has a certain momentousness, because Depew's account of the confrontation in effect displaced Sumner from his cherished stand on Plymouth Rock, much as President Grant had removed him from the chairmanship of the Committee on Foreign Relations. When the cigar smoke faded away, there was the Rock and there also was General Sherman, a Puritan for a new generation of Republicans, of which Chauncey Depew was representative. Because General Sherman, like the ghost of Miles Standish evoked by Depew, will haunt the next couple of chapters, being a familiar, if often silent, figure at banquets celebrating the Pilgrims, and cited even when he was absent, we should perhaps at this point give some consideration to Depew's posthumous tribute.

William Tecumseh Sherman, like Charles Sumner, was a direct descendant of Puritans who arrived in Massachusetts during the first years of Winthrop's colony, but his military fame would have admitted him to circles like the New England Society in New York in any event. Unlike Sumner, however, Sherman was no radical Republican, for in the words of Depew he was a Whig "brought up and trained in the school of Hamilton, of Webster, and of Henry Clay" and believed "slavery to have guarantees in the Constitution" (133). According to Depew he "would have unsheathed his sword as readily against a John Brown raid as he did upon Fort Sumter." Thus when offered a commission in the

Confederate army, Sherman not only refused but resigned from "the superintendency of the State Military School of Louisiana, so ardent was his loyalty to the Republic."

Most important in Depew's estimation, though Sherman was "a superb specimen of the pure Puritan stock," the general had been "born and bred in the West," and his was a western and expansive vision, inspired by the "grandeur" of the westering Republic. The Whig prospect of growth and prosperity "captured and possessed his heart and mind," so that as a young graduate of West Point, Sherman spent his time in lonely frontier forts "building railroads across the continent on paper, and peopling those vast regions with prosperous settlements, long before they had any roads but the paths of the buffalo, and any inhabitants but roving tribes of wild Indians" (133–34). According to Depew, Sherman never could understand "the lamentation, so common, over the extermination of the buffalo," and his antipathy to Native Americans was famous: he regarded their idle tenancy of fertile lands and their warlike propensities as having "retarded the development and checked the majestic march of his country to the first place among the nations of the earth" (133–34). If ever a latter-day Puritan matched Lowell's description of a man with empire in his brain, it was General Sherman.

The date of Depew's tribute (and Sherman's death) coincided with the Columbian Exposition, which would celebrate four centuries of westward-moving progress. It was that occasion, also, that in 1893 inspired Frederick Jackson Turner's famous celebration of the frontier as a distinctly American experience, a liminal process and a virtual avatar of progress in the abstract as well as particulars. Sherman, a product of and participant in that process, was a Puritan transformed into a Pioneer and by Depew's account was a new kind of American man. Thus where Curtis had celebrated Charles Sumner as a modern-day Puritan whose sterling virtue in the service of reform was the last gleam of a glory identified with the emergence of the Republican Party, Depew celebrated William Tecumseh Sherman as a type of leader needed for the postwar years: "Quick, nervous, intelligent, pugnacious . . . with his Indian warrior name" he was a hybrid, born to fill the duties of the new occasion, chiefly witnessed by his paper dreams of railroads spanning the great West and the hardheaded utilitarianism regarding buffalo and Indians. He was, though Depew did not acknowledge the precedent, just such a transmogrified Yankee as Lowell had thought of in 1864 as an ideal champion for an emerging new order, where Charles Sumner was associated invariably with Boston and the exclusive Brahmin spirit.

In considering these contrasts and transformations, we need also to pay some attention to the character of the celebrants of Sumner and Sherman, for Curtis and Depew were very much part of the process we are defining. George

William Curtis was younger than Sumner by some dozen years and a full decade older than Depew, which placed him at a critical midpoint between two generations of Republicans, the radical and the reactionary. Born in 1824, Curtis as a young man spent two years at Brook Farm, where he came under the influence of Emerson and transcendentalism. Though much of his professional life was spent in New York City, he never really left Concord, to which he would periodically return to visit his mentor. Curtis, however, was no dreamy idealist but very much a man of the world—and *for* the world, in the most positive sense of that conjunction.

As a writer, editor (of *Harper's Monthly*), and a worker for reform, Curtis spent his adult life acting out the injunction made in his first public oration, *The Duty of the American Scholar to Politics and the Times* (1856), that informed virtue should not be closeted but become a force for change. Curtis in belles lettres was one of many American writers who continued the Irving tradition of good-hearted sentimentality, which he used his editorial position to perpetuate, but unlike Irving he also enlisted his pen in political action: an abolitionist in the fifties, he later spoke out for the education of women and female suffrage and was a prime mover during the 1880s for the establishment of the civil service under the administration of the federal government.

In contrast to Charles Sumner's outspoken and therefore often ineffective championship of reform, Curtis's was ever a mediating and therefore a successful presence. As we have seen, when in 1864 he had pointed out Hawthorne's failure to respond in literature to the enormity of slavery, Curtis preferred to ask leading questions, not make denunciatory moral judgments, with a characteristically gentle touch laying bare the stony heart of the man. Thus it was a gentler kind of reforming spirit that Curtis carried forward into the last half of the nineteenth century, and the man who as a boy had attended the school taught by Margaret Fuller differed from his fellow radicals in other ways as well. Because of his emphasis on moderation and balance, he was more a prototypical liberal than a bona fide radical, essentially uncomfortable with the uncompromising postures of the true-blue Puritan, as his anecdote about Sumner reveals.

If the career of George Curtis marks that line of radical Republicanism that points toward modern liberalism, then the career of Chauncey Depew delineates the branch of conservative Republicanism that became in his case the New York Central Railroad. Where Curtis was a product of New England, who flourished as a citizen of the New York world of letters, Depew was a native New Yorker, of Huguenot and New England ancestry, and like his hero, Sherman, was something of a hybrid, though without the western heritage. Ten years younger than Curtis, he belonged to a later generation of Republicans and shared a different, if not antithetical, vision, progressive perhaps but hardly in the political sense. Depew certainly shared Curtis's lightness of touch and deftness of address, to which he added a boisterous sense of humor, but the depth of moral commitment was generally missing, along with the liberal sentiments.

And yet, at the start, the career of Chauncey Depew was identified with the rise of radical Republicanism. Yale educated (Class of 1856, the year in which Wesleyan graduates were listening to Curtis's lecture on their responsibilities to politics and the times), Depew was born into a wealthy Democratic household but was early on attracted to the Free-Soil movement, and by the time he was admitted to the bar (1858), he had joined the newly formed Republican Party. He became a willing part of Thurlow Weed's New York machine, and his service during the Civil War was limited to representing his district in the state legislature.

Depew's committee assignments brought him into personal contact with Lincoln, whose body he would escort on the long train trip from New York to Springfield, Illinois. It was a symbolic journey for Depew, for the next stage of the lawyer's career took him out of Republican politics (at least as an elected official) and into railroading, that increasingly powerful force with which Lincoln's own legal career had been identified. In 1866, Depew declined to serve as President Johnson's minister to Japan and instead went to work as an attorney representing the railroad interests of Commodore Vanderbilt, in effect a lobbyist.

In 1872, at Vanderbilt's request, Depew ran on the Liberal Republican ticket as candidate for lieutenant governor of New York, which is not to say that he shared Horace Greeley's opinions. He went down to defeat with Greeley but continued to prosper as a lawyer representing Vanderbilt and continued likewise to run and be defeated for political office, this during a time when railroads were becoming symbolic of vested interests and corruption in high places, despite Vanderbilt's attempts to associate himself with reformist politics. By 1885, Depew was president of the New York Central, a powerful position he resigned when finally elected to the U.S. Senate in 1899, though he remained chairman of the board until his death, in 1928.

Like Curtis, Depew was a perennial favorite at dinner parties hosting the rich and famous, whose popularity as a public speaker was attributable less to his moral earnestness than to his wit and humor. Though he never rid himself of the odor of commercial entanglements, Depew was a person of great charm, who circulated among those people for whom his business associations were no discredit—indeed, many of them were the plutocrats of his day. Because of his New England origins (his mother was descended from Roger Sherman of Connecticut, and he and the general were distant cousins) Depew was a regular at the Forefathers' Day dinners given by the New England Society in the City of

New York, one of the many organizations to which Depew belonged whose function was largely social and celebratory. And because of his New York heritage, his humorous remarks on these occasions continued the Irving tradition of twitting Yankees and stressing the Dutch influence in the New World.

And yet, as his eulogy for General Sherman suggests, when Depew was inclined to speak favorably of the Puritans, he did so in terms that took the militant outlines associated with the rhetoric of New England abolitionists before the war. Nor was George Curtis, despite his debt to Emerson, immune to the Puritan afflatus, as witnessed by his praise for Senator Sumner. We will have frequent occasion in chapters that follow to sample the oratory of Chauncey Depew, but in this chapter we come to closure with a consideration of an address delivered by his counterpart, on an occasion that provided Curtis an opportunity to step forward yet again as a champion of stern and unyielding Puritan virtue.

The year was 1885, a critical moment during which the forces of radicalism and reaction gathered for the explosion in Chicago's Haymarket Square. It was also the year in which Saint-Gaudens created his stalwart Puritan caught in midstride, an avatar of rectitude that catches the spirit Curtis strove to celebrate, inspired by a statue of a similar shape and implication. As in his speech on Puritan pluck and principle two years earlier, Curtis in 1885 revealed the latent conservatism that underlies the liberal impulse, not the enlightened love of compromise and mediation reflected in his role in the Tilden-Hayes dispute, but something much deeper by way of a defensive mechanism when he sensed a threat to the social status quo. At such times, he and Chauncey Depew were kith, if not kind, much as Senator Sumner and General Sherman were both Puritans under their very thin skins.

IV

The statue at whose dedication Curtis spoke in 1885 was the representation of a Pilgrim Father placed that year in Central Park. It was the work of John Quincy Adams Ward, whose career by that date was well advanced, and the statue joined several other figures in the Park by Ward, including *The Freedman* (1865), his *Indian Hunter* (1868), and a bronze *Union Soldier* (1869). The addition of Ward's *Pilgrim* to this symbolic group of muscular male icons had been commissioned by the New England Society in New York, and though the original proposal suggested either "one of the Pilgrim Fathers of Plymouth or one of the Puritans of Massachusetts Bay," it was the former the society decided to honor—not surprising given their fealty to the Landing (*Unveiling*, 6). There is nothing save the title of Ward's statue to convey the distinction, but the various speeches given at the dedication made it clear that the man in the steeple-crown hat is to be taken as representative of that "band of homeless

FIGURE 25. John Quincy Adams Ward's *Pilgrim* (1885), one point in a militant vector that terminates at the far southern end of Central Park in Saint-Gaudens's statue of General Sherman. It is worth noting that Ward gives the traditional bell-crown hat a Stetson-like look, which with the Pilgrim's musket and boots conflates with the figure of a U.S. cavalry-man or guide, types that by 1885 were associated with the conquest of the Far West. (Courtesy Archives of New York City Parks and Recreation)

exiles" and was to be imagined as looking down the centuries to "catch a glimpse of the golden future beyond," even as he remained stolidly fixed in place (14).

In effect, he was to represent in bronze that perpetual visitor evoked at so many of the society's dinners, a ghostly figment of the Pilgrim past called up to confront the modern moment. S. L. Woodford, president of the society, whose words these are, strove to give the statue an immediacy, using the oratorical trick of ventriloquism made familiar by Webster. He made as he claimed "those bronze lips speak," and they spoke "of heroic endurance, of obedience to the voice of duty, of loyalty to justice, truth, and right. The shadow of Plymouth Rock steals across the centuries. May it not fall over us in vain! Yonder figure stands as the Pilgrim of old stood, with his back to his friends and flatterers, and with his face to his foes and duty" (14).

These words suggest a guardian shape, and unlike Saint-Gaudens's Puritan (see fig. 23), Ward's Pilgrim holds a musket, not a staff, with no book in sight. Moreover, where Saint-Gaudens's Puritan is caught in motion, Ward's Pilgrim is fixed, legs somewhat apart and musket "at rest," a less imaginative but still an effectively equivalent expression of physical strength. Yet it is a stance that suggests not an actively militant ideology striding out of the past into the present but a defensive, even reactionary posture. It is that of a sentinel, challenging the present generation to emulate him as he guards against perceived adversaries, precisely the point made by Curtis in his address.

In effect, he expanded on his remarks regarding Puritan pluck and principle two years earlier, with a similar emphasis on rectitude and vigilance, but with his characteristic impulse toward mediation, he developed a "Puritan" acceptable to his liberal cast of thought, denoting a class of men whose very name came from their "demand for reform" and who were never fanatics, save in the "high sense of unchangeable fidelity to a sublime idea" (*Orations*, 1:377). Otherwise, like so much said in praise of the Pilgrims immediately following the Civil War, Curtis's was an elegant restatement of earlier wisdom, bringing together both the radical and the conservative reading of the Puritan, compounded as a libertarian who set in motion that tidal wave of progress that would result in the American Revolution.

But he extended the Puritan errand into the era of Reconstruction, carrying it across that "irrepressible conflict" that was the War for the Union: "Chiefly from New England came the moral appeal, penetrating and persistent, disdaining political argument and party alliance . . . with all the ancient fervor of the Puritan faith" (390). Such work was never finished, and Curtis looked to Ward's statue both as an inspiration for future generations and as an "imperishable and relentless censor," for "no man shall stand unrebuked in the sculpted presence of departed greatness." Curtis's was the most recent updat-

ing of the need of monuments as an adjunct to rhetoric, and in these sentiments, he came close to the spirit of the jeremiad, a form with which he was
not particularly comfortable but which the present occasion, given the times,
seemed to warrant.

Curtis's Puritan as inspired by Ward's statue is a facsimile of his tribute to
Charles Sumner's principled pluck. It is an icon of alert militancy, defensive of
hard-bought liberties and ardent in promoting the freedom of others, whose
eagle-eyed vigilance was "often flouted and traduced [by] history and tradition" but which as pure principle "walked undismayed the solitary heights of
duty and of service to mankind": "The unspeaking lips shall chide our un-
worthiness, the lofty mien exalt our littleness, the unblenching eye invigorate
our weakness; and the whole poised and firmly planted form reveal the unconquerable moral energy—the master-force of American civilization" (390). This
last is the central phrase and notion in the quotation. For in evoking the
Carlylean notion of "master-force," Curtis is yet again revealing the golden
wire connecting him with Concord, defining the Pilgrim spirit as "a divine
energy underlying human society, manifested in just and equal laws, and
humanely ordering individual relations."

His definition of the Puritan is shot through with Enlightenment ideology,
giving "faith" a thoroughly secular focus, in terms once again reminding us of
the influence on him of Emerson, and there is something also of Longfellow's
John Alden in his evocation of a Pilgrim musing "in the rapt sunset hour on
the New England shore, his soul caught up into the dazzling vision of the
future, beholding the glory of the nation that should be." In sum, his is a
Pilgrim who could be enlisted in Sumner's prophetic company, foreseeing the
time when the United States would "stand forever and forever, the mighty
guardian of human liberty, of God-like justice, of Christ-like brotherhood."

But the date was 1885, a time threatened by adversaries that neither Emerson
nor Sumner dreamed of, and something further by way of elucidation of
Curtis's sentinel Pilgrim may be derived from his earlier speech, in which
Sumner was put forth as a modern-day Puritan. For the immediate context of
his response to the toast "Puritan Principle and Puritan Pluck" was the revelation of corruption at the national and metropolitan levels that was pandemic
in the 1880s and inspired the civil service reforms led by Curtis himself. Thus,
though the modern Puritan was no longer threatened by "wild beasts" and
"savage men," he was faced by "abuses of every kind . . . in our administrative
systems national or state or municipal . . . [that] have accumulated into Augean
heaps of fraud and corruption" (260).

Having cleared a continent and "founded a free Church and a free State, and
decreed the equal rights of the people, it is the business of . . . Puritan principle
and pluck . . . now to keep the Church and the State free, the government pure,

[and] politics honest" (259). Curtis called for "Puritan principle firmly [to] hold the light of investigation and exposure in the darkest places, and Puritan pluck with a broom of fire [to] sweep them clean" (260). In effect, he had turned from praise for Sumner's heroic stand on civil rights to the very cause to which he was devoting his own energies, converting, as it were, the sword to a broom, a domestic but no less effective weapon—if associated with cleanliness perhaps more than with godliness.

Curtis had closed his 1883 address by bidding the sons of New England there present to "consecrate" the Puritan spirit by their deeds, so that "America will indeed tower aloft—incarnate Liberty enlightening the world—Puritan principle and Puritan pluck will still go around the globe conquering and to conquer." We need to focus on that central phrase, set off by dashes, for in 1883 Bartholdi's colossus had yet to be erected in New York Harbor, but in advance of its advent Curtis was busy associating that essentially Enlightenment configuration with Puritan zeal, in effect projecting upon it Webster's beaconlike monument on Bunker Hill. Equally significant, he gave the process of revelation a militant language—"conquer, conquering"—suggesting that Pluck and Principle can raise a sword as well as a beacon light as a signal to countries yet laboring in darkness. That is, like the Rock itself, Curtis's notion of the Puritan has a guardian shape, holding back the forces that threaten what was then the modern United States.

In 1882, Congress had authorized the construction of the first steel warships that would make up the famous White Squadron, which would become symbolic of the reinforcement of the Monroe Doctrine in the waters of the Western Hemisphere. And this should serve to remind us that between Ward's statue of the guardian Pilgrim and Bartholdi's *Liberty Enlightening the World* stands Saint-Gaudens's General Sherman on horseback, already setting out toward the South in Victory's van, but aimed, shall we posit, at Cuba and Puerto Rico. Much as we can trace a vector of muscular Christian vigor and militancy by aligning Lowell's essay of 1864, Sumner's address in 1873, and the orations of Curtis in 1883 and 1885, so a line may be traced by means of the statues by Ward, Bartholdi, and Saint-Gaudens that reinforces an equivalent militancy.

"This Statue of Liberty," pronounced Chauncey Depew in 1886, "rises toward the heavens to illustrate an idea . . . which charged with Cromwell and his Ironsides . . . which fired the farmer's gun at Lexington, and razed the Bastille in Paris; which inspired the charter in the cabin of the *Mayflower*, and the Declaration of Independence from the Continental Congress" (*Orations*, 1:107). Where an obelisk "except as a monument of antiquity," Depew declared, "conveys no meaning and touches no chord of human sympathy . . . this statue will grow in the admiration and affections of mankind . . . for unnumbered centuries to come, as Liberty levels up the people to higher standards and a broader life."

The obelisk to which Chauncey Depew referred was the Egyptian relic recently set up in Central Park and not the one on Bunker Hill, but the resonance is definitive. For the net effect of Depew's remark was to displace that earlier symbol of Liberty broadcast to the world by another and greater, removing the omphalos of Freedom from New England to New York. In so doing, Depew gave final and definitive shape to that "third monument" called for in 1859 by Senator Hale, who could hardly have had Bartholdi's statue in mind, even though its general shape and meaning were foreshadowed by Billings's design.

Thus Faith as in the conventional Pilgrim metamorphosis becomes Liberty at the last, and by the end of the century the idea of Liberty would share, at least in New York, its meaning with both General Sherman's memorial statue and the nearby colossus, twin points on a vector indicated by Sherman's sword. It is a diagram suggesting that as the United States approached the Columbian anniversary, the Puritan errand would next operate in proximity to the place where the idea of America began.

V

Much as James Russell Lowell after the Civil War operated well beyond the influence of Maria White, so the image of the Puritan he was in large part responsible for generating was decidedly male in gender and stern in profile. It is perhaps notable that when Lowell married for the second time, in 1857, it was to a far different kind of woman, hardly strong-minded however much supportive. Frances Dunbar served her husband much as the most famous governess in literature served her former master, bringing order and tranquillity to his life but hardly acting as a muse manqué. It was a sign of changing times to come, for after the war the feminization of the Pilgrims that characterized oratory and poetry of the 1850s seems to have disappeared from public discourse. Though, as with the popular depictions by George Henry Boughton, the influence of Longfellow most certainly lingered on, the figure of Miles Standish dominated the annual celebrations of the Landing during the Gilded Age.

Thus in his oration of 1870 Robert Winthrop put his heavy stamp of approval on Longfellow's "'stalwart captain of Plymouth,'" whose sword had been carried in the late war by "the late venerable Judge Davis," also of Plymouth, albeit on a nightly patrol of Boston (*Proceedings*, 45). Nonetheless the point was made, the doughty captain having been pressed into service yet again, as Judge Davis "walked the midnight round with that . . . trusty and all-sufficient companion." Winthrop thereby made straight the way for latter-day celebrants of Forefathers' Day who like Chauncey Depew would see in Standish a diminutive Sherman or Grant, whose Rubicon talents were still needed in the troublesome, postwar years. Certainly the poet's carefully encoded feminism seems entirely to have escaped his contemporaries, who in bearing testimony to the poem's continued popularity, revealed a somewhat skewed understanding of its message.

In 1875, at the Forefathers' Day dinner of the New England Society in New York, Chauncey Depew responded to a toast to "Woman" with an extended allusion to Longfellow's poem that reveals the shift of emphasis. Depew celebrated Priscilla's challenge to Standish's errand boy as the epitome of Yankee initiative, "audacious, self-reliant, and irrepressible. . . . That motto has been the spear in the rear and the star in the van of the New Englander's progress" (*Orations*, 4:2). But Depew then retreated into the sentimental attitude that was Priscilla's target in her subsequent attack on Alden's vaporings: "Woman has been the source of all that is pure, unselfish, and heroic in the spirit and life of man" (3).

In effect, it was as if the strong-minded woman had never existed or had been chained with fetters of sentimentality to "the hearthstone around which linger the recollections of our mother," a fireside altar "where our wife awaits us" and from which comes "all the purity, all the hope, and all the courage with which we fight the battle of life." These objects of "tribute and homage" are by Depew's account specimens of that "perfect Woman" who shines with "angelic light." But they are hardly the kinds of women to effect changes in the gendered balance of power, and if they acted as a spear in the rear, it was with a gag on the mouth.

A like yet different use of Longfellow's poem on an identical occasion was made by Joseph H. Choate, a close contemporary of Depew and like him a representative figure of his day, whose background provides a key to their dissimilar views. Born in Salem, Massachusetts, in 1832, Choate was a first cousin once removed of Rufus Choate, and when in 1854 the younger Choate decided to pursue a legal career in New York, the older man provided him with a letter of introduction to William M. Evarts, another transplanted New Englander and a lawyer of rising fame and influence. As Joseph Choate much later recalled, "When I handed that letter to Mr. Evarts he took me by the hand and said 'Join the New England Society, and come into my office.' And my fortune was made! My first steps were most effectively smoothed by him" (*Arguments*, 1137). The order of priorities is significant: the entanglements between politics and business that characterize the careers of many rising men of the 1870s and 1880s were facilitated by the social contacts provided by the New England Society in New York and similar organizations.

Choate therefore, like Depew, became a joiner, and with the native New Yorker also he became a popular after-dinner speaker. In other ways his career was different, for where Depew's conservative Republicanism drew him into railroading, Choate became an advocate for liberal Republican causes and donated his energies and talents to a number of benevolent organizations. Nor was he ever a career politician, for like his cousin Rufus, Joseph Choate preferred the practice of trial law. But in time Choate's liberal Republicanism recommended him to President McKinley, who in 1899 launched him on a new career at the age of sixty-seven by appointing him ambassador to the Court of St. James. An effective agent of a burgeoning national imperialism, Choate secured treaties that opened the way for trade with China and cleared the way for the Panama Canal. In sum, Choate like Depew was an influential actor in post–Civil War affairs, and though like Curtis he devoted himself to promoting reform, he was foremost in following the pointer provided by the sword of General Sherman, becoming associated with the kind of Republicanism that sought to expand American energies into the Caribbean.

Though no champion of female suffrage, Choate did support the admission of women to colleges and universities, on the practical ground that demographics indicated a surplus that needed to be usefully employed. This was the logic of the marketplace, not the argument of someone sensitive to women's rights, but it does place Choate, as always, on the side of reform. Thus his response to a toast to "The Pilgrim Mothers," given at the 1880 Forefathers' Day banquet of the New England Society in the City of New York, conveys a different emphasis when compared with Depew's remarks in 1875. We cannot discount in that regard the fact that the society in 1880 broke precedent by inviting the wives of members to attend the celebration, a move that in a very small way reflected the changing status of "ladies" in society during a critical period that saw the formation of national organizations seeking the vote for women.

Like Depew, Choate began with an allusion to Longfellow's *Courtship*, quoting with approval the lines "As unto the bow the cord is, / So unto the man is woman," and then, after a number of humorous digressions on the subject of the opposite sex, he finally got around to the topic of the toast: "Mr. Chairman, I believe you said I should say something about the Pilgrim mothers. Well, sir, . . . when you go back to the stern terrors of the Pilgrim rule, when you contemplate the rugged character of the Pilgrim fathers, why you give credence to what a witty woman of Boston said—she had heard enough of the glories and virtues and sufferings of the Pilgrim fathers; for her part, she had a world of sympathy for the Pilgrim mothers, because they not only endured all that the Pilgrim fathers had done, but they also had to endure the Pilgrim fathers to boot. [Laughter.]" (*Arguments*, 1054). That "woman of Boston," we can recall, made her remark at the women's rights convention in Worcester in 1853, Choate's account of which is somewhat garbled, but his repetition of it in 1880 before quite a different audience does suggest a slight advance in approval for improving woman's lot among representative men of position and power.

Still, Choate's final stress was on the image of the Pilgrim Mothers not as heroic individuals but as long-suffering companions, equivalents to the women of the *Mayflower* celebrated by Pierpont in 1855. And his allusion to the tyranny of Pilgrim Fathers—modern and antique—was considerably more facetious than that of the delegate from California to the Worcester convention, never mind that of Elizabeth Oakes Smith. Notably, though wives had been invited to attend the celebration, they were kept in their places, as Choate noted, as "occupants of the galleries," overlooking but not participating in the festivities, an elevation that enhanced their status as angels, of the guardian as much as domestic variety.

Choate went on to reverse Oakes Smith's perspective emphatically, noting that the Pilgrim Fathers "were afraid of woman. They thought she was almost too refined a luxury for them to indulge in. Miles Standish spoke for them all, and I am sure that General Sherman, who so much resembles Miles Standish, not only in his military renown but in his rugged exterior and in his warm and tender heart, will echo his words when he says:—'I can march up to a fortress, and summon the place to surrender, / But march up to a woman with such a proposal, I dare not'" (1065). Here again, Choate's tone is facetious, save the aside regarding the character of General Sherman, and the power he was granting the ladies present was hardly what radical women were seeking in 1880. It is notable, moreover, that Choate in closing his remarks evaded the marital for the maternal frame, raising his glass to his own mother, who like all mothers was "the holiest thing alive; and if I could dismiss you with a benediction tonight, it would be invoking upon the heads of you all the blessing of the mothers that we left behind us." This sentiment, met with "prolonged cheers," put women in their proper place: "behind us."

On another occasion, Choate spoke out in favor of admitting women to medical schools, a controversial topic of the day, so we can hardly dismiss him as simply a reactionary male. In this, as in other matters, he was in favor of progressive change—reform. But the gist of his remarks in 1880 reinforces the point that Choate's humor, like Depew's, was used to establish distance from, not intimacy with, the opposite sex, suggesting that both of these lawyers were most comfortable in the fraternal company of men who shared their station and professional status. This was the masculine norm in an age of private clubs and other social groups exclusively male in membership, a living chain of associations that stretched from college days to old age and from Boston to San

FIGURE 26. A pencil sketch (*top*) by Edward Percy Moran (ca. 1912), known for his depictions of events from American history, which further testifies to the overwhelming influence of Longfellow on the continuing iconography of the Pilgrims. Thus the figures identified by Moran are John Alden, Priscilla, and Miles Standish, here being pointed ashore by "Governor Winthrop." This last is a chronological enjambment testifying to the overshadowing of the Pilgrim advent by Boston and to Moran's ignorance of the facts of the Landing, shared with another prominent New Yorker, Theodore Roosevelt. (See chapter 22.)

Moran's tableau seems never to have been completed, but in 1920 Henry A. Ogden, a painter known for historical and military subjects, produced a remarkably similar composition (*bottom*), commissioned by Chase and Sanborn to accompany a booklet illustrated by Ogden, *The Story of the Pilgrim Fathers*. The author, A. V. Lally, stuck to the line that the Landing on the Rock was made by the exploring party led by Miles Standish, while Ogden, in order to produce a conventional icon, chose to depict the Pilgrims coming ashore on Cape Cod, a compromise anticipated by the great debate of the 1850s.

Francisco. These were men whose commitment to the Protestant ethic was not only shaped by but was eager to bend to Lowell's image of the Puritan/Pilgrim as delineated in bronze by Saint-Gaudens and Ward.

It is not, therefore, surprising that between Depew's saucy Priscilla and Choate's doughty but woman-shy Miles Standish, Longfellow's uxorious ancestor somehow dropped from sight, in effect granting the captain's wish without fulfilling his desire. It was a process in which General Sherman would continue to play a dominant role, as a figurehead who decorated and warranted such sentiments in New York, as ubiquitous and sacred a guest as Lafayette a half century earlier. Depew's eulogistic association of Sherman and Miles Standish in 1892 is a summary statement of a lengthy association between those militant males, whether in terms of domestic or frontier affairs, a continuity that reinforced the exclusive masculinity of celebrations of the Pilgrims during the Gilded Age.

At the same time, paradoxically, we find as in the remarks above of Depew and Choate an increased levity associated with celebrations of the Pilgrims, at least in New York and its environs, which was the region after all where the Puritan had never been taken seriously, not from the days of Washington Irving. As we shall have an opportunity to observe at length, Irving as New York's model humorist, as demonstrated by Curtis's genteel geniality, would be replaced in the 1880s by Mark Twain, whose platform monologues and after-dinner speeches were characterized by an abiding irreverence. It was an emerging tradition that may not explain the disjunctive yoking of high hilarity and equally high seriousness where the Puritan heritage was concerned, but which was very much in evidence in that time and at that place, much as wives, mothers, and daughters continued to stay at home.

CHAPTER 20

Brooklyn Nights—Something by Way of Lighter Fare

*Whatever the opinion of the Dutchman may be
of the Yankee, this dinner of Brooklyn Pilgrims on
the anniversary of the day on which Bradford and his
comrades passed over from Clark's Island and made the
first landing upon Plymouth soil, and the dinner of our
brethren, the New York Pilgrims, tomorrow night, on the
anniversary of the day on which there was not a Pilgrim
within thirty miles of Plymouth Rock, both show at least
the Yankee's just estimate of himself. He is so vast, so
important a personage in American history that he
naturally supposes that it took him two days to come
ashore, and with perfect propriety he devotes two
consecutive dinners to celebrating that event.*
—George W. Curtis

I

For extensive examples in kind of both hilarity and seriousness we can turn to the annual Forefathers' Day celebrations of the New England Society in the City of Brooklyn, a brother organization originally founded in 1847. We have an oration delivered before the society by James Humphrey in 1848, which ended on Rufus Choate's mortuary note, the burial of the dead at Plymouth during the cruel winter of 1621, "the first seed-field of a New World . . . planted in sorrow and in tears!" (40). The society seems itself to have soon died and been forgotten, for when a new version was founded in 1880, no mention of the old was made. We may attribute the decline and death of the original organization to its proximity to the New England Society in the City of New York, and given that their purpose was identical, it might well be asked—

and it occasionally was—why the felt need in 1880 for two associations dedicated to the same functions in such close quarters?

But the question is shaped by modern notions of urban geography, in which Brooklyn is a borough of New York City, when in 1880 it was an independent and thriving city. Roebling's great bridge was making its slow way over the East River, providing suspense in terms of public drama as well as cables, but the only connection between the two urban centers was still Walt Whitman's celebrated ferry. Moreover, although, as Alan Trachtenberg has shown us, the Brooklyn Bridge was a structure beautiful in form and iconic in signification, in the eyes of some Brooklynites, who feared for the loss of their autonomy, it was a dubious blessing. Indeed, we may regard the founding of the competing society in 1880 as an assertion of civic integrity, a hegemonic act in keeping with the emergence of Forefathers' Day earlier in the century as a celebration of regional sovereignty.

Certainly brotherhood between the twin societies was complicated by sibling rivalry, and the building of the bridge, with the consequent threat of civil consolidation, was responsible for a considerable amount of occasionally tense chaffing. Expressions of competitiveness were permitted, even encouraged, by the fact that while the members of society in New York continued to meet on December 22, their brothers in Brooklyn observed the corrected date of the 21st, allowing an exchange of members back and forth over the estuarine moat. Both Joseph Choate and Chauncey Depew were among a number of commuters who regularly made this convivial trip, and along with Generals Grant and Sherman, the Reverends Henry Ward Beecher and Edward Everett Hale, and Choate's partner in law, William Evarts, they were present at the first meeting of the Brooklyn society, on Forefathers' Day in 1880.

Choate, who as a New Yorker was in favor of making the two cities one, was also careful to keep his opinion carefully veiled by the good-natured ripostes for which he was famous. In his remarks he styled Brooklyn "the dormitory of New York" but also set the tone by urging his auditors "to eat and drink your way back to Plymouth Rock. It is the true way to celebrate the Pilgrim Fathers. Do not have any long orations. They nearly killed the parent society" (*Proceedings*, 56). Choate's advice seems not to have been necessary, for all the speeches that evening were brief and by the standards of the day humorous and were limited to responses to toasts, in effect duplicating the after-dinner festivities enjoyed by the brother society without featuring an orator of the evening. This established a tradition that would be followed thereafter, with the high seriousness of the celebrations in New York being preceded by hilarity in Brooklyn.

The humor heard across the East River was aimed not only at the celebrants but the Saints being celebrated. New Englanders at least once removed from their native region, the Brooklyn diners apparently felt less constrained to observe the pieties, and undoubtedly the flow of liquors helped lift them toward hilarity, if not Heaven. The effect was not unlike that which characterized the Feasts of Shells almost a century earlier, but without the consequent discharge of bile. These after all were not Federalists after the Fall but Republicans in the fullness of their postwar affluence and power. The jokes aimed at their own overstuffed bodies were in themselves a register of their supreme self-confidence, even when cited in reference to the starving time of the Pilgrims.

Much of the levity may be credited to the impromptu comic team of Choate and Depew, who were frequent guests in Brooklyn. In 1899, Mark Twain was the honored guest of the Whitefriars' Club in London, and among the diners was "an old and valued friend," Chauncey Depew, whose acquaintance Mark Twain traced back to those "delightful days . . . more than twenty-five years ago . . . when I was taking lessons in oratory . . . [and] who was my master in the art" (*Writings*, 28:180–81). Twain credited Ambassador Joseph Choate with being his "other master," for "under these two gentlemen I learned to make after-dinner speeches, and it was charming."

The school kept by Depew and Choate was "the New England dinner," which is "a great occasion on the other side of the water. Every year those people used to meet at a great banquet in New York . . . to celebrate the landing of the Pilgrims . . . and these masters of mind [*sic*] in oratory had to make speeches. It was Doctor Depew's business to get up there and apologize for the Dutch, and Mr. Choate had to get up later and explain the crimes of the Puritans, and grand, beautiful times we used to have" (181–82). We may doubt Twain's statement of indebtedness, but the point about the complementary roles played by Choate and Depew at New England Society dinners should be well taken, functions they filled at banquets in both New York and Brooklyn.

Thus on the occasion of the first dinner in 1880, Depew explained that he was "a representative" to the Yankees of Brooklyn "of the Dutch. I attend your dinner because it is the only opportunity we have to get even for your long occupation of our State. (*Laughter*.) I am like the famous temperance lecturer who was detected by one of his disciples taking a hot whiskey toddy before going to bed. 'I thought you were a total abstainer,' said his shocked disciple, 'and so I am, said the lecturer, 'but not a bigoted one.' (*Laughter*.)" (63). Depew also noted the disparity of the dates celebrated in New York and Brooklyn, which he attributed less to scholarly differences than an example of Yankee "thrift and smartness," enabling celebrants "to get one dinner here this evening, and another in New York tomorrow." True to his word, Depew attended the dinner hosted by the rival society in New York and reported on the "extraordinary meeting of the Pilgrims in Brooklyn last night. . . . As I understood the Yankee-Brooklyn idea, that city is the metropolis and New York is the suburb" (*Orations*, 4:8). If Brooklyn would survive into the next century as something of a joke, Chauncey Depew undoubtedly gave initial impetus to the tradition.

And yet his wisecrack about the Yankee-Brooklyn idea was hardly original with him, having been set in motion by the opening remarks of the president of the new society at its initial meeting the night before, when he characterized New York City as "our ambitious suburb that lies across the river" and noted "the distinction to which it aspires of being considered a part of Brooklyn. (*Laughter.*)" (22). The point was picked up and elaborated upon by General—formerly President—Grant, there that night in Brooklyn, who defended "carpet-baggers" as expessing an essentially Yankee impulse: "It requires a little stirring up, a little going away, a little going abroad—going from the place of one's nativity—to bring out one's best energies. You may take this city, you may take the suburbs across the East River (*laughter*) or elsewhere, wherever you like, and . . . you find hardly any thing that is new in the way of enterprise that is not started by someone who has come among you. So I am decidedly in favor of the principles of New England" (25). Indeed, in reading through the collected *Proceedings* of the Brooklyn celebrations one encounters any number of jokes that recur on subsequent celebrations, much in the manner of Choate's stumbling version of the story about the sufferings of Pilgrim Mothers.

One example of this chain reaction can be traced to the celebration in Brooklyn in 1881, which Depew again addressed; having credited "all there is of glory, strength, and prosperity, of progress, civilization and liberty" to the New Englander, he went on to allude to the diners seated before him, who had consumed so much food that "they will be thinking in their sleep that instead of their forefathers having come over in the Mayflower, the Mayflower came over on them. (*Laughter and applause.*)" (26). The following year, Depew's joke took on a more familiar shape, thanks to the efforts of a guest from New Jersey, who thought it a shame that the Pilgrims had not landed on the Jersey coast "instead of having been cast upon that barren and inhospitable rock." This reminded him of a remark by "an irreverent friend who said, 'What a pity instead of the Pilgrim Fathers landing on Plymouth Rock, Plymouth Rock had not landed on the Pilgrim Fathers' " (49). Whatever its original point of origin, this joke was perpetuated as a well-known line in Cole Porter's bumptuous *Anything Goes* and a wisecrack by Dorothy Thompson. Though not all such evolutionary matters were necessarily improvements on the original remark, this evidence of the subterranean life of American humor is related to the subversive function it performed during those festive nights in Brooklyn.

We should here recall Mark Twain's remark about the functions performed by the team of Choate and Depew at celebrations of the Landing of the Pilgrims. Twain went on to characterize the Forefathers as "a lot of people who were not needed in England . . . and they were persuaded to go elsewhere. . . . They fell in over there with the Dutch from Rotterdam, Amsterdam, and a lot of other places with profane names, and it is from that gang that Mr. Depew is descended. On the other hand, Mr. Choate is descended from those Puritans who landed on a bitter night in December" (181). Contrary to Twain's recollection, Depew was not of Dutch descent, but neither was Washington Irving, with whom he sided in giving the Dutch their due. His was not, however, the conventional Knickerbocker image of the Netherlander as a fat burgher in kneebreeches with pipe and floppy Flemish hat, conceived as a drowsy counterpart to the ambitious, restless Yankee. Instead of posing the Dutch as the Puritan's antithesis and antagonist, Depew celebrated Holland as the source of the Pilgrim's liberal ideology, in effect asserting the hegemony of New Netherlands over New England.

In 1881 he observed that "if it had not been for Holland there would have been neither Puritans or Pilgrims; for when bigotry and despotism had crushed out conscience and freedom everywhere else, they were cherished and protected in Holland; and that little land, which had dyked out the sea, was the sole asylum for years of civil and religious liberty. (*Applause.*)" (26). This, we will recall, was the message of the Reverend George Washington Bethune to the New England Society in New York in 1850, and thanks to John Lothrop Motley's influential history of the Dutch Republic, first published in 1856, it became conventional wisdom that their interlude in Leyden had been influential in liberalizing not only the Pilgrims' Calvinism but their notion of government. Thus in his Forefathers' Day address in 1895, Senator George Frisbie Hoar, who chose the occasion to celebrate the Pilgrims as apostles of political freedom, gave full credit to their sojourn in Holland, where the Forefathers witnessed "the best example ever seen in [their] time, or before, of municipal Republican government. The compact signed on board the Mayflower was the necessary and natural result of what [they] had learned in the Low Countries" (*Proceedings*, 27).

Depew put it in his usual off-handed way, insisting that the Pilgrims' Puritanism had been "softened" by "the comforts and amenities of Dutch hospitality." But Depew became increasingly serious in his list of improvements made to the Pilgrims by their sojourn in Holland, which included "the benefits of universal popular education," so often claimed for their ancestors by celebrants of the Puritans. Moreover, the Republican spirit of the United Netherlands had inspired the famous Compact, whose principal emphasis on "just and equal laws" was responsible for "establishing and maintaining liberty" in the new country (28). And as for the persecution of Quakers and the "burning" of witches, "the Puritans who did these things were subsequent arrivals, who had never been in Holland. (*Laughter and applause.*)" Over the years, a number of subsequent speakers in Brooklyn would forward Depew's emphasis on the differences between the Pilgrims and the Puritans of Boston (as had Robert Winthrop in Plymouth in 1870), but not always with a nod toward the Dutch connection, nor with Depew's characteristically deft touch.

Despite these occasional digressions into serious matters, one gets the impression that the speakers addressing the diners in Brooklyn resembled a succession of stand-up comedians following one another to the dais. This was the era after all of platform "humorists" like Bill Nye, the most famous of whom from our present perspective was Mark Twain, whose tongue-in-cheek tribute to Choate and Depew in 1899 made the necessary connection. Though Twain seems never to have been either a guest or a speaker at the festivities in Brooklyn, his spirit of irreverence was constantly in attendance. Twain's hilarious after-dinner speeches when placed in the context of those "extraordinary" nights in Brooklyn begin to lose their singulariness, if not their superiority. For these were occasions when the kind of rich and powerful men of the sort Twain liked to associate himself with proved themselves nearly his equal in turning a joke, and when even General Sherman could raise a laugh.

If General Sherman was characterized by his celebrants as having carried the spirit of New England into the West and South, then Twain (who lacked Puritan credentials) may be seen as having carried the spirit of the Southwest into New England, with not always happy results. Where Sherman could generally be counted on to deliver his blessing on the mounting heaps of dead buffalo and Indians that characterized the advance of Civilization in the West, Mark Twain predictably would perpetrate an outrage entirely his own.

Thus his unfortunate speech delivered on the occasion of Whittier's birthday celebration in 1877 notoriously revealed the humorist's problematic attitude toward the literary saints of New England: in a burlesque travesty Twain had cast the beloved and elderly Whittier, Longfellow, and Emerson as rascally cardsharps and con men operating in a western mining camp, a romp that the author had thought was hilarious, but Boston was not amused. Like Holmes in 1855, Twain writhed apologetically, but he was more ignored than forgiven, save by his fellow westerner William Dean Howells.

The year before, as a guest on Forefathers' Day of the New England Society in New York, Twain had risen to the occasion handily, limiting his remarks to the subject about which one talks rather than risk deeper waters—the weather. Therefore, given his disastrous experience in Boston in 1877, it is surprising that when, on one of the few subsequent occasions Twain spoke in public about the Pilgrims, he once again risked offending his audience by impishly displaying his propensity for the perverse.

The occasion was the first meeting of the New England Society in Philadelphia, on December 22, 1881, an exercise in filiopiety the very purpose of which Twain chose to challenge by questioning the need for observing the anniversary date at all: "Celebrate their landing?" he asked. "What was there remarkable about it, I would like to know?" He pointed out that "those Pilgrims had been at sea three or four months" and that "coming ashore" was not only the natural but the inevitable thing to do: "If they hadn't landed, there would be some reason for celebrating the fact" (*Writings*, 28:87).

Following the line of Artemus Ward thirty years earlier, Twain defined the Pilgrims as "a mighty hard lot," who were guilty of persecuting his own "ancestors," among whom were an Indian, several Quakers, and Roger Williams. Even when he praised the Pilgrims it was to damn them: "Your ancestors broke forever the chains of political slavery, and gave the vote to every man in this wide land, excluding none!—not except those who did not belong to the orthodox church. Your ancestors . . . gave us religious liberty to worship as they required us to worship, and political liberty to vote as the church required" (89). This was a familiar paradox, if not often stated so bluntly on such occasions, but Twain went on to embellish it with his own impudent embroidery work:

> O my friends, hear me and reform! I seek your good not mine. You have heard the speeches. Disband these New England societies—nurseries of a system of steadily augmenting laudation and hosannaing, which, if persisted in uncurbed, may some day in the remote future beguile you into prevarication and bragging. No, stop, stop, while you are still temperate in your appreciation of your ancestors! Hear me, I beseech you; get up an auction and sell Plymouth Rock! The Pilgrims were a simple and ignorant race. They never had seen any good rocks before, or at least any that were not watched, and so they were excusable for hopping ashore in frantic delight and clapping an iron fence around this one. But you, gentlemen, are educated; you are enlightened; you know that in the rich land of your nativity, opulent New England, overflowing with rocks, this one isn't worth at the outside, more than thirty-five cents. Therefore, sell it, before it is injured by exposure, or at least throw it open to the patent-medicine advertisements, and let it earn its taxes. (90–91)

Unfortunately, the standard text of Twain's Forefathers' Day speech includes no parenthetical clues to its reception, but since nothing by way of contrition was forthcoming from the speaker, we must conclude that it was politely, if not hilariously, received.

On that same Forefathers' Day, George Curtis in New York was holding up the Puritans as moral exemplars against which present-day corruption should be measured, while Twain in Philadelphia was reversing the convention, assuring his audience that they were "better than their predecessors. . . . Yes, those among you who have not been in the penitentiary . . . are better than your fathers and grandfathers were" (88). Where Curtis (and Robert Winthrop and Sumner before him) presumed that the societies to which they addressed their remarks shared their high moral purpose, Twain mockingly characterized such groups as "hotbeds of vice, of moral decay—perpetuators of ancestral superstition" (91).

Speaking as "a Connecticut Yankee by adoption," a hybrid mixture of "Missouri morals" and "Connecticut culture," hence as "the perfect man," Twain spoke in self-mocking hyperbole. But he used this facetious height as a mock pulpit from which to call for the disbanding of "these New England societies," the renunciation of "these soul blistering saturnalia," a cessation of "varnishing the rusty reputations of your long vanished ancestors—the super-high-moral old iron-clads of Cape Cod, the pious buccaneers of Plymouth Rock—go home, and try to learn to behave!" (88, 91).

Twain's carnival of incrimination may be considered only an extreme instance of the general irreverence with which the Pilgrims and their Rock were treated during the Gilded Age, as exemplified by the remarks aired at the annual dinners in Brooklyn. In 1891, St. Clair McKelway, like Twain a journalist from Missouri, carried on the southwestern tradition by informing the assembled Brooklynites that "on a conglomerate occasion like this every one has the right to claim and celebrate as his special possession and legitimate pride all the virtues that have dawned on the race since the Pilgrims first planted their considerable feet on Plymouth Rock": "It has been declared of them that the first thing they did was to fall on their knees; the next thing they did was to fall on the aborigines. (*Oh!*)" (12).

Despite the parenthetical expression of festive shock, this became a well-worn joke also: its source is credited by the *Oxford Dictionary of Quotations* to William M. Evarts with the late date of 1913, but even McKelway's use suggests an earlier point of origin. And in the year following the Missouri-born journalist's appearance in Brooklyn, the mayor of that city graced the annual celebration of the New England Society with a garbled version of the joke, to wit: " 'The first thing that the early settlers of New England did was to fall upon their knees, and the next thing they did was to fall upon the Indians' " (65). The mayor seems to have been counting on the society's shortness of collective memory, when in fact it was his own powers of retention that were in need of repair, resulting in a version of the joke that seems not to have survived the telling.

The witty Wendell Phillips, like Mark Twain, may never have been a guest at the Brooklyn dinners, but like Twain he had his representative, in this instance Frederic Taylor of New York. At the dinner in 1893 Taylor spoke to the toast "The Puritan and his Mission Today" and in so doing updated Wendell Phillips's catalog of 1855 and Senator Wilson's list of 1870 without, however, acknowledging their priority: "It is our habit," noted Taylor, "to think of Plymouth Rock always as being at Plymouth, and nowhere else. Well it was there once [but] when the Pilgrims' feet pressed that boulder at Plymouth it became instinct with life and began to broaden at its base; and its base has ever since been spreading out, till now Plymouth Rock underlies the continent." Interrupted by frequent applause, suggesting that time-worn themes are easily swallowed, Taylor went on to recite "a record of the times and ways and places in which the rock has cropped out," which was tantamount to "a history of the country."

> Dear old Tecumseh Sherman rested his pad upon it, when, a college professor down in Louisiana, he wrote, in reply to the offer of a Confederate command, that for nothing in this world would he ever think a thought or do an act against the Government of the United States. [Applause.] Worden had it for ballast in that little Monitor when he sailed out to tackle the Merrimac. Grant stood upon it when he dictated the dispatch to Buckner that no terms but immediate and unconditional surrender would be accepted. [Applause.] Glorious old Ward Beecher carried a jackstone of it in his pocket for luck. When only a citizen of the Republic he crossed the Atlantic, and grappling, single-handed and alone, with English greed and English envy, he cried them hold off their hands till we had fought out our fight. [Great applause.] It was with a rough and jagged piece of Plymouth rock in his big, bony right hand that Abraham Lincoln shattered the manacle of the slave. [Loud applause]. (47)

Scanting Beecher's much more famous efforts on behalf of abolition, Taylor's reference was to his wartime visit to Great Britain in 1863, where he preached movingly (if perhaps not so effectively as Taylor allows) the cause of the North.

But then, Taylor's context was the Civil War, illustrating his point that "the rock and the Puritan—they go together" and pairing likewise the Puritan with the Republican Party. He included in his list of latter-day saints Beecher's sister, who defeated the monster Slavery "by pointing at it with her pen," thereby directing toward it the killing "stare of the civilized world" (50–51). To Taylor's way of thinking, the printing press was "the mightiest engine on the globe," for it is through "the power of public opinion that the Puritan works toward accomplishment of his mission today" (50). This was essentially Webster's line, that "nearly all the nations of the earth, responding to the pressure of the Puritan idea, are today surely, though in instances slowly, moving toward a larger liberty and better conditions for their peoples" (49). But it was Phillips's great catalog of radical worthies that was Taylor's model.

In imitation of Phillips, also, Taylor noted that Bradford and Carver were "with us today," not, however, "clad like the statue in our Central Park—grim of feature and saturnine of manner." Nor were they in the manner of Phillips's

Pilgrims shipping out to radicalize the West but might be found among the guests there assembled, for even though they "wear sharply creased trousers and display boutonnieres of appalling dimensions, part their hair in the middle and sport the conventional mustache, [they] are 'thoroughbreds clean down to the ground.' [Laughter.]" (48). In elaborating on the modern and improved version of the Puritan, Taylor evoked "the erstwhile slimy rock at Plymouth [which] had been cleaned up, as there is now a gilded railing around and a mansard roof above it."

Taylor's reference to Hammatt Billings's canopy was intended to emphasize his point that the essential spirit of Puritanism remained intact, ready like the Rock itself to "rise from the lap of artificial life, fling away its softness and startle you with [the] sight of a man. [Applause.]" Which is to say that beneath the levity and irreverence displayed during those Brooklyn dinners, there lay a bedrock of continuity with earlier and entirely serious depictions of the updated Puritan, as instanced by Taylor's notion of Ward's severe Pilgrim in modern dress, the signal characteristic of which was manliness in muscular form. This brings us to the following section, which might be entitled "The Statue and the Man."

II

The speaker who had immediately preceded Frederic Taylor that evening in 1893 was the Reverend Richard Salter Storrs, the venerable minister of the Church of the Pilgrims in Brooklyn and the son of the same Richard Salter Storrs who had in 1826 celebrated Forefathers' Day in Plymouth with an orthodox sermon commemorating "the Spirit of the Pilgrims." In 1857, likewise, Storrs the son had celebrated the Pilgrim Fathers at the Forefathers' Day celebration of the New England Society in New York, the last such before the Civil War put a temporary halt to such ceremonies. He was then a young minister who had given up the practice of law for the profession—and Trinitarianism—of his father and grandfather and proved as popular as his counterpart in the Plymouth church, preaching a much tighter orthodox line than Beecher and walking the same where his female parishioners were concerned.

The jeremiad was second nature to the Reverend Storrs, and in 1857 he had pointed to the moral backslidings of New England, calling for a return of old-fashioned family values. But in 1893, having spent nearly a half century in his Brooklyn pulpit, Storrs aimed his criticism nearer to home, pointing to the decline of the neighboring metropolis. Willing to indulge in some mild clerical humor for the sake of the evening's fun, Storrs used the ready example of "our friend Mr. Choate" to make his point that the modern Puritan differed from the original in terms of exterior appearance: Choate, whose plumpness was a regular target of dinner-table humor, was "the old Puritan modified" (40). But where Taylor would maintain that the heroic hearts of the old Puritans were hidden beneath the rotund exteriors of their descendants, Storrs's anatomy lesson found something lacking within.

By 1893, thanks to the efforts of Chauncey Depew, among others, the beneficial effects of their sojourn in Holland on the Pilgrims had become a commonplace, but Storrs maintained that the Dutch influence in New York was responsible for encouraging "a sensibility to pleasure which the [old] Puritans had missed" (40–43). This was not, to Storrs's way of thinking, a transformation devoutly to be desired, nor was it identified with true progress: "it must always be remembered there were, and are, grand elements which no one can dispute in the Puritan character," which are quite distinct from modern "grace and polish" (43). The Puritans' "strength" and "steadfastness" and their "power of endurance," along with their "heroic faith," were the undeniable elements "of great character in persons or in peoples." Echoing Lowell in 1864 and the Emerson of 1861 and 1870, Storrs declared that the original Puritan was a man of granite, not marble, of iron, not silver, materials that "may not take as easy or as fine a polish" but serve uses "to which the marble and the silver are altogether inadequate. And it was the work of the Puritan to put the iron and the granite into the public life of New England, and largely of the country of which New England is such a memorable and important part" (43).

Storrs's terms suggest monuments, and Storrs at the age of seventy-two was himself a statuesque presence. He might well have seemed Elder Brewster himself in modern dress, the very personification of the living Puritan spirit of which he and Frederic Taylor would speak, an illustrative example of the man of granite and iron. And where Taylor alluded to Ward's *Pilgrim* in Central Park, Storrs went on to describe a figure that not a little resembled Saint-Gaudens's *Puritan*, that other epitome of the Gilded Age idea of stern and zealous manhood:

> The Puritan was not a sentimentalist, in any sense; he was not a dainty, artistic person; he had a great work to do, constructive, and not merely destructive; he had a time of manifold, troubled perplexity in which to do that work; he required qualities that were apt to the times and adequate for the work; and he no more needed the fine polish of the dilettante diplomats of feebler peoples than the stiff and stubborn Alpine climber requires a pair of shining roller-skates. He needed the stout alpenstock, the hobnails in his shoes, and that was his sufficient equipment, and in that equipment he appears in history, marching up the steeps of difficult problems and reaching their summit, looking upon the landscape behind and far off upon the landscape in the future. [*Applause.*] (43–44)

The resemblance was not coincidental: in December 1889, Storrs had delivered in Boston before the Congregational Club an oration entitled "The Puritan Spirit" that covered similar ground, if in wider compass, and drew the same comparison between the stern, unyielding Calvinist and the effete, luxury-loving modern habitué of salons. When published as a book in 1890, the address was illustrated by a frontispiece photograph of the Reverend Storrs as well as one at midtext of Saint-Gaudens's statue. It was an association with which we may be sure the Reverend Storrs was familiar.

There was, it can be said, not much of the Pilgrim in Storrs's Puritan, in whom intolerance was to righteousness closely allied, and the minister himself let fly his remarks without concern for their effect on his auditors, there being, as he noted in 1889, "a lack of affectionate sympathy in the Puritan spirit," which is likewise "comparatively careless of pleasant things on earth" (*Puritan Spirit*, 32, 44). Storrs's contrast between men of granite and iron and "dainty, artistic persons" recalls Lyman Beecher's sarcastic blast at Unitarian dilettantes in 1827, degenerate dandies who would not have lasted ten minutes in the Plymouth of the Pilgrims.

Despite Henry Ward Beecher's doctrinal disagreements with his father and his colleague in the pulpit of the Church of the Pilgrims in New York, he had mounted a similar argument in his remarks to the first gathering of the New England Society in Brookyn in 1880. He defined "the radical idea of Puritanism" as a matter of "manhood," which was forged in the fires of repression in the Old World, where "every attempt to make himself a larger . . . and stronger man was met with buffet and even with persecution, unto death often times. Nevertheless, this was the purpose—a purer, a deeper, a stronger, a nobler manhood. That was the radical idea" (27). Beecher thanked God for having sent the Puritans to the best possible region for further hammering out their manhood, a place "by nature sterile, with an uncompromising winter, with a short, penurious summer, with a thin soil" (31).

As Edward Everett had observed more than fifty years since, such an environment provided a marvelous opportunity for cultivating virtue, but Beecher's argument ran closer to that of Lowell, for central to his argument was the celebration of hard physical work: "There was not a boy that was born to the Puritans that did not understand the moment that he got out of the cradle that he had to go to work and earn a living. There is not a river in New England that does not understand that it has got to go to work and earn a living before it has emptied into the sea. (*Applause*)."

Beecher developed the traditional comparison between the relative effects of soil and climate on the New Englander and on the southerner. But this was a parting curtain that was drawn to reveal the stalwart figure of Puritan manhood personified, General Sherman, who had carried "the type of New England manhood" with him "throughout the West" and thence, "beginning at the old Mason and Dixon's line," ran it clear through to the Atlantic Ocean: "Wherever you will find institutions that imply regularity, accuracy, steadfastness, you will find Yankees. If not Yankees that are presidents or managers then they married Yankee wives (*laughter and applause*); for I say of the men of the South and the West that they know a good thing when they see it. (*Laughter.*) We tried to send out . . . Yankee schoolmistresses, but they took them off our hands faster than we could get them out there; but they very soon opened their own schoolhouses and supplied their own scholars. (*Great laughter.*)" (32).

Beecher's emphasis on the restless spread of Puritan institutions by means of Yankee migrations is a constant feature of New England Society speeches, indeed is inescapable, given the very nature and spirit of those organizations. His chosen vessel here is certainly unusual, given his earlier commitment to the instrumentality of the Sharp's rifle, but he was celebrating the spirit of Reconstruction. Moreover, it is here that we find the seed of Owen Wister's subsequent celebration of a reconstructive marriage between East and West involving a cowboy from Virginia and a Vermont schoolmistress, women in the West performing a civilizing function similar to barbed wire. In 1885, five years after Beecher's remarks, Wister took his first trip west and, having arrived in Wyoming, noted in his diary that "every man, woman, and cowboy I see comes from the East—and generally from New England, thank goodness" (Wister, 32). Reassured by the eastern origins of the westerner, Wister predicted that "it won't be a century before the West is simply the true America, with thought, type, and life of its own kind."

Moreover, the emergence of the cowboy as a popular American icon during the 1880s suggests that the muscular, hardworking ideal celebrated in Brooklyn as the Puritan in his steeple-crown hat rather easily translated into the westerner in a Stetson, who like Sherman at the southern end of Central Park took his defining shape from a horse and his sense of mission from an idealized notion of true womanhood, not a schoolteacher perhaps, but surely an agent of civilization on the Victorian plan.

In 1893, as Wister was beginning to turn out his first Western stories, something equally militant by way of muscular Christianity was presented to the assembled members of the New England Society in Brooklyn at their annual dinner. The speaker was the president of the organization, Robert D. Benedict (LL.D.), a lawyer given to joining such ceremonial militia groups as the Society of Colonial Wars, the Military Order of Foreign Wars, and the Order of Settlers and Defenders of America, who took the opportunity of Forefathers' Day to revise the image of the Landing so that it would better conform to his embattled sense of the Protestant ethic.

By Benedict's lights, "the prevalent idea as to the attitude of the Pilgrims when they landed is not an accurate one," thanks to the baneful influence of Felicia Hemans's poem: thus the popular notion has it that, "as soon as the Pilgrim Fathers had . . . set foot on Plymouth Rock, they gathered around it, and, though 'the heavy night hung dark, the winds and waters o'er,' they 'shook the depths of the desert gloom' with hymns till the 'sounding aisles of the dim wood rang,' while the one thought which was in the minds of all was the exultant thought that they had reached a land where they had 'found freedom to worship God'" (27).

We will remember that Hemans's image of the singing Pilgrim gained considerable currency in the 1850s, part and parcel of the ongoing feminization of America promoted by Unitarians. But in harmony with the prevailing masculinity of the Gilded Age, Benedict (as his name suggests) would have none of it. Though he had no quarrel with the notion of a rock-bound coast, yet with the committee of 1850, with Robert Winthrop in 1870 and John Goodwin in 1876, he pointed out that there were no women or children present at the first Landing, only "ten men who wore coats of mail and were armed with muskets and cutlasses" (28). Nor did they pray or sing hymns but "marched into the land, saw divers cornfields and running brooks, with a place they judged fit for habitation, and then returned to the ship."

For those who sought for a tableau emphasizing expressions of piety, Benedict recommended the first landfall made by the Pilgrims, a month earlier, on Cape Cod. But here again the group, he insisted, was made up only of "armed men," who, having offered up a brief prayer of thankfulness, "proceeded to business" (28). At this critical juncture in their history (following Lowell and Lowell's Emerson), Benedict maintained that the Pilgrims "were busy, not with the singing of anthems or with rejoicing that they had found a place where they could have freedom to worship God. The chief subject of their thoughts that day was not worship but work; not the next world, but this; not religion, but law. . . . And what was their first business? It was to combine into a body politic, by a solemn contract to which they set their hands in the cabin of the Mayflower." We could expect no less from the compiler of ten volumes of *Reports of Cases Argued and Determined in the District Courts of the United States within the Second Circuit* and the editor of *Benedict's Admiralty*.

But the net effect was to defeminize (or remasculinize) the Pilgrims, a reversionary revisionism that by association also defrocked Beecher's notion of New England's present mode of progress, that missionary schoolroom presence who civilized westerners by marrying them. Benedict's militant, no-nonsense Pilgrims thereby moved forward into the 1890s not only Lowell's image of the Puritan as a businessman but Senator Wilson's ideal of a succession of "brave men" who would carry on the Pilgrim heritage of making "equal and just laws for the general good": "That was," concluded Benedict, echoing Wilson, "the determination with which the Pilgrim Fathers landed," not to pray and sing hymns, but "to make just and equal laws for the general good and to obey them" (29). In sum, the Pilgrim was a legislator, which is to say a lawyer, the profession not only of Robert Benedict but of many men in his audience.

Once again, beneath and beside all the hilarity engendered by the dinners given by the New England Society in Brooklyn, we can find a serious agenda being pursued, a corporate consensus that brought forward the idea set in motion by Lowell in 1864 that the main business of the Pilgrims was business and that their chief order of business was to frame not only a meetinghouse and a schoolhouse but a system of laws. By equating the drafting of the Compact with "business," Benedict drove home the nail that fastens that sacred document to the law-office door, the threshold to which was Plymouth Rock.

As fellow businessmen and lawyers, the Puritans and their modern celebrants were brothers under their antique and modern costumes, forming the far and near end of a long line of descent that stretches back in the manner of the militia companies evoked by the Reverend Greenwood in 1826. And upon occasion the diners at the annual celebrations in Brooklyn were given an opportunity to display the armor-clad side of the Puritan inheritance, lying just beneath the heavy cloak and smallclothes of Saint-Gaudens's marching man and expressed by the watchful pose of Ward's guardian statue in Central Park.

III

In 1886, Edward L. Pierce, Charles Sumner's protégé and biographer, a New England native and resident of Massachusetts who had served in the Civil War (chiefly in administrative posts) and afterward filled many public (but not elected) offices, spoke in Brooklyn to the sentiments "The Puritan Spirit: A Mighty Force in Human Progress." In the manner of his mentor, Pierce pushed aside historical instances so as to grapple with the present crisis and dismissed the need to make a "distinction between Pilgrims and Puritans," from which last group he was himself descended. He pointed not to the Rock but to the threat being faced by the descendants of both groups, "when so many of our New England cities and populous towns are passing under the control of crowds who have no connection, by blood or training or ideas, with that early history we commemorate" (35).

That was the worry also of the Reverend Blagden, who in 1834 had been prophetic in so many unpleasant ways, and the Reverend Storrs, in his 1857 jeremiad delivered to the New England Society in New York, had warned against "promiscuous immigration" that was creating a "polyglot" nation within a nation that is "only a casual human sandbar, accidentally heaped together"

(*NESO*, 2:363). In 1886, in Brooklyn, General Sherman had preceded Pierce in the order of speakers and reminisced about the pioneers whose westward trek he had witnessed in his boyhood, the living avatars of the spirit of the settlers who had "landed at Plymouth Rock, and began that series of events which has gone on, is still going on, and which, I trust, will go on to the end of time . . . bound upon that same general pupose to open up new lands and create a new civilization" (*Proceedings*, 22–23). But Pierce gloomily predicted that "the time may not be far off when you will have to seek on the farms of the West . . . for the best realization of the Puritan influence and character" (35).

Sumner's biographer shared his mentor's penchant for cries of hyperventilated alarm, and while acknowledging the ability of the "Puritan spirit" to survive "all mingling of blood, all changes in manners, all new departures in theology, all reconstructions of government," he felt that the time had come to draw a shining line in the sand at the water's edge (35–36). It was not that the Puritan tradition "of good government, of pure administration, of honest money, of equal laws for all men" should not be extended to people "of every race within our borders." But the descendants of the Puritans faced a threat to the selfsame tradition of "freedom" for all men, and, as in the time of the American Revolution, the loyal sons of New England needed to come "to the defense of the old cause," which was now being "assailed from a new direction" (38). Among the unalienable rights of Americans, by Pierce's reckoning, was "the right of men and women to labor for themselves and their families," now being "assailed by terrorism and violence."

Where Sumner was dedicated to extending civil rights to African Americans, Pierce added to that list of assured blessings "the right of every man to work for whom he pleases, and as long as he pleases, and for what wages he pleases—with a corresponding right in every man who wished to employ him." This was "a fundamental, an original, a primordial right . . . just as essential as the right of every man to own himself, born with us and derived from nature herself. [*Applause.*]" (38). The parameters of Nature's Nation do not always coincide with those of Memory's Nation, and Pierce seems to be addressing an issue not thought of by the drafters of the Constitution or *The Federalist*. We need not doubt the new occasion that inspired new rights, for Pierce was of course alluding to the rise of labor unions and the violent agitation that accompanied that rise. His discourse was haunted by specters difficult to distinguish from the dark outlines looming above Brooklyn of Anarchy and Communism, which by 1885 were inevitably associated with the dangers of uncontrolled immigration.

"Why," asked Judge Noah Davis, who followed Pierce on the program in 1886, "should we take to our bosoms and nourish and cherish the enemies of our system; ready to poison and destroy the principles we love?" (43). Davis had two years previous been nominated by reform Republicans to the state supreme court and had sat in judgment on Boss Tweed, emerging as a paragon of judicial virtue in the eyes of persons eager to flush corruption from the local government. He had been introduced to the society as "a voice for the right of no uncertain sound," a man welcome "in this hour, when some of the fundamental principles of liberty seem to be threatened . . . if not endangered" (39).

Davis was not reluctant to aim his pointer at what he perceived to be the greatest threat to the American way of life: "The Socialist, the Communist, the Nihilist, the Anarchist, in so far as they are enemies of our government and its principles, have no right to the protection of what they seek to destroy" (43). Chief culprit in his ideological gallery was "the wretched dynamiter, who seeks to hide his crimes behind the shelter of our Constitution and laws." Judge Davis was speaking to a toast to "AMERICAN LAW AND LIBERTY," which with John Winthrop and James Russell Lowell he regarded as one and inseparable, hence the threat of the Anarchist who appealed to the one for protection while destroying the other.

The year, once again, was 1886, and the immediate provocation for the outcries of Pierce and Davis was the Haymarket Riot in Chicago and the subsequent trial of the men accused of throwing a bomb into a group of policemen attempting to control the rioters. Out of this incident arose the caricature of the Anarchist as a bearded fanatic with a bomb in one hand and the Communist Manifesto in the other. Like the Abolitionist before him, he was a symbol of misrule and a threat to the American way of life, an image invariably associated not with hordes of freed slaves but with the floods of immigrants lured to America as cheap labor, the supply of which now exceeded demand. "The sanctuary we afford to the oppressed of all lands," declared Judge Davis, "cannot be truly sacred when we allow its protection to yield opportunity to those enemies of the human race who strike blindly at all order and law, and aim to overthrow the principles of justice that protect them. [*Applause.*]"

Of like purport were the remarks of the Reverend John R. Paxton, who followed the judge: "If the cabin of the Mayflower had been filled with a crowd of hungry peasants fleeing starvation and thinking only of bread, then the Declaration of Independence would never have been signed, and Bunker Hill would never have been fought. [*Applause.*] People who emigrate on their belly never found great States. [*Laughter.*]" (44–45). It is perhaps needless to add that champions of Labor's cause were not included among the members and their guests at the Brooklyn dinners, being the kinds of specters liable to give the diners indigestion, resulting in nightmares of a very heavy presence not represented by the *Mayflower* or Plymouth Rock but by an incubus of subhuman form.

The great, unifying shape of the Brooklyn Bridge now seemed dwarfed by the specter of the Dynamiter, who threatened the structure of the Constitution itself. But Joseph Choate, who had traveled to the dinner that evening by means of the recently opened span, felt it was necessary to celebrate Roebling's engineering marvel: "That teeming tide of life that pours over the Bridge at every hour of the day, and demonstrates that each city is always in full possession of its sister, proves that the swift river that divides them is only the thread that binds their fortunes together. The cars that keep flying across it with the swiftness of steam, bearing the living streams of humanity across, are but the shuttles that are weaving these two great municipalities into one—one and ineseparable, forever" (27). These Webster-derived sentiments drew applause from the diners, but Choate steered away from any serious proposition regarding incorporation, instead lapsing into the kind of facetiousness that inspired "Great merriment." It needs to be noted, however, that Choate's celebration of union and good fellowship came early in the evening, which increasingly darkened with the dire prophecies of less merry men.

Judge Davis was also a celebrant of the "American Union" and proposed thanks to General Sherman for having clothed it "with the purified garment of universal liberty." He too had crossed over to Brooklyn on "the beautiful and monumental roadway of art" and declared himself eagerly looking foward to the "consummation of that union" that was sure to follow, which would "give to the world a single city, unsurpassed in wealth and power, intelligence and influence, amongst the peoples of the earth" (40–41). But like Webster in Washington twenty-five years earlier, Davis was a celebrant of bridges and union because he feared for the future, and though he was certain that like the great bridge itself "American law and liberty today rest upon solid bases . . . we are in danger of forgetting that in all essential elements they are AMERICAN, and as such must be preserved and maintained for ourselves and our posterity against all that threatens their existence and perpetuity, either at home or abroad" (42).

Yet another visitor from New York, Granville P. Hawes, praised Davis as a judge with "the true Puritan conscience," with "iron enough in his blood to do his whole judicial duty, as he understands it. . . . By such honesty and courage alone is there safety to the commonwealth" (55). Hawes was less concerned, however, about the threat of anarchists than over the long-standing ills of political and commercial corruption, citing "the golden age of New England, when vice was crushed, especially oppression and extortion in prices and wages, which is injustice done to the public" (53). Like Whittier in 1870, Hawes wondered if in setting aside the "simple laws" of the Puritans, "which seem to govern the individual too strictly," that perhaps "we have not gone too far the other way."

"It might be very healthy if old Cotton Mather could come back once more with all his power," bringing with him that "community" of "principle" in which the "audacity of Wall street would be impossible," setting things to rights in an age when "stock-watering and cotton-gambling [are] legal enterprises" and "our newspapers [try] our criminals and terrorize our Courts" (54). Hawes alone seems to have sensed the parallel between his times and those "golden" days, much as we can hear modern resonances in his call for a return to the "good old ways" of dealing with civic problems, and half expect to hear a demand for a return of corporal punishment, until we remember that it was still being practiced in 1886, both in schoolrooms and behind prison walls.

Given the consanguinity of the members of the New England Society in the City of Brooklyn and its brother across the bridge—Choate noted that the diners at both celebrations were "the same Salem men, and Boston men, and New London men, and Worcester men"—the variety of responses to contemporary problems in 1886 was wide, from disgust over the continued corruption on Wall Street to dismay over the threat to American institutions of unchecked immigration, which brought with it the added dangers of Anarchy posed with its bomb, the chief target of which was the very same Wall Street Hawes attacked for its corruption. But most of the speakers did seem unanimous in their sense that the Republic was in danger, and like New Englanders during the Revolution and before the Civil War they looked back at the Puritan past for heroic exemplars worthy of imitation.

The Reverend John Paxton had celebrated the "stern Puritan," dismissing modern cavils against the type by "lavender little fellows" and describing him in statuesque terms as "masterly, wonderful, colossal," a tower of virtue who believed "that a little distinct universe walked around under [his] steeple crowned hat. . . . That is the legacy of Plymouth Rock; and God grant that the billows of passion, the strife of parties, the conflict of classes, the despair of hunger, the rage of atheism, or the greed of corporate power never submerge Plymouth Rock" (48).

The earnest self-righteousness of Hawes and Paxton, along with the anxieties and outrage expressed by the other speakers that evening, certifies that 1886, like 1776, was a revolutionary year in the United States, but the issues were conflicted and difficult to define, more confused than during the War for Independence and hardly the schematic diagram of opposed right and wrong used to precipitate the recent conflict. The decade had undeniably seen great reforms, including the institutionalization of the civil service, which kept it out of the hands of crooked politicians and their cronies. But this did not mean an end to crimes against the public weal, and as the vulture shape of Boss Tweed flapped fatly off the stage, from the other wing crept the gaunt shape of the "wretched dynamiter," with the Constitution for a shield.

THE HIGH TIDE OF IMMIGRATION—A NATIONAL MENACE.

"TO THEE I CLING."

FIGURE 27. A triptych from the 1880s, which provides commentary sufficient unto itself.

There was much work to be done by Puritan pluck and principle, in this "time of manifold, troubled perplexity," a job requiring a hero capable of Herculean efforts, who combined the righteous dedication to reform of the Pilgrim with the emerging ideal of the Puritan as an avatar of hard work. When the times are truly out of joint, a hero like Hamlet is not sufficient to set things right but requires a large measure of Fortinbras in his makeup, balancing idealism with a well-muscled arm. As in *Richard III*, what was needed was a Richmond, a hero recently arrived from the wars with a horse firmly beneath him, a General Sherman set in motion out of Central Park. As we shall discover, one such was already waiting in the wings, a man, however, not of Puritan but Dutch descent, a living reminder that while the Pilgrims were being tutored in Holland regarding democratic institutions, the United Netherlands were busily expanding their empire in distant climes, including the very place toward which the *Mayflower* was originally intended to sail.

IV

If the specter of Anarchy summoned up by the Haymarket Riot of 1886 haunted the Booklyn festivities thereafter, that dread presence was given greater power by the absence from the annual dinners of General Grant, whose death in 1885 left a space at the table seemingly impossible to fill. Despite his disgrace in the eyes of many Americans because of the corruption associated with his second administration, the general remained popular among conservative Republicans, his wartime exploits and general friendliness toward businessmen making him a local saint in New York and Brooklyn.

Grant's complement in these regards was the Reverend Beecher, that other solid presence at the Brooklyn celebrations, who despite the stain left on his reputation by the Tilton affair regularly blessed those occasions with one of his energetic, good-humored performances. It was entirely fitting, therefore, that the first speaker on the program in Brooklyn in 1885, following a silent toast to the late president, was Beecher himself, "whose brawny frame," in the words of the president of the society, "and brawny brain, and untiring force, bespeak his race, and the land from which he came" (21).

With his trial now a decade behind him, Beecher rose to define a "Puritan" as a man who has "predominantly in his constitution the moral sense" and could distinguish "between lie and truth, between virtue and vice, between liberty and oppression. [*Applause.*]" (23). If Beecher was indeed, as Mark Twain had early attested, a "brick," by 1885, as Twain later observed in a letter to Howells, it was one that had been slathered with "whitewash," lending the appearance of purity, if not the reality, to which the popular preacher added a projectile force.

Nor need we have any doubt as to the "Puritan" Beecher had in mind, described as having "a will power to make himself the champion of the cause of rectitude in whatever shape, in what ever nation he lived." Though on the present occasion it was the late General Grant that Beecher was supposed to be enlisting in the ranks of Puritanism, in public obsequies a certain amount of self-interestedness is to be expected, instance *Lycidas* or Marc Antony over Caesar's bier. But then, to cheers and applause, Beecher praised "the silent, deep, widespread manhood" of General Grant, a quality that made him "grander and greater than any of his deeds. . . . He was a man who believed in the right and hated wrong, and was willing to lay down his life for its sake" (26).

Within two years, Beecher himself would be dead, dual symbol with the president he extolled of the clay feet upon which so many great men of the Gilded Age were mounted, whatever the massive weight of granite or bronze above. But in 1885, as he stood before the gathered members of the society and their guests, Beecher with his own massive presence must have seemed himself that ideal he was celebrating, much as in 1891 John Quincy Ward would memorialize him by means of another thoroughly masculine monument, given particular solidity by rendering the preacher draped in his characteristic overcoat, which had the added advantage of concealing his weaker part.

For if Beecher (posed with Negro children in whose cause he had labored) was militant Christianity personified, a modern version of the Puritan cleric, so he was a joint symbol with General Grant of what could lie beneath the gilt of the Gilded Age, the fleshly man beneath the armor of Soldier or Saint. Like Grant, he was an equivalent Webster, who could never quite shake off the shadow of having sold himself to the cotton interests, nor Grant the charges of corruption, nor he the suspicion of adultery. But like Webster and Grant, the Reverend Beecher continued to be supported by his own, those Republican celebrants in Brooklyn, where his church was located, but where the likes of Wendell Phillips and celebrations of insurrection were no longer welcome.

And, as in 1852, the departure of Beecher and Grant left a large hole in what was now a Republican consciousness, but one essentially similar to that Whig sensibility that likewise maintained such solid faith in national union and personal righteousness at whatever price. What was needed was a new champion, who would combine Grant's inflexible presence with Beecher's moral message, but a man purified of the dross of human weakness, whose "own character was absolutely pure," a compound of General Sherman's "courage of tempered steel" and the "noble and true-heartedness" of George Curtis.

Just such a man was at present available, a former state legislator who for his active support of Benjamin Harrison was brought to Washington as a civil service commissioner in 1889, a post he filled with the zeal of an evangelist for public virtue. Back in New York City by 1895, he served in a reform administration as an activist president of the police commission and was celebrated in newspapers as a courageous fighter of crime. In 1896, he returned to Washington during McKinley's first term, serving as assistant secretary of the navy, where again he took a highly active role, pushing for war with Spain and helping to advance the career of one of the officers who would emerge as a hero of that conflict, Admiral (to be) George Dewey.

When the war itself broke out, he resigned his navy post and became a hero himself. As the officer central to the regiment of Rough Riders he had organized, Colonel Theodore Roosevelt became the militant western spirit incarnate, a role given additional warrant by the youthful years he had spent in the

Dakota Territory, where as a U.S. marshal he had hunted down and brought in his man. Roosevelt's short ride up San Juan Hill on the only horse available was the stuff of Frederic Remington's West and had a lengthy trajectory, taking him all the way to Albany and beyond. For having become a reform governor of New York in 1899, by 1900 he thought himself ready for national office, a notion shared by a number of politicians in Albany, for all the right but different reasons. In 1901, Roosevelt ran as vice president on the Republican ticket with McKinley, thereby rising to that fabled heartbeat away from the highest public office in the land, and when the other heart was stopped by an assassin's bullet, Roosevelt ascended an even bullier pulpit than that enjoyed by Henry Ward Beecher.

The hero of the Spanish-American War was "the exponent of all that is most vigorously and characteristically American in our national life," who boasted of his "intimate" associations with "ranchmen, cow-punchers, and game hunters," the very men with whom he surrounded himself in Cuba (*Works*, 13:359). As Wister was at pains to demonstrate, and as Roosevelt argued at length, it was the western spirit that inevitably absorbed the civilizing ideals of the East, for "it is perfectly obvious that it is the West which will shape the destinies of this nation." But the chronicler of the Winning of the West would celebrate as "the healthiest type" of American "a thoroughly sincere, earnest, hard-working old Christian," just the kind of rugged old Puritan so often praised by the celebrants in Brooklyn, embodied in Richard Salter Storrs and even (with some forgiving forgetfulness) Henry Ward Beecher himself (356, 370).

Roosevelt was not descended from the Puritans of Massachusetts but traced his line back to those Dutchmen Chauncey Depew was always being asked to celebrate, yet there was between him and the Puritan spirit an intimate and human connection, a vital political umbilicus, as it were, with Boston, Massachusetts. For if Roosevelt brought to Cuba in 1898 and to Washington in 1900 that western spirit associated by so many after-dinner speakers with General Sherman, his presence there was only incidentally the work of President McKinley of Ohio.

It may be chiefly attributed to the machinations early and late of Roosevelt's great and good friend Henry Cabot Lodge, who was responsible for his appointment in 1896 to the Navy Department and who masterminded his career thenceforth. A perennial celebrant of the Puritan spirit, Lodge seems to have seen in Roosevelt a modern Webster who lacked the great Whig's faults, and since the New Yorker's sudden ascension to the presidency in 1901 was made possible by the act of an immigrant anarchist, the hero of San Juan Hill may be said to have ridden the whirlwind of 1886 into the highest and most powerful political position in the land.

Though the connections are coincidental, it cannot be denied that Roosevelt fitted easily into the armor fashioned by many hands those many Brooklyn nights. If at times he would seem as much Quixote as Galahad, it was despite the efforts of the senator from Massachusets who rode by his side. A lean, dapper figure that to many observers resembled less Sancho Panza than Mephistopheles in tandem with Roosevelt's Faust, Lodge was in truth an avatar of the old Puritan spirit, beaten out into that finer stuff associated with the Brahmins of Beacon Hill. This made him nonetheless Roosevelt's evil genius, as we shall see, warrant and witness of the long association of the Puritans with their working partner, the Devil, as celebrated by Nathaniel Hawthorne. Of Roosevelt we shall hear something more in the chapters to come, but our chief attention thenceforth will be on Henry Cabot Lodge, the biographer of Daniel Webster and not coincidentally his counterpart throughout the remainder of this book, being a celebrant of the Puritans whose strength was his greatest flaw.

CHAPTER 21

The Stern and Rock-Bound Lodge

As a pilgrim father that missed th' first boats, I must raise me
claryon voice again' th' invasion iv this fair land be th' paupers an'
arnychists iv effete Europe. Ye bet I must—because I'm here first.
—Mr. Dooley

I

Born in 1850, Henry Cabot Lodge was the generational successor to the kind of citizen scholar represented by George W. Curtis, having left a teaching post at Harvard in order to enter politics. A Republican virtually at birth, Lodge shared with Curtis a commitment to reform, and he revered the figure of Charles Sumner, a familiar in his father's home. While a Harvard undergraduate, he came under the spell of Henry Adams, who was his mentor during his postgraduate years as well. But James Russell Lowell was also teaching at Harvard when Lodge was a student there and seems likewise to have left his mark, much as Lowell's revisionary Puritan provided a definitive profile for celebrants of the Pilgrims during the Gilded Age. In sum, these influences ensured that even as a liberal Republican Henry Cabot Lodge would be no George W. Curtis.

In 1886, at the start of his long career in Congress, Lodge delivered an address to the students of his alma mater entitled "The Uses and Responsibilities of Leisure," the subject of which was equivalent to the burden of Curtis's address to Wesleyan students thirty years earlier. Notably, Lodge began with a tribute paid by James Russell Lowell to Edmund Quincy, as a man who " 'early in life . . . devoted himself to the arduous profession of gentleman,' " no easy task according to Lowell, " 'in a country where we have business in the blood, and where leisure is looked down upon as the larceny of time that belongs to other people' " (*Speeches*, 14).

Quincy, as Lodge observed, went on to become a writer and speaker for reform, leaving "a noble record of well-doing," the secret of which was simple: "He used his leisure, that was all. Leisure well employed is of high worth" (14).

Lodge's point in 1886 was a reprise of Curtis's declaration thirty years earlier concerning the responsibilities of the American scholar, and though Lodge made no mention of Curtis, he certainly followed his lead, in effect erecting a span between the two generations of reformers, and what he said is revelatory of the differences occasioned by the intervening war.

Thus where Curtis had spoken of "duty," Lodge spoke, like Lowell, of "work," and especially of "working for the public," which could take several forms: literature was one, but it should be the kind of writing that "commands a market"—that is, makes money—and there were opportunities also in "public education and public charities," where there was "a vast and growing demand for intelligent work" (18). A man of leisure "can win wide reputation in these departments, and render incalculable service to his fellow-men," a notion of public life that unlike Curtis's was firmly anchored in the cash nexus.

Lodge saved politics for last, an "honorable calling" and not deserving of the "sneers" with which it is often regarded, but it is also "a very practical" profession, no place for an amateur, who is likely "to do harm by mistaken efforts to do good. Take hold of politics as you would of any other business, honorably and respectably, but take hold hard" and "work for the highest and best measures always. When the question is between right and wrong, work for what you believe to be right without yielding a jot" (19). Much as Lodge's address begins with a quotation from Lowell, so the whole is filled with the spirit of the older man, and in sentiments it shares nothing of Henry Adams's pervading cynicism regarding personal engagement in public affairs—including that of his former protégé, Lodge, whose defection from scholarship to politics he seems never to have understood.

By the time he spoke to those Harvard students, Lodge had been active in public life for seven years, a career marked by several reversals and disappointments: even as he urged his auditors to "stand for the right . . . against the wrong always," he cautioned against "insisting on the unattainable" where no moral question is involved and thereby risking the loss of "everything" (19–20). We should pair this caution with Lodge's caveat against the hypocrisy of "treating public questions as moral questions when they are not so," because Lodge's warning provides an ironic gloss on his subsequent career, in which he did not always follow his own good advice. It is an easy game to hold a politician up against some early speech made to a youthful audience, but this is the Henry Cabot Lodge who in 1883 had condemned Daniel Webster for betraying his own early promise, and though his were never Webster's faults, they have been read as equally serious in their consequences.

The occasion for his evaluation of Webster was Lodge's biography of the Great Man, timed for the anniversary of Webster's birth, nor was it the only centennial event. But where the ceremonies sponsored by agencies like the

Webster Historical Society chiefly resurrected the Whig pieties of 1852, Lodge took a highly critical view of his subject. Though willing to give credit where it was due, acknowledging that Webster "stands today as the preeminent champion and exponent of nationality" (which would provide a substantial, if to some eyes piratical, plank in Lodge's own platform), the disciple of Henry Adams could not forgive Webster his "moral failure. His moral character was not equal to his intellectual force" (*Webster*, 361, 360). But Lodge regarded as Webster's greatest "failing" his profligate way with money and his "indifference to debt" (357).

It can safely be said that Webster's faults were not Lodge's: never guilty during a time of widespread corruption of sharing Webster's confusion of the public weal with his own well-being, Lodge was removed by his own inherited wealth from any such temptation. But if Henry Cabot Lodge is remembered today, it is for his championing the Spanish-American War and defeating President Wilson's attempts to bring the United States into the League of Nations, achievements not now generally regarded as to his or the nation's credit. Moreover, the status that came with Lodge's wealth brought a measure of pridefulness and intransigency, an arrogant inflexibility similar to that of his childhood hero, Charles Sumner, for whom moral postures (and posturing) were second nature.

Like Sumner he was undeniably an honest man, with the courage of his convictions, and was fittingly characterized upon his death by one who knew him well as "a man of absolute sincerity," a quality defined by his memorialist as his "foundation rock" (Lawrence, 125). But like Sumner, also, his self-righteousness included a corresponding tendency to self-destruct. He was given to vituperative outspokenness and a slashing wit when crossed, opportunities for which seemed to increase, not lessen, as he grew older and abandoned his early commitment to reform. For with the turning of the century new occasions revised his sense of duty: Lodge became a champion for the imperial presence in the Caribbean that his hero Sumner had opposed, and by opposing, had lost his beloved chairmanship of the Senate Committee on Foreign Relations, which Lodge would eventually inherit.

There is very little in Henry Cabot Lodge's public life, including the ardent nationalism that gradually replaced his zeal for reform, that cannot be traced back to heredity and the circumstances of his childhood and youth. Unlike his model, Sumner, and his mentor, Adams, Lodge could not claim a direct line to the Puritans, for although his mother was descended from the fabulously taciturn Cabots of Boston, the family was relatively new to the area, their common ancestor having arrived in Salem in 1700. Anna Cabot Lodge was the granddaughter of George Cabot, a much respected Federalist senator during Washington's administration. Grandfather Cabot dropped out of active politics thereafter, though he would remain until his death in 1823 a force among Massachusetts politicians loyal to Hamilton's memory. There for the time the political legacy stopped, and young Cabot (as he was called) grew up in a family dominated by a very different heritage—business. His father, John Ellerton Lodge, was the son of an Englishman who had fled to America from Santo Domingo during the 1791 uprising. Finding himself by chance in Boston, Grandfather Lodge founded a shipping firm that was carried on after his death by John Ellerton until his own death, in early middle age, in 1862.

Lodge was twelve at the time, and though he preserved fond memories of his father and the good times they enjoyed together at the family's summer home on Nahant, he spent his adolescence in the even fonder company of his mother, resulting in something akin to Lord Fauntleroyism, but with a decidedly spoiled edge. He was, however, by his own account very much a man's boy, given to sports and mischief, and he spent his undergraduate years at Harvard enjoying himself immensely, following pursuits in no way connected with his studies. His youth was in general characterized by a desultory indolence, a quality of indifference that was extended into an early and very tentative career in law.

In this Lodge resembles the young Wendell Phillips, whose brand of radicalism he detested, much more than the admired Sumner, who had been born into a tradition of active reform. But Lodge's sudden decision to abandon Harvard and Henry Adams for politics has never been attributed to the influence of his cousin-wife, Anna Cabot Davis; it seems, rather, to have been a delayed explosion of ancestral genes. Though Adams opposed his protégé's change of career, it must be said that Lodge never gave up his interest in scholarship and writing, although his pursuit of an alternative career as an author of books intended for a popular audience, like his biography of Webster, habitually let his view of the past yield to the political issues of the moment.

Lodge's drift toward politics was first indicated by his Ph.D. thesis, which was not in history but political science, a scrupulously researched account of Anglo-Saxon land laws that reflected the new, German-inspired scholarship fostered by Professor Herbert Adams at Johns Hopkins. And his most substantial contribution to scholarship during this early period was his *Life and Letters of George Cabot*, first published in 1878. The book may not have inspired his coincidental impulse to enter public life at that time, but it certainly put the author through an extended baptism in Federalist ideals, requiring total submersion in Hamiltonian economics.

Lodge in his memoirs credits an emotional episode in a postgraduate year abroad for his entrance into politics, which we shall consider in a later place, but certainly the coincidental threshold provided by his extended recovery of ancestral Federalism may be credited with having its effect. Lodge's choice in 1886 of Edmund Quincy as an admirable example of leisure put to good use could hardly have been made in ignorance of Quincy's own Federalist background, and Lodge's commitment to moral purity—though typical of the Victorian age—was certainly in the old Federalist spirit. And yet he espoused political specifics that were not obvious manifestations of the Federalist tradition, being in synchronization with contemporary reforms.

He worked in Congress to continue Curtis's good work on behalf of purifying the civil service and forwarded Sumner's legacy of granting civil rights to southern Negroes. And Lodge by the turn of the century had joined his friend Roosevelt in taking on the trusts, backing legislation that would curb the monopolistic tendency of big business. This drawing of power toward the center of government was hardly what Hamilton had in mind, and even Lodge's fight to preserve the gold standard was a ploy to establish bimetalism internationally. In sum, Lodge was something of a mutant Federalist, which is to say he was a Republican during an age of ideological transition, which necessitated a certain flexibility.

For example, in his attempts to forward the imperialist annexation of the Philippines in 1900, Lodge cited the priority of Jefferson's purchase of Louisiana, without mentioning that it had been an act exceeding the constitutional powers granted the president that had inspired paroxysms of outrage in Federalist New England and was regarded by Henry Adams as the defining paradox of Jefferson's administration. And yet in many other ways Lodge continued to champion the letter of Federalism, evincing a definitive paranoia regarding foreign influences, including not only international matters but the perceived threat of immigration. And by the early years of the twentieth century he would become increasingly concerned with international matters, with extending the sphere of American influence well beyond the limits implicit in the Monroe Doctrine. During this later phase of his career, Lodge would abandon the reformist tradition associated with Sumner and Curtis.

His friend and fellow expansionist during those transition years, Theodore Roosevelt, would do otherwise, lending great physical power and psychic energies to further attacks on the ills of American capitalism, espousing reforms that he took much further than Lodge wished to go. Roosevelt became famous even in defeat as a man of courage and determination to do right, in effect practicing what Lodge had preached to Harvard students in 1886. He was, like those other profiles carved on the side of Mount Rushmore, a colossus of rectitude, if carefully self-sculpted in advance.

Lodge, by contrast, for all his ferocious energy, wit, and intelligence, even during his lifetime—as his good friend Barrett Wendell regretfully observed— became a bitter and diminished thing, for reasons and with consequences we shall be considering thenceforth. Because when Lodge was the orator of the day on the occasion of the Pilgrim tercentenary, he brought to Plymouth Rock the sum total of what he had been, what he was, and what in many ways his New England had become. Nor was it difficult to detect in Lodge in 1920 a ghostly presence, the perturbed spirit of Federalism that Webster had thought to lay to rest a century before.

II

In 1888, Lodge was a guest of the New England Society in Brooklyn, and responding to the traditional toast "THE DAY WE CELEBRATE," he began with a rhapsodic paean to New England in a Websterish vein—"It is but a little corner of the great land which we call our own, and yet we love it"—and then inspired a cry of horror by threatening to deliver "a discourse on the tariff. ('No! No!') I see your eagerness; I see how anxious you are to hear it. . . . [*Laughter.*]" (*Proceedings*, 24–25). As a public speaker, Lodge was the master of a certain dry humor, few instances of which survived subsequent revision for the volumes of his collected speeches. But the burden of his remarks in 1888 made the cut and were the occasion for very little laughter, being a discourse not on the blessings of the tariff but on the true meaning of "Americanism."

Lodge's speech in Brooklyn was an early expression of what would become an emerging reactionary and jingoistic spirit that colored the militant imperialism for which he is best known. Unlike his economic agendas, which in replacing his early commitment to reform reflected the ongoing evolution of the Republican Party, Lodge's rightward shift had a primarily internal logic. As we have seen, he was hardly alone in voicing concern in the wake of the Haymarket Riots, but it was the subsequent combination of his exclusivist posture regarding immigration with his advocacy of imperialistic adventuring that provided a unique blend of his inherited Federalism and the expansive, seaborne commercial spirit evinced by the paternal line. For it was increased trade with China that Lodge hoped to draw to America by his advocacy of annexation, first of Hawaii in 1895, then of the Philippines in 1900. Still, the connection with his celebration of the Puritan spirit in 1888 is definitive of his character and was put forward in identifiably Federalist terms, for whatever the cause to which Lodge turned his not inconsiderable powers, it was always in the service of what he deemed was right.

In 1884, Lodge had addressed the New England Society in New York at its anniversary dinner and struck a chauvinist and neo-Federalist note in celebrating the Puritans' "Independent Spirit." In denouncing America's "dependence on foreign ideas" in artistic matters, Lodge declared that "the past is across the water," in the Old World, while "the future is here in our keeping," and that "when nature does not lend itself to art it is because there is no art able to borrow. Let the right men come in the right spirit and they will have no trouble with nature" (*Speeches*, 5, 10). This is the old Whig notion updated, which drew a distinction between ruins and railroads, but it also shares Emerson's contempt for the dead hand of the past. Though trained as a historian, Lodge seems to have been well advised to leave the academy for the political arena, for his passion was to seize the present moment, a point to keep in mind as we consider his reaction to contemporary "social and labor problems."

For Lodge in 1884, the important thing about the Puritans was their "spirit of hostility to foreign control and foreign influence," in effect an updated Hamiltonianism. Lodge's was a nativist emphasis that urged a national literature that "must accept . . . our own conditions": "of 'Americanisms' of the right sort we cannot have too much." In Brooklyn in 1888, Lodge went on at greater length to define what he meant by "the right sort," a handily ambiguous term that, like Roosevelt's "right stuff," lent itself to any number of connections, in Lodge's case the link in the celebrations of the Pilgrims between Puritan exclusivism and the anti-immigrant bias that had been accelerated to hysteria by the Haymarket Riot.

Lodge took great pains to separate his brand of Americanism from that of the Know-Nothings, which "had a brief political existence more than thirty years ago" and which was based "on race and sect," an emphasis that was "thoroughly un-American. . . . True Americanism says, 'Hands off!' " (25–26). Indeed, "Hands off!" would in its many applications characterize Lodge's national and international policies over the next thirty years, as open (and closed) an expression as "the right sort." In time, that "spirit of hostility to foreign control and foreign influence" would extend far beyond the water's edge.

But the present problems of 1888 were internal and required a hands-on policy, and in rising that year at the Forefathers' Day dinner in Brooklyn, Lodge did not tarry long on conventional themes. Having lumped together the "Pilgrim and the Puritan" as Lowell's men who "did a great work in the world," he moved on in the manner of someone (say Sumner) impatient with history to contemporary concerns (*Proceedings*, 24). For there was great work yet to do, evinced by "the enormous gravity of the social and labor problems which confront us," which "True Americanism recognizes," and for which it seeks solutions "without rest and without stay" (26). "True Americanism" as Lodge defined it, while believing "the safety of the Republic depends upon well-paid labor, and the highest possible average of individual well-being," was utterly opposed to "the doctrine of the Anarchist and the Communist, who seek to solve the social problems not by patient endeavor, but by brutal destruction" (26).

In 1884, Lodge had urged men of wealth to achieve sympathy "with the American people and with American ideas," to give up "living in Europe, by mimicking foreign habits, by haunting well-appointed clubs, or by studying our public affairs in the columns of a Saturday Review." They should, as he would urge Harvard graduates in his Lowell-inspired address, "go to work." Lodge had pointed the way by outlining a program of legislation that would promote "the welfare of . . . working men and women," an agenda that was consistent with his subsequent career after his election to Congress and which not a little resembles a campaign speech laden with the kind of lumber from which political platforms are made: "Practical measures are plentiful enough: the hours of labor; emigration from our over-crowded cities to the lands of the West; economical and energetic municipal governments; proper building laws; the rigid prevention of adulteration in the great staples of food; wise regulation of the railroads and other great corporations; the extirpation of race and class in politics; above all, every effort to secure to labor its fair and full share of the profits earned by the combination of labor and capital" (7, 9).

This list is a calendar of progressive measures, in line with the liberal Republicanism of the day, and would seem about as far from the stringent simplicity of the Federalists as one could go. Surely to extend the role of government well past protective tariffs and deep into the private sector—while conscientiously protecting the rights and well-being of labor—is a policy that could never have entered Hamilton's hive of a head. This last, however, was chiefly inspired by the interests of the large working-class population in Lodge's Essex County constituency, a political consideration with which no Federalist of Hamilton's generation had to deal. The people might still be a mob, but the mob now had the vote.

And Lodge's progressive view of the opening opportunities of the West was in line with his friend Roosevelt's enthusiasm for ranch life and the hunting trail, as well as a late expression of the idea, originating with Edward Everett, that the West served as a safety valve for social pressures. But the Lodge who was capable of making these liberal Republican sounds in 1884 was by 1888 preaching a vehement, hard-line sermon against an alien menace, in synchronization with his nativist animadversions against foreign influence surely, but enforcing a perimeter suddenly shrunk to correspond with the continental limits of the United States. In other ways also, Lodge's liberal coloration would fade, revealing a palimpsestic Federalism underneath, as well as a closer resemblance to the exclusionist position of the American Party than Lodge was willing to admit.

Between his appearance in New York in 1884 and that in Brooklyn in 1888, Lodge spoke before the New England Society of Philadelphia, which had survived despite Mark Twain's efforts to disband it. In 1887, at the usual occasion, Lodge responded to the toast "The Puritans," and his sentiments provide a useful waymark to the emergence of his underlying Federalism. He stressed the capacity of Puritanism for change—"Has [New England] not freed herself from the narrowing influence of her early creeds, and turned her intellect to broader and nobler works?" (*Speeches*, 35). It was a leading question that carries forward John Robinson's famous farewell advice, but it can be easily translated to explain both the changes in and the consistency of Lodge's ancestral heritage.

In 1885–86 there had appeared Lodge's nine-volume edition of Hamilton's works, scholarly labors that like his filiopietistic tribute to George Cabot may be seen as occupying an important juncture in the author's public life. These scholarly works were liminal thresholds, the first of which was published as he entered politics, and now a second one as he was at last successful in his attempts to be elected to national office. The year 1886, once again, was a frightening one for establishmentarians, the events of which may have acted to reinforce in Lodge a Hamiltonian distrust of the populace, which if given too much liberty would revert to anarchy. Certainly his tribute to the Puritan delivered in Philadelphia is not difficult to translate into equivalent terms: "The Puritan," he declared, "stands out in history as distinctly as a Greek temple on a hilltop against the brightness of the clear twilight sky. It is a stern figure enough, lacking many of the ordinary graces, but it is a manly figure withal, full of strength and purpose" (34).

This stark outline of the Puritan "as he really was" was familiar enough by 1887, a statuesque apparition equivalent to the figures cast in bronze by Ward and Saint-Gaudens and in rhetoric by the Reverends Storrs and Beecher and any number of honorables attending Forefathers' Day celebrations of the period. But it is a figure evocative also of the Federalists: "They were an able, strong, hard-headed, and rather dogmatic body," Lodge wrote of them in his biography of Hamilton, "most of them holding high places in the republic" (*Hamilton*, 278). Highest of all in profile, of course, was Alexander Hamilton himself: Lodge quotes Jefferson as calling his chief antagonist the "Colossus of the Federalists," a monumental metaphor that matches Lodge's "Greek temple on a hilltop" (276).

The same Federalist fealty to right angles can be detected deep within Lodge's legislative agenda in 1884, because if it is heavily weighed with measures reforming the ills of capitalism, those measures not only purified the institution central to the Federalist idea, the very basis of the system of checks and balances, the Constitution, but they were intended to curb the excesses associated by aristocrats of inherited wealth like Lodge with the vulgar class of plutocrats then emerging from the social substrata. In effect, he was driving the money changers from the Federalist temple on a hill.

But perhaps the strongest line of continuity with his Federalist antecedents can be found in Lodge's emphasis on declaring independence from foreign influences, even while reviving "the high and self-respecting spirit of the Puritan" among Americans of wealth and privilege. For this was a modern equivalent not only to the nationalistic spirit of the revolutionary period but to the xenophobia of the Federalists aroused by the French Revolution, given particular point by Jefferson's perceived friendliness toward the excesses of Jacobinism. And it would eventually prove to be the chief armament in Lodge's imperialist arsenal, when the time came to convert the Monroe Doctrine into Roosevelt's big stick.

The Haymarket Riot may be said to have played, albeit in a minor key, the same role among conservatives that the Reign of Terror performed nearly a century earlier. For it aroused that latent paranoia regarding an alien presence in the land that was the dark inheritance of New England Federalism as personified by Jedidiah Morse and Timothy Pickering. It had resulted in the Alien and Sedition Acts and the first stirrings of secession east of the Hudson River. Thus where in 1884 in New York Lodge had regarded "the idle, the worthless, and the criminal" as forming "but a small element of the community," vastly outnumbered by "honest, God-fearing working men and women," in 1888 in Brooklyn he changed his emphasis, if he did not reverse his proportion.

"In the great public lands of the West," declared Lodge, "an American policy sees one of the safeguards of the Republic. It opposes the further use of these lands to invite immigration or to attract speculation. They should be the heritage of the American people, and not a bait to draw a surplus population that we do not want. [*Applause.*] The true American policy goes further, and believes that immigration should not only not be stimulated but that it should be restricted. The pauper and the criminal, the diseased and the vicious, the Anarchist, the Communist, and the Mormon should be absolutely shut out, while the general flow of immigration should be wisely and judiciously checked" (27).

Lodge's sudden shift regarding the use of western territories has a familiar Federalist sound, being a revival of opposition to unchecked western expansion that the Federalists associated with rampant real estate speculation and the sapping of the political power (and labor pool) of established eastern centers. Lodge shared the Federalists' objections regarding speculation but updated their latter concern, the problem not being insufficient laborers but too many.

The appearance of the Mormons on Lodge's list of the great unwanted, the result of polygamous Utah seeking admission to the Union as a state, brings forward to the Gilded Age earlier animadversions against the equivalent Quakers of the day, not those modern paragons of respectability and family values but, as Lodge expressed it, "a people who defy our laws and maintain a barbarous and corrupting system of marriage." At best, as in Artemus Ward's monologues or Mark Twain's *Roughing It* (1872), the Mormons were a butt for ribaldry because of their household harems. At worst, as in Joaquin Miller's popular melodrama of the period, *The Danites* (1877), they were regarded as a kind of frontier Mafia, licensing bands of "avenging angels" to destroy their enemies. Lodge would not be the only speaker addressing the New England Society in Brooklyn who would lump Mormons with anarchists as enemies of America, and at the end of his celebration of Americanism as exclusionism, he was greeted by "*tremendous applause*," an indication of the popularity of his argument among the members and their guests.

Though Lodge maintained that he had no sympathy with the American Party of the 1850s, by substituting "Roman Catholic" for "Mormons" the similarity is revealed. Like Lodge, the Know-Nothings were aroused to action by what they feared was "the encroachment of foreigners on the sacred rights of American citizens" (*Sons of the Sires*, 28). Their spokesmen described the ambitions of the Roman Catholic Church as operating subversively, seeking to undermine "our noble Constitution," by "ulterior designs to substitute for it the tyranny of the Inquisition" (29). Lodge attempted to "shut out" undesirable immigrants, on grounds similar to the Know-Nothings' plan to delay the process of naturalization, for "unless some radical change takes place in relation to the admission of foreigners to citizenship, they will work disastrous ruin to our institutions" (*Sons of the Sires*, 65). But, once again, the common thread of paranoia and xenophobia may be traced back to the Federalist hysteria regarding the subversive threat from "foreign" influences.

Guarding the gates to America would remain one of Lodge's obsessions, and after his elevation to the Senate in 1893, the same year that Frederick Jackson Turner announced the closing of the frontier, hence the turning off of the safety valve, Lodge mounted legislation that would restrict immigration, introducing a bill to that effect in 1896. Lodge's speech proposing his bill was an elegant literary performance that, in warning that "the quality of our citizenship is endangered by the present course and character of immigration to the United States," quoted Carlyle's famous passage on the Promethean cargo of the *Mayflower* (*Speeches*, 251, 257). But to the credit of the Congress Lodge's bill was defeated.

Ironically, George Cabot had opposed the extremes of reaction expressed by the Alien and Sedition Acts, as Lodge knew full well. But his great-grandfather's correspondence is filled with expressions of hatred and loathing toward France and Jacobinism, and in his commentary Lodge revealed his deep sympathy for Cabot's position. He likewise shared his great-grandfather's aversion to Jefferson, an attitude that his association with Henry Adams could only have encouraged. But as his subsequent use of Jefferson's expansionist priority suggests, Lodge was quite capable of learning from the lessons of history, and he framed his remedy to the modern, if equivalent, problem accordingly.

Thus, the Alien and Sedition Acts, as George Cabot predicted, had proved to be counterproductive, inspiring a popular backlash against the Federalists because of their persecution of "subversives" who were American citizens for the most part, guilty only of voicing incautious Republican sentiments. But Lodge's proposal for restrictive immigration would have stopped undesirables at the gate, thereby avoiding the noise and consequent public scrutiny occasioned by the repression of internal subversion. As a tactic, it was an epitome of Brahmin tact, for the closed-door policy had long been in effect on Beacon Hill and in Harvard Yard, where only the "right sort" were let in through the door.

III

Lodge's xenophobia was shared by many men of his class and political convictions. On Forefathers' Day in Brooklyn in 1892, the perennially open-minded and good-natured Joseph H. Choate conjured up a group of Pilgrim Fathers from "their forgotten graves" and sent them traveling westward "to see how their descendants are getting along" (*Proceedings*, 31–32). "Westward" in this regard meant the east bank of the East River, and Choate felt the Pilgrims would feel right at home among the residents of Brooklyn, "but they would not feel quite so sure of that medley of strange voices and that din of foreign customs that is echoed from across the East River, and so here they would pitch their tents and here they would set up their Ebenezer."

On the other hand, exclusivist sentiments were not universal among the celebrants of the Puritan spirit in Brooklyn. Thus Lodge was followed on the program in 1888 by the Reverend T. De Witt Talmage, a Dutch Reform minister who, in speaking for "the descendants of the men who embarked off Delft Haven for this promised land of America," chose to celebrate them as an early instance of immigrants, being "foreigners from a foreign land" (32). At the New England Society dinner in New York in 1855, Richard O'Gorman of the St. Patrick's Society had delivered an impassioned appeal on behalf of the contributions of immigrants to American progress and prosperity, during which he styled the Pilgrims as "those fearless few—the earliest immigrants to the shores of New England," a very early instance of that inclusive notion (*Report of the Semi-Centennial Dinner*, 106). O'Gorman's remarks were undoubtedly inspired by the Know-Nothing agitation, and in updating his metaphor Talmage likewise urged his auditors to "set yourselves against the stupid and asinine cry of 'America for Americans,'" advice that can only be taken as a corrective of Lodge's equivalent nativism.

Talmage was an exceedingly popular preacher who in 1882 had taken on Robert G. Ingersoll, the spellbinding advocate of agnosticism, and did not fear Congressman Lodge. While agreeing that "we want none of the thieves and scoundrels and Anarchists of other lands, for we have enough of our own,"

Talmage called for an open door to America "for all men who will come and be genuine Americans, swearing loyalty to our government, and working for the public good": after all, he observed, "the only Americans in this country who are not descendants of foreigners are the Indians. And what an interesting spectacle it would have been if, on the morning of December 20, 1620, on the shores of Cape Cod had assembled the Modocs, and the Cherokees, and the Mohicans, and the Chippewas, and the Ottawas, and the Tuscaroras crying, 'Go back with that ship; keep off our soil; home with you to England and the Netherlands; America for Americans.' Drive from our American merchandise and American law and American theology and American art the foreigners, and you would set this country back half a century" (32–33).

The terms of Talmage's remarks have a distinctly modern ring, but over the years that followed, his sentiments were not much echoed in Brooklyn on the occasion of Forefathers' Day. When in 1892 Ellis Island replaced Castle Garden as the entranceway to the United States, it put in place a mechanism intended to filter out what that stalwart gatekeeper General Horace Porter defined in his remarks in 1887 as "a vicious element, men who were Godless, conscienceless, who sneered at holy things and blasphemed against Heaven" (41). A decorated veteran of the Civil War and a longtime associate of President Grant, Porter would allow only "a wholesome, vigorous immigration." Thus Ellis Island could be regarded as carrying on "the work of the staunch, sturdy, brave old Puritan" as figured by so much rhetoric mounted during these occasions, terms suggesting the guardian figure in Central Park, as opposed to the welcoming woman in New York Harbor.

Where Roebling's great bridge during the celebrations in Brooklyn through the decade of the eighties was often cited as a symbol of union between the two cities, the Statue of Liberty was alluded to only once, in 1884, two years before its completion. The reference was made by Professor Theodore William Dwight, of the Columbia Law School, in a formal address entitled "No Law Without Liberty; No Liberty Without Law." Dwight's paper focused on the English Puritan martyr William Prynne, and he got around to America only in his closing remarks, in which he observed that "lynch law and Mormon Law must go the way marked out by the final extinction of slave law," for "Liberty will not associate with barbarism—it will have no consort with the sons of Belial" (36–37). This brought to Dwight's mind the proposed "erection in a conspicuous place in our harbor, crowning a majestic pedestal, of a magnificent statue of liberty lifting a flaming torch enlightening mankind."

The professor allowed that such a figure was certainly appropriate as a symbolic presence, but he deemed it "an imperfect conception" by itself and proposed adding "a companion statue of Justice, with her scales weighing all things, even the claims of liberty itself, determining whether it is a bastard liberty or a true and glorious liberty, the precious inheritance of freemen made free by the truth, liberty united with law, 'now and forever, one and inseparable' " (37). Despite the echoes of Webster, Dwight was operating in the spirit of Lowell, in his indirect, academic way suggesting that a certain narrowness of entrance was still advisable and that the statue proposed for New York Harbor was perhaps too generous and wide-open a conception: "The question comes home, Whither is the human race marching, and for what purpose *does it need light?* The answer is, it needs to be lighted to the judgment seat of an impartial justice," which though in harmony with Charles Sumner's pairing in 1873 was hardly Bartholdi's notion.

Much more in keeping with the sculptor's intention were the remarks of Chauncey Depew, who was one of the many speakers at the dedication of the Statue of Liberty in the troubled year 1886. Himself of French descent, despite his frequent celebrations of the Dutch heritage, Depew stressed the long history of amicable Franco-American relations, obligatory given the source of the gift now decorating the harbor. But in summing up its message, that "American liberty has been for a century a beacon light for the nations," Depew did not get much further than Webster had in 1825 (*Orations*, 1:105). Like the Bunker Hill Monument, the Statue "rises toward the heavens to illustrate an idea," the progress of Liberty over the ages, inspiring "the charter in the cabin of the Mayflower, and the Declaration of Independence from the continental Congress" (107).

Depew made no mention of Plymouth Rock, which hardly made a show when placed against the Statue, but his remarks were otherwise completely in sympathy with the sentiments traditionally offered during the dinners of the New England Society in Brooklyn. The occasion, however, mandated an emphasis on the optative, Depew assuring his listeners that "the problems of labor and capital, of social regeneration and moral growth, of property and poverty, will work themselves out under the benign influences of enlightened lawmaking and law-abiding liberty, without the aid of Kings and armies, or of anarchists and bombs."

For "Liberty levels up the people to higher standards and a broader life," a truth that brought Depew to a sentiment not originally intended by Bartholdi but which had been added to the meaning of his statue by the now famous poem affixed to its base: "The rays from this beacon, lighting this gateway to the continent, will welcome the poor and the persecuted with the hope and promise of homes and citizenship. It will teach them that there is room and brotherhood for all who will support our institutions and aid in our development; but that those who come to disturb our peace and dethrone our laws are aliens and enemies forever."

This was not exactly in the spirit of Emma Lazarus but did express a balance between her famous welcoming lines and those often belligerent notes of warning sounded by Lodge and other guardian spirits of the age. It was a reminder perhaps that the promise held out by the torch was one thing and the apparatus soon in place on Ellis Island was another. The dream of Professor Dwight in 1884 had in effect by then been answered, the Statue of Liberty being balanced by an architectonic expression of Law. And, in 1902, Depew addressed himself to the meaning of Ellis Island also, when he rose at the Forefathers' Day celebration of the New England Society in New York to respond to the toast "If Miles Standish Were Here," sentiments quite in keeping with Dwight's desire.

Depew was certain that the resurrected Pilgrim would be pleased by the moral reforms recently initiated in "our cities," the work of "a descendent of the Puritans" (he apparently had the Reverend Charles Henry Parkhurst in mind), but a "visit to Ellis Island would shock and startle the gallant Captain beyond all his experience" (*Orations*, 4:43). Standish would be informed that "our immigration as a whole has deteriorated. The less we need of foreign importations for the development of our industries the poorer grows the quality," and what followed by way of solution was in keeping with Depew's message in 1886, but there was a detectable shift in emphasis.

"We should not put up any impassable barrier, but we should raise high the bars. . . . The enemies of government and society should be excluded. We do not want our labor demoralized and society endangered by such dense masses of ignorance that it is almost impossible to absorb them into and make them worthy citizens of our body politic" (43). Where the Reverend Talmage had declared himself content with handing incoming immigrants "copies of the Constitution of the United States and the Declaration of Independence, the Ten Commandments, and the Sermon on the Mount, and then tell[ing] them to go whither they will, and do the best they can for themselves and their families," Depew maintained that a literacy test should come first: "To be able to read our Constitution in their own tongue is not a hard requirement."

Depew gave the closing words to Miles Standish, yet another instance of rhetorical ventriloquism, and the captain, having toured the United States and had his worries about " 'the destructive threats of anarchists and the distributive theories of socialists' " put to rest " 'by an interview upon these same subjects and the future of the country with President Roosevelt,' " pronounced himself well satisfied with the "virile race" of which he was the "mighty progenitor." For the benefit of the members gathered, Standish delivered a final benediction and prophecy, the sort of thing associated with Elder Brewster before the Civil War had set up military men as models of masculine governance, not excepting President Roosevelt.

"'You have dispersed the Indians and occupied their lands. You are so isolated and powerful that you are placed beyond the possibility of assault from any foreign nation. You have made nature your slave; you have subdued the forces of the air, the water and the earth to your will and made them the ministers of your progress; your problems are all within yourselves and in your own household. The charter framed in the cabin of the Mayflower for just and equal laws is as competent to solve the difficulties of the United States of America as it was to form into a political community the little company which landed upon Plymouth Rock'" (44). Standish was convinced that that the problems of the sprawling nation were "'insignificant before the difficulties we, your ancestors, faced,'" and in his opinion popular education was the remedy for the nation's ills, supported by the teachings of the church: "'The State House and the Court House are safe only in proportion as they are inspired by the church and the school house.'"

It is easy enough to dismiss such solutions as simplistic and to mock the xenophobic fears of Depew and Lodge, of General Porter and Professor Dwight, but they were shared by many intelligent and well-informed men of the day, who never graced the precincts of the New England Society in Brooklyn. They included even William Dean Howells, whose openness to European culture and ideas, including Tolstoy's social theories, could not accommodate the swarms of immigrants he encountered in the streets of New York, to which he had moved in 1889 to take over the editorship of *Harper's*.

Thomas Bailey Aldrich, who succeeded Howells as editor in Boston of the *Atlantic*, in 1892 wrote his bigoted *caveat canaille* "The Unguarded Gates," an exclusivist exercise that served as a corrective to the welcoming lines by Emma Lazarus. Aldrich's poem pointedly characterizes Liberty as a "white Goddess!" and warns in an apocalyptic vein about the "wild motley throng" flooding unchecked into America and bringing with it "unknown gods and rites": "In street and alley what strange tongues are loud, / Accents of menace alien to our air, / Voices that once the Tower of Babel knew" (*Writings*, 2:71–72). Not coincidentally, Lodge's speech in the Senate urging the restriction of immigration ended with a lengthy quotation from Aldrich's caveat.

In a letter to a friend, Aldrich alluded to his just completed poem "in which I mildly protest against America becoming the cesspool of Europe. . . . I'm much too late, however. I looked in on an anarchist meeting the other night . . . and heard such things spoken by our 'feller citizens' as made my cheek burn. These brutes are the spawn and natural result of the French Revolution; they don't want any government at all. . . . My Americanism goes clean beyond yours. I believe in America for the Americans; I believe in the widest freedom and the narrowest license, and I hold that jail-birds, professional murderers, amateur lepers . . . and human gorillas generally should be closely questioned at our Gates. Or the 'sifting' that was done of old will have to be done over again" (Greenslet, 168).

Though Aldrich is not known as a celebrant of the Puritans, his allusion to "sifting" evokes the traditional notion and phrase associated with the winnowing process by which the "choicest grain" of the Puritans was sifted to produce the founders of Massachusetts—a figure first coined by the Reverend (later Governor) William Stoughton in his election sermon of 1668—but here he seems to be alluding to the rigorous policies and severe punishments by which "undesirables" were kept out of the colony.

That the exclusionary ideal was generally shared by men of high position and influence in the 1890s is further borne out by the testimony of Phillips Brooks, the popular Episcopalian priest of Boston and a man of great doctrinal generosity. Though of Puritan origins, Brooks at a young age accompanied a parental shift from Unitarianism to the faith that was proving increasingly attractive to residents of his native Boston, a tendency that Brooks rose upon with great success. Avoiding theological wrangles and ecclesiastical disputes, Brooks was gifted with a large frame and radiant personality that projected a spirit entirely Christian, an energetic and benevolent presence that did much to identify Episcopalianism with the evangelical energies of the day.

Son of a businessman, Brooks combined spirituality with a Lowell-like sense of the realities of the world, and in 1890 as the rector of Boston's Trinity Church he presided over the Lenten services of Trinity Church in New York, carrying his exuberant love of Christ deep into the precincts of Wall Street. Perhaps as a consequence of this extended demonstration of piety in a practical guise, the Right Reverend Brooks—now bishop of Massachusetts—was entertained as a guest in 1892 of the New England Society in Brooklyn, where he rose to respond to the toast "THE DAY WE CELEBRATE," giving yet another voice to sentiments common to those celebrations at that time.

For Bishop Brooks, Puritanism was not narrowly limited to the Forefathers but was identified with "the great public spirit which meddles with the things of all the earth, and which will show its force when that force is called for. It stands like a rusty gun in the corner of the room; but let no man ever fool with Puritanism, thinking the thing is not loaded, for bye and bye it will go off. It is the essential positiveness of the thing that has force and life that is going to show itself whenever needed" (32). Brooks then passed on to the idea of "trusteeship" inherited from the Puritans, "with which every nation and every age holds the earth on which it lives for all humanity and for the posterity that is to come, and by which it is to make fit for the purposes of its trust and fit to bestow the great life which is in it for the blessing of mankind. . . . We are never going to lose that conception; it may be, it must be, in order that we may make our land the blessing that it should be to all the world, that we shall stand guard over it from time to time. It may be that some day we shall receive into it the lives of the oppressed, the lives of the degraded. We shall exclude them for the moment, and it may be stand guard over the quantity in order that we may make more sure of the quality of that to which we shall welcome all the world" (35–36).

Such exclusions, Brooks emphasized, should not be enforced for selfish ends but only "because we feel so profoundly the trust that God has given to us in this America of ours, that we desire to keep her pure and to receive into her that which she has abundant power to assimilate, so that she shall be able forever to receive into a higher life, a life higher than theirs, those who come to us out of the darkness of other lands." Bishop Brooks would be dead within a year, a sudden passing at fifty-seven that left Boston in a state of shock and grief, so these must be accounted among his final words, the ambivalence of which is revealed in the twisted logic that contorts his syntax: "It is simply keeping the home of the oppressed so that the oppressed may come to her and shake their chains off upon the beach and live the full lives of intelligent and well-grown citizens within her borders."

Brooks in 1892 echoed Whittier in 1870 by insisting that "what the world needs today is more Puritanism and not less Puritanism," that there was a great need to elevate the "standards of our national life, and to do in new ways, precisely the same thing which it has been necessary to do in the old ways in other days" (37). But in declaring that "there is in Puritanism the force waiting at the door, touching the springs of action of the world at all times," the bishop in effect delineated a doctrine that keeps the door shut and the bolt thrown in the name of preserving America and the institutions handed down from the past.

As we pass over an equivalent (and centennial) threshold to that of the 1890s, encountering the tormenting question once again concerning the "right sort" of people to allow into the United States, we should perhaps check our impulse to laugh these speakers to scorn who thought to block undesirable aliens from entry and to convert the rest by "enlarging the curriculum of popular education according to the requirements of the age." It is important that we recognize our contemporary kinship with these men, who were celebrants of what Alfred Kazin in his magisterial *On Native Grounds* identifies as the "ancestral Puritanism" in American thought. For Kazin, the Puritanism of the age was epitomized by the "rasping intolerance" and the "middle-class" intelligence of Irving Babbitt, but Babbitt in Kazin's view was but a latter-day representative of a prior continuity, a narrowness of vision he attributes as well to Aldrich and Lodge (289).

Certainly, what Kazin says about Babbitt seems to fit Henry Cabot Lodge like a well-tailored riding habit, who with "his herculean energy and his talent for domination . . . belonged to the age of 'heroic enterprise' " in America: "He was a Force. . . . He knew what he knew so absolutely and insisted upon it so inflexibly that the very passion which gave him such moral authority exposed his temperamental rigidity" (298). Like Babbitt, also, Lodge maintained a faith "in the political principles of Alexander Hamilton," carrying the spirit of Federalism into the twentieth century, the ills of which Babbitt identified with a moral syphilis traceable (like modern radicalism) to Rousseau, which in Federalist terms meant Thomas Jefferson.

Had it been designed by the confraternity represented by Aldrich and Lodge, the Statue of Liberty Enlightening the World would have had a sword in one upraised hand and the "Battle Hymn of the Republic" under his arm, the song Theodore Roosevelt felt should be the national anthem. But then by 1903 the statues of the guardian Pilgrim and General Sherman were also in place, certifying the latest revision of the Republican plan, even then being acted out in the distant Philippine Islands. It is notable that when, in 1898, Lodge had stood up in the U.S. Senate for "intervention in Cuba," he opposed to the Spanish colonial tradition of "oppression, bigotry, cruelty, and terror" those "principles of liberty and of free government" associated with Holland and England (*Speeches*, 305). For in American veins ran conjointly "the blood of Holland and the blood of England," no more so than in the vessels of those very good friends Theodore Roosevelt and Cabot Lodge, counterparts to Chauncey Depew and Joseph Choate, who likewise contributed their very active support to the manifestarian mood of the age.

IV

We return now to Plymouth, the Pilgrims, and the Rock and pose as an alternative icon to Bartholdi's great statue a reading updated to the 1890s of Hammatt Billings's Forefathers monument, topped by the giant figure of Faith, who in posture and symbolism not a little resembles the much more famous figure. Where Bartholdi's colossus holds a torch aloft, Billings's points toward Heaven, and instead of a tablet commemorating the Fourth of July, Faith holds a Bible, yet both wear diadems of a sort, the one radiating a spiked halo, the other set with a single star, suggesting perhaps Hesperus, the heavenly guide that rises in the West. The Statue of Liberty was an Enlightenment ideal in human form, a secular icon, where Faith is its counterpart, Piety personified, with Enlightenment virtues relegated to supporting figures.

Equally important, like the Brooklyn Bridge beyond, which Chauncey Depew in 1886 had called "the latest and grandest result of science, invention, and industrial progress," Bartholdi's statue was a marvel of technology. Its great height was made possible by Eiffel's innovative use of iron girders, and it dwarfs not only the bridge but Billings's conception, which utilized traditional and delimiting materials. Moreover, though the meaning of the Statue of Liberty was complicated by the addition of Lazarus's poem, it remains a relatively simple icon when compared with Billings's complex assemblage of personifications and is thereby a much more effective presence, enhanced by its position as an official greeter of all who enter America by way of New York.

By contrast, as Oliver Wendell Holmes predicted, the Forefathers monument because of its isolation in Plymouth became something of a folly and was further obscured by not being completed until 1889, three years after Bartholdi's was in place. Moreover, by that late date Billings's iconography provided coincidental coordinates with the efforts of politicians and preachers to reinforce a national policy of limiting immigration, a campaign associated with and affirming the Anglo-Saxon Protestant heritage of New England, though specifically asserting the "institutions" traceable to the Pilgrims. If Bartholdi's statue became a reasonable equivalent to the colossal Clinton proposed by Henry A. S. Dearborn for the entrance to the Erie Canal at Buffalo, a beacon indicating the way to the land of opportunity, Billings's Statue of Faith could be thought of—when it *was* thought of—as a humanoid steeple of exclusivist implication.

Though in the mind of its creator the idea of Faith was coupled with Liberty, an association warranted by a great deal of Forefathers' Day oratory, Billings's monument was in effect a strictly Protestant aggregate of symbols, authenticating New England's claims for moral ascendancy that emerged during the abolitionist crusade. But after the Civil War that iconic argument began to lose force because it no longer had much point. As we have seen, Billings's concept of Liberty as an armed Roman slave was as a symbol limited to a specific issue of the day and in any event was placed in a subordinate position to Faith, which endowed the monument with an unmistakable aura of theocracy.

Bartholdi's iconography was hardly ambivalent, but it did lend itself to a conversion from Webster's Enlightenment ideal to a generally humanitarian notion, while Billings's monument became a rhetorical gesture covered over and enclosed by time, a limitation reinforced by the canopy Billings had designed for the Rock itself. Executed in the Tuscan manner, the smaller of the two monuments was fitted with gates limiting access to the sacred stone, and the attic in the overhead dome was used as a repository for the Pilgrim bones authenticated by Dr. Holmes. The result was a combination of exclusivism and ancestor worship that was inherent to the conservative impulse as expressed by Senator Lodge.

We must not forget that Billings conceived his great project during the heyday of the Know-Nothings, that nativist phenomenon with which such diverse Republicans as Senator Henry Wilson and Senator William Seward had flirted but which Lodge was anxious to detach from his own chauvinist notion of Americanism. In their publications, the Know-Nothings repeatedly invoked the Pilgrims along with George Washington and the Revolution as validating their bigotry. In their gift book *The Wide Awake*, published in 1855, there appeared a lengthy quotation from the *New York Mirror* that discussed the erection of the Forefathers monument, declaring that the Pilgrims were a "worthy object for a national monument—column, obelisk, pyramid, or temple!" (158–59).

That the Know-Nothings were concerned with adding "to the immortality of our Pilgrim Fathers" does suggest a link between exceptionalism and exclusionism: it was in that same gift book that Elizabeth Oakes Smith's essay on the women of the *Mayflower* appeared. But much as Smith's essay was in no way nativist in its emphasis, so there is nothing about Billings's design that indicates specific sympathies with the American Party. And yet the circumstances by which the artist emerged as the choice of the Pilgrim Society to execute its monument are suggestive. They certainly point forward to the exclusivist sentiments that distinguished so many remarks delivered during those Brooklyn nights in the 1880s and 1890s.

As James O'Gorman relates it, the society's competition was won by a New York firm of artists, Asboth & Zucker, immigrants from Hungary. Hearing the news, Billings objected to the prize committee that a "National Monument" should be designed by a "native," not a foreign-born, artist. We do not know the particulars of the winning design, about which the records of the Pilgrim Society (which apparently thought of "history" as stopping well short of its own activities) tell us little. Billings had apparently already given some thought to the project, because he quickly proposed the idea of two monuments, giving sufficiently attractive terms so that the committee felt his offer was not only patriotic but financially advantageous. Determined to do what they considered was only fair, the committee paid Asboth & Zucker their prize money, and the Hungarians obligingly dropped from sight.

Whatever his own politics, Billings's opinion regarding the qualifications for artists of national monuments has a nativist ring. And in the *Illustrated Pilgrim Memorial*, which contains the speeches given at the laying of the cornerstones on August 2, 1859, there is a relevant section that seems otherwise out of place in a booklet celebrating the Pilgrim experience and delineating Plymouth landmarks. Entitled "Immigration into the United States," it is accompanied by a picture of foreign nationals standing on the deck of an immigrant ship as it approaches the American shore. It is a scene that would become very familiar in time and would eventually have in the background the shape of Bartholdi's statue, with the immigrants regarding it with expectant, smiling faces. But Lady Liberty was not in any picture in 1863, the year the booklet was published, nor do the immigrants have the rapt expressions so often associated with the promise held out by the Statue. Instead, their faces wear frowns, suggesting a certain well-warranted apprehension of what awaits them at Castle Garden or perhaps a certain stubborn reluctance to submerge themselves in the great Protestant republic.

This is not to say that the essay betrays the usual hysteria of nativist paranoia, with its virulent anti-Catholic bigotry. Indeed, it borrows the anti–Know-Nothing conceit of Richard O'Gorman in 1855 by casting modern immigrants in the Pilgrim mold, as persons escaping "the intolerance of European Governments" and willing to add their strength to forwarding progress in America. They seek only a decent income and the security hard work can provide, and as workers, the writer points out, they have helped build railroads, public works, even cities, and some have followed the frontier, assisting in the settling of new states. They are populating a vast space never dreamed of by the *Mayflower* passengers, who likewise could not have conceived of the "grand and crowded emigrant ships of the present day" (27). But, despite the value of immigrants to the growth of the Republic, cautions the writer, "their social and political influence, and the impression they have made upon the mental and moral character of our institutions, have been by no means in the ratio of their numbers. Only a comparatively small proportion of those arriving here are even naturalized, while the vote is only about one-fourth of that of a native population of the same number."

Thus, where the Know-Nothings of 1855 and cautionary speakers thirty years later would be fearful about the influence of immigrants on American institutions, the writer in 1863 seems worried that they are not influential enough but are remaining detached from the country at large, becoming a rapidly growing nation-within-the-nation without vital connections to the body politic. What the writer shares in common with later, xenophobic commentators is a sense that there exists within the boundaries of the United States a large foreign population ignorant of American institutions. After 1886, by which time this intestine growth had become immense, it would be associated with that unholy trinity Anarchism, Communism, and Socialism, "anti-American" creeds that were submerged and undetected in the foreign-born mass, subversive equivalents to the Roman Catholicism that aroused the paranoia of the 1850s.

Coming as it does in the *Illustrated Pilgrim Memorial* just before a description of Billings's Forefathers monument, the essay can be seen as a prelude of sorts, attaching its message to the colossus at Plymouth in the manner of Lazarus's poem but to a contrary end. Whatever Billings's original intention may have been, this revised iconography was written in very large letters for those readers who, like the architect-artist, were defensive about the priorities of "native-born"—which is to say Anglo-Saxon Protestant—Americans. Monuments, as Archibald Alison and William Tudor suggested in 1819, could serve an educational function, but as Webster declared in 1825 and the *New York Mirror* maintained in 1855, they needed a national memory in order to work effectively, without which any monument is meaningless. And to the extent that immigrants were without such a memory, to that degree were monuments without the desired effect. Increasingly, then, erections like the Bunker Hill obelisk cried "Here!" to a diminished population.

In 1893, an ornately sumptuous volume appeared entitled *American Landmarks*, a collection of photogravures depicting historic sites throughout the North and South. Published in Boston, *American Landmarks* was a massive response to Archibald Alison's associationist aesthetic and may be regarded as an elaborate contribution to the growing American penchant for tourism, but it is also evidence as to the ideological basis for not only monument building but the necessity for preserving famous historical places. Notably, it opened with an account of Plymouth, " 'the American Mecca,' " along with a picture of the Rock, but the first photogravure of many shows Billings's Forefathers monument with admiring tourists at its base.

The editors referred in their preface to the current "fashion to sneer at the Puritan as a canting, carping hypocrite, a disturber of established institutions, the relentless opponent of all innocent amusement, a hard, angular, dogmatic revolutionist" (vii). But they suggested that a visit to "the first meetinghouse of the Puritans at Salem," with its "ancient timbers" and "rugged simplicity," would correct this attitude, by "telling another tale," bringing the visitor "face to face with men who have been, under God, the mightiest force in Anglo-Saxon history, driving their will, like a wedge, through every difficulty," a will, moreover, "dominated by their conscience, and harmonizing with that 'increasing purpose, which through the ages runs.' "

And finally, the editors proposed that their production would act to "promote a purer patriotism, and foster a stronger faith in the future of our country. We are confronted to-day by tremendous political and social problems; problems constantly increasing with the flotsam and jetsam of foreign immigration, swept upon our shores by every in-coming wave of either ocean; problems not less vital, and not less difficult of solution, than those which our fathers faced." The editors voiced no hope that their collection, expensively produced and bound in leather, would have its effect on that alien influx, but rather it would itself act as a monumental tribute to "our fathers' spirit," an inspiration to the kind of Americans celebrated by Henry Cabot Lodge.

"Let us rest for a moment" they wrote, "from the mad excitement of our on-rushing civilization, with its material aims and ignoble indifference to all that is heroic in human life, while we stand with heads uncovered in the presence of these national shrines. Let us listen, for they are resonant with the voice of all that is sacred in our country's past." What we have in *American Landmarks* is a sanctuary of sorts, enclosed within the "historic boundaries" traced within, a collection or museum of monumental structures, Memory's Nation expressed in architectonic terms, exclusivism in stone—or upon occasion in American pine given neoclassical forms.

Much as it gave strength to celebrants of Americanism, who could draw inspiration from its contents, so also the book can be read as spurring the construction of reminders of the New England priority. It was an activity that, when it reached the commemorative stage, generally found Lodge available to bless the occasion with appropriate words, as at the celebration of the long-delayed completion of Billings's monument, with which we shall be presently concerned. It was an occasion that once again certified that whatever the contemporary constructs given such monoliths, new contexts eventually revise them.

CHAPTER 22

Wherein the Rock Gets Reconstructed

Plymouth Rock is the corner-stone in the cellar wall of
our republican structure, paregorically speaking, and the
spirit of Liberty sits upon it with a drawn sword in one
hand and the torch of freedom in the other. The monument
to the Pilgrim Fathers, upon Plymouth Rock, will be three
thousand feet above the level of the sea, and can be easily
seen from New Haven, the place the Pilgrims came from,
with the naked eye.
—Ike Partington

I

Memorial Day, instituted in 1868 in remembrance of the sacrifices engendered by the Civil War, has its stone equivalents in thousands of marble and granite upthrustings located throughout the land in the years following the defeat of the Rebellion. In a report of 1910 on the Civil War monuments in Massachusetts, it was determined that there was "an easy average of more than a single tribute for every one of the three hundred and fifty-four parts into which the Commonwealth is divided," from the Soldiers' and Sailors' Monument in the Boston Common ($150,000) to a "humble record placed upon the inner wall of a rustic town hall" ($50) (Roe, 5). In making an inventory of the monuments in Plymouth County, the compiler noted of Duxbury that "it is hardly to be expected that any memorial to the soldiers of the Rebellion could rival the imposing monument to the memory of Miles Standish, a figure that dominates many miles of Massachusetts coast," and though the citizens of that town had also put in place "a very beautiful shaft" with suitable inscriptions, the Standish monument at its conception was associated with the Civil War (47).

Standish was honored as one of the original settlers of Duxbury, but the idea for a monument was undoubtedly influenced by the rising profile of the captain that resulted from his prominence in Longfellow's poem. Still, John

534

FIGURE 28. Miles Standish comes ashore on the American strand, a print by the maritime artist J. Steeple Davis (1895) that attests to the increasing dominance after the Civil War of the captain as an American icon, an emergence that accompanied the ascendancy of the United States as an imperial power, associated (as here) with amphibious assaults. (Courtesy American Antiquarian Society)

Alden was another of the town's founders, so we may add the erection of Standish's monument in Duxbury to the results of that liminal wartime process by which Alden's rival emerged as the dominant figure in the poem. As rhetoric in stone, it provides an enduring equivalent to the many comparisons with the Pilgrim captain that Generals Grant and Sherman had to endure as the price of admission to celebrations of Forefathers' Day in New York and Brooklyn.

Not coincidentally, it was on the occasion of the 250th year of that anniversary that the founding members of the Standish Memorial drew up their articles of incorporation, declaring in 1870 their intention to "erect a suitable and proper Memorial Monument . . . on or near Captain's Hill" (Allen, 17). They anticipated, in the words of their corresponding secretary, that "members of the Grand Army of the Republic alone would cheerfully erect [such] a monument," but that need was gainsaid by the generosity of "our first merchants and citizens . . . too sensible of the great service of our soldiers to allow them to be at this expense," and who therefore offered the generous sum of fifty thousand dollars to speed the monument's construction (16).

We may assume that the citizens of Duxbury were animated by other considerations besides national patriotism, for local pride was surely aroused by the rival erection across the bay, the prospect of which had been a focus of the Plymouth celebration in August of that same year. But that the recent war was foremost in the minds of the moving spirits behind the idea is borne out by the tenor of the ceremonies at the dedication in August 1871 of the as yet unconstructed monument. For the orator of the day was General Horace Binney Sargent, who, having been honorably wounded in the late Rebellion and brevetted with the rank of brigadier general because of conspicuous gallantry under fire, brought to the podium the martial postures of his grandfather's depiction of Governor Carver and his armed escort as they posed with their families on the Rock.

A practiced public speaker, Sargent gave his auditors what they expected, a thoroughly militaristic celebration of Miles Standish's achievement in America, which took its meaning from the recent conflict. Sargent celebrated Miles Standish as the prototypical "citizen soldier," defined as "skilled military force in loyal subordination to the civil authority." What Grant and all his armies had been for the United States, that "single heroic person" had been for the future of America, for had the doughty Miles not been with the Pilgrim Fathers, "the reverend heirs [*sic*] of the elders of the little church of Leyden would probably have adorned the wigwams of 'the Massachusitts'" and "Plymouth Rock would have been of no importance except to some leisurely antiquarian."

But most important, "even this beautiful headland," on which the monument was to be erected, "might have been tilled by Virginian slaves today" (33–34). We may forgive Sargent his anachronisms regarding the scalping proclivities and housing arrangements of Woodland Indians and his easy way with geopolitics for the main point he wished to make, which was to derive from Standish's example of "public service, vigorous fidelity, and trained fitness" a definition of the Pilgrim idea: "Special fitness for special work" (31, 34). The general's was a pragmatic and utilitarian notion of value in keeping with the detectable influence of James Russell Lowell on postwar oratory, and the monument intended to honor Standish was conceived in a similar spirit, in that it would serve "as a sighting point to navigators in entering Massachusetts Bay" (17).

By 1872 the design of the Standish monument had been determined, a shape presumably dictated by its intended function as a landmark for navigators, since it strongly resembled the outlines of a lighthouse, with the figure of Standish in place of a beacon. A tower rising one hundred feet, it showed to the world the heroic captain, looking eastward as if on guard, one hand resting on the hilt of his famous sword, the other holding out toward Plymouth a scroll supposedly representing the charter of the colony—or perhaps the bill for his services. The monument's simplicity and utility were not, however, sufficient to guarantee its rapid completion, which took a full thirty years, despite the promised generosity of Duxbury merchants. Oratory, as Webster had hinted in 1825, may have been a form of commemoration superior to structures of stone, but it was undeniably less expensive.

Thus during the several decades that it took to build the Duxbury monument, an address by Judge Arthur A. Putnam, of Worcester, Massachusetts, helped fill the available space. First delivered in 1877, Putnam's lecture on "Myles Standish" proved so popular that "it was subsequently given several times nearly every year until 1909, before historical societies and literary clubs in various parts of the State" (Putnam, 15). The author had been an army officer in the Civil War, had subsequently served in the state legislature, and was during his day an important force in local Republican politics. As a boy he had attended the "demonstration on the occasion of the completion of Bunker Hill Monument" and understood the importance of "the effect upon the youth of the land who may see [its] monuments rise, witness their dedication, and be thereby led to a closer study and understanding of the history they point to and illustrate" (110–11).

In his lecture, Judge Putnam, like Webster, spoke of monuments, but it was the sword of "the Defender of the little Plymouth Colony" that was the artifact chiefly celebrated, that weapon of Damascus steel described by Longfellow and used to such good, if entirely symbolic, effect by Judge Davis in patrolling Boston streets during the Civil War. "Curved at the point and inscribed with its mystical Arabic sentence," the sword contained "hieroglyphics" that "antiquarians and scientists" were unable to decipher (41). Putnam wondered if the sword was a veteran of earlier wars or if it had remained "in its scabbard, awaiting a mission greater than that of the sword of a Cortez, a Coeur de Lion or the Maid of Orleans," which began when it was placed in the hand "of the spunky little Captain whose sabre is this memento of the Pilgrims!" (41–42).

For Judge (formerly Captain) Putnam, as for Generals Porter and Sargent, the most memorable sentence to emerge from the record of the Pilgrim's first days in America was: "We chose Myles Standish our Captaine" (29). Not only did this validate the importance of a military presence on the threshold to a new state and nation, but it was "the first formal act of the Pilgrims in town meeting assembled" and was as vivid a testimony to their democratic spirit as was the Sabbath observance to their simple piety.

Hence the importance of the captain's cabalistic sword, which, by touching, we touch "this man of the Mayflower," thereby grounding the lightning and absorbing the electricity of the captain who was so terribly swift in his actions in defense of the Pilgrims of Plymouth. Putnam's lecture may be added to General Sargent's oration as signals of the failure of Longfellow's message to survive the passage of the Civil War. It should, however, be noted that for all his soldier worship, the judge left the Republican Party in protest against what he regarded as the abandonment of "its principles in entering upon the policy of colonial empire," not the liberation of Cuba in 1898, but the subsequent annexation of the Philippines as a protectorate, which last was chiefly the business of men who had missed Lieutenant Putnam's war.

II

Meanwhile, back in Plymouth, the arched canopy designed by Hammatt Billings to protect that part of the Rock still embedded in the wharf had been completed in 1867, and in 1880, the top part of the Rock was rejoined to its base. This reunion took place approximately a century after they had been separated, and at this time also the date 1620 was chiseled into the granite, replacing painted numerals. This significant event took place without the usual parade and ceremonies, a silence that seems inexplicable, given the epochal nature of the restoration and its relevance to contemporary events. Where the Patriots of 1775 had read the splitting of the two parts as prophetic of separation—disunion—citizens of Plymouth in 1880 could have interpreted the conjunction of the twain as expressing the spirit of Reconstruction, the "northern" half having been replaced on top of the "southern," but such a signification, if observed, was not recorded at the time.

In 1882, the reuniting of the two halves of the Rock was noted by Herbert B. Adams, a collateral cousin of the famous Adamses and the Johns Hopkins professor who had introduced the germ theory of cultural evolution to American historiography. In "Plymouth Rock Restored," a two-part article in the *Magazine of American History*, Adams addressed himself to several matters, bringing together "a few old facts," in effect a summation of all that was known about the Landing, including the problematic but "pleasing tradition" about the "ancient stepping-stone" at Plymouth (pt. 1:789–90).

Adams seems to have been inspired to undertake his retrospective essay by a resolution passed by the Pilgrim Society that year reinstating the 22d as the official date of the Landing, not because the society had any quarrel to pick with the decision of the committee in 1850 regarding the true anniversary but, as the resolution put it, because the 22d " 'has been hallowed by an observance during a period of over one hundred years, and consecrated by the words of Winslow, Webster, Everett, Adams, Seward, and other eminent orators of our land' " (641). As the editor of the *Magazine of American History* had observed, in conveying this information to his readers, it appeared as though "the orators were 'consecrated' by the day," rather than the day by the orators, precisely the emphasis the committee's report had argued against.

This matter was picked up by E. L. Godkin's *Nation*, preeminently the journal promoting reconstruction and reform but not a likely place for an

FIGURE 29. Hammatt Billings's baldachino for the Rock, designed in 1855 but not completed until 1867. The scallop shells dominating the Gothicized design are traditionally associated with the Pilgrims, dating from the Feasts of Shells in the early years of the nineteenth century. In 1820, Daniel Webster had one placed on a chain around his neck by a group of young women of Plymouth.

extended debate over the correct date of the Landing. Nevertheless, the *Nation* managed to stir up considerable antiquarian controversy with an article maintaining that December 22 Old Style was the Forefathers' Day first celebrated in Plymouth in 1769, the date that saw, as Adams quoted from the article, " 'a general landing of men, women, and children from the Mayflower upon Plymouth Rock' " (803). That, the *Nation* maintained, was the Landing originally commemorated by the Old Colony Club, whose members had simply ignored the difference between the old and new calendars.

With the energetic punctiliousness of an Admiral Morison, Adams set out

to disprove the *Nation's* notion, relying on *Mourt's Relation* and, most significant to his mind, a recently discovered survey map of Plymouth drawn in 1774,
with notes written on it that tradition attributed to Edward Winslow Jr. This
last document seemed in Adams's very certain opinion to demonstrate that the
members of the Old Colony Club knew the difference between Old Style and
New Style and that the Landing celebrated in 1769 and thereafter was that of
the exploring party in the shallop and not the passenger list of the *Mayflower*.
Adams maintained that there was never any such "general landing," beloved of
iconmongers, but rather a "gradual" process by means of which the Pilgrims
came ashore. Plymouth had a perfect right, opined Adams, to celebrate whatever day it wished and for whatever reason, but facts were facts and should be
distinguished finally from "myth" (803). This, we should recall, was James
Goodwin's point in 1876.

But in the end Adams pronounced the whole matter of dates entirely relative. More important was the sequence of "stepping-stones" by which the
Pilgrims made their way from Provincetown to Plymouth, much as "Germany,
England, and New England have been stepping-stones for the Aryan race in its
colonial progress westward" (790). These thresholds signified a "process" of
"self-governing village communities" that made "Teutonic land" an ever extending empire, identified in America with the "Pilgrims and Puritans," who
were "imbued with the same old English spirit of independence and self-
government in religious forms" and who "peopled a New England with Teutonic village life, strengthened by English parish experience" (790). In a figure
that recalls the metaphors of Wendell Phillips and his cousin Holmes, Adams
identified these stepping-stones with "outcroppings of that old red sandstone
of Germanic self-government which underlies all dividing seas between Germany, England, and New England" (pt. 2:41).

Adams's geology was more poetic than scientific, as Robert Arner has observed, but it was chiefly enlisted in the service of his own ur-myth, which had
to do with the Germanic continuities in English institutions and which traced
the American Revolution back to the "old Saxon right and might to tax and
rule themselves by customary law." The Revolution and the "removal of Plymouth Rock" to the town square were "surface upheavals caused by underlying
historic forces," and for years the Rock remained a "symbol of disruption,"
asserting "ideas of historic separation and local independence for Pilgrim
Fathers and Sons."

By a process of "accretion," involving "memorial sermon and public oration, local pride, New England reverence, and national respect," Plymouth
Rock became an American equivalent to the "Holy Sepulchre" or the "Caaba
of Mecca" (41, 44). As a force acting upon "the popular imagination," Adams
maintained, the reverence accorded Plymouth Rock "is beyond estimate. . . .

To be descended from, or to be associated with . . . even remote kindred of those who came over in the Mayflower, is, for a New England man, as great an honor as for an Englishman to be able to trace his lineage to those who came over with William the Conqueror, or to those who sailed the seas with a Saxon pirate" (42).

But now, with the return of the top part of Plymouth Rock "to its old bedrock near the quickening, world-uniting sea," Adams thought that the time was right to set aside the old spirit of "disruption" and assert its counterpart, the process of "healing," a principle found in both nature and history, which "restores the damaging effects of revolution and reformation without losing their healthful results" (1:789; 2:41). The reuniting of Plymouth Rock "stands for an upbuilding of local history upon the basis of a past which antedates the spirit of disruption. . . . A new era of historical restoration has begun, not an era of destructive criticism, but an era of constructive truth built upon the foundations of historic fact, good judgment, good taste, and the common sense of most" (2:48). But the "reconstruction" Professor Adams had in mind was not the process by which the South had been forced into the nineteenth century; it was of much greater scope, a "union with the great past, upon the experience of which our nation is really building to-day as upon a cornerstone" (51).

Having freed themselves "from the tyranny of the Old World," Americans now needed "to clasp hands with the English and with all good Teutons over common and quickening memories of an illustrious past. . . . Disruption is sometimes necessary in order to achieve civil or religious independence but, with independence achieved, a generous union is vital to the highest progress of nations." Of a reconstructive reunion between North and South Adams said not a word but devoted the weight of his laborious scholarship to encouraging rapport between the United States, Germany, and Great Britain, an emphasis that reinforces the truth that men who study the lessons of the past are seldom able to predict the future with any accuracy. Over the next twenty years, powerful men in America, including a student of Anglo-Saxon law, would be extending the peripheries of U.S. influence by way of ensuring that neither Germany nor Great Britain would have colonial leverage in either the Caribbean or the eastern Pacific.

Yet on another level Adams's thesis was prophetic, in that it enforced the exclusivist idea in New England. His ur-myth about the origins of American institutions gave scholarly validation to the traditional WASP hegemony at just the moment when it was about to find itself besieged by the threat posed by unrestricted immigration. He thereby gave his own measure of power to Plymouth Rock as an icon of race purity and institutional integrity: at the start of his essay, Adams acknowledged with his kinsman John Quincy Adams the uniqueness of "this traditional and actual landing-place" that "is different from all others," a "conviction" that steals over the "modern pilgrim" as he stands below Cole's Hill and "contemplates that low-lying wharf by the sea" (1:789).

But Adams at midpoint introduced a different view, the one obtainable "on a clear day" from the higher ground of the village itself, from which "one can look straight across the Bay to the sands of Cape Cod," and so also "in the clear light of history the student can look across the sea from New England to Old England and restore to his consciousness the various landing-places of his Teutonic forefathers" (806). And he closed by insisting that "the best of New England institutions really rest upon Old English foundations," maintaining in his concluding sentence that not only was the colony of Plymouth "built upon an English substructure, [but] it is no sacrifice of American independence to admit the fact" (2:52).

This bifurcated argument, which coupled the uniqueness of the Forefathers with the common inheritance of their Old World forebears, would, as Adams insisted, prove much more important than the hotly debated matter as to which was the true date of whatever Landing was celebrated in 1769. But it would have immediate consequences that Adams surely did not intend, much as he did not allude to the more recent "disruption" in the United States, which in the minds of the leaders of the Confederacy was a reassertion of the old idea of "historic separation and local independence" that surfaced with Plymouth Rock in 1776, the "sacred right of Liberty, which makes reformations and revolutions possible" (41). And testimony that that spirit had not been quelled by the Union victory would soon be brought to Plymouth Rock, which even in its reconstructed form still showed its dividing line, which no mortar made by man could conceal.

III

Among the "restorations and local improvements" that Professor Adams listed as ongoing in Plymouth, and which would make "the environment of Plymouth Rock . . . a thing of beauty and a joy forever," was the monument to the Forefathers, work on which was "progressing slowly but surely toward completion, like the Washington Monument and the [un]finished Cathedral of Cologne" (2:48–49). Where Billings's canopy was completed in something more than ten years, the most ambitious of his two projects took three times as long to build, for the colossus in Plymouth, like the Brooklyn Bridge, seemed peculiarly dogged by the vicissitudes of fate. The first major impediment was the war that the artist's Unionist iconography silently validated, but other delays followed the cessation of hostilities between North and South, most of them caused by the slowness of voluntary contributions to defray the tremendous cost of Billings's project.

Though no accidental deaths resulted from the monument's construction, the natural closures of old age slowed the work. Billings himself died in 1874, but not before he was forced to scale back his original scheme to a more realistic and economical eighty-one feet—thus removing the possibility of an interior room and tower—and his brother took over the project until his own demise in 1880. The project was further delayed by the death that same year of the Reverend Willard M. Harding, who had served as the chief fund-raiser and administrator of the project, halting construction for another four years until a committee was formed by the Pilgrim Society to replace Harding, whereupon the monument once again continued to be very slowly assembled.

It was a piecemeal process, as the cost of each of the supporting figures was donated by wealthy persons or agencies—the most of whom were not residents of Plymouth. Though reduced nearly by half, the monument when finished in 1889 was pronounced the largest granitic structure in the world, and the figure of Faith was constructed of fifteen separate sections, to a total weight of 180 tons, a fact widely circulated, perhaps in the hope of compensating for the loss in height. And when the colossus was at last completed, Adams's oversight regarding the relevance of the reconstruction of Plymouth Rock to Reconstruction in the United States was rectified, for the monument originally conceived as an assertion of the sanctity of national union served as the centerpiece for ceremonies attesting to the newfound brotherhood of North and South.

The celebration was from the start thought of as national in scope and implication, and as in 1870 letters of invitation went out to prominent persons across the United States, including the president of the United States, and as previously regrets came back from most, including the president of the United States. Thus the affair ended up pretty much a regional event, with guests limited to New England notables, including as always a number of political hopefuls. An important exception was the orator of the day, who, in an explicit nod toward the spirit of national reunion, was the Honorable William C. P. Breckinridge, a former journalist but now a congressman from Kentucky. Breckinridge, though the son of an ardent Unionist, had served as an officer in the Confederate army, commencing in July 1862, until he made up part of Jefferson Davis's bodyguard during his retreat from Richmond in the spring of 1865. His presence in Plymouth surely attested that the war was over, but as we shall see, the spirit of the Confederacy took a long time dying.

The plan had been to pair the Democrat Breckinridge with Senator George Frisbie Hoar, the liberal Republican from Massachusetts. Hoar had been active with his father and older brother in antislavery politics before the war and by 1889 was forwarding civil service and like reforms in Washington, but though the senator allowed his name to be listed among the day's speakers, he declined the honor of delivering a major address. That particular void was filled by the

Irish-born poet John Boyle O'Reilly, a Fenian hero and a journalist much loved in Boston, whose presence in Plymouth was yet another testimony to the broad-gauge views of the organizing committee.

O'Reilly did what was expected of him, in the kind of occasional poem that has occasionally happy moments delivering a flowery tribute to the land of his adoption. But this left the forensic field entirely to Breckinridge, who took double advantage of the opportunity, in terms of both duration and tactic. Aside from its length, the Kentuckian's performance is a curious document, learned in burden and politely circumspect in manner, and in terms of wit a featureless blank. Rhetorically speaking, Breckinridge was courtesy itself, but in the mode, if not manner, of Richard Yeadon in 1853, he conveyed a message in all ways contrary to his intended function.

Breckinridge touched on a number of topics in 1889, and it is impossible to do justice to his amplitude in short compass. But something of his duplicity is suggested by his insistence that the idea that the men who had drawn up the sacred Compact were innovators was a notion that contained neither "historic nor philosophic truth" (*Proceedings*, 67). Though the image of the Pilgrims gathered in the cabin of the *Mayflower* was "a captivating picture and attracts the heart," the idea that they had actually forged a "new and original governmental mode," that they had put behind them the "old forms and institutions" of Europe and "consciously" formed "new institutions, based on new principles," was a pleasing fiction only (68).

All such institutions, Breckinridge argued, are the product of slow growth, determined by preexisting conditions and forms, and thereby leave little room for radical innovation: "Each generation finds that what has been done before it comes into power, has limited its action and shut it up in quite straitened lines of choice." Lowell among others had emphasized that the Pilgrims as a group were not innovators, but Breckinridge's notion of institutional growth went much further, and like Hawthorne's story of the *Mayflower* and the Reverend Thomas Winthrop Coit's account of the Puritans, it acted to desanctify the Pilgrim experience by dismissing the exceptional implications of the Landing and discounting the Rock as a unique and liminal zone.

Breckinridge characterized the Compact as "a thoroughly English paper, simple, compact, limited, and yet comprehensive and flexible," but he noted also that the settlers of Virginia had already demonstrated "that on the shores of this continent Englishmen could make homes and might also erect in some form a Commonwealth" (91, 87). Thus the Compact is chiefly valuable as a "demonstration that they were planting the seeds of the old truths, not attempting to make some new and unknown harvest from untried seeds" (92). For it is an observable truth that "emigrants do not leave their country behind them, they carry it with them, with all that 'country' means, with their faith, custom, tradition, these are the true emigrants, which remain permanent citizens in the new land; men die, these survive" (91).

Repeatedly, Breckinridge returned to what Perry Miller called the "Virginian priority," and when in the spirit of reunion he noted that there was an "affecting link connecting the settlers of Jamestown with the Plymouth Fathers," what he had in mind was the fact that "John Smith had given to the place to which adverse winds drove the Mayflower, the name so dear from the associations with England" (94). This not only extended the Virginian priority to New England but in so doing managed to point out that the Pilgrims had not planned on landing where they did, which reinforced Emerson's point that the whole thing was a vast mistake.

Though Breckinridge's notion of the Pilgrims as a conduit of Old World ideas was quite in keeping with Professor Adams's germ theory, which was already influencing American historians, he ignored the mythic qualities of the Landing. Instead, the congressman placed the *Mayflower* passengers in their familiar tableau, "on and around that rock—the Rock of the ocean's shore," the scene so often "painted by the brush of the artist, in the song of the poet, by the pen of the historian, and the tongue of the orator." But if Breckinridge's "exiles" are endowed with an "immortal vigor," it is not derived from a unique relationship with God; rather, it was drawn through a golden wire that linked "the unseen shores of far off Europe with the untrodden wilderness of unconquered America" (96). As Herbert Adams had insisted in 1882, "it was English liberty, English independence of character, English colonial enterprise, English capital, English maritime experience, an English ship, manned by English sailors familiar with the New England coast, that brought the Pilgrims safely from old Plymouth to New Plymouth" (1:790).

But where Adams was careful not to discount the traditional Pilgrim "difference," Breckinridge insisted that there was nothing exceptional about the experience of the Forefathers, whose meaning derived from the conservative nature of institutions, which in America were derived from "the Teutonic gift to mankind of delegated power exercised by representatives." Breckinridge was willing to "gratefully admit that humanly speaking American liberty was impossible without New England" but then added the devastating qualification, "even if it were impossible to New England alone" (102). Again, we are inevitably reminded of the performance of Richard Yeadon in 1853, but Breckinridge was far more subtle in his demolition efforts, smilingly and courteously destroying any number of the sacred icons of New England, like a man with a cane held under his arm, bowing his way through a china shop.

Perhaps the congressman's most ingenious display of ingratiating insult involved his insistence on drawing a comparison between the hard facts of the Pilgrims' arrival and the humble circumstances of Christ's birth. Both events were, of course, associated with the same date, but Christmas was an anniversary that the Pilgrims were famous for having not celebrated. The coincidence was one steadfastly avoided by their celebrants in Plymouth; indeed, the holiday was not much celebrated in New England until the benign influence of Irving and Dickens began to have its effect.

But Breckinridge, even while acknowledging the Separatists' doctrinal avoidance of "all human holidays and all ceremonies not warranted by their interpretation of the Scriptures," went blithely and cheerily along, associating "the sweet morning when angels proclaimed that new birth, which meant 'Glory to God in the Highest, and on earth peace, good will toward men,' with that bleak week when those who loved the master were in exile and poverty and winter, laying the foundations of a temple to Him . . . on which have been built liberty in state and freedom in religion. . . . From the manger came the soul of that disembarkation" (95). Again, the orator's Dickensian note was in harmony with the times, and by the 1880s New England was beginning to celebrate Christmas, but the Pilgrims had not, and to insist on bringing them ashore in company with "the wise men of the East," along with their "gifts, gold and frankincense and myrrh," was in terms of the occasion a sacrilege, yet it was perfectly consistent with what had gone before.

The congressman finally got around to acknowledging the chief purpose of the celebration and ended his oration by pointing to "this monument of granite with its symbolic statues and entablatures," the completion of which had been made possible by gifts from rich and poor, from "States in their sovereignty, the Union in its national spirit" (103). Implicitly, the monument, like the United States, is a cumulative phenomenon, the slow growth of which involved "the labor of years, the hopes of thousands," all now brought to closure: "At last it is completed."

But, alas, Breckinridge's oration was not. He went on to enlarge upon the suitableness of the monument's allegory, assisted by the subsidiary figures, but then ended by demolishing it as a sudden wave destroys a sand castle: "Noble as is this lofty shaft, with its figures and inscriptions," it does not sufficiently "commemorate" the occasion it was designed to memorialize: in words strangely echoing those of Senator John P. Hale at the dedication of the Forefathers monument thirty years earlier, Breckinridge declared that the "best" monument to the Pilgrims is still "incomplete," even though it had been under construction for nearly three hundred years: "We may not be able to see its exact proportions, for the scaffolding is not yet entirely removed, and the hammer of the artisan is still heard on the walls" (104).

This was the familiar argument that promoted institutions over monuments as the most effective memorial to the Pilgrims, but Breckinridge was heading in a somewhat different direction, once again with an ulterior motive: "My countrymen, the chiefest merit of those to whose memory this monument has been erected was their loyalty to the truth as they saw the truth. For its sake they separated themselves from the communion of the church of their fathers and surrendered the sympathy of brothers with whom they agreed in most matters; for it they tore in twain the dear ties which bind men to their country and became exiles. . . . To the untrammeled pursuit and fearless advocacy of truth; to that freedom of the intellect and of the soul, which knows no other limitation than allegiance to truth, in the name of the Fathers we dedicate this monument and ourselves" (105).

As an accompaniment to these words we may imagine the rising sound of the band playing "Dixie," because by compounding the idea of separation with "loyalty to the truth as they saw the truth," the orator of the day pulled, as it were, an invisible cord dropping a curtain not from Billings's monument but from the meaning entire of his oration. It was a cord the end of which could have been detected in his earlier pairing of "the Union in its national spirit" with "the States in their sovereignty," the very issue over which, above and beyond the matter of slavery, the Civil War had been fought.

Breckinridge's oration must be accounted quite a display of audacity. Not only had he corrected the mistaken notion that the Pilgrim advent was a version of special creation; not only had he demonstrated that the Pilgrims even with the help of Boston were not capable by themselves of setting a new nation in motion; not only had he in effect reduced Billings's colossus to its component parts; but throughout his oration the Democrat from Kentucky was laboring to convert the religious impulse of Separatism to a statist equivalent of Secession. For what was the South's situation in 1860 but a glorious example of "loyalty to the truth as they saw the truth," one that necessitated the separation of brother from brother—at least in the mind of the South? As for the mind of the North, in the form of William T. Davis, the Plymouth antiquarian whose fund-raising efforts had made possible the monument's completion, it thanked Breckinridge for having "earnestly reconsecrated" himself "to the welfare and glory of our Beloved Union," suggesting either a very quiet irony or absolute uncomprehension of what had just been said (*Proceedings*, 116).

Breckinridge's performance was followed by a number of shorter speeches, only two of which need to be considered here. The first of these was by Senator Hoar, who had declined the invitation to share the honors with the congressman from Kentucky and who seemed to have some difficulty focusing on the colossus looming overhead. Though his speech was both elegant and moving, it began by celebrating not the Pilgrims but their earlier celebrants, Daniel Webster and Edward Everett, and only after the usual demurrer about the impossibility of rivaling such paragons did Hoar get around to the monument: "Faith, law, freedom . . . are the essence of New England Puritanism. From this root has grown what we call New England" (*Proceedings*, 128).

That the senator would feel it necessary to follow the time-honored custom of bowing before the forensic talents of Webster and Everett is explainable in part by his age, in terms of both years and era. Born in 1826, Hoar had entered politics at about the time that Robert C. Winthrop had left the Senate, and by 1889 he was about to replace that octogenarian as an august, white-haired presence at such ceremonies, who brought to them learning, eloquence, and the wisdom presumed to come with elder years. In 1895, on the occasion of the 275th anniversary of the Landing, Senator Hoar would be orator of the day at Plymouth and, as we have earlier had occasion to note, would expand on the superior qualities of the Pilgrim character, noting that Plymouth was never guilty of the crimes committed against humanity in Boston and Plymouth: "The Pilgrim had none of the Puritan's harshness, intolerance or religious bigotry" (*Proceedings* [1896], 29). Hoar went so far as to regret that his ancestors were among the founders of Boston, not Plymouth, though it is clear from his career as well as his oration that, despite his reservations regarding William Lloyd Garrison, his own "pedigree of the spirit" as he called it was traceable to the radical reading of the Pilgrims that emerged in the early 1850s (44).

The following year, Senator Hoar made his association with the Pilgrims all the more concrete when he took advantage of a trip to England to press the ecclesiastical authorities for the return to America of the manuscript of Bradford's *History of Plimoth Plantation*, to which Robert Winthrop had referred so reverently in 1870. Long missing, the precious document had been discovered in 1855 in the library of the bishop of Oxford by American antiquarians, and though the bishop had allowed a copy to be made and the complete text of Bradford's book had been published by the Massachusetts Historical Society shortly thereafter, the original remained in the Fulham Library.

Senator Hoar had consulted Bradford's great work in preparing his address of 1895, and becoming convinced that the manuscript was a sacred American icon, he set out to recover it. His appeal went through a complicated series of channels that by necessity reached Queen Victoria (as Defender of the Faith and Stolen Property) before it was granted by chiefly extralegal procedures. With much powwow and ceremony, the leather-bound manuscript was placed in a glass case in the Massachusetts State House, where it was left open at the page recording the words of the Mayflower Compact.

But in 1889 Senator Hoar avoided antiquarianism entirely, and rather than emulate Winthrop by engaging in scholarly discourse, he began with a rhapsodic paean to the beauties and historical associations of his native Massachusetts, centered by the town in Massachusetts that had long been his place of residence, Worcester, though animated by the spirit of his birthplace, Concord. The senator's tender home feelings had been intensified by his recent return from a journey that had taken him through the western territories all the way to the Pacific coast, a great and "marvelous region," surely, but one that contained "no fairer vision" than a Sunday morning in New England: "Ah, my friends, there is no loveliness like that of the blossom of the vine whose root is by the Rock of Plymouth" (*Proceedings*, 130).

And Hoar looked forward to that moment, now thirty years hence, when "the people of Plymouth will be getting ready to celebrate their third centennial" and conjectured (correctly) that he would not be there to witness that event. Echoing Tennyson, Hoar declared that it would "be no cycle of Cathay that they will celebrate. . . . It will be three centuries of America. It will be three centuries, which are still but the early childhood of the life of that nation born at Plymouth, which shall abide so long as God shall give faith, law and freedom to endure among men" (131). This forecast was modeled after Webster's prediction in 1820, but it may also have been intended as a mild rebuke from the liberal Republican of his congressional colleague from Kentucky, by way of restoring the regional piety regarding the Pilgrim exception. On the other hand, Hoar shared with Breckinridge a sense that the United States was only in its infancy, an optimism that would not be voiced by the orator of the day in Plymouth on the occasion of the tercentenary celebration.

It is one of those small coincidences that lend ironic spice to events that the speaker who followed Hoar on the program in 1889 would head the list in 1920. Henry Cabot Lodge was in his third year as a congressman and as we have seen was already well rehearsed in celebrating the Puritans in speeches that, like his books, were infiltrated by current concerns and were characterized also by the outspokenness that only radical zeal or the privilege of birth and the assurance of inherited wealth can bring. Where Congressman Breckinridge had indulged in a lengthy subversive circumlocution, Lodge went straight to the point, but what he had to say was no less revisionist than Breckinridge's thesis about institutional innovation.

However, what Lodge sought to discredit was not the exceptionalism of the Landing but the time-honored truism, dating from John Quincy Adams's oration in 1802 and celebrated in Felicia Hemans's famous hymn, that the Pilgrim Fathers did not come as conquerors but as men of peace. "The little handful of God-fearing men who landed here on that December day," Lodge asserted, "and that other band of adventurous Englishmen who built their cabins in Virginia, were the heads of two great columns which came for the conquest of the American continent" (*Proceedings*, 133).

The inspiration for Lodge's bellicosity is not hard to find, for that very year his friend Theodore Roosevelt had published the first two volumes of *The*

Winning of the West. Dedicated to Francis Parkman, Roosevelt's first volume takes up where Parkman's account of the French and Indian War had ended, but his opening chapter, "The Spread of the English-Speaking Peoples," like Breckinridge's account of English institutions, reaches back to "Teutonic" origins, not Adams's self-governing villages, however, or Breckinridge's representative governments, but warlike "wanderings."

Westward expansion in the form of violent spasms of territorial aggrandizement was the inheritance of the English people, whose career in America was but a repetition of earlier conquests: "The English had exterminated or assimilated the Celts of Britain, and they substantially repeated the process with the Indians in America; although of course in America there was very little, instead of very much, assimilation" (*Works*, 8:5, 10–11). In sum, an Englishman loves a Celt but cannot abide an Indian, and thus American history is a centuries-long "career of conquest," the end result of which was to bring "the whole of this great domain within the control and use of civilized man. History records no conquest vaster than this" (133).

So also Lodge in 1889, not that he needed his friend's authority. In his own *History of the English Colonies in America*, published in 1881, he described the Landing at Plymouth as "the vanguard of a great column, bearing a civilization and a system of government which was to confront that other system founded far away to the south on the rivers of Virginia, and which, after a conflict of two centuries and a half, was destined to prevail throughout the length and breadth of a continent" (342). By 1889, Lodge was no longer interested in promoting the Civil War as a climactic encounter and instead followed Roosevelt by characterizing the conquest of America as a binary but finally uniform inheritance. He also acknowledged Breckinridge's emphasis on "the principle of representation," which was "planted here by the Pilgrim Fathers, as it was planted in Virginia by the London adventurers, and spreading from these points it has reached a wider extension and a greater influence in the United States than in any other country in the world" (134).

But where Breckinridge stressed separation and secession, Lodge declared that the principle of representation gave the American empire "cohesion"—a vital third added to the inherited imperial policies of "subjugation and incorporation." Representation was a great "binding force," and in stressing it the Republican Lodge stressed union, less in response perhaps to the Democrat Breckinridge than in leading up to his main point, which was to bring the force of history down upon the House of Representatives, which had become a "travesty of representative government" (135).

Where other speakers had at least made a passing reference to the colossus looming nearby, Lodge did not, and having converted the Pilgrims into berserkers, he turned upon the House of Representatives in an equivalent guise.

His attack was on "the distribution of offices," the chief evil besetting "public life," destroying "the usefulness of parties and public men. . . . It is utterly unAmerican" (136). At the time, Lodge, like Senator Hoar, was battling for civil service reform and now identified un-Americanism with the patronage system (tacitly identified in turn with the Democratic Party), a betrayal of "the great principle of representation planted on the shores more than two hundred and fifty years ago by the men who landed on Plymouth Rock."

Lodge ended by calling to his fellow Americans to cleanse the House of Representatives and to "restore it again to the position that should be occupied by a great representative body which on this continent traces its high descent from Jamestown and Plymouth Rock" (137). It is difficult to ascertain the relevance of Lodge's remarks to the celebratory occasion, but they do testify to his ardent and Sumner-like dedication to whatever business was at hand, in this case civil service reform, a purification of those institutions that were by Breckinridge's accounting (by way of Herbert Adams) the heritage of Teutonic tribes.

Moreover, the apparent disparity between the latter part of Lodge's speech and his opening celebration of the imperial tradition in America is explained, if not resolved, by pointing to the subsequent career of the man from Massachusetts and his friend from New York, which likewise combined reform of the perceived ills of American capitalism with efforts to speed along the third phase of imperial conquest defined by Roosevelt, collateral rather than tangential lines of advance. Thus if the celebration in Plymouth was intended in part as an expression of national reunion, of which Breckinridge was both symbol and subverter, then it was Lodge who prophetically foresaw its fulfillment, figured as those two columns of conquerors, not ending as in 1861 on the battlefield opposing one another but as in 1898 extending conjointly the forefront of civilization still further, an expedition that also furthered the unifying process.

"Not the least of its many good features," wrote Colonel Roosevelt of the Spanish-American War, "was the unity it brought about between the sons of the men who wore the blue and of those who wore the gray," with the result that "the country at large is growing more and more to take pride in the valor, the self-devotion, the loyalty to an ideal, displayed alike by the soldiers of both sides in the Civil War. We are all united now" (*Works*, 13:356). It was toward that harmonious resolution that Lodge's remarks at the completion of the Forefathers' Monument were aimed, which acted to reaffirm Hammatt Billings's assertion of the sacredness of the Union but in a way hardly anticipated by the artist.

As for the other festivities in Plymouth on August 15, 1889, they followed the traditional pattern, with a "procession," marching bands, decorative arches and banners, celebratory mottoes, and the rest. One innovation should be noted, and that was the illumination of the monument "by a powerful electric focus light . . . during the evening of the celebration," which perhaps made up for the postponement of the planned pyrotechnics (because of rain) until the next night (*Proceedings*, 37). By then the dignitaries and honored guests had departed and missed the "display of fireworks . . . given near the northwesterly slope of Monument Hill, closing with set pieces representing the Mayflower, the Landing, and the National Monument with the legend 'Faith crowns the work' " (36).

The rain dampened other events as well, but in most respects the celebration was a great success, with a large crowd in attendance. The anticipated problem of pickpockets did not finally amount to much, thanks to the alertness of the local police, who were quick to recognize upon their arrival "a few noted criminals from Boston and New York" who were "either held in confinement until the next day or sent to Boston by steamboat or rail" (146). It was a proceeding the Pilgrim Fathers would most certainly have understood, whatever its coordinates with the principle of representation and equal rights under the law.

IV

As we have seen, Plymouth was from early on a tourist center, a function abetted by the regional guides written by Theodore Dwight and essential to the monument-building impulse. As John Sears has declared, tourism became a widespread and popular phenomenon after the Civil War, and the attempts of William S. Russell before the war to encourage and facilitate pilgrimages to Plymouth Rock were primitive compared with the industriousness of A. S. Burbank during the 1880s and 1890s to profit from the town's historic associations. Burbank, who ran the Pilgrim Book Store in Plymouth, was a publisher of inexpensive guidebooks and "views" of Plymouth and sold a line of Pilgrim souvenirs, including a miniature model of Miles Standish's sword, "designed for use as a scarf or hat pin," and glass paperweights in the shape of Plymouth Rock. He also commissioned a line of pictorial dishware, enabling those who so desired to dine off plates and drink from cups decorated with historic scenes, thereby absorbing depictions of the Pilgrims with their food.

This manufacture and sale of artifacts obviously benefited from the enclosure of Plymouth Rock, forcing tourists in search of souvenirs to reach for their wallets and purses instead of a sledgehammer. But it was a sign of the times generally, as the evidence of similar kinds of artificial mementos associated with other famous historic sites attests. Memory's Nation was busily commodifying itself into merchandise suitable for triumphant display in America's parlors, companion pieces to *Pilgrim's Progress*, *The Faerie Queene*, *Paradise Lost*, and *Robinson Crusoe*, as evidence of the close interrelationship between travel and piety. Still, Burbank must be accounted a pioneer in the range of items he offered, close equivalents to those decorated handicrafts sold at anti-slavery fairs in Boston during the antebellum years, and he served as a potent reminder to shopkeepers elsewhere in New England of the commercial potential of historical associations.

The expressed interest of the merchants of Duxbury in promoting (if not actually funding) the memorial to Miles Standish was hardly incidental to its function, and across Massachusetts Bay the village of Provincetown seems by the turn of the century to have heard the sound of the cash register from afar. For many years a fishing port, and visited by Thoreau in the 1850s as a remote bastion of the old Yankee spirit, by the turn of the century the town now associated with theatrical displays at several levels began to make its first stirrings in the direction of becoming a vacation spot. Its seaside location, connected to metropolitan centers by steamboat, recommended Provincetown's potential, and as the place where the Forefathers first came ashore, in whose harbor their famous Compact was written and signed and their laundry washed, it boasted sufficient historical associations to lure modern pilgrims as well.

As early as 1852, coincidental (in terms of year only) with similar activities in Plymouth, interested persons in Provincetown proposed to construct a monument on High Pole Hill, yet another of those exclamation marks designed to call attention to a historic place. Presented to the state legislature in hopes of gaining public funding, the proposal failed of approval, but even the mere prospect of a rival monument was not well received in Plymouth. In its columns for August 20, 1859, the *Old Colony Memorial* noted nervously that the *Barnstable Patriot* had revived the scheme of 1852 and was encouraging its readers to "apply their gifts not to the Plymouth but the Provincetown monument." But Plymouth's worries were needless, for Barnstable had to wait fifty years before the editor's hopes were realized, and in the meantime it contented itself with a tablet erected in front of the town hall at the expense of a native son, Chief Justice Lemuel Shaw of the state supreme court. Put in place in 1853, the tablet reminded passersby of the Pilgrims' early presence there until 1877, when it was destroyed when the building itself burned down.

Provincetown for its part continued to boast a landfall not much different, as its residents pointed out, from that which greeted the Pilgrims upon their arrival. H. A. Scudder, representing the Cape Cod Association at the 1853 celebration in Plymouth, had described in lyric terms the "bleak and dreary sand-peaks" that lifted themselves along its shore, "doubtless the same this hour as in that memorable day when first our fathers sought and found a shelter within their cheerless embrace" (*An Account*, 55). It was an assumption that ignored the Pilgrims' description of the trees and seafowl they claimed to have found there but accorded well (as Thoreau sourly noted) with Captain John Smith's less enthusiastic account of Cape Cod.

Scudder went on to insist that "such impressive mementos of the past . . . aided by the associations which they suggest" invariably carry "our minds . . . back to that ancient period," a sentiment entirely in keeping with Oliver Wendell Holmes's objection to placing any such monument as Billings had proposed in Plymouth. But in Provincetown as in Plymouth, local opinion differed with this standpoint, and in 1892 the idea of a monument on High Pole Hill was again revived, in the traditional form of an organization and an act of incorporation, efforts that resulted as in Plymouth and elsewhere in slim returns, a meager sum that was put out to gather interest and await the event.

That occurred in 1901, in the person of Captain J. Henry Sears, vice president of the Pilgrim Club of nearby Brewster, who committed himself to the proposed memorial and became a tireless worker on its behalf. Within four years, he had headed a fund-raising effort that garnered from the state legislature the promise of twenty-five thousand dollars, to be matched by an equivalent sum guaranteed by the Pilgrim Memorial Association, which, with Captain Sears at the helm, was shortly forthcoming also, thanks to the generosity of individuals and like-minded organizations.

Sears next made himself a lobbyist in the halls of Congress, this time securing a commitment of forty thousand dollars, also contingent on matching funds, using as his strategy the one adopted by Duxbury in 1871. For Sears proposed that a monument of sufficient height be raised on High Pole Hill in Provincetown (whose very name suggests some sort of slim erection with a similar purpose) that "could be seen from every town on Cape Cod and . . . from every vessel, in any reasonably fair weather, coming in or going out of Massachusetts Bay" (Carpenter, 53).

In proposing this landmark, Sears was indefinite in terms of design but did suggest that nothing elaborate was required for his purpose, only a tower constructed of "plain, rough stone, just as high as possible," or, in other words, "just as high as we have money to build." Perhaps having learned from the sad precedent provided by Mills and Billings that form in America should hew closely to function, Sears forwent elaborate iconography and aimed for height, for clearly the taller the structure, the better the landmark, and with rival monuments perhaps in mind, the more the tourist attraction. At the start, the captain proposed a structure perhaps two hundred feet tall, the cost of which would be around one hundred thousand dollars. He counted on High Pole Hill to add an additional hundred feet of elevation, that site having recently been deeded to the Monument Association by the town fathers of Provincetown.

Sears also stressed the educational value of such a tower, being of incalculable value not only to the U.S. government and "descendants of the Mayflower pilgrims" but as "an excellent object lesson to those coming into the country, both as a landmark which shall point out the place of the first landing of the

New England settlers and as well as a commemoration of the execution of the first charter of a true democratic government known in human history" (56, 54). Sears's emphasis suggests that he had the Statue of Liberty in mind, the alternative greeting to America that celebrated the heritage of Freedom but without the advantage of local landmarks to enhance its meaning. Perhaps, as Sears suggested, there was "no rivalry nor ill-feeling between Provincetown and Plymouth," but we cannot discount monument envy between Massachusetts and New York, whose port city by the turn of the century had become the main point of entry to the United States, leaving rival Boston far behind.

There is some irony, then, in the fact that when in 1907 the committee of arrangements was successful—where its counterparts in Plymouth in 1859, 1870, and 1889 were not—in securing the presence of the president of the United States not only as a guest at the ceremonies observing the laying of the cornerstone to the Provincetown monument but as the orator of the day, the chief executive was Theodore Roosevelt, whose connection to New England was largely limited to his college degree. Roosevelt was famously from New York, even though it was his rustication in the Far West and his subsequent ride up San Juan Hill that had accelerated his political career, with some help from his friend Lodge and an anarchist's bullet.

Moreover, despite a warning from Senator Lodge, who had seen a copy of Roosevelt's speech in advance, the president managed to offend some New Englanders by confusing the Pilgrims with the Puritans, "an almost unpardonable sin," as Lodge remarked, "in the eyes of the descendants of the former" (Roosevelt and Lodge, Selections, 2:277). Much of what Roosevelt had to say was in exclusive praise of the Puritan character: "His hearers listened in vain for a contrast between the Pilgrims of the Plymouth Colony and the Puritans of the Massachusetts Colony," and the "squalls" that Lodge predicted soon followed: "There was considerable dismay in this part of the country" (Matthews, 294). Heeding Lodge's warning, the president did preface his prepared speech with a brief, impromptu apology for having "mixed up the Pilgrim and the Puritan," explaining that "in a remote region like New York we tend to confound men," but this was not included in the version published in the press, nor did it help matters much in Plymouth "when it became known that the President had only just learned of the existence of such a distinction." In a subsequent revision of his opening remarks, Roosevelt noted the difference between the Pilgrims and "their sterner kinsmen, the Puritans," who had followed them over "in far larger numbers," but the horse had long since left the barn (Carpenter, 76; cf. Matthews, 294–95).

Still, the people of Provincetown were enthralled by Roosevelt's presence among them, and his advent gained considerable éclat by having the president arrive aboard the presidential yacht, the Mayflower (a coincidence inspiring any number of happy journalistic remarks), whose passage into the harbor was greeted by the cannonades of eight battleships drawn up in parallel columns, down which the yacht passed in review. The building of these floating fortresses—the famous White Fleet that supplanted the White Squadron—was largely Roosevelt's doing, but as the assembled guests surely realized the initial impetus had come from their own senator, who had spoken so fervently in Plymouth eighteen years earlier about the nation's imperial heritage and who was generally regarded as Roosevelt's guiding (some said "evil") genius in such matters. Proceeding by that other modern marvel the motorcade through Provincetown's narrow and winding streets, the president was greeted by an enthusiastic crowd, which perhaps encouraged him to seize the moment on behalf of government intervention in business affairs, though of course his speech had not only been written but set into hard print by the time he rose to deliver it.

"The Puritan's task was to conquer a continent," Roosevelt pronounced, echoing Lodge's remarks in 1889, "not merely to overrun it, but to settle it, to till it, to build upon it a high industrial and social life; and while engaged in the rough work of taming the shaggy wilderness, at that very time also to lay deep the immovable foundations of our whole American system of civil, political, and religious liberty achieved through the orderly process of law. This was the work allotted him to do; this is the work he did; and only a master spirit among men could have done it" (76). Roosevelt's Puritan was just such an example of muscular Christianity as the present moment demanded, who shuns "ease and rest and pleasure for the joys of a job well done": "The lesson above all others which Puritanism can teach this nation is the all-importance of the resolute performance of duty" (77).

Roosevelt's *The Strenuous Life*, serialized in *Century Magazine* in 1899, was published as a book in 1900, with a frontispiece photograph showing the vice president on horseback jumping over a split-rail fence as he enjoyed his daily gallop through the Maryland countryside. It was an iconic leap in that ride from San Juan Hill to the White House and an illustration that he was truly the "master spirit" needed to fill the vacancy in American life left by General Sherman. For both book and oration put forth the Roosevelt who could be seen as personifying the admirable qualities of the Puritans as defined by Lowell and Curtis and the Reverends Storrs and Beecher, put forward, however, not by a sere and rock-bound profile but, as a newspaper account of the Provincetown event had it, with a "bronzed face" radiating confidence and warmth (Carpenter, 69). For Roosevelt, after all, the key word was not "virtue" but "effort," a term that combined the ideals of duty and work in a kind of package that the president embodied in his person and displayed in his record of achievement on the personal and public levels.

Governor Curtis Guild, just before introducing the president to the members and guests assembled, had quoted Lowell's memorable lines, beginning "New occasions teach new duties," which conveniently served as Roosevelt's text, as he laid out his agenda for the descendants of the Puritans, who, no longer confronted by the necessity of "taming the wilderness . . . must try to shape the life of our complex industrial civilization by new devices, by new methods, so as to achieve in the end the same results of justice and fair dealing toward all" (79). By Roosevelt's definition, the notorious narrowness of the Puritan was that sword shape celebrated by Lowell: the "spirit of the Puritan was a spirit which never shrank from regulation of conduct if such regulation was necessary for the public weal; and this is the spirit which we must show today whenever it is necessary" (80).

What Roosevelt meant by "regulation" had a somewhat different application than did the codes enforced by the Puritans, as corporate America had already learned to its sorrow, and regarding which his friend Lodge had increasingly imperfect sympathies. Senator Lodge would address that troublesome difference, but when he followed Roosevelt to the podium, he first applied himself to getting the dedication ceremony back on its intended course. He made it his business to emphasize the blessed singularness of the "little band of English people [who] anchored in yonder bay" in 1620 (thereby making up for Roosevelt's omission) and who though "humble folk" were inspired by "the adventurous spirit of the Elizabethans" that had motivated their Jamestown counterparts (Carpenter, 100). But they were a group distinct from "the great Puritan colony" to the north, as well as from the Dutch in New York and the Swedes on the Delaware, and what distinguished them was the document they signed aboard the *Mayflower*, "a very simple deed" but one with tremendous consequences, being "the first in the long line of written constitutions with which modern times have become so familiar" (102–3). This was a tack calculated to flatter his Provincetown hosts, for whom the document was an equivalent Rock, yet Lodge managed in relatively short order to swing about in line with Roosevelt's imperial emphasis, much as he celebrated the Compact as the first small step in what became "a conquering march, which in three centuries would reach over all the world of western civilization, and which is even yet unstayed."

That, of course, was the stress of Lodge's opening lines in 1889, but where he then had followed Breckinridge by associating the Mayflower Compact with the principle of representative government, Lodge now qualified that position, noting that the Compact did not institute popular representation, which would come later. What was important about the Compact was, first, that it was both "organic" and "democratic," having been signed by all the "people" of their own free will, and, second, that it could not be changed save by "the entire body politic and with the utmost precaution" (104). Lodge used the notion of "organic law" as a stick with which to belabor socialism, that "new Theory which is to solve all problems and wipe away all tears!" (106).

Like Roosevelt—indeed, like everyone on the platform and probably in the audience—Lodge deemed that "Socialism is bad," but he also had "no sympathy with those who blindly and bitterly resist all efforts to deal with the corporations. . . . New and complex conditions have arisen, demanding new laws" (107). Lodge then quoted the lines by his old college teacher with which Governor Guild by way of Scripture had opened the program, to which he added a somewhat less ringing phrase, "and new problems must receive new answers." That was the simple beauty of "organic law," the gradualist formulation that George Bancroft had regarded as central to the growth of institutions and which is so nobly represented by the Mayflower Compact. Organic law is a growing, changing force and "has never barred the march of progress, and never will" (110).

And that same ideal of organicism translates to the Constitution, with its mechanism of amendments accommodating the need for growth and change, which guarantees that progress will as Bancroft also insisted take an orderly and legal form—the kind of progress equated with due process. If socialism was a modern version of inorganicism, an attempt to force upon the people an artificially contrived system of governance, its counterpart fifty years earlier was abolitionism in its radical aspects, which accomplished "great work, no doubt," but if those advocates of abolition like Wendell Phillips "who had denounced the Constitution and favored northern secession had had their way, the Union would be in fragments and slavery would still survive" (108). Lodge's reservations regarding the kind of reformers identified with radical movements in America were entirely in keeping with Roosevelt's own, who in *The Strenuous Life* had also criticized Phillips for having "denounced Abraham Lincoln as 'the slave-hound of Illinois,' " and by doing so "did not show himself more virtuous than Lincoln, but more foolish. Neither did he advance the cause of human freedom" (45).

Yet by 1907 Lodge was no longer in complete accord with Roosevelt's campaign for reform and expressed in his speech doubts concerning the lengths to which the government should reach in its exercise of central powers, particularly when they are identified with a single, powerful figure whose program may outrace the capacity of the Constitution to accommodate change. In attempting to solve "our new questions," Lodge declared, Americans must "hold fast to the great and underlying principles which have been our stay and salvation," the organicism traceable to the Compact that frames laws "adopted by all the people which cannot be overridden by any less authority and to which all laws and all officers of the government shall be subject," presumably including the commander in chief (108). Opening his speech by quietly correcting his friend's oversight regarding the difference between the Pilgrim and the Puritan, Lodge devoted the burden of his remarks to a gentle but firm chiding of Roosevelt's tendency not only to get up on his high horse but to leap over established barriers as if they were split-rail fences in Chevy Chase.

In Lodge's eyes, perhaps, Roosevelt in abnegating principles essential to Republicanism in order to pursue reform was verging close not only to socialism but to Wendell Phillips. Certainly, to some minds Roosevelt's conception of new "duties" were worse than the "occasions" they were supposed to solve, the encroachments of central government on private concerns being, like the problems of railroads and patronage, something the framers of the Constitution had not anticipated. Therefore, although he was willing to the extent he was able in 1907 to guide his reckless friend into safe harbor, Lodge soon after (in a manner best illustrated by Du Maurier's famous cartoon of Kaiser Wilhelm dropping Bismarck as his pilot) took his leave of the presidential *Mayflower*, which sailed on into uncharted and increasingly radical seas. The friendship (and letters) between the two men endured until Roosevelt's death, but the political partnership faded until the mutual hatred of Woodrow Wilson caused it to flare up anew, a hot and a destructive fire fueled by just that spirit of aggressive nationalism that had kept the two men on course together for so many years.

V

As with the raising of funds, the erection of the Provincetown tower was accomplished with amazing speed, especially compared with the slow progress of so many equivalent monuments. It seems a marvel of even greater luster when one realizes that when the cornerstone had been set in place in 1907, the design of the structure had not yet been decided upon, beyond its intended function as a landmark and a viewing platform. The commission had long deliberated the problem, rejecting an obelisk as neither original nor pertinent to the Pilgrims, to whose memory no Egyptian associations were attached. Indeed, the commission finally despaired of finding any "distinctive Pilgrim monumental architecture" for a model and opted for the Italianate "campanile, or bell tower," that still dominates the Provincetown skyline. A distinctly phallic shape that draws from contemporary wags associations with the intensely male summer population of the town, it has no obvious connection with the Pilgrim idea, indeed seems more directly associated with the Maypole that was their notion of an Old World abomination.

In architectural terms the structure was conventional, for the Florentine style had long been popular for public structures and factories in New England, and it certainly loaned itself to the simple functionalism that Captain

FIGURE 30. The Provincetown monument, intended as a navigational landmark and a regional omphalos. (From Carpenter, *The Pilgrims and Their Monument*)

Sears had primarily in mind. It may have lacked any of those exterior iconic features relevant to the Pilgrims devised by Hammatt Billings, but in terms of its final height it exceeded even the captain's expectations: looming 250 feet above its reinforced concrete foundation, it dwarfed the figure of Faith and put Captain Miles Standish into proper perspective. Moreover, where the Standish monument advertised its regional character by having built into its arches stones from each county of Massachusetts and the states of New England, the Provincetown tower had incorporated into its walls "memorial stones . . . from the shrines of the Pilgrims across the sea," souvenir rocks from England and Holland that were supplemented by two blocks of marble from Siena, Italy, "in recognition of the fact that the design of the monument was copied from the tower of their municipal building" (Carpenter, 153).

Added to these exotic souvenirs were memorial stones "presented by societies of Mayflower descendants," all of which were recent creations, formed in reaction to the perceived threat to the purity of American institutions by the influx of latter-day "pilgrims," many of which were from the same place of origin as the two blocks of marble and the tower's Florentine design. That is, Italian immigrants entering the United States by way of Boston would be greeted by a sight perhaps more reminiscent of home than a reminder of the advent of the Pilgrims and the writing of the Mayflower Compact, which increasingly became sacred icons to persons of Anglo-Saxon origins even as they despaired over the hugeness of the task of amalgamating whole boatloads of Columbuses.

The votary stones sent by *Mayflower* descendants were mortared in place with the other specimen rocks so as to have their inscriptions readable by persons climbing to the viewing room above, resulting in a conduit of sorts, so that climbers could read the writings on the walls as they mounted toward the view obtainable from the top of this upended tunnel commemorating Memory's Nation. Whatever the message sent, the Provincetown bell tower was an impressive pile of rough-cut granite, and at its final dedication in 1910 it was graced with the presence of an equivalent avoirdupois, for like the man he followed into the White House, President William Howard Taft attended the dedication. He followed his predecessor's example also by bringing with him a flotilla of eight battleships, their presence presumably attesting to the efficacy of the tower as an aid to navigation.

Theodore Roosevelt was certainly a hard act to follow, and yet if Taft as president, despite his bulk, was a mere shadow of the man he succeeded, as a speaker in Provincetown in 1910 he succeeded where his predecessor had failed. Brief as his remarks may have been, and coming late in the day, following a half dozen other speeches, Taft said what the descendants of the Separatists had come to hear: "The differences between the Pilgrims and the Puritans emphasize the heroism of the Plymouth colony," an emphasis to which he devoted a full paragraph (Carpenter, 241). As a descendant of New England Puritans, the Ohio-born Taft did not need prompting to make the distinction, and in 1914 he would expiate at length on the subject in observing Forefathers' Day in Cleveland. But on that occasion he put a decided stress on the heroism of the founders of Boston, a shift perhaps dictated by the looming shadows of war.

The main speaker of the day in Provincetown in 1910 was Charles W. Eliot, the recently retired president of Harvard University, who over the four decades of his administration brought the institution forward yet again, in the grand tradition of his predecessors Kirkland and Quincy. Where in 1907, to convenience Governor Guild, who had a previous commitment, the ceremonies had occurred on a date of no particular significance, in 1910 the dedication took place on August 5, the anniversary increasingly in vogue for outdoor festivities honoring the Pilgrims. That it was the Departure that was celebrated underwrote the presence on the platform of Jonkheer H. M. Van Weede, secretary of the Netherlands legation, who spoke about the fond relations and close resemblances in their histories of Holland and the United States, as well as the now familiar Dutch connection regarding those Pilgrim institutions, "free religion, free education, and a free press" (207). By contrast, President Eliot chose to repeat the familiar story of the lasting effect of those institutions over the interval since the Pilgrims' arrival, a progressive chronicle associated not only with the "advance of science" but with the reciprocal increase in "liberality of spirit," first signaled by Pastor Robinson's farewell words and most recently witnessed by government reforms, set in motion by "small groups of disinterested, public-spirited persons" (179).

Eliot insisted that the system of governance put in place by the Forefathers in 1638 had "clearly anticipated by more than two centuries and a half the much discussed initiative and referendum of recent times"—proposals associated with Roosevelt's most recent and radical attempts to derive government directly from the people (200). Eliot, moreover, held up the Pilgrims as ideal exemplars in yet another respect, noting that "twentieth-century industrial and trading corporations have not yet attained in all respects to the standard of the Plymouth stock company," which gave not only food and apparel to "their employees" but a share in the company profits as well. The primitive communism that conservatives, from John Quincy Adams onward, had seen as a false direction for the Plymouth colony Eliot obviously thought was worthy of emulation: "Democracy and community of interest could no further go" (190–91). This last was a statement with which any number of persons present could agree, whatever their reservations regarding Eliot's sentiment.

Among that group might be counted Senator Lodge, who sat with the president's party as a last-minute substitute for the secretary of war, who was busy in the Philippines attending to matters Senator Lodge had been responsible for setting in motion and President Taft for administering in the years prior to his election. The senator had been an undergraduate at Harvard when Eliot was installed as president, and not all that he attempted or accomplished was to Lodge's liking. On Eliot's part, there lingered an element of resentment over the fact that, upon his father's sudden death during a time of financial embarrassment, the Eliot mansion had been acquired by Lodge's father. There was, in short, nothing but the politest kind of conversation between the Eliots and the Lodges, and in that spirit Lodge refrained from attacking what he must have regarded as the drift of the president emeritus toward socialism. He stuck instead to his hastily prepared script, celebrating the Pilgrims once again in Lowell's terms as "men with empire in their brains," that imperial shape that Roosevelt had so closely approximated in 1900.

But now Lodge warned against "the shadow of the savior of society, of the strong man, or the man on horseback," which falls "darkly across the pages of history when the representative principle fails" (216). In so doing, he brought forward William Sullivan's fears in 1829 concerning that other military man on horseback, General Andrew Jackson, the American Napoleon and the Federalist's worst nightmare, now updated to suit new occasions. Lodge also predicted "woe to that man or that nation which makes wealth its god" and waxed uncharacteristically Emersonian by insisting that "high ideals in the conduct of life are what survive," a truth that explains the importance of the Pilgrims, whose arrival "stands forth in the pages of every history as one of the great events of the time" (219). To the greedy plutocrat he added that other bad example, men who have been unsuccessful in their pursuit of wealth and who attempt to disguise their "envy and malice" in political doctrines which "would destroy the more fortunate and involve the prosperity of guilty and innocent alike in a common ruin" (218). He did not mention the several "isms" associated with what Eliot had thought of as a fair and just division of profits, but perhaps in 1910 he felt he did not have to.

Yet another point of view was offered by the Honorable James T. McCleary, a congressman from Minnesota who was in Provincetown because he had helped forward the bill of appropriation that had made possible the building of the monument. What McCleary emphasized was not the Compact itself but its modern equivalent, a mechanism for universal and worldwide peace that he called "the United States of the World," constructed like the United States of America "on the two great principles of representation and federation, which our history has shown to be practicable over a vast area" (234). These were principles that Lodge himself had championed, and which at about this same time he had also planned to work into some system of international order not too far different from McCleary's, which would thereby extend those "American institutions" identified with the Pilgrims and their Compact throughout the civilized world.

By such means, as McCleary declared, "international difficulties" would be "settled without resort to war," and "this great federal-representative idea" would truly extend "from pole to pole and from the rising to the setting of the sun" (236). McCleary's speech drew frequent bursts of applause, as indicated in the published account and which are missing from the transcriptions of the orations of Eliot and Lodge, for internationalism was very much in the air in 1910. Notably, the congressman's scheme in broad outlines resembled that worldwide system of checks and balances offered as a mechanism of world peace to the American people by the man who succeeded Taft in the presidency, thanks in large part to Roosevelt's all too well named Bull Moose Party. And of course it would be Senator Lodge who, despite his own friendliness toward such a scheme in 1910, would ten years later devote all of his energies, intelligence, and savage wit to defeating President Woodrow Wilson's proposal for a League of Nations when it was presented to the U.S. Congress.

Something by way of an illustrative anecdote seems useful here, intimately connected with the construction of the Provincetown tower and prophetic of events to come, the nature of which would considerably modify Senator Lodge's faith in representative federalism as a solution to international conflicts. Given the size of the campanile and the weight of its materials, the historian of the monument noted the "great satisfaction" that was "felt by all that no fatality or even injury to any workman occurred during the progress of the work," unlike the tragic chronicles of the bridge in Brooklyn (257). Yet during the building of the monument one death did occur that was incidentally related to the technology used in its construction.

On August 5, 1908, the 288th anniversary of the Pilgrims' departure from England (a coincidence not noted by the chronicler), Mrs. Rosilla Bangs, aged eighty-five, was killed when during a severe thunderstorm the heavy steel car used to haul great granite blocks up Town (vice High Pole) Hill broke loose. The car was pulled up on rails "by means of an engine at the top," and having been left "empty and unused upon the level space on the top of the hill," it was set in motion downward "probably through the medium of a lightning stroke" (258). Gaining "terrific velocity" as it descended, the iron car demolished "a heavy structure of timbers, well braced," which had been built at the bottom of the hill "in anticipation of such an event." The juggernaut continued on, "with fearful force, across the street at the foot of the hill," landing squarely on the unfortunate Mrs. Bangs, who was "at that instant passing" and who had been paralyzed with fear at the sight of the great car rushing toward her. "This fatality was the cause of much regret to the directors of the association and to all the town's people" and would cause, even today, great pain and suffering to any tort lawyer that he had not been alive and practicing his profession at the time.

By 1914, the implications of the freak accident in 1908, which occurred despite all the precautions and planned obstacles to the dread event, might have been read by a person of the Puritan persuasion as both prophetic and valuable as a lesson that man's proposals do not always coincide with the divine dispensation. To such a sensibility the bell tower thenceforth might be imagined as casting a shadow on all sunny imaginings by liberal leaders like President Eliot and Congress McCleary that history is a record of steady progress and improvement and that men by instruments of enlightened governance may ensure universal prosperity and peace worldwide. Such, certainly, were the very similar conclusions drawn by Senator Henry Cabot Lodge from the lessons of history when it was his turn, yet once more, to celebrate the Landing of the Forefathers.

CHAPTER *23*

The Pilgrim Fathers, Where Are They?

> *No, sir, masheens ain't done much f'r man. . . . We do make*
> *pro-gress but it's the same kind Julyus Caesar made an' ivry man*
> *has made befur or since an' in this age iv masheenery we're*
> *still burrid be hand.*
> —Mr. Dooley

I

In what he styled "A Tercentenary Reverie," Fred Lewis Pattee in 1920 paid perverse tribute to "the *Mayflower* and the Pilgrim Fathers and Plymouth Rock," which "do not move me as they once did" (161). He felt that it was "time perhaps to change the subject" yet admitted that "the episode" still had a power to enthrall: "They sought no port, no definite land: they sailed simply into the west and the first landfall they made was to be their home." But however courageous this act, it was stripped by Pattee of the idealism traditionally associated with it, for though "the Pilgrim said it was the hand of God on the tiller . . . we say today that sheer chance flung them [upon] the New England coast" (162). In effect, Pattee discountenanced Emerson's objection to Everett's emphasis in 1824, desacramentalizing the Pilgrim errand by removing the element of Providence, along the way placing a handful of dirt on Emerson's grave as well.

There is a quality of nihilism in Pattee's remarks, inherent in the spirit of his age, but he spoke also as a New England native who despaired of his region's future, for rather than a blessed land it seemed now "the country that God forsook. A curse seems to have fallen upon it" (173). Pattee's was the New England of Edith Wharton, Robert Frost, and Sarah Orne Jewett, a region of cellar holes and second-growth forests where farms once had stood, its former inhabitants long gone away toward the West, leaving behind elderly people only, waiting to occupy a hard-earned place in the graveyard: "The native race is swiftly dying out," replaced by persons "born of foreign parentage" (174). The "epic," as Pattee called it, of New England was over, four generations of which the greatest was the most recent, "that marvelous single generation that burst from its borders . . . and tamed a raw continent."

The point to be derived from Pattee's pessimistic reverie is the peculiar appropriateness of Henry Cabot Lodge as the celebrant of the Pilgrim tercentenary at Plymouth, for the senator was most certainly in 1920 the representative man of a New England long fallen from the flower celebrated by Van Wyck Brooks. "The rock-bound coast was stern no longer," observed Brooks in his sequel volume; "the Boston mind appeared to have lost its force," and Lodge as the heir of the golden age of statesmen, the "scion of all the old patricians . . . seemed oddly small and shrunken in their light . . . and one felt in him the end of a spent tradition" (412–13). Moreover, where Daniel Webster, a century earlier, spoke at the start of a great public career, Lodge would be dead by 1924, and in 1920 his greatest accomplishments lay behind him. Behind him also was the First World War, and where Webster had been buoyed up by the energies released after the War of 1812, his performance in 1820 being a pluperfect expression of the Era of Good Feelings, Lodge in 1920 stood on the threshold to what has been called the Lost Generation, a phrase implying both confusion and impotence, characteristics of old age in men.

Webster brought to the Bicentennial an assertion of New England's centrality to the expanding nation's moral force, which he and John Quincy Adams would go on as emerging Whigs to embody and thereby redeem for a time the region's political eminence. Lodge brought to the Tercentenary a quality of despair, at the end of his own career approximating one of those specters traditionally called up by Forefathers' Day orators, a validation not of the region's great future but its demise as a vital center. His final triumph, as he saw it, was the defeat of Woodrow Wilson's League of Nations on the Senate floor, an assertion of antique notions of nationalism that drew upon the old Federalist fear of involvement with foreign powers. Xenophobia was still very much alive deep inland in midwestern, rural America, albeit taking new, populist energies from the regional paranoia regarding the interlock between capitalism and internationalism.

Lodge was hardly a spokesman for the West, that democratic stronghold from which William Jennings Bryan had emerged in 1896, who threatened to break the long Republican hegemony that had ruled the United States from the East. It had been Lodge who placed the gold-standard plank in the Republican platform that year, thereby giving Bryan the materials from which to fashion his notorious cross, and though by 1920 this battle was as far distant as the Spanish-American War, it was still fresh in the memory of Vachel Lindsay.

In 1896 a sixteen-year-old in Springfield, Illinois, and an ardent Democrat, Lindsay in 1919 celebrated Bryan's campaign as the natural forces of the West summoned up by the "Boy Orator of the Platte" against the political machinery of Boss Hanna and the eastern Plutocrats. Lindsay described the western spirit in terms of a revolutionary wildness, a whirlwind "of men and . . . flowers and beasts," which Bryan, "the bard and prophet of them all," rode toward the East:

> Prairie avenger, mountain lion,
> Bryan, Bryan, Bryan, Bryan,
> Gigantic troubadour, speaking like a siege gun,
> Smashing Plymouth Rock with his boulders from the West. (99)

But mere animal strength and courage can always be outmatched by guile backed by wealth, and the victory went to men "With dollar signs upon their coats, / Diamond watchchains on their vests." It was a victory, also, of the "custodians" of "Plymouth Rock, / And all that inbred landlord stock," a "victory of the neat" (103). It was, that is to say, a battle won by the kind of easterner epitomized in the West by Henry Cabot Lodge, perennial celebrant of Plymouth Rock and an epitome of "the neat."

In recalling in 1919 the "Defeat of my boyhood, defeat of my dream," Lindsay chiefly had McKinley in view, a "respectable" man, "without an angle or a tangle," as the representative of neatness. But his catalog of villains, including "Roosevelt, the young dude cowboy, / Who hated Bryan, then aped his way," was a list of once powerful men now all dead and in Lindsay's opinion damned. Lodge, though the most obvious representative of Bryan's eastern adversaries, did not qualify for inclusion in Lindsay's list, perhaps by virtue of being still alive.

By 1920 Lodge was also very much alone, a veteran of party battles and issues that were no longer relevant save as memories sacred both to himself and to Vachel Lindsay, if for different reasons. His great friend Roosevelt had died in 1919, and Bryan himself would survive Lodge by only a year. Woodrow Wilson, Lodge's nemesis ever since the Democrats had seized the White House in 1912, would also die in 1924, but Wilson's vision, like Theodore Roosevelt's, had a long trajectory into the future, while Lodge was a champion of Memory's Nation, still a celebrant of the Puritan spirit at a time when Puritanism was definitely out of popular favor.

In 1900, Wilson, then a member of the faculty at Princeton, had taken his turn on Forefathers' Day before the New England Society in New York. He spoke as a descendant of Scotch-Irish settlers and as a son of Ohio-born parents, a heritage that, with his Virginia nativity and southern upbringing and education, placed considerable distance between himself and the Puritans and their descendants. But Professor Wilson did what he could to extend credit to his hosts, humorously acknowledging the country's need for "a certain degree of intolerance," even an occasional healthy expression of "hatred" (Wilson, 1:102). His definition of the Puritan not a little resembled that of George Frisbie

Hoar in 1895, who in drawing out his lengthy comparison between the Pilgrims of Plymouth and their neighbors to the North noted that "the Puritan had a capacity for an honest, hearty hatred, of which I find no trace in Pilgrim literature. Indeed a personal devil must have been a great comfort to our Massachusetts ancestors, as furnishing an object which they could hate with all their might, without violation of Christian principles" (*Proceedings* [1896], 18–20).

By Wilson's much more subtle accounting the Puritan stood upon "the single principle of discipline of order, of polity," a "splendid principle" but a single one nonetheless, which "was for the discipline that pulls in harness; it was for subjection to authority; it was for crucifixion of the things that did not comport with a fixed and rigid creed" (105). By contrast, his own Scotch-Irish ancestors, who had pushed the frontier across the southern mountains along the path blazed by Daniel Boone, had followed "another principle than that of discipline to do—the principle of aspiration, the principle of daring, the principle of unrest, the principle of mere adventure, which made the level lines of the prairie seem finer and more inviting than the uplifted lines of the mountains; that made it seem as if the world were bigger on the plains, and as if the feet of young men were the feet of leaders" (107).

This was the same frontier spirit that Theodore Roosevelt had celebrated, defined by Wilson as an Emersonian expression of "that expansion of power . . . that fine elevation and expansion of nature which ventures everything may go with us to the ends of the earth," identified with "the spirit of progression . . . which has led us into new conditions and to . . . a new destiny. [Applause.]" (108). Both Roosevelt and Lodge had something similar in mind at the time, associated with the opportunities presented by the Philippines, but where Roosevelt and Lodge thought of Puritanism in expansionist terms derived from Lowell, Wilson did not and associated the Puritan principle with "restraint," which opposed the "progressive" spirit. While Wilson welcomed "that mechanical combination, that poise, that power of union, which is the spirit of discipline," "without which the national spirit would have simply set the world on fire," it is clear which of the "principles" he most favored, the expression of energy over the restrictive "forms of our lives," the "national" as opposed to the localized "New England spirit" (109, 108).

In sum, Wilson on the threshold to a new century carried forward the worst features of the Puritans. His were the kind of people who, according to H. L. Mencken (for whom, ironically, "the Archangel Woodrow . . . was a typical Puritan"), were haunted by the "fear that someone, somewhere, may be happy" (*Chrestomathy*, 248, 624). They were Senator Hoar's angry vessels of bigotry and repressiveness, soon to be identified with censorship and prohibition, and with an unwholesome (post-Freudian) hatred of physical pleasure, the whole an expression of mean-spirited envy masquerading as moral rectitude. "Show me a Puritan," wrote Mencken, "and I'll show you a son-of-a-bitch," a vernacular pungency lacking in the definitions of either Hoar or Wilson yet reflecting an attitude for which both men made straight the way (625). Together, the old Republican and new Democrat constructed a profile that would provide a perfect fit for Senator Lodge in his later years, as Wilson would learn to his regret.

Using another Emersonian figure, Wilson called for Americans to forget "all the things which might restrain us, not going with with faces averted over our shoulder, but going with faces to the front, faces that will scorn to face a shame but will dare to face a glory" (111). But as Wilson would eventually learn, it sometimes pays to look behind you when advancing, for the Puritan spirit, as he noted, is forever hunting for someone to crucify and thereby help along to glory, and one such was following in his van, like Hawthorne's Roger Chillingworth willing to bide his time. That man was Henry Cabot Lodge.

Opposed to Wilson on party grounds, and angered by the president's reluctance to enter the war, by 1920 Lodge seems to have seen in that idealistic southern Democrat a frightening resurrection of Thomas Jefferson. For beneath the feelings of personal insult that had aroused Lodge's antagonism toward the president, who seldom consulted the powerful Republican member of the Senate Foreign Relations Committee, there was a family inheritance that naturally distrusted utopian schemes put forth with a southern accent, coupled with an uneasiness that resulted when such persons began to talk of alliances with foreign nations. That is, the line is straight and narrow from *The Life and Letters of George Cabot* to that volume of documents and speeches that Lodge gathered together as justification of his fight to defeat Wilson's League of Nations.

Pique, then as now, is a powerful agent provocateur in Washington, but to argue, as some have done, that Lodge's personal animosity toward Wilson provided his only motive in opposing him seems too simplistic for a complex occasion. The president stood for everything that Lodge was against, from his southern birth to his advocacy of reduced tariffs. Senator Lodge's feelings of being ignored by the president stirred up his ready wrath, hatred shared by Roosevelt even on his deathbed, to which Lodge regularly repaired to cast imprecations upon the head of the Democratic administration. As Hoar had observed, the Puritan was a good hater, and Wilson provided a very convenient Devil.

But as a Puritan, once again, Lodge was mostly a Federalist and a wily strategist remarkably able to channel his anger along lines he wished to promote. Even if we ignore the matter of separating the terms of Germany's surrender from machinery establishing the League of Nations—Lodge's chief reason for opposing Wilson in the Senate—there was good reason (at least to his way of thinking) for setting aside his earlier commitment to world peace through arbitration and to bring all his flag-waving energies to bear on the defeat of Wilson's scheme.

Essential to Lodge's single-minded championing of national sovereignty was the threat that the United States would be subject to the whim of third-rate principalities should the Senate ratify Wilson's treaty. It is a powerfully emotional and nationalistic argument interwoven with xenophobic bigotry, and it can still be used in the U.S. Congress to great effect today. Then as now, it was an argument set against the terrible fact of a war, not one of limited focus, if interminable extension, but a worldwide conflict that was hitherto unmatched in extent and destructiveness. That war was the result of a complex interlock of treaties ensuring mutual defense in case of aggression that approximated the kind of cooperation Lodge seems to have had in mind before hostilities commenced and was certainly what Wilson proposed after the armistice was declared.

In Plymouth in 1920, Senator Lodge made no mention of Wilson or the League of Nations—having won his war, there was no need. But in his tercentenary oration he did refer to the world war and in a frame that made his celebration of the Pilgrims at once startlingly different in emphasis from all others that preceded it and remarkably consistent with sentiments stated by Lodge prior to 1914. Once again, where Webster had used the occasion of 1820 to launch himself from Plymouth Rock on a national career, Lodge took advantage of the Tercentenary to bring closure to forty years of public life. In terms of oratory, there is no comparison between the two speeches, for Henry Cabot Lodge was no Daniel Webster. But then that was the main point of his remarks in Plymouth in 1920.

II

His trig figure defiantly erect—Lodge was not a small man in stature but was always slender and appears almost dainty when photographed standing alone—his manicured beard a hedge of antique fashion in a sea of clean-shaven faces, the senator must have seemed as he took his place on the stage a version of Lafayette at Bunker Hill a century earlier, a visitor from a distant age. His anachronistic presence was set off as well by Calvin Coolidge, who shared the platform, a visible token of a new age of politicians, who sat perched uncomfortably in Governor Bradford's great chair. Present on the occasion as the governor of Massachusetts, Coolidge was also vice president–elect of the United States, an office he owed to the efforts of Senator Lodge to deny him the Republican nomination for the presidency, on the stated grounds that a man who lived "in a two-family house" was not deserving of the faith of Massachusetts (Fuess, 257).

Even Claude Fuess, who puts the best construction possible on an uneasy

FIGURE 31. Henry Cabot Lodge with Calvin and Grace Coolidge, posed in 1920 alongside an elevated Rock, which was being stored against the long-delayed completion of its new canopy. (From *Cape Cod and All the Pilgrim Land*)

relationship, allows that Lodge and Coolidge "were precise opposites," and there is a photograph of the two men with Grace Coolidge standing by Plymouth Rock—presumably taken in connection with their appearance on December 21—that says it all (349). The Rock itself was in a process of transition, and so was the Republican Party once again, an evolution signified by the contrast between the patrician smile of self-mockery inspired by the occasion on Lodge's face and the expressionless blank of Coolidge's sharply shrewd features. Though of rural origins, Coolidge was no Webster either, and his famous gift of Yankee understatement contrasts markedly with Webster's forceful powers of expression. And next to the patrician Lodge, Coolidge seems a reasonable facsimile of a village pundit, celebrated for his cracker-barrel wit, the last, as it were, of the Hosea Biglows, where Lodge stands in for the running-out of the Homer Wilbur line, "the Brahmin of Brahmins" as Feuss calls him, reinforcing Brooks's notion of a generational loss.

Coolidge led off the speeches on Forefathers' Day in 1920 in his characteristically forthright manner, pointing to the "material and spiritual" increase that had followed the advent of the Pilgrims and was traceable to their influence: "Plymouth Rock does not mark a beginning or an end. It marks a revelation of that which is without beginning and without end, a purpose, shining through eternity with a resplendent light" (Bittinger, 11). He was followed by LeBaron R. Briggs, president of Radcliffe College, who had written a poem for the occasion and who seems to have been touched upon his lips by Kipling's muse, not the celebrant of empire but the morose, even contrite spirit of "Recessional." For Briggs's poem was something of a jeremiad, aimed at that traditional target, the rising generation, and where Coolidge had sounded the note of triumph mandated by the occasion and the necessities of public office, Briggs, who enjoyed the security of tenure, did not. Having celebrated the Allied victory as somehow the work of the "Pilgrim's sons," he turned to the problems of the postwar years.

This Side of Paradise was published that year, and the Jazz Age was under way, characterized by Briggs as a "carnival of death," a ceaseless "revel" of mad laughter and dance. Briggs denounced this desperate spirit of hedonism and urged the "slaves of sloth and the senses" to rejoin "the Pilgrim's army" in a war for "Freedom and Truth." He ended his poem with an anthem echoing Lowell's "The Crisis," sending "the spirit's Mayflower into seas unknown. . . . The port is Freedom! Pilgrim heart, sail on!" (Bittinger, 14). Where Coolidge had brought the *Mayflower* "up out of the infinite," Briggs sent it back into the spirit world, yet of the two, it was the poet who established contact with the emerging modern world, even while remaining studiously vague as to what new duties the new occasions might dictate.

The details were supplied by Senator Lodge, who generally took advantage of such occasions to prescribe specifics for societal ills. He began, however, with a theatrical reversal of audience expectations, a bid for attention that dismissed the centennial occasion as a merely chronological event, the passage of three hundred years being nothing in itself. "The act of commemoration," Lodge asserted, "must be justified by its subject," and he wondered aloud whether in commemorating the Landing "we celebrate something of world effect or an incident of the past which merely touches the memories or the pride of a neighborhood" (*Pilgrims*, 4–5). This was the same stress on consequences by means of which Webster had compared the Landing with other great historical events, and we must assume that Lodge's audience was confident the speaker would, like his great predecessor, eventually assure them that they (like the Pilgrims) had not come all the way to Plymouth for nothing.

Lodge did not disappoint them, but first he emphasized the point that few events in history meet the test of "decisiveness," such in the grand perspective of world history being "solitary light-towers set above reefs and shoals in lonely seas" (7). Lodge went on to list a handful of such events, like the signing of Magna Carta and the voyage of Columbus, "momentous alike to the Old World and the New," before coming back to his initial question regarding the importance of "what happened here at Plymouth." He then laid to rest the anxiety of his audience by assuring them that "Jamestown and Plymouth were the cornerstones of the foundations upon which the great fabric of the United States has been built up, and the United States is today one of the dominant factors in the history and in the future of the world of men. . . . There is no need to go further to find the meaning in history of what the Pilgrims did."

But in evoking Jamestown and Plymouth, Lodge made no mention of those twin arms of conquest he had celebrated in 1889. Instead he moved on to consider "what has come from the work of the Pilgrims who . . . influenced history and affected the fate of Western civilization," with the purpose of finding out "what lessons they teach which will help us in the present and aid us to meet the imperious future ever knocking at the door." Lodge wasted little time evoking the Landing but rather hurriedly carried his audience to the present moment, giving his oration a certain urgency by noting that Western civilization, whose "entire course" was affected by the Landing of the Pilgrims, had recently been "shaken and clouded by the most desolating of wars," and was now "trembling in the balance" (9).

It was time once again to "consider the lessons of the Past," to look to the Pilgrims for "light and leading, for help in facing the known and in shaping the best we may the forces which govern the unknown" (13). But first, Lodge sought to put the Pilgrims' accomplishments into perspective by assessing their importance with a survey of "the movement of opinion in regard to them and what they did." As we have seen, a ritual bow in the direction of the great orators who preceded the speaker at or on Plymouth Rock was a convention of the genre, but Lodge expanded this tradition to a lengthy consideration of those orations as revealing the changing image of the Forefathers. In effect he bypassed the Pilgrims for their celebrants, of which he was the most recent and hence the last in the line.

Self-consciousness can go no further, and Lodge carried it a very long way, starting out with the Lowell of the second series of *The Biglow Papers*, for whom the Forefathers were "stern men with empires in their brains." Lodge credited the Pilgrims with "a profound consciousness that they were engaged in a vastly greater task than establishing a colony. They felt in the depths of their being that they were laying the foundation of an empire—of a mighty nation" (14–15). Lodge defined the Pilgrims as "eponymous and autochthonous heroes, as the Greeks would have called them if they had come up out of the darkness where myths are born and history never written," but the archetype had faded when "the pioneers passed away," and the Forefathers had been succeeded by lesser men (15).

Yet the original spirit remained in subterranean form and "deep down in their very being guided and led the succeeding generations," until it surfaced once again in 1769, on the occasion of the first of the public commemorations of the Landing. This event, on the eve of Revolution, signified New England's realization that "here in Plymouth something had once happened which merited celebration and made such demand for the outward signs of remembrance as to insist upon a visible manifestation" (17). From that starting point there had sprung a sequence of celebrations "beyond enumeration," which spread westward with the "migrations . . . of the children of New England across the continent, until now in ever-increasing numbers the anniversary of the landing in 1620 is marked and celebrated with each recurring year from the Atlantic to the Pacific" (18–19).

Like Webster at Bunker Hill in 1825, Lodge in 1920 declared his faith in ceremonial rhetoric as the vestal flame of memory, those "endless acts of commemoration" to which must be attributed "the development of public opinion about the results of the Plymouth landing" (19). Again, the Landing in itself was not the thing; it was the celebrations of the event that counted, "the addresses made by well-known men upon the coming of the Mayflower," which provided a chart of evolving attitudes toward the event, indeed were responsible far more than the historical circumstances surrounding the Landing for creating what we have received as the Pilgrims. Rhetoric can do no more in the service of rhetoricians.

Echoing the logic of those who attempted in 1883 to restore the traditional anniversary of December 22, Lodge pointed out that those speakers were a roster of men "who in our history have attained high distinction in the pulpit, at the bar, in literature, and in public life. You will find there orators and poets, philosophers and historians, Presidents, Governors of States, Senators, and leaders of the House of Representatives." It was "an imposing list not without significance," whose commemorative orations, in effect, provide a reasonable equivalent to Ruskin's Venetian stones, icons of memory revealing the cultural evolution of a nation.

But instead of attempting to render a reprise of the entire process, impossible within the scope of an hour, Lodge chose to demonstrate the potential of such a study by concentrating on one celebration and the speaker on that occasion, "who made that particular day famous, and who was at once interpreter of the past and prophet of the future. That occasion and the man who then spoke stand out very distinctly and very radiantly against the background of the dead years, charged with much deep meaning to all who consider them and above all competitors however eminent" (20). The man was Daniel Webster, the occasion the Bicentennial, and by citing Webster in such honorific language, Lodge seemed about to revise his own opinion of the great Whig, whom in 1883 he had defined as greatly flawed. We must remember, however, that Lodge was never inconsistent, and the audience might have been fore-warned when the speaker began by bringing the mighty Daniel down from the Rock and placing him in the midst of events in the process of unfolding in 1820, which included the ongoing career of Daniel Webster.

Memory, Lodge emphasized, whether personal or national, is a cumulative process, and when we "picture to ourselves at a given moment a certain man," we tend "to treat him as if his life was at that instant complete as we now know it." Thus, in the popular memory Webster in 1820 is also the Webster of 1830, the great defender of the Union, and the Webster of 1850, the infamous com-promiser, when in fact he was not yet either of those Websters: "If we are to judge rightly and really draw forth the lesson we perchance are seeking, we must force ourselves to remember just what sort of world it was at the historic moment which is in our thoughts, and not confuse the actors or the occasion with after years familiar in history to us, but an unknown future to them." In modern terms, Lodge was a contextualist, a method he had undoubtedly borrowed from his mentor, derived from that tour de force with which Henry Adams opened his multivolumed history of the administrations of Jefferson and Madison, rendering in six chapters the complexity of a single year, 1800, by way of preparing the way for a lengthy deconstruction of the Democratic tradition.

Lodge's target here was not Jefferson but Webster, whose bicentennial ad-dress was given in the year in which George III died, old, blind, and crazy, "almost forgotten, a pathetic figure not without suggestion to the moralist." Nor were there signs in America in 1820 that the nineteenth century was truly under way, for the great changes that would be brought about by invention and technology during Webster's lifetime had hardly started, witnessed chiefly by a "little steamboat" that had appeared on the Hudson River in 1807. But the "world's traffic" was still carried over the oceans by sail, and the first steam-powered railroad "was still ten years in the future, and twenty years were to elapse before the coming of the telegraph—the two discoveries which were to make a greater change in human environment than anything which had hap-pened since the wheel, the hollow boat, and the alphabetical signs for language had broken upon the world of men" (22–23). Thus "it was with an eighteenth-century atmosphere about him that Webster rose to speak at Plymouth, as much so as the coach which had brought him to his destination" (23).

So Webster's great moment was essentially an eighteenth-century event, nor was the speaker "the Webster so familiar to us, who looms so large during the succeeding thirty years of the country's history" (24). Impressive in appear-ance and imposing in presence in his later days, with deep-set and burning eyes, Webster's face at thirty-eight was smooth, lacking those crags and fissures that characterize the "tragic aspect of the latest portraits" of the elder states-man. Nor did Webster bring to the Rock a personal history rich in famous accomplishments, including those orations "which so added to his fame, and which generations of schoolboys were fated to recite." Indeed, it was the very absence of any notable past that undoubtedly reinforced the audience's sense, when Webster was finished, that "they had listened to an unusual man making a speech quite beyond anything they had ever heard before" (25). Lodge saw no need "to criticise or analyse the speech," for his purpose was only to learn from it, if possible, "Webster's attitude of mind in 1820, and what meaning the anniversary had to him, representing as he did the best thought of the time."

Lodge began by quoting entire "the fine and stately sentences with which he closed, for they are addressed directly to us, and it is for us to reply," not coincidentally the paragraphs carried down through the years in Pierpont's and other class readers. But Lodge had got only to the end of the first para-graph of three—in which Webster had predicted that a century hence there would be heard at Plymouth "the voice of acclamation and gratitude," which, commencing at the Rock, would be "transmitted through millions of the sons of the Pilgrims, till it lose itself in the murmurs of the Pacific seas"—when he (and Webster) were interrupted. A telephone placed on the platform rang, and the local manager of the phone company stepped forward, and having in-formed the audience that the call was from the governor of California, he introduced the man on the other end of the line to his Massachusetts counter-part and handed the instrument to Governor Coolidge. What followed is recorded in the account of the tercentenary celebration, a conversation that marvelously fulfilled "the prophetic utterances of Webster a century previous": " 'Governor Stephens, Yes. This is Governor Coolidge of Massachusetts. Yes, I am seated in the chair of Governor Bradford at Plymouth. I wish to say that Massachusetts and Plymouth Rock greet California and the Golden Gate, and send the voice which is not to be lost in the waves and roar of the Pacific. I'll do so. Goodbye' " (Bittinger, 22).

Senator Lodge assured the audience that "it was the merest accident that I read that sentence" just before the telephone rang, and we need not doubt his sincerity. Yet such coincidences are the stuff of stagecraft, as was the fact that the man on the far end of the line was not Governor Stephens of California but his secretary, for the governor was away hunting at the time, and yet, as the tercen-tenary report affirmed in confessing that fact, "the Webster prophecy had been fulfilled, nevertheless" (16). Certainly the theatrical moment dramatized the technological changes that had taken place in the nineteenth century, but where in 1850 the Reverend Kendall had drawn a like comparison between Webster's prophecy and the power of the telegraph to carry words with lightning speed across the continent, part and parcel of Kendall's celebration of the wonders of progress, this jiggery-pokery was not at all in the spirit of Lodge's subsequent remarks. Whatever his willingness to go along with the joke, what Lodge went on to say was quite different from what Governor Coolidge had said, earlier and then over the phone, though it was not uncomplimentary to the man sitting in Bradford's big chair. It was, however, not at all what Webster had expected from the orator who would succeed him in Plymouth a century hence.

III

Having gone on to read the last two of Webster's famous paragraphs, Lodge proposed to respond to that call to the "future generations," when in 1820 Webster had welcomed the people of 1920 to "the immeasurable blessings of rational existence, the immortal hope of Christianity, and the light of everlasting truth!" But first he asked his audience a series of leading questions: "What have we to say in answer? What message do Webster's words convey to us? What meaning did he find in the work of the Pilgrims, and how did he interpret their simple and momentous story? How far do we go with him, where do our time and belief agree, and where do they contrast with his?" (27). Though Webster had risen to speak in "the still lingering atmosphere of the eighteenth century," his voice was that of the nineteenth century, which spoke in large and confident terms about "the progress of the country" (28). It was a theme inextricable from the idea, relatively new in Webster's day, that asserted "the continuous progress of man." Thus the major question to be answered, and which Lodge left unasked, was whether or not the twentieth century still shared that faith in progress, which had been reaffirmed by Professor Wilson of Princeton in 1900 and President Emeritus Eliot of Harvard in 1910.

Lodge did not ask the question, but he did answer it, and his response took the vivid form of deconstructing Webster himself, a process that began by pointing out a distinction that the great orator had failed to make, between "the fact of progress" and the "law of progress," which were quite different things. The idea that progress was an immutable law emerged during the eighteenth century and was inseparable from a notion of "posterity," as testified by the closing paragraph of Webster's oration. That declared expectation of the approval of a century hence, frozen in the amber of a hundred thousand schoolbooks, was a "capstone of the edifice" that testified "how completely the idea of a law in progress and a belief in the evolution of mankind had . . . taken possession of Webster's mind and heart" (29).

That is, the idea of progress carries with it a faith in the future, which is the sum and ongoing product of a cumulative process: thinking about tomorrow produces a consciousness that tomorrow will be better than today in part *because* of today. Such was "the ruling principle of the nineteenth century, the spirit of the century just ended." Lodge cited Herbert Spencer, "who asserted that progress was a universal law," and Charles Darwin, whose work was regarded as scientific proof of the law's "immutability" (36). But these savants, like Webster, tended to confuse what they called "progress" with improvements that were essentially "material" in nature, mechanisms that had transformed the conditions of mankind's daily life: "Steam, electricity, and the unresting labors of applied and mechanical science" were responsible for a "profound alteration in human environment," greater than any equivalent change since the writing of history began (37).

In 1870, Robert Winthrop had pointed to the difference between material and spiritual improvements, and like Winthrop also Lodge observed that along with these great and transforming inventions came an increase in personal wealth. This was an aspect of materialism that reduced "the spirit of progress" to its "cash basis," an emphasis that was balanced, if not compensated, by the complementary belief "that the movement of mankind was ever upwards and onwards." This in turn had brought about great social reforms, promoting the idea that "if you could give every man a vote, an opportunity for education, set men free, and call the government a republic, all would be right with the world" (38). Well, of course, such was not the case: "We now know that there is no such panacea for human ills."

To the contrary, what have the emerging sciences of anthropology and archaeology shown us but "the astonishing permanence of human nature and human desires," that the actual improvement of society, when taken on the scale of the ages, seems as slow as "geologic changes in the earth's surface" (39)? No one any longer believes "that by environment and education a Hottentot can be turned into an Englishman," and though no one would deny either that we possess more knowledge than our forebears, "there is no evidence that we have better brains or greater unassisted intellectual power."

Indeed, the historical record since 1820 demonstrated otherwise, and the faith in the "law" of progress expressed by Webster and his contemporaries suggested that they "neither completely understood the lessons of the past nor perceived the limitations which the laws of nature set to the possible accomplishment of their own brief lives" (40). Perhaps their greatest fault was their inability to imagine that "the progress of mankind in all directions" might not go on indefinitely, that "the destiny of man" might suffer reverses, even decline. This blind "faith" persevered during the early years of the twentieth century, for signs of onward movement were still evident (here Lodge could have cited President Eliot's progressive message in 1910), and "the extended application of international arbitration," demonstrated by the court at Hague (in which Representative McCleary had put such hope), encouraged the expectation that mankind had so far advanced that there would be no wars, or if war came, that its worst horrors "would be either avoided or mitigated" (41).

"Then suddenly, without warning, there broke upon the Western World the greatest and the worst war ever known in a recorded history of six thousand years which had been filled with wars. Not only was it the greatest of wars, but when it came the powerful conventions of society, the comfortable fictions of daily existence, were rent and flung aside, and primitive man, even the savage of the Neanderthal period, began to show himself lurking behind the demure figure of nineteenth-century respectability. The difference was that the primitive instincts and passions were now equipped with all the methods of destruction which the latest and most advanced science could furnish." Germany, as the aggressor, was the chief culprit, having "carried her purely materialistic conception of organization at home and dominion abroad to the highest state of perfection," but all the nations involved in the war "were largely under the materialistic influences which were so powerful in that phase of nineteenth-century progress, and which had forgotten the real and informing spirit of the time; confounded material progress with that of intellect and character, and made the cash basis loom large upon man's horizon" (41–42).

As a boy watching men only slightly older than himself marching off to do battle for the salvation of the Union and the emancipation of slaves, Lodge in 1861 was wrought into a savage frenzy of war fever and aroused to a hatred of the South that long endured. As a congressman during the period of Reconstruction, he was widely reputed to be the author of the "force bill" that would have placed federal troops at southern polling places to ensure access by black Americans. The Civil War also influenced his summary history of the colonial period, resulting in his image of those two conquering armies set in motion by the founding of Jamestown and Plymouth that would ultimately oppose each other at Gettysburg. And, finally, his armchair role as scholar-soldier was responsible for his enthusiasm for a war with Spain that would considerably widen his nation's territorial periphery, extending into the orient its sphere of imperial interests.

It was a war, to borrow a phrase from Perry Miller, for those who had missed their war, and it was very much the war of Henry Cabot Lodge. It had been, as his friend and his wife's lover John Hay had expressed it, a "splendid little war," and as celebrated by its hero, Colonel Roosevelt, it was a conflict in which best of American youth sailed off to wrest control of islands essential to the nation's strategic interests. Lodge's son, George Cabot, namesake of his Federalist forebear, was a hero of that war, as a young naval officer aboard the *Dixie* effecting the easy surrender of a town in Puerto Rico and raising the Stars and Stripes over city hall. That act was a paradigm of national righteousness, seizing from a corrupt and dying empire a long neglected prize ripe for Christianity and civilization, in the form of Protestant, Anglo-Saxon continuity.

But the First World War was not that kind of conflict of all, not a struggle between a young and healthy and an old and ailing state but a collision of young or renewed empires that had been steered by men like Henry Cabot Lodge and Theodore Roosevelt, leaders who were masters of the intricacies of commerce and treaties and who put great faith in the efficacy of floating fortresses and island outposts to authenticate their nationhood. Lodge, of course, had played no great part in the most recent conflict; instead, he was famous for having defeated Wilson's plan for preventing another such. But now, in 1920, he took advantage of the occasion to point to a new threat, a "savage despotism" that, having "replaced the autocracy of the czars[,] is threatening the destruction of all civilization," menacing a world "exhausted and almost prostrate" because of the cost in treasure and lives paid during the late Great War.

Out of the First World War arose the communist menace, a familiar enough theme for Lodge, who had been sounding the tocsin of alarm ever since 1886. Then it was the Anarchist with his bomb concealed in the mobs allowed access to America by unrestricted immigration; now it was the new Neanderthal man in Russia waving about a scarlet but no Harvard flag. And the menace was made even more frightening by the weakness of the Western world, not only the physical but the psychic exhaustion, which had resulted in a widespread pessimism in Europe, "a flat negation of what the nineteenth century devoutly believed." Lodge found evidence of this nihilism in recent books coming out of France, Italy, and Germany (Spengler's serialized *Decline of the West* began to appear in 1918), and even in the United States, where there were signs of a universal malaise arising "among those who think and who are the first to see and to weigh the chances of the future" (45). Among these we may even number Lodge himself, who, as he turned finally to read "the message of the Pilgrims," which for Webster had been one in "harmony with the spirit of progress," intimated that he, unlike his great predecessor, did not "largely embody" the optimism of the previous century.

"What do they say to us, not in the dawn of a young hope everywhere for a new and better world, not in the heyday of the idea of continuous progress, but after six years of trial marked by an intensity and severity hitherto unknown, in an hour of darkness and doubt beset with perils which no man can measure or foresee?" In 1820, the idea of the Landing brought inspiration and hope to Webster, but what is its message to Americans "as we look about in this troubled and desolate world," what solace or encouragement can be passed on to a generation brought up in an abiding faith in material progress, "looking no further than the physical effects and thinking too little of the higher meaning?" (46). Well, as his audience might reasonably expect, Lodge despite his own pessimism was able to rise to the occasion from the murky depths of a "troubled and desolate world" with something golden gleaming in his hand.

What the Pilgrims had to offer the twentieth century was that "stern and austere look" on the faces of the statues by Ward and Saint-Gaudens, that unsmiling visage testifying that "life was very serious," a kind of visored evidence of the Pilgrims' "unfailing courage," their "very strong and active sense of public duty" (46). Surely such seriousness was preferable to the easy assurance that "money and amusement and restless movement" are what life is all about, a stark contrast that calls to mind Professor Briggs's finger-shake at carousing college couples. Echoing Whittier's sentiments in 1870, Lodge drew together two postwar evaluations of an uneasy peace: "Just at present there seems [to be] a great deal of concern about rights, and a tendency to forget the duties which rights must always bring with them, and without which rights become worthless and cannot be maintained" (47).

This reflection brought Lodge back to 1620, for it was the principle inherent in the Compact. As the Pilgrims set up their outpost of civilization on the edge of a vast wilderness, they realized "that there could be no organized society unless laws made by the state were obeyed by all, and this mighty principle they planted definitely in the soil of their new country, where it has found its latest champion in a successor of Bradford and Winslow, the present Governor of Massachusetts" (49). What a sudden spin this was, dramatized perhaps by a gesture toward the slim figure perched in Bradford's great grandfather of a chair, an arrangement whereby magistrate met magistrate across the centuries, a union far more fundamental than that recent conversation over the phone to California.

Nor was Lodge merely paying a ritual compliment to the man he had recently tried to keep from the White House, for the popular enthusiasm for Coolidge's candidacy, which swept him virtually by acclamation onto the national ticket, had been the governor's response in 1919 to a police strike in Boston. Having delayed taking action until crime was rampant citywide, Coolidge called out the National Guard to enforce the peace and then refused to rehire the strikers. Nowhere, Coolidge declared, was it written in the Constitution that persons entrusted with the public safety were permitted to strike against the well-being of the state. These sentiments elevated an otherwise lackluster politician to national notice, sailing like the *Mayflower* itself out of "the infinite" of anonymity and displaying a profile equivalent to those stern Puritans cast in heroic bronze by Quincy Ward and Saint-Gaudens.

We can also, Lodge continued, perhaps with President Eliot's message of 1910 in mind, learn from the Pilgrims that communism as a system of government does not work. For their own experiment had determined that holding property in common was "an obstacle to advancement and in conflict with human nature," that mankind's true happiness is achieved by protecting "the right of men to private property honestly obtained" (50). This time-tested truth, along with Governor Coolidge's use of militiamen in putting down a strike deemed a threat to the public safety, should be kept in mind during a time "filled with the noise of destructive, clamorous, and ancient remedies for all human ills" (50). These, then, were the lessons to be learned from the Pilgrims as their arrival on the American shore "towers ever higher as a decisive event in history," a tower that like the one recently raised in Provincetown had a shape not a little resembling the golden trophy the speaker brandished as he emerged from troubled and murky depths—a replicated police baton. In sum, the Pilgrim celebrated by Senator Lodge in 1920 was a reasonable facsimile of those Puritans celebrated by him in New York and Brooklyn in the 1880s, avatars not of the liberal spirit credited to the founders of Plymouth by Senator Hoar in 1895 but of the hard-handed repressiveness associated by Hoar with the Puritans of Salem and Boston.

Lodge returned one last time to Webster, resurrected for the occasion from the obloquy-filled grave into which he had placed him nearly forty years earlier, only to bury him one last time, guilty now not of too much drink and too easy a way with gifts but of being incapable of drawing "the distinction between historic progress in arts, science, and knowledge and a law of progress," which was not really a law but "a state of mind" (53, 43). As such, it was both relative and irrelevant, nor was it essential to the Pilgrim idea, which in 1620 was not far advanced from the view of the universe entertained by men of the Middle Ages, which placed earth at the center and heaven above. So much for the notion, promulgated by so many orators over the past centuries, that the Pilgrims were borne to America on the leading edge of the Reformation, carrying with them a boatload of ideological baggage. Henry Adams's disciple proved once more that he was Lowell's student as well.

His Pilgrims, like Lowell's, were but English rustics, not men of ideas but a simple folk whose lot as they saw it was "to do their best on earth and to make it, so far as they could in their short existence, a better place for their fellowman" (55). This, finally, was the modest lesson to be learned from the Pilgrims, which is not (let us now add) much different from the skeptic lesson of *Candide*, that "there can be no nobler purposes for man than thus to deal with the only earth he knows and the fragment of time awarded him for his existence here." It is a humble enough creed, if subvertly pagan in its way, rather much in the mode of Virgil, who expressed in poetry a similar truth as his contribution to maintaining the stability of empire, attesting once again to Senator Lodge's abiding love of the classics and his hope of enforcing a Roman peace. Where Webster, in 1820, had spoken as a nascent Whig, Lodge, a century later, spoke as a recrudescent Federalist, who brought to Plymouth Rock not a great hope for but a terrible fear of the future.

IV

We are told by Lodge's unkindest biographer that the oration at Plymouth was regarded by his audience as a "masterpiece of sophistication and disillusionment," a Bridge of Sighs over which an entire generation may be seen as passing into the turbulence of the twenties (Shriftgeisser, 359). As such, it was an expression of the very pessimism that Lodge decried. We cannot doubt that the war had its effect on Lodge, but his evocation of that terrible event was in the service of a skepticism he had long entertained regarding the universal faith in human progress that was the Enlightenment's gift to the nineteenth century. If his address was a "masterpiece," it was because it contained truths so well rounded through constant use that they rattled like the shingle on Dover Beach, for virtually all that Lodge had to say in 1920 regarding the *ignus fatuus* of the nineteenth-century faith in progress can be found not only in earlier speeches but, more important, in his autobiographical recollections, *Early Memories*, published in 1913, on the eve of the Great War.

Even the eighteenth-century frame that Lodge placed around Webster's Plymouth address was anticipated by the portentousness with which Lodge surrounded the year of his own birth. For though by 1850 the United States was well into the revolutionary changes in transportation and communication that occurred after 1820, modern America had not yet emerged from its chrysalis, "and the ideas of the earlier time—the habits, the modes of life, although mortally smitten and fast-fading—were still felt, still dominant. . . . Thus it happened that the year 1850 came at the dawn of a new time, at the birth of new forces now plainly recognized, but the meaning and scope of which are as yet little understood, and the results of which can only be darkly guessed, because the past has but a dim light to throw upon the untried paths ahead. Yet, none the less, that which was first apparent to the child born in 1850, as he came to consciousness during the next ten years, was the old world which still surrounded him, for a child, happily for himself, sees only what is near to him—his present seems to have existed always and is haunted with no shadow of change" (16–17).

Lodge by his own account grew up in a home in which the tastes of the eighteenth century were still in place, thanks to his father's literary preferences and his maternal grandfather's status as a living relic, a survivor from a time "when Horace Walpole was writing letters and Gibbon was telling the story of the Roman Empire" (41). This abiding sense of having been born into the atmosphere of an earlier and no longer relevant period is clearly derived from his mentor's *Education*, which had first appeared privately in 1907 and which Lodge would edit for publication in 1918. Much like Adams, Lodge observed that he had come "upon the stage of life just as the remarkable group of men who had made New England and Boston famous in the middle of the nineteenth century were passing off" (276). If he had been born into a cultural museum, it was also a living mortuary, haunted in memory by the ghosts of men like Charles Sumner and Rufus Choate, two of many famous men who passed through the boy's neighborhood, looming like giants in his recollections but long gone now to their graves.

There is an *ubi sunt* quality to Lodge's autobiography, given added force by the author's ending it in 1880, the moment he himself entered public life. It is pervaded by a sense of loss, both personal and generational, that is coupled with an equivalent ambivalence in recording the impact of the many inventions that had emerged after the Civil War, which vastly accelerated the pace of civilized life: "The sleeping-car, the parlor-car, the fast through trains, the huge steamships . . . which now cross the Atlantic in less than a week. . . . In the world upon which I opened my eyes, and in which I lived and played contentedly for many years, there were no ocean cables and only a very limited supply of telegraphs" (201). But then "street railways" broke upon the scene and by applying electricity "as a motive power have revolutionized . . . local communications," to which Lodge added the telephone, now "an integral part of our existence," the wireless, the electric light, and the automobile, and he reckoned "if I should live a few years longer I shall, I suppose, behold, with the indifference born of familiarity, the outlines of flying machines dark against the sky."

All these accelerated communications "have changed radically human environment and the conditions of life, thereby affecting the evolution of the human race as only a changed environment can effect it," and though he stopped short of declaring whether or not these "alterations" had a good or a bad effect—"That is a matter of personal taste"—the drift of his own inclination is clear (202). Lodge's opinion that "the vast development of communication and transportation," along with the constant impact of foreign immigration, had transformed the "English" character of the America in which he grew up to one distinguished by "cosmopolitanism" surely points toward a forlorn conclusion (205).

More pertinent perhaps to his tercentenary oration was Lodge's criticism of the material emphasis in America that had been promoted by increasing the rate of communication, which brought with it "not only general prosperity, but huge and quickly acquired riches" (206). Here was that specter familiar to Lodge's earlier orations, the "plutocrat," a breed of "lawless" men, who "disregard the rights of others" in their quest for riches and who "have taken complete possession of the fashionable world in some places" (211, 210). To

Lodge's way of thinking it is the pervading presence of wealth that has inspired "agitation" by men claiming to represent the discontent masses, whose goal is "to take money by means of legislation . . . from those who have it . . . and give it to those who have not earned it, and especially to those who are unable or unwilling to earn it" (212). Here are more echoes from those nights in Brooklyn, along with the complaint that old-fashioned "individualism" like honestly earned "success" is thought of as "almost purely evil, to be curbed, if not wholly extinguished" (212). In these latter days, even hard work "appears to be considered a misfortune."

These are forever the complaints of the privileged classes, often reinforced by the anxieties of old age, for Senator Lodge's world seems very close at times to Mr. Sammler's planet. And in concluding that "the faiths of my youth . . . are now in many quarters not only denounced, but cast aside as only fit for the dust heaps of history," Lodge went on to make what is by now a familiar point: "If it be assumed that all movement is good, merely as movement, without regard to its direction, we must have made great advances, if advances are measured merely by distance" (216). Lodge's is an axiom loaded with the kind of ammunition provided for riot guns, for looking back through "the glare and noise of the twentieth century" to the "very plain and simple world" of the Boston he knew as a boy, Lodge concluded that only a "cheerful temperament" could assert the familiar "creed of the nineteenth century, that mankind is steadily advancing and that we are moving slowly upward to perfection" (203). And this is the essential message, beyond the various articles of Pilgrim furniture mandated by the occasion, of Lodge's tercentenary oration. His autobiography attests that by the eve of the First World War all the attitudes were in place, that the horrors that followed only confirmed but did not inspire his pessimism.

Lodge lost no one to that war, his great losses having come much earlier, and most are recorded in his book of recollections, which is literally a Book of the Dead, overshadowed at the beginning by the death of his father, who died suddenly, worn out at midcareer at the start of the Civil War when his son was only twelve. But equally poignant were two other deaths that touched young Lodge deeply, far more influential than the passing away of the great men of his youth—who were after all old and nothing more than cardboard cutouts placed around the room—the loss of two young men who had influenced him at critical points in his passage to adulthood.

The first was Constant Davis, his cousin and a recent Harvard graduate who accompanied the boy and his mother as a tutor when they went abroad in 1866, getting him away from the distractions of Boston so that he might prepare for the entrance exams for Harvard. But having aroused in Lodge his love of the classics, Davis, whose sister Lodge would marry, shortly thereafter died. The other was a college classmate, Michael Henry Simpson, the son of a wealthy Boston manufacturer he had known at Harvard and who, the young men meeting in Rome while Lodge was on his honeymoon, became his companion and friend, only to die within the year. Simpson had planned to dedicate himself to public service, and Lodge claimed he was moved by his example and death to do the same.

Lodge's most sympathetic biographer has questioned the literary convenience of these losses, but it is probably a mistake to dismiss these recollections out of hand, if only because they are in keeping with the kinds of intensity same-sex relationships could engender in the nineteenth century. Where Phillips and Lowell were famously inspired by the urgings of their wives, Lodge belonged to a later generation, and his intense rapport with other men, like Roosevelt, gave impetus to his life. There is in that regard one more death that needs to be reckoned with here, which is not in Lodge's autobiography because of his chronological limits but surely is reflected there.

This was the sudden passing of his beloved son, George Cabot Lodge, familiarly known as "Bay," that young hero of the Spanish-American War who went on to marriage and fatherhood and became something of a poet, made much of as such by his father's circle of influential friends. Bay died at thirty-six, stricken in 1909 while he and his father were vacationing on isolated Tuckernut Island, literally in his father's arms, and with him there must have passed away something bright and hopeful from Lodge's heart. Both parents were staggered by the loss, and Anna Cabot Lodge did not long outlive her son. It was during the terrible aftermath that Lodge began to write his memoirs, and it is not difficult to comprehend the possibility that he deflected the intensity of his grief through the deaths of those other young men, his friends and mentors, so full of promise too soon extinguished.

Once again, Lodge lost no one in the war that followed, but then he didn't have to. By 1920, most of the men who had been particularly close to him were dead, Roosevelt the last in the long funeral procession. We can therefore read Lodge's oration in Plymouth as containing personal resonances reflected in his obsequies for Webster and the nineteenth century, being something by way of a eulogy for his generation and an elegy for himself. In that speech, by way of celebrating the Pilgrims in terms of Greek mythology, Lodge quoted a line from Edwin Arlington Robinson, a modern poet who retained respect for form and thereby earned Lodge's respect as well, and there is that in his final oration that conveys the spirit of Robinson's "The Man against the Sky."

For Lodge posed defiantly against the background glare of a world war, infused with a Enlightenment skepticism tantamount to a faith, his silhouette compounded with that lone figure on a hilltop, "the last god going home unto his last desire," in effect placing himself among those Puritans he had compared to a Greek temple outlined against the fading light of day, which in turn had been shaped by his piety for the lost Federalist cause. Once again, he was the best possible candidate, all things considered, to deliver the tercentenary address in Plymouth in 1920, a moment that signaled the passing away of a New England that would not return. The occasion of Lodge's funeral, a scant four years later, inspired an admiring journalist to style him "the noblest Roman of them all," rather ironic praise, all things considered, there being less Brutus in Lodge and more Cassius. But if he was not finally the noblest Roman of his time, he was certifiably the last.

CHAPTER 24

The Rock Impounded

> On Roanoke Island, there is no enduring symbol for the first
> "permanent" English settlement in America like the rock at Plymouth,
> Massachusetts. In place of a symbol, Roanoke has mystery . . . a shadowy
> sense of an older time that Plymouth Rock, surrounded, dwarfed, and
> protected in stone and steel, has lost.
> —William Least Heat Moon

I

Senator Lodge's contribution to the Tercentenary differed from Webster's bicentennial oration in terms of proportion as well as emphasis, for where the celebration in 1820 was largely limited to Webster's oration, in 1920 it was a massive and extensive production, long in planning and almost a year in duration. It included suggestions published by various public and private agencies for local celebrations, including dramas and other events suitable for presentation for and by children, all aimed at educating Americans concerning their history and institutions, in effect preparing them for citizenship in Memory's Nation.

The effort is exemplified by the project of the Society of Colonial Dames, which had continued the good work of the "Southern Matron" by devoting itself to saving historic buildings and when necessary resurrecting them. This last activity resulted in the restoration of the ancient church in Jamestown, Virginia, a project timed to coincide with the anniversary date of 1607 but with the forthcoming Tercentenary of Plymouth clearly in mind: "You cannot stop the mouth of Chesapeake Bay with Plymouth Rock," noted a Richmond editorial of the day, sentiments suggesting that despite the grand reunion of Civil War veterans in Cuba some reconstructive surgery was still in order (Lamar, 116).

The Colonial Dames conceived itself a "national" organization, at least in spirit, a generous purview attested by the fact that the resurrection of the Jamestown church originated with the Massachusetts chapter of the society,

589

and the project went forward under the leadership of the chapter president, Edith Greenough (Mrs. Barrett) Wendell. Completed by May 11, 1907, the church at Jamestown in effect fulfilled the proposal made by the Honorable Salmon Chase in 1889 that a memorial equivalent to the Forefathers monument be erected in that "cradle" (as Thomas Nelson Page insisted upon its completion) "not only for the Commonwealth of Virginia, but of the Republic" (128). But, in effect, the project in Jamestown seems to have been by way of achieving balance to the intended work to be done in Plymouth that would contribute to the Tercentenary a shape equivalent to the Greek temple associated by Lodge with the Puritans.

Among its several differences from Jamestown, Plymouth lacked a ruin to be restored, necessitating that the Colonial Dames break with its own infant tradition and erect the elegant beaux arts canopy over the place where New England and, in New England's eyes, the Republic began. But whereas the Jamestown project took only three years to complete, the much simpler structure in Plymouth took more than a decade, not for lack of enthusiasm or funds but because of problems outside the Colonial Dames' control. Jamestown at the turn of the century was little more than a desert island, occupied by a crumbling Confederate fort and the ruined tower of its seventeenth-century church, whereas Plymouth was a crowded, if decaying, seaport, with little left from its early years save street names and the fabled Rock. Despite the preliminary clearing undertaken prior to the construction of Billings's canopy, the waterfront was still "disfigured with walls, wharfs, coal sheds and all the sordid accompaniments of commerce" (Lamar, 133). Much had to be undone before anything could be started.

The Pilgrim Society resolved in the spirit of the occasion to restore the shoreline to approximately what it had been in 1620, thereby relieving orators from the necessity of calling up the scene in the imaginations of their auditors. This was not simply a matter of removing the remaining evidences of "commerce" that had so offended the sensibilities of the reporter from New York in 1853, but involved the talents of landscape as well as structural architects. It was an extended effort that included the destruction of what was now deemed an "inartistic" structure sheltering the Rock, to make way for the neoclassical portico designed by McKim, Mead, and White.

Professor Herbert Adams had long ago found fault with Hammatt Billings's "colossal, pretentious canopy of granite . . . this baldacchino, which reminds the beholder of the canopy over the altar of St. Peters . . . this mausoleum, under the leaky roof of which now lie Pilgrim bones, taken from the kindly shelter of mother earth upon Cole's Hill, to which some day they will probably be returned, just as Plymouth Rock has been restored to its original bed" (pt. 2, 46). He suggested that the canopy might be "removed to Cole's Hill, where it

FIGURE 32. The original architectural drawing for the elegant McKim, Mead, and White canopy, which diminished even as it guarded the Rock, seen as a lump centered in the openings designed to admit the waters of the bay. The canopy as completed differs some-what from this sketch, including the installation of bars across the openings to prevent entrance at low tide, but its effect on the Rock remained consistent, illustrating the expo-nential law of petrapiety: as worship intensified, so did rhetorical grandiloquence and iconic grandiosity, the which, along with depredations by souvenir hunters, reduced the object of attention proportionately. In sum, inflation by increased volume reduces mass. (Courtesy Pilgrim Society)

will serve for a monument, if such a thing is desirable," but instead it was reduced to rubble (49).

These activities took time as well as money and were interrupted by the world war, as well as by subsequent problems, so that when Senator Lodge rose to speak on Forefathers' Day in 1920, the canopy was not yet in sight, and the seawall designed as its protective base had not been completed. The Rock, as the photograph of Lodge with the Coolidges testifies, had been removed until the work was completed, and only late in November 1921 was the portico finished and the Rock returned. Thus the dedication ceremony proved to be the penultimate (and wintry) event of the Tercentenary, the capstone, as it were, to a number of prior events and dedications of less ambitious but note-worthy monuments.

Sundry statues, plaques, and like concrete memorials were set in place, including a bronze figure representing Massasoit, which was unveiled with becoming reluctance by his last living descendant, a Native American princess of advanced years and severely reduced circumstances, who stood surrounded by Red Men from the fraternal order so named, which had given the statue to Plymouth. There was also cast a bronze "Pilgrim Maid," who was given a rough rock pedestal for her sturdy feet, an obvious allusion to Mary Chilton, though for tourists not in the know she could pass easily for Priscilla Mullins staring John Alden back to the beach.

A new, stone facade in the Greek Revival style replaced the wooden porch to Pilgrim Hall (the gift of the ever generous New England Society in New York). And on Cole's Hill there was constructed a large sarcophagus to hold the handful of Pilgrim bones recovered in poor condition from the upper chamber of Billings's demolished canopy, in effect fulfilling Professor Adams's prediction, at least in part. Among other structures erected for the occasion was a log cabin intended to represent the first dwellings of the Pilgrims, the mistaken fruit of James Goodwin's good work, and a replicated *Mayflower* was built in Boston, using the hull of a former coasting schooner, the *Fannie Hall*.

This effort did not sail into Plymouth Harbor under its own power but was towed down by the tug *Nellie*, causing the ship's dinghy to founder en route, so that it had to be bailed out before the landing party could be embarked. But at last, despite these adversities and the prevailing opinion of strict antiquarians over the years, the people dressed as Pilgrims came ashore on the riprap protecting the beach at Plymouth, and a facsimile of Mary Chilton was helped ashore by an equivalent version of John Alden. This photo opportunity was captured by the "movie men" (as the tercentenary record calls them), who were everywhere with their hand-cranked machines during the extended event, signifiers of the times. But perhaps the greatest evidence of the modern age were the traffic jams caused by the narrow streets of the old town when visitors ignored the availability of rail and steamboat transport for the mistaken convenience provided by their internal combustion engines. If Lodge's emphasis on the impact of automobiles on New England needed validation, it got it in 1920 in Plymouth.

During these activities the sacred Rock was moved about as a participant in events, before being stored under guard to await its final resting place. Preparations for the new canopy included not only building the seawall but digging a channel that would let the ocean reach the Rock, thereby authenticating the tradition. And lest souvenir hunters take advantage of low tide, a heavy steel grill was installed in the granite wall, protecting the threshold of a nation from further depredations. But the net effect of placing the Rock in this elegant cage was counterproductive, reducing it still further in terms of relative proportions and forbidding the continuation of the time-honored custom of standing on the Rock, which Billings's gate allowed.

FIGURE 33. The Landing reenacted for the cameras, August 1921, observing the wrong date but the Chilton priority. The Pilgrim hats, a convention that emerges obscurely from the nineteenth century, as in the statue by Ward (see fig. 24), reinforce the western connection, albeit (unlike the tercentenary log cabin erected at Plymouth) not intentionally so. (From *Plymouth Tercentenary Illustrated*)

There is a photograph of Governor Coolidge doing just that at some point prior to the old canopy's destruction, and he may therefore be accounted the last in the succession of famous steppers-upon, a line stretching back at least to Dr. Thacher, never mind the Forefathers, to whose use of that stepping-stone Elder Faunce had testified. Coolidge was accompanied on this occasion by a group of schoolchildren, who took their turns admiring the Rock, a familiarity one would think devoutly to be desired, in that it maintained an intimate connection with that moment made meaningful by Pilgrim feet.

But the design of the new canopy cut off all access, permitting only visual contact with a boulder set at the water's edge, in the manner of a seal in its pen at the zoo. Not only did this eliminate the personal touch, but the beautiful canopy elevated against the sky drew attention away from the humble Rock, while it advertised in large letters the generosity of the Colonial Dames. Still, the new enclosure was petite compared with the pavilioned "temple" originally proposed by the architectural engineer hired for the project, which would have virtually wrapped the Plymouth shoreline in a neoclassic curtain or fence, an extended series of colonnaded porticoes centered by an extended dock designed to accommodate the motor launches of the affluent devout. This ambitious expression of filiopiety would have swallowed up the object it was intended to enhance, so that as at Mecca the chief object of awe and worship would be the cenotaph and not the stone. Celebration can go no further, but it is perhaps fortunate that there were not sufficient funds for this massive display of beaux arts revivalism, and other ambitious plans for the Tercentenary were also revised downward and reduced in size.

There were, however, sufficient structures erected to fulfill the desire of the city fathers that whatever money was raised for the celebration would be invested not in frivolous and ephemeral displays of momentary veneration— the slogan-bearing banners and green bowers of the past—but on lasting monuments that would enhance the improvements to what, in the words of a tercentenary commissioner, resembled less a town than a town dump. One no longer heard about the Pilgrims being their own best monument, and that a desire to profit from tourism was intimate with this strategy—a pioneering attempt to rescue a downtown area by razing it—is implicit.

Nor was the ephemeral element, the bread and circuses, entirely missing, there being sufficient events to attract motion picture cameras and visitors, in quantities seldom lured by dedications of memorials and slow improvements to a civic profile. These included the grand procession commemorating the Departure that was held on August 1, 1921, which drew a crowd of visitors estimated at one hundred thousand, and the Shriner's Parade of August 10, which caused a traffic jam of monumental proportions. But the chief attraction, in part responsible for the huge crowds of people and streams of auto-

FIGURE 34. (*Top*) Coolidge on the Rock in the soon-to-be-demolished canopy designed by Billings; (*bottom*) children in close proximity to the Rock, now no longer possible save by stealth.

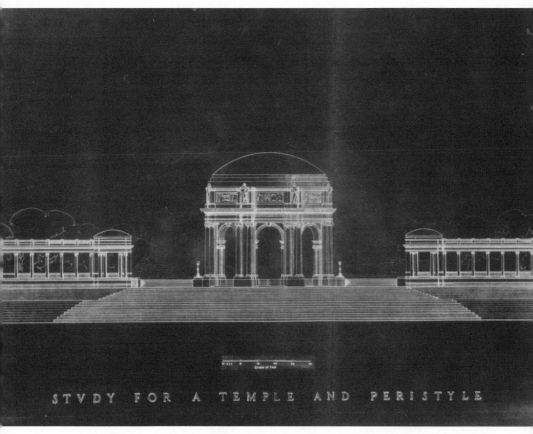

STVDY FOR A TEMPLE AND PERISTYLE

FIGURE 35. The temple designed to shelter the Rock in the projected plan of 1916, to be flanked by porticoes leading to a boat landing on the one side and a waterfall on the other; (*opposite*) the architect's sketch of the whole, literally devouring the Rock with a plan dominated by the projected harbor for visitors to the site. Any such would be privileged persons wealthy enough to afford waterborne transportation, as opposed to those who came ashore by way of the equally ornate but contradistinctive structure at Ellis Island. (Both photos courtesy Pilgrim Society)

mobiles on August 1 and 10, was a mammoth outdoor drama, *The Pilgrim Spirit*, which had opened in the middle of July and drew ever larger audiences with each succeeding performance, until it closed a month later.

This pageant was written and staged by Professor George P. Baker of Harvard University, who had introduced courses in playwriting at that institution and whose students would include Eugene O'Neill and Thomas Wolfe. The innovative Baker proved quite able also in managing the kind of complex spectacle usually associated with his younger contemporary Paul Green of North Carolina and with a much later period. July and August were chosen as

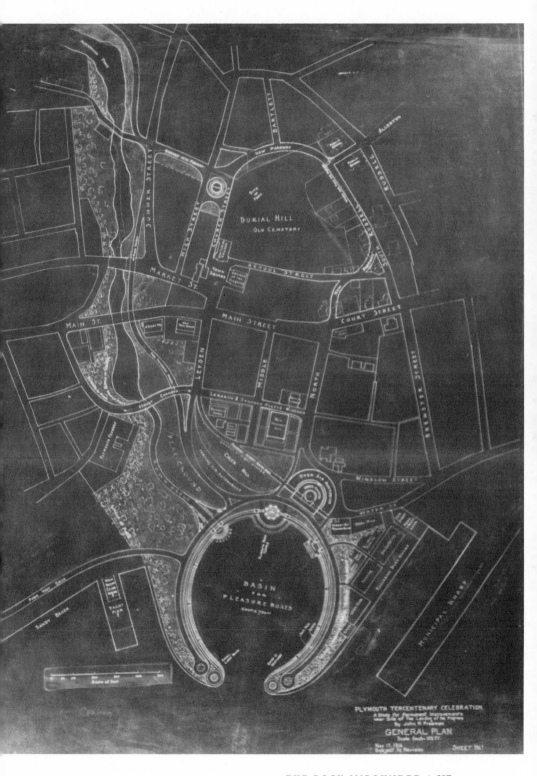

the months for the pageant for the usual reasons, but good weather in New England, as Mark Twain fabulously observed, is a sometime thing, and as the great moment approached, so did thunderstorms. The field that was the theater was drenched on July 10, canceling the first weekly production, and rain threatened subsequent performances as well, of which there were twelve in all. But the most important night was the evening of August 1, the anniversary of the Departure, and "Plymouth Day," as it was called, turned out to be picture-book perfect, a sequence of blessings that included Plymouth's luck in at last luring a U.S. president to town, the first, as the chronicler of the Tercentenary noted, in three hundred years.

Warren G. Harding while still a senator from Ohio had served as chairman of the Massachusetts Tercentenary Commission and could hardly have refused the invitation, so the president and Mrs. Harding graced the day, a dinner, and the drama and provided as well a centerpiece for the parade. Harding's party arrived aboard the *Mayflower* (the presidential yacht, not the refurbished schooner), thereby carrying on the great Republican tradition, but Harding was accompanied by a strategically reduced naval fleet, suggesting a subtle shift in Republican priorities. As on those earlier occasions, Senator Lodge was in attendance, but in attendance only, perhaps another signifier of changing times.

President Harding acquitted himself handsomely, if not profoundly, giving New England the expected credit for its founding role in "rearing new standards of freedom," even while warning that "the one outstanding danger of today is the tendency to turn to Washington for the things which are the tasks or the duties of the forty-eight commonwealths which constitute the American Union" (Bittinger, 81). This is a message familiar to our own times, affirming the iron continuities in the Republican platform.

Harding ended his brief address on a positive, even a cheery note, by informing his auditors that the country was "solvent financially, sound economically, unrivalled in genius, unexcelled in industry, [and] resolute in determination and unwavering in faith." Such assurances became the very ground that his sudden successor (who on that day was home minding the store, as it were) would stand upon, and which would endure until he stepped off, suggesting that Calvin Coolidge in more ways than one enjoyed the favors of Grace, as well as the blessings of divine as well as popular Election. For the twenties turned out to be the most ephemeral of decades, much as its hysterical gaiety was an intensified equivalent to the equally evanescent Era of Good Feelings exactly a century earlier.

Equally short lived was Professor Baker's drama, albeit of sober mien and featuring a minimal amount of dancing. Though published as a small book by way of a souvenir, the pageant was one of those literary efforts defined as "occasional," meaning an artifact designed for a moment it seldom outlives.

The production was a considerable achievement, however, and gave Plymouth Rock and the Pilgrims a contemporary and therefore available setting, in heft and emphasis providing an extended complement to Harding's presence, if not his speech. Senator Lodge had opened the centennial year with a wintry performance in the Puritan mode, and it closed with the snow-swept dedication of Plymouth Rock's new enclosure, but Professor Baker's was a summertime thing, affirmative as any such pastoral moment, and it celebrated the Pilgrims in the spirit of "normalcy," a neologism that Lodge is on record as having detested, even though he led the fight to give the man who coined it the Republican nomination.

II

Professor Baker's was not the first pageant staged at Plymouth that celebrated the Pilgrim adventure: in 1896 there was presented a "Historical Festival" so successful that a second was given in 1897 under the directorship of "Miss Margaret MacL. Eager, of New York," which dramatized in nine "scenes" the familiar story, ending with the fabled courtship of John and Priscilla in three parts (*Old Plymouth Days and Ways*, 32–58). To these were added five more scenes depicting "the Later History of Plymouth," and featured during the matinees were "children's scenes," the most elaborate of which, "The First Spring," depicted "the Pilgrims finding the Wild Flowers of Plymouth," personified by children in appropriate costumes (64). Though scheduled for the summer months (July 28 to August 3), the festival was enacted in the Plymouth Armory, whereas the *Pilgrim Spirit* was not, and "Pageant Master" Baker may be given an edge with a wide margin on the score of length, his production having a total of four episodes, each with from two to eight scenes, as well as length of score, there being considerable music involved.

There were, as we shall see, other innovations, but though in many respects a pioneering effort, the Pageant Master's production unrolled like an old-fashioned panorama, those mile-long canvases depicting set scenes in a spatial or chronological sequence. Even in dramatic terms it was something of an antique, for the first part was taken up by a series of tableaulike episodes done in pantomime, mute actions that served to tell the story of the earlier arrivals to the Plymouth shore, from the Norsemen to Captain John Smith. On the other hand, the audience may well have accepted the soundless scenes as theatrical equivalents to the silent screen, that modern miracle whose representatives were ubiquitous during the tercentenary celebration. It was certainly a clever and economical device, not only allowing for considerable historical material to be covered quickly but permitting the display of the many local talents demanded by the sheer size of the spectacle without putting an undue strain on same.

For if Plymouth is a celebrated instance of the Local, then Baker made great use of the tradition, enlisting the services of resident seamstresses and carpenters for costumes and sets. Included among the hundreds of actors listed were many names of Italian derivation, most of whom were undoubtedly recruited from the local cordage works, Plymouth's largest employer. According to the factory's most recent historian, Samuel Eliot Morison, its workers were immigrants eager to be absorbed into the existing culture, and participation in the pageant may have been seen by them as a giant step toward that ideal goal. By participating in historical events their forebears had not been able to witness, they became, as it were, honorary members of Memory's Nation. Still, having Italians filling the roles of sailors aboard Captain Bloch's *Onrust* may have necessitated a strenuous suspension of disbelief among those playgoers unwilling to accept the possibility that the Dutch explorer had hired Columbus's original crew.

The historian of the tercentenary celebration put the best possible construction on this necessity, noting the representation not only of Italy on the program but of "Portugal, France, Holland, Sweden, Russia," as well, which made it truly "an international affair." It was as if Ellis Island had been moved to Plymouth for the occasion, which was hardly the purport of Baker's drama (Bittinger, 52). Along with the presence in Plymouth of motion picture cameras and automobiles, the modernity of the moment was testified to by the technology involved in the production: "The electric lighting plant for the pageant field was reputed to be the largest and most complete of anything of that kind ever erected in this country," making possible in the grand finale "a wondrous blaze of illustration from electric-fed projectors which dazzle the eye and fulfill the demand of the old Pilgrim pastor, John Robinson, for 'more light'" (52, 43). The chronicler seems to have confused Robinson's farewell sermon with Goethe's dying words, the authenticity of which is likewise somewhat in doubt. But certainly those evidences of material progress questioned by Senator Lodge must have impressed any of those present—like Lodge—who had witnessed the puny spectacle of that single spotlight in 1889.

The pageant also allowed for the display of New England's luminaries in the arts. Composers of the stature of Henry F. Gilbert, Edgar Stillman-Kelley, F. S. Converse, Lee Sowerby, Chalmers Clifton, and George W. Chadwick contributed music for poetic interludes, which were written by the likes of Edwin Arlington Robinson, Josephine Preston Peabody, and Hermann Hagedorn. But the penultimate poetic moment was taken up by the work of Robert Frost, who in words set to the music of John Powell raised a song from the region itself as it greeted the Pilgrims. Of this effort two stanzas suffice, the brackets being the poet's device:

As freely of it as was yours to give
You gave it to us to be ours to hope again,
[Your hope of landing was your gift to men.
And hope forever to be free and live.]

Come in a Second Coming to the West,
Coming in a Second Coming to the land
Where once you left the print of feet impressed
As deep in rock as others have in sand. (Baker, 135)

Frost was so disappointed by this his first attempt to write poetry on commission that he swore never to do the like again, and his contribution to Baker's pageant has not been included in his collected poems. This omission perhaps facilitated Frost's second, much more successful attempt at occasional verse, read by him forty years later, which contains detectable echoes of his contribution to Baker's production.

But in Plymouth on the night of August 1, the pageant went smoothly despite the threat of showers, although the play of powerful searchlights from the battleships in the harbor gave the Pageant Master more light than he wanted, and he requested that they be shut off as distractions drawing the attention of his audience. Certainly the spectacle required the viewer's collective concentration, for Baker's drama was comprehensive, and like so many orations that had celebrated the Landing, it devoted considerable time to prior events transpiring in the Old World. Baker traced the Pilgrim Spirit all the way back to Lydgate's translation of the Bible, and the persecution that that bold act of the Reformation inspired.

The Departure is the central moment in the pageant, as befits the anniversary date, with the text of John Robinson's fabulous farewell being rendered in full. The pastor's words were followed by a poem by his namesake, E. A. Robinson, "The Pilgrims' Chorus," which expresses the sermon's spirit: "Though God may leave our reaping unto others who come after, / He has called us, and we follow, to the new and the unknown" (78). Due acknowledgment to Longfellow's influence was made by having Alden and Priscilla exchange calf-eyes while still aboard the *Mayflower*, but the role of Standish was severely reduced to one voice among those in authority—chiefly expressing defensive caution in all ventures. The fiery captain's adventures among the Indians were excised, perhaps because of the terrible recent war, and certainly the play had a pacifist emphasis, for the region's inhabitants were presented as a gentle, even fearful people.

Maintaining a continuity with the stress of Joseph Croswell's drama of 1802, the controversy involving the rebellious John Oldham and the subversive

Lyford was given a prominent place toward the end of the action, suggesting that Baker's liberalism had a limit similar to that of the Pilgrims. In 1921, once again, subversion as in 1621 was in the air, and emphasis was given to the signing of the Compact as a regulatory mechanism guaranteeing the civic peace. Women had at last been suffered the vote, and the initial putting ashore on Cape Cod provided an occasion for a tribute to the Pilgrim wives and maidens, shown washing clothes as Standish and the men of the exploring party set off on their expedition.

This left the distaff side behind, who revived Hemans's idea of Pilgrims singing in the wilderness, raising their voices in a lyric by Josephine Preston Peabody. The writer, herself famous as the author of poetic dramas, suffered from chronic illness, and her efforts on behalf of war refugees had reduced her to invalidism. Within two years, Peabody would be dead at forty-eight, and her song turns on a prophetic note of foreboding, framed as a debate between the hopeful sentiments of the "Young Girls" and the doubts and fears of the "Older Voices" among the women. Thus the former voice a happy optimism for the future—"And some day, from our sowing, / Midsummer overflowing;— / Ways of brightness, for our feet unknowing! (All, all unknowing)"—but the parenthetical tag at the end of their song is picked up by the older women, with an italicized resonance that gives it a second, somber implication: "(*All, all unknowing*)" (93). In the last verse, the women put their reliance on God—"Thou wilt see / Beyond our poor discerning," but as they sing, Dorothy Bradford is seen standing apart from the rest, "*shading her eyes*" and looking off "*toward the place where her husband has disappeared*," an ominous final moment given that she will mysteriously drown during his absence (96–97). In effect, Dorothy replaces Rose Standish as the focus of pathos, given a setting that denies sentimentality—a subtle shift of emphasis.

For the scene underwrites the tragic outcome of the Pilgrims' first year, but it also stresses the theme of work, which, commencing with Lowell's revision of the Puritan idea, dominates much of the oratory during the last years of the nineteenth century. Notably, no sooner have the Pilgrims landed at Plymouth (the exploring party first, followed by the main body of the passengers, a division honoring the report of 1850) and knelt to sing the "Hymn of Praise" written by Hagedorn (who would become the editor and biographer of the celebrant of the Strenuous Life) than men in the background are shown with "*axes, hammers, adzes, saws*" (96). For having fallen on their knees, the Forefathers "*set to work felling trees*," a safe substitute for the antagonists in the traditional rhyme. Though the Rock itself (the real one) figures prominently in the scene, it is as a stage prop, not the actual threshold across which the passengers from the *Mayflower* step, for reasons made clear by the photograph of Lodge and the Coolidges standing next to it. Done in pantomime, the Landing was rather much minimized, equal time being given in the scene that followed, which was devoted to "THE INDIAN QUESTION." Again, rather than emphasize Standish's violent solution, we are shown Carver and Massasoit coming to terms of mutual amity and accord, with the Rock once again standing passively nearby.

Nor did Plymouth Rock serve only as a mute witness to the action, for at crucial moments it is given lines to speak, in "a rich, powerful voice," very much in the spirit of Walt Whitman as perhaps modified by Carl Sandburg. The pageant opens with a prologue spoken by the Rock, which emphasizes the predestinarian idea, reinforcing the conceit that the speaker itself is part of the action, even as a static participant: "I, the rock of Plymouth, speak to you Americans":

> Here I rested in the ooze
> From the ages primordial
> Men came and went: Norsemen,
> Seamen of England, voyagers of France, Dutch adventurers;
> Over and round me
> The Indians worked, played, lived.
> I was a rock of millions along the shore,
> Waiting,—for what? (5)

The question, repeated throughout the prologue, is one of those leading kinds favored by orators, and the pageant provided an answer familiar to the audience. But that is always the underlying premise of Forefathers' Day celebrations, being a ritual reassertion of what is already known by way of providing certainty in the face of the unknown future, thereby validating the essential conservatism of memory. "Here," the Rock asserts of the Pilgrims, "they will work out their salvation. . . . Of me the rock in the ooze, they have made a cornerstone of the Republic" (6). Old news, by and large, is good news, which Baker apparently felt his audience needed in large doses. Thus the Rock speaks again, later in the action, as the Pilgrims depart for the New World, anticipating the Compact, "Liberty's fabric" that will be wrought by "artisan farmers," and what the Compact will assert is very much in harmony with the transmutation of Lowell's message over the years. In effect, absent English grain, the Pilgrim "farmers" brought with them the seeds of the Protestant ethic: "Gain must be theirs / At the price of their labor" (78).

What immediately follows from the Rock is in keeping with Lodge's Americanism, for we are told that the Pilgrims will "punish the traitor" even as they pity "the culprit," a balance that weights the scales of justice heavily against subversion: "This is your heritage. All you Americans. Do ye maintain it?" (79). Such tough talk, suitable for a granite boulder, sets the stage, as it were, for the treatment accorded the rebellious faction toward the end of the drama. Thus, when the "Stranger," John Oldham, troubles the peace of the settlement with his cantankerous demurrers, arousing the discontent of a number of Pilgrims, Governor Bradford uses the Compact as a kind of limbo stick: "Return to England, whoever wishes and can. But let him who remains know this: no man who works shall starve, but he who has, must work for what he gets, and must share in the common defense" (117). This plain speaking inspires "*grumbling, discontent*" from Oldham's group, the kind of rhubarb that the Pilgrim Fathers knew how to sweeten. Uncovering the plot against the colony, Bradford, waving incriminating letters seized by him from the *Charity*, "full of slanders and false accusation," brings Oldham to heel and Lyford to tears (126).

Expelling Oldham forthwith and giving Lyford six months to correct his thinking, Bradford delivers the final word: "Let this be for a warning that what we establish here for personal liberty and self-government, that will we hold as a heritage for our children and our children's children" (131). The scene ends with an anthem made up of words from Bradford's great chronicle, as the governor is revealed "*sitting at a table writing his history, his only illumination a tallow dip.*" Thus the drama's final moment validates authorship, much as the packet of purloined letters had been the critical lever dislodging the party of discontent, with the Compact serving as fulcrum. Behind Bradford can be seen the spirit presences of the men who figure prominently in his book, standing "like statues, near at hand," in effect monumental witnesses, like the Rock. It is with this scene that the Pilgrim part of the drama ends, but the action continues, as Washington and Lincoln make brief appearances, quoting from the farewell and Gettysburg addresses.

Then two men appear in modern dress, who approach the Rock and look away toward the sea, obviously choric representatives of the author. The first man to speak calls Plymouth Rock "the granite wharf prepared for them" at this "the port of entry of our freedom. . . . I wonder," continues the speaker, "what the Pilgrims if they came / Would say to us as freemen. Is our freedom / Their freedom as they left it to our keeping—Or would they know their own in modern guise?" (133). The question is followed immediately by a clash of cymbals and a roll of drums, signifying "*War*," not one of the many colonial conflicts but *the* war, so recent in the audience's collective memory:

Across the back of the Field, to march music, pass the flags of the allies, so lighted that they show brilliantly, but not their bearers. Nearer move the French and British flags, and then all wave and beckon. There follows a hush. Suddenly from far out on the Mayflower a bugle calls in the darkness, and light begins to glow on the vessel, but very faintly.

VOICE OF THE ROCK

"The path of the *Mayflower* must forever be kept free."

This declaration brings in, by means of sequential waves, the entire cast of earlier "adventurers," whose torches are virtually extinguished by having the stage lighting gradually increased. Meanwhile, the speaker in modern dress "wishes" for a song to "call them back today," in terms echoing John Masefield, an "off-shore song / Wide as an off-shore wind, but not so hard / For a ship to beat into port against," sentiments bringing to mind the perverse rill in Frost's "West-Running Brook" and heralding that poet's contribution, "THE RETURN OF THE PILGRIMS" (134).

Frost's line "a Second Coming to the West," already quoted, serves as a signal for the Pilgrims to return to the field, "*convoying forty-eight young women bearing the State flags*," as the other actors part to make way, opening an avenue that directs their gaze toward the *Mayflower*, which now is fully illuminated, the entire cast of the pageant and the harbor "*ablaze with light, and great searchlights are sweeping the sky*" (136). But with the final line of Frost's hymn, all the lights are extinguished save those on the *Mayflower*, and the last speech is given to the "VOICE FROM THE ROCK," which, as the light fades from the Pilgrim ark, intones the memorable words from Lincoln's address: "With malice toward none and charity for all it is for us to resolve that this nation under God shall have a new birth of Freedom." With that the pageant ends, having made quite literally a line direct from Plymouth to Gettysburg and, by evoking the recent war, updating the relevance of both to the modern occasion.

As in that war, the enlistment of modern technology was used to spectacular effect, the massive installation of electrical apparatus a regnant symbol of the complex coordination required by the infrastructure that made the pageant possible. The light show with which the drama ended was a logical, if novel, extension of the traditional pyrotechnics, but by epitomizing the mechanics of the pageant, which like the lighting was a marvel of engineering, it added a definitive element producing the vague outlines of an art deco production, of a kind soon to be associated with the Radio City Music Hall and Nuremberg.

Despite his emphasis on law and order and the kind of regimentalization associated with militant patriotism, the Pageant Master was hardly a chauvinistic ideologue. But he did express a definably subdued liberalism that was alert to the dangers of subversion, regarded as a threat best dealt with by strict laws and a ready access to other people's personal papers—not force of arms. Once again, the multinationalism of the characters and cast worked toward a mood of mutual tolerance and understanding, the flags of the allies woven in with those of the states. Baker's was a quiltlike fabric that perhaps gave vague support to the ideal of a League of Nations but which in no way posed any specific challenge to the national status quo. In sum, the pageant was just what one might expect of an academic writer with creative ambitions in 1920, theatrical rhetoric posing no threat to the Republic.

We need not argue with the contemporary enthusiasm of the "High Authority" quoted by the chronicler of the event concerning Baker's contribution, that it was "the greatest pageant ever given by any people since the beginning of the art . . . an immortal classic" (Bittinger, 97). Critical opinions, like critical reputations and cheap dyes, tend to fade with time, and the evaluation by Francis Trevelyan Miller, author of *America: The Land We Love* and *American Hero Tales*, editor of *The Photographic History of the Civil War* and the *Journal of American History*, may be credited to the excitement of the moment. President Harding was more restrained, if also positive, in his response, declaring himself "impressed" with the pageant and calling it a credit to the community and to "those who were more or less directly responsible for its success." This presidential praise may not have increased Professor Baker's pulse rate but was certainly, if carefully, well meant. From this distance, Baker's intended masterpiece seems in no risk of a revival, but there was another drama being staged nearby that would prove an enduring classic of sorts, a virtual pageant the revisionary retelling of which has only validated its mythic status, so that it shares the noumenous quality of the autochthonous event evoked by Lodge in his commemoration of the Pilgrims.

III

The backdrop to the alternative drama unfolding in Plymouth in 1920 was the source for so many members of his gigantic cast, the Plymouth Cordage Works, located north of town. Founded in 1824, by 1920 the Cordage Works was the largest factory in the world producing binder twine, rope, and whatever else could be woven from imported hemp and other fibers by the complex machinery developed for that purpose. According to Samuel Eliot Morison, the works was one of those innovative, worker-friendly factories, a benevolent presence that over the past quarter century had been a pioneer in providing pension plans, decent and inexpensive housing for its employees, a lunch room, and other facilities for worker comfort and convenience. In short, like the machines they tended, the workers themselves were symbols of enlightened progress.

But the administrative officers of the Cordage Works had somehow in their rush to better the lot of their workers overlooked the disparity between what they were paying them and salaries earned elsewhere. As a result, during the height of the war effort in 1916, when demand for hemp products was great, the factory was crippled by a strike declared by those workers for whom fringe benefits were not a substitute for a living wage. The strikers were not unionized and refused the overtures of the AFL and IWW organizers to help them, preferring as Morison notes to keep the matter in the "family." And in the end the strikers settled for an increase deemed fair by their employers, though it was much less than what they had demanded. For their part, the factory owners were surprised and not a little hurt by the sudden action taken by workers they had tried to make happy.

In the official history written to commemorate the centennial of the Cordage Works in 1924, it was hinted that the strike was the work of a "Red" agitator, presumably with a view toward crippling the war effort, to which the greatest producer in the world of binder twine (used in the harvest of western grain) was making a vital contribution. Morison some thirty years later did not buy this thesis and, having noted that the offers of the Wobblies to agitate further unrest had been rejected by the strikers, defined the affair as strictly nonpolitical.

The agitator hinted at in the official history of 1924 was not named, but his identity was already written in capital letters on the factory wall, in large part because of his own much publicized claim that he had been a leader in the strike, had been blacklisted as a result, so that he had to seek elsewhere for work. The facts were otherwise, for by 1916 Bartolomeo Vanzetti had quit his job at the Cordage Works and gone to work with the gang of men building up the breakwater at Plymouth intended to protect the site of the new canopy for the Rock. By 1920, Vanzetti had opted for free enterprise and, while regularly participating in the meetings and other activities of local anarchist groups, peddled fish from a cart through the Italian district of North Plymouth. It was this occupation he claimed he was busily pursuing on the morning of December 24, 1919, when a failed payroll robbery took place in nearby Bridgewater, a crime for which he was later tried and convicted, in a trial that took place in June and July 1921, as Baker's pageant began its month-long run.

This was but one in a chain of events, largely circumstantial, that were preludial to the main drama, in which Vanzetti and his friend and fellow anarchist Nicola Sacco were charged with the much more serious crime of murdering a paymaster and his guard in South Braintree, near Boston, on the afternoon of April 15, 1920, and making off with fifteen thousand dollars. It was after his arrest in May that Vanzetti was accused of the earlier robbery attempt, for which he was convicted and sentenced to prison, a hurried-up and peremptory procedure that was prejudicial to the proceedings of the second trial, which began more than a year after the two men had first been arrested.

Professor Morison stated in his history of the Cordage Works that Sacco and Vanzetti were indeed innocent, an opinion shared by many liberals at the time of the trial, who protested that the two men were being tried as anarchists, not bank robbers. Whatever the truth of the matter, the two men were declared guilty by a jury of well-informed peers (thanks in both respects to the unrelenting efforts of the prosecutor and presiding judge) on Bastille Day, 1921, but it would not be until 1927, in the month of August, sacred to the memory of the

Pilgrim Departure from Delft-Haven, that Sacco and Vanzetti suffered death in the electric chair. Their champions made much at the time of the anguish of the two men as they waited out the years in the Charlestown jail, and certainly the wheels in whose gears the two men were caught turned painfully slow, but the process was retarded because of the legal appeals and petitions mounted on behalf of the accused by their champions.

If indeed the Pilgrims had brought freedom of political conscience to America from England in 1620, the parallel and alternative spectacle in which Sacco and Vanzetti played central roles indicates that the persecutory spirit associated with colonial Salem and Boston was very much alive with paranoid electricity in Massachusetts. Equally in evidence, moreover, was the eagerness of radicals to promote martyrs to the cause of freedom, the kind of activities we associate with that latter-day Puritan saint William Lloyd Garrison. Only this time around it was the Bill of Rights that was cited, that subversive (indeed to some minds infernal) engine concealed within the Constitution, intended to protect individuals from the unjust workings of the rule of law, the very refuge sought by those anarchists denounced by Lodge in 1888.

And it was the rule of law, exemplified by the Mayflower Compact and the "trial" and expulsion of John Oldham, that was celebrated in Professor Baker's drama. Though most of the planned ceremonies and festivities of the tercentenary celebration attempted to be politically neutral, there is an ideological conservatism virtually inherent in most publicly sponsored activities of this kind, as the drift of previous celebrations of the Landing demonstrate. Further evidence of the conservative, even reactionary impulse underlying the events is provided by a solicitation for donations put out late in 1920 by the Pilgrim Tercentenary Memorial Fund of the New England Historic Genealogical Society on letterhead bearing the names—along with others—of J. P. Morgan and Henry Cabot Lodge. In a note accompanying the engraved invitation to become a Pilgrim Tercentenary Member by donating three hundred dollars, the society emphasized its good work in forwarding "Americanization," through virtue of being "the source of the information upon which that of the patriotic societies in America have been founded." In America, at least until very recently, genealogical research has chiefly nurtured those twin trees whose roots (in the parodic words of Orpheus C. Kerr) are "firm bound" in Plymouth Rock and Bunker Hill.

Thus those patriotic societies cited by the letter sent out by the Pilgrim Tercentenary Memorial Fund Committee were mostly founded in the closing decade of the nineteenth century. Borne on the rising tide of Lodge's "Americanism," they registered a reaction to the perceived threat to the United States that was posed by subversives with foreign names and associated with violent acts against the establishment. The letter refers to a recent bomb explosion on

Wall Street, which did extensive damage to the House of Morgan and was, as we now know, intended as retaliation for the Sacco-Vanzetti "persecution." The letter made no such connection, but did view with alarm "an element in our country which has a false idea of liberty and a perverted understanding of the free democracy upon which the country was established by our fathers."

We might attribute these words to Lodge were not such attitudes by 1921 as conventional as the pieties expressed on Forefathers' Day, among which they had been increasingly enlisted. The writer went on to insist that "the inculcation of American ideals and traditions and the creation of a respect for law and order in this unassimilated element are . . . vital to our continued existence and prosperity." Therefore, moneys donated to the society would forward that advancing line of defense against un-Americanism and lawlessness by maintaining "a free source of authoritative knowledge of American ideals and traditions," just such a purpose as Professor Baker's celebration of *The Pilgrim Spirit* was designed to effect.

IV

If "amalgamation" was in the 1830s a major, if not always explicit, signal of alarm over the consequences of granting freedom to black Americans, so "assimilation" was the signifier in 1920. In this particular case it was a consummation devoutly desired by New Englanders who sought to process the raw material of immigration into the kinds of stuff produced by the Plymouth Cordage Works—that is to say pliable fibers woven into material dedicated to the ideal of hard work at a wage determined by employers. We may not doubt Professor Morison's assurance that the majority of the immigrants employed by the Cordage Works were—unlike the man caught up in the carpet machinery in Mark Twain's twice-told tale—glad to become part of the weave. But much as there were a few who sought to effect radical changes in the structure of American society, so there were in New England as elsewhere a number of powerful individuals who expressed a deep uneasiness over the consequences should efforts toward assimilation fail, a fear that may be traced back to the Reverend Blagden's brief statement of concern in 1834.

Thus the idea of using the tercentenary occasion as an instrument of public education was central to the planning that went into the event and undoubtedly assisted in obtaining state funds for various related projects, including plays and readings to be used in schools. We may be sure, once again, that this complex motive lay behind the large number of Italians enrolled in the pageant's enormous cast. Vanzetti was not among them, but then he was detained elsewhere, his efforts at entrepreneurship so essential to the American way of life not having been sufficient to save him from the taint of his political ideology.

In the back pages of the book containing Professor Baker's play there are a number of titles advertised by the publisher as having historical and political interest, including a "Bilingual Series for New Americans." This was another of the projects underwritten by the Society of Colonial Dames, including a book entitled *The Story of America*, available in alternative Italian and English (and Polish and English) and written by one Alberto Pecorini. Likewise, on Forefathers' Day in 1920 the orations of Coolidge and Lodge were followed in the afternoon by another program, sponsored by the citizens of Plymouth, that also featured songs and orations, and among the latter was "The Immigrant's Share in Our Heritage—What Part May He Fairly Expect?" by Vittorio Orlandi of Boston, and "For the Rights Accorded the Immigrant, What May America Justly Expect of Him?" by Dr. Frank V. Thompson, Boston superintendent of schools (Bittinger, 17).

Unfortunately, the texts of these speeches were not preserved in the official history of the celebration, but included there is another address bearing on the same subject, delivered during the Ninth General Congress of the General Society of Mayflower Descendants which met in Plymouth on September 6, 1921. An organization founded in 1896, and a virtual contemporary of the Society of Colonial Dames, the Society of Mayflower Descendants had as its icon not the Rock but the Ship, and its members devoted themselves to honoring "the vessel and the voyage, rather than the landing and settlement" (*General Society*, 5). They customarily, as in 1921, held their annual meeting in September, when the historic voyage was well—if slowly—under way.

Toward the same end, the speaker on that occasion, the society's deputy governor-general, Asa P. French, chose to celebrate Captain Christopher Jones of the *Mayflower*, a man who from the days of Cotton Mather had suffered obloquy at the hands of the celebrants of the Forefathers. According to ancient authority, Jones had been in the pay of the Dutch, who were averse to the Pilgrims' original plan to land on the banks of the Hudson River, a place in which they themselves had an active interest. It was this fact, not adverse winds, that resulted in the *Mayflower's* dropping its hook off Cape Cod, a tradition that like Jones's reputation as a pirate was mostly gossip, and which Deputy Governor-General French converted to praise, thanking Jones for not having landed the Pilgrims in the vicinity of Coney Island. Rather than blaming the captain, the descendants of the *Mayflower* passengers should be eternally grateful to him, or so went French's reasoning, intended by him as one of those heavy-handed jokes that had become increasingly obligatory on such occasions.

After a few more such pleasantries, French got down to the serious part of his speech, which addressed the undeniable truth that "many of our fellow citizens take no special pride, and have no special interest in or sentiment about the Pilgrim fathers" (Bittinger, 106). Natives of many foreign nations, all "on their way to citizenship, jostle each other in the streets of our large cities, and are scattered throughout the land. Can we hope to inculcate in them any deep-rooted respect or enthusiasm for the devoted band which settled this Colony and helped to found this nation?" Here again we hear amplified Blagden's warning nearly a century earlier about "foreigners unacquainted with the nature of our institutions," a tinkling bell of alarm that the events of recent years seemed to validate, the dull thump of anarchists' bombs providing reasonable equivalents to sounding brass.

What, French wondered aloud, might be the results of keeping these alien people inside the gates, should armed conflict with their native countries erupt? Would they, "if put to the test, prove unswervingly faithful to the land of their adoption, undisturbed by the consequences to the land of their birth?" As German Americans could attest, their loyalties were very much in question during the recent war, nor would their hardworking advocacy of the American way of life protect Japanese Americans twenty years later. "Frankly," said Deputy Governor-General French, "none of us can help feeling apprehensive as to the answer to this question," and in the background we can hear the ghost of Thomas Bailey Aldrich whisper "Amen."

Like Aldrich, and like Lodge as well, French felt that the United States had "perhaps been unwisely hospitable," but he despaired, given the political climate, of changing the immigration laws. Nor was he very hopeful over the possibilities of educating "ignorant foreigners within the comparatively short space of time in which they can become citizens, both in our language and in the machinery of our government and to inspire them with adequate comprehension of and respect for the fundamental principles of its origin." French's remarks were uniformly in keeping with the sentiments expressed in Brooklyn in the 1880s in pointing to signs of national decline, the "diminishing" spirit of the Forefathers "among the people," so many of whom were beyond the reach of the traditional jeremiad. The deputy governor-general ended by reading Webster's famous concluding paragraphs that had been addressed to posterity, but with a different purpose from that of Senator Lodge. For French had no desire to discredit Webster's optimism but borrowed it so as to assure all Americans that the Society of Mayflower Descendants was not "grounded upon any spirit of exclusiveness or upon any feeling that our blood is purer . . . because it flows from the Pilgrims" (107).

We may give French due credit for honesty and view the efforts of his Descendants along with those of the Colonial Dames and the New England Historic Genealogy Society as sincere attempts to assist the formation of what they conceived to be patriotic Americans, shaping immigrants into upright citizens speaking a uniform language. They, and other organizations, including the Tercentenary Commission, sought to "instil" in resident aliens the "principles" of the Pilgrims, not out of hatred and fear but with "love and reverence." The problem, however, was not the benevolent aim of such societies; it was "the method of accomplishment. The obstacle is the immensity of the task": time is short, but the lines at Ellis Island were very long.

Toward the end of forwarding the society's good work, its annual congress that year entertained a motion to require throughout the country a yearly reading of the Mayflower Compact, to take place in all "city and town schools of the United States on the last school day before Thanksgiving of each year" (108). The resolution was not adopted, though the congress assembled did vote to have its presiding officer read the Compact aloud to the Descendants there present before the meeting adjourned, an apt demonstration of the difficulties that lay ahead.

V

A number of American writers and artists were participants in the demonstrations protesting the conviction of Sacco and Vanzetti, including Katherine Anne Porter and John Dos Passos. Of the two young writers, Dos Passos's was the most significant literary contribution to the movement to save Sacco and Vanzetti, Porter's being limited to transcribing the letters of the two martyrs— still something of a classic in primitivist prose—while Dos Passos compiled a maledictory on the eve of the dual execution in 1927. Entitled *Facing the Chair*, it is a collection of documents and transcriptions interwoven with his own commentary that ends with the claim "If the truth had been told they would be free men today" and with the plea "Save Sacco and Vanzetti" (127). When, ten years later, Dos Passos published the concluding volume of his massive trilogy, *U.S.A.*, entitled *The Big Money*, he used the Sacco and Vanzetti protests as a paradigm of the problematics of radicalism in America, a preludic hint of his eventual disillusionment with the Communist Party. More pertinent to our concerns here, he reworked the material of his pamphlet into one of the most memorable of the autobiographical "Camera Eye" sections of the novel.

The episode in *The Big Money* was based on a visit he made to Plymouth on a muddy spring day in 1921, the purpose of which can be found in *Facing the Chair*: there, Bartolomeo Vanzetti is depicted "peddling fish in the pleasant little Italian and Portuguese town of North Plymouth," the details of which are informed by local color gathered by the writer:

He was planning to go into fishing himself in partnership with a man who owned some dories. Early mornings, [he pushed] his cart up and down the long main street, ringing his bell, chatting with housewives in Piedmontese, Tuscan, pidgin English. . . . Between the houses he could see the gleaming stretch of Plymouth Bay, the sandy islands beyond, the white dories at anchor. About three hundred years before, men from the west of England had first sailed into the grey shimmering bay that smelt of woods and wild grape, looking for something; liberty. . . . freedom to worship God in their own manner. . . . space to breathe. Thinking of these things . . . as he pushed the little cart loaded with eels, haddock, cod, halibut, swordfish, Vanzetti spent his mornings making change, weighing out fish, joking with the housewives. It was better than working at the great cordage works that own North Plymouth. Some years before he had tried to organize a strike there and been blacklisted. The officials and detectives at the Plymouth Cordage Works, the largest cordage works in the world, thought of him as a Red, a slacker and troublemaker. (58)

This is a clever propaganda piece, evoking sympathy for the hardworking, popular seller of fish, a man who is enterprising and intelligent, speaking several Italian dialects, "schooled" in anarchism, as Dos Passos points out, but ambitious to succeed by hard work.

Though victimized by corporate capitalism, Vanzetti retains his faith in America, his idealism sanctioned by the Pilgrim example: he too wants "space to breathe." As journalism, Dos Passos's account is nothing more than an imaginative, even subjective presentation of Vanzetti's own account of things, with no mention of the violent specifics of his brand of anarchy, which involved the use of dynamite to open up breathing space. It was written in the hope of enlisting last-minute sympathy for the condemned men, using Vanzetti as a case in point, who, because of his handsome features as well as his interest in intellectual matters and a superior command of English, had emerged as the most appealing of the two men.

When Dos Passos came to work this material into *The Big Money*, he converted the point of view from that of Vanzetti to his own, translating the earlier plain, journalistic prose into the mannered, stream-of-consciousness style then in vogue, thanks to the influence of James Joyce. It is the "Camera Eye" of the writer that looks out past "the grey framehouses under the robins-egg April sky across the white dories anchored in the bottleclear shallows across the yellow sandbars and the slaty bay ruffling to blue to the eastward" (435). Those imagined reflections of Vanzetti about the Pilgrims are now returned to their proper point of origin and expanded into a lengthy meditation, more complex than the simple irony of contrasts established by the earlier version: "this is where the immigrants landed the roundheads the sackers of castles the kingkillers haters of oppression this is where they stood in a cluster after landing from the crowded ship that stank of bilge on the beach that belonged to no one between the ocean that belonged to no one and the enormous forest that belonged to no one that stretched over the hills where the deertracks were up the green rivervalleys where the redskins grew their tall corn in patches forever into the incredible west."

In the 1937 version, Dos Passos introduced a new, nativist note, in harmony with the drift of American literature and art in the thirties, an emphasis integral to reactionary as well as radical ideologies. As his tone suggests, Dos Passos felt no intimate connection with the Pilgrims, who merely serve as ideological icons of convenience, nor does he stress the religious nature of their errand as he had earlier. They are, as in Richard O'Gorman's sense eighty years earlier, the first "immigrants," but they are also J. R. Lowell's "stern men with empire in their brains," in search of available space, not "freedom to worship" as they please. Their search for liberty is put forth in militant terms, resulting in that time-honored conflation with Cromwell's Ironsides that had served radical ends a century earlier but had little to do with the Pilgrims (or they with it).

But again, Dos Passos's emphasis here is less on the Landing than on the promise held out by a continent "belonging" to no one, including the resident "redskins," a racist term engendered by the frontier experience of the nineteenth not the seventeenth century. For the next "threehundred years," Dos Passos tells us, these "immigrants" will "toil into the west," for his is a delayed observance of the Tercentenary, which couples the Pilgrim errand with Manifest Destiny (*Big Money*, 435). Ironically, and to say the least unintentionally, Dos Passos echoes Webster's prophecy in 1820, thereby conflating the Pilgrims with the ancestors of Woodrow Wilson.

A contrasting figure is permitted by the looming shape of the great Plymouth Cordage Works, now occupying the space once taken up by "tall corn in patches," evidence that the Industrial Revolution had displaced the old, Agrarian dream, which had once stretched "forever into the incredible west." Turning his back on the preindustrial, postcard New England of quaint gray houses and white dories, Dos Passos aims his camera eye at "huge sheds and buildings companyhouses all the same size all grimed the same color a great square chimney long roofs sharp ranked squares and oblongs cutting off the sea" (436). This is not the architecture of individual opportunity but expresses the oppression and exploitation associated with the later class of "immigrants" who followed the Pilgrims' pathway of hope to America.

Here in the cordage plant worked a man who like those earlier immigrants was a "hater of oppression who wanted a world unfenced" and who after being blacklisted for his activities on behalf of his comrades took to peddling fish to his fellow immigrants, people who when confronted with questions about Vanzetti are "scared to talk of Bart scared because they knew him scared eyes narrowing black with fright." Only a little boy among them is unafraid, who, walking "shyly browneyed beside me to the station talks about how Bart helped him with his homework wants to get ahead why should it hurt him to have known Bart? wants to go to Boston University we shake hands don't let them scare you," says Dos Passos boarding the train back to Boston (436–37).

Seated in the smoking car, the author self-consciously refers to his notebook, bemoaning the inadequacy of the "pencil scrawls . . . the scraps of recollection the broken halfphrases the effort to intersect word with word to dovetail clause with clause to rebuild out of mangled memories unshakably (Oh Pontius Pilate) the truth" (436–37). But as the confused syntax of Dos Passos's stream of consciousness suggests, the "truth" remains stubbornly disjunct, indeed may be most truthful because so out of joint. The writer's notes are also a kind of scripture (much as Vanzetti is a kind of Christ), a divinely inspired but therefore often unintelligible message, a code that must be unscrambled.

Regarding his fellow passengers, the familiar "jumble of faces" that "rumble cozily homelike . . . through the gathering dark," Dos Passos wonders "how can I make them feel how our fathers our uncles haters of oppression came to this coast how say Don't let them scare you how make them feel who are your oppressors America." The problem of communication is made worse by the decay of language, the older testament now "ruined words worn slimy in the mouths of lawyers districtattorneys collegepresidents judges without the old words the immigrants haters of oppression brought to Plymouth how can you know who are your betrayers America . . . or that this fishpeddler you have in Charlestown Jail is one of your founders Massachusetts?" (437).

In 1937, Dos Passos in retrospect bends 1920 back upon 1620, and like the abolitionists of 1837 who imposed the occasion of Lovejoy's death on Forefathers' Day he makes radicals of the Pilgrims and Pilgrims of the radicals. Both are conceived as "immigrants" and hence both are feared and detested by "lawyers districtattorneys collegepresidents judges" who in the manner of (and often as) Forefathers' Day orators twist and pervert the original words of the Forefathers in order to force them into place as timbers holding up a rotten establishment, against which the anarchist-immigrants of 1620 or 1920 pose such a destructive threat.

Again, the notion of immigrants as Pilgrims dates from 1855, although, as we will soon see, Dos Passos had a much closer and more likely source for his compound metaphor. His concluding focus, moreover, is linguistic, as he faces the problem of how to proceed on his own errand without having first to "rebuild" the "old words" with which Plymouth Rock and the Pilgrims had so long been endowed, words now grown foul in mouths slimy with corruption. His is a conundrum much like that put forward a century earlier by James Russell Lowell when he accused the overstuffed celebrants of Forefathers' Day of betraying the spirit of the people they were celebrating.

To these troubled sentiments, which by expressing a conflict define it, we can add a subsequent section of the "Camera Eye" that immediately follows the chapter in the novel in which a group of radicals are beaten and hauled off to jail for protesting the execution of Sacco and Vanzetti. The "words" used here are familiar to the rhetoric employed by radicals of the 1920s and are defiant in acknowledging defeat: "all right you have won you will kill the brave men our friends tonight" (462). Clubbed down and thrown in jail, the radicals have been "beaten by strangers who have turned our language inside out who have taken the clean words our fathers spoke and made them slimy and foul." Here Dos Passos repeats the meditation made after his journey to Plymouth but gives it more point by associating it with the thoughts of the radicals, who see themselves as embodying the true spirit of the Pilgrim Fathers.

In the author's eyes the modern agitators and dissidents make up one of what is now "two nations," a separatist and secessionist theme that runs throughout Dos Passos's great trilogy. He thereby reestablishes the dialectic of the Garrisonites, enforcing a division that is no longer geopolitical but is a matter of the privileged and underprivileged classes in America, the employers and the workers. The former have the district attorneys and judges on their side, the latter have the radicals who seek to find words "to make you feel who are your oppressors America," to convince Americans that "the old words of the immigrants" of 1620 are "being renewed in blood and agony tonight" and will not be "forgotten in our ears tonight" (563).

These assumptions are at the heart of what Lodge defined as "unAmericanism," being the apologetics of a radical insurgency that seeks to replace capitalism with communism, but the point to be reinforced here is that Dos Passos is repeating the argument of Garrison and Wendell Phillips, making over radicals into the party of Memory, resurrecting through words the spirit of the Pilgrims. Notably, it is not with the words of Robinson or Bradford that the episode ends, or the language of the Mayflower Compact, but the famous message of Bartolomeo Vanzetti, "the old words made new" by the men "in the deathhouse . . . before they died": "*If it had not been for these things, I might have lived out my life talking at streetcorners to scorning men. I might have died unknown, unmarked, a failure. This is our career and our triumph. Never in our full life can we hope to do such work for tolerance, for justice, for man's understanding of man as we do by an accident.*"

There are a number of ironies framing this statement, which has taken on the luster and resonance of American scripture, along with the farewell and Gettysburg addresses, and which, given Dos Passos's implicit context, could be included among those speeches associated by Wendell Phillips with Plymouth Rock. It might even, following Professor Baker, be given to the Rock itself, for without the Landing of the Pilgrims, that compound fracture of an accident, the Rock would have been nothing, also.

The first irony is a matter of translation, for what appeared in *The Big Money* was somewhat revised from the original words written at the time by a reporter, which in turn were transcribed from shorthand notes hastily taken down on the margins of a newspaper during an interview with Vanzetti in his cell. Vanzetti did acknowledge making some such statement, with the intention of comforting the reporter, who was disconsolate over the certainty of the good man's death. But his testimony made the words not an expression of disinterested valor but strategic to a specific and highly personal moment.

None of this discounts the nobility and resonance of the sentiments, which became famous long before Dos Passos used his slightly revised version in *The Big Money*. But regarded as facts surrounding the origin of the words, they do mitigate somewhat the power of Vanzetti's statement. Moreover, by voicing these sentiments, Vanzetti in effect sanctioned the strategy of the Communists, the cynical opportunism that Katherine Anne Porter would by 1970 find so reprehensible. And the final irony is derived from the use of Vanzetti's words as an epigraph to the collected letters of the two anarchists, which Katherine Anne Porter transcribed (a labor for which she received no credit), thereby sealing the whole with an apparent gesture of willing, even eager martyrdom. Coming as they do toward the end of the penultimate book of *U.S.A.*, these words likewise enlist the massive weight of Dos Passos's great novel in the Communist cause he would soon after disavow, rolled like a stone emblazoned with Vanzetti's final words over the tomb of the martyred anarchists.

It is an act equivalent to that desire voiced by Garrison a century earlier, who in 1837 wished that the body of the martyred printer, Lovejoy, could be borne into Faneuil Hall by black men in chains, as his grieving widow followed after. And Vanzetti's famous words, spoken in the prison in Charlestown, Massachusetts, call to mind the sentiments of Captain John Brown, spoken in the prison in Charlestown, Virginia, towns whose names are resonant with the name of a king whose martyrdom was the work of Cromwell and the regicides. Thoreau felt that Brown's last words to his accusers would be remembered forever, but where Brown himself sanctioned his own martyrdom, Vanzetti seems to have been thinking chiefly of comforting not the Communists but the reporter to whom he was speaking. By taking his words out of context, Dos Passos forwarded a myth equivalent to that of John Brown kissing the slave mother's child, a coupling whereby the two Charlestown jails become one.

The similitude is given further sanction by Ben Shahn's famous tryptich, which celebrates Sacco and Vanzetti not in the traditional form of a historical tableau but in the disjunct, askew manner of surrealism, a stylistic equivalent to Dos Passos's prose. When completed in 1932, the composition was flanked on either side by the words transcribed by the reporter in 1927, linking them forever with the iconic portrayal of the two noble anarchists, the Communist-led protests, and the savagely satiric third panel of the two men in their coffins as the Lowell committee with Judge Thayer in the background extend funeral lilies of tribute. By such means were Sacco and Vanzetti immortalized as willing martyrs to a cause they never supported, becoming in a sense not meant by Dos Passos the equivalents to the Pilgrims posed on Plymouth Rock, who like many such mythologized icons took their meaning from ideologies they never shared.

CHAPTER 25

The Statue and the Rock

Part he was of New England stock
As stubborn, close guarded as Plymouth Rock...
He would call New England his place and his creed
But part he was of an alien breed
Of a breed that had laughed on Irish hills
And heard the voices in Irish rills.
—*Jacqueline Kennedy*

I

"Let us fear no emigration from the one side or the other. This country is emphatically the asylum for the oppressed of all nations. Welcome them on either shore, the Atlantic or the Pacific. . . . Accepting the responsibilities of the hour which Providence has placed on this Nation, let it ever continue in the fulfilment of its great mission. . . . Then shall it literally inherit the divine promise: 'I will give the heathen for an inheritance and the uttermost parts of the earth for a possession' " (*Proceedings*, 119–20). These were the generous sentiments of the president of the Pilgrim Society, Edward S. Tobey, at the 250th celebration of the Landing in 1870, who proposed that the missionary efforts of the Forefathers be continued by converting the "heathen" who came in increasing numbers to the land of the Pilgrims, "moulding" them "to Christianity through the influence of our institutions as well as by direct teachings of the Gospel."

As we have seen, Tobey's was distinctly a minority view during the annual celebrations of Forefathers' Day during the Gilded Age, and coming when it did, before the problems of immigration because of an oversupply became severe, it perhaps sprang as much from his need as a prominent industrialist for cheap labor as from his sincere devotion as an orthodox Congregationalist to missionary endeavors. And yet his argument was essentially one of assimilation, which was the stated aim of those many patriotic organizations founded during the last two decades of the nineteenth century. Thus if so liberal a spirit as Senator Hoar could observe in his Forefathers' Day address of 1895 that the "great stream" of immigrants "which has poured into our State" had "on the whole [a] favorable influence upon her history," he was led to that opinon by his faith that "Massachusetts has educated the foreigner. She is making an American of him. She is surely . . . impressing upon him what is best of the Pilgrim and the Puritan quality and the Pilgrim and the Puritan conception of a State" (*Proceedings*, 42).

"The Pilgrims," observed Hoar, echoing a refrain that was by then a century old, "were Englishmen," and their descendants were "Englishmen still," testifying to the old Anglo-Saxon continuity that was celebrated by his predecessors over the years at earlier Forefathers' Day anniversaries (43). "English aptness for command, habit of success, indomitable courage, unconquerable perseverance have been, are, and are to remain the American quality. The men of other blood who come here acquire and are penetrated with the English, or perhaps without boasting or vanity we may say, the American spirit" (43–44). Despite the senator's generous sentiments regarding persons with national origins other than English, there was no confusing recent immigrants with the Forefathers, and though "the portrait of our Irish hero, Sergeant Plunkett," was "hung on the walls of Mechanics' Hall" in Hoar's hometown of Worcester, it was John Winthrop whose portrait hung in the halls of the American Antiquarian Society in the same city (42).

Those who followed the logic of Richard O'Gorman in 1855 and conflated the Pilgrim with the Immigrant were like O'Gorman of recent foreign extraction and by 1920 were more often than not radicals like John Dos Passos, himself the grandson of a naturalized Portuguese, who sought to displace the old hegemonies. Sacco and Vanzetti had certainly learned "the Puritan conception of a State," albeit not in the sense meant by Senator Hoar. But then, they were not the kind of foreigners associated with assimilation to an essentially English culture but alien presences, who sought to import foreign ideologies and force them on Americans by violent means. They were associated with "anarchists and bombs" and were the kind of people that Chauncey Depew in 1886 wanted to see separated at the gates from "the benign influences of enlightened law-making and law-abiding liberty" (*Orations*, 107). Toward that end had the mechanism on Ellis Island been constructed, a vast machine that gave definition to the Statue at whose dedication Depew had spoken.

But by 1920, also, thanks to the poem written by the daughter of immigrants, Bartholdi's monument was not Depew's sentinel but a welcoming presence, no longer projecting the spirit of Liberty worldwide but holding out a

The "Pilgrim Fathers" of 250 Years Ago.   **JUST AS DANGEROUS NOW AS THEN.**   The "Pilgrim Fathers" of To-Day.

FIGURE 36. Frederick Burr Opper, cartoon from *Puck*, ca. 1885. The iconography of the Landing yields to nineteenth-century demographics, here humorously sympathetic to the conflation of Pilgrims and immigrants, a minority notion at Forefathers' Day celebrations of the 1880s. The structure visible in the right-hand side of the cartoon is Castle Garden in New York Harbor, before the construction of Ellis Island as the receiving point for immigrants, a process so unregulated as to allow the kinds of swindles depicted by Opper, which, along with the admission of undesirable aliens, the new facility was designed to prevent.

torch that lit the way for all who wished to share the blessings of freedom. Once again, its iconography was different in implication from that otherwise similar shape dominating Hammatt Billings's Forefathers monument, largely because of the poem affixed to its base, which extended an invitation easily distinguished from those issued on the letterhead of the Pilgrim Tercentenary Memorial Fund Committee. Bartholdi's great work became a symbol of inclusion even as Plymouth Rock, protected behind granite columns, became a symbol of exclusion, much as New York is thought of as the most cosmopolitan of American cities while Boston is not.

But as always with such neat divisions and dichotomies there are exceptions, and one very powerful example can be found in Mary Antin's little book *They Who Knock at Our Gates*, published in 1914, as the Colonial Dames were making their plans for the tercentenary occasion, and which can be classed with that and other preparations for the great event, albeit with a defining difference. For it was Mary Antin who provided Dos Passos with the connection he commemorated between Vanzetti and the Pilgrims, the link so obviously missing from the sequence of events that made up the extended celebration in 1921.

Though an immigrant herself, Antin was no revolutionary like Dos Passos but wrote in a spirit of assimilation similar to that of a number of documents purposely produced for the three hundredth anniversary of the Landing. Born in Russia of Jewish parents, Antin came to America as a child, entering through Boston, not New York. Hers was mostly a positive experience, for she regarded life in the New World as a happy contrast to the bigotry and persecution suffered by Jews in the Old, and she devoted her career and craft to promoting understanding and acceptance of the foreign-born who sought admittance to the United States.

In 1912, her autobiographical *The Promised Land* had appeared and exemplified her essentially melioristic, assimilative line, an argument not universally accepted by the Jewish population for whom she presumed to speak. While acknowledging that she had encountered anti-Semitism in the United States, Antin also expressed her eagerness to become in all ways an American, sentiments that should have reassured people who were worried that the digestive powers of the Republic were inadequate to the occasion. They should also have been comforted by Antin's praise of the public system of education, associated by her with a joyous liminal experience, which included early recognition by her teachers of Mary's promise as a writer.

They Who Knock at Our Gates is a complementary publication, subtitled *A Complete Gospel of Immigration*, a kind of secular New Testament, intended, however, not for immigrants themselves but for native-born Americans. The book is divided into three parts, each devoted to "answering" one of the three "main questions" generally asked in regard to the perceived threat (or implicit promise) of immigration. The first lays down, as it were, the law upon which the remaining two are based: "The fundamental American law . . . the law of the Fathers," as immutable as the tablets brought down from Sinai, is the Declaration of Independence (3). And in its opening statements regarding the self-evident truths upon which the new nation was founded, the Declaration does not exclude any class or place of origin from its glorious generalities but "accords to all men an equal share in the inherent rights of humanity," which translates into the inherent right of all men to come to America, where that equal share is guaranteed.

Antin's logic is hardly perfect, and she conveniently ignores the fact that the Declaration of Independence is a statement of principles, not a body of laws, but then hers is a radical though not a revolutionary purpose. Like Garrison during his abolitionist crusade, Antin aims at a higher truth, holding up the ideals of the Declaration as a standard against which the modern instance may be measured and by which "the true Americans—the spiritual heirs of the founders of our Republic" may be found: "To such a test we are put, both as a nation and as individuals, every time we are asked to define our attitude on immigration" (7). It is not sufficient, Antin declares, for American citizens "to maintain our own independence," selfishly hugging "that vision to our own bosoms. If we sincerely believe in the elevating power of liberty, we should hasten to extend the reign of liberty over all mankind" (16). Moreover, in preaching this good news, the evangels of the "goddess Liberty" need not travel afar: they "are saved the trouble of carrying our gospel to the nations, because the nations come to us," logic anticipated by that earlier celebrant of immigration, Edward S. Tobey, in 1870.

But where Tobey had in mind conversion not only to citizenship but Christianity, presumably producing workers sufficiently meek to inherit the earth by and by, Antin's is an Enlightenment religion, despite her frequent references to the Old and an occasional mention of the New Testament. The figure central to her evangelism is that Athena-like colossus standing at the entrance to America: "The most precious piece of real estate in the whole United States is that which supports the pedestal of the Statue of Liberty," a work whose significance is enhanced by the fact that it was conceived by a Frenchman and made a reality by "the pennies of the poor" (25). And the meaning of that figure is glossed by "the verses graven on a tablet within the base," which were "the inspiration of a poetess descended from Portuguese Jews," sentiments that explicate the meaning of the Statue, which is that "the love of liberty unites all races and all classes of men into one close brotherhood, and that we Americans, therefore, who have the utmost of liberty that has yet been attained, owe the alien a brother's share" (26).

Though Antin comes close to championing the melting-pot idea—pennies melded into a "mountain-weight of copper," all classes and races unified into one brotherhood—her final section, entitled "The Fiery Furnace," avoids the obvious connection and returns to her central point: our attitude toward immigration reveals the extent to which we are true Americans by testing our willingness to put our ideals into action, a definition that challenges the exclusiveness inherent in the "Americanism" of Henry Cabot Lodge, never mind the closing gates of T. B. Aldrich: "Here, in the trial at Ellis Island, we are put to the test of the fiery furnace. It was easy to preach democracy when the privileges we claimed for ourselves no alien hordes sought to divide with us. But today, when humanity asks us to render up again that which we took from the English in the name of humanity, do we dare to stand by our confession of faith?" (141–42).

In this same chapter, Antin confronts head-on the cynical "restrictionists" who frightened workers into opposing open immigration by suggesting that wages would be lowered if foreign-born labor enters the workforce, hysteria fed by bigotry that blinds Americans to the benefits of competition. It discourages "idealism" in the workers and inspires instead cynicism and selfishness: "Is there anything brotherly about a monopolization of the labor market?" (109). The notion of an "over-supply of labor" is a "myth of the restrictionist imagination that vanishes at one glance around the country" (111). It is the dream child of the "rich men . . . who ransack ancient chronicles to establish their connection with the heroes of the Revolution" (104).

Antin's attack on the establishment parallels that of both Vachel Lindsay and Dos Passos, but it is not in the service of either Populism or Communism but forwards the ideal of opening the gates to America indiscriminately. Like Garrison, she repeatedly calls on patriotic Americans, which include workers and union organizers, to acknowledge by their actions the principles of the Forefathers and to "unite in a practical recognition of the rights of their belated brothers who are seeking to enter the kingdom of liberty and justice" (103–4). As for those who fear the failure of assimilation, Antin points to the fact that "race-blending has been going on here from the beginning of our history," much as "none of the great nations of Europe that present such a homogeneous front today arose from a single stock" (119–20).

Antin's refutations of the various "myths" that fuel the restrictionist hysteria are many and complex, but it is the central and pivotal section of her book that speaks directly to the matter we are concerned with here. Because it is in that second chapter that she mounts an extended comparison between modern Pilgrims and "the Mayflower stock," and, perhaps not surprisingly, Antin's typical immigrant turns out to be a Russian Jew like herself, who also turns out to be superior to the original model (36).

Rating the newcomers in terms of "the predominant virtue of the Pilgrims," which Antin defines as an embattled "Idealism," she maintains that "it takes a hundred times as much steadfastness and endurance for a . . . Jew [in Russia] today to remain a Jew as it took for an English Protestant in the seventeenth century to defy the established Church" (37). As for that hallowed threshold to nationhood, the American Revolution, Antin countered with the Russian Revolution of 1905, which enlisted the energies of "the Jews of Eastern Europe" (39). And when measured on the score of heroic rebellion and suffering for the sake of freedom, by Antin's system of bookkeeping "many of the Russian refugees of today are a little ahead of the Mayflower troop," a ratio that tends to hold throughout her assessment (40).

It must be said that if Antin really thought to convert the Anglo-Saxon establishment to her gospel of immigration, hers was the wrong way to go. As Werner Sollors has demonstrated, Antin's Boston heard her preaching from afar and was not pleased. Among her critics was Professor Barrett Wendell of Harvard, husband of the president of the Massachusetts chapter of the Society of Colonial Dames and a literary critic associated by Van Wyck Brooks with Henry Cabot Lodge as symbols of the decline of Brahmin culture. Barrett had been impressed by Antin as a child—"miraculously precocious"—and had granted her access to the Athenaeum, but by 1917 he was less charmed, having been put off by her "irritating habit of describing herself and her people as Americans, in distinction from such folks as Edith and me, who have been here for three hundred years" (Howe, 281–82; cf. Sollors, 289).

Agnes Repplier, writing for the *Atlantic*, was offended by Antin's use of James Russell Lowell, from whom she had taken her notion of the Pilgrims as monopolists of virtue. Repplier was also put off by comparisons between the Pilgrims and modern immigrants, noting that there had been no army of well-wishers and hospitable civil servants, as at Ellis Island, attending the Landing in 1620. Moreover, as Sollors also points out, the idea of assimilation had its ideological opponents among Jews as well, who were not eager to sacrifice their religion and culture to the Americanization process.

In evaluating the response by the Boston literary establishment to Antin's book, we cannot discount an element of anti-Semitism, but the dominant note seems to be that traditional Brahmin hostility toward the noisy newcomer, and in the opinions of Barrett and Repplier we hear faint echoes of the Puritans who were outraged when a female Quaker invaded the pulpit of a Congregational church. Antin had gone so far as to echo the words of John Robinson, for in responding to those who would discount the modern relevance of the Declaration of Independence, she asked the leading question, "If our Fathers did not foresee the whole future, shall we therefore be blind to the light of our own day?" (24).

Moreover, if Jewish immigrants were the new Pilgrims, then the Puritans were by way of the Old Testament the first American Jews, the mark of "Hebrew" wisdom being "plainly stamped on the works of the Puritans" (28–29). And if the Puritans placed great faith in education as the only sure way of salvation, so also "on the East Side of New York, 'Teacher' is a being adored" (47). Thus the much vaunted "New England invention of compulsory education is more eagerly appropriated by the majority of our immigrants than by native[-born] Americans of the corresponding level" (50).

Once again, none of this seems very likely to convert the Anglo-Saxon Protestant establishment to Antin's gospel, which shares with Garrison's rhetoric not only the use of American ideals as a club with which to beat the unconverted into the church but the same quality of self-destructive perversity, being counterproductive in its effect. Yet we may doubt if Antin's claim was her intention, for the logic of her argument is one of competitive replacement, not equivalency, and by emphasizing the vitality and intelligence of these new immigrants Antin is validating the opinion of such as Fred Lewis Pattee, that the spirit of old New England is dead and gone, leaving a vacancy to be filled by the very people Antin is celebrating.

Aside from such matters of interpretation, the point to be taken from Mary Antin's gospel is her proposition that the Pilgrims, removed from the familiar tableaux of "signing compacts or . . . effecting a historic landing," can be conceived simply as immigrants, as "strangers come to establish themselves in a strange land," and as such are no different from "other immigrants" who would follow them to America. In effect, she is ripping the Pilgrims out of the frames of reference carefully crafted and gilded during the course of the nineteenth century. Instead of standing in a tight little group on Plymouth Rock, they are shoved into line with all the other homeless and tempest-tossed arrivals, indistinguishable from the wretched refuse, those huddled masses waiting at the gate. This, then, was Mary Antin's gift to the tercentenary occasion, her declaration that "the ghost of the Mayflower pilots every immigrant ship, and Ellis Island is another name for Plymouth Rock" (98). It is a reading of American history that provided the gloss with which Dos Passos gave meaning to the drama unfolding near Plymouth during the tercentenary celebration and for six years thereafter.

A similar displacement is effected by the terms Antin used in depicting her "new pioneers," who are shown "awaiting God's miracle of human happiness in the grisly darkness of the mine, in the fierce glare of the prairie ranch, in the shrivelling heat of coke-ovens, beside roaring cotton-gins, beside blinding silk-looms, in stifling tailor shops, in nerve-racking engine-rooms,—in all the places where the assurance and pride of the State come to rest upon the courage and patience of the individual citizen" (56–57). Gone is the traditional "winnowing" process, the exodus of adversity, the dreadful starving winter on an inhospitable shore. Gone also is Longfellow's pastoral, rural imagery of springtime promise. A new postindustrial iconography is now in place, and Antin's text is accompanied by Joseph Stella's illustrations, celebrations of the strong, open countenances of immigrants. This is "The Sinew and Bone of All the Nations," as one caption reads, who in the terms of another bring "A Fresh Infusion of Pioneer Blood" to America, thereby evoking that frontier spirit traditionally associated with the Pilgrim heritage, but absent the Anglo-Saxon tie and the agrarian setting.

Moreover, Stella's idealized immigrants not a little resemble those subsequent items of propaganda, the photographs of Sacco and Vanzetti, and the paintings they inspired from Ben Shahn. This natural nobility is echoed in the inspiring sentiments of immigrants whom Antin interviewed, whose voices are described as joining in "an anthem in praise of American ideals, a passionate glorification of the principles of democracy," which anticipates Dos Passos's use of that quotation from Bartolomeo Vanzetti: "Volumes might be filled with the broken sayings of the humblest among the immigrants which, translated into the sounding terms of the universal, would give us the precious documents of American history over again. . . . What nobler insistence on the rights of manhood do we find in the writings of the Puritans?" (74).

What are these but the "new words" Dos Passos sought with which he could displace the "old words" grown slippery and foul in the mouths of the corrupt understrappers of a rotten establishment? It is a parallelism that couples Antin's notion of a new gospel with those noble ideals given expression in Vanzetti's acceptance of his martyrdom. Moreover, the purport of her argument and example discounts the necessity promoted by the descendants of the *Mayflower* passengers that these newcomers needed to be subjected to a conversion process in order to become true Americans. As for Lowell's much celebrated call in his poem "The Crisis," Antin's gospel declares that the spirit of the *Mayflower* now takes the shape of immigrant ships arriving daily, sailing past the Statue of Liberty and debarking their passengers on Ellis Island, sufficient pilgrims for the new occasion, who teach Americans new duties by their example.

Once again, by generalizing the notion of the Pilgrims, Antin robbed them of their singularity as newcomers, much as the Reverend Coit in 1835 had stripped the Forefathers of their exceptionalness, much as Senator Breckinridge in 1889 had stolen their sacred fire by tracing it back to the flickering flames of Teutonic tribal councils. In so doing, Antin realized the worst fears of New England's exclusivists, that demographics would devour their most sacred icon, by her rhetoric transferring the Pilgrims from that templed cabin in their sacred ark to the steerage of the latest immigrant ship.

It is a conceit, moreover, that like Hawthorne's complex miscegenetic metaphor in 1862 acted to desacramentalize the Pilgrims and Plymouth Rock, by claiming kinship not between African and Anglo-Americans but between modern immigrants and the Pilgrims. It was a process of transmogrification given terrific genesis by the martyrdom of Sacco and Vanzetti, transformed into enduring literature and art through the agency of Dos Passos and Ben

Shahn, among others, but it originated with Mary Antin's little book, which in protesting its Americanism proved to be the most subversive engine of all.

II

Finley Peter Dunne rose to fame by way of the ruminations of his spokesman, Mr. Dooley, an immigrant saloon keeper in Chicago who served much the same function anent the McKinley and Roosevelt administrations as Seba Smith's Major Jack Downing served during the Jacksonian years. Mr. Dooley was given to sly observations about "Hinnery Cabin Lodge," as he called him, usually in contexts that made a mockery of the senator's opportunistic imperialism, in which "hands across the ocean" generally ended up in someone else's pocket. And Dooley's remarks concerning the threat of foreign immigration were also undoubtedly inspired by Lodge's xenophobic fulminations.

When Shaugnessy, the barkeeper's friend and frequent butt, expressed a desire to bar from American shores "th' off-scourin's iv Europe" because they are "arnychists" who won't "assymilate with th' country," Mr. Dooley dismissed his fears as irrelevant: "If immygrants is as dangerous to this counthrey as ye an' I an' other pilgrim fathers believe they are, they'se enough iv thim sneaked in already to make us aborigines about as infloointial as the prohibition vote in the Twinty-ninth Ward. They'll dash again' our stern and rockbound coast till they bust it" (Dunne, 53).

This is a trenchant and unintentionally prophetic observation, because now, nearly a century after Mr. Dooley made it, the journalist-geologist John McPhee writes of the efforts in Plymouth to save the Rock from deterioration, the act in 1921 of placing it at the ocean's edge in effect doing more harm to its surface than had the former depredations by tourists. Moreover, even as the objective correlative of Felicia Hemans's imaginary stern and rockbound coast threatens to disintegrate without the constant application of the stonemason's craft, the Statue of Liberty and Ellis Island have become the regnant symbols of entry, prioritized by several generations of immigrants who passed by the first and through the second as they heeded the call of the New World. In a sense not meant but surely hoped by Mary Antin, the Immigrant is now the Pilgrim.

The ceremonies celebrating the centennial of the Statue and the subsequent conversion of Ellis Island to a historical landmark and a museum provided the occasion for any number of self-conscious analogies between the Island and the Rock, but the emphasis was always on the Island, not the Rock. Moreover, now that Ellis Island no longer serves its threshold function as a liminal zone of transformation, so it becomes increasingly sacramentalized both by the testimony of persons who actually passed through it and by the activities of their descendants, busily converting those exiles into ancestors and thus repeating the rituals of so many Forefathers' Days of a century hence. Memory's Nation is no longer a private club for white, Anglo-Saxon protestants, yet the process of exclusion goes on, and as they wander through the exhibits at Ellis Island, the descendants of Pilgrims do not have to be told that this is a society to which they need not apply.

Our business, however, has been with Plymouth Rock, a transaction we now bring to a close, with the Tercentenary and its events serving as a convenient and symbolic terminus. It is a pivot of sorts signaling the swing of demographic forces celebrated in Mary Antin's gospel of immigration toward the reversal of proportion and emphasis we can now observe as nearly complete. As the elderly Lodge was given to declare, echoing the wisdom of Solomon and James Russell Lowell, one generation is succeeded by another, a younger and always different group dedicated to propositions determined by its own interests and ideals. It is a genesis resembling the system of checks and balances we call dialectic, which is inevitably associated with progress by some and degeneration by others, but which most certainly has been very hard over the years on Plymouth Rock.

The 375th anniversary of the Landing recently passed by, virtually unnoticed outside the purlieus of Plymouth. Some account of the ceremonies follows in the concluding coda to this book, but the point to be derived from the Rock's present state of national neglect is its symbolic persistence. Where, during the nineteenth century, the actual size of the Pilgrim threshold was diminished by souvenir hunters, a reduction that reflected exponentially the increase in devout interest, now the Rock serves chiefly as a disillusioning focus of encounter, its reduction enhancing the stark contrast between the myth that visitors bring to the shrine and the reality with which they depart.

From its initial appearance as a public icon, Plymouth Rock has been associated with New England, first as a political and then as a moral force in the emerging Republic, and like the Rock, New England is now a diminished and fractured entity. No longer the bastion of white, Anglo-Saxon, and Protestant purity, its rural landscape is chiefly characterized by farmlands dotted with vacation condominiums and townships centered by empty factories, whose best hope is conversion to a shopping mall, outlets for products manufactured far from New England's long-deserted mills. The political dynasty of the Adams family has been succeeded by the Kennedys, a complete process attended by the kind of confusion contained in the epigraph to this chapter.

The Yankee, once a universal figure in the American mythology, retains his profile in the sharp features and goatee, the stirrup trousers, Congress gaiters, and nappy top hat of Uncle Sam, that familiar figure in political cartoons. But to most newspaper readers the regional connection is lost, along with the basis for those other icons that survive from the nineteenth-century tradition of symbolic caricature, the Republican elephant and Democratic donkey. And as for the association of Massachusetts with the ideal of national union, celebrated by the oratory of Daniel Webster and the monument created by Hammatt Billings, that too is long forgotten, along with the oratory and monuments it inspired.

Indeed, the South has fulfilled its long-kept promise and has risen again, a periphery of political expansion associated with the place from which General Sherman set out for the sea. The notion of returning power to the states, over which so much internecine blood was shed, lumbers unimpeded through the corridors of Congress, nor can African Americans look as before to the Republican Party for support and sustenance. Radicalism in America, which William Lloyd Garrison and Wendell Phillips were ardent to associate with the Pilgrims, is now traced to Thoreau's secessionist shack on Walden Pond, where he assembled that infernal engine of anarchy that came to be known as "civil disobedience." And Thoreau, as we have seen, was no celebrant of the Pilgrims.

So where does that leave Plymouth Rock?

Well, the easiest response is also the quickest, being the kind of tautology for which the Yankee is famous: it remains where in the local memory it has always been, long before it was known as Plymouth Rock. As for its present place in the national memory, let me here turn to a brief consideration of another memorial stone, within view of the tourists on the Plymouth shore but beyond their reach—or what, to paraphrase Browning, is private property for? On Clark's Island there is a monument that is perhaps the least known and most seldom visited by Americans save for the tablet on Iwo Jima's Mount Suribachi, yet one that has an unmatched power to impress and in its very isolation possesses the sanctity of mystery that accessible memorials lack.

It has been forty years since I was privileged to stand before the bas-relief on Iwo, as below stretched that brief and fatal zone, the keeping and taking of which was a bloody pivot in the war but which was nothing but a heap of volcanic ash, a wasteland dotted with the shattered pillboxes of defeat, in which could still be found human bones. Only the Vietnam Memorial in Washington has such a power to convey the essential futility of warfare, carried in the constant winds that blow over the imperfect cone of a still active but slumbering volcano.

It has not, however, been my privilege to visit Clark's Island, so we must here depend on the impressions of another, who has rendered an account of the monument there, the idea for which originated in a suggestion made by Robert C. Winthrop in his oration of 1870: having recounted the story as told in *Mourt's Relation* of the Pilgrim's first month in the New World, Winthrop came to the account of how the exploring party under Captain Miles Standish spent December 20 (New Style) on Clark's Island before landing the following day on the Massachusetts shore. He quoted the statement "On the Sabboth day wee rested," which struck him as revealing a "fine and characteristic picture," a tableau matching the familiar grouping of the *Mayflower* passengers coming ashore at Plymouth (*Proceedings*, 71).

Having enlarged on the implications of that pious interlude, Winthrop declared that "no monument on the face of the earth, ancient or modern . . . would appeal more forcibly to the hearts of all who reverence an implicit and heroic obedience to the commandments of God, than would an unadorned stone on yonder Clark's Island, with the simple inscription '20 Dec. 1620—On the Sabbath day we rested.' There is none to which I would myself more eagerly contribute" (72). Hammatt Billings was among the invited guests that day, and we can only imagine his reaction to Winthrop's proposition, which would mean siphoning money away from his unfinished colossus for the sake of another (and pointedly much simpler) monument, but as it turned out, Winthrop's proposed "stone" required no extensive fund-raising effort.

The story is told by Judge Arthur Putnam, in his lecture on Miles Standish, of how Winthrop and some others were carried to Clark's Island in a revenue cutter for the purpose of selecting a site for the proposed marker, but then, "as they stood on the isle and noted near its centre a massive ledge reaching down, down into the earth, they said, 'Here is the monument already erected. Let us inscribe it.' And in deep-set letters they chiseled thereon the simple words" (quoted by Winthrop, 25). This is surely the least expensive of American monuments of comparable size, save perhaps for the equivalent ledge known as "Redemption Rock," which marks the place near Princeton, Massachusetts, where Mary Rowlandson was redeemed from captivity and which, thanks to the generosity of George Frisbie Hoar—a descendant of the man who redeemed her—bears a like legend carved into its face.

But unlike Redemption Rock, the one on Clark's Island cannot be visited by the general public, and even the privileged Judge Putnam experienced "considerable trouble in reaching the island" when he sought out "the great ledge, almost perpendicular for some fifteen feet, the surface . . . about as smooth as rough board, clothed more or less with moss and shaded somewhat by wild wood . . . the scene as natural as nature itself" (25). In a spot kept remote from the intrusive gaze of the populace, Memory's Nation coincides with Nature's Nation, just offshore from the point where the dual process began.

It is, moreover, a site marked by the kind of a monolith so much oratory celebrating the Landing called up, sublime in size, integral to the native granite, and given great power by the simplicity of its setting, the whole rounded with a grace taken from the pious inscription. How different from Plymouth Rock, the sanctity of which is negated by the pompous granite canopy surrounding it, which is in turn surrounded by the tawdry commerce in souvenirs and like tourist businesses that characterize the waterfront street.

Judge Putnam, however, did not indulge in invidious comparisons but merely observed, as he subsequently "paused to stand on Plymouth Rock," that persons not familiar with that boulder but with Hemans's poem are inclined to imagine "that the Rock is some manner of ledge extending down into the sea as part and parcel of the 'stern and rock-bound coast.' Whoever is not disabused of this notion before making his pilgrimage is doomed to a bewildering surprise or disappointment" (26). The judge here defined the problem of Plymouth Rock, aesthetically considered, though he was hardly the first to do so. He then turned from his vantage point, looking up from under Billings's canopy to Billings's "monument to the Forefathers looking down . . . from yonder height," that granitic colossus intended to compensate for the inadequacy to the occasion of Forefathers' Rock (28).

Under the "arm of Faith uplifted to the heavens, your footrest the same whereon stepped, perchance one after another, the disembarking adventurers when the breaking waves dashed on the solitary shore," Putnam placed himself in a kind of signifying sandwich, bearing witness to the power of art to elicit the feelings once ascribed to the Rock alone. But the awkwardness of his language, abstracted from the very poem that the reality of place devalued, suggests that a kind of contortion was necessary, rather much like those cramping postures required to make an ill-tailored suit fit its ill-fated buyer.

Billings's canopy is now landfill, and his ambitious monument is no longer visible from the site of Plymouth Rock, but even if that colossus still towered over Plymouth Rock, it is doubtful if a witness like Judge Arthur Putnam could be found, who would arrange himself in such a way as to serve as a conduit of emotion. Once again, the iconic clutter of the Forefathers monument has lost its meaning, and its ambitious height even before it was completed was shadowed by the far greater and still impressive Statue in New York Harbor.

And as for Plymouth Rock, Putnam's judgment still holds true, for its effect on most who first view it is diminished by the expectations brought to the site, a perpetual problem whose remedy so much rhetoric and artwork was intended to effect but which only increased the disparity. Perhaps the Pilgrims' best monument remains the institutions they first established in America, as so many orators insisted, much as it was what the Pilgrims were credited with accomplishing that gave meaning to the boulder on which they were supposed to have landed.

But my preference is for that great ledge rising from bedrock on Clark's Island, with its simple piety, in terms of both the statement inscribed and the sentiments that inspired it, kept forever remote from the tourist presence, inviolate and forgotten, epitomizing the benign neglect that the greatest orator of his day associated with the growth of a nascent republic, best identified with the region still called New England.

That you can't get there from here, as the Yankee farmer put it, is the crochet that expresses the moment past recovery that is essential, finally, to the meaning of the Pilgrims' arrival in America. Perhaps, therefore, it would be best to let the equivalent processes of nature take their course, allowing the threshold famously celebrated in Plymouth to be reduced by time and tides to a framed bit of pebbly beach and the slow wash of waves, a zone that visitors may stare at uncomprehendingly (though no more so than they do now), but which will possess more meaning than was ever carried by that sacred stone.

For if Plymouth Rock in its busiest century did indeed symbolize Liberty, both religious and political, then it stood for a force that cannot be contained by walls of granite or bars of steel, and when asked what had happened to the Rock, the watcher by the gates of memory could truthfully reply, "It escaped."

Sanct Graal

A Forwarding Address

Remember the Maine, Plymouth Rock, and the Golden Rule!
—The Music Man

I

The weekend falls between Valentine's Day and what, for that year, 1986, will serve as Washington's Birthday, and though the visiting scholar had anticipated that Plymouth at midwinter would be abandoned by tourists, the abandonment he encountered was defined by the "Valentine's Day Package" offered by the local Sheraton Hotel. There were, that evening, no vacancies available, and through the lobby there strolled young couples in various stages of *bas couture* (in which vinyl figured largely) maintaining the sort of friendly yet restrained conversation that is different from the austere yet understanding silences observed by wedded persons whose marriage has been of some duration.

The impression received by the weary traveler was uncomfortably complex, confronted as he was by a hotel that had no room for him, having instead converted itself for the long weekend sandwiched between saint's days of considerable contrast into a trysting place catering to young lusts. This was a hotel, moreover, that had been erected at the cost of some historic, if not Pilgrim-era, buildings to accommodate the national urge to pay homage to the Forefathers, the subject of the middle-aged scholar's own inquiry. He was reminded of the antipathy of the Pilgrims to the goings-on at Thomas Morton's nearby Merrymount.

The Governor Bradford Inn was likewise filled, but space was still available in the Governor Carver, with its boasted facilities for the comfort of "Hungry Pilgrims," "Thirsty Pilgrims," and the like, but here, too, the pilgrims most in evidence seemed votaries of Venus and moved about with hands clasping some mutual secret between them. Where the scholar was interested in the Landing of 1620, and its celebration down through the years, these young people appeared to be in a holding pattern awaiting departure for that modern equivalent to Cithera, a Loveboat, about to take place collectively in the rooms above.

At breakfast the next morning, the scholar was relieved to find the dining room peopled with overweight persons of his own generation taking full advantage of the Sunday brunch, the younger clientele still absent upstairs, presumably taking some advantage of their own. Outside, the ground was covered with aging, dirty snow, and the sun shown brightly over the bay, so that Clark's Island and the Gurnett were clearly outlined, and the shaft commemorating Miles Standish in Duxbury elevated its diminutive captain in the fashion of a guardian angel against the blue morning sky.

The tourist shops were boarded up along Water Street, the *Mayflower* was likewise battened down for the winter, and as the day wore on, young beneficiaries of the Valentine package made their appearance, strolling about aimlessly from tourist point to tourist point, evincing polite curiosity but chiefly, it would seem, using up the less interesting part of their package in lieu of pursuing what appeared to be a decided lack of animated conversation.

Plymouth is not a pleasant place to visit at midwinter, those boarded-up storefronts witness to the seasonal decline, yet, as the scholar strolled about, it occurred to him that this was indeed the best of times to visit that particular shrine. The crowds of tourists, the shops bursting through their windows with garish merchandise, the hustle, the bustle, all were gone, and the snow-covered height of Cole's Hill with its massive sarcophagus was an immaculate casket for Pilgrim bones. The advent of the Forefathers was moreover a wintry one, begun on the very first day of the season of adversity, and was followed by a time of terrible hardship, compounded of disease, near starvation, uncertainty, death.

The scholar noticed that here and there a solitary young person could be standing, as he stood, looking out at the palely gleaming winter sea from the vantage point of the hill, their postures suggesting contemplation, presumably along lines similar to his own. Whatever desires had brought them there, they were now absorbed as he was in attempting to recapture the long lost yet forever memorialized moment when the former parishioners from Scrooby stepped ashore to become Americans, not the first, assuredly, but perhaps the most famously so.

The Rock, the putative threshold of arrival, lay squat in its imposing shrine, that immaculate arrangement of columnar certitude, so different from the haphazard arrangement of circumstances that brought the Pilgrims here. The tide was out and left behind a detritus of frozen, salty slush and crumpled tourist brochures that some angry because presumably disillusioned visitor had hurled down at the disappointing cynosure. On and around it gleamed dozens of coins of small denominations pitched at the Rock, not as a votary gesture but in a contest to see if a pitched penny, nickel, or dime would remain on its slightly sloping surface.

It was not a sight to arouse piety, yet the young couples who strolled about the vacant parkway stopped each in turn to lean against the cold rail and behold the Rock. As the scholar walked away, a young man was taking its picture, an obligatory gesture but one that, given the circumstances, seemed to betray a certain degree of genuine respect. These young people had to come to worship at the shrine of a pagan goddess who had been borne landward on a scallop shell, yet they lingered in the cold Sunday morning air to ponder the secret of a much different kind of desire, also symbolized by the scallop because of a quite different association, borne landward in 1620 to a sandy beach whose distinguishing feature was this solitary glacial boulder.

Something of the original geography yet remains, the Town Brook and the Jones River that would bracket and certify the tiny settlement, indeed were instrumental in the Pilgrims' decision to set up their community here, but nothing else is the same. Only the seaward view remains a constant, bleak and austere, while the inland scene, once that sere and hard-visaged wilderness that greeted the Pilgrims, is now crowded with buildings and monuments, including a cold bronze Massasoit, clothed only in feather and loincloth, his eyes fixed on Miles Standish across the bay, less a memorial to the departed Indians, however, than a tribute to their instrumentality in assisting the settlers in their grimly determined struggle to survive.

What truth there is in the landward view has to do with the spirit that replaced the Pilgrim piety, even in their first decade in America, the terrific, at times terrible energy released by the commercial necessity. If you wish to recapture something of the original afflatus, you must turn away from what they faced and look backward, as it were, in the direction from which they came. But then, that is the traditional way of viewing the Pilgrims, standing slightly before them on the shore as they clamber up from the shallop onto America.

Of all the features on the beach in 1620, only the Rock endures, at once a disillusionment and something of a mystery, a humble and diminished thing, yet stubborn and solidly final. Abused, scorned, reviled, scarred by the glacier that carried it there and bearing the faint traces of graffiti imperfectly removed, even on the cold winter's day the Rock maintained its dignity, as do dumb creatures in the lowliest zoo, stoic and aloof from the stares of the curious, which seek to penetrate the small secrets given to each species. Stones, save those with fossils, contain no hint of life, no meaning except what we subjectively endow them with, and the Rock at Plymouth is no more or less than what the beholder wants it to be, contains nothing except a date inscribed on its surface and all that its celebrants have associated with the moment.

Yet on that wintry afternoon the persistence of the Rock suggested that perhaps, after all, there was something here still worth the visit, whatever the disappointment, that the young couples now uncoupled for the moment could not escape the paradox of the unstated terms of the Valentine package, which confronted them with the cold witness of a desire fixed higher than the hotel or even the hill behind them, fixed rather on the perfect blue dome of New England's winter sky, the same today as then, as ever, forever.

II

Ten years later on a day late in July the scholar returned to Plymouth, his labors now almost completed, research that endowed the site with the kind of meaning that awareness promoted by prolonged exposure to a subject brings. The occasion was the celebration of the 375th anniversary of the Landing, promoted by the usual committees and historical societies, different only in degree from those earlier occasions that had been the chief subject of his study. Intimate with matters of degree was the weather, always a permissible topic in New England, where there is great variety, if little to praise. It was hot with thunderstorms threatening, in all ways a contrast to that cold day in February 1986, and the town was crowded with tourists dressed less for the occasion than the season.

The scholar had been unable to attend the embarkation from Delft-Haven that had been reenacted as the starting event, but which, because of a mistake in the local newspaper, was witnessed by no more persons than those who attended the original departure from Holland of the Pilgrims. The replicated *Mayflower*, a much more authentic vessel than that of 1920, having sailed back to Provincetown to enable it to make its centennial appearance, came in on the morning of the 22d with the assistance of a tugboat, thereby reenacting not the event of 1620 but that of 1920. Further disappointment was occasioned by the failure of certain advertised Hollywood luminaries to make the trip, who now grace such celebrations where once political figures of national prominence came.

Later that day the Landing was effected by means of the *Mayflower*'s longboat, after considerable debate among officials over whether it or the replicated shallop should be used, the final decision based on the greater depth of water drawn by the shallop, which would make the main event awkward, if not impossible, to execute. As a loudspeaker blared solemnities suitable to the occasion, a replicated Mary Chilton was helped into the water and onto the shore, her authentic costume apparently considered warrant enough to validate the occasion. This followed closely upon the parade, or rather procession, a spare but therefore effective march of militia companies. These were not civilians dressed in the depressing uniformity of camouflage clothing that conceals but hardly hides the smoldering groundfire of militant paranoia. They were costumed in the historical regalia traditionally worn by organizations whose roles were now entirely ceremonial, indeed had been so for more than a century.

Marching in step to fife and drum, brief wave after wave of militiamen passed through Plymouth. They were followed by men dressed in Civil War garb, even to the obligatory Confederate gray, who were followed in turn by African Americans in Union blue, living equivalents to the stone ranks carved by Saint-Gaudens on the tablet in Boston Commons. Then came a crowd of persons dressed as Pilgrims, mingled with people in modern dress. Last but thereby occupying the place of honor was a float bearing on it an effigy of the Landing upon the Rock, a *tableau vivant* that observed the convention insisted upon by the committee in 1850, that the event in question was the one in which a handful of men, not the entire passenger list of the *Mayflower*, took part.

Thus the two landings, the one by sea and the other by float, achieved a compromise but hardly provided an answer to the eternal question as to actual priority, nor was this the only dysfunctional aspect of the celebration obvious to the visiting scholar. Immediately following the Landing, a number of recent immigrants to the United States were sworn in as citizens by Justice Souter of the Supreme Court of the United States, their number (104) intended to correspond to the passenger list of the *Mayflower*, a mistake not of computation but generosity, a few last-minute future citizens having been allowed on the platform.

The naturalization ceremony had considerable meaning to the scholar witness, quite aside from the moving spectacle of these persons bearing testimony to the importance to them of this liminal crossing of a threshold to citizenship. Here again were exiles being made over into the material of ancestors, but what had seemed a problem to a number of prominent Americans in 1920 now seemed to the promoters of such events in Plymouth as part of the solution: "It is most appropriate for us now," as the program read, "to recognize the continuing contribution of ALL immigrants to the American way of life," including "those first Mayflower immigrants of 1620."

Where once a very sharp and occasionally edged distinction was made between the descendants of the *Mayflower* passengers and their modern equivalents, so as to emphasize the priority and with it the superior virtue of the former, now the celebrants of the Pilgrims were eager to associate their ancestors with these modern exiles, by way, one must conclude, of rectifying the increased marginality that demographics had brought about for persons with Anglo-Saxon antecedents. That old Yankee virtue of pragmatism still had hold of the New England psyche, and the display of patriotic fervor occasioned a decade ago by the anniversary of the completion of the Statue of Liberty apparently impressed upon the people who claim descent from *Mayflower* passengers a few salient truths. Not only had the system worked, making over immigrants into loyal and productive citizens like themselves, but if they themselves wanted to be considered as something other than a living equivalent to a historic display of waxworks, they had better climb aboard the immigrants' ship.

Moreover, and of equivalent interest to our visiting scholar, the large crowd in attendance at these events, who crowded by the hundreds to the railings to watch the longboat come ashore and lined the streets to cheer the ranks of costumed militiamen, suggested like those random couples he encountered ten years ago that there yet remains in the American heart an enduring affection for the event of 1620. The day was hot, the weather threatening, yet the people came and stood and waited and applauded each wave of marching men. The crowds then waited at the rail, dozens deep, to cheer the replicated Pilgrims ashore.

Why this particular date was chosen, with no connection to the historical calendar of Departure and Arrival, may lie more in the strategies of tourist bureaus and chambers of commerce than in the desire to honor a specific moment and place in Memory's Nation, but then the person who wishes to cut a line between the phenomenon of tourism and the popularization of historic sites will need an instrument sharper than any yet known to medical science. If the scholar's researches had taught him anything, it was that such confusion was ever thus.

Of a similar order and category were the extensive plans afoot to rearrange the waterfront of Plymouth, not as in 1920 by acquiring land, tearing down existing buildings, and erecting monuments and like structures, but a kind of interior redecorating, a moving about of furniture for a new effect, the sort of thing with which most families are familiar. The various statues and memorial stones are to be shifted into a more useful pattern, and most significantly, the beaux arts canopy over the Rock is to be relocated to the top of Cole's Hill, where it will be placed over the sarcophagus containing the Pilgrim bones authenticated by Oliver Wendell Holmes.

This was, our scholar recalled, the fate once suggested for the previous canopy, validating the cyclical, not the germ, theory of historical advance. Once again the harbor fronting the area where the Landing took place will be reworked in the name of authenticity, restoring the beach to its former condition and setting the Rock where it presumably rested awaiting that epochal arrival. The shallop will remain anchored just offshore as a testimonial witness to the nature of the event that took place here, and informational tablets will be erected at the viewing site, informing the visitor as to the significance of the event, providing in small what orators of the past supplied in large amounts.

Central to the new plan for Plymouth will be a stairway leading up from the waterfront and the site of the Landing to the sarcophagus with its relocated canopy. It is a rearrangement that is both an expression of filiopiety and a witness to the condign hope of the merchants of Plymouth that tourists, once having climbed to the top of Cole's Hill, will be tempted to follow the footsteps of the Pilgrims even farther into town, visiting the shops and restaurants and increasing the revenues therein. As the visiting scholar knew, this was a time-honored tradition not only in Plymouth but in hundreds of communities in New England and elsewhere that have increasingly viewed tourism as a productive industry, replacing factories like the old and long defunct Cordage Works, which now serves as that sign of the times, a mall. But in confronting the realities that often follow such plans, the scholar could not help wondering if the forty millions of dollars the project is to cost were put out at interest, with the profits divided equally among the merchants of Plymouth, it would not effect the same and perhaps a more lucrative end.

But this was only a fugitive and skeptical thought. Certainly relieving the Rock of its overbearing canopy was an inspired idea, and though relocating it as the centerpiece of a restored shoreline would do nothing to rectify the problem of proportion, it could do no harm, at least not to the Rock's reputation. Two centuries of disillusionment had become something of a tradition in any event, the kind of thing that is endemic to the American experience, where great expectations are often followed by small returns. The Rock is never as big as the uninformed visitor expects, nor will it ever be, absent some considerable diminution in the size of the American citizen.

What is important about the Rock has nothing finally to do with its dimensions, the visiting scholar had long since concluded, but is entirely a matter of the way in which it has served generations of its celebrants as a noumenous signifier of arrival. Much as the Pilgrims are thought of as being changed by their passage over the Rock, so the Rock itself has undergone transformations as a symbol of translation, of passage, always in conjunction with reevaluations of the Pilgrims standing upon it. This revisionary process not coincidentally began with the American Revolution and is essential to the function of memory in times of conflict or radical change, which ratifies revision even as it is affected by the process of revising.

Whether or not the Pilgrims actually came ashore on the Rock struck the scholar as having no more importance than the question regarding the identity of the persons first ashore. Defenders of the Rock's authenticity do not cease their efforts to prevail and were bolstered these fifty years since by the authority of Admiral Morison. In violation of all known rules of seamanship, Morison opined that the Rock had indeed been of service to the Pilgrims, who effected the "beachhead at Plymouth" by lashing a seventeenth-century equivalent of a rhino barge to it.

The admiral's was a notion derived from the ingenuity of engineers during the Second World War he had chronicled, but it violates all known rules of invention, which is almost never associated with the initial stages of settlement. Thus the Pilgrims were quite content to accept the name of the place given to it by John Smith, which provided a nostalgic tie to the country of their origin, and set about erecting houses made from wattles and mud modeled after rural sheds in England, instead of erecting those log cabins with which for so long they were associated, structures with as little validity as the admiral's barge.

The scholar would not have the people of Plymouth give up their Rock, if only to honor Thoreau's observation that the Rock was all that Plymouth had, this at a time when the town was in decline and tourism a fledgling industry in New England. Plymouth has its Rock and has certainly made much of and from it, and even if you were able to remove the Rock from the history books, you will never dislodge it from its bed in the popular memory. Desecration, from those early tourists who availed themselves of a blacksmith's sledgehammer to break off specimen souvenirs, to modern graffiti, which from a swastika to a dismissive "Fake" to a uniform coat of blue paint continue to involve the Rock in controversy, suggests that it remains a very live symbol, which is after all what one wants of it.

Recently John McPhee has demonstrated that the Rock as a relic of great tectonic plate movements was not only a Pilgrim carried southward by the glacier but was a fragment of a great land mass that was once part of Africa. As such, it was doubly the captive of huge, necessitarian forces, carried to the New World well in advance of the first slave ship whose voyage to America in 1620 helped define the difference between New England and Virginia for antebellum orators on Forefathers' Day. McPhee's was hardly Hawthorne's intention when he mischievously repeated the story that the *Mayflower* had subsequently served as a slave ship, but it most certainly works against the notion associated with the Rock of Anglo-Saxon exceptionalism.

For this knowledge opens the Rock to an entirely new range of iconic meanings connoting and enforcing the idea of Exile, not, however, associated with Liberty but certainly intimate with the idea that there are energies operating well beyond our ability to control. Innovation is forever a giver of energy and an enlivener thereby, unlike the delimiting spirit associated with historical inquiry and definition. We may cite, for example, the pieties observed by the directors and staff of Plimoth Plantation, the living museum. In their attempts to rescue the settlers of Plymouth from the Pilgrim myth, they maintain the illusion that 1627, extended indefinitely and revised periodically to suit political as well as historical correctness, is the Pilgrim Year, that being the date when an early tourist made extensive notations as to the way of life of Plymouth's settlers. Such specificity, mused our visiting scholar, often works against the intended effect. How much more elastic is the Rock that, until the recent anniversary event, to which they donated costumes and actors, the experts at Plimoth Plantation pretty much agreed to ignore.

Smooth and featureless save for its inscribed date, the Rock is not only our oldest monument but the most flexible, and having first emerged to serve the needs of New England patriots at a time when few memorials of the colonial past could be found, it survives into a time when historical mementos—not excluding theme parks—abound, yet it transcends them all in its lack of specificity. In its humble plainness, the Rock lacks the particularized furniture of other monuments, which as in the instance of the colossus standing on a height in Plymouth can by their complex iconography become often meaningless to witnesses from a later generation, who do not possess the necessary information enabling them to decipher the meaning of what they behold.

In its way, the Rock associated with the Pilgrims resembles those people themselves, humble and earth-bound yet with terrific powers of endurance, being made of the granite that is the region stone and is often associated with the character of the people of New England. Once again, it was moved there by the geological equivalent to the ideological force that drove the Pilgrims to leave England for Holland and Holland for America, a commitment that enabled them not only to survive but endure, and not only endure but, to borrow from William Faulkner's praise of rural people in the South, to prevail.

III

In making these observations, the visiting scholar thought once again of Bartholdi's great statue, as modified upon its dedication by Emma Lazarus's open-armed poem, and remembered how yet a third modification was made to Lady Liberty's iconography during its recent centennial, this time quite by accident. Thus it was observed that a verdigris tear had appeared just below one of the Statue's eyes, a phenomenon thought rather much a miracle but which proved to be the irreverent result of urine discharged by workers from the scaffold erected to correct the ravages of time.

But until the truth was determined, symbolic sensibilities pondered the signification of this tear, remembering the observation of African Americans that the symbolism of the Statue was a cruel irony for them. Their ancestors had not come to America of their own free will, nor was liberty a goal of the voyage, quite the reverse. Nor was the tragic conclusion of many hopeful voyages to America being made at the time in pathetically inadequate vessels putting out not only from nearby Caribbean islands but from faraway Vietnam irrelevant to the meaning of that tear.

So the Statue at least for the moment proved itself capable of a new and complex meaning, thanks to ribald circumstances that emphasize the comic potential of even the most serious set of symbols. It brought to the scholar's mind an anecdote of an illustrative kind, which involved a friend, a professor of medieval literature in an eastern university, who claimed descent from the Pilgrims and who grew up in Duxbury, across the harbor from Plymouth. As a teen, he and another boy slipped into the canopy sheltering the Rock late one night and with a hammer and cold chisel attempted to obtain a souvenir fragment of the sacred stone. What they got for their pains were some granitic specks in their eyes, of sufficient quantity and size to satisfy their desires.

The scholar once recounted this story to a bartender in a private club in Worcester, Massachusetts, a young man of Italian descent, who laughed and told the scholar that he too had had a youthful adventure involving the Rock. Having consumed overmuch beer in a Plymouth saloon, he had climbed up on the wall of the canopy and discharged his bladder on the boulder below. To give these stories meaningful closure, we need only imagine both events occurring simultaneously, resulting in a truly Chaucerian moment for the scholar's medievalist friend and giving Plymouth Rock a latter-day voice, unsuitable to ceremonial pageants yet pungent with the true Anglo-Saxon sound. But even without this imagined jointure there is meaning in these parallel tales, the mischievous piety of the son of the Pilgrims matched by the impudent gesture of the son of Italian immigrants, the both bearing witness to the breach that the recent ceremonies in Plymouth were intended to heal.

And so it goes. However hard its surface, this granite boulder has served for more than two centuries as a tabula rasa upon which was inscribed a changing and forever revised sequence of meanings, becoming a veritable Moby-Rock of subjective interpretation. From the Melvillean point of view, this range of meanings validates the arbitrariness of all and any signifiers in this round and cypherlike globe. But rather than surrender to the nihilism implicit in the doubloon worldview, the scholar preferred to draw strength and comfort from the story of yet another rock on the Massachusetts shore, northwest of Plymouth and near Rhode Island.

Long before the Rock at Plymouth became the object of so much ceremony, Dighton Rock in Taunton received a century of scrutiny and conjecture and was regarded as a relic of truly ancient times, so old as to predate the national memory. Where Plymouth Rock was associated with the arrival of the Pilgrims, its counterpart bore hieroglyphic evidence of much earlier visitors, Phoenicians some thought, but Vikings or Norsemen surely, voyagers shrouded in the autochthotonous darkness of prehistoric time. Scribbled upon with graffiti overlaid by subsequent graffiti, the mysterious rock bore obvious evidence also of aboriginal inscriptions, petroglyphs equivalent to those found across the American continent.

Dighton Rock drew the interest of colonial antiquarians, of which Cotton Mather was the most prominent, who sent a transcription of its markings to the Royal Society, and a later drawing was made by Bishop Berkeley's protégé, the artist John Smibert, presumably at the behest of his employer. By the early years of the nineteenth century, scholars had given a reading to the petroglyphs that told a tale of the arrival of great winged creatures from which strange-looking men emerged and took captives away who were never seen again, suggesting equivalents to modern stories of extraterrestrial visitors but connected by historians of the day with the habit of English explorers to seize specimen Indians as living souvenirs—and slaves. This process of interpretation would undoubtedly have continued except for the dedicated labors of one man, trained not as an anthropologist but a psychologist, who during the 1920s by means of photographs and other devices determined that lying beneath all the other hieroglyphs so intriguing and mysterious was an arrow pointing up the stream that flows by the rock to a spring that was its source with a simple message in English that fresh water was obtainable there.

The psychologist determined to his satisfaction that all the other writing had been added by passing Indians, who were challenged by this message—undecipherable to them—to add their own, the most of which are the kinds of gibberish associated even now with graffiti by those to whom the codes are not known. The conclusion our scholar was led to by this story is that the arrow and message informing the traveler about the spring of fresh water is the equivalent to the truth underlying so many myths that humankind in its quest for belief has engendered. And so also there remains that date carved into Plymouth Rock, an equivalent arrow and message, conveying the undeniable fact that in 1620 a group of English Separatists along with persons pursuing their own, nonsectarian interests came ashore in this place. In order to establish community amongst themselves, these people had signed a compact, and they likewise drew up a treaty with the region's Indians.

Writing was of the very essence of their experience, the record of which became Governor Bradford's great but unfinished book, which ends in blank entries headed by dates signifying the failure of the Separatist utopia, which was succeeded by errands of a more practical and profitable sort. It is an ending inspiring skepticism toward idealistic human endeavor, but the record kept by Bradford endures as an expression of the heroism high ideals can inspire. It is, moreover, related in the simplest and purest of English, containing passages suitable for inscription on the pediments of monuments but which are much better left in the context of the whole. As Wendell Phillips insisted in 1855, in summoning up a catalog of persons associated with the radical and Separatist spirit symbolized by the journey to America of the Pilgrims, Plymouth Rock has proven invaluable as a writing desk, whatever the function it filled in 1620.

And that, for the visiting scholar, was the message from the Rock in 1995, which he conveyed with mixed results to the members of the Pilgrim Society gathered to celebrate Forefathers' Day and the 375th anniversary of the Landing that year.

BIBLIOGRAPHY

What follows is intended to serve as a combination of a catalog of texts quoted and cited and a reference list to which quotations and citations refer. For convenience, it is divided into primary and secondary texts. In general, title listings in the first category are foreshortened and do not include publishers, unless a listing is a recent and edited version. Items published under the auspice of a society are listed by title, that being the source of the key word that follows quotations parenthetically in the body of this book; the same is true of anonymous publications. The one exception is the annual publications of the New England Society in the City of Brooklyn, because the titles do not vary over the many years to which my own text has frequent reference. When faced with a choice between bibliographical conventions and the need to key this bibliography to references in my text, I have given priority to the second of the two.

The list of primary sources is limited to the texts to which I refer or from which I have drawn quotations, again with one exception. I have included here every Forefathers' Day oration or sermon that I was able to locate, in the hope that the labor I went through will not have to be repeated by others. Not even major collections of American imprints, like the American Antiquarian Society or the Huntington Library, catalog these important documents under the classification by which they are best known. And, aside from Albert Matthews's incomplete listing, there is no inclusive bibliography available, nor do I claim to have located every Forefathers' Day address that was published during the nineteenth century. But it is a start.

Finally, the list of secondary sources includes not only texts alluded to in this book but those that contributed to remedying deficiencies in my own historical background, most notably the complex matter of agitation for and against abolition. It seems the most economical way of registering a very large indebtedness to the scholarly community.

PRIMARY TEXTS

Abbot, Abiel. *A Discourse Delivered at Plymouth December 22, 1809, at the Celebration of the 188th Anniversary of the Landing of Our Forefathers in That Place.* Boston, 1810.

An Account of the Pilgrim Celebration at Plymouth, August 1, 1853, Containing a List of the Decorations in the Town, and Correct Copies of the Speeches Made at the Dinner-Table. Revised by the Pilgrim Society. Boston, 1853.

"An Account of the Tercentenary Celebration of the Landing of the Pilgrims, Plymouth, Massachusetts, July and August, 1921." Compiled by William Woodward, 1925. [A scrapbook.]

Adams, Hannah. *An Abridgment of the History of New England, for the Use of Young Persons.* Boston, 1807.

Adams, Herbert. "Plymouth Rock Restored. I." *Magazine of American History with Notes and Queries* [New York] 8, pt. 2 (1882). "Plymouth Rock Restored. II." 9, pt. 1 (1883).

Adams, John. *Works*. Ed. Charles Francis Adams. 10 vols. Boston, 1850–56.

Adams, John Quincy. *An Oration, Delivered at Plymouth, December 22, 1802. At the Anniversary Commemoration of the First Landing of Our Ancestors, at That Place*. Boston, 1802.

Adams, Samuel. *Writings*. Ed. Harry Alonzo Cushing. 4 vols. New York, 1906.

Albro, John A. *The Fathers of New England. A Discourse Delivered at Cambridge, December 22, 1844*. Boston, 1845.

Alden, Timothy. *Collection of American Epitaphs and Inscriptions, with Occasional Notes*. 5 vols. New York, 1814.

Aldrich, Thomas Bailey. *Writings*. 9 vols. Boston, 1907.

Alger, William Rounseville. *The Genius and Posture of America: An Oration Delivered before the Citizens of Boston, July 4, 1857*. Boston, 1857.

——. *The Historic Purchase of Freedom: An Oration Delivered before the Fraternity, in the Music Hall, Boston, Dec. 22, 1859, the Two Hundred and Thirty-ninth Anniversary of the Landing of the Pilgrims at Plymouth*. Boston, 1859.

Alison, Archibald. *Essays on the Nature and Principles of Taste*. 2d American ed. Hartford, 1821.

Alison, Archibald, Sir. "National Monuments." *Miscellaneous Essays. The Modern British Essayists*. Vol. 2. Philadelphia, 1853.

Allen, Stephen M., ed. *Standish Monument on Captain's Hill, Duxbury . . . Breaking Ground [and] Laying Corner-Stone, Oct. 7, 1872, by the Grand Lodge of Massachusetts*. Boston, 1873.

Allyn, John. *A Sermon, Delivered at Plimoth, December 22, 1801, Commemorative of the Pious Ancestry, Who First Imigrated to That Place, 1620*. Boston, 1802.

American Landmarks: A Collection of Pictures of Our Country's Historic Shrines. With descriptive text by George A. Cleaveland and Robert E. Campbell. Boston, 1893.

American Sketches, by a Native of the United States. London, 1827.

Antin, Mary. *The Promised Land*. Boston, 1912.

——. *They Who Knock at Our Gates: A Complete Gospel of Immigration*. Boston, 1914.

Apess, William. *On Our Own Ground: The Complete Writings of . . . a Pequot*. Ed. Barry O'Connell. Amherst: University of Massachusetts Press, 1992.

Awful Beacon, The. See Coverly, Nathaniel.

Bacon, Leonard. *The Genesis of the New England Churches*. New York, 1874.

——. *A Plea for Africa*. New Haven, 1825.

——. *The Providential Selection and Training of the Pilgrim Pioneers of New England. A Paper Read to the Connecticut Congregational Club, December 21, 1880*. Hartford, 1880.

Baker, George P. *The Pilgrim Spirit*. Boston, 1921.

Baldwin, Joseph G. *The Flush Times of Alabama and Mississippi*. New York: Hill and Wang, 1957.

Baldwin, Samuel. *A Sermon, Preached at Plymouth, December 22, 1775. Being the Anniversary Thanksgiving, in Commemoration of the First Landing of the Fathers of New-England There; Anno Domini, 1620*. America, Massachusetts-Bay; Boston, 1776.

Bancroft, George. *A History of the United States, from the Discovery of the American Continent*. 6 vols. Boston, 1879.

———. *Literary and Historical Miscellanies*. New York, 1855.

Bartlett, W. H. *The Pilgrim Fathers; or, the Founders of New England in the Reign of James the First*. London, 1853.

Baxter, James Phinney. *The Tercentenary of the Landing of the Pilgrims. How Can It Be Made Worthy of the People of New England*. Portland, 1916.

Baylies, Francis. *An Historical Memoir of the Colony of New Plymouth*. 2 vols. Boston, 1830.

Beecher, Lyman. *The Memory of Our Fathers. A Sermon Delivered at Plymouth, on the Twenty-Second of December, 1827*. Boston, 1828.

———. *The Spirit of the Pilgrims*. Vols. 1–6. Boston, 1828–33.

Berkeley, George, Bishop of Cloyne. *Works*. Ed. A. A. Luce and T. E. Jessop. 9 vols. London, 1948–57.

Bisbee, M. D. *Songs of the Pilgrims*. Boston, 1887.

Bittinger, Frederick W. *The Story of the Pilgrim Tercentenary Celebration at Plymouth in the Year 1921*. Plymouth, 1923.

Blagden, George W. *Great Principles Associated with Plymouth Rock. An Address Delivered before the Pilgrim Society of Plymouth, December 22, 1834*. Boston, 1835.

———. *The Influence of the Gospel upon the Intellectual Powers. A Sermon Preached in the Central Church, Philadelphia, May 25, 1835*. Philadelphia, 1835.

———. *Remarks, and a Discourse on Slavery*. Boston, 1854.

———. See also *Pastor's Memorial*.

Bloomingdale, H. *Plymouth Tercentenary Illustrated. With a Brief History of the Life and Struggles of the Pilgrim Fathers*. ["Including original program of the 'Pilgrim Spirit' by Professor George P. Baker, President Harding's visit, all scenes, episodes and official photographs of the Tercentenary Celebration."] New Bedford, Mass., 1921.

[Boynton, Charles Brandon]. *Oration Delivered before the New England Society of Cincinnati, on the Anniversary of the Landing of the Pilgrims*. Cincinnati, 1848.

Bradford, Alden. *A Sermon Delivered at Plymouth, December 21st, 1804; the Anniversary of the Landing of Our Fathers in December 1620*. Boston, 1805.

Bradford, William. *Of Plymouth Plantation*. Ed. Samuel Eliot Morison. New York, 1953.

Breck, Samuel. *Discourse before the Society of the Sons of New England of the City and County of Philadlephia, on the History of the Early Settlement of Their Country; Being Their First Anniversary. Delivered December 21, 1834, by Their President*. Philadelphia, 1835.

Breckinridge, C. P. "Oration." See *Proceedings at the Celebration . . . August 15, 1889.*

Brewer, Daniel Chauncey. *The Conquest of New England by the Immigrant*. New York, 1926.

Brooks, Charles. *See* Cape Cod Association.

Brown, Rev. Hugh Stowell. *The Pilgrim Fathers: A Lecture . . . Delivered October 25 & 27, 1853. Illustrative of the . . . Picture, by Charles Lucy, The Departure of the Pilgrim Fathers (A.D. 1620)*. Manchester, 1854. [Contains a key to the principal figures in the painting.]

[Browne, Charles Farrar]. *Artemus Ward's Best Stories*. Introduction by William Dean Howells. New York, 1912.

Browning, Mrs. [Elizabeth Barrett]. *The Complete Poetical Works of Mrs. Browning*. Boston, 1900.

Buel, Alexander W. *Oration, Delivered before the New England Society of Michigan, at Detroit, December 22d, 1846, On the Landing of the Plymouth Pilgrims; Being upon the Occasion of Its First Anniversary Celebration*. Detroit, 1847.

Bushnell, Horace. *A Discourse on the Slavery Question. Delivered in the North Church, Hartford, Thursday Evening, Jan. 10, 1839*. Hartford, 1839.

Cape Cod and All the Pilgrim Land. A Monthly Magazine Devoted to the Interests of Southeastern Massachusetts. 4.10 (1921).

Cape Cod Association. *Constitution of . . . with An Account of the Celebration of Its First Anniversary at Boston*. November 11, 1851. Boston, 1852.

Carlyle, Thomas. *Works*. Edinburgh ed. 30 vols. New York, 1903–4.

Carpenter, Edmund J. *The Pilgrims and Their Monument*. New York, 1911.

Cass, Lewis. *Address Delivered before the New England Society of Michigan, December 22, 1848*. Detroit, 1849.

Chamberlain, Daniel Henry. *The Character and Work of the Pilgrims of New England: Speech at the Annual Dinner of the New England Society of Charleston, S.C., in Response to the Toast, "Our Country." December 23, 1889*. Charleston, [1890].

Chandler, Joseph R. *"The Pilgrims of the Rock." An Oration, Delivered in the First Congregational Church, before the Society of the Sons of New England of Philadelphia, at Their Second Anniversarry, on the 22d December, 1845*. Philadelphia, 1846.

Channing, William E. *The Works of William E. Channing, D.D.* Boston, 1895.

Channing, William H., ed. *Memoir of William Ellery Channing, with Extracts from His Correspondence and Manuscripts*. 3 vols. Boston, 1848.

Chapin, Stephen. *The Duty of Living for the Good of Posterity. A Sermon, Delivered at North-Yarmouth, December 22, 1820, in Commemoration of the Close of the Second Century from the Landing of the Forefathers of New-England*. Portland, 1821.

Cheever, G. B. *The American Common-Place Book of Prose . . . from the Writings of American Authors*. Boston, 1833.

[Cheney, Harriet Vaughan]. *A Peep at the Pilgrims in Sixteen Hundred Thirty-Six: A Tale of Olden Times*. Boston, 1824.

Chester, John. *A Sermon, in Commemoration of the Landing of the New-England Pilgrims, Delivered in the 2d Presbyterian Church, Albany, December 22d, 1820: On the Completion of the Second Century, since That Event . . . "Qui Transtulit Sustinet."* Albany, 1820.

Child, Lydia Maria. *Hobomok, and Other Writings on Indians*. Ed. Carolyn L. Harcher. New Brunswick, N.J.: Rutgers University Press, [1986].

Choate, Joseph Hodges. *Arguments and Addresses*. Ed. Frederick C. Hicks. St. Paul, Minn., 1926.

Choate, Rufus. *Addresses and Orations*. Boston, 1878.

Chorley, Henry F. *Memorials of Mrs. Hemans with Illustrations of Her Literary Character from Her Private Correspondence*. 2 vols. London, 1836

Clark, Joseph S. *Repairing the Breach. A Historical Discourse, Preached in Plymouth, Mass., at the Twenty-Fifth Anniversary of the Pilgrim Conference of Churches, May 16, 1855*. Boston, 1855.

Clemens, Samuel L. *See* Twain, Mark.

Cobb, Alvan. *God's Culture of His Vineyard. A Sermon, Delivered at Plymouth before the Robinson Congregation, on the 22d of December, 1831*. Taunton, 1832.

Codman, John. *The Faith of the Pilgrims. A Sermon Delivered at Plymouth, on the Twenty-second of December, 1831*. Boston, 1832.

Coit, Thomas W. *Puritanism: or, a Churchman's Defence against Its Aspersions, by an Appeal to Its Own History*. New York, 1845.

Conant, Sylvanus. *An Anniversary Sermon Preached at Plymouth, December 23, 1776. In Grateful Memory of the First Landing of Our Worthy Ancestors in That Place, An. Dom. 1620*. Boston, 1777.

Conway, Moncure Daniel. *Autobiography, Memoirs, and Experiences*. 2 vols. Boston, 1904.

Coolidge, Calvin. *Have Faith in Massachusetts: A Collection of Speeches and Messages*. Boston, 1919.

Cotton, John. "An Account of the Church of Christ in Plymouth, the First Church in New-England, from Its Establishment to the Present Day. By a Member of Said Church. (Written in 1760)." *Collections of the Massachusetts Historical Society, for the Year M, DCC, XCV*. [Vol. 4, 1st ser.] Boston, 1795. Reprinted, Boston, 1835.

[Coverly, Nathaniel Jr., a.k.a. Mrs. Eliza Bowen Webb]. *The Awful Beacon, to the Rising Generation of Both Sexes*. Boston, 1816.

Crafts, William. *Address, Delivered before the New-England Society of South Carolina, on the 22nd December, 1820, Being the Two Hundreth Anniversary of the Landing at Plymouth of the Ancestors of New England*. Charleston, 1820.

The Crisis, No. 1; or, Thoughts on Slavery, Occasioned by the Missouri Question. New Haven, 1820.

"Criticism on the Landing of the Fathers, a Picture by Henry Sargent Esq," and "Another Paper on the Same Subject." *Collections of the Massachusetts Historical Society*. Vol. 3, 2d ser. Boston, 1815. Reprinted, Boston, 1846.

Croswell, Joseph. *A New World Planted; or, the Adventures of the Forefathers of New-England; Who Landed in Plymouth, December 22, 1620. An Historical Drama—in Five Acts*. Boston, 1802.

Cummings, Thomas Harrison, ed. *The Webster Centennial. Proceedings of the Webster Historical Society*. Boston, 1883.

Curtis, George W. "Nathaniel Hawthorne." *Essays from the North American Review*. Ed. Allen Thorndike Rice. New York, 1879.

——. "Oration." *Proceedings at the Centennial Celebration of the Concord Fight, April 19, 1875*. Concord, 1876.

——. *Orations and Addresses*. 3 vols. New York, 1894.

——. See also *Unveiling*.

Cushman, John. *Self Love: . . . . "The First Sermon Preached in New England; and the Oldest Extant of Any Delivered in America."* New York, 1857.

Davis, John. *A Discourse before the Massachusetts Historical Society, Boston, December 22, 1813. At Their Anniversary Commemoration of the First Landing of Our Ancestors at Plymouth, in 1620. Collections of the Massachusetts Historical Society*. Vol. 1, 2d ser. Boston, 1814.

[Davis, Samuel]. "Notes on Plymouth, Mass." Article XX. *Collections of the Massachusetts Historical Society*. Vol. 3, 2d ser. Boston, 1815. Reprinted, Boston, 1846.

Davis, William T. *History of the Town of Plymouth, with a Sketch of the Origin and Growth of Separatism*. Philadelphia, 1885.

——. *Plymouth Memories of an Octogenarian*. Plymouth, 1906.

Dearborn, Henry A. S. *Letters on the Internal Improvements and Commerce of the West*. Boston, 1839.

Depew, Chauncey M. *My Memories of Eighty Years*. New York, 1922.

——. *Orations Addresses and Speeches*. Ed. John Denison Chapman. 8 vols. New York, 1910.

Description of the Engraving of Plymouth Rock, 1620 [the *Landing* by Peter Rothermel]. *To which Is Prefixed an Outline of the Occurrences Connected with the Landing of the Forefathers*. Boston (n.d.), ca. 1869.

Dewey, Orville. *The Claims of Puritanism. A Sermon Preached at the Annual Election, May 31, 1826, before His Excellency Levi Lincoln, Governor, the Honorable Council, and the Legislature of Massachusetts*. Boston, 1826.

——. *Discourse on Slavery and the Annexation of Texas*. New York, 1844.

Dinner of the New England Society: With the Speeches . . . Celebrated at the Astor House, December 23, 1850. New York, 1851.

Dodge, Josua. *A Sermon, Delivered in Haverhill, December 22, 1820; Being the Second Centesimal Anniversary, of the Landing of New England Fathers at Plymouth*. Haverhill, 1821.

Dos Passos, John. *The Big Money*. New York, 1936.

——. *Facing the Chair: Story of the Americanization of Two Foreignborn Workmen*. Boston: Sacco-Vanzetti Defense Committee, 1927. New York: Da Capo Press, 1970.

Douglass, Frederick. *Narrative of the Life of . . . an American Slave Written by Himself* (1845). Ed. Houston A. Baker Jr. New York: Penguin, 1982.

[Draper, Andrew Sloan]. *The Pilgrim and His Share in American Life. . . . An Address at Forefathers' Convocation, Sunday, December 13, 1896*. Champaign: University of Illinois, n.d.

Dunkin, Benjamin Faneuil. *Address, Delivered before the Members of the New-England Society, in Charleston [S.C.], at Their Anniversary Meeting, December 20th, 1819*. Charleston, 1820.

Dunne, Finley Peter. *Observations by Mr. Dooley*. New York, 1906.

Dutton, Samuel W. S. *The Fathers of New England.—Religion Their Ruling Motive in Their Emigration. A Sermon Preached on the Lord's Day, December 22d, 1850, the Two Hundredth and Thirtieth Anniversary of the Landing of the Pilgrims*. New Haven, 1851.

[Dwight, Theodore, Jr.]. *The Northern Traveller: (Combined with the Northern Tour.) Containing the Routes to Niagara, Quebec, and the Springs. With the Tour of New-England, and the Route to the Coal Mines of Pennsylvania. . . .* 3d ed., revised and extended. New York, 1828.

[——]. *Things as They Are: Or, Notes of a Traveller through Some of the Middle and Northern States*. New York, 1834.

Dwight, Timothy. *Travels in New England and New York*. Ed. Barbara Miller Solomon. 4 vols. Cambridge: Harvard University Press, 1969.

The Eighty-Second Anniversary of American Independence: Being a Full Report of the Events of the Day in the City of Boston, Together with the Revised Orations of Rufus

Choate and John S. Holmes, and the Speeches at the Faneuil Hall and Revere House Banquets. July 5, 1858. Boston, 1858.

Ely, Alfred. *A Sermon, Delivered at Monson, Massachusetts, December 22, 1820; the Second Centurial Anniversary of the Landing of the Fathers of New England, at Plymouth*. Hartford, 1821.

Emerson, Ralph Waldo. *The Complete Works*. Centenary ed. Ed. Edward Waldo Emerson. 12 vols. Boston, 1903–4.

——. *The Early Lectures*. Ed. Robert E. Spiller et al. 3 vols. Cambridge: Harvard University Press, 1966–72.

——. *The Journals and Miscellaneous Notebooks*. Ed. William H. Gilman et al. 15 vols. Cambridge: Harvard University Press, 1960–78.

Emmons, Nathanael. *A Sermon, Delivered Dec. 31, 1820. The Last Lord's Day in the Second Century since Our Forefathers First Settled in Plymouth*. Dedham, 1821.

Everett, Edward. *Orations and Speeches on Various Occasions*. 3 vols. Boston, 1850.

——. See also *Eighty-Second Anniversary*.

Flint, James. *A Discourse Delivered at Plymouth, December 22, 1815, at the Anniversary Commemoration of the First Landing of Our Ancestors at That Place*. Boston, 1816.

Francis, Convers. *A Discourse Delivered at Plymouth, Mass., Dec. 22, 1832, in Commemoration of the Landing of the Fathers*. Plymouth, 1832.

Freeman, John R. "General Scope of Drawings to Accompany Report. Plymouth Tercentenary Celebration. Site for Permanent Improvements Near Site of the Land of the Pilgrims." November 17, 1916. Mimeographed.

French, Jonathan. *A Discourse, Delivered at North-Hampton, N.H., December 22, 1820. A Day Religiously Observed by Many, in Commemoration of the Landing of the First Settlers of New-England, Two Hundred Years Having Elapsed since That Event*. Portsmouth, 1821.

Garrison, Wendell P., and Francis J. Garrison. *William Lloyd Garrison, 1805–1879*. 4 vols. New York, 1885–89.

Garrison, William Lloyd. *An Address Delivered before the Free People of Color in Philadelphia, New-York, and Other Cities during the Month of June, 1831*. Boston, 1831.

——. *An Address on the Progress of the Abolition Cause*. Delivered before the African Abolition Freehold Society of Boston, July 16, 1832. Boston, 1832.

——. *Annual Report of the Board of Managers of the Massachusetts Anti-Slavery Society*. Boston, 1836–57.

——. *Letters*. Ed. Walter M. Merrill. 6 vols. Cambridge: Harvard University Press, 1971.

——. *Liberator*. Vols. 1–35. Boston, 1831–65.

——. *Proceedings of the American Anti-Slavery Society at Its Second Decade*. New York, 1854.

The General Society of Mayflower Descendants: Meetings, Officers and Members in State Societies, Ancestors and Their Descendants. The General Congress, 1901.

Goodwin, Rev. Ezra Shaw. "The Providence of God in the Settlement of New England" [Preached at Plymouth, December 22, 1816]. *Sermons by the Late . . . Pastor of the First Church and Society of Sandwich Mass. With a Memoir*. Boston, 1834.

Goodwin, John A. *The Pilgrim Fathers. Oration Delivered before the City Council and Citizens of Lowell, December 22, 1876*. Lowell, 1877.

——. *The Pilgrim Republic: An Historical Review of the Colony of New Plymouth.* Boston, 1886.

Grand Review of Historic Regiments Celebrating the 375th Anniversary of the Landing of the Mayflower, Plymouth Massachusetts, July 23, 1995. (Pamphlet, n.p., n.d.)

Green, Samuel. *A Discourse, Delivered at Plymouth, Dec. 20, 1828, on the Two Hundred and Eighty Anniversary of the Landing of the Pilgrim Fathers.* Boston, 1829.

Greenough, Horace. "Aesthetics at Washington." *A Memorial of Horatio Greenough.* Ed. Henry T. Tuckerman. New York, 1853. (Cited in Somkin, *Unquiet Eagle*, 109.)

Greenwood, F. W. P. *Character of the Puritans. A Sermon Preached before the Ancient and Honourable Artillery Company, June 5th, 1826, Being the 188th Anniversary.* Boston, 1826.

Harris, Thaddeus Mason. *A Discourse Delivered at Plymouth, Dec. 22d, 1808, at the Anniversary Commemoration of the Landing of Our Ancestors at That Place.* Boston, 1808.

Hawes, Joel. *A Tribute to the Memory of the Pilgrims, and a Vindication of the Congregational Churches of New England.* Hartford, 1836.

Hawthorne, Nathaniel. *The Centenary Edition of the Works.* Vols. 17–18, *Letters.* Ed. Thomas Woodson et al. Columbus: Ohio State University Press, 1987.

——. *The Complete Works.* Ed. George P. Lathrop. 12 vols. Boston, 1883.

Hemans, Felicia. *The Complete Works of Mrs. Hemans.* Ed. by Her Sister. 2 vols. New York, 1853.

——. *Poems.* Ed. Andrews Norton. Vol. 1. Boston, 1826. Vol. 2. Boston, 1827.

Henry Cabot Lodge: Memorial Addresses Delivered in the Senate and House of Representatives of the United States in Memory of Henry Cabot Lodge Late a Senator from Massachusetts. Washington, D.C., 1925.

Hitchcock, Gad. *A Sermon Preached at Plymouth, December 22d, 1774. Being the Anniversary Thanksgiving, in Commemoration of the First Landing of Our New-England Ancestors in That Place, Anno Dom. 1620.* Boston, 1775.

Hoar, George Frisbie. "Address." *Bradford's History "Of Plimoth Plantation." From the Original Manuscript. With a Report of the Proceedings Incident to the Return of the Manuscript to Massachusetts.* Boston, 1898.

——. *Autobiography of Seventy Years.* 2 vols. New York, 1903.

——. *Oration.* See *Proceedings at the Celebration . . . 1895.*

——. *Speech . . . December 22, 1902, at the Banquet of the New England Society, of Pennsylvania, at Philadelphia.* Washington, D.C., 1903.

Holmes, Abiel. *A Discourse, Delivered at Plymouth 22 December 1806, at the Anniversary Commemoration of the First Landing of the Fathers, A.D. 1620.* Cambridge, Mass., 1806.

——. *Two Discourses on the Completion of the Second Century from the Landing of the Forefathers of New England at Plymouth, 22 Dec. 1620, Delivered at Cambridge 24 Dec. 1820.* Cambridge, Mass., 1821.

Holmes, John S. See *Eighty-Second Anniversary.*

Holmes, Oliver Wendell. *Works.* 13 vols. Boston, 1891.

——. See *Report of the Semi-Centennial Dinner.*

Homes, William. "Oration." *Proceedings at the Anniversary of the Landing of the Pilgrims. St. Louis, December 22, 1845.* St. Louis, [1846].

Hopkins, Mark. *A Sermon, Delivered at Plymouth, on the Twenty-Second of December, 1846.* Boston, 1847.

Howe, M. A. DeWolfe. *Barrett Wendell and His Letters.* Boston, 1924.

Howe, U. Tracy, and Charles Hess. *The Pilgrims of 1620. An Oratorio . . . Respectfully Dedicated to the New-England Society of Detroit.* Detroit, 1849.

Hume, Harrison. *Address . . . Delivered at the 250th Dinner of the New England Club, December 21, 1889.* Boston, 1890.

Humphrey, Heman. *The Character and Sufferings of the Pilgrims. A Sermon, Delivered at Pittsfield [Mass.], December 22, 1820; Being Just Two Centuries from the Landing of the Pilgrims at Plymouth. With an Appendix.* Pittsfield, 1821.

——. *Discourses and Reviews.* Amherst, 1834.

——. *Parallel between Intemperance and the Slave Trade: An Address Delivered at Amherst College, July 4, 1828.* Amherst, 1828.

Humphrey, James. *An Address, Delivered before the New England Society of the City of Brooklyn, N.Y., December, 1848. On the Anniversary of the Landing of the Pilgrims at Plymouth.* New York, 1849.

Hunt, Rev. T[imothy] Dwight. *Address Delivered before the New England Society of San Francisco, at the American Theatre, on the Twenty-second Day of December, A.D. 1852.* San Francisco, 1852.

Hunt, William Gibbes. "The Landing of the Fathers at Plymouth, New England, December 22ds, 1620." *Western Review and Miscellaneous Magazine.* Vol. 3, from August 1820 to January 1821, inclusive. Lexington, 1821.

Huntington, Daniel. *A Discourse, Delivered in the North Meeting-House in Bridgewater, on Friday, Dec. 22, 1820. Being the Second Centurial Anniversary of the Landing of the Pilgrims at Plymouth.* Boston, 1821.

Hyde, Alvan. *A Sermon Delivered at Lee [Mass.], December 22nd, 1920: Being the Two Hundredth Anniversary of the Landing of Our Ancestors at Plymouth.* Stockbridge, 1821.

Illustrated Pilgrim Memorial, The. Boston, 1863.

Irving, Washington. *History, Tales, and Sketches.* Library of America. New York: Literary Classics of the United States, 1983.

[Johnson, Algernon Sidney]. *The Memoirs of a Nullifier; Written by Himself.* Columbia, S.C., 1832.

Journal of Debates and Proceedings in the Convention of Delegates, Chosen to Revise the Constitution of Massachusetts . . . November 15, 1820 . . . to January 9, 1821. Boston, 1821.

Judson, Adoniram. *A Sermon, Preached in the New Meeting House, Plymouth, December 22, 1802, in Memory of the Landing of Our Ancestors, December 22, 1620.* Boston, 1803.

"Junius Americanus." *A Review of "A Discourse Occasioned by the Death of Daniel Webster, Preached at the Melodeon on Sunday, October 31, 1852, by Theodore Parker, Minister of the Twenty-Eighth Congregational Society in Boston."* Boston, 1853.

Kendall, E. A. *Account of the Writing or Dighton Rock; in a Letter to the Hon. John Davis, Esq. Recording Secretary of the American Academy of Arts and Sciences. Memoirs of the American Academy of Arts and Sciences.* Vol. 3, pt. 1. Cambridge, Mass., 1809.

Kendall, James. *A Discourse Delivered January 1, 1850, upon the Fiftieth Anniversary of His Ordination as Pastor of the First Church in Plymouth*. Plymouth, 1850.

Kingsley, Darwin P. *The Pilgrims: The Most Successful Adventurers in All History. New England Society of the City of New York: 114th Annual Festival, December 22, 1919*. New York, 1920.

Kirkland, Rev. John Thornton. *See* Morse, Jedidiah, and Elijah Parish, *History*.

Knapp, Samuel L. *A Memoir of the Life of Daniel Webster*. Boston, 1831.

Know-Nothing Token. See Wide-Awake Gift.

Lally, A. V. *The Story of the Pilgrim Fathers*. Illustrated by H. A. Ogden. N.p.: Chase and Sanborn, 1920.

Lamson, Alvan. *The Memory of John Robinson: A Discourse Delivered at Dedham, Mass. On Sunday, Dec. 21, 1851*. Boston, 1852.

Lemay, J. A. Leo, ed. *An Early American Reader*. Washington, D.C.: United States Information Agency, 1988.

The Liberty Bell. By Friends of Freedom. Boston, 1839–58.

Lindsay, Vachel. *Collected Poems*. New York: Macmillan, 1930.

Lodge, Henry Cabot. *Alexander Hamilton*. Boston, 1896.

——. *Certain Accepted Heroes and Other Essays in Literature and Politics*. New York, 1897.

——. *Daniel Webster*. Boston, 1892.

——. *The Democracy of the Constitution and Other Addresses and Essays*. New York, 1915.

——. *Early Memories*. New York, 1913.

——. *A Fighting Frigate and Other Essays and Addresses*. New York, 1907.

——. *A Frontier Town and Other Essays*. New York, 1906.

——. *George Washington*. 2 vols. Boston, 1889.

——. *Historical and Political Essays*. Boston, 1892.

——, ed. *Life and Letters of George Cabot*. Boston, 1878.

——. *One Hundred Years of Peace*. New York, 1913.

——. *The Pilgrims of Plymouth*. Boston, 1921.

——. *Sea Power of the United States*. Washington, 1895.

——, ed. *Selections from the Correspondence of Theodore Roosevelt and Henry Cabot Lodge, 1884–1918*. New York, 1925.

——. *The Senate of the United States and Other Essays and Addresses Historical and Literary*. New York, 1921.

——. *The Senate and the League of Nations*. New York, 1925.

——. *A Short History of the English Colonies in America*. New York, 1886.

——. *Speeches and Addresses, 1884–1909*. Boston, 1909.

——. *The Story of the Revolution*. 2 vols. New York, 1898.

——. *Studies in History*. Boston, 1884.

Lodge, Henry Cabot, and Theodore Roosevelt. *Hero Tales from American History*. New York, 1895.

Longfellow, Henry Wadsworth. *Complete Poetical and Prose Works*. 11 vols. Boston, 1886.

——. "Longfellow's *The Courtship of Miles Standish*: Some Notes and Two Early

Versions." Ed. Edward L. Tucker. *Studies in the American Renaissance: 1985*, ed. Joel Myerson. Charlottesville: University Press of Virginia, 1985.

Longfellow, Samuel, ed. *Life of Henry Wadsworth Longfellow.* 2 vols. Boston, 1886.

Lord, Arthur. *Plymouth and the Pilgrims.* Boston, 1920.

Lothrop, S. K. "Remarks." *Report of the Dinner at the Semi-Centennial Anniversary of the New England Society in the City of New York. At the Astor House, December 22d, 1855. Semi-Centennial Celebration in the City of New York.* New York, 1856.

Love, William De Loss. *Obedience to Rulers.—The Duty and Its Limitations. A Discourse Delivered December 22d, 1850, the Two Hundred and Thirtieth Anniversary of the Landing of the Pilgrims.* New Haven, 1851.

Lowell, James Russell. *The Anti-Slavery Papers of James Russell Lowell.* 2 vols. Boston, 1902.

[——]. *Class Poem.* Cambridge, Mass., 1838.

——. *The Complete Writings.* Ed. Charles Eliot Norton. 16 vols. Boston, 1904.

——. *Letters of James Russell Lowell.* Ed. Charles Eliot Norton. 2 vols. New York, 1894.

[Lyman, S. P.]. *Life and Memorials of Daniel Webster. From The New-York Daily Times.* 2 vols. New York, 1853.

Mann, Horace. *See* Mann, Mary.

Mann, Joel. *A Discourse Delivered in Bristol, December 22, 1820, on the Anniversary of the Landing of Our Ancestors at Plymouth.* Warren, 1821.

Mann, Mary. *Life of Horace Mann.* [1888.] Miami: Mnemosyne Publishing, 1969.

Marshall, John. *A History of the Colonies Planted by the English on the Continent of North America, from Their Settlement, to the Commencement of That War Which Terminated in Their Independence.* Philadelphia, 1824.

Martin, Edward Sandford. *The Life of Joseph Hodges Choate: As Gathered Chiefly from His Letters, Including His Own Story of His Boyhood and Youth.* 2 vols. New York, 1920.

Matthews, Albert. *The Term Pilgrim Fathers and Early Celebrations of Forefathers' Day.* Publications of the Colonial Society of Massachusetts. Vol. 17. Boston, 1914.

May, Samuel J. *Discourse on Slavery in the United States, Delivered in Brooklyn, July 3, 1831.* Boston, 1832.

——. *Letters to Rev. Joel Hawes, D.D. in Review of His Tribute to the Memory of the Pilgrims.* Hartford, 1831.

Memoir of the Life and Writings of Mrs. Hemans. By Her Sister. Philadelphia, 1839.

Memorial of Daniel Webster from the City of Boston. Boston, 1853.

Mencken, H. L. *A Mencken Chrestomathy.* New York: Alfred A. Knopf, 1949.

Mentor 8.17 (1920). [Entire issue devoted to the Pilgrims.]

Moon, William Least Heat. *Blue Highways: A Journey into America.* Boston: Little, Brown and Co., 1982.

Morse, Jedidiah. *The American Gazetteer . . . of the American Continent.* 2d ed. Boston, 1804.

——. *The American Geography; or, a View of the Present Situation of the United States of America.* Elizabethtown, 1789.

——. *The American Universal Geography. . . . In Two Parts. . . . Part I. Being a New Edition of the "American Geography," Corrected and Greatly Enlarged.* Boston, 1893.

Morse, Jedidiah, and Elijah Parish. *A Compendious History of New England, Designed for Schools and Private Families.* Charlestown, 1804.

Morton, Nathaniel. *New England's Memorial.* Ed. John Davis. Boston, 1826.

National Monument to the Forefathers. Broadside, dated January 1, 1859.

Nebraska: A Poem, Personal and Political. Boston, 1854.

New England Society in the City of Brooklyn. *Proceedings at the First and Subsequent Annual and Spring Meetings and First and Subsequent Annual Dinners from 1880 to 1895 Inclusive.* Vols. 1 and 2. Brooklyn, 1896.

———. *Proceedings of the Seventeenth Annual Meeting and Seventeenth Annual Festival of the New England Society in the City of Brooklyn. Officers, Directors, Council, Members, Standing Committeees, and By-Laws of the Society.* Brooklyn, 1897.

———. *Twenty-first Annual Report.* Brooklyn, 1901.

———. *Twenty-third Annual Report.* Brooklyn, 1905.

———. *Thirtieth Annual Report.* Brooklyn, 1910.

———. *See also* Humphrey, James.

New England Society in the City of New York. *Eighty-First Anniversary Celebration at Delmonico's. December 22, 1886.* New York, 1887. See also *New England Society Orations; Dinner; Kingsley; Report of the Semi-Centennial Dinner.*

New England Society of Charleston, South Carolina. *Sixty-First Anniversary . . . December 22, 1880.* Charleston, n.d. *See also* Chamberlain, Daniel Henry; Crafts, William; Dunkin, Benjamin Faneuil; Way, William; Whitridge, Joshua Barker.

The New England Society Orations. Ed. Cephas Brainerd and Eveline Warner Brainerd. 2 vols. New York, 1901.

New York State Anti-Slavery Society. *Proceedings of the First Annual Meeting . . . , Convened at Utica, October 19, 1836.* Utica, N.Y., 1836.

Norton, Andrews. Letterbook C. Shelf List Number: bMS AM 1089. Used by permission of the Houghton Library, Harvard University.

Obituary Addresses on the Occasion of the Death of the Hon. Daniel Webster, of Massachusetts, Secretary of State for the United States. Washington, D.C., 1853.

Old Plymouth Days and Ways. Handbook of the Historic Festival in Plymouth Massachusetts July 28, 29, 30, 31 August 2 and 3 MCCCCXCVII. Plymouth, 1897.

The Out-Line: An Historic Poem. Montpelier, Vt., 1821.

Page, Walter Hines. *An Address at Plymouth, August 4, 1917.* Privately printed, 1920.

Parker, Theodore. *Centenary Edition* [running title of his works]. 15 vols. Boston, 1907–13. (Separate volumes are unnumbered except in the final, index volume. The memorial sermon for Webster is in vol. 8, *Historic Americans,* ed. by Samuel A. Eliot.)

Pastor's Memorial. Twenty-Fifth Anniversary of the Installation of George W. Blagden, D.D. as Pastor of the Old South Church and Society in Boston. N.p., 1862.

Pattee, Fred Lewis. *Side-Lights on American Literature.* New York, 1922.

Peabody, Oliver W. B. *A Discourse, Delivered in the Church of the First Congregational Society in Burlington, Sunday, December 21, 1845, the Anniversary of the Sabbath, Which Preceded the Landing of the Pilgrim Fathers. . . .* Burlington, Vt., 1846.

Phillips, Wendell. *Speeches, Lectures, and Letters. First Series.* Boston, 1894. *Second Series.* Boston, 1894.

Picture of the Embarcation of the Pilgrims from Delft-Haven in Holland; Painted by Robt. W. Weir . . . at Washington. New York, 1843.

Pierce, John. *A Discourse Delivered at Dorchester, on 17 June, 1830, to Commemorate the Completion of the Second Century from Its Settlement by Our Pilgrim Fathers.* Boston, 1830.

Pierpont, John. *The National Reader; a Selection of Exercises in Reading and Speaking, Designed to Fill the Same Place in the Schools of the United States, That Is Held in Those of Great Britain.* Boston, 1828.

Pilgrim Memorial State Park. Prepared for Commonwealth of Massachusetts Department of Environmental Management, June 1994. Prepared by the Halvorson Co.; Freeman/Brigham/Hussey; Parsons Brinkerhoff Quade and Douglas.

Pilgrims, or First Settlers of New England, The. [Poetry: a child's book. Illustrated.] Baltimore, [1825].

Pilgrim Society. *Naturalization Ceremony, July 23, 1995. Pilgrim Memorial State Park, Plymouth, Massachusetts.* [Program for the ceremony.]

Pilgrim Tercentenary Memorial Fund. Engraved invitation to subscribe, accompanied by T.L.S. from F. Conant Hawes, Secretary for the Committee. Collections, American Antiquarian Society.

The Pilgrim Tercentenary 1620–1920. Suggestions for Observance in the Schools, Giving Specimen Programs, Pilgrim Stories, a Pageant and a Bibliography. Prepared by the Special Committee on the School Observance of the Pilgrim Tercentenary. The Commonwealth of Massachusetts: Bulletin of the Department of Education. 1920, no. 10, whole no. 119.

Plymouth Church Records, 1620–1859. 2 vols. New York, 1920.

Plymouth Cordage Company. *Golden Anniversary Celebration . . . in Honor of Gideon Francis Holmes.* Cambridge, Mass., 1909.

Plymouth Cordage Company: One Hundred Years of Service. Plymouth, 1924.

Plymouth Tercentenary Illustrated. New Bedford, 1921.

Porter, Charles S. *The Paramount Claims of the Gospel. A Semi-Centennial Discourse, Delivered October 1, 1851, Commemorative of the Organization of the Third Church, Plymouth, Mass.* Boston, 1851.

Porter, Katherine Anne. *The Never-Ending Wrong.* Boston: Little, Brown and Co., 1977.

Porter, Noah. *A Discourse, on the Settlement and Progress of New-England. Delivered in Farmington [Conn.], on Friday Evening, December 22, 1820.* Hartford, 1821.

Prentiss, S[eargent] S. *The Constitution of the New England Society of Louisiana, with An Oration Delivered before the Society, February [sic] 22, 1845.* New Orleans, 1851. Also in *A Memoir of S. S. Prentiss.* Vol. 2. New York, 1858.

Prime, Nathaniel S. *The Year of Jubilee; But Not to Africans: A Discourse, Delivered July 4th, 1825, Being the 49th Anniversary of American Independence.* Salem, N.Y., 1825.

The Proceedings at the Celebration by the Pilgrim Society at Plymouth, August 15, 1889, of the Completion of the National Monument to the Pilgrims. Plymouth, 1889.

The Proceedings at the Celebration by the Pilgrim Society at Plymouth, December 21, 1870, of the Two Hundred and Fiftieth Anniversary of the Landing of the Pilgrims. Cambridge, Mass., 1871.

The Proceedings at the Celebration by the Pilgrim Society, Plymouth, December 21, 1895, of the 275th Anniversary of the Landing of the Pilgrims. Plymouth, 1896.

Putnam, Arthur A. *A Selection from the Addresses, Lectures, and Papers, with a Biographic Sketch, of Arthur A. Putnam of Uxbridge, Mass.* Cambridge, Mass., 1910.

Quincy, Josiah. *An Address to the Citizens of Boston, on the XVIIth of September M DCCCC XXX, the Close of the Second Century from the First Settlement of the City.* Boston, 1830.

Records of the Old Colony Club. Proceedings of the Massachusetts Historical Society. Vol. 3, 2d ser. Boston, 1887.

Redpath, James. *The Public Life of John Brown . . . with an Auto-Biography of His Childhood and Youth.* Boston, 1860.

Reese, David M. *A Brief Review of the "First Annual Report of the American Anti-Slavery Society with the Speeches Delivered at the Anniversary Meetings May 6th, 1834." Addressed to the People of the United States.* New York, 1834.

Report of the Pilgrim Tercentenary Commission . . . January 3, 1917. Boston, 1917.

Report of the Semi-Centennial Dinner of the New England Society in the City of New York in Commemoration of the Landing of the Pilgrim Fathers of New England at Plymouth in 1620 . . . December 22d, 1855. New York, 1856.

Report on the Expediency of Celebrating in Future the Landing of the Pilgrims on the Twentyfirst Day of December, Instead of the Twentysecond Day of That Month. By a Committee of the Pilgrim Society. Boston, 1850.

Ripley, Charles. *An Oration on the Colonization of New England, Delivered December 22, 1838, before the Pilgrim Society of Louisville.* Louisville, Ky., 1839.

Robbins, Chandler. *A Sermon Preached at Plymouth, December 22, 1793; Being the Anniversary of the Landing of Our Ancestors in That Place, in 1620. Published at the Request of Those Who Heard It, and Others; with Some Enlargements, and Particular Anecdotes Relating to Their Sufferings before They Left England; Never Before Published.* Boston, 1794.

Robbins, Philemon. *A Sermon Preached at the Ordination of the Reverend Mr. Chandler Robbins, to the Pastoral Office over the First Church and Congregation in Plymouth, January 30th, 1760.* Boston, 1760. Includes "An Appendix, Containing an Account of the Church of Christ in Plymouth, the First Church in New-England, from Its Establishment to the Present Day. By John Cotton, Esq. Member of Said Church." *See also* Cotton, John.

Roe, Alfred S. *Monuments, Tablets, and Other Memorials Erected in Massachusetts to Commemorate the Services of Her Sons in the War of the Rebellion—1861–1865.* Boston, 1910.

Romeyn, John B. *The Duty and Reward of Honouring God. A Sermon, Delivered in the Presbyterian Church, Cedar-Street, New-York, on the 22d of December, 1821, the Anniversary of the Landing of the Pilgrims of New-England.* New York, 1822.

Roosevelt, Theodore. *The Strenuous Life.* New York, 1900.

——. *Works.* National ed. 20 vols. New York, 1926.

Roosevelt, Theodore, and Henry Cabot Lodge. *See* Lodge, Henry Cabot, ed.

Root, David, Rev. *A Sermon Delivered before the Anti-Slavery Society of Haverhill, Mass., Aug. 1836.* Andover, 1836.

Rowland, William F. *A Sermon, Delivered at Exeter, December 22d, 1820. Being the*

Second Centennial Anniversary of the Landing of the Pilgrims of New-England. Exeter, 1821.

The Royal American Magazine, or Universal Repository of Instruction and Amusement. Vols. 1 and 2 (all published). January 1774–March 1775.

Russell, William S. *Guide to Plymouth, and Recollections of the Pilgrims*. Boston, 1846.

———. *Pilgrim Memorials, and Guide to Plymouth*. Boston, 1855.

Sabine, James. *The Fathers of New England. A Sermon, Delivered in the Church in Essex-Street, Boston, December 22, 1820, Being the Second Centennial Celebration of the Landing of the Fathers at Plymouth*. Boston, 1821.

Sanborn, F. B. *The Life and Letters of John Brown, Liberator of Kansas, and Martyr of Virginia*. Boston, 1891.

Sanford, Enoch. *Sketch of the Pilgrims Who Founded the Church of Christ in New England*. Boston, 1831.

Sawyer, Joseph Dillaway. *History of the Pilgrims and Puritans: Their Ancestry and Descendants, Basis of Americanization*. 3 vols. New York, 1922.

[Sedgwick, Theodore]. *Hints to My Countrymen*. By an American. New York, 1825.

Seward, William H. *Works*. Ed. George Baker. 4 vols. New York, 1861.

Sherwood, Samuel. *The Church's Flight into the Wilderness: An Address on the Times*. New York, 1776.

Smibert, John. *The Notebook*. With essays by Sir David Evans, John Kerslake, and Andrew Oliver. Boston: Massachusetts Historical Society, 1969.

Smith, Elizabeth Oakes, ed. *The Mayflower for M DCCC XLVIII*. Boston, 1848.

———. *Selections from the Autobiography of Elizabeth Oakes Smith*. Ed. Mary Alice Wyman. Lewiston, Maine, 1924.

———. "The Women of the Mayflower." See *Wide-Awake Gift*.

Sons of the Sires, The; a History of the Rise, Progress, and Destiny of the American Party, and Its Probable Influence on the Next Presidential Election. By an American. Philadephia, 1855.

Spooner, Allen. *Speech . . . before the Pilgrim Society at Plymouth, Dec. 22, MDCCCLI*. Boston, n.d. [Contains the poem "The Faith of the Puritans."]

Spooner, Zilpha H., ed. *Poems of the Pilgrims*. Boston, 1882.

Sprague, Charles. *The Poetical and Prose Writings*. Boston, 1850.

Sprague, Peleg. *An Address Delivered before the Pilgrim Society of Plymouth, December 22, 1835*. Boston, 1836.

Sprague, William. *Annals of the American Pulpit*. 9 vols. New York, 1857–69.

Stearns, John M. *The Puritan as a Character in History. An Address at the Celebration of the Landing of the Pilgrims: At the New England Congregational Church, December 22d, 1875*. Brooklyn, E.D., 1876.

Stetson, Seth. *The Substance of a Discourse, Preached in the Second Parish, Plymouth, December 22, 1806 in Memory of the Landing of Our Forefathers, 22 December, 1620*. Boston, 1807.

Stoddard, Charles A. *A Discourse Commemorative of the Rev. George Washington Blagden, D.D., Delivered in the Old South Church, Boston, February 22nd, 1885*. Boston, 1885.

Storrs, Richard S. *The Spirit of the Pilgrims. A Sermon Delivered at Plymouth, December the Twenty-second, 1826*. Plymouth, 1827.

Storrs, Richard Salter. *The Puritan Spirit. An Oration before the Congregational Club, Boston, 18 December 1889.* Boston, [1890].

Story, Joseph. *A Charge Delivered to the Grand Jury of the Circuit Court of the United States, at Its First Session in Portland, for the Judicial District of Maine, May 8, 1820.* Portland, 1820.

——. *A Discourse Pronounced at the Request of the Essex Historical Society, September 18, 1828, in Commemoration of the First Settlement of Salem, Mass.* Boston, 1828. Also in *The Miscellaneous Writings, Literary, Critical, Juridicial, and Political.* Boston, 1835.

Stowe, Harriet Beecher. *The May Flower, and Miscellaneous Writings.* Boston, 1855.

Street, Alfred B. *A Poem Delivered before the . . . Phi Beta Kappa Society at Yale College.* New Haven, 1851.

Strong, Jonathan. *A Sermon, Delivered at Plymouth, December 22, 1803, at the Anniversary Commemoration of the First Landing of Our Ancestors at That Place.* Boston, 1804.

Sullivan, William. *A Discourse Delivered before the Pilgrim Society at Plymouth, on the Twenty Second Day of December, 1829.* Boston, 1830.

Sumner, Charles. *Complete Works.* Intro. George Frisbie Hoar. 20 vols. Boston, 1900.

——. *A Finger-Point from Plymouth Rock.* Boston, 1853.

——. *Prophetic Voices Concerning America. A Monograph.* Boston, 1874.

Taft, William Howard. *Address . . . Delivered Saturday Evening, November 21st, 1914, [before] the New England Society of Cleveland and the Western Reserve.* [Cleveland], 1915.

Thacher, James. *History of the Town of Plymouth; from Its First Settlement in 1620, to the Present Time.* 3d ed. [Facsimile, from Boston, 1835]. Ed. Peter Gomes. Yarmouthport, [Mass.]: Parnassus Imprints, 1972.

——. *Military Journal of the American Revolution from the Commencement to the Disbanding of the American Army.* Hartford, 1862.

Thompson, George. *Letters and Addresses by . . . during His Mission in the United States, from Oct. 1st 1834, to Nov. 27, 1835.* Boston, 1837.

[Thomson, Mortimer N.]. *Plu-Ri-Bus-Tah. A-Song-That's-by-No-Author. Perpetrated by I. K. Philander Doesticks.* New York, 1856.

Thoreau, Henry David. *Writings.* 20 vols. Boston, 1906.

Ticknor, George. *Life, Letters, and Journals.* Ed. George S. Hillard. 2 vols. Boston, 1876.

[——]. *Remarks on the Life and Writings of Daniel Webster, of Massachusetts.* Philadelphia, 1831.

Torrey, William T. *A Sermon, Delivered in Plymouth, Dec. 23, 1821, on the Lord's Day after the Anniversary of the Landing of the Fathers.* Boston, 1822.

Tudor, William. *Letters on the Eastern States.* 2d ed. Boston, 1821.

Turner, Charles. *A Sermon, Preached at Plymouth, December 22d, 1773. Being the ANNIVERSARY THANKSGIVING, in Commemoration of the Landing of the FATHERS There, A.D., 1620.* Boston, 1774.

Twain, Mark. *Writings.* Ed. Albert B. Paine. Stormfield ed. 37 vols. New York, 1929.

Unveiling of the Pilgrim Statue by the New England Society in the City of New York at Central Park, June 6, 1885. New York, 1885.

Ward, Artemus. *See* Browne, Charles Farrar.

Washington Society. *An Historical View of the Public Celebrations of the . . . and Those of the Young Republicans. From 1805, to 1822.* Boston, 1823.

Way, William. *History of the New England Society of Charleston, South Carolina, 1819–1919.* Charleston, 1920.

Webster, Daniel. *Writings and Speeches.* National ed. Ed. J. McIntyre. 18 vols. Boston, 1903.

———. See also *Journal of Debates and Proceedings.*

Weeks, Robert P. *Commonwealth vs. Sacco and Vanzetti: A Book of Primary Source Materials.* Englewood Cliffs, N.J.: Prentice-Hall, 1958.

Weir, Robert W. See *Picture.*

Wendell, Barrett. *See* Howe, M. A. DeWolfe.

West, Samuel. *An Anniversary Sermon, Preached at Plymouth, December 22d, 1777. In Grateful Memory of the First Landing of Our Pious New-England Ancestors in That Place, A.D. 1620.* Boston, 1778.

Whitridge, Joshua Barker. *An Oration Delivered on the Anniversary of the New-England Society, Charleston, S.C., December 22d, 1835; in Commemoration of the Landing of the Pilgrims, upon the Rock of Plymouth, December 22d, 1620.* Charleston, 1836.

Whittier, John Greenleaf. *Writings.* Ed. Horace E. Scudder. 7 vols. Boston, 1892.

Wide-Awake Gift, The: A Know-Nothing Token. New York, 1855.

Wilbur, Hervey. *The Pilgrims. A Sermon, Preached in Wendell, Dec. 22, 1820, It Being the Second Centennial Anniversary of the Landing of Our Ancestors at Plymouth.* Wendell, 1821.

Willis, N. Parker. *Hurry-Graphs; or, Sketches of Scenery, Celebrities and Society, Taken from Life.* 2d ed. New York, 1851.

Willison, George F. *The Pilgrim Reader: The Story of the Pilgrims as Told by Themselves and Their Contemporaries Friendly and Unfriendly.* Garden City, N.Y.: Doubleday, 1953.

Wilson, Woodrow. *Selected Literary and Political Papers and Addresses.* 3 vols. New York, [1925].

Winthrop, Robert C. *Addresses and Speeches on Various Occasions.* Boston, 1852.

———. *Addresses and Speeches on Various Occasions, from 1852 to 1867.* Boston, 1867.

Wisner, Benjamin B. *Influence of Religion on Liberty. A Discourse in Commemoration of the Landing of the Pilgrims, Delivered at Plymouth, December 22, 1830.* Boston, 1833.

[Wister, Owen]. *Owen Wister Out West.* Ed. Fanny Kemble Wister. Chicago: University of Chicago Press, 1958.

Woodbridge, John. *The Jubilee of New England. A Sermon, Preached in Hadley, December 22, 1820, in Commemoration of the Landing of Our Fathers at Plymouth; Being Two Centuries from That Event.* Northampton, 1821.

Woodward, William. "An Account of the Tercentenary Celebration of the Landing of the Pilgrims." Scrapbook, ca. 1925.

Worcester, Samuel M. *New England's Glory and Crown. A Discourse, Delivered at Plymouth, Mass., December 22, 1848.* Salem, 1849.

Young, Alexander. *Chronicles of the Pilgrim Fathers of the Colony of Plymouth, from 1602 to 1625.* Boston, 1841.

Abrams, Ann Uhry. "National Paintings and American Character: Historical Murals in the Capitol Rotunda." *Picturing History: American Painting, 1770–1930*. Ed. William Ayres. New York: Rizzoli, 1993.

Abzug, Robert H. *Passionate Liberator: Theodore Dwight Weld and the Dilemma of Reform*. New York: Oxford University Press, 1980.

Agulhon, Maurice. *Marianne into Battle: Republican Imagery and Symbolism in France, 1789–1880*. Trans. Janet Lloyd. Cambridge: Cambridge University Press, 1981.

Allibone, S. Austin. *A Critical Dictionary of English Literature and British and American Authors*. 3 vols. Philadelphia: J. B. Lippincott, 1874.

Appelbaum, Diana Karter. *Thanksgiving: An American Holiday, an American History*. New York: Facts on File, 1984.

Arner, Robert. "Plymouth Rock Revisited: The Landing of the Pilgrim Fathers. *Journal of American Culture* 6.4 (1983).

Avrich, Paul. *Sacco and Vanzetti: The Anarchist Background*. Princeton: Princeton University Press, 1991.

Bailyn, Bernard. *The Ideological Origins of the American Revolution*. Cambridge: Harvard University Press, 1967.

Barnes, Gilbert Hobbs. *The Antislavery Impulse, 1830–1844*. New York: Harcourt, Brace and World, 1964.

Bartlett, Irving H. *Daniel Webster*. New York: Alfred A. Knopf, 1978.

——. *Wendell and Ann Phillips: The Community of Reform, 1840–1880*. New York: W. W. Norton and Co., 1979.

——. *Wendell Phillips: Brahmin Radical*. Boston: Beacon Press, 1961.

Bemis, Samuel Flagg. *John Quincy Adams and the Union*. New York: Alfred A. Knopf, 1970.

Bercovitch, Sacvan. *The American Jeremiad*. Madison: University of Wisconsin Press, 1978.

——. *The Office of the Scarlet Letter*. Baltimore: Johns Hopkins University Press, 1991.

Berens, John F. *Providence and Patriotism in Early America, 1640–1815*. Charlottesville: University Press of Virginia, 1978.

Billington, Ray Allen. *The Protestant Crusade, 1800–1860: A Study of the Origins of American Nativism*. New York: Rinehart and Co., 1938.

Blackwell, Alice Stone. *Lucy Stone: Pioneer Woman Suffragist*. Boston: Little, Brown and Co., 1930.

Boyer, Richard O. *The Legend of John Brown: A Biography and a History*. New York: Alfred A. Knopf, 1973.

Boynton, Robert S. "God and Harvard." *New Yorker*, November 11, 1996, 64–73.

Branch, E. Douglas. *The Sentimental Years, 1836–1860*. New York: D. Appleton-Century, 1934.

Briggs, Rose T. *Plymouth Rock: History and Significance*. Boston: Nimrod Press, Pilgrim Society, 1968.

Brooks, Van Wyck. *New England: Indian Summer, 1865–1915*. E. P. Dutton, 1940.

Brown, Norman D. *Daniel Webster and the Politics of Availability*. Athens: University of Georgia Press, 1969.

Brown, Thomas. *Politics and Statesmanship: Essays on the American Whig Party*. New York: Columbia University Press, 1985.

Buell, Lawrence. *New England Literary Culture from Revolution through Renaissance*. Cambridge: Cambridge University Press, 1986.

Burgess, Walter H. *The Pastor of the Pilgrims: A Biography of John Robinson*. New York: Harcourt, Brace and Howe, 1920.

Cohen, Daniel A. " 'The Female Marine' in an Era of Good Feelings: Cross Dressing and the 'Genius' of Nathaniel Coverly, Jr." *Proceedings of the American Antiquarian Society* 103 (1994).

Cowie, Alexander. *The Rise of the American Novel*. New York: American Book Company, 1951.

Craven, Wesley Frank. *The Legend of the Founding Fathers*. New York: New York University Press, 1956.

Cuckson, John. *The First Church in Plymouth, 1610–1901*. Boston: Beacon Press, 1920.

Current, Richard N. *Daniel Webster and the Rise of National Conservatism*. Boston: Little, Brown and Co., 1955.

Dahl, Curtis. *Robert Montgomery Bird*. New York: Twayne, 1963.

Dalzell, Robert F., Jr. *Daniel Webster and the Trial of American Nationalism, 1843–1852*. Boston: Houghton Mifflin, 1973.

Dangerfield, George. *The Era of Good Feelings*. New York: Harcourt, Brace and Co., 1952.

Dauer, Manning J. *The Adams Federalists*. Baltimore: Johns Hopkins Press, 1953.

Delabarre, Edmund Burke. *Dighton Rock: A Study of the Written Rocks of New England*. New York: Walter Neale, 1928.

Delbanco, Andrew. *William Ellery Channing: An Essay on the Liberal Spirit in America*. Cambridge: Harvard University Press, 1981.

Dickey, Dallas C. *Seargent S. Prentiss: Whig Orator of the Old South*. Baton Rouge: Louisiana State University Press, 1945.

Donald, David. *Charles Sumner and the Coming of the Civil War*. New York: Alfred A. Knopf, 1961.

Douglas, Ann. *The Feminization of American Culture*. New York: Alfred A. Knopf, 1977.

Duberman, Martin, ed. *The Antislavery Vanguard: New Essays on the Abolitionists*. Princeton: Princeton University Press, 1965.

——. *Charles Francis Adams, 1807–1886*. Stanford: Stanford University Press, 1960.

——. *James Russell Lowell*. Boston: Beacon Press, 1966.

Ekirch, Arthur A., Jr. *The Idea of Progress in America, 1815–1860*. New York: Columbia University Press, 1944.

Elkins, Stanley M. *Slavery: A Problem in American Institutional and Intellectual Life*. Chicago: University of Chicago Press, 1976.

Erickson, Paul D. *The Poetry of Events: Daniel Webster's Rhetoric of the Constitution and Union*. New York: New York University Press, 1986.

Filler, Louis. *The Crusade against Slavery, 1830–1860*. New York: Harper and Row, 1960.

Finkelman, Paul, ed. *His Soul Goes Marching On: Responses to John Brown and the Harpers Ferry Raid*. Charlottesville: University Press of Virginia, [1995].

Finley, Ruth E. *The Lady of Godey's: Sarah Josepha Hale*. Philadelphia: Lippincott, 1931.

Fliegelman, Jay. *Prodigals and Pilgrims: The American Revolution against Patriarchal Authority, 1750–1800*. Cambridge: Cambridge University Press, 1982.

Friedman, Lawrence J. *Gregarious Saints: Self and Community in American Abolitionism, 1830–1870*. Cambridge: Cambridge University Press, 1982.

——. *Inventors of the Promised Land*. New York: Alfred A. Knopf, 1975.

Fuess, Claude M. *Calvin Coolidge: The Man from Vermont*. Boston: Little, Brown and Co., 1940.

Garraty, John A. *Henry Cabot Lodge: A Biography*. New York: Alfred A. Knopf, 1965.

Gaustad, Edwin S. *George Berkeley in America*. New Haven: Yale University Press, 1979.

Geertz, Clifford. *The Interpretation of Cultures*. New York: Basic Books, 1973.

Gillett, Frederick H. *George Frisbie Hoar*. Boston: Houghton Mifflin, 1934.

Gomes, Peter. *See* Boynton.

Greenhouse, Wendy. "The Landing of the Fathers: Representing the American Past, 1770–1860." *Picturing History: American Painting, 1770–1930*. Ed. William Ayres. New York: Rizzoli, 1993.

Greenslet, Ferris. *The Life of Thomas Bailey Aldrich*. Boston: Houghton Mifflin, 1908.

Griffin, C. S. *The Ferment of Reform, 1830–1860*. New York: Thomas Y. Crowell Co., 1967.

Grossman, Carl L., and Charles R. Strickland. "Early Depictions of the Landing of the Pilgrims." *Antiques* 98.5 (1970).

Haroutunian, Joseph. *Piety versus Moralism: The Passing of the New England Theology*. New York: Henry Holt and Co., 1932.

Hatch, Alden. *The Lodges of Massachusetts*. New York: Hawthorn Books, 1973.

Hatch, Nathan O. *The Sacred Cause of Liberty: Republican Thought and the Millennium in Revolutionary New England*. New Haven: Yale University Press, 1977.

Heimert, Alan. *Religion and the American Mind: From the Great Awakening to the Revolution*. Cambridge: Harvard University Press, 1966.

Henry, Stuart. *Unvanquished Puritan: A Portrait of Lyman Beecher*. Grand Rapids, Mich.: William B. Eerdmans, 1973.

Higginson, Mary Thacher. *Thomas Wentworth Higginson: The Story of His Life*. Boston: Houghton Mifflin, 1914.

Holland, F. Ross. *Idealists, Scoundrels, and the Lady: An Insider's View of the Statue of Liberty–Ellis Island Project*. Urbana: University of Illinois Press, 1993.

Howard, Leon. *Victorian Knight-Errant: A Study of the Early Literary Career of James Russell Lowell*. Berkeley: University of California Press, 1952.

Howe, Daniel Walker. *The Political Culture of the American Whigs*. Chicago: University of Chicago Press, 1979.

——. *The Unitarian Conscience: Harvard Moral Philosophy, 1805–1861*. Cambridge: Harvard University Press, 1970.

Johnson, Paul E. *A Shopkeeper's Millennium: Society and Revivals in Rochester, New York, 1815–1837*. New York: Hill and Wang, 1978.

Joughin, Louis, and Edmund M. Morgan. *The Legacy of Sacco and Vanzetti*. Princeton: Princeton University Press, 1948.

Kammen, Michael. *A Season of Youth: The American Revolution and the Historical Imagination*. New York: Alfred A. Knopf, 1978.

Kazin, Alfred. *On Native Grounds: An Interpretation of Modern American Prose Literature.* New York: Reynal and Hitchcock, 1942.

Kerber, Linda K. *Federalists in Dissent: Imagery and Ideology in Jeffersonian America.* Ithaca, N.Y.: Cornell University Press, 1970.

———. *Women of the Republic: Intellect and Ideology in Revolutionary America.* Chapel Hill: University of North Carolina Press, 1980.

Klyn, Mark Stephen. "Webster on the Seventh of March: A Study in the Theory and Practice of Rhetorical Criticism." Ph.D. diss. Northwestern University, Evanstan, Illinois, June 1966.

Knupfer, Peter B. *The Union as It Is: Constitutional Unionism and Sectional Compromise, 1787–1861.* Chapel Hill: University of North Carolina Press, 1991.

Koch, G. Adolf. *Republican Religion: The American Revolution and the Cult of Reason.* New York: Henry Holt and Co., 1933.

Lamar, Mrs. Joseph Rucker. *A History of the National Society of the Colonial Dames of America from 1891 to 1933.* Atlanta: Walter W. Brown, 1934.

Lathem, Edward Connery, ed. *Meet Calvin Coolidge: The Man behind the Myth.* Brattleboro, Vt.: Stephen Greene Press, 1960.

Lawrence, William. *Henry Cabot Lodge: A Biographical Sketch.* Boston: Houghton Mifflin, 1925.

Liberty: The French-American Statue in Art and History. Ed. Barbara Bergeron and William Zeisel. New York: Harper and Row, 1986.

McCaughey, Robert A. *Josiah Quincy, 1772–1864: The Last Federalist.* Cambridge: Harvard University Press, 1974.

McKivigan, John R. *The War against Proslavery Religion: Abolitionism and the Northern Churches, 1830–1865.* Ithaca, N.Y.: Cornell University Press, 1984.

McPhee, John. "Travels of the Rock." *New Yorker,* February 26, 1990, 108–17. Also in *Irons in the Fire.* New York: Farrar, Straus & Giroux, 1997.

Marling, Karal Ann. *George Washington Slept Here: Colonial Revivals and American Culture, 1876–1986.* Cambridge: Harvard University Press, 1988.

Marsden, R. G. "The 'Mayflower.' " *English Historical Review* 19 (October 1904): 669–80.

Martin, Terence. *Parables of Possibility: The American Need for Beginnings.* New York: Columbia University Press, 1995.

Marty, Martin E. *Righteous Empire: The Protestant Experience in America.* New York: Dial Press, 1970.

Minner, Marty. "Pilgrims and Migrants: American Myth and Cultural Conversion." *Excursus* 3.1 (1990): 7–14.

Monagan, Charles. "The Rock." *Yankee* 49.9 (1985): 172–75.

Mordell, Albert. *Quaker Militant: John Greenleaf Whittier.* Boston: Houghton Mifflin, 1933.

Morgan, Edmund S., and Helen M. Morgan. *The Stamp Act Crisis: Prologue to Revolution.* Chapel Hill: University of North Carolina Press, 1953.

Morison, Samuel Eliot. "The Pilgrim Fathers: Their Significance in History. Why Are the Pilgrim Fathers Significant?" *By Land and by Sea: Essays and Addresses by Samuel Eliot Morison.* New York: Alfred A. Knopf, 1953.

——. "Plymouth Colony Beachhead." *United States Naval Institute Proceedings* 80 (December 1954): 1344–57.

——. *The Ropemakers of Plymouth: A History of the Plymouth Cordage Company, 1824–1949.* Boston: Houghton Mifflin, 1950.

——. *The Story of the "Old Colony" of New Plymouth, 1620–1692.* New York: Alfred A. Knopf, 1956.

Mott, Frank Luther. *A History of American Magazines.* 3 vols. Cambridge: Harvard University Press, 1938.

Mulford, Carla. "Radicalism in Joel Barlow's *The Conspiracy of Kings* (1792)." *Deism, Masonry, and the Enlightenment: Essays Honoring Alfred Owen Aldridge.* Ed. J. A. Leo Lemay. Newark: University of Delaware Press, 1987.

Nagel, Paul C. *One Nation Indivisible: The Union in American Thought, 1776–1861.* New York: Oxford University Press, 1964.

Nathans, Sydney. *Daniel Webster and Jacksonian Democracy.* Baltimore: Johns Hopkins University Press, 1973.

Nelson, William E. *Dispute and Conflict Resolution in Plymouth County, Massachusetts, 1725–1825.* Chapel Hill: University of North Carolina Press, 1981.

Nye, Russel B. *Fettered Freedom: Civil Liberties and the Slavery Controversy, 1830–1860.* East Lansing: Michigan State University Press, 1963.

——. *William Lloyd Garrison and the Humanitarian Reformers.* Boston: Little, Brown and Co., 1955.

O'Connor, Thomas H. *Lords of the Loom: The Cotton Whigs and the Coming of the Civil War.* New York: Charles Scribner's Sons, 1968.

O'Gorman, James F. "The Colossus of Plymouth: Hammatt Billings's National Monument to the Forefathers." *Journal of the Society of Architectural History* 54.3 (1995).

Olson, Lester C. *Emblems of American Community in the Revolutionary Era: A Study in Rhetorical Iconology.* Washington: Smithsonian Institution Press, 1991.

O'Toole, Patricia. *The Five of Hearts: An Intimate Portrait of Henry Adams and His Friends, 1880–1918.* New York: Ballantine Books, 1991.

Pattee, Fred Lewis. *The Feminine Fifties.* New York: D. Appleton-Century, 1940.

Paulson, Ronald. *Representations of Revolution (1789–1820).* New Haven: Yale Univeristy Press, 1983.

Peterson, Merril D. *Democracy, Liberty, and Property: The State Constitutional Conventions of the 1820's.* New York: Bobbs-Merrill, 1966.

Phillips, Joseph W. *Jedidiah Morse and New England Congregationalism.* New Brunswick, N.J.: Rutgers University Press, 1983.

Pickard, Samuel T. *Life and Letters of John Greenleaf Whittier.* Boston: Houghton Mifflin, 1894.

Richards, Leonard L. *"Gentlemen of Propriety and Standing": Anti-Abolition Mobs in Jacksonian America.* London: Oxford University Press, 1970.

Ruchames, Louis, ed. *A John Brown Reader: The Story of John Brown in His Own Words, in the Words of Those Who Knew Him, and in the Poetry and Prose of the Literary Heritage.* New York: Abelard-Schuman, [1959].

Russell, Francis. "The Pilgrims and the Rock." *American Heritage* 13.6 (1962).

——. *Sacco and Vanzetti: The Case Resolved.* New York: Harper and Row, 1986.

reference services, Keith Arbour, Joanne Chaison, and Thomas Knowles, along with Marie Lamoureux of that department. The late Joyce Tracy and her assistant Dennis Laurie were especially helpful in my researches into ancient newspapers. I should like to thank as well John Hench, vice president for academic activities at the society, for lending his support in a number of ways, nor let me forget Alan Dugutis, head of cataloging, who at the start of the project gave me a precious specimen of the Rock itself, long held in safe keeping by his family, evincing the spirit of generosity that is so typical of that place.

But I return to Georgia Barnhill, once again, who has been my main contact at the society over the years, dating from the early sixties, and who has been of great help regarding matters far beyond her responsibilities. It was she, for example, who introduced me to James O'Gorman of the art department at Wellesley College, because of our mutual interest in the iconography of the Pilgrims, a meeting from which came a long and rewarding exchange of ideas and information. For these and other favors and suggestions over the years, I am greatly in her debt.

Let me here also thank Barbara Hanrahan, then with the University of North Carolina Press, who at the start of the process of publication was instrumental in seeing the manuscript through the first stages of what proved to be a lengthy voyage. I am grateful also to those professional colleagues and friends who obliged me by taking the time to give this manuscript their helpful attention. James Baker, Giles Gunn, Wayne Franklin, John Sears—all were willing to take on a huge task in reading a draft that was close to a third longer than the present version, and though their strictures were often longer than their enthusiasm, I am in their debt for both. Indeed, had I been able to read all of the former, I have no doubt but that this would have been a far better book in the opinion of many besides themselves. I am particularly grateful to Professor William R. Taylor, whose generous comments as a reader for the University of North Carolina Press came at a critical point in the process and gave both the editors and the author a necessary measure of encouragement.

In that latter regard I should like to express my gratitude to Lewis Bateman of the Press, who first solicited this study and who, along with his assistant, Mary E. Laur, spent the better part of a year helping me accomplish what I could not do myself, by providing the distance and perspective that allowed the reduction of the manuscript to present proportions. That it might still be shorter is the proposition with which I began this book, and I end it with a similar acknowledgment. But then it would have been a different study, whereas this comes as close as reason allows to what the subject seemed to me to dictate, to which a certain expansiveness was essential. My thanks also to Townsend Ludington, once my colleague at the University of North Carolina and ever my friend, whose faith in both my abilities and the Press on whose board he sat helped hold this project on course through a thankfully brief moment when all seemed lost, a maneuver to which another good friend, Alan Trachtenberg, lent his weight as well.

The index, let me add, was compiled by Roberta Engleman, through arrangement with the Press.

Here at the University of Florida I have benefited greatly from my position as graduate research professor, which has allowed me considerable free time to pursue my study and which provides a small stipend that has been of considerable help in

Schriftgiesser, Karl. *The Gentleman from Massachusetts: Henry Cabot Lodge*. Boston: Little, Brown and Co., 1945.

Scudder, Horace Elisha. *James Russell Lowell: A Biography*. 2 vols. Boston: Houghton Mifflin, 1901.

Sears, John F. *Sacred Places: American Tourist Attractions in the Nineteenth Century*. New York: Oxford University Press, 1989.

Shenkman, Richard. *Legends, Lies, and Cherished Myths of American History*. New York: William Morrow and Co., 1988.

Sherwin, Oscar. *Prophet of Liberty: The Life and Times of Wendell Phillips*. New York: Bookman Associates, 1958.

Shields, David S. *Oracles of Empire: Poetry, Politics, and Commerce in British America, 1690–1750*. Chicago: University of Chicago Press, 1990.

Silverman, Kenneth. *A Cultural History of the American Revolution*. New York: Thomas Y. Crowell, 1976.

Simpson, Lewis P. *Mind and the American Civil War: A Meditation on Lost Causes*. Baton Rouge: Louisiana State University Press, 1989.

Slotkin, Richard. *Regeneration through Violence*. Middletown, Conn.: Wesleyan University Press, 1973.

Sollors, Werner. " 'Of Plymouth Rock and Jamestown and Ellis Island'—Or, Ethnic Literature and Some Redefinitions of 'America.' " *Multiculturalism and the Canon of American Culture*. Ed. Hans Bak. Amsterdam: VU University Press, 1993.

Somkin, Fred. *Unquiet Eagle: Memory and Desire in the Idea of American Freedom, 1815–1860*. Ithaca, N.Y.: Cornell University Press, 1967.

Starobinske, Jean. *1789: The Emblems of Reason*. Trans. Barbara Bray. Charlottesville: University Press of Virginia, 1982.

Stauffer, Vernon. *New England and the Bavarian Illuminati*. New York: Columbia University Press, 1918.

Stout, Harry S. *The New England Soul: Preaching and Religious Culture in Colonial New England*. New York: Oxford University Press, 1986.

Taylor, William R. *Cavalier and Yankee: The Old South and American National Character*. New York: George Braziller, 1961.

Tilton, Eleanor M. *Amiable Autocrat: A Biography of Dr. Oliver Wendell Holmes*. New York: Henry Schuman, 1947.

Tocqueville, Alexis de. *Democracy in America*. Ed. J. P. Mayer. Garden City, N.Y.: Doubleday, 1969.

Tompkins, Jane. *Sensational Designs: The Cultural Work of American Fiction, 1790–1860*. New York: Oxford University Press, 1985.

Trachtenberg, Alan. *Brooklyn Bridge: Fact and Symbol*. New York: Oxford University Press, 1965.

Trachtenberg, Marvin. *The Statue of Liberty*. New York: Viking Press, 1976.

Treuttner, William H. "The Art of History: American Exploration and Discovery Scenes, 1840–1860." *American Art Journal* 14.1 (1982): 4–31.

Tucker, Edward L. *The Shaping of Longfellow's John Endicott: A Textual History*. [Charlottesville]: University Press of Virginia, 1985.

Turner, Victor. *Dramas, Fields, and Metaphors: Symbolic Action in Human Society*. Ithaca, N.Y.: Cornell University Press, 1974.

——. *The Ritual Process: Structure and Anti-Structure*. Ithaca, N.Y.: Cornell University Press, 1977.

Tuveson, Ernest Lee. *Redeemer Nation: The Idea of America's Millennial Role*. Chicago: University of Chicago Press, 1968.

Tyack, David B. *George Ticknor and the Boston Brahmins*. Cambridge: Harvard University Press, 1967.

Vartanian, Pershing. "The Puritan as a Symbol in American Thought: A Study of the New England Societies, 1820–1920." Ph.D. diss. University of Michigan, 1971.

Villard, Oswald Garrison. *John Brown, 1800–1859: A Biography Fifty Years After*. Boston: Houghton Mifflin, 1910.

Walzer, Michael. *Exodus and Revolution*. New York: Basic Books, 1985.

Warner, Marian. *Monuments and Maidens: The Allegory of the Female Form*. New York: Atheneum, 1985.

Warren, Austin. *The New England Conscience*. Ann Arbor: University of Michigan Press, 1966.

Wecter, Dixon. *The Hero in America: A Chronicle of Hero Worship*. New York: Charles Scribner's Sons, 1941.

Welch, Richard E., Jr. *George Frisbie Hoar and the Half-Breed Republicans*. Cambridge: Harvard University Press, 1971.

Whitridge, Arnold. *No Compromise!: The Story of the Fanatics Who Paved the Way to the Civil War*. New York: Farrar, Straus and Cudahy, 1960.

Wiecek, William M. *The Sources of Antislavery Constitutionalism in America, 1760–1848*. Ithaca, N.Y.: Cornell University Press, 1977.

Willison, George F. *Saints and Strangers*. New York: Reynal and Hitchcock, 1945.

Wyatt-Brown, Bertram. *Yankee Saints and Southern Sinners*. Baton Rouge: Louisiana State University Press, 1985.

Wyman, Mary Alice. *Two American Pioneers: Seba Smith and Elizabeth Oakes Smith*. New York: Columbia University Press, 1927.

ACKNOWLEDGMENTS

Memory's Nation was inspired at the start by a humorous p[...] magazine, a New England–based and –focused periodical designed chie[...] living elsewhere. The article emphasized the essential absurdity of Plym[...] tourist attraction and aroused my postmodernist sensibilities to the id[...] book about a subject the very nature of which was both dubious an[...] native New Englander, who at a youthful age was exposed to the di[...] viewing the Rock, I also was inspired by the perverse necessity that is to[...] of making something of nothing—perhaps even an article of trade.

This notion occurred simultaneously with an extended stay in 198[...] ican Antiquarian Society, funded by the National Endowment for the[...] the intended purpose of completing work on another project, no[...] lished. The unavailability of a study carrel for several months, alon[...] able rush of enthusiasm that attends a new idea, combined to o[...] initial research on the subject of the Rock, and necessarily Plymou[...]

There is no collection in the world better suited to such an inqu[...] to a very large extent upon ephemeral materials and which was sp[...] not only of the society's staff but of other scholars resident there: [...] my attention to items he came across while pursuing his own re[...] papers; Karen Halttunen in an informal lecture provided inform[...] workings at Plimoth Plantation that suggested doctrinal dispute[...] in that place; and Deborah Van Broekhoven supplied importan[...] ences used here. These are but several of many generous coll[...] only materials but insights. Georgia Barnhill, curator of the [...] especially helpful in locating depictions of the Landing, and by[...] acquired sufficient slides to mount a lecture on the many w[...] had been presented between the Federalist era and the tercen[...] the skeleton of what is now a completed book.

Subsequent visits of shorter duration to Worcester were[...] work, right up to the final revisions, and a summer fell[...] Library in San Marino, California, provided leisure and m[...] research further. Both the Pilgrim Society and the Library[...] helpful, and I owe Peggy and James Baker a personal debt [...] the Metropolitan Museum of Art has been of invaluable[...] many other projects involving graphic materials. J. A. Le[...] ware) and Kenneth Silverman (N.Y.U.) responded genero[...] as did Michael Meyer (University of Connecticut) and W[...]

Yet it is finally to the American Antiquarian Society t[...] debt is due, not only to the director during my term[...] Corison, whose genial skepticism regarding this proje[...] ambience, but to the helpful members of the staff who[...] upon which so much can depend. I cite in particula[...]

Schriftgiesser, Karl. *The Gentleman from Massachusetts: Henry Cabot Lodge*. Boston: Little, Brown and Co., 1945.

Scudder, Horace Elisha. *James Russell Lowell: A Biography*. 2 vols. Boston: Houghton Mifflin, 1901.

Sears, John F. *Sacred Places: American Tourist Attractions in the Nineteenth Century*. New York: Oxford University Press, 1989.

Shenkman, Richard. *Legends, Lies, and Cherished Myths of American History*. New York: William Morrow and Co., 1988.

Sherwin, Oscar. *Prophet of Liberty: The Life and Times of Wendell Phillips*. New York: Bookman Associates, 1958.

Shields, David S. *Oracles of Empire: Poetry, Politics, and Commerce in British America, 1690–1750*. Chicago: University of Chicago Press, 1990.

Silverman, Kenneth. *A Cultural History of the American Revolution*. New York: Thomas Y. Crowell, 1976.

Simpson, Lewis P. *Mind and the American Civil War: A Meditation on Lost Causes*. Baton Rouge: Louisiana State University Press, 1989.

Slotkin, Richard. *Regeneration through Violence*. Middletown, Conn.: Wesleyan University Press, 1973.

Sollors, Werner. " 'Of Plymouth Rock and Jamestown and Ellis Island'—Or, Ethnic Literature and Some Redefinitions of 'America.' " *Multiculturalism and the Canon of American Culture*. Ed. Hans Bak. Amsterdam: VU University Press, 1993.

Somkin, Fred. *Unquiet Eagle: Memory and Desire in the Idea of American Freedom, 1815–1860*. Ithaca, N.Y.: Cornell University Press, 1967.

Starobinske, Jean. *1789: The Emblems of Reason*. Trans. Barbara Bray. Charlottesville: University Press of Virginia, 1982.

Stauffer, Vernon. *New England and the Bavarian Illuminati*. New York: Columbia University Press, 1918.

Stout, Harry S. *The New England Soul: Preaching and Religious Culture in Colonial New England*. New York: Oxford University Press, 1986.

Taylor, William R. *Cavalier and Yankee: The Old South and American National Character*. New York: George Braziller, 1961.

Tilton, Eleanor M. *Amiable Autocrat: A Biography of Dr. Oliver Wendell Holmes*. New York: Henry Schuman, 1947.

Tocqueville, Alexis de. *Democracy in America*. Ed. J. P. Mayer. Garden City, N.Y.: Doubleday, 1969.

Tompkins, Jane. *Sensational Designs: The Cultural Work of American Fiction, 1790–1860*. New York: Oxford University Press, 1985.

Trachtenberg, Alan. *Brooklyn Bridge: Fact and Symbol*. New York: Oxford University Press, 1965.

Trachtenberg, Marvin. *The Statue of Liberty*. New York: Viking Press, 1976.

Treuttner, William H. "The Art of History: American Exploration and Discovery Scenes, 1840–1860." *American Art Journal* 14.1 (1982): 4–31.

Tucker, Edward L. *The Shaping of Longfellow's John Endicott: A Textual History*. [Charlottesville]: University Press of Virginia, 1985.

Turner, Victor. *Dramas, Fields, and Metaphors: Symbolic Action in Human Society*. Ithaca, N.Y.: Cornell University Press, 1974.

——. *The Ritual Process: Structure and Anti-Structure*. Ithaca, N.Y.: Cornell University Press, 1977.

Tuveson, Ernest Lee. *Redeemer Nation: The Idea of America's Millennial Role*. Chicago: University of Chicago Press, 1968.

Tyack, David B. *George Ticknor and the Boston Brahmins*. Cambridge: Harvard University Press, 1967.

Vartanian, Pershing. "The Puritan as a Symbol in American Thought: A Study of the New England Societies, 1820–1920." Ph.D. diss. University of Michigan, 1971.

Villard, Oswald Garrison. *John Brown, 1800–1859: A Biography Fifty Years After*. Boston: Houghton Mifflin, 1910.

Walzer, Michael. *Exodus and Revolution*. New York: Basic Books, 1985.

Warner, Marian. *Monuments and Maidens: The Allegory of the Female Form*. New York: Atheneum, 1985.

Warren, Austin. *The New England Conscience*. Ann Arbor: University of Michigan Press, 1966.

Wecter, Dixon. *The Hero in America: A Chronicle of Hero Worship*. New York: Charles Scribner's Sons, 1941.

Welch, Richard E., Jr. *George Frisbie Hoar and the Half-Breed Republicans*. Cambridge: Harvard University Press, 1971.

Whitridge, Arnold. *No Compromise!: The Story of the Fanatics Who Paved the Way to the Civil War*. New York: Farrar, Straus and Cudahy, 1960.

Wiecek, William M. *The Sources of Antislavery Constitutionalism in America, 1760–1848*. Ithaca, N.Y.: Cornell University Press, 1977.

Willison, George F. *Saints and Strangers*. New York: Reynal and Hitchcock, 1945.

Wyatt-Brown, Bertram. *Yankee Saints and Southern Sinners*. Baton Rouge: Louisiana State University Press, 1985.

Wyman, Mary Alice. *Two American Pioneers: Seba Smith and Elizabeth Oakes Smith*. New York: Columbia University Press, 1927.

ACKNOWLEDGMENTS

Memory's Nation was inspired at the start by a humorous piece in *Yankee* magazine, a New England–based and –focused periodical designed chiefly for persons living elsewhere. The article emphasized the essential absurdity of Plymouth Rock as a tourist attraction and aroused my postmodernist sensibilities to the idea of writing a book about a subject the very nature of which was both dubious and dull. But as a native New Englander, who at a youthful age was exposed to the disillusionment of viewing the Rock, I also was inspired by the perverse necessity that is to the region born of making something of nothing—perhaps even an article of trade.

This notion occurred simultaneously with an extended stay in 1984–85 at the American Antiquarian Society, funded by the National Endowment for the Humanities, with the intended purpose of completing work on another project, now long since published. The unavailability of a study carrel for several months, along with the undeniable rush of enthusiasm that attends a new idea, combined to open up a period of initial research on the subject of the Rock, and necessarily Plymouth and the Pilgrims.

There is no collection in the world better suited to such an inquiry, which depended to a very large extent upon ephemeral materials and which was sped along by the help not only of the society's staff but of other scholars resident there: Robert Winans called my attention to items he came across while pursuing his own research in early newspapers; Karen Halttunen in an informal lecture provided information about the inner workings at Plimoth Plantation that suggested doctrinal disputes are not yet at an end in that place; and Deborah Van Broekhoven supplied important W. L. Garrison references used here. These are but several of many generous colleagues who shared not only materials but insights. Georgia Barnhill, curator of the graphics collection, was especially helpful in locating depictions of the Landing, and by the end of the year I had acquired sufficient slides to mount a lecture on the many ways in which that subject had been presented between the Federalist era and the tercentenary occasion, in effect the skeleton of what is now a completed book.

Subsequent visits of shorter duration to Worcester were helpful in continuing the work, right up to the final revisions, and a summer fellowship at the Huntington Library in San Marino, California, provided leisure and materials to supplement my research further. Both the Pilgrim Society and the Library at Plimoth Plantation were helpful, and I owe Peggy and James Baker a personal debt of gratitude. Barbara Burn of the Metropolitan Museum of Art has been of invaluable assistance, with this as with many other projects involving graphic materials. J. A. Leo Lemay (University of Delaware) and Kenneth Silverman (N.Y.U.) responded generously to queries along the way, as did Michael Meyer (University of Connecticut) and Werner Sollors (Harvard).

Yet it is finally to the American Antiquarian Society that my greatest and continuing debt is due, not only to the director during my term of residence, Marcus A. McCorison, whose genial skepticism regarding this project set the proper New England ambience, but to the helpful members of the staff who can locate those obscure trifles upon which so much can depend. I cite in particular the continuity of directors of reference services, Keith Arbour, Joanne Chaison, and Thomas Knowles, along with Marie Lamoureux of that department. The late Joyce Tracy and her assistant Dennis Laurie were especially helpful in my researches into ancient newspapers. I should like to thank as well John Hench, vice president for academic activities at the society, for lending his support in a number of ways, nor let me forget Alan Dugutis, head of cataloging, who at the start of the project gave me a precious specimen of the Rock itself, long held in safe keeping by his family, evincing the spirit of generosity that is so typical of that place.

But I return to Georgia Barnhill, once again, who has been my main contact at the society over the years, dating from the early sixties, and who has been of great help regarding matters far beyond her responsibilities. It was she, for example, who introduced me to James O'Gorman of the art department at Wellesley College, because of our mutual interest in the iconography of the Pilgrims, a meeting from which came a long and rewarding exchange of ideas and information. For these and other favors and suggestions over the years, I am greatly in her debt.

Let me here also thank Barbara Hanrahan, then with the University of North Carolina Press, who at the start of the process of publication was instrumental in seeing the manuscript through the first stages of what proved to be a lengthy voyage. I am grateful also to those professional colleagues and friends who obliged me by taking the time to give this manuscript their helpful attention. James Baker, Giles Gunn, Wayne Franklin, John Sears—all were willing to take on a huge task in reading a draft that was close to a third longer than the present version, and though their strictures were often stronger than their enthusiasm, I am in their debt for both. Indeed, had I been able to heed all of the former, I have no doubt but that this would have been a far better book in the opinion of many besides themselves. I am particularly grateful to Professor William R. Taylor, whose generous comments as a reader for the University of North Carolina Press came at a critical point in the process and gave both the editors and the author a necessary measure of encouragement.

In that latter regard I should like to express my gratitude to Lewis Bateman of the Press, who first solicited this study and who, along with his assistant, Mary E. Laur, spent the better part of a year helping me accomplish what I could not do myself, by providing the distance and perspective that allowed the reduction of the manuscript to its present proportions. That it might still be shorter is the proposition with which I began this book, and I end it with a similar acknowledgment. But then it would have been a different study, whereas this comes as close as reason allows to what the subject seemed to me to dictate, to which a certain expansiveness was essential. My thanks also to Townsend Ludington, once my colleague at the University of North Carolina and forever my friend, whose faith in both my abilities and the Press on whose board he serves helped hold this project on course through a thankfully brief moment when all seemed lost, a maneuver to which another good friend, Alan Trachtenberg, lent his weight as well.

The index, let me add, was compiled by Roberta Engleman, through arrangement with the Press.

Here at the University of Florida I have benefited greatly from my position as graduate research professor, which has allowed me considerable free time to pursue this study and which provides a small stipend that has been of considerable help in funding travel and related expenses. I am grateful to the institution and to my department, and to colleagues like David Leverenz and Bertram Wyatt-Brown for sympathy and scholarly support. Greg Cunningham and the photographics staff in the Office of Instructional Resources were very helpful in providing reproductions of many of the illustrations used here, often on short notice.

I want also to thank Charles F. Purro of the Yankee Book and Art Gallery in Plymouth, who specializes in materials relevant to the early history of that town, for having supplied me over the years with scarce books and pamphlets—some previously unknown to me—that related to the Pilgrims and their Rock. As I have in other places made clear, my debt to dealers in rare and used books is ongoing, but Mr. Purro was singular in that regard relative to this project.

During the more than ten years taken up in researching and writing this book, I have enjoyed alternative summers teaching at Dartmouth College, and my colleagues there have also contributed in general terms to the work, notably Robert McGrath, with whom I have jointly taught in the MALS program and from whom I have learned much of what I know about American art in the nineteenth century, and Donald E. Pease, who was instrumental in seeing that one section of chapter 17, somewhat revised, would appear in *Annals of Scholarship* 12.3 and 12.4 (1998).

I close with a statement of specific indebtedness to William C. Spengemann and James M. Cox, both coincidentally and sequentially on the Dartmouth faculty, long-time friends and colleagues in the best sense of the word. The first I have depended on for hard questions regarding the nature and shape of this project, and though the result is not at all what Bill Spengemann thought it should be, neither is it what it would have been without his help. The second contributed in what was at once a lesser and a greater way, for if this book has an underlying ideology, it may be traced back to a point Jim Cox made long ago, that Thoreau was in effect a secessionist, which at the time brought with it a flash of recognition equivalent to a bolt of lightning in a greenhouse, and the terms of which may be seen working in direct and oblique ways throughout much of this narrative.

For what was new Secessionist but old Separatist writ in blood, the both deeply rooted in notions of exceptionalism and exclusion, still sadly and ferociously at work amongst us even at this moment, as a cabin about the size of Thoreau's at Walden is being carried westward to California with the intention of proving yet another political perfectionist mad in the hope of saving his life.